# Great Dishes
## of the World in Colour

**HAMLYN**
LONDON · NEW YORK · SYDNEY · TORONTO

Illustrations by *John Scott-Martin*

Photography by
*Eric Carter*
*Christian Délu*
*Irwin Horowitz*
*Arne Krüger*
*John Lee*
*John Miller*

**Edited by Jennifer Feller**

Published by
The Hamlyn Publishing Group Limited
London · New York · Sydney · Toronto
Astronaut House, Feltham, Middlesex, England
© Copyright The Hamlyn Publishing Group Limited 1976
Reprinted 1978

Some material in this book has already been published
in *The World of Food* series:
*Provincial France* (First printing 1972)
*Italy*          (First printing 1973)
*China*          (First printing 1973)
Published by
The World Publishing Company, New York
Published simultaneously in Canada by
Nelson, Foster & Scott Ltd.

Printed and bound in Spain by Graficromo, S. A. – Córdoba     ISBN 0 600 31927 X

# CONTENTS

# USEFUL FACTS AND FIGURES

## Note on metrication

In this book quantities have been given in both imperial and metric measures. It is essential that either the imperial or the metric column is followed, not a combination of both, as they are not interchangeable. Exact conversion from imperial to metric does not usually give very convenient working quantities and so for greater convenience metric measures have been rounded off into units of 25 grams. The table below shows recommended equivalents.

| Ounces | Approximate grams to nearest whole figure | Recommended conversion to nearest unit of 25 |
|---|---|---|
| 1 | 28 | 25 |
| 2 | 57 | 50 |
| 3 | 85 | 75 |
| 4 | 113 | 100 |
| 5 | 142 | 150 |
| 6 | 170 | 175 |
| 7 | 198 | 200 |
| 8 | 226 | 225 |
| 9 | 255 | 250 |
| 10 | 283 | 275 |
| 11 | 311 | 300 |
| 12 | 340 | 350 |
| 13 | 368 | 375 |
| 14 | 396 | 400 |
| 15 | 425 | 425 |
| 16 | 454 | 450 |
| 17 | 482 | 475 |
| 18 | 510 | 500 |
| 19 | 538 | 550 |
| 20 | 567 | 575 |

When converting quantities over 20 oz, first add the appropriate figures in the centre column, then adjust to the nearest unit of 25. As a general guide, 1 kg (1000 g) equals 2.2 lb or 2–2¼ lb.

### Liquid measures
The millilitre being a very small unit of measurement, decilitres (units of 100 ml) have been used for liquid measures. For quantities of 1¾ pints and over, litres and fractions of a litre have been used.

### Linear measures
The metric unit of length is the metre which is roughly equal to 3 feet 3 inches. There are 100 centimetres (cm) to the metre, 10 millimetres to the centimetre and 1 inch is 2.54 cm. Measurements have been rounded up or down to the nearest whole centimetre, so a 9-inch cake tin has been converted to a 23-cm tin (exactly 22.86 cm).

## OVEN TEMPERATURES

Oven temperatures on modern electric cookers are marked in degrees Celsius (formerly Centigrade). The following chart shows the recommended conversions from degrees Fahrenheit to degrees Celsius, together with the Gas Mark.

| Description | Fahrenheit | Celsius | Gas Mark |
|---|---|---|---|
| Very cool | 225 | 110 | ¼ |
|  | 250 | 120 | ½ |
| Cool | 275 | 140 | 1 |
|  | 300 | 150 | 2 |
| Moderate | 325 | 160 | 3 |
|  | 350 | 180 | 4 |
| Moderately hot | 375 | 190 | 5 |
|  | 400 | 200 | 6 |
| Hot | 425 | 220 | 7 |
|  | 450 | 230 | 8 |
| Very hot | 475 | 240 | 9 |

# INTRODUCTION

Today people have broadened their horizons through travel and this has had an immense influence over their food habits. It is not surprising, therefore, that in kitchens and on tables everywhere exotic foods and foreign dishes are making their appearance where two or three decades ago they would have been unknown and unthought of. As horizons narrow, all the world becomes one's heritage.

The shapes and colours of the four corners of the earth are being fed into our senses through the media almost every hour of the day. But it is only in the kitchen that we have the complete freedom to experiment and concoct and bring home the flavours of distant lands. For the adventurous and the romantically inclined, these experiments and experiences are ones which can hardly be denied. It can give great pleasure and satisfaction to dine off dishes normally served in hot desert lands or cooked by the lagoons of the Pacific islands. Or to prepare Soochow Melon Chicken or Peking Duck for a special celebration. The long winter months are ideally suited to provide the time and opportunity to enliven our existence by creating the flavours and foods of places and holidays we have known, and preparing for places we intend to go to and the holidays we dream about. Dreams, after all, give life its silver lining. Although we cannot go everywhere, we can cook the food of many countries.

In this book the food and cooking of many regions of the world are brought between two covers, an unrivalled culinary 'package tour' of famous and fabled areas with all their intriguing colour, history, geography and traditions.

In the dishes of the United States one can sense that vast territory, spreading from 'sea to shining sea' across the grain-laden plains of the Middle West, and feel the vitality of the teeming cities, from New York to New Orleans, from Philadelphia to San Francisco. In the dishes of Scandinavia one can feel the North Sea swelling off the rocky shores of Norway and see the Baltic lapping against that inimitable seafront at Copenhagen and the countless islands which cluster around the approaches to Stockholm, where the fish and seafoods hauled in from the shallows are as fresh as they are sweet. In the classical and regional dishes of France, one cannot help but feel a sense of history – that flavour of the Grand Siècle – which reflects the grandeur of Europe's recent past. The same applies to the more robust German dishes – which must beckon continually to all with healthy appetites – culled from the many picturesque regions of Germany. Equally, the Spanish, Italian, Jewish dishes and those from the Eastern Mediterranean are steeped in the history and geography of all those famous and colourful countries.

In China one has an entirely different continent, with a distinct culinary history and tradition of its own, which perhaps because of its range, unique refinement and unparalleled vigour, has engendered a momentum which is only now being felt throughout the five continents of the world. In the Far Eastern dishes one becomes aware of the immensity of the Pacific and the life-styles of its many peoples. Not least of all are the food and cooking of these islands, especially those dishes which have been least influenced by French and other continental practices, and are genuinely reflective of the taste of Elizabethan times and the spacious days of the Victorian and Edwardian eras.

Kenneth H. C. Lo

# AMERICAN

Ann Seranne

*Photography by Irwin Horowitz*

The United States is a land of many moods and many cultures. Within its fifty states reside first and second generation ethnic groups from almost all the other countries of the world. Since the first Pilgrim ships arrived with their cargo of religious and political refugees from England, the United States has become a melting pot of immigrants. All these groups – and the original settlers, the American Indians – have contributed to American cooking to make it nutritious, varied and interesting.

Once the problems of survival were solved, and after the horrendous 'Starving Times' of Jamestown and Plymouth, American women fed their families remarkably well. They dealt ingeniously with native food products, and made the best of whatever was available from land, forest, lake or sea, until permanent settlements were established and the soil was cultivated to produce truly American crops such as maize or Indian corn. It was corn that sustained the Pilgrims and nourished those adventuresome frontiersmen who crossed the plains and moved west in covered wagons to conquer new territories. Beans and peas, pumpkins and many varieties of vegetable marrow, water melon and other types of melons, sweet potatoes and cranberries are other native foods which have played an important role, not only in the cooking of America but in the cooking of the world.

The Pilgrims learned from the Indians how to use these crops and today some favourite dishes are still based on those original recipes, most of which have been improved over the years and modified to meet the demands of more sophisticated palates.

Generally speaking, a cook in any part of the United States can duplicate the typical dishes of any area in her home kitchen; dishes such as Louisiana gumbo, Boston baked beans, Texas barbecued beef, California Crab Louis salad or Minnesota wild rice casserole. She has at her fingertips not only a bewildering assortment of American food products, but the best from almost every country in the world.

The American cook is quick to embrace new combinations of flavours and to experiment with different herbs and spices, exotic fruits and vegetables. She has learned to be creative with fish and the inexpensive cuts of meat, and has become proficient in the preparation of many so-called 'gourmet' dishes. Classic methods of food preparation have been simplified by the use of electric appliances designed to take the work out of cooking. Imaginative substitutions are used for obscure ingredients. Such prepared foods as soya sauce, canned water chestnuts and bean sprouts have become staples in many American kitchens, taking their place beside the many convenience foods such as canned broths, gravies, tomato products, dried cereals and pastas.

American cooking has come a long way from the 'meat and potato' era, to a knowledgeable age of curiosity in cooking, resulting in an enormous variety of dishes. Despite American food manufacturers who spend billions of dollars on new products devised to 'keep the cook out of the kitchen', American women and a surprising number of men live to cook rather than cook to live, and it is they who have been instrumental in raising the standard of cooking in the United States to an all-time high. The recipes in this section represent the best to be found in American homes across the nation.

# SPARE RIBS WITH MONTANA SAUCE

*Serves 4*

| | |
|---|---|
| 4–4½ lb/about 2 kg spare ribs | ½ oz/15 g castor sugar |
| **for the sauce:** | 1½ teaspoons salt |
| 1 small onion | 2 teaspoons chilli powder |
| 1 clove garlic | ¼ teaspoon cayenne pepper |
| 4 oz/100 g butter | 2 teaspoons Worcestershire sauce |
| scant ½ pint/2·5 dl water | ½ teaspoon Tabasco sauce |
| 3 tablespoons vinegar | 1 teaspoon black pepper |
| 1 teaspoon dry mustard | 1 teaspoon paprika |

To precook the spare ribs and make them moist and juicy, spread the spare ribs in a large roasting tin, cover tightly with aluminium foil and bake the ribs in a moderate oven (350°F, 180°C, Gas Mark 4) for 1½ hours. Meanwhile, prepare the sauce. Peel and finely chop the onion and garlic. Place in a saucepan with the butter, water and vinegar. Add the mustard, sugar, salt, chilli powder, cayenne pepper, Worcestershire sauce, Tabasco sauce, black pepper and paprika. Bring to the boil and simmer for 30 minutes.

When the spare ribs have cooked for the required time, remove the foil and baste the ribs with the sauce. Continue cooking for a further 30 minutes, turning the spare ribs from time to time in the sauce.

*Note:* This sauce may be used to baste steaks, chops or chicken during roasting or barbecuing.

# OYSTERS ROCKEFELLER

*Serves 4*

| | |
|---|---|
| 1 stick celery | 1½ tablespoons Pernod or anisette |
| 6 spring onions | 1 tablespoon Worcestershire sauce |
| 1 small clove garlic | salt |
| 8 oz/225 g butter | freshly ground black pepper |
| small bunch parsley, chopped | cayenne pepper |
| 1½ lb/700 g chopped cooked spinach | rock salt (see recipe) |
| ¼ teaspoon aniseed | 24 freshly opened oysters on half shell |
| 2 oz/50 g toast crumbs | |

Chop the celery very finely, chop the spring onions and peel and crush the garlic. Melt the butter in a frying pan and sauté the celery, spring onions, garlic and parsley for about 4 minutes, or until the vegetables are softened. Transfer the mixture to a liquidiser and add the spinach, aniseed, toast crumbs, Pernod and Worcestershire sauce. Add salt, pepper and cayenne pepper to taste. Liquidise until the sauce is thoroughly puréed. If a liquidiser is not available, rub the ingredients through a sieve or pound in a mortar until reduced to a pulp.

Spread a thick layer of rock salt on each of 4 individual gratin dishes. Arrange 6 oysters on each dish. Spread 1 tablespoon of the sauce over each oyster, spreading it to the edge of the shell. Place the dishes in a very hot oven (450°F, 230°C, Gas Mark 8) and bake for 5 minutes, or until the sauce bubbles.

# ISLAND SHRIMPS

*Serves 4*

1 lb/450 g uncooked shrimps or prawns
3 cloves garlic
3 fresh or dried chillies
6 tablespoons lime juice or generous ¼ pint/1·5 dl lemon juice
1 teaspoon salt

Put the shrimps or prawns into a saucepan with salted water to cover. Bring to the boil and simmer gently for 5 minutes. Drain and put the shrimps immediately into iced water. Peel and remove the dark vein running down the back of each shrimp. Peel and finely chop the garlic and finely chop the chillies.

Put the shrimps into a glass bowl and sprinkle with the garlic, chillies, lime juice and salt. Marinate the shrimps in the refrigerator for several hours before serving. Impale each shrimp on a cocktail stick and serve very cold as an appetiser.

# OLYMPIA OYSTER COCKTAIL

*Serves about 10*

1¾ pints/1 litre freshly opened oysters
4 sticks celery
6 tablespoons chilli sauce
1½ tablespoons lemon juice
2 teaspoons Worcestershire sauce
¼ teaspoon Tabasco sauce

Rinse the oysters well. Pick out any little bits of shell. Finely chop the celery and combine with the chilli sauce, lemon juice, Worcestershire sauce and Tabasco sauce. Stir in the oysters. Spoon the mixture into individual glasses and chill well before serving.

# GUACAMOLE

*Makes about ½ pint (3 dl)*

1 large avocado
1 small clove garlic
1 tablespoon olive oil
1 tablespoon lemon juice
2 teaspoons finely chopped onion
¼ teaspoon salt
¼ teaspoon freshly ground pepper
Tabasco sauce to taste

Peel the avocado, remove the stone and set it aside. Place the flesh in a bowl. Peel and crush the garlic. Mash the avocado coarsely with a silver fork to prevent discoloration and mix in the garlic, olive oil, lemon juice, onion, salt and pepper. Season the mixture generously with Tabasco sauce to taste. Place the stone in the mixture until ready to serve to prevent discoloration. Cover the bowl and place in the refrigerator until chilled. Discard the stone and serve the avocado as a dip with crisp uncooked vegetables or small savoury biscuits.

*Island shrimps*

# FLORIDA FROGS' LEGS

*Serves 2–3*

12 pairs frogs' legs or 1 (7¼-oz/
    205-g) can frogs' legs
2 oz/50 g plain flour
½ teaspoon salt
¼ teaspoon pepper
bacon dripping

2 oz/50 g butter
1 small clove garlic
1½ tablespoons lemon juice
watercress
radish roses

Soak the frogs' legs in lightly salted water for 2 hours. Combine the flour, salt and pepper. Drain the legs, dry on kitchen paper and then roll in the seasoned flour. Sauté the legs in hot bacon dripping in a frying pan for about 7 minutes, turning frequently. Arrange on a heated serving dish.

Pour off all the bacon dripping and add the butter to the pan. Peel and finely chop the garlic and sauté in the butter over moderate heat. As soon as the butter bubbles and begins to turn brown, stir in the lemon juice. Pour the sauce immediately over the frogs' legs and garnish with watercress and radish roses. (To make radish roses see Danish Blue Cheese and Radish open sandwich, page 80.)

# DAKOTA CORNED BEEF SAUERKRAUT BALLS

*Makes 50 balls*

1 (1-lb/454-g) can sauerkraut
generous ½ pint/4 dl water
1 small onion
1 (12-oz/340-g) can corned beef
2 oz/50 g butter
1 oz/25 g plain flour
¼ teaspoon dry mustard
1 teaspoon grated fresh
    horseradish root

generous ¼ pint/2 dl milk
2 oz/50 g dried breadcrumbs
2 eggs
flour (see recipe)
fine dried breadcrumbs for
    coating
oil for deep-frying

Empty the sauerkraut into a saucepan and add the water. Bring to the boil and simmer for 15 minutes. Peel and quarter the onion. Drain the sauerkraut thoroughly and put through the medium blade of a food shredder or chop with a sharp knife, together with the corned beef and the onion.

Melt the butter in a saucepan. Stir in the flour, mustard and horseradish. Gradually stir in the milk and cook, stirring constantly, until the sauce is smooth and very thick. Add the sauerkraut mixture and cook over low heat for 10 minutes, stirring occasionally. Stir in the breadcrumbs and cook for a few minutes longer. Chill for several hours or overnight.

Whisk the eggs. Form the sauerkraut mixture into 1-inch (2·5-cm) balls. Roll the balls in flour, dip in the beaten egg then roll in breadcrumbs. Heat the oil in a deep saucepan to 365°F (185°C) and fry the balls for 3–4 minutes, or until crisp and golden brown. Drain on kitchen paper. Serve as an appetiser.

*Note:* These may be made before required and refrigerated or frozen. Reheat in a moderately hot oven (400°F, 200°C, Gas Mark 6) for 10 minutes before serving.

# COLD CREAM OF CUCUMBER SOUP

*Serves 6*

1 large cucumber
1 medium-sized onion
scant ½ pint/2·5 dl water
½ teaspoon dried dill weed or mint
½ teaspoon salt
pinch pepper
1 oz/25 g plain flour
¾ pint/4·5 dl chicken stock

generous ⅓ pint/2 dl double cream
2 drops green food colouring

**for the garnish:**
4 oz/100 g cucumber
1 (5-oz/141-g) carton soured cream
fresh dill or mint

Peel and slice the cucumber. Peel and dice the onion. Place the cucumber and onion in a large saucepan and add the water, dill weed or mint, salt and pepper. Bring to the boil and simmer for 20 minutes, or until the cucumber and onion are tender. Blend the flour with a little of the chicken stock to make a thin paste and stir into the cucumber with the remaining chicken stock. Bring to the boil and simmer for 30 minutes. Press through a sieve or blend, half at a time, in a liquidiser to make a purée. Cool and chill. Before serving, stir in the cream and food colouring and correct the seasoning with salt and pepper.

Serve in individual soup plates garnished with unpeeled, thinly sliced cucumber, 1 tablespoon of soured cream for each serving and a sprinkling of chopped dill or mint.

# CORN CHOWDER

*Serves 4*

1 large onion
4 large potatoes
2 slices salt pork
1¼ pints/7·5 dl water
6 cream crackers
scant ½ pint/2·5 dl rich milk (half cream, half milk)

8 oz/225 g fresh or frozen sweet corn kernels or 1 (11½-oz/326-g) can sweet corn kernels, drained
salt and pepper
paprika

Peel and chop the onion. Peel and dice the potatoes. Cut the pork into small cubes and sauté in a large saucepan until crisp and golden brown. Add the onion and cook until soft and transparent. Add the potatoes and water. Bring to the boil and simmer for 20 minutes, or until the potatoes are tender.

Meanwhile, crumble the cream crackers into the rich milk and set aside to soften. When the potatoes are tender, add the softened crackers and the sweet corn. Season with salt and pepper to taste and cook over low heat for 5–10 minutes without boiling. Serve each portion with a sprinkling of paprika on top.

*Note:* The first corn chowder was made in Massachusetts. Now, in some parts of the country, chopped green sweet pepper is added; in other parts bits of tomato are added for flavour and colour.

*Corn chowder*

# NEW ENGLAND CLAM CHOWDER

*Serves 6*

| | |
|---|---|
| 1½ pints/9 dl fresh clams or 2 (7½-oz/212-g) cans shelled clams (see note) | 3 medium-sized potatoes |
| | 2 slices salt pork |
| | 1 small onion |
| 1 stick celery with leaves | 1 stick celery |
| 1 medium-sized onion | salt and pepper |
| 1 small bay leaf | ¾ pint/4·5 dl single cream |
| pinch thyme | 1 oz/25 g butter |
| 2 pints/generous litre cold water | paprika |

Scrub the clams and place in a large saucepan. Chop the celery coarsely, peel and dice the onion. Place in the pan with the clams and add the bay leaf, thyme and water. Bring to the boil, cover the pan tightly and cook for 10 minutes, or until the shells open. Remove the clams and discard the shells. Strain the clam liquid into a large saucepan through a sieve lined with muslin. Discard the strained vegetables and the bay leaf. Peel and cube the potatoes and simmer in the clam liquid for 20 minutes, or until tender.

Meanwhile, peel back the tough outer sheath from the soft belly of each clam and cut away the connecting cord. Dice the bellies and mince the tough outer sheaths. Cover with a little of the hot clam liquid and set aside.

Chop the salt pork and fry in a large saucepan until crisp and golden brown. Chop the onion and thinly slice the celery, add to the salt pork and cook over low heat for 10 minutes, or until the vegetables are tender. Add the clam liquid and potatoes, then simmer for 5–10 minutes longer. Season with salt and pepper to taste. Heat the cream. Just before serving, stir in the clams, butter and hot cream. Heat, but do not boil. Serve immediately in large heated soup bowls, sprinkling each serving with paprika. Serve with water biscuits.

*Note:* To make a chowder with canned shelled clams, drain the liquid from the clams into the saucepan, reserving the clams, and follow the recipe, adding a little water for additional liquid to cover the potatoes as they cook.

# PHILADELPHIA PEPPERPOT SOUP WITH DUMPLINGS

*Serves 8*

| | |
|---|---|
| **for the soup:** | salt and pepper |
| 2 lb/1 kg dressed honeycomb tripe | generous pinch cayenne pepper |
| 1 veal knuckle with meat | **for the dumplings:** |
| 1 large onion | 8 oz/225 g plain flour |
| 1 carrot | ½ teaspoon salt |
| 4 medium-sized potatoes | 4 oz/100 g shredded beef suet |
| 1 bay leaf | about ¼ pint/1·5 dl water |
| few sprigs parsley | 1 tablespoon finely chopped parsley |
| ½ teaspoon dried thyme | |
| ½ teaspoon crushed red chilli | |

The preparation of this dish should be commenced the day before it is required. Ask your butcher how much longer the tripe needs to be cooked. Put it into a heavy saucepan with 5¼ pints (3 litres) water and bring to the boil. Reduce the heat, cover and barely simmer for the required length of time, or until the tripe is tender. Let the tripe cool in the stock. When cool enough to handle, remove the tripe and cut into small pieces. Strain and reserve the stock, which should measure about 3 pints (1·5 litres).

While the tripe is cooking, wash the veal knuckle and put it into another heavy saucepan with water to cover. Bring the water to the boil and remove any scum that rises to the surface. Reduce the heat and simmer for 3 hours. Cool, then remove the meat from the veal bone and cut into small pieces. Add the veal meat to the tripe. Strain the veal stock into the tripe stock. Place the meat and stock in the refrigerator overnight.

Next day, remove any solidified fat from the surface of the stock and return the stock to the saucepan. Peel and dice the onion and carrot and add to the stock. Bring to the boil and simmer for 1 hour. Peel and dice the potatoes. Add the tripe and veal, potatoes, bay leaf, parsley, thyme, crushed chilli, salt and pepper to taste and cayenne pepper. The soup should be quite peppery. Continue to simmer for 45 minutes.

While the soup simmers, make the dumplings. Sift the flour and salt into a bowl. Add the suet and mix with a pastry blender or 2 knives or rub in with the fingertips until evenly mixed. Stir in just enough water to make a soft dough that can be rolled with floured fingers into nuggets the size of walnuts. Drop the dumplings into the simmering soup, cover the pan tightly and simmer for 10 minutes. Pour into a heated soup tureen, sprinkle with chopped parsley and serve.

# BRUNSWICK STEW

*Serves 8*

| | |
|---|---|
| 1 chicken, about 5 lb/2·25 kg | 12 oz/350 g fresh okra or 1 (13-oz/369-g) can okra |
| salt and pepper | |
| 5 pints/3 litres water | 1 lb/450 g fresh or frozen sweet corn kernels or 2 (11½-oz/326-g) cans sweet corn kernels |
| 2 medium-sized onions | |
| 1 lb/450 g potatoes | |
| 1½ lb/700 g tomatoes | 2 teaspoons salt |
| 1½ lb/700 g shelled broad beans | ½ teaspoon pepper |
| | 1 tablespoon castor sugar |

Cut the chicken into eight portions and season well. Place in a large saucepan, add the water and bring to the boil. Simmer the chicken for 1½ hours, or until the flesh is easily removed from the bones. Remove the chicken with a perforated spoon and when cool enough to handle, discard the bones and cut the meat into bite-sized pieces. Set aside.

Peel and slice the onions, peel and dice the potatoes and peel and chop the tomatoes. Add to the broth remaining in the pan with the broad beans and okra. Bring to the boil and cook over low heat until the vegetables are tender, stirring occasionally. Pour in a little hot water if necessary, to make a total of at least 2½ pints (1·5 litres) of liquid. Add the reserved chicken meat, the sweet corn, salt, pepper and sugar. Simmer for 15 minutes. Serve hot.

# LOBSTER STEW

*Serves 3*

| | |
|---|---|
| 4½ pints/2·5 litres water | 4 oz/100 g butter |
| 2 tablespoons salt | 1½ pints/9 dl hot rich milk (half |
| 1 live lobster, about 1½ lb/700 g | milk, half cream) |

Bring the water and salt to a rapid boil in a large saucepan. Plunge the live lobster head first into the water. Cover and cook for 8 minutes. Remove from the water and set aside to cool. When the lobster has cooled sufficiently to handle easily, split the body in half lengthwise and crack the claws. Remove the meat, discarding the gills, the intestinal vein that runs down the tail and the sac lying in the back of the head. Cut the meat into good-sized chunks. Save the green liver and the pink coral, if any.

Melt the butter in a heavy saucepan and simmer the liver and coral for 6 minutes. Add the lobster pieces and cook over very low heat for 5–10 minutes. Remove the pan from the heat and cool slightly. Slowly trickle in the milk, stirring constantly. Stirring is the most important part of this recipe, since curdling can take place unless the stew is stirred while adding the milk. Continue to stir until the stew becomes an attractive pink. Remove from the heat, cool, cover and refrigerate for 5–6 hours before reheating and serving.

# GRAND CENTRAL STATION OYSTER BAR STEW

*Serves 4–6*

| | |
|---|---|
| generous ¾ pint/5 dl single cream | 1 oz/25 g butter |
| ¾ pint/4·5 dl milk | salt and pepper |
| 1¼ pints/7·5 dl freshly opened | celery salt |
| oysters with their liquid | paprika |

Heat the cream and milk together in a saucepan but do not boil. Heat the oysters and their liquid with the butter in another saucepan until the oysters plump and the edges begin to curl. Remove from the heat immediately. Combine the hot cream mixture with the hot oysters and liquid. Season with salt, pepper and celery salt to taste. Pour into heated soup bowls and sprinkle with paprika. Serve with water biscuits.

*Note:* The Oyster Bar in Grand Central Station opened in 1912. It is still a favourite stopping-off place for commuters who enjoy this dish made according to the original recipe.

*Lobster stew*

# ALASKAN SALMON SUPPER LOAF

*Serves 6–8*

| | |
|---|---|
| 4 (7½-oz/212-g) cans salmon | ¼ teaspoon pepper |
| 1 large onion | 2 tablespoons chopped parsley |
| 4 sticks celery | 4 teaspoons grated lemon rind |
| 2 oz/50 g butter or margarine | 6 tablespoons lemon juice |
| 8 oz/225 g mushrooms | 2 eggs |
| 6 oz/175 g fine fresh breadcrumbs | 6 tablespoons milk |
| ½ teaspoon salt | 1½ lb/700 g potatoes |

Flake the salmon, reserving the liquid. Peel and chop the onion and chop the celery. Heat the butter in a frying pan and sauté the celery and onion in the butter for 10 minutes, or until tender. Peel and coarsely chop the mushrooms and sauté for 5 minutes with the celery and onion, stirring frequently. Combine the cooked vegetables with the breadcrumbs in a mixing bowl. Add the salmon, the reserved salmon liquid, salt and pepper, parsley, lemon rind and lemon juice. Lightly whisk the eggs and add to the salmon mixture with the milk.

Grease a large loaf tin or line the base with buttered greaseproof paper. Fill with the salmon mixture. Bake in a moderately hot oven (375°F, 190°C, Gas Mark 5) for 50 minutes.

Meanwhile, peel the potatoes and boil in salted water to cover until tender. Drain and cream with a little milk and butter. Keep warm until required.

Turn out the salmon loaf on to a heated serving platter. Remove the paper (if used) and garnish the top with creamed potato. Place under a hot grill for about 3 minutes, or until the potato topping is tinged with brown.

# SHRIMP CREOLE

*Serves 6*

| | |
|---|---|
| 1 large onion | 1 bay leaf, crushed |
| 2 cloves garlic | 1 large green sweet pepper |
| 4 tablespoons cooking oil | 3 tablespoons finely chopped |
| ½ oz/15 g plain flour | parsley |
| 4 tablespoons tomato purée | 2 tablespoons chopped spring |
| 1 (1-lb 12-oz/793-g) can tomatoes | onion tops |
| 1 teaspoon salt | 2 lb/1 kg uncooked shrimps or |
| ¼ teaspoon pepper | prawns, peeled and deveined |
| pinch cayenne pepper | |

Peel and very finely chop the onion and garlic. Heat the oil in a heavy saucepan and sauté the onion and garlic for about 5 minutes until transparent but not brown. Mix in the flour and cook, stirring constantly, until the mixture becomes lightly browned. Add the tomato purée, the tomatoes with their liquid, salt, pepper, cayenne pepper and the bay leaf. Bring to the boil, cover and simmer for 20 minutes. Halve the sweet pepper, remove the seeds and finely chop the flesh. Place in the pan with the parsley, spring onion tops and shrimps. Cover and simmer for 15 minutes longer. Serve over cooked rice with a tossed green salad.

# LOBSTER NEWBURG

*Serves 2–3*

| | |
|---|---|
| 1 oz/25 g butter | cayenne pepper |
| 12 oz/350 g cooked lobster meat in large chunks | generous ¼ pint/2 dl double cream |
| | 6 tablespoons sherry or Madeira |
| salt | 3 egg yolks |

Heat the butter in a heavy saucepan and sauté the lobster meat for several minutes, or until heated through. Sprinkle with salt and cayenne pepper to taste. Add the cream and sherry and bring the liquid to simmering point. Lightly whisk the egg yolks and combine with a little of the hot liquid, then stir into the lobster mixture. Cook over very low heat for about 2 minutes, stirring constantly, but do not boil. Serve on hot buttered toast or with cooked rice.

# FILLETS OF SOLE MARGUERY

*Serves 6*

**for the fish:**

| | |
|---|---|
| 6 fillets of sole or flounder | 12 uncooked shrimps or prawns, peeled and deveined |
| salt and pepper | **for the sauce:** |
| 1 oz/25 g melted butter | 3 oz/75 g butter |
| 6 tablespoons clam juice or fish stock | ½ oz/15 g plain flour |
| scant ¼ pint/2·5 dl dry white wine | scant ½ pint/2·5 dl milk |
| 1½ tablespoons lemon juice | 3 tablespoons double cream |
| **for the garnish:** | salt |
| 12 freshly opened oysters with their liquid | 2 egg yolks |

Arrange the fillets side by side in a buttered frying pan and sprinkle with salt, pepper and the melted butter. Pour the clam juice, wine and lemon juice around the fillets. Cover and poach over low heat for 10 minutes, basting occasionally. With a broad spatula carefully transfer the cooked fillets to a heated ovenproof serving dish; cover and keep warm. Bring the poaching liquid to the boil and boil until the liquid is reduced to about 6 tablespoons.

Meanwhile, in a separate pan poach the oysters in their own liquid, just until they plump and the edges curl. Drain the oyster liquid into the frying pan and boil again to reduce the volume of liquid in the pan. Arrange the oysters on top of the fillets. Poach the shrimps or prawns in water to cover for 5 minutes, drain and arrange around the fillets.

Melt one-third of the butter for the sauce in a heavy saucepan. Stir in the flour. Gradually stir in the milk and cook, stirring, until the sauce is smooth and thickened. Stir in the cream and add the reduced liquid. Cook over low heat for 5 minutes, stirring occasionally. Correct the seasoning with salt to taste. Combine the egg yolks with a little of the hot cream sauce, then stir into the remaining sauce. Stir over low heat while adding the remaining butter, little by little. Do not let the sauce boil. Pour the sauce over the fillets and put under the grill for 2–3 minutes, or until the sauce becomes tinged with brown.

# BAKED RED SNAPPER OR SEA BASS

*Serves 4*

| | |
|---|---|
| 1 red snapper or sea bass, about 3 lb/1·5 kg | 1 large onion |
| | 1½ lb/700 g tomatoes |
| salt and pepper | 2 tablespoons finely chopped parsley |
| ¼ teaspoon dry mustard | |
| 3 tablespoons bacon dripping | ½ teaspoon castor sugar |
| 1 tablespoon plain flour | |

Gut, wash and thoroughly dry the red snapper or bass. Rub the fish inside and out with salt, pepper and mustard. Place in a greased roasting tin and brush with 1 tablespoon of the bacon dripping. Sprinkle with the flour. Bake in a moderately hot oven (375°F, 190°C, Gas Mark 5) for 15 minutes, then reduce the heat to moderate (350°F, 180°C, Gas Mark 4).

Meanwhile, peel and finely chop the onion and sauté in the remaining bacon dripping in a frying pan until transparent. Peel and chop the tomatoes and add with the parsley and sugar to the pan. Bring to the boil and simmer for 5 minutes. Season the tomato mixture quite highly with salt and pepper and pour over the fish. Continue to bake for 40 minutes, basting occasionally with the sauce in the tin and adding a little boiling water, if necessary, if the sauce reduces too much. Transfer the fish to a heated serving dish and pour over the sauce.

# PLANKED LAKE SUPERIOR WHITEFISH

*Serves 4*

| | |
|---|---|
| 1 whitefish or grey mullet, about 3½–4 lb/1·5–1·75 kg | 1 egg yolk |
| | **for the sauce:** |
| salt and pepper | 4 oz/100 g melted butter |
| 2 oz/50 g butter | 1½ tablespoons lemon juice |
| 1½ tablespoons water | 2 tablespoons finely chopped parsley |
| 1 tablespoon lemon juice | |
| 2 lb/1 kg potatoes | |

Oil a hardwood plank about 2 inches (5 cm) thick or a large ovenproof plate and put it into a hot oven (450°F, 230°C, Gas Mark 8) for 10–15 minutes. Meanwhile, fillet the whitefish (see note). Place the fish fillets, skin side down, on the hot plank and sprinkle generously with salt and pepper. Dot with half the butter. Melt the remaining butter and stir in the water and lemon juice. Bake the fish in the hot oven for about 25 minutes, basting several times with the melted butter mixture.

Meanwhile, peel the potatoes and boil in salted water to cover until tender. Drain and cream with a little milk and butter.

Remove the plank from the oven and make a ring of potatoes around the fish, or pipe the creamed potatoes in swirls. Whisk the egg yolk with 1 tablespoon water and brush over the potatoes. Return the plank to the oven for 5 minutes, or until the potatoes are lightly browned.

To make the sauce, combine the melted butter, lemon juice and parsley and pour into a sauceboat. Serve the fish from the plank and serve the sauce separately.

*Note:* Gut and clean the fish and cut off the head. Cut along the backbone from head to tail. Insert the blade of the knife at a slight angle to the backbone. Keeping the sharp edge towards the tail, ease the flesh gently away from the bone with slicing movements. When the whole fillet is freed, open out the fish and cut off the fillet at the tail. Using the tip of the knife, ease off the backbone from the other fillet and cut off the tail. Cut the fillets into serving-size portions.

# POACHED HALIBUT WITH EGG SAUCE

*Serves 6*

3 pints/1·5 litres water
1 medium-sized onion
1 medium-sized carrot
2 sticks celery with leaves
few sprigs parsley
1¼ tablespoons lemon juice or
    vinegar
1 bay leaf
4 cloves
½ teaspoon peppercorns

2 teaspoons salt
3 lb/1·5 kg fresh halibut steaks
**for the sauce:**
1½ oz/40 g butter
1½ oz/40 g plain flour
generous ¾ pint/5 dl hot rich milk
    (half milk, half cream)
salt and pepper
3 hard-boiled eggs

Pour the water into a saucepan large enough to hold the halibut. Peel and coarsely chop the onion, carrot and celery and place in the saucepan with the parsley. Add the lemon juice, bay leaf, cloves, peppercorns and the salt. Bring to the boil and simmer for 20 minutes.

Carefully lower the fish into the simmering water. Bring the water to simmering point again, lower the heat and poach the fish until cooked. Allow 5 minutes per pound (per half kilo). Do not let the water boil.

When cooked, set aside the fish in the liquid and make the sauce. Melt the butter in a saucepan, add the flour and cook for a few moments, stirring constantly. Remove the pan from the heat. Add the milk all at once. Return the pan to the heat and cook, whisking or stirring rapidly, until the sauce is smooth and thickened. Add salt and pepper to taste. Cook over low heat for 5 minutes, stirring occasionally. Shell and chop the eggs and stir into the sauce. Remove the fish from the pan, place on a heated serving platter and pour the egg sauce over the fish.

*Planked Lake Superior whitefish*

*Oregon celery vinaigrette*

# CRAB LOUIS SALAD

*Serves 2*

| | |
|---|---|
| 1 lettuce | 1 tablespoon chilli sauce |
| 1 lb/450 g crab meat | 1 teaspoon lemon juice |
| 1 small green sweet pepper | pinch salt |
| 3 spring onions | **for the garnish:** |
| 6 green olives | 2 tomatoes, quartered |
| scant ½ pint/2·5 dl mayonnaise | 2 hard-boiled eggs, sliced |
| 3 tablespoons double cream | |

Wash and shred the lettuce and arrange on 2 individual plates. Divide the crab meat between the 2 plates. Place in the refrigerator to chill. Halve the green pepper, remove the seeds and very finely chop the flesh. Finely chop the spring onions and olives. Combine with the mayonnaise, cream, chilli sauce, lemon juice and salt.

Pour the dressing over the chilled crab meat and garnish with the tomato quarters and egg slices.

# OREGON CELERY VINAIGRETTE

*Serves 4*

| | |
|---|---|
| 4 large celery hearts | 1 tablespoon chopped green sweet |
| 1½ tablespoons vinegar | pepper |
| 4 tablespoons salad oil | 1 tablespoon chopped canned |
| ¼ teaspoon paprika | pimento |
| 1 teaspoon salt | |

Split the celery hearts lengthwise. Trim and wash thoroughly under cold running water. Place in a large saucepan and barely cover with lightly salted water. Simmer for 30–40 minutes, or until the celery is tender but still firm. Drain and cool.

Combine the vinegar, salad oil, paprika, salt, green sweet pepper and pimento. Pour the dressing over the cooked celery. Chill for at least 30 minutes before serving.

# CAESAR SALAD

*Serves 6–8*

| | |
|---|---|
| 1 clove garlic | ½ teaspoon salt |
| generous ¼ pint/2 dl olive oil | 2 eggs |
| 4 oz/100 g stale French bread, | 3 tablespoons lemon juice |
| diced | 8 anchovy fillets |
| 2 Cos lettuces | 2 oz/50 g fresh Parmesan cheese, |
| freshly ground black pepper | grated |

Peel and crush the garlic and add to the olive oil. Let stand overnight. The next day, heat a third of the garlic-flavoured oil in a small frying pan and sauté the bread cubes until golden. Drain on kitchen paper and set aside. Strain the remaining oil to remove the garlic.

Wash the lettuces and tear the leaves into a salad bowl. Sprinkle the black pepper and salt over the leaves. Add the remaining oil and toss until each leaf is glossy with the oil. Lower the eggs into a small saucepan of boiling water and boil for 1 minute. Remove the eggs and break them into the middle of the salad. Squeeze the lemon juice over the eggs and toss again until the lettuce leaves look creamy. Add the anchovy fillets and correct the seasoning of the salad with salt and lemon juice. Sprinkle with the Parmesan cheese, add the bread cubes and toss again lightly before serving.

# NEW ENGLAND BOILED DINNER

*Serves 8*

| | |
|---|---|
| 4 lb/1·75 kg salt brisket of beef | 2 lb/1 kg potatoes |
| 1 large bay leaf | 3 lb/1·5 kg small onions |
| 1 teaspoon peppercorns | 3 lb/1·5 kg small raw beetroot |
| 1 lb/450 g carrots | 1 large cabbage |

Wash the beef well and place in a large heavy saucepan with cold water to cover. Add the bay leaf and peppercorns. Bring to the boil, partially cover and simmer for 2½ hours, adding water if necessary to keep the meat covered all the time.

Peel and halve the carrots and peel the potatoes; add to the pan and simmer for 30 minutes. Peel the onions, add to the pan and simmer for a further 30 minutes. Meanwhile, steam or boil the beetroot in their skins for 45 minutes, or until tender. Peel and keep hot.

Transfer the beef from the pan to the centre of a large serving platter and keep hot. Discard the coarse outer leaves of the cabbage and cut away the hard centre core. Cut the head into 8 wedges. Add the wedges to the pan with the liquid and vegetables and simmer for 15 minutes.

Drain the vegetables and arrange around the beef. Alternatively, slice the meat across the grain into thin slices. Place a wedge of cabbage in the centre of each individual plate and cover with several slices of meat. Surround with the vegetables. Serve with mustard and creamed horseradish and, if liked, a sauceboat of melted butter with chopped parsley.

# POT ROAST WITH SOURED CREAM

*Serves 8*

| | |
|---|---|
| 6 lb/2·75 kg topside of beef | 2 (5-oz/141-g) cartons soured |
| 1 teaspoon salt | cream |
| freshly ground black pepper | 1 bay leaf |
| 2 tablespoons plain flour | 1 oz/25 g soft brown sugar |
| 2 small onions | 7 tablespoons tomato purée |
| 2 oz/50 g beef dripping or | 1½ pints/9 dl water |
| cooking fat | cornflour (see recipe) |

Rub the roast with the salt and pepper, then sprinkle with the flour. Peel and chop the onions. Heat the bacon dripping or fat in a large flameproof casserole and brown all sides of the beef evenly over moderate heat. Add the onions, soured cream, bay leaf, brown sugar, tomato purée and water. Cover tightly and roast in a moderate oven (350°F, 180°C, Gas Mark 4) for 3 hours, or until the meat is very tender.

Discard the bay leaf and transfer the meat to a heated serving platter. Allow 1½ teaspoons of cornflour per ½ pint (3 dl) liquid in the casserole. Blend the cornflour with cold water and stir into the casserole juices. Bring to the boil and cook, stirring constantly, until the gravy has thickened. Pour into a gravy boat and serve with the meat.

*New England boiled dinner*

# TAMALE CASSEROLE

*Serves 6*

8 oz/225 g *chorizos* (hot Spanish sausage)
1 large onion
2 cloves garlic
2 medium-sized green sweet peppers
8 oz/225 g lean beef, minced
4 oz/100 g fresh or frozen sweet corn kernels

2 oz/50 g black olives, sliced
1 tablespoon olive liquid from a can or jar of olives
½ teaspoon salt
1 tablespoon chilli powder
4 oz/100 g Cheddar cheese, grated
2 (15-oz/423-g) cans *tamales* in chilli gravy

Brown the sausage in a large frying pan. Meanwhile, peel and chop the onion and garlic very finely. Halve the green pepper, remove the seeds and dice the flesh. Remove the sausage from the frying pan and place on kitchen paper to drain. Pour off all but 3 tablespoons of the sausage dripping in the frying pan. Sauté the onion, garlic and the green pepper in the pan until tender and the onion is golden brown. Stir in the minced beef and cook, stirring frequently, until the meat loses all red colour. Break or crumble the sausage and add to the beef with the sweet corn, olives, olive liquid, salt and chilli powder. Mix well and simmer for 15 minutes. Spoon the mixture into a large shallow baking dish.

Remove and discard the corn husks from the *tamales* and arrange them on top of the meat mixture in the baking dish. Pour over any extra gravy from the cans of *tamales*. Bake uncovered in a moderate oven (350°F, 180°C, Gas Mark 4) for 20 minutes. Sprinkle with the cheese and return the dish to the oven for a further 15 minutes, or until the cheese has melted and the sauce is bubbling. Serve immediately.


# ROAST LEG OF LAMB WITH APRICOTS

*Serves 8–10*

1 tablespoon salt
2 teaspoons dry mustard
1 tablespoon plain flour
¼ teaspoon pepper
1 leg of lamb, about 6 lb/2·75 kg

2 (15½-oz/440-g) cans apricot halves in syrup
1 stick cinnamon, about 2 inches/5 cm
mint jelly (see recipe)
mint leaves (optional)

Combine salt, mustard, flour and pepper in a small bowl. Wipe the lamb with a damp cloth and arrange it meaty side up on a rack in an open roasting tin. Sprinkle with the mixed seasonings and roast in a very hot oven (475°F, 240°C, Gas Mark 9) for 30 minutes. Reduce the temperature to moderate (350°F, 180°C, Gas Mark 4) and continue to roast for an additional 1 hour for medium rare, or 1½ hours for well done.

Meanwhile, place the apricot halves and syrup in a saucepan. Add the cinnamon stick, bring to the boil and simmer for 3 minutes.

Remove the roast from the tin and place on a heated serving plate. Surround with the apricot halves cut side up. Place 1 teaspoon mint jelly in each apricot half. If fresh mint leaves are available, garnish each half with a mint leaf in addition to the jelly.


# SMITHFIELD HAM COOKED WITH APPLES

*Serves a party*

1 cured ham, about 14 lb/6·5 kg
1½ lb/700 g cooking apples
1 lb/450 g soft brown sugar
¾ pint/4·5 dl cider vinegar

**for the glaze:**
4 oz/100 g soft brown sugar
4 tablespoons French mustard
1½ tablespoons dry sherry
whole cloves (see recipe)

Soak the ham for up to 24 hours, changing the water at least 3 times to remove the salt. Wash in cold running water and scrub with a stiff brush. Put the ham in a large saucepan, cover with water and bring to the simmering point. Peel and quarter the apples and add to the pan with the brown sugar and the vinegar. Partially cover the pan and simmer for 18 minutes per pound (per half kilo), or until the small bone at the shank end can be easily removed. The ham should be completely covered with water throughout the cooking time.

When the ham is cooked take it out of the pan, discard the liquid and when the ham is cool enough to handle, remove the skin and trim off the excess fat. Score the remaining fat deeply into diamonds.

For the glaze, mix the brown sugar, mustard and sherry to a paste. Spread the mixture evenly over the fatty surface of the ham. Stud each diamond with a whole clove and bake in a moderate oven (350°F, 180°C, Gas Mark 4) for about 40 minutes, or until the crust is well browned, basting occasionally with the juices. Cool and serve very thinly sliced.


# OREGON HAM SLICE WITH FRUIT

*Serves 4*

1 large slice gammon, about 1 inch/2·5 cm thick
1 teaspoon butter or margarine
8 oz/225 g crushed strawberries, with juice
1½ tablespoons water

few cloves
4 oz/100 g castor sugar
1½ tablespoons lemon juice
2 canned pineapple rings
4 whole strawberries

Cut the ham into quarters. Melt the butter in a heavy frying pan, brown the ham lightly on both sides then transfer to a shallow baking dish. Add 2 tablespoons of the strawberry juice and the water to the juices remaining in the pan. Swirl the pan over moderate heat until the liquid simmers, then pour the liquid over the ham. Cover the baking dish with aluminium foil and bake in a moderately hot oven (375°F, 190°C, Gas Mark 5) for 45 minutes. Remove the ham from the oven and stud the fatty parts with cloves.

Meanwhile, combine the crushed strawberries, sugar and lemon juice in a saucepan and bring to the boil. Pour the hot fruit over the ham and return to the oven, uncovered, to bake for 20 minutes longer. Baste occasionally with the juices. Place the pineapple rings under a hot grill for 2–3 minutes. Transfer the ham and sauce to a heated serving platter and garnish with halved pineapple rings. Place a whole strawberry in the groove of each pineapple half.

*Crown roast with sweet corn stuffing*

# CROWN PORK ROAST WITH SWEET CORN STUFFING

*Serves 8*

6–7 lb/2·75–3·25 kg
   crown roast of pork
   (12–14 ribs)
salt and pepper
**for the stuffing:**
1 egg
1 medium-sized onion
1 small green sweet pepper

6 oz/175 g fresh or frozen sweet
   corn kernels or 1 (11½-oz/326-g)
   can sweet corn kernels, drained
1 (10-oz/283-g) can cream style
   sweet corn
3 oz/75 g fine fresh breadcrumbs
1½ teaspoons salt
pinch pepper
preserved kumquats (see recipe)

Ask the butcher to prepare the crown roast, forming the rib chops into a neat ring. Sprinkle with salt and pepper and place in a shallow roasting tin. Wrap pieces of aluminium foil around the bone ends to keep them from charring. Roast in a moderate oven (325°F, 160°C, Gas Mark 3) for 1½ hours.

Meanwhile, prepare the corn stuffing. Lightly whisk the egg. Peel and very finely chop the onion. Halve the green pepper, remove the seeds and finely chop the flesh. Combine the egg, onion and green pepper with the whole kernel sweet corn, cream style sweet corn, breadcrumbs, salt and pepper. Mix well.

Remove the roast from the oven and fill the centre of the ring with the stuffing, piling it up high in the centre. Return to the oven and roast for a further 1½ hours, or until the meat is well cooked. Transfer to a heated serving platter. Remove the foil from the bone tips, and either place paper frills over the tips before serving or place a preserved kumquat over each bone tip.

# PUERTO RICAN PORK LOIN ROAST

*Serves 8*

6 lb/2·75 kg loin of pork
2 large cloves garlic
2 teaspoons oregano
½ teaspoon coarsely ground black
   pepper
2 teaspoons salt

6 tablespoons olive oil
6 tablespoons unsweetened orange
   juice or lime juice
¾ pint/4·5 dl hot water
1 oz/25 g plain flour
pinch cayenne pepper

Make deep cuts between the ribs of the loin. Peel and finely chop the garlic and mix with the oregano, pepper, salt and olive oil. Thoroughly rub the mixture into the cuts and all over the surface of the meat. Place the meat in the refrigerator overnight. Put the loin, meat side up, on a rack in a shallow open roasting tin and roast in a moderate oven (350°F, 180°C, Gas Mark 4) for about 3 hours. Baste with the orange juice and the hot water, a little at a time, during roasting. When the meat is brown and well roasted, remove from the oven and transfer to a heated serving platter. Pour the juices from the tin into a large measuring jug and allow the fat to rise to the surface.

Return 3 tablespoons of the fat to the roasting tin and discard the rest of the fat. The remaining liquid should measure 1¼ pints (7·5 dl). If not, add hot water to make up this amount. Place the roasting tin over direct heat and stir in the flour. Cook, stirring, until the mixture bubbles. Gradually stir in the hot liquid, stirring constantly while scraping the bottom and sides of the tin with a wooden spoon to loosen all the brown particles. When smooth and thickened, add a pinch of cayenne pepper and correct the seasoning with salt. Strain into a gravy boat and serve with the roast.

# CHICKEN OKRA GUMBO

*Serves 6*

1 chicken, about 4–5 lb/
   1·75–2·25 kg
3 oz/75 g margarine or cooking
   fat
1 large onion
12 oz/350 g tomatoes
1 clove garlic
2 sticks celery

1 oz/25 g plain flour
1½ lb/700 g fresh okra
6 pints/3·5 litres water
2 bay leaves
½ teaspoon dried thyme
salt and pepper
cayenne pepper

Cut the chicken into serving portions. Heat the margarine in a large heavy saucepan and sauté the chicken until browned on all sides. Meanwhile, peel and chop the onion and tomatoes. Finely chop the garlic and chop the celery. Drain the chicken pieces and set aside. Stir the flour into the hot fat remaining in the pan. Cook over moderate heat, stirring constantly, until the mixture becomes golden brown. Add the onion, garlic and celery to the flour mixture. Cover and cook over low heat for about 10 minutes, or until the vegetables are tender.

Slice the okra and add to the pan. Cook for about 10 minutes or until the ingredients are well blended. Add the chicken pieces, water, bay leaves, thyme and the salt, pepper and cayenne pepper to taste. Bring to the boil and simmer for about 1½ hours, or until the chicken is tender. Serve with cooked rice.

# MARYLAND FRIED CHICKEN WITH CREAM GRAVY

*Serves 4*

**for the chicken:**
1 chicken, about 3 lb/1·5 kg
2 oz/50 g plain flour
1 teaspoon salt
¼ teaspoon pepper
4 oz/100 g butter

scant ½ pint/2·5 dl water
**for the gravy:**
1½ oz/40 g plain flour
generous ¾ pint/5 dl single cream
salt and pepper

Cut the chicken into quarters. Wash and dry each portion thoroughly. Combine the flour, salt and pepper in a paper bag and shake the chicken portions in the seasoned flour until well coated. Melt the butter in a heavy frying pan and brown the chicken quickly on all sides. Reduce the heat to low, add the water, cover and cook for 30 minutes. Remove the lid and continue to cook for 20–30 minutes, or until the chicken is very tender and crisp. Transfer to a serving dish and keep warm.

To make the gravy, stir the flour into the dripping remaining in the frying pan. Gradually stir in the cream. Add salt and pepper to taste. Cook over moderate heat, stirring constantly, until the gravy is smooth and thickened. Simmer for 3 minutes then pour into a heated sauceboat.

Garnish the chicken pieces with fried bananas and bacon rolls and serve with the cream sauce and Dutch Welshkorn oysters (see page 28).

# CREAMED CHICKEN

*Serves 4*

1 chicken, about 3½ lb/1·5 kg
1 medium-sized onion
3 sticks celery with leaves
½ lemon
2 teaspoons salt
½ teaspoon peppercorns
1 large clove garlic

1 fresh or dried chilli
1 bay leaf
½ teaspoon dried thyme
2 egg yolks
3 tablespoons lemon juice
2 oz/50 g butter
1 oz/25 g plain flour

Place the chicken, breast down, in a large heavy saucepan. Add enough water to come about three-quarters of the way up the sides of chicken. Peel and slice the onion, coarsely chop the celery and slice the lemon. Add the onion, celery, lemon, salt, peppercorns, garlic, chilli, bay leaf and thyme to the pan. Place the pan over high heat and bring the liquid to simmering point, lower the heat, partially cover and simmer for 1½ hours, or until the chicken is very tender. Add

*Maryland fried chicken with cream gravy*

additional salt to the broth to taste, seasoning it rather highly.

Whisk the egg yolks and lemon juice in a cup or small bowl. Set aside. Melt the butter in a heavy saucepan. Stir in the flour and cook, stirring, until the mixture bubbles. Remove from the heat. Remove the chicken from the broth and keep warm. Strain the broth through a sieve into a bowl and reserve 1½ pints (9 dl). Discard the vegetables and spices. Any excess broth may be used in another recipe or for soup. Add the reserved broth to the butter mixture, return to the heat and stir constantly until the sauce is smooth and slightly thickened. Add a little of the hot sauce to the egg yolk mixture and stir the egg yolk mixture into the hot sauce. Cook, stirring, for 1 minute, being careful not to allow the sauce to boil. Remove immediately from the heat.

Slice the chicken breast and thigh meat on to a heated serving plate and coat generously with the sauce. Serve with cooked rice.

# CHICKEN JAMBALAYA

*Serves 4*

| | |
|---|---|
| 1 chicken, about 4 lb/1·75 kg | 1 bay leaf |
| 1 large onion | few drops Tabasco sauce |
| 2 cloves garlic | pinch powdered saffron |
| 6 spring onions | 2 pints/generous litre water |
| 1 green sweet pepper | 1 lb/450 g long-grain rice |
| 6 tablespoons olive oil | 1 canned pimento |
| 1 (14-oz/396-g) can tomatoes | 1 (10-oz/283-g) packet frozen |
| 1 tablespoon salt | *petits pois* |

Cut the chicken into four portions. Peel and finely chop the onion and garlic. Trim and chop the spring onions. Halve the green pepper, remove the seeds and slice the flesh. Heat the olive oil in a large flameproof casserole and sauté the chicken until well browned. Remove the chicken and set aside.

Add the onion, garlic, spring onions and the green pepper to the hot oil remaining in the casserole. Sauté for about 5 minutes, or until lightly browned, adding a little more oil if necessary. Drain the tomatoes and reserve the liquid. Add the salt, bay leaf, Tabasco sauce, powdered saffron and drained tomatoes to the casserole. Cook over low heat for 6–7 minutes. Add the browned chicken, tomato liquid, water and rice. Stir to mix and bring the liquid to a rapid boil. Remove from the heat, cover tightly and bake in a moderately hot oven (400°F, 200°C, Gas Mark 6) for about 45–50 minutes, or until the rice is tender and most of the liquid has been absorbed.

Cut the pimento into thin strips. Heat the peas, drain and sprinkle over the rice. Garnish with strips of pimento.

# POLYNESIAN CHICKEN

*Serves 4*

| | |
|---|---|
| 6 oz/175 g fresh coconut, grated | 1 teaspoon ground coriander |
| ½ pint/3 dl boiling water | 1 chicken, about 3–4 lb/1·5 kg |
| 1 small onion | 1 tablespoon castor sugar |
| 2 cloves garlic | 1 tablespoon vinegar |
| 1½ tablespoons groundnut oil | scant ½ pint/2·5 dl coconut milk |
| 1 teaspoon salt | (see recipe) |
| ½ teaspoon turmeric | |

To make the coconut milk, pour the boiling water over the grated coconut and let stand for 20 minutes. Strain through a fine sieve or muslin, pressing out as much 'milk' from the coconut as possible. Reserve the amount required for the recipe.

Meanwhile, peel and finely chop the onion and garlic. Heat the groundnut oil in a large saucepan and sauté the onion with the garlic until the onion is tender but not brown. Stir in the salt, turmeric and coriander. Cut the chicken into four portions and sauté in the spice mixture about 5 minutes on each side, or until the chicken is lightly browned. Add the sugar, vinegar and coconut milk. Simmer very gently over low heat for 20 minutes.

Before serving, remove the chicken from the sauce and grill under an electric or gas grill or barbecue over glowing coals until brown and tender, basting frequently with the remaining sauce. Serve with cooked rice.

# ROAST GOOSE WITH FRUIT STUFFINGS

*Serves 8*

1 goose, about 10–12 lb/
   4·5–5·5 kg
1 teaspoon salt
1 orange
2 tablespoons lemon juice
**for the apricot stuffing:**
4 oz/100 g dried apricots
1 stick celery
1 tablespoon finely chopped
   parsley
5 oz/150 g dried breadcrumbs
1 oz/25 g cream cracker crumbs
¾ teaspoon salt

¼ teaspoon paprika
1 oz/25 g melted butter or melted
   goose fat
**for the wild rice and chestnut
stuffing:**
8 oz/225 g chestnuts
7 oz/200 g wild rice or brown rice
1¼ pints/7·5 dl water
1 teaspoon salt
½ small onion
4 oz/100 g melted butter or
   melted goose fat
¼ teaspoon pepper

Wipe the goose with a damp cloth and sprinkle inside and out with salt. Grate the orange rind and squeeze the orange. Mix together the orange rind and juice and lemon juice.

To make the apricot stuffing, cover the apricots with water and bring to the boil. Simmer for 20 minutes, or until plump and tender. Drain the apricots and reserve the liquid. Chop the celery. Chop the apricots and combine with the celery, parsley, breadcrumbs, cream cracker crumbs, salt, paprika and melted butter. Moisten with the apricot liquid. Set aside.

To make the wild rice and chestnut stuffing, slit the skins of the chestnuts, place in a saucepan, cover with water and bring to the boil. Simmer gently for 30 minutes, or until the chestnuts are tender. Set the chestnuts aside to cool, then remove the skins. Wash the rice well and put into a saucepan with the water and salt. Bring to the boil and simmer for 40 minutes, or until tender. Drain. Peel and chop the onion very finely. Combine the rice, chestnuts, onion, melted butter and pepper. Mix well and set aside.

Lightly fill the neck cavity of the goose with apricot stuffing and the body cavity with wild rice and chestnut stuffing. Sew up or skewer together the openings and truss the goose. Prick the skin generously with a fork, paying particular attention to the fatty areas around the legs and wings. Place the goose, breast down, on a rack in a shallow roasting tin and roast in a moderate oven (325°F, 160°C, Gas Mark 3) for 3 hours, removing the fat from the tin as it accumulates. Turn the goose breast up and pour the orange juice mixture over it. Continue to roast for 2 hours longer for a 10 lb (4·5 kg) goose, or 3 hours longer for a 12 lb (5·5 kg) goose. For a smaller goose roast for a total of 30 minutes per pound (per half kilo). Baste occasionally with the juices in the tin during the rest of the roasting period. Remove the trussing strings or skewers before serving.

*Roast goose with fruit stuffings*

# ROAST TURKEY WITH YAQUINA OYSTER STUFFING

*Serves 14–16*

**for the stuffing:**
8 oz/225 g turkey fat, chopped
1 large onion
4 sticks celery
1–1½ lb/450–700 g dried breadcrumbs
3½ teaspoons salt
1 teaspoon pepper
1 teaspoon dried sage

24 freshly opened oysters with their liquid
**for the turkey:**
1 turkey, about 10–12 lb/ 4·5–5·5 kg
salt
8 oz/225 g butter
1 oz/25 g plain flour
6 tablespoons boiling water

For the stuffing, heat the turkey fat in a frying pan until the fat is rendered and the bits of tissue are crispy. Peel and chop the onion. Chop the celery. Add the onion and the celery to the pan and sauté for about 10 minutes, or until tender but not brown. Combine the onion and celery in a mixing bowl with the breadcrumbs, salt, pepper and sage. Fold in the oysters and their liquid.

Loosely stuff the filling into the turkey cavity and neck area allowing enough space for expansion. Sew up or skewer together the openings and truss the turkey. Place the turkey on its side on a rack in a large open roasting tin and sprinkle with salt. Cream half the butter with the flour and spread the breast, legs and wings with this mixture.

Roast in a hot oven (450°F, 230°C, Gas Mark 8) for 30 minutes, then reduce the oven temperature to moderate (350°F, 180°C, Gas Mark 4). Roast for 3 hours longer. Melt the remaining butter in the boiling water and pour a little over the roasting turkey at half-hour intervals. After 1 hour, turn the turkey to the other side. After 2 hours, turn the bird breast side up for the remainder of the roasting time. If the turkey browns too quickly, cover the breast and thighs with aluminium foil or a buttered cloth. Remove the trussing strings or skewers before serving.

# MINNESOTA WILD RICE CASSEROLE

*Serves 6*

14 oz/400 g wild rice or brown rice
2 teaspoons salt
1 green sweet pepper

2 small onions
8 sticks celery
4 oz/100 g butter

Wash the rice thoroughly in several changes of water, then soak in cold water for 2 hours. Drain, place in a saucepan and cover generously with boiling water. Add the salt, bring to the boil and cook, uncovered, for 30 minutes. Drain thoroughly and set aside.

Halve the green pepper and remove the seeds. Peel the onions. Finely chop the pepper, onions and the celery. Melt the butter in a frying pan and sauté the vegetables for about 10 minutes, or until partially soft but not brown. Stir the vegetables and butter into the rice. Transfer to a buttered 3-pint (1·5-litre) casserole. Cover and bake in a moderate oven (350°F, 180°C, Gas Mark 4) for 1 hour.

# SUCCOTASH

*Serves 6*

1 (8-oz/226-g) packet frozen broad beans
generous ¼ pint/2 dl water
8 oz/225 g fresh or frozen sweet corn kernels or 1 (11½-oz/326-g) can sweet corn kernels
1 oz/25 g butter
½ teaspoon salt
freshly ground black pepper
6 tablespoons single cream
2 tablespoons chopped parsley

Place the frozen broad beans and water in a saucepan. Bring to the boil and simmer until the beans are easily separated with a fork. Cover and cook over low heat for 3 minutes. Drain and retain the beans in the pan. Add the sweet corn kernels, butter, salt and pepper to taste and then the cream. Cook over low heat for 20–30 minutes, but do not allow the cream to boil. Transfer to a heated dish, garnish with the chopped parsley and serve.

# LOUISIANA RED BEANS

*Serves 8*

1 lb/450 g dried red kidney beans
1 ham bone with a generous amount of meat
1 teaspoon salt
1 large onion
1 clove garlic
1 stick celery
¼ green sweet pepper
1 large bay leaf
1 tablespoon castor sugar
pinch cayenne pepper
2 tablespoons chopped parsley
cooked rice (see recipe)

Wash and pick over the beans. Place in a bowl, cover with cold water and soak overnight.

Place the beans and the water in which they were soaked in a saucepan, add the ham bone and salt and bring to the boil. Cook over low heat for 1½ hours, adding a little boiling water from time to time if the beans become too dry. Peel and finely chop the onion and garlic. Chop the celery and the green pepper. Crush the bay leaf. Add the onion, garlic, celery, green pepper, bay leaf, sugar, cayenne pepper and parsley to the pan and continue cooking for 30 minutes–1 hour, or until the beans are very tender and moist. Serve over mounds of cooked rice.

# BOSTON BAKED BEANS

*Serves 6*

1 lb/450 g haricot beans
8 oz/225 g salt pork
1 medium-sized onion
1½ teaspoons salt
1 teaspoon dry mustard
1 teaspoon black pepper
6 tablespoons black treacle

Pick over the beans and soak overnight in plenty of cold water. Drain, place in a saucepan and cover with fresh water. Bring slowly to the boil and simmer gently for 1¼ hours, or until tender but not overcooked. Add boiling water, if necessary, to keep the beans covered with liquid.

Soak the salt pork in boiling water for 10 minutes. Drain and cut off two thin slices. Put one slice on the bottom of a 3-pint (1·5-litre) casserole and slice the other into slivers. Score the remaining salt pork deeply at frequent intervals, but without cutting all the way through. Set aside.

Using a perforated spoon, transfer the beans from their cooking liquid to the casserole. Stir in the slivered salt pork. Peel the onion and bury it in the centre of the beans. Combine the salt, mustard, pepper and black treacle with ½ pint (3 dl) of the bean liquid and pour over the beans. Add enough additional bean liquid or boiling water to just cover. Push the scored piece of salt pork into the centre of the beans. Cover and bake in a very cool oven (250°F, 130°C, Gas Mark ½) for 6 hours. Uncover during the last half hour to brown the beans on top and add more liquid from time to time, if needed, to keep them moist.

# LOUISIANA CANDIED SWEET POTATOES

*Serves 4*

4 medium-sized sweet potatoes, about 2½ lb/1·25 kg
6 oz/175 g soft brown sugar
2 oz/50 g castor sugar
¼ teaspoon salt
½ teaspoon freshly grated nutmeg
3 oz/75 g butter
4 paper-thin slices lemon
3 tablespoons water

Peel the sweet potatoes and cut into strips similar in size to potato chips or ½ inch (1 cm) wide by 2 inches (5 cm) in length. Place in an 8- by 12-inch (20- by 30-cm) ovenproof dish. Sprinkle with the brown sugar, castor sugar, salt and nutmeg, then dot with butter. Place the lemon slices on top and add the water to the dish. Bake in a moderately hot oven (400°F, 200°C, Gas Mark 6) for 1 hour, or until the sweet potatoes are tender and the sugar and butter have become the consistency of thick syrup. During baking, baste occasionally with the syrup in the dish.

# DEEP-FRIED OKRA

*Serves 4*

1 lb/450 g young fresh or frozen okra
¾ pint/4·5 dl water
¼ teaspoon salt
1½ tablespoons lemon juice
1 egg
1 tablespoon cold water
pinch salt
pinch cayenne pepper
cracker or fine bread crumbs (see recipe)
cooking fat for deep-frying

If using fresh okra, wash and trim the stalks. Do not cut into the pods or the juice will be lost. Place the water, salt and lemon juice in a saucepan and bring to the boil. Drop in the pods and simmer for 10 minutes. Drain well.

Whisk the egg with the cold water and add the salt and cayenne pepper. Dip each okra into this mixture and roll in the fine crumbs. Deep-fry until golden brown in cooking fat heated to 365°F (185°C). Drain on kitchen paper and serve hot.

*Succotash*

# BAKED BANANAS

*Serves 6*

2 lb/1 kg bananas, not too ripe
2 oz/50 g melted butter

2 oz/50 g soft brown sugar
3 tablespoons rum

Peel and split the bananas lengthwise and arrange them in a buttered shallow ovenproof dish. Sprinkle the melted butter, brown sugar and rum over the bananas. Bake in a moderate oven (350°F, 180°C, Gas Mark 4) for 20 minutes. Serve hot or flambé with rum for special occasions.

# SPICED PEACHES

*Makes 4 lb (1·75 kg)*

6 lb/2·75 kg fresh clingstone
   peaches
3 lb/1·5 kg castor sugar
generous ¾ pint/5 dl water
1 stick cinnamon, about 4 inches/
   10 cm

12 cloves
1 oz/25 g whole ginger
scant ¾ pint/4 dl wine vinegar

Drop the peaches into rapidly boiling water for 1 minute, remove and strip off the skins. Put half the sugar with the water in a saucepan. Bring to the boil and boil rapidly for 5 minutes. Lower the heat, drop the peeled peaches into the syrup and simmer for 5 minutes. Take the pan off the heat and let the peaches stand in the syrup for 2–3 hours.

Remove the peaches. Tie the cinnamon, cloves and ginger in a muslin bag and add to the syrup. Add the vinegar and remaining sugar. Bring to the boil and boil rapidly for 10–15 minutes. Return the peaches to the pan and simmer for about 20 minutes, or until the peaches are tender and the syrup is thick.

Remove the pan from the heat and let the peaches stand in the syrup overnight. Discard the spice bag and pack the peaches into sterilized jars. Bring the syrup to the boil and pour over the peaches to fill the jars. If preferred, a stick of cinnamon and a few cloves may be added to each jar. Seal the jars and store. This is an excellent preserve to serve with roast meats or poultry.

*Baked bananas*

26

# FROZEN RUM CREAM

*Serves 6–8*

4 egg yolks
2 oz/50 g castor sugar
3 egg whites

generous ½ pint/3 dl double cream
6 tablespoons dark rum

Whisk the egg yolks and sugar in a mixing bowl until thick and pale in colour. Whisk the egg whites in another bowl until stiff and glossy and fold into the egg yolk mixture. Whip the cream and fold into the mixture. Stir in the rum. Turn into a refrigerator tray and freeze for 8 hours before serving.

# BURNT CREAM

*Serves 6*

2 oz/50 g castor sugar
2 teaspoons cornflour
6 egg yolks

1 pint/6 dl double cream
2 teaspoons vanilla essence
6 oz/175 g soft brown sugar

Gradually beat the sugar and cornflour into the egg yolks and continue to beat for 2–3 minutes, or until the mixture is thick and pale in colour. Heat the cream to simmering point and gradually pour it into the egg yolk mixture, stirring constantly.

Strain the mixture into a saucepan and cook over gentle heat, stirring rapidly and constantly with a wooden spoon, reaching all over the bottom and sides of the pan, until the cream thickens enough to coat the spoon. Be careful not to let it boil. Remove from the heat and continue to stir rapidly for 2 minutes to cool the cream. Stir in the vanilla essence and pour the cream into a heat-resistant serving dish. Chill for several hours or overnight.

Put the bowl in a shallow tin containing cracked ice. Sprinkle the brown sugar evenly over the top of the cream and place under the grill for 4–5 minutes, or until the sugar melts and caramelises. Be careful not to let the sugar burn. Serve immediately or chill again for several hours before serving.

# LEMON CHEESECAKE

*Serves 6*

**for the crust:**
6 oz/175 g digestive biscuits
4 oz/100 g castor sugar
¼ teaspoon grated nutmeg
2 oz/50 g melted butter
**for the filling:**
1 lb/450 g cream cheese

2 eggs
1 tablespoon lemon juice
2 (5-oz/141-g) cartons soured
  cream
4 oz/100 g castor sugar
1 oz/25 g melted butter

To make the crust, crush the digestive biscuits and mix with the sugar, nutmeg and melted butter. Line a buttered 9-inch (23-cm) flan dish with the crumb mixture.

To make the filling, allow the cream cheese to soften at room temperature. Whisk the eggs lightly with the lemon juice in a mixing bowl. Stir in the soured cream and the sugar. Gradually beat in the cream cheese to make a smooth mixture. Stir in the melted butter. Pour the mixture into the lined flan dish and bake in a moderate oven (325°F, 160°C,

Gas Mark 3) for 30–40 minutes, or until set in the centre. The filling will be very soft but will become firmer as the cake cools. Chill thoroughly before serving.

# KEY LIME PIE

*Makes 1 8-inch (20-cm) pie*

**for the crust:**
6 oz/175 g digestive biscuit
  crumbs
4 oz/100 g castor sugar
4 oz/100 g melted butter or
  margarine
**for the filling:**
½ oz/15 g powdered gelatine
6 tablespoons lime juice
2 eggs
1 tablespoon castor sugar
12 oz/350 g sweetened condensed
  milk (1 large can)
½ teaspoon grated lime rind

To make the crust, combine the crumbs and the sugar. Mix in the melted butter. Press the mixture into a buttered 8-inch (20-cm) flan dish. The crust may be well chilled or, if preferred, baked in a moderately hot oven (400°F, 200°C, Gas Mark 6) for 10 minutes before the filling is added.

To make the filling, soak the gelatine in the lime juice in a double saucepan for 5 minutes, then stir over simmering water until the gelatine is completely dissolved. Separate the eggs. Whisk the yolks until pale in colour. Whisk the egg whites until fluffy, add the sugar slowly and continue to whisk to make a stiff, glossy meringue. Stir the lime mixture and egg yolks into the condensed milk and beat thoroughly. Fold the meringue carefully into the lime mixture and pour into the prepared pie case. Allow to set and sprinkle with grated rind before serving.

# LEMON CHEESE PIE

*Makes 1 9-inch (23-cm) pie*

**for the pastry:**
4 oz/100 g plain flour
1 egg yolk
2–3 teaspoons water
¼ teaspoon salt
4 oz/100 g cold butter
**for the filling:**
4 oz/100 g butter
10 oz/275 g castor sugar
3 eggs
6 tablespoons lemon juice
scant ½ pint/2·5 dl double cream
1 teaspoon grated lemon rind

Prepare the pastry as for Southern Pecan Pie, see following page.

On a lightly floured board, roll out the pastry to about ⅛ inch (3 mm) thick and about 1½ inches (3·5 cm) larger than the diameter of a 9-inch (23-cm) fluted flan dish. Line the flan dish with the pastry.

For the filling, cream the butter and sugar until fluffy. Add the eggs one at a time, beating well after each addition. Stir in the lemon juice. Pour into the uncooked pastry case and bake in a moderate oven (350°F, 180°C, Gas Mark 4) for 35–40 minutes. Remove from the oven and set aside to cool.

When the pie is cool, whip the cream and pipe in a decorative border round the edge of the filling. Sprinkle with the grated lemon rind.

# SOUTHERN PECAN PIE

*Makes 1 9-inch (23-cm) pie*

**for the pastry:**
4 oz/100 g plain flour
1 egg yolk
2–3 teaspoons water
¼ teaspoon salt
4 oz/100 g cold butter
  (see recipe)

**for the filling:**
1 oz/25 g butter
7 oz/200 g castor sugar
3 large eggs
12 oz/350 g dark corn syrup or
  golden syrup
1 teaspoon vanilla essence
¼ teaspoon salt
4 oz/100 g pecan nuts, halved

To make the pastry, put the flour into a mixing bowl and make a well in the centre. Put the egg yolk, water and salt into the well. Cut in the butter, which should be firm and cold but not directly out of the refrigerator or freezer. Begin working the ingredients in the centre to a smooth paste, then gradually work in the flour until all the ingredients can be gathered into a rough dough. A few drops of water may be necessary, depending upon the size of the egg yolk. If the pastry is too soft to roll out easily, chill in the refrigerator for 30 minutes.

On a lightly floured board, roll out the pastry to about ⅛ inch (3 mm) thick and about 1½ inches (3·5 cm) larger than the diameter of a 9-inch (23-cm) fluted flan dish. Line the flan dish with the pastry and bake blind in a moderately hot oven (400°F, 200°C, Gas Mark 6) (see note).

Cream the butter and sugar together thoroughly. Whisk the eggs and add to the creamed mixture with the corn syrup, vanilla essence and salt. Beat well. Sprinkle the halved pecan nuts in the cooked pastry case. Pour the mixture over the pecan nuts. Bake in a hot oven (450°F, 230°C, Gas Mark 8) for 10 minutes. Reduce the oven temperature to moderate (350°F, 180°C, Gas Mark 4) and bake for 30–35 minutes longer. Cool and serve with whipped cream.

*Note:* To bake a pastry case, line it with foil or greaseproof paper and weigh down with dried beans or rice. Bake in the centre of the oven for 15 minutes.


# CREAM WAFFLES

*Makes 4 waffles*

6 oz/175 g plain flour
2 teaspoons baking powder
¼ teaspoon salt

3 eggs
¼ pint/1·5 dl double cream

Sift the flour, baking powder and salt into a mixing bowl. Separate the eggs. Whisk the egg yolks vigorously and gradually whisk in the cream. Stir the egg yolk mixture into the flour mixture, and whisk with a rotary whisk, electric mixer or fork until the batter is smooth. Whisk the egg whites until stiff and fold into the batter. Chill the batter for 30 minutes.

Lightly grease and heat a waffle iron. Pour a little of the batter into the heated waffle iron, cook for 3–4 minutes then turn out and keep warm. Repeat with the rest of the mixture.


# DUTCH WELSHKORN OYSTERS (CORN FRITTERS)

*Serves 4*

4 eggs
8 oz/225 g fresh or frozen sweet
  corn kernels, or 1 (11½-oz/
  326-g) can sweet corn kernels

4 tablespoons plain flour
1 teaspoon salt
¼ teaspoon black pepper
¼ teaspoon cayenne pepper

Separate the eggs. Combine the sweet corn kernels and egg yolks in a mixing bowl, and whisk well. Sift in the flour, salt and the peppers, and mix to a batter. Whisk the egg whites until stiff but not dry and fold into the sweet corn mixture. Drop spoonfuls (the size of oysters) on to a well-greased hot griddle or frying pan and fry until golden brown on both sides. Serve hot.

*Note:* In inland regions of the Middle Atlantic states, fresh oysters were not always available. This dish, looking very much like batter-fried oysters, was devised to 'fool the eye' and please the palate.


# CORN FLAPOVERS

*Makes 24*

generous ¼ pint/2 dl milk
2 oz/50 g yellow corn meal
6 oz/175 g plain flour
3 teaspoons baking powder

1 teaspoon salt
2 oz/50 g melted butter
soft butter (see recipe)

Scald the milk in a saucepan. Remove from the heat and stir in the corn meal. Set aside. Combine the flour, baking powder and salt in a mixing bowl. Stir in the melted butter and the corn meal mixture. Turn out on to a well floured board and knead gently with floured fingers until the dough holds together. Knead in a little more flour, if necessary. Roll out ¼ inch (5 mm) thick on a lightly floured board and cut with a 2-inch (5-cm) floured biscuit cutter. Score the rounds slightly off centre with the back of a knife and brush each with soft butter. Fold over each round envelope-style and arrange on a baking tray. Bake in a hot oven (425°F, 220°C, Gas Mark 7) for 15 minutes.


# WHEAT GERM MUFFINS

*Makes 12 medium-sized muffins*

8 oz/225 g plain flour
3 teaspoons baking powder
1 teaspoon salt
1 oz/25 g castor sugar

2 oz/50 g wheat germ
1 egg
scant ½ pint/2·5 dl milk
2 oz/50 g melted butter

Combine the flour, baking powder, salt, sugar and wheat germ in a mixing bowl. Whisk the egg into the milk and add to the mixing bowl. Mix lightly until all the dry ingredients are moistened, then stir in the melted butter. Grease a tray of bun tins and fill the moulds two-thirds full of batter. Bake in a moderately hot oven (400°F, 200°C, Gas Mark 6) for 20–25 minutes. Remove the muffins and serve warm.

# CHEESE SCONES

*Makes 16 2-inch (5-cm) scones*

8 oz/225 g plain flour
2½ teaspoons baking powder
½ teaspoon salt
3 oz/75 g margarine or cooking
  fat

¼ pint/1·5 dl milk
4 oz/100 g Cheddar cheese, grated
4 oz/100 g butter

Combine the flour, baking powder and salt in a mixing bowl. Cut in the margarine with a pastry blender or two knives, or rub in with the fingertips until evenly mixed. Add the milk and stir gently with a fork until the dough holds together. Gather the dough into a ball, turn it on to a lightly floured board and knead gently with floured fingers, about 12 kneading strokes.

Roll the dough out ½ inch (1 cm) thick on a lightly floured board and cut with a 2-inch (5-cm) floured plain cutter. Melt the cheese and butter in a double saucepan until the mixture is smooth, stirring occasionally. Dip the top of each scone into the butter and cheese mixture and place on a baking tray 1 inch (2·5 cm) apart with the cheese side up. Alternatively, place the scones in a baking tin and spoon the cheese sauce on top of each one. Bake in a hot oven (425°F, 220°C, Gas Mark 7) for 12–15 minutes. Serve hot. These scones are excellent with baked ham for lunch.

# SPOON BREAD

*Serves 4*

¾ pint/4·5 dl milk
6 oz/175 g yellow corn meal
1 teaspoon salt

2 oz/50 g melted butter
4 eggs

Heat the milk to simmering point in a saucepan. Gradually stir in the corn meal and cook, stirring constantly, until the mixture is smooth and thick. Stir in the salt and melted butter. Set aside to cool.

Separate the eggs. Whisk the egg yolks and stir into the corn meal mixture. Whisk the egg whites until stiff and fold in. Pour into a buttered 3-pint (1·5-litre) casserole and bake in a moderately hot oven (375°F, 190°C, Gas Mark 5) for 35–40 minutes, or until lightly brown. Serve hot and spoon the bread from the casserole at the table.

*Spoon bread*

# BOSTON BROWN BREAD

*Makes 3 small loaves or 2 large loaves*

| | |
|---|---|
| 6 oz/175 g yellow corn meal | generous ¼ pint/2 dl black treacle |
| 4 oz/100 g wholemeal flour | ½ oz/15 g castor sugar |
| 4 oz/100 g rye flour | ¾ pint/4·5 dl soured milk or |
| 1 teaspoon bicarbonate of soda | buttermilk |
| 1 teaspoon salt | 4 oz/100 g seedless raisins |

Combine the corn meal, wholemeal flour, rye flour, bicarbonate of soda and salt in a mixing bowl. Stir in the black treacle, sugar, soured milk or buttermilk and raisins and stir until well mixed. Place rounds of greaseproof paper in the bottom of 3 1-lb (450-g) coffee tins or 2 large pudding basins. Grease the tins or basins and fill two-thirds full of mixture. Cover with aluminium foil tied tightly over the tops.

Place the tins upright on a rack in a large saucepan and add water to reach halfway up the sides. Cover the pan and bring the water to the boil. Boil gently for 2 hours or until the bread is firm and dry on top, adding more boiling water from time to time if needed. Remove from the pan and cool slightly before turning the bread out on to a wire rack. Let stand until cold.

# ANADAMA BREAD

*Makes 2 loaves*

| | |
|---|---|
| 2½ oz/65 g white or yellow corn meal | ¾ pint/4·5 dl boiling water |
| 1 oz/25 g butter or cooking fat | 2 oz/50 g fresh yeast or 1 oz/25 g dried yeast |
| 6 tablespoons black treacle | 4 tablespoons warm water |
| 2 teaspoons salt | about 2 lb/1 kg plain flour |

Measure the corn meal, butter, black treacle and salt into a large mixing bowl. Pour in the boiling water and stir until the butter is melted. Let stand until lukewarm. Blend the yeast with the warm water and stir it into the corn meal mixture. Beat in two-thirds of the flour, a little at a time, then work in enough additional flour to make a soft dough. Grease the surface of the dough, cover lightly with a tea towel and let stand in a warm place for 1 hour, or until the dough has doubled in bulk. In cold weather, or if the kitchen is cool, rising time might take a little longer.

Knock back the dough, turn it out on to a floured board and knead until smooth. Form into a long thick roll and cut in half crosswise. Put each half into a greased loaf tin, cover with a tea towel and set aside to rise for 1 hour, or until the dough is well rounded over the edge of the tin. Bake in a moderately hot oven (375°F, 190°C, Gas Mark 5) for 55 minutes–1 hour. Remove the loaves from the oven, turn out and cool on wire racks. To obtain a shiny crust, brush the tops of the loaves with melted butter while still hot.

# SALLY LUNN BREAD

*Makes 2 loaves*

| | |
|---|---|
| scant ½ pint/2·5 dl milk | 5 tablespoons lukewarm water |
| 4 oz/100 g butter | 2 lb/1 kg plain flour |
| 1½ oz/40 g castor sugar | 3 eggs |
| 2 teaspoons salt | 1 tablespoon soft butter |
| 1 oz/25 g fresh yeast or ½ oz/15 g dried yeast | |

Put the milk and butter into a small saucepan. Heat until the butter melts and the mixture simmers, then pour into a large mixing bowl to cool. Stir in the sugar and the salt. Soften the yeast in the lukewarm water.

When the milk mixture is lukewarm, beat in about one-third of the flour, then the yeast mixture. Lightly whisk the eggs and stir them into the mixture. Gradually beat in another third of the flour to make a smooth elastic dough. Finally, knead in enough of the remaining flour to make a dough that is quite soft but not sticky. Cover lightly with a tea towel and let rise in a warm place for 1½ hours, or until the dough has doubled in bulk.

Knock back the dough and turn out on to a lightly floured board. Knead until smooth and elastic, form into a ball and cut in half. Shape each half into a long narrow loaf and put into 2 greased or oiled loaf tins. Brush the surface of the dough lightly with the soft butter, cover with a tea towel and set aside to prove for about 1 hour, or until the dough is well rounded above the top of each tin. Bake in a hot oven (425°F, 220°C, Gas Mark 7) for 30–40 minutes, or until golden brown. Remove from the tins and cool on a wire rack. Serve with butter and jam. Sally Lunn bread is delicious toasted.

# PINEAPPLE BREAD

*Makes 2 loaves*

| | |
|---|---|
| 1 lb/450 g plain flour | 3 oz/75 g butter |
| 4 teaspoons baking powder | 12 oz/350 g soft brown sugar |
| ½ teaspoon bicarbonate of soda | 2 eggs |
| ½ teaspoon salt | 1 (13¼-oz/376-g) can crushed |
| 6 oz/175 g macadamia nuts, pecan nuts or walnuts, coarsely chopped | pineapple |

Combine the flour, baking powder, bicarbonate of soda and salt in a mixing bowl. Stir in the nuts. Cream the butter and brown sugar together in another mixing bowl. Beat in the eggs, one at a time, and continue beating until the mixture is smooth. Stir in half the flour mixture, the crushed pineapple with its juice, then the remaining flour mixture. Divide the mixture between 2 large well-oiled loaf tins. Bake in a moderate oven (350°F, 180°C, Gas Mark 4) for 50 minutes–1 hour, or until a skewer inserted in the centre comes out clean. Cool for 5 minutes, then turn out on a wire rack to cool completely before slicing. Serve thinly sliced with butter.

*Boston brown bread*

# HONOLULU BARS

*Makes 25 bars*

6 oz/175 g melted butter or margarine
1 lb/450 g soft brown sugar
3 eggs
12 oz/350 g plain flour
2½ teaspoons baking powder
½ teaspoon salt
4 oz/100 g macadamia nuts, pecan nuts or walnuts, coarsely chopped
6 oz/175 g plain chocolate chips

Cream the melted butter and brown sugar in a mixing bowl. Add the eggs, one at a time, beating well after each addition. Sift together the flour, baking powder and salt into another bowl. Stir the chocolate and nuts into the flour mixture. Add the ingredients to the egg mixture and mix until smooth. Spread the mixture in a large greased oblong baking tin. Bake in a moderate oven (350°F, 180°C, Gas Mark 4) for 30–35 minutes. Cool and cut into bars before serving.

# PHILADELPHIA STICKY BUNS

*Makes 12*

1 oz/25 g fresh yeast or ½ oz/15 g dried yeast
3 tablespoons lukewarm water
½ pint/3 dl milk
1¼ lb/600 g plain flour
3 oz/75 g melted butter
3 oz/75 g castor sugar
2 egg yolks
1 teaspoon salt
2 teaspoons grated lemon rind
1 teaspoon ground cinnamon
3 oz/75 g currants
2 oz/50 g butter
4 oz/100 g soft brown sugar

Sprinkle or crumble the yeast into the lukewarm water to soften. Scald the milk, empty it into a large mixing bowl and cool to lukewarm. Stir in 6 oz (175 g) of the flour, add the yeast mixture and beat until the mixture is smooth. Cover lightly and let stand in a warm place until bubbles form on the surface. Stir in two-thirds of the melted butter and two-thirds of the sugar. Whisk the egg yolks and add with the salt and the grated lemon rind.

Stir in the remaining flour, then knead until the dough is smooth and springy, adding a little more flour if necessary. Cover and set aside to rise in a warm place for about 1 hour, or until doubled in bulk.

Knock back the dough and turn out on to a floured surface. Roll out into a long rectangle about ¾ inch (1·5 cm) thick. Brush the surface with the remaining melted butter and sprinkle with the remaining sugar mixed with the cinnamon. Sprinkle with the currants. Roll lengthwise into a long roll and cut into 1-inch (2·5-cm) slices. Place a heavy 9- or 10-inch (23- or 26-cm) baking tin over direct heat and in it melt the 2 oz (50 g) butter. Remove the tin from the heat and sprinkle the base with the brown sugar. Place slices of dough, cut side down, on top of the sugar, cover and let rise again in a warm place until puffy and almost doubled in bulk. Bake in a moderate oven (350°F, 180°C, Gas Mark 4) for 25–30 minutes, or until nicely brown on top. Turn the buns out to cool.

# LOUISIANA PECAN PRALINES

*Makes about 40 pralines*

12 oz/350 g soft brown sugar
7 oz/200 g castor sugar
scant ½ pint/2·5 dl water
generous ¼ pint/2 dl single cream
1 lb/450 g pecan nuts, halved

Combine the brown sugar, castor sugar, water and cream in a saucepan. Bring to the boil and cook to the soft ball stage (238°F, 113°C on a sugar thermometer). Remove from the heat and beat the mixture until creamy. Stir in the nuts. Drop spoonfuls on to a greased baking tray and let stand until cool.

# LADY BALTIMORE CAKE

*Makes 1 8-inch (20-cm) cake*

**for the cake:**
8 oz/225 g butter
14 oz/400 g castor sugar
1 lb/450 g plain flour
6 teaspoons baking powder
½ teaspoon salt
scant ½ pint/2·5 dl milk
7 egg whites
½ teaspoon rose water

**for the icing and filling:**
1¼ lb/600 g castor sugar
generous ¼ pint/2 dl water
¼ teaspoon cream of tartar
4 egg whites
2 oz/50 g seedless raisins, chopped
3 dried figs, chopped
4 oz/100 g nuts, chopped
4 oz/100 g glacé cherries, chopped
3 oz/75 g glacé pineapple, diced

In a large mixing bowl, cream the butter and sugar together thoroughly until the mixture is fluffy. Combine the flour, baking powder and salt and stir into the creamed mixture alternately with the milk. Whisk the egg whites until stiff enough to hold a peak and fold gently into the mixture. Fold in the rose water. Divide the mixture between 3 7-inch (18-cm) round cake tins lined with greaseproof paper. Bake in a moderate oven (350°F, 180°C, Gas Mark 4) for 30–35 minutes, or until an inserted skewer comes out clean. Leave in the tins for 5 minutes, then turn out on to wire racks to cool.

For the icing and filling, combine the sugar, water and cream of tartar in a heavy saucepan. Bring to the boil and boil rapidly until the syrup spins a short thread (236°F, 113°C on a sugar thermometer). Whisk the egg whites until they stand in stiff peaks. Gradually add the syrup, whisking constantly until the icing is thick and shiny. Fold the chopped raisins and figs into the icing with the nuts, cherries and pineapple. Sandwich the cakes together with part of the icing and cover the top and sides of the cake with the remaining icing.

*Lady Baltimore cake*

# BRITISH

## Marguerite Patten

*Photography by John Miller*

The variable climate of Britain, with its comparatively mild winters and ample rainfall, is ideal for the growing of a wide variety of fruits and vegetables and the raising of cattle. The dairy produce is excellent, with numerous local cheeses, Cheddar, Stilton, Cheshire, Leicester and Sage Derby being only a few of the best known. British meat is of exceptional quality—tender lamb from the South Downs, Wiltshire, Suffolk and York hams and, of course, beef, the most highly prized being Scotch. Roast beef with roast potatoes, Yorkshire pudding and creamed horseradish must be to many the supreme classical English dish.

Fish and shellfish are plentiful—lobster and mackerel from the West Country, the famous sole from Dover, oysters from Whitstable and the Welsh coast, salmon from Scotland and Ireland and the many varieties of North Sea fish such as cod, haddock and herring. The countries and counties of Britain all offer their own specialities to enrich the national cuisine. Kent and the Vale of Evesham in Worcestershire vie with each other for the title of 'the garden of England'. Their orchards of cherries, apples and pears present a wonderful picture in the spring. Norfolk is renowned for its fine turkeys, much in demand for the traditional Christmas dinner. In the north of England where high tea, a combination of tea and supper, is a main meal of the day, baking comes into its own, giving the British cuisine excellent recipes for teacakes, breads and cakes.

Some of the most fertile and productive farming land in Britain is to be found in the Lowlands of Scotland. It is particularly suitable for the growing of oats and barley, both of which appear frequently in Scottish cooking, and for soft fruits—jams and jellies are a national speciality which perfectly complement the many varieties of bread, rolls and oatcakes served for breakfast and tea.

Scotland is perhaps particularly noted for the excellence and variety of its fish, two of the most well-known being herring and salmon, and for its beef. Scotch beef is expensive and a great deal of mutton is therefore used in traditional dishes—sheep are reared for both wool and meat throughout Scotland. There is a wide variety of game in the remote Highlands. The season for deer lasts from June to January, but probably the most prominent date in the shooting calendar is August 12, the traditional start of the grouse season.

The cuisine of Wales is plain and wholesome rather than exotic. The staple meat is mutton, for the hill country is ideally suited to sheep farming. Potatoes, root vegetables and, of course, leeks, the national emblem, are the most common accompaniments. Griddle baking is a speciality, and Welsh cakes, the round fruited girdle scones, are a real treat eaten freshly baked and lavishly buttered. As in all parts of Britain, fish and shellfish are excellent, one speciality of the Gower coast being oyster soup, and the hill streams and rivers abound in salmon and trout. Wales also has its own cheeses, the most famous being Caerphilly, a mild, white cheese.

Traditional food in Ireland also has simplicity as its keynote. The climate and soil of Ireland is ideal for the potato which is the staple food, often combined with pork, bacon or ham, the most popular meat. The Irish are also great bread makers. The seafood is excellent and salmon, eel and trout are plentiful, forming the basis for some of Ireland's best recipes.

# POTTED SHRIMPS

*Serves 4*

2–2½ lb/1–1·25 kg fresh shrimps or prawns, unshelled
4 oz/100 g butter
grated nutmeg (see recipe)
pinch black pepper
½ lettuce
2 lemons, sliced

If using freshly caught shrimps, boil them until pink in colour and peel while still warm. If buying cooked shrimps, put into hot water, let stand for 1 minute and then drain and peel them.

Put half the butter into a saucepan and heat until melted but not brown. Add the shrimps with a generous pinch of nutmeg and the pepper. Heat gently, shaking the pan frequently, until the shrimps are warm. Prolonged heating will make them tough. Spoon into 4 small pots and let stand until the butter cools and sets. Melt the remaining butter, pour over the shrimps and let stand until the butter is quite firm. Cover and store in a cool place or freeze until required.

Loosen the layer of butter on the surface of each pot, using the top of a knife, and unmould the shrimps on to serving plates. Garnish with lettuce leaves and lemon slices and serve with thinly sliced brown bread and butter.

# SCALLOPED CRABS

*Serves 4*

2 cooked crabs, about 1½–2 lb/700–900 g each
few drops olive oil
1 (1¾-oz/50-g) can anchovy fillets
3 oz/75 g butter
3 oz/75 g fine fresh breadcrumbs
2 teaspoons distilled or pure malt vinegar
½–1 teaspoon cayenne pepper
1 lemon, cut into wedges
few sprigs parsley

Remove the legs and claws of the crabs by twisting gently in a circular motion. Place each crab on its back with the tail flap towards you. With the fingers of both hands on the shell and both thumbs under the tail flap, push upwards until the body breaks away from the shell. Discard the greyish-white stomach bag, which lies behind the head in the shell, and the grey feathery 'dead men's fingers' from each body. Crack the legs and claws and remove all the white meat. Reserve the small claws. Tap sharply along the false line on the underside of each shell and it should come away quite neatly. Scrub the shells, dry them well and rub lightly with the olive oil to make them shiny.

Drain the anchovy fillets, chop half of them and reserve the remainder. Heat the butter in a frying pan, add the breadcrumbs and sauté until pale golden brown. Mix both the white and dark meat of the crabs together in a bowl with the chopped anchovy fillets, one-third of the breadcrumbs and the vinegar. Season to taste with the cayenne pepper, adding it sparingly as it is very hot. Press the crab meat mixture back into the shells (see note). Sprinkle with the remainder of the sautéed breadcrumbs and heat in a hot oven (425°F, 220°C, Gas Mark 7) for about 10–12 minutes, or brown under the grill. Top the crabs with a lattice of the remaining whole anchovy fillets. Garnish with the lemon, parsley and small crab claws.

*Note:* If there is too much mixture for the crab shells, put the surplus into scallop shells and arrange round the crabs.

# POTTED CHEESE

*Serves 4*

12 oz/350 g cheese, white
   Cheshire, Lancashire or
   Cheddar
5 oz/150 g butter

2 teaspoons dry mustard
2 tablespoons dry sherry
3 oz/75 g walnuts, finely chopped
   (see note)

Finely grate the cheese. Soften it by pounding in a mortar with a pestle, rubbing through a sieve or beating with a wooden spoon until it is the consistency of butter. Cream half the butter until very soft and fluffy. Add the cheese to the butter and cream again. Blend the mustard with the sherry and gradually stir into the cheese mixture. Beat in the walnuts. Put the mixture into 4 small pots. Melt the remaining butter, cool and then spoon over the top of each pot of cheese. Cover and keep in a cool place or in the refrigerator. Slice and serve with crackers, bread or fresh fruit.

*Note:* Fresh, dried or pickled walnuts may be used. The brown skins on fresh walnuts should be removed by blanching. Fresh walnuts enhance while preserving the original colour and flavour of the cheese, but many people enjoy the distinctive 'bite' of the black pickled walnuts.

# COCK-A-LEEKIE

*Serves 4–6*

12 prunes
½ pint/3 dl water
1 boiling chicken
3 pints/1·5 litres chicken stock or
   water

salt and pepper
1½ lb/700 g leeks
few sprigs fresh parsley,
   chopped

Soak the prunes overnight in the water. Drain before using.

Wash the chicken and put into a very large saucepan with the stock. Add the giblets but omit the liver as it darkens the stock. Bring the liquid to the boil and skim the surface. Lower the heat, add salt and pepper to taste, cover tightly and simmer gently for 2½ hours, or until the chicken is very tender. Remove the chicken from the pan, discard the giblets and set the chicken aside. Strain the stock, return it to the pan and boil rapidly until reduced by half. Skim the fat from the surface of the liquid and discard (see note).

Remove the meat from the chicken breasts and dice finely. Reserve the remainder of the chicken flesh for another dish. Trim the leeks and rinse thoroughly under cold running water. Cut into very small rings and add to the chicken stock together with the prunes. Simmer over moderate heat for 40 minutes. Add the chicken flesh and heat for a few minutes. Taste, and adjust the seasoning. Pour into a heated soup tureen and garnish with the parsley. Alternatively, a little grated cheese sprinkled in at the last minute adds extra flavour.

*Note:* The stock may be cooled and refrigerated until the fat hardens. The fat can then be lifted away from the surface of the stock.

*Cock-a-leekie*

# OYSTER SOUP

*Serves 4*

| | |
|---|---|
| 12 oz/350 g scrag end of mutton | pepper |
| 3 medium-sized onions | 2 oz/50 g butter |
| 1 lb/450 g mutton bones | 2 oz/50 g plain flour |
| 3 pints/1·5 litres water | 24 small oysters (see note) |
| 1 blade mace or $\frac{1}{4}$ teaspoon ground mace | 1 leek or 2 tablespoons chopped fresh parsley |

Cut the mutton into pieces. Peel and slice the onions. Place the mutton and onions in a saucepan with the bones, water, mace and pepper. Do not add salt as the oysters are salty. Bring to the boil over high heat. Skim the surface of the liquid, cover the pan and simmer for about 1½ hours. Strain the stock carefully through a muslin cloth until clear. Discard the bones, meat and vegetables. Return the stock to the pan and boil until it is reduced by half.

Heat the butter in a saucepan over moderate heat. Stir in the flour and cook gently, stirring constantly, until pale golden brown. Add the stock gradually, mixing well after each addition. Bring to the boil, stirring constantly until the mixture becomes smooth and thickened. Trim the leek and discard the coarse outer leaves. Rinse thoroughly under cold running water and then slice thinly. Remove the oysters from their shells and add any oyster liquid to the soup. Put the oysters into heated soup bowls. Check the seasoning of the soup and then pour over the oysters. (A generous pinch of cayenne pepper and a little lemon juice may also be added before serving for more flavour.) Garnish with the parsley or thinly sliced leek and serve.

*Note:* This soup may also be made substituting sliced scallops, mussels or clams.

# WINDSOR SOUP

*Serves 6–8*

| | |
|---|---|
| 8 oz/225 g stewing steak | salt and pepper |
| 3 lb/1·5 kg beef bones | $\frac{1}{4}$–$\frac{1}{2}$ pint/1·5–3 dl Madeira or |
| 1 calf's foot | sweet red wine |
| 3 pints/1·5 litres water | 1 tablespoon chopped fresh |
| *bouquet garni* (see recipe) | parsley |

Cut the beef into ½-inch (1-cm) cubes and place in a large saucepan. Rinse the beef bones and calf's foot thoroughly under cold running water. Add to the pan with the water, *bouquet garni* (3 bay leaves, 3 sprigs parsley, 1 sprig thyme, tied together) and salt and pepper to taste. Bring to the boil and skim the surface. Lower the heat, cover the pan and simmer gently for 2½ hours.

Discard the bones, beef and *bouquet garni*. Strain the soup, add the wine, reheat and adjust the seasoning. Pour into heated soup bowls and garnish with the parsley or a more elaborate garnish such as tiny pieces of lobster or chopped anchovy fillets.

*Note:* The flavour of shellfish blended into this soup is very pleasant and may be achieved by adding small pieces of flaked lobster when reheating the soup.

# COD STEAKS AND BACON

*Serves 4*

| | |
|---|---|
| 4 cod steaks, about 8 oz/225 g each | 1 teaspoon grated lemon rind |
| salt and pepper | 1 tablespoon chopped fresh parsley |
| 1½ tablespoons lemon juice | salt and pepper |
| 4 rashers streaky bacon | 1 egg |
| 1½ oz/40 g butter | 1½ tablespoons lemon juice |
| **for the stuffing:** | **for the garnish:** |
| 4 oz/100 g fine fresh breadcrumbs | few sprigs fresh parsley |
| 2 oz/50 g shredded suet or melted butter | 8 tomatoes |

Rinse the fish under cold running water and dry well. Sprinkle each side with salt and pepper to taste and the lemon juice. Remove any rind from the bacon. Grease the bottom of a shallow ovenproof dish with half the butter.

To make the stuffing, mix together the breadcrumbs, suet, lemon rind, parsley and salt and pepper to taste. Lightly whisk the egg and stir into the mixture together with the lemon juice to make a moist stuffing. Divide the stuffing into 4 equal portions and press one portion on top of each piece of fish. Wrap the bacon around the fish and lift carefully into the dish. (The cod steaks may be placed on buttered foil for stuffing and then lifted on to the dish.) Melt the remaining butter and brush over each piece of stuffed fish. Bake in a moderately hot oven (375°F, 190°C, Gas Mark 5) for approximately 20 minutes, or until the fish is tender. Do not overcook. Transfer the fish to a heated serving dish and garnish with parsley and baked or grilled tomatoes.

# SALMON PATTIES

*Serves 4*

| | |
|---|---|
| 8 oz/225 g salmon, cooked | salt and pepper |
| 8 oz/225 g potatoes, cooked and mashed | 1 egg |
| ½ teaspoon grated lemon rind | **for the batter:** |
| 2 teaspoons lemon juice | 4 oz/100 g plain flour |
| 1 teaspoon chopped chives or grated onion | pinch salt |
| 2 teaspoons chopped fresh parsley (or use half parsley and half fresh tarragon) | 1 egg |
| | ¼ pint/1·5 dl milk |
| | 4 tablespoons single cream |
| | oil for deep-frying |
| | 1 lemon, sliced |

Flake the salmon and place in a mixing bowl with the mashed potatoes, lemon rind, lemon juice, chives, parsley and salt and pepper to taste. Lightly whisk the egg and add to the mixture. Mix thoroughly to a stiff consistency. Turn out on to a lightly floured board and shape the salmon mixture into 8 small round flat cakes. Set aside in a cool place or in the refrigerator while making the batter.

To make the batter, sift the flour and salt into a mixing bowl and make a well in the centre. Whisk together the egg, milk and cream. Pour the egg mixture into the well and beat with a wooden spoon to form a smooth batter.

Dip the salmon cakes into the batter, drain off the surplus and deep-fry in hot oil until crisp and golden brown. Drain on kitchen paper and arrange on a heated serving plate. Garnish with the lemon slices and serve hot.

# MACKEREL WITH GOOSEBERRY SAUCE

*Serves 4*

| | |
|---|---|
| 4 mackerel | 3 oz/75 g sugar |
| 1 sprig fennel | ¼ pint/1·5 dl water |
| 3 oz/75 g butter | 1 oz/25 g butter |
| salt and pepper | 3 teaspoons chopped fresh parsley (optional) |
| **for the sauce:** | |
| 1 lb/450 g gooseberries | few sprigs fennel or parsley |

Gut the mackerel, discard the heads and rinse the fish under cold running water. Remove the backbones, taking care to maintain the shape of the fish. Finely chop the fennel. Spread the insides of the fish with half the butter, season well with salt and pepper to taste and sprinkle with half the fennel. Fold the fish back into shape. Melt the remaining butter in a small saucepan. Brush the melted butter over the fish and sprinkle with the remaining fennel. Grill the fish under moderate heat, turning over once, until the flesh is tender.

Meanwhile, wash the gooseberries without removing the stalks. Place in a large saucepan with the sugar and water. Simmer over moderate heat until the fruit is reduced to a pulp. Rub the fruit and juice through a sieve to make a purée and discard the seeds and skins. Return the purée to the pan, add the butter with the chopped parsley and reheat. Arrange the fish on a heated serving dish and garnish with sprigs of fennel or parsley. Serve with the hot gooseberry sauce and new potatoes.

# DOVER SOLE WITH ORANGE OR LEMON BUTTER

*Serves 2*

| | |
|---|---|
| 2 Dover sole, about 8–12 oz/225–350 g each | salt and pepper |
| ½ pint/3 dl water | 2 teaspoons grated orange or lemon rind |
| 1 bay leaf | 2 oz/50 g butter |
| ¼ pint/1·5 dl fish stock (see recipe) | 1 orange or lemon, cut into wedges |
| ¼ pint/1·5 dl white wine | |

To make the fish stock, remove the skins of each fish and reserve. Leave the fish whole. Put the skin into a saucepan with the water and the bay leaf and simmer gently for 15 minutes. Strain the stock into a clean saucepan and then reboil until reduced to ¼ pint (1·5 dl). Put the fish stock, whole fish and wine into a large saucepan. Season lightly with salt and pepper. Poach the fish gently for 10 minutes, spooning the liquid over the fish once or twice.

Meanwhile, blend the orange or lemon rind with the butter. Remove the fish from the liquid and place on a buttered heated flameproof dish. Spread the flavoured butter over the fish and cook for 5–6 minutes under a hot grill. Garnish with the orange or lemon wedges and serve.

# FINNAN HADDIE IN CREAM SAUCE

*Serves 4*

2 lb/1 kg smoked haddock
about ¾ pint/5 dl milk
1 bay leaf
pepper
2 oz/50 g butter

1½ oz/40 g plain flour
2 teaspoons dry mustard
½ pint/3 dl single cream
pinch cayenne pepper
1 lemon, sliced

Cut off the tail and fins of the smoked haddock and cut the fish into 4 portions. Place in a large shallow saucepan or frying pan and cover completely with the milk. Add the bay leaf and a little pepper. Bring just to the boil, then lower the heat and simmer until the fish is cooked but not broken. Carefully remove the fish from the liquid, drain thoroughly and place on a heated serving dish. Cover with buttered paper or foil and keep hot.

Strain the milk and, if necessary, add more milk to make a scant ¾ pint (4 dl). Heat the butter in a saucepan, stir in the flour and mustard and cook for 2–3 minutes. Remove from the heat and add the flavoured milk and the cream, a little at a time, mixing well after each addition. Bring to the boil over moderate heat, stirring constantly until the mixture thickens. Pour some of the sauce over the fish and serve the remainder in a sauceboat. Sprinkle the fish with cayenne pepper and garnish with the lemon. Finnan haddock prepared in this way is particularly good accompanied by young carrots and new potatoes.

*Dover sole with lemon butter*

*Cheese pudding*

# STEAK AND KIDNEY PIE

*Serves 4–5*

**for the filling:**
1½ lb/700 g stewing steak
4 oz/100 g ox kidney
1 oz/25 g plain flour
½ teaspoon salt
pinch pepper
2 oz/50 g lard or dripping
1 pint/6 dl water
1 large onion (optional)
4 oz/100 g button mushrooms
   (optional)

8 oysters (optional)
**for the flaky pastry:**
8 oz/225 g plain flour
pinch salt
6 oz/170 g butter or 4 oz/110 g
   butter and 2 oz/60 g cooking
   fat
about ¼ pint/1·5 dl cold water
**for glazing:**
1 egg
1 tablespoon water

Cut the beef into 1-inch (2·5-cm) cubes and discard any excess fat. Discard any membrane and fat from the kidney and cut into pieces the same size as the beef. Blend the flour with the salt and pepper on a plate. Coat the meat thoroughly in the seasoned flour. Melt the lard in a saucepan, add the meat and fry over moderate heat for 5 minutes. (If using the onion, mushrooms or oysters, see note.) Gradually blend in the water and bring to the boil, stirring constantly until thickened. Lower the heat, cover the pan and simmer gently for about 2 hours, or until the beef is tender. Taste, and adjust the seasoning.

Meanwhile, prepare the flaky pastry. Sift the flour and salt together into a mixing bowl. Soften the butter on a plate, reshape it into a rectangle and divide it into 3 equal portions. Add one portion of the butter to the flour mixture. Rub the mixture lightly between the fingertips, allowing it to

fall back into the bowl. When evenly mixed, add the lemon juice and enough water to make a smooth, elastic dough.

Turn the dough out on to a floured board, knead lightly and roll out to a rectangle. Cut the second portion of the butter into small pieces and dot over the top two-thirds of the rectangle. Fold the lower third of the rectangle up over the centre third and the top third down to enclose the butter completely between the layers. Give the dough a quarter-turn to the right so that an open end is towards you. Seal both ends by pressing down firmly with a rolling pin, then 'rib' the pastry by pressing the dough with a rolling pin at regular intervals.

Roll the dough out carefully to a rectangle again and repeat the above process using the remaining portion of butter. Turn, seal the ends and 'rib' the pastry. Let the pastry stand in a cool place or in the refrigerator for several hours before the final rolling.

Roll out the pastry to about 1 inch (2·5 cm) larger all around than a 9-inch (23-cm) pie dish. Grease the rim of the pie dish and place on it a narrow strip cut from the pastry. Spoon the hot meat mixture into the dish. Reserve most of the gravy. Moisten the top of the pastry strip with a little water and cover the pie with the pastry lid. Press the edges firmly together to seal, cut off any surplus pastry with a sharp knife and knock up the pastry edges by making horizontal cuts along the edge. Make a slit in the lid to allow the steam to escape during cooking. Cut any leftover pastry into decorative shapes such as leaves, a rose or a tassel and arrange on the pastry. Whisk the egg and water together and brush over the pastry. Bake in a hot oven (450°F, 230°C, Gas Mark 8) for 25 minutes, then lower the heat to 375°C (190°C,

Gas Mark 5) for a further 10–12 minutes. Reheat the reserved gravy and serve separately in a gravy boat with the pie.

*Note:* If using the onion, mushrooms or oysters, add as follows. Slice the onion thickly and sauté with the meat in the saucepan. Add the mushrooms to the saucepan during the last 5 minutes cooking time. Blend the oysters with the cooked meat before spooning the meat mixture into the pie dish.

# CHEESE PUDDING

*Serves 4*

3 oz/75 g fine fresh breadcrumbs
6 oz/175 g Cheddar cheese, grated
¼ pint/3 dl milk
1½ oz/40 g butter

¼ pint/1·5 dl single cream (see note)
pinch dry mustard
salt and pepper
3 eggs

Put the breadcrumbs into a bowl with the cheese. Heat the milk in a saucepan with three-quarters of the butter, the cream, mustard and salt and pepper to taste. Do not allow to boil. Whisk the eggs lightly. Whisk the hot milk into the beaten eggs. Strain the mixture over the breadcrumbs and cheese and set aside for 15–20 minutes to allow the breadcrumbs to absorb the liquid. Grease a 2-pint (1-litre) pie dish or soufflé dish with the remaining butter. Pour the cheese mixture into the dish and bake in a moderately hot oven (375°F, 190°C, Gas Mark 5) for about 45 minutes, or until well risen and golden brown. Serve at once with a crisp green salad.

*Note:* For a less rich pudding, substitute milk for the cream.

# ROAST BEEF WITH ROAST POTATOES

*Serves 6–8*

1 rolled sirloin, about 3 lb/1·5 kg
2 oz/50 g beef dripping (see recipe)

salt and pepper
6 large potatoes

Place the beef in a large roasting tin. If the beef is very lean, spread the dripping over the top and sides. Sprinkle lightly with salt and pepper. Roast in a hot oven (425°F, 220°C, Gas Mark 7) for 15 minutes per pound (per half kilo) plus an additional 15 minutes. At the end of this time the beef will be slightly underdone and red in the centre. For a well done roast, allow 20 minutes per pound (per half kilo) plus an additional 20 minutes.

Peel and rinse the potatoes. Dry thoroughly with kitchen paper, cut into halves and sprinkle very lightly with salt. Place in the tin with the beef about 1 hour before the end of the roasting time. Baste the potatoes with the fat in the tin and turn them several times so they become crisp and evenly browned on the outside but soft in the centre.

Remove the potatoes and drain well. Place the meat in the centre of a large heated meat dish and arrange the potatoes around the sides. Serve immediately with Yorkshire pudding and creamed horseradish (see below). Traditionally, the beef is carved at the table.

*Note:* Other vegetables such as parsnips or onions may be roasted and served with beef in the same way as the potatoes. Allow 1¼–1½ hours roasting time for onions. Parsnips should be boiled for 20–25 minutes, well drained and then roasted for 35–40 minutes.

# YORKSHIRE PUDDING

*Serves 4–6*

4 oz/100 g plain flour
pinch salt
1 egg
¼ pint/1·5 dl water

¼ pint/1·5 dl milk
1 oz/25 g cooking fat or meat dripping

Sift the flour and salt into a mixing bowl. Using a wooden spoon, beat in the egg and gradually beat in about one-third of the liquid, or just enough to make a thick batter. Beat vigorously until the batter is smooth, then gradually add the remaining liquid. Set aside in a cool place until required.

About 30–40 minutes before the end of the roasting time for the meat, heat the cooking fat or meat dripping in a Yorkshire pudding tin or roasting tin about 7 by 5 inches (18 by 13 cm). Pour in the batter. Place the tin on the top shelf of a hot oven (425°F, 220°C, Gas Mark 7) and bake for about 30–40 minutes, or until well risen and golden brown.

*Note:* To cook a Yorkshire pudding in the traditional way, lift the meat from the roasting tin about 45 minutes before the end of the roasting time for the meat. Pour off nearly all the meat dripping, reserving 1–2 tablespoons in the tin. Pour in the batter and replace the tin in the oven. Place the meat on a trivet over the roasting tin or on a shelf above the tin so the juices from the meat will drip on to the Yorkshire pudding during cooking.

# CREAMED HORSERADISH

*Serves 4–6*

¼ teaspoon dry mustard
¼ teaspoon salt
pinch pepper
pinch sugar
¼ pint/1·5 dl double cream

2 tablespoons grated fresh horseradish root
1 tablespoon white vinegar or lemon juice

Mix together the mustard, salt, pepper, sugar and cream. Add the grated horseradish, then very gradually beat in the vinegar. Serve as an accompaniment to roast beef.

*Melton Mowbray pie*

# WILTSHIRE HAM IN CIDER

*Serves 4–6*

1 piece gammon, about
    4 lb/1·75 kg
about 1½ pints/9 dl cider, dry or
    sweet according to taste
12 small onions

4 cloves
*bouquet garni* (see recipe)
pepper
2 oz/50 g fine dried breadcrumbs

If the ham is well salted, cover with cold water and soak overnight. The next day, discard the water and place the ham in a large saucepan. Add enough cider to cover. Bring to the boil over moderate heat, skimming the surface occasionally. Lower the heat and simmer for 1 hour. Peel the onions and add them whole to the ham with the cloves, *bouquet garni* (3 bay leaves, 3 sprigs parsley, 1 sprig thyme, tied together) and pepper to taste. Continue simmering for a further 40 minutes, or until the onions are tender but unbroken.

When the ham and onions are tender, carefully remove them from the pan.

Strip off and discard the rind from the ham and sprinkle the fatty surface with the breadcrumbs. Serve the ham with the onions, broad beans, young carrots and mashed potatoes. The cider in which the ham was cooked may be served separately as an unthickened sauce.

# MELTON MOWBRAY PIE

*Serves 5–6*

**for the filling:**

1½ lb/700 g lean boneless pork, cut
    from the leg
8 oz/225 g belly of pork
6–8 anchovy fillets or 1 teaspoon
    anchovy essence
pinch pepper
3 tablespoons chicken or veal
    stock

**for the hot water crust pastry:**

12 oz/350 g plain flour
pinch salt
¼ pint/1·5 dl water
4 oz/100 g lard or cooking fat
1 egg
1 tablespoon water

**for the jelly:**

generous ¼ pint/2 dl chicken or
    veal stock
1 teaspoon powdered gelatine

The following recipe gives two methods of preparing the pie mould. See note for the alternative method.

Cut the pork into ½-inch (1-cm) cubes and chop the anchovies. Mix the pork and anchovies together in a mixing bowl and add the pepper and the stock. Do not add any salt. If using anchovy essence instead of anchovies, blend it with the pepper and stock and add to the pork mixture. Set the mixture aside until required.

Sift the flour and salt into a mixing bowl. Make a well in the centre. Place the water and lard in a saucepan and heat until the lard melts and the water boils. Remove from the heat and immediately pour the hot liquid into the flour. Blend the mixture with a knife to make a rough dough. Turn out on to a floured board and knead lightly while the dough is still warm.

Divide the pastry into thirds. Cover one-third of the dough and set aside in a warm place until required. Roll out one-third of the dough to a 7-inch (18-cm) circle and place in the bottom of a lightly greased 7-inch (18-cm) deep cake tin. Roll out the remaining third of the pastry into a rectangle the depth of the tin being used and long enough to go around the circumference of the tin. Line the inside of the tin, pressing the seams firmly together. If necessary, brush with a little water to make sure the joins are firmly sealed. Turn the rim of the pastry down slightly to make a firm base for the pastry lid. Pack the reserved pork and anchovy filling into the pastry case.

Roll out the reserved one-third of the pastry into a circle to fit the top of the pie. Put the pastry lid over the filling, trim off the surplus and seal the edges firmly. Make a hole or slit in the pastry lid. Make leaves or a rose with the surplus pastry, moisten the decorations with a little water and press on to the pastry. Whisk the egg with the water and brush over the pie surface and decoration to glaze. Bake in a moderate oven (350°F, 180°C, Gas Mark 4) for about 2½ hours. Lower the heat to 325°F (160°C, Gas Mark 3) after 1½ hours if the pastry becomes too brown. Remove the pie from the oven and cool completely. For the jelly, measure the stock into a saucepan, sprinkle in the gelatine and allow to soak for a few moments. Stir over low heat until dissolved. Remove from the heat and cool until almost setting. Pour the mixture into the pie through the hole or steam vent in the pastry lid. Set aside in a cool place for several hours until the jelly sets. Serve the pie with a green salad.

*Note:* An alternative method of preparing a 'raised' pie is to raise or mould the pastry by hand around a 7-inch (18-cm) deep cake tin which has been greased and floured. Roll two-thirds of the pastry into a large circle. Place the cake tin in the centre of the pastry and mould the warm dough firmly around it. Wrap a double layer of greaseproof paper around the pastry for additional support. Let stand until cool then remove the greaseproof paper and the cake tin. Proceed as above, reducing the baking time by 15 minutes.

# SALTED BEEF

*Makes 4–6 lb (1·75–2·75 kg)*

1 gallon/4·5 litres water
1 lb/450 g salt
6 oz/175 g soft brown sugar
½ oz/15 g saltpetre

4–6 lb/1·75–2·75 kg silverside
    or rolled brisket of
    beef

Place the water, salt, sugar and saltpetre in a very large saucepan. Stir over low heat until the sugar is dissolved, then add the beef. Bring to the boil, lower the heat then simmer steadily for 5 minutes. Remove the beef, skim the surface of the liquid, strain into a very large enamelled bowl or earthenware jar and let stand until cold. Wipe the beef carefully, trim away any excess fat and put into the brine. Cover and let stand in a cold place for a minimum of 7 days to obtain mildly salted beef, or about 10 days for a stronger flavour. Turn the beef in the brine each day. Use as required.

# FAGGOTS

Serves 4–6

| | |
|---|---|
| 1 large onion | pinch chopped fresh thyme or |
| 12 oz–1 lb/350 g–450 g pig's | dried thyme |
| liver or 1 pig's heart, about | 2 oz/50 g fine fresh breadcrumbs |
| 8 oz/225 g | or oatmeal |
| 4 oz/100 g belly of pork | 1 egg |
| salt and pepper | about 6 tablespoons stock |
| pinch ground ginger | 1 pig's caul (optional) |
| pinch chopped fresh sage or | |
| dried sage | |

Peel and slice the onion. Rinse the liver and pork under cold running water. Discard any tough fibrous parts. Place the onion, liver and pork in a saucepan, cover with cold water and season with salt and pepper. Place over high heat and bring to the boil. Lower the heat and simmer for 45–50 minutes, or until the meat is tender. Drain off and reserve the stock.

Finely mince the liver and pork and mix in the ginger, sage, thyme, breadcrumbs and egg. Add enough of the reserved stock to form a moist mixture and add salt and pepper to taste. Form the mixture into 2- to 3-inch (5- to 7·5-cm) balls and wrap each ball in a piece of the caul. Place the balls fairly close together in a lightly greased tin. Alternatively, spread the mixture into a greased 8-inch (20-cm) square tin, mark into squares and cover with a sheet of greased cooking foil. Cook in a moderately hot oven (400°F, 200°C, Gas Mark 6) for about 1 hour. Serve the faggots hot with brown gravy and pease pudding (see page 52) or mashed potatoes.

# GAMMON IN WHISKEY AND CREAM

Serves 4

| | |
|---|---|
| 2 large potatoes | 2 medium-sized cooking apples |
| salt and pepper | 1 tablespoon soft brown sugar |
| 1 egg yolk | 2 oz/50 g butter or bacon |
| 1 oz/25 g butter | dripping |
| 1 oz/25 g plain flour | ¼ pint/1·5 dl beef stock |
| 4 slices lean gammon, about | ¼ pint/1·5 dl Irish whiskey |
| 8 oz/225 g each | 4 tablespoons double cream |

Peel the potatoes and cut into quarters. Cook in salted water to cover until tender. Drain, mash and season well with salt and pepper to taste. Beat the egg yolk and butter into the mashed potato and set aside in a warm place until required.

Meanwhile, mix the flour with a little pepper. Remove any rind from the gammon slices and coat the gammon on both sides with the seasoned flour. Peel, core and thinly slice the apples, then sprinkle with the sugar. Heat the butter in a large frying pan over moderate heat and fry the gammon slices for 2–3 minutes on each side, or until tender. Place the slices on a heated serving dish and keep hot.

Pour the stock and whiskey into the frying pan and bring to the boil. Put the apples into the hot liquid and simmer gently for 5 minutes. Lower the heat and stir in the cream. Return the gammon to the pan and heat gently for 2–3 minutes, but do not boil.

Using a large star tube in a piping bag, pipe the mashed potato mixture in a border around the edge of a large ovenproof serving plate and place under a hot grill until lightly brown. Arrange the gammon in the centre of the plate and carefully spoon the sauce over the slices. Serve immediately.

# ROAST LAMB AND ACCOMPANIMENTS

Serves 4

| | |
|---|---|
| leg or shoulder of lamb, about | 2 tablespoons distilled or pure |
| 4 lb/1·75 kg (see note) | malt vinegar |
| salt and pepper | **for the cucumber sauce:** |
| **for the mint sauce:** | 1 medium-sized cucumber |
| 2–3 tablespoons chopped fresh | salt and pepper |
| mint | 2 oz/50 g butter |
| 3 teaspoons castor sugar | ½ pint/3 dl white stock or water |
| 2 teaspoons boiling water | ¼ pint/1 5 dl double cream |
| (optional) | |

Place the lamb in a roasting tin and season lightly with salt and pepper. Unless the lamb is very lean, there is no need to add any fat. Roast, uncovered, in a hot oven (425°F, 220°C, Gas Mark 7), allowing 20 minutes per pound (per half kilo) plus an additional 20 minutes. If the joint is wrapped in aluminium foil or a covered roasting tin is used, then allow an additional 15–20 minutes cooking time.

To make the mint sauce, rinse the mint under cold running water, dry well and strip the leaves from the stalks. Finely chop the leaves on a board with the sugar. Place the mixture in a bowl and stir in the water and vinegar. Alternatively, put the water and vinegar into a liquidiser, then add the sugar and the mint leaves. Blend for a few moments until finely chopped.

To make the cucumber sauce, peel the cucumber. If a little of the skin is left on the cucumber it will give a pale green colour to the sauce. Cut the cucumber into ½-inch (1-cm) pieces, then cut each piece into fine strips. Season lightly with salt and pepper to taste. Set aside for about 30 minutes to draw the excess water from the cucumber. Melt the butter in a saucepan, add the cucumber and sauté for several minutes. Add the white stock and simmer until tender. Rub the mixture through a sieve or use a liquidiser to make a purée. Return the purée to the pan and stir in the cream. Reheat gently but do not allow to boil. Taste and adjust the seasoning.

Serve the hot roast lamb with the sauces, peas and new potatoes.

*Note:* A crown roast may also be served with these sauces. The centre of the crown may be stuffed before roasting, or filled with young vegetables just before serving. Protect the ends of the bones with aluminium foil to prevent burning. Garnish each bone with a paper frill, olive or glacé cherry.

*Roast lamb and accompaniments*

# JUGGED HARE

*Serves 4–6*

1 (3-lb/1·5-kg) hare, with the
  blood, if possible
3 teaspoons vinegar
1½ pints/9 dl water or hare stock
  (see recipe)
salt and pepper
2 oz/50 g plain flour
2 medium-sized onions
3 medium-sized carrots (optional)
3 oz/75 g cooking fat
*bouquet garni* (see recipe)
1 lemon (optional)
3 tablespoons redcurrant jelly
¼ pint/1·5 dl port or claret

**for the forcemeat balls:**

4 oz/100 g fine fresh breadcrumbs
1½ tablespoons chopped fresh
  parsley
salt and pepper
½ teaspoon finely grated lemon
  rind
2 teaspoons lemon juice
pinch mixed dried herbs
2 oz/50 g shredded suet or melted
  butter
1 egg

The blood of the hare gives a rich flavour to the sauce. Cut
the hare into pieces, place in a large saucepan, cover with
water and add the vinegar. Soak the pieces of hare for 1 hour
to whiten the flesh.

Meanwhile, to make the hare stock, put the liver and head
of the hare into a second large saucepan with water to cover
and salt and pepper to taste. Cover tightly and simmer for a
minimum of 30 minutes. Strain the stock and add water to
make 1½ pints (9 dl). Reserve the liver.

Mix the flour with ½ teaspoon salt and a pinch of pepper.
Drain and dry the hare pieces and coat with the seasoned
flour. Peel and slice the onions and carrots, if used. Carrots
give a sweeter flavour to the sauce. Melt the cooking fat in a
saucepan over moderate heat and sauté the hare pieces for 5
minutes. Remove the hare and set aside until required.

Add the onions and carrots to the hot fat in the pan and
sauté for 3–4 minutes. Add the stock gradually, stirring well
after each addition, and bring to the boil, stirring constantly
until thickened and boiling. Place the hare pieces and the
liver in the sauce with the blood and *bouquet garni* (3 bay
leaves, 3 sprigs parsley, 1 sprig thyme, tied together). Halve
the lemon, remove the seeds and add the lemon halves to the
pan. Lemon flavour gives bite to the sauce. Cover the pan
and simmer the hare for 2 hours.

Remove the hare pieces and keep hot. Discard the lemon
and *bouquet garni*. Rub the vegetables and liquid from the
pan through a sieve, or use a liquidiser to make a purée and
return to the pan. Add the redcurrant jelly and wine and heat
gently until the jelly dissolves. Taste and adjust the
seasoning. Return the hare to the sauce, cover the pan and
simmer for a further 1 hour. Alternatively, the hare and
sauce may be put into a casserole, covered and cooked in a
moderate oven (325°F, 160°C, Gas Mark 3) for 1¼–1½ hours.

To make the forcemeat balls, mix together the breadcrumbs, parsley, salt, pepper, lemon rind, lemon juice, dried
herbs, suet and the egg. Shape into 12 small balls and bake
on a greased baking tray near the top of a moderate oven
(325°F, 160°C, Gas Mark 3) for 20–30 minutes. Serve the
jugged hare with the forcemeat balls. Garnish with fried
bread croutons or glacé cherries and serve redcurrant jelly
separately.

*Jugged hare*

# CASSEROLE OF PORK

Serves 4

| | |
|---|---|
| 1 cabbage, about 1 lb/450 g | ½ teaspoon chopped fresh sage |
| 3 large onions | 2 teaspoons chopped fresh parsley |
| 2 oz/50 g butter | pinch grated nutmeg |
| salt and pepper | **for the garnish:** |
| 4 large pork loin chops, about | 2 medium-sized cooking apples |
|     8 oz/225 g each | 1 oz/25 g butter |
| ½ pint/3 dl sweet cider | 1 oz/25 g soft brown sugar |

Discard the coarse outer leaves of the cabbage, reserving just the heart. Cut in quarters lengthwise, cut away the hard centre core and finely shred. Peel and thinly slice the onions. Melt the butter in a saucepan and sauté the cabbage and onions for 2–3 minutes. Season well with salt and pepper and place in a large, shallow casserole. Arrange the pork chops over the cabbage mixture, pour the cider over the chops and sprinkle with the sage, parsley and nutmeg. Cover the casserole tightly and cook in a moderate oven (350°F, 180°C, Gas Mark 4) for about 1–1½ hours, or until the meat is very tender.

Meanwhile, prepare the garnish. Peel, core and cut the apples into thin rings. Melt the butter in a heavy frying pan, add the apple rings and sauté until just tender. Sprinkle with the sugar and arrange the apple rings around the edge of the pork chops in the casserole before serving.

# CORNISH PASTIES

Serves 4

| | |
|---|---|
| **for the filling:** | **for the shortcrust pastry:** |
| 12 oz/350 g rump steak | 12 oz/350 g plain flour |
| 2 medium-sized potatoes | pinch salt |
| 2 medium-sized onions | 4–6 oz/110–175 g butter or |
| small piece swede or turnip |     cooking fat (see recipe) |
|     (optional) | about 3 tablespoons water |
| salt and pepper | 1 egg |
| 1 tablespoon water or beef stock | 1 tablespoon water |

To make the filling, cut the beef into ½-inch (1-cm) cubes and place in a mixing bowl. Peel and finely dice the potatoes, onions and swede, and add to the beef. Season well with salt and pepper to taste and blend with the water.

Prepare the pastry as for Mince Pies, page 53. Use the smaller quantity of butter if a less rich pastry is desired. Roll out to ¼ inch (5 mm) thick and cut into 4 circles, about 7 inches (18 cm) in diameter. (In Cornwall, if the pasty is to be served hot for a family meal, one large pasty is traditionally made instead of several small ones.)

Place the circles on a baking tray. Place the filling across the centre of the pastry, moisten the edges of the pastry with water and bring the opposite edges together to enclose the filling completely. Press the pastry edges firmly together to seal in the filling and flute them. Lightly whisk the egg with the water. Brush the pastry with the egg mixture. Bake in a moderately hot oven (400°F, 200°C, Gas Mark 6) for 20 minutes, then lower the heat to 325°F (160°C, Gas Mark 3) and bake for a further 25–30 minutes for small pasties, or a further 45 minutes for a large pasty. Serve hot or cold.

*Note:* For a sweet filling use apples, sugar and sultanas.

# MUTTON PIES

*Serves 4*

**for the filling:**
12 oz/350 g boneless mutton, cut
    from the shoulder or loin
salt and pepper
6 oz/175 g currants or raisins
3 oz/75 g soft brown sugar

**for the hot water crust pastry:**
12 oz/350 g plain flour
pinch salt
5 oz/150 g cooking fat or
    margarine
¼ pint/1·5 dl water
1 egg

To make the filling, coarsely mince the meat. Season well with salt and pepper and set aside until required. Wash the currants, soak in boiling water for a few minutes, drain and dry. Mix the currants and brown sugar together.

Prepare the pastry as for Melton Mowbray Pie, page 43. Roll out to ⅛ inch (3 mm) thick on a lightly floured board while still warm. Cut out 8 small circles and press into lightly greased deep patty tins. Cut the remaining dough into slightly smaller circles for the lids. Place the lids in a warm place until ready to use so the pastry remains pliable.

Put the mutton and raisins in alternate layers in the lined patty tins, starting and finishing with the mutton. Press down lightly, as the filling should be fairly compact. Brush the edges of the pastry with water and cover each pie with a pastry lid. Make a slit in the centre of each pie and decorate with pastry roses and leaves made from the pastry trimmings. Lightly whisk the egg and brush over the surface of each pie. Bake in a moderately hot oven (400°F, 200°C, Gas Mark 6) for 20 minutes, then lower the heat to 375°F (190°C, Gas Mark 5) and bake for a further 15 minutes, or until the pastry is golden brown and the meat is tender. Serve the pies hot, with salad or cooked leeks.

# KENTISH CHICKEN PUDDING

*Serves 5–6*

**for the suet pastry:**
11 oz/300 g self-raising flour
pinch salt
4½ oz/125 g shredded suet
about ¼ pint/1·5 dl water

**for the filling:**
1 boiling chicken with giblets,
    about 4½ lb/2 kg

¾ pint/4·5 dl water
3 medium-sized onions
6 medium-sized carrots
½ oz/15 g plain flour
salt and pepper

To make the suet pastry, sift the flour and salt together in a large mixing bowl. Add the suet. Stir in enough of the water to form a soft dough. Turn the dough on to a floured board and knead lightly. Roll into a large circle, cut out a quarter of the circle in a wedge shape and set aside for making the pastry lid. Lower the remaining three-quarters of the circle into a greased 3-pint (1·5-litre) heat-resistant bowl or pudding basin. Bring the cut edges of the dough together and press on to the sides and bottom of the bowl, sealing the edges together. Trim any surplus dough from the top. By lining the bowl in this way you avoid any uneven pleats in the dough. Wipe the chicken. Put the giblets into a saucepan with the water and simmer for a minimum of 30 minutes to make a good stock. The heart may be diced when partially cooked and added to the filling.

Discard the skin from the chicken. Joint the chicken, remove the flesh from the bones and cut into large pieces. Peel and slice the onions and carrots and mix with the chicken flesh and heart. Sprinkle with the flour and salt and pepper to taste. Place the prepared chicken mixture in the bowl or pudding basin. Add enough of the giblet stock to half cover the filling. Reserve any remaining stock.

Roll the reserved dough into a circle the same size as the top of the bowl. Brush the rim of the pastry with water and press the lid into position. Traditionally, a linen pudding cloth is used to cover a steamed pudding. It is first dipped into boiling water, then into flour, so it becomes moisture-proof. To cover the pudding, make a fold down the centre of the cloth to allow the pudding to rise as it steams, place it over the pudding and tie securely with string around the edge of the bowl. Then bring up the four corners and tie them neatly together over the pudding. Make a handle with the string. Alternatively, lightly buttered greaseproof paper or aluminium foil may be used, in which case simply trim away the spare paper or foil below the string and make a handle as before. Place the pudding in a steamer over boiling water (see note). Steam for at least 3½–4 hours. Keep the water boiling constantly throughout the cooking time and replenish with additional boiling water when necessary.

When the pudding is cooked, remove the bowl from the steamer with the string handle or with tongs and remove the covering. Dry the outside of the bowl. Fold a napkin lengthwise, so that it is as wide as the bowl is high. Wrap the napkin around the bowl and secure the ends with a small safety pin or tuck them into the fold of the napkin. To serve, remove the first slice of pudding and pour in the reserved stock which has been reheated.

*Note:* When a steamer is not available, the pudding may be put into a large saucepan with boiling water reaching halfway up the sides of the bowl. Cover the pan and boil steadily throughout the cooking time. Replenish with boiling water when necessary.

# LANCASHIRE HOT-POT

*Serves 4*

1½ lb/700 g middle or best end
    lamb
salt and pepper
2 large potatoes
2 carrots

1 small turnip
1 large onion or 2 leeks
about ¾ pint/4 dl water
meat dripping (see recipe)

Season the lamb with salt and pepper to taste. Peel and thickly slice the potatoes, carrots, turnip and onion. If using leeks instead of onion, trim, rinse thoroughly under cold running water and cut into 1-inch (2·5-cm) pieces. Place the lamb, potatoes, carrots, turnip and onion in layers in a deep casserole, adding additional salt and pepper to taste. End with an overlapping layer of potatoes. Add enough of the water to reach about one-third of the way up the casserole. Place small pats of meat dripping on top of the potatoes. Cover the casserole and cook in a cool oven (300°F, 150°C, Gas Mark 2) for 2½–3 hours. Remove the cover about 30 minutes before the end of cooking and increase the temperature to 400°F (200°C, Gas Mark 6) to brown the top layer of potatoes. Serve with pickled red cabbage.

# HAGGIS

*Serves 10–12*

| | |
|---|---|
| 1 sheep's pluck (liver, heart and lights) | 2 medium-sized onions |
| salt and pepper | 8 oz/225 g oatmeal |
| ½ pint/3 dl stock (see recipe) | 8 oz/225 g shredded suet |
| | pinch cayenne pepper |

Rinse the pluck thoroughly under cold running water. Open the heart and cut away the gristle and vessels. Put the pluck into a saucepan and cover with cold water. Season lightly with salt and pepper and simmer over moderate heat for 1¼ hours. Remove the pluck from the pan and reserve ½ pint (3 dl) of the stock. Discard the remainder. Mince the pluck. Peel and grate the onions. Mix together the reserved stock, pluck, onions, oatmeal and suet. Season well with salt and pepper and the cayenne pepper. Put the mixture into a greased heat-resistant bowl or pudding basin. Do not fill more than three-quarters full as there must be room for the haggis to swell during cooking. Cover the bowl with buttered greaseproof paper or aluminium foil. Place in a steamer over boiling water, and steam for at least 4 hours. Keep the water boiling constantly throughout the cooking time and replenish with additional boiling water when necessary. (If no steamer is available, see Kentish Chicken Pudding, page 48, for an alternative method of steaming.)

Remove the haggis from the bowl and serve at once with mashed neeps (turnips). Whisky is generally served with haggis, and a little whisky is sometimes poured over it.

*Note:* The true haggis is difficult to make at home as the various ingredients must be put into a sheep's stomach bag. Apart from the problem of obtaining this, there is the rather unpleasant and lengthy task of cleaning the bag. Modern Scottish cooks, however, often make haggis in a bowl, and while it may not look the same, the flavour is excellent.

# ROAST VENISON

*Serves 6*

| | |
|---|---|
| 2 medium-sized onions | 4½–5 lb/about 2·25 kg haunch of venison |
| ½ pint/3 dl red wine | |
| *bouquet garni* (see recipe) | 8 oz/225 g lard or cooking fat |
| pinch salt | **for the game chips:** |
| 8 peppercorns | 3 medium-sized potatoes |
| 2 teaspoons prepared mustard | oil for deep-frying |
| 2 tablespoons olive oil | 3 oz/75 g fried breadcrumbs |

To make the marinade, peel and thickly slice the onions and place in a large bowl with the wine, *bouquet garni* (3 bay leaves, 3 sprigs parsley, 1 sprig thyme, tied together) and salt. Add the peppercorns, mustard and olive oil. Rinse the venison under cold running water and dry thoroughly with kitchen paper. Place the venison in the marinade. Cover and set aside in a cool place for 2–3 days. Turn the meat once or twice a day so the marinade soaks into the meat.

When ready to cook, remove the venison from the marinade and place in a roasting tin with the lard. Roast in a moderately hot oven (400°F, 200°C, Gas Mark 6), allowing 20 minutes per pound (per half kilo) plus an additional 20 minutes. Baste frequently with the fat in the tin.

At the end of the cooking time, strain the marinade and reserve for making the game sauce (see page 52) or gravy.

To make the game chips, peel the potatoes, cut into wafer-thin slices and dry well. In a deep saucepan, heat the oil to 365°F (185°C). Put the potato slices into a frying basket and fry for 1–2 minutes. Lift out and drain on kitchen paper. Reheat the oil, fry the chips for a further 30 seconds and drain again. Game chips should be very crisp.

Serve the venison with the fried crumbs, game chips, watercress, redcurrant jelly and either game sauce (see page 52) or gravy.

*Roast venison*

# ROAST TURKEY WITH CHESTNUT STUFFING

*Serves 12–14*

1 turkey, about 12–16 lb/
  5·5–7·5 kg
turkey giblets
4 oz/100 g melted butter or
  12 oz/350 g streaky bacon
2 lb/1 kg pork sausages
12 oz/350 g streaky bacon rashers
  for bacon rolls

**for the stuffing:**
1½ lb/700 g chestnuts or 1
  (15½-oz/440-g) can unsweetened
  chestnut purée
giblet stock or salted water (see
  recipe)
1 lb/450 g pork sausage meat
4 oz/100 g walnuts, finely
  chopped
salt and pepper

Wipe the turkey inside and out with a damp cloth or kitchen paper. Place the heart, gizzard and neck in a small saucepan, cover with water and simmer for 1–2 hours. Add the liver for the last 10–15 minutes of the cooking time. Strain and reserve the giblet stock.

If using fresh chestnuts, make a cut in the flat end of each chestnut with the point of a sharp knife, place the chestnuts in a large saucepan, cover with water and simmer for 10 minutes. Drain, and remove the skins while the chestnuts are still warm. Replace the nuts in the pan and cover with the giblet stock or salted water. Bring to the boil and simmer for a further 20 minutes, or until tender. Drain the chestnuts well and rub through a sieve to make a purée.

Mix the puréed chestnuts or the canned chestnut purée with the sausage meat and walnuts. Season well with salt and pepper. Lightly press a little of the stuffing into the neck cavity of the turkey. Pull the neck skin over the stuffing and secure at the back with a skewer. Twist the wings under the bird so they lie flat with the tips together. Stuff the body cavity with the remainder of the stuffing, but do not pack tightly to allow for expansion. Tie the drumsticks together with string or secure under the band of skin next to the tail.

Brush the turkey well with the melted butter, or cover with the streaky bacon, particularly over the breast. Alternatively, cover tightly with aluminium foil. To calculate the cooking time for a turkey weighing up to 12 lb (5·5 kg), allow 15 minutes per pound (per half kilo) and an additional 15 minutes at the end of the cooking time. For a turkey over 12 lb (5·5 kg), allow 12 minutes per pound (per half kilo) and an additional 12 minutes at the end of the cooking time. Place the turkey on a rack in a shallow roasting tin. Roast in a moderately hot oven (375°F, 190°C, Gas Mark 5) for the calculated time. If using bacon, remove for the last 12–30 minutes to brown the bird. If cooking the turkey in aluminium foil, allow about 30 minutes extra time. The foil should be removed for the last 30–40 minutes to brown the turkey.

Place the sausages in the tin with the turkey for the last 30–40 minutes of the cooking time. Roll up the bacon fairly tightly and thread on to metal skewers. Place in a separate tin and cook in the oven with the turkey for about 15 minutes.

Serve the turkey garnished with sausages and bacon rolls and accompanied by Brussels sprouts, chestnuts, roast potatoes and bread sauce (see page 52).

*Note:* If using canned chestnut purée, the texture and taste of the stuffing will differ slightly.

# ROAST DUCKLING WITH SAGE AND ONION STUFFING AND APPLE SAUCE

*Serves 4*

2 small ducklings, about
  3 lb/1·5 kg each
salt and pepper
**for the stuffing:**
2 large onions
½ pint/3 dl water
salt and pepper
2 teaspoons chopped fresh sage or
  1 teaspoon dried sage

1 oz/25 g melted butter or
  shredded suet
2 oz/50 g fine fresh breadcrumbs
1 egg (optional)
**for the sauce:**
1 lb/450 g cooking apples
¼ pint/1·5 dl water
about 2 oz/50 g sugar
1 oz/25 g butter
  (optional)

Place the ducklings in a roasting tin and season the skin very lightly with salt and pepper.

To make the stuffing, peel and coarsely chop the onions and simmer in the water with a pinch of salt for 10 minutes. Drain and reserve the liquid. Chop the onions more finely, place in a mixing bowl and add pepper to taste. Add the sage,

butter and breadcrumbs and mix well. Adjust the seasoning. Either use the egg and a little onion liquid, or use only the reserved liquid to make a moist stuffing. Put the stuffing into a lightly greased ovenproof dish and cover with foil.

Place the ducklings and the stuffing in a moderately hot oven (400°F, 200°C, Gas Mark 6). Roast the ducklings for 15 minutes per pound (per half kilo) plus an additional 15 minutes. If the birds are unequal in weight, adjust the roasting time for each one accordingly. For an older duck, roast at the same temperature as for the ducklings, allowing 20 minutes per pound (per half kilo) plus an additional 20 minutes. Prick the skin of each duckling very lightly with a fine skewer after the first 30 minutes, so the excess fat is released and the skin becomes crisp.

To make the sauce, peel and slice the apples. Simmer in a small heavy saucepan with the water and sugar until very soft. Rub the apples through a sieve, or liquidise. Beat a little butter into the sauce, if desired. Pour into a heated sauceboat. Serve the ducklings with new potatoes, peas seasoned with a small sprig of mint and the apple sauce.

*Note:* To give extra crispness to the skin, cook the ducklings as above until the last 15 minutes of the cooking time. Then pour off the fat from the tin. Blend 2 tablespoons of honey with 1 tablespoon hot water, brush over the ducklings and continue cooking.

*Roast game birds with game chips; trifle (see page 56)*

# DEVILLED POULTRY OR GAME

*Serves 4*

| | |
|---|---|
| 4 joints cooked chicken, turkey or game | 3 drops Worcestershire sauce |
| | pinch cayenne pepper |
| 6 oz/175 g butter | pinch salt |
| 2 teaspoons prepared mustard | 2 tablespoons sweet chutney |
| 1–2 teaspoons curry powder | |

Make several cuts in the chicken to enable the devilled mixture to penetrate the flesh. Cream the butter with the mustard, curry powder, Worcestershire sauce, cayenne pepper, salt and chutney (see note). Spread the mixture evenly over the chicken and place on a rack in a grill pan. Grill under moderate heat for 10–15 minutes on each side. The devilled mixture which drips into the grill pan may be used to baste the chicken. Serve with boiled rice and a crisp green salad.

*Note:* The addition of 1½ oz (40 g) fine fresh breadcrumbs blended with the butter gives an interesting texture to the devilled mixture.

# ROAST GROUSE

*Serves 4*

| | |
|---|---|
| brace of young grouse (see note) | giblets of the grouse |
| 2 oz/50 g butter (see note) | 4 slices white bread |
| salt and pepper | 3 oz/75 g fried breadcrumbs |
| 4–8 rashers streaky bacon or 3 oz/75 g butter | watercress |

Wash the grouse and dry well. Put half the butter inside each bird (this helps to keep the flesh moist). Season the grouse with salt and pepper and cover with the bacon rashers or butter to prevent the flesh from excessive drying. Set aside until required.

Place the giblets in a small saucepan, cover with water and simmer until tender. Strain and reserve the stock for the port wine gravy (see page 52). Mash and season the liver from the giblets. Trim and discard the crusts from the bread slices. Toast the bread and spread with the mashed liver. Place in a roasting tin and put the grouse on top. Place the tin in a moderately hot oven (400°F, 200°C, Gas Mark 6) and roast for 15 minutes per pound (per half kilo) plus an additional 15 minutes at the end of the cooking time. Rinse the watercress under cold water and set aside until required.

To serve the grouse, cut each bird in half and place the halves on the slices of toast. Garnish with game chips (see Roast Venison, page 49), fried crumbs and watercress. Serve with redcurrant jelly or bread sauce, and port wine gravy (see page 52).

*Note:* This recipe may be used for other game birds, provided they are young and tender. If roasting pheasant, allow 20 minutes per pound (per half kilo) plus an additional 20 minutes at the end of the cooking time.

# REDCURRANT JELLY

*Makes about 3 lb (1·5 kg)*

2 lb/1 kg redcurrants      preserving sugar (see recipe)
1 pint/6 dl water

Wash the redcurrants, place in a large saucepan with the water and simmer slowly to obtain a thick pulp. Strain through a jelly bag or several thicknesses of muslin.

Measure the liquid into a saucepan and add 1 lb (450 g) sugar to each 1 pint (6 dl) of liquid. Stir over low heat until the sugar dissolves then boil rapidly without stirring until a few drops, placed on a cold plate, set and crinkle when pushed with the finger.

Skim the surface and pour the jelly into hot clean jars to within ½ inch (1 cm) of the top. Tap the jars lightly to remove any air bubbles. Cover the surface of the jelly immediately with greaseproof paper discs. When cold, cover securely with a lid or cling film and store in a cool dry place away from strong light.

# PORT WINE GRAVY

*Serves 4*

¼ pint/3 dl giblet stock      salt and pepper
2 oz/50 g clarified game dripping      pinch soft brown sugar
   or butter      ¼ pint/1·5 dl port
1 oz/25 g plain flour

Strain the stock through a layer of muslin. Heat the dripping or butter in a saucepan. Stir in the flour and cook gently for several minutes, or until the flour begins to turn golden brown but does not burn. Stir in the stock and bring to the boil, stirring constantly until thickened. Add salt and pepper to taste, the brown sugar, port and any sediment from the roasting tin. Heat the gravy and strain it through a sieve before pouring into a gravy boat. Serve with roast grouse (see page 51) or any other roasted game.

# GAME SAUCE

*Serves 4–6*

1 medium-sized onion      salt and pepper
1 large tomato      2 tablespoons dry sherry
2 medium-sized mushrooms      ¼ pint/1·5 dl red wine or Madeira
2 oz/50 g butter or dripping      1 tablespoon malt vinegar
1 oz/25 g plain flour      about 2 tablespoons sugar
½ pint/3 dl meat stock      about 6 oz/175 g redcurrant jelly
   (see note)

Peel and chop the onion and tomato. Rinse and chop the mushrooms. Heat the butter in a saucepan over moderate heat. Add the onion, tomato and mushrooms and sauté for a few minutes. Stir in the flour and cook over low heat for 1–2 minutes, stirring frequently. Gradually add the meat stock and bring to the boil, stirring constantly until thickened.

Strain the mixture and season with salt and pepper to taste. Return the mixture to the pan and add the sherry, wine, vinegar, sugar and redcurrant jelly. Heat gently until the jelly melts. Taste, and adjust the seasoning if necessary.

Serve the sauce hot as an accompaniment to roast game birds or roast venison (see page 49).

*Note:* If preferred, a little brown ale may be substituted for part of the meat stock.

# BREAD SAUCE

*Serves 6–8*

1 large onion      1½ oz/40 g butter or margarine
3 cloves      salt and pepper
4 oz/100 g fine fresh breadcrumbs      4 tablespoons single cream
generous ¾ pint/5 dl milk

Peel the onion and stick with the cloves. Put the onion and breadcrumbs into a saucepan. Add the milk, butter and salt and pepper to taste and bring to the boil. Remove from the heat and let stand in a warm place for 20–30 minutes to allow the onion flavour to penetrate the sauce.

Just before serving, remove the onion, stir in the cream and reheat without boiling. This sauce should be the consistency of a thick cream and should be well seasoned. Serve as an accompaniment to roast turkey (see page 50).

# PEASE PUDDING

*Serves 8–10*

1 lb/450 g dried yellow split peas      2 oz/50 g butter
1 ham bone, about 2 lb/1 kg      salt and pepper
1 large onion      1 egg (optional)

Soak the peas overnight in plenty of cold water. Put the ham bone in a large saucepan, cover with cold water and soak overnight.

Drain the peas and the ham bone. Place the ham bone in a large saucepan and cover with fresh cold water. Simmer gently over moderate heat for about 1 hour. Discard the bone and reserve the stock. Finely chop the onion. Place the peas and onion in a second saucepan and cover with the reserved ham stock. Simmer gently over moderate heat for about 2 hours, or until the peas are very tender. The peas should absorb all the liquid. Add the butter. Taste, and season with salt and pepper. Whisk the egg and add to the peas.

Put the mixture into a heat-resistant bowl or pudding basin and cover with buttered aluminium foil or greaseproof paper. Place the bowl in a steamer over rapidly boiling water and steam for about 45 minutes. Keep the water boiling constantly throughout the cooking time and replenish with additional boiling water when necessary. (If no steamer is available, see Kentish Chicken Pudding, page 48, for an alternative method of steaming.) Turn the pudding out of the bowl on to a heated serving dish and serve hot with faggots (see page 44) or with pork. To reheat pease pudding, either resteam or cut into slices and heat gently in bacon dripping.

*Note:* A little chopped or dried sage may also be added to flavour the pudding.

Mincemeat: Many of the original recipes for mincemeat contained minced beef with the fruits and spices, which is the reason for the rather odd name of this traditional sweet filling for Christmas pies. Mince pies were originally oval in shape, not round, to represent the manger, and Christmas fare is not complete without them. They are easy to freeze. Leave on the baking trays in the quick-freeze compartment until frozen firm. Pack carefully in rigid polythene containers with foil between the layers. Overwrap, seal and label. Store in the freezer until required.

# MINCEMEAT

Makes about 2½ lb (1·25 kg)

| | |
|---|---|
| 1 cooking apple | 1 teaspoon finely grated lemon |
| 1 lb/450 g mixed dried fruit | rind |
| 4 oz/100 g shredded suet or | ½ teaspoon ground cinnamon |
| melted butter or margarine | 1 teaspoon ground mixed spice |
| 4 oz/100 g demerara sugar | ½ teaspoon grated nutmeg |
| 4 oz/100 g chopped mixed | 3 tablespoons lemon juice |
| candied peel | 4 tablespoons brandy, whisky or |
| 4 oz/100 g blanched chopped | rum |
| almonds | |

Peel, core and grate the apple. Place in a large mixing bowl with the remaining ingredients. Mix thoroughly until all the ingredients are evenly distributed. Pack the mixture into clean, dry jars. Cover and seal. Store in a cool, dry place until required. The mincemeat can be used at once but the flavour improves if left to mature for at least 1 month.

# MINCE PIES

Makes 12 pies

| for the shortcrust pastry: | for the filling: |
|---|---|
| 8 oz/225 g plain flour | about 8 oz/225 g mincemeat |
| pinch salt | 1 oz/25 g castor sugar |
| 4 oz/110 g butter | |
| about 3–4 tablespoons cold water | |

To make the shortcrust pastry, sift the flour and salt into a mixing bowl. Cut the butter into pieces and add. Rub the mixture lightly between the fingertips, allowing it to fall back into the bowl. When the butter is evenly distributed and the mixture is like fine breadcrumbs, add the water and mix to a dough. Turn out on to a lightly floured board and knead until smooth.

Roll out the pastry to about ¼ inch (5 mm) thick and cut into 2½-inch (6-cm) circles using a floured round cutter. Place half of the circles on a greased baking tray. Place 1 teaspoon of the mincemeat in the centre of each circle. Moisten the edges of the pastry circles with cold water. Cover each one with a pastry lid and press the edges firmly together to seal. Cut two small slits in each lid to allow the steam to escape during baking. This helps to keep the pastry crisp. Bake in a moderately hot oven (400°F, 200°C, Gas Mark 6) for 20 minutes. Sprinkle with sugar and serve hot or cold.

Note: Flaky pastry may also be used for mince pies. Prepare the pastry as for Steak and Kidney Pie, page 40, and make up the mince pies as above. Bake in a hot oven (425°F, 220°C, Gas Mark 7) for 15 minutes, then reduce the heat to 400°F (200°C, Gas Mark 6) and bake for 5 minutes. Sprinkle with sugar and serve hot or cold.

# CHERRY COBBLER

*Serves 4*

1½ lb/700 g black cherries or 2 (15-oz/425-g) cans
3 tablespoons water
3 oz/75 g sugar

**for the cobbler:**
6 oz/175 g self-raising flour
1½ oz/40 g butter or margarine
3 oz/75 g castor sugar
3–4 tablespoons milk (see recipe)

If using fresh cherries, wash them and remove the stalks but do not stone them. If using canned cherries, drain the juice from the cans and reserve 2–3 tablespoons. Place the cherries in a 9-inch (23-cm) pie dish and add the water and sugar or, for the canned cherries, the juice, substituting this for the sugar and water in the recipe. If using fresh cherries, put a piece of aluminium foil or greaseproof paper over the fruit and bake in a moderately hot oven (375°F, 190°C, Gas Mark 5) for 15 minutes.

Meanwhile, prepare the cobbler. Sift the flour into a mixing bowl. Cut the butter into pieces and add to the flour. Rub the mixture lightly between the fingertips, allowing it to fall back into the bowl. When the butter is evenly distributed, stir in two-thirds of the sugar. Add enough milk to form a soft dough. Turn the dough out on to a lightly floured board and roll until ½ inch (1 cm) thick. Cut the dough into 2-inch (5-cm) circles using a floured round cutter. Brush the circles with the remaining milk and sprinkle with the remaining sugar.

Arrange the circles on top of the hot cherries. Raise the oven heat to 425°F (220°C, Gas Mark 7) and bake for a further 15–20 minutes, or until the cobbler is well risen and golden brown. Serve hot with cream.

# CHRISTMAS PUDDING

*Makes 4 small or 2 large puddings*

4 oz/100 g glacé cherries
4 oz/100 g dried apricots
8 prunes
4 oz/100 g blanched almonds
1 medium-sized carrot
1 large cooking apple
4 oz/100 g plain flour
½ teaspoon ground cinnamon
½ teaspoon ground nutmeg
½ teaspoon ground mace
½ teaspoon ground allspice
8 oz/225 g fine fresh white breadcrumbs
8 oz/225 g soft dark brown sugar
6 oz/175 g shredded suet or melted butter
6 oz/175 g currants
12 oz/350 g sultanas
1½ lb/700 g seedless raisins
6 oz/175 g chopped mixed candied peel
1 teaspoon grated lemon rind
2 teaspoons grated orange rind
4 eggs
2 tablespoons golden syrup
2 tablespoons lemon juice (see note)
5 tablespoons orange juice (see note)
2 tablespoons sweet sherry
scant ½ pint/2·5 dl dark beer (see note)

Coarsely chop the glacé cherries, dried apricots, prunes and blanched almonds. Peel and grate the carrot. Peel, core and grate the apple.

Sift the flour, cinnamon, nutmeg, mace and allspice into a large mixing bowl. Add the breadcrumbs, brown sugar, suet, currants, sultanas, seedless raisins, mixed candied peel and the lemon and orange rind. Add the prepared cherries, apricots, prunes, blanched almonds, carrot and apple. Mix the ingredients thoroughly and make a well in the centre. Lightly whisk the eggs and pour into the well with the golden syrup, lemon and orange juice if used, sherry and beer. Stir well until the ingredients are thoroughly moistened. Cover with a cloth and set aside overnight to mature in flavour.

Grease and lightly flour 4 1-pint (6-dl) or 2 2-pint (1-litre) heat-resistant bowls or pudding basins, and divide the mixture equally among them. Press firmly into the bowls, filling each one to within 1 inch (2·5 cm) of the top. To make a light crumbly pudding, pack the mixture less tightly. Cover with greaseproof paper, buttered on each side, then aluminium foil or another piece of greaseproof paper.

Steam the larger puddings for 6–7 hours or the smaller ones for 4–5 hours, or allow 1–2 hours in a pressure cooker at 15 lb pressure. (If no steamer is available, see Kentish Chicken Pudding, page 48, for an alternative method of steaming.) When the puddings are cooked, remove them from the water, uncover and set aside until cold. Cover each with a clean dry cloth or greaseproof paper, tie securely and store in a cool dry place. Allow the puddings to mature for at least 3 weeks before using.

When required for use, cover the pudding with fresh buttered greaseproof paper and resteam for 2–3 hours. Turn the pudding out of the bowl and serve hot with Cumberland rum butter (see below).

*Note:* To make a very moist pudding, include the lemon and orange juice. For a drier pudding omit the lemon and orange juice or use half the quantity of beer.

# CUMBERLAND RUM BUTTER

*Makes approximately 1¼ lb (600 g)*

8 oz/225 g unsalted butter
12 oz–1 lb/350–450 g demerara or soft brown sugar (see recipe)
pinch ground cinnamon
pinch grated nutmeg
about 2 tablespoons rum

Cream the butter until very soft and light. Gradually beat in the sugar. The amount of sugar added depends upon how sweet a butter is desired. Beat in the cinnamon and nutmeg and gradually add the rum, beating thoroughly after each addition to prevent the mixture from curdling.

Put into attractive serving pots, seal tightly and store in a cool place. Serve as an accompaniment to Christmas pudding (see above) or on bread or toast.

# SNOWDON PUDDING

*Serves 4–6*

1½ oz/40 g butter
6 oz/175 g seedless raisins
4 oz/100 g shredded suet
6 oz/175 g fine fresh breadcrumbs
1 oz/25 g cornflour
pinch salt
1 teaspoon grated lemon rind
4 tablespoons orange marmalade

**for the sauce:**
1 large lemon
scant ½ pint/2·5 dl water
½ oz/15 g cornflour
½ pint/3 dl sweet red wine
4 oz/100 g castor sugar

Butter a 2-pint (1-litre) heat-resistant bowl or pudding basin with 2 tablespoons of the butter. Press half the raisins against the bottom and sides of the bowl. Place the remaining raisins in a mixing bowl and add the suet, breadcrumbs, cornflour, salt, lemon rind and marmalade. Mix to a stiff consistency, then spoon the mixture into the bowl and press down firmly. Butter a sheet of greaseproof paper or aluminium foil, using the remaining butter. Cover the bowl and secure with string. Place the bowl in a steamer over rapidly boiling water and steam for 1½–1¾ hours. Replenish with boiling water when necessary. (If no steamer is available, see Kentish Chicken Pudding, page 48, for an alternative method of steaming.)

To make the sauce, thinly pare the rind from the lemon and put into a saucepan with the water. Simmer for 15 minutes to extract the lemon flavour. Strain, discard the lemon rind and return the liquid to the pan. Squeeze the lemon and add the juice to the pan. Blend the cornflour with the wine and stir into the lemon liquid. Add the sugar, place the pan over low heat and bring to the boil, stirring constantly until thickened and smooth.

When the pudding is cooked, remove the paper and turn out of the bowl on to a heated serving plate. Serve immediately with the hot sauce.

# SWEET FANTASY

*Serves 4*

3 egg yolks
4 oz/100 g castor sugar
1 teaspoon grated lemon rind
¾ pint/4·5 dl double cream
4 tablespoons lemon juice

Whisk the egg yolks in a mixing bowl with the sugar and lemon rind. Gradually add the cream. Place the bowl over a saucepan of hot, but not boiling water and whip until the mixture begins to thicken.

Divide the lemon juice between 4 small glass dishes and spoon the cream mixture carefully on top. Serve immediately.

# ORANGE CUSTARDS

*Serves 4*

2 Seville oranges (see note)
¼ pint/1·5 dl water
2 oz/50 g castor sugar
4 eggs
½ pint/3 dl single cream
½ pint/3 dl milk
few blanched pistachio nuts or blanched almonds

Thinly pare the rind from the oranges, taking care not to include any white inner skin which will give a bitter taste to the custard. Put the rind with the water and sugar into a saucepan, cover tightly and simmer for 10 minutes. Strain the orange flavoured liquid into a small bowl and set aside to cool slightly. Add the eggs and whisk well.

Meanwhile, warm the cream and milk together in a saucepan. Stir the cream mixture into the egg mixture. Taste and add a little sugar if necessary. Strain the custard into 4 individual moulds and place them in a pan or ovenproof dish with cold water to come halfway up the sides of the moulds. Place the pan in a moderate oven (325°F, 160°C, Gas Mark 3) and bake for about 1 hour. Decorate with the pistachio nuts and serve hot or cold.

*Note:* When Seville oranges are out of season, the custard may be made with sweet oranges, but the amount of sugar should then be slightly decreased.

*Orange custards*

# TRIFLE

*Serves 6–8*

**for the custard:**
4 eggs
1 egg yolk
2 oz/50 g castor sugar
¼ pint/1·5 dl single cream
1 pint/6 dl milk
1 lemon
**for the base:**
4–6 individual sponge cakes or
    1 sponge cake
3 tablespoons raspberry jam or
    redcurrant jelly
24 ratafias

¼ pint/1·5 dl sweet sherry
2 tablespoons Drambuie or
    brandy
2 oz/50 g blanched almonds
**for the decoration:**
½ pint/3 dl double cream
1 egg white (optional)
2 oz/50 g blanched almonds
8 small pieces crystallised
    fruits or glacé cherries
12 ratafias
1 oz/25 g blanched pistachio nuts

To make the custard, whisk the eggs and egg yolk with the sugar in a mixing bowl. Stir in the cream and the milk. Pour the mixture into the top of a double saucepan or stand the bowl over a saucepan of hot, but not boiling water. Thinly pare the rind from the lemon and add a few strips of the rind to the custard mixture. Cook over low heat, stirring constantly, until the mixture is thick enough to coat the back of a spoon. Remove from the heat, discard the lemon rind and let stand until cool. Stir the custard frequently to prevent a skin from forming on the surface.

For the base, split the prepared sponge cake in half, spread with the jam and cut into pieces. Arrange in a shallow glass serving bowl with the ratafias. Blend the sherry with the Drambuie and spoon it over the cake and ratafias to soak them. For a moister texture, extra sherry may be used or the sherry and liqueur diluted with a little fruit juice. Sprinkle the almonds over the sponge cake. Pour the custard over the sponge cake and almonds to cover completely and let stand until the custard sets.

To make the decoration, whip the cream until it just holds its shape. If desired, whisk the egg white until very stiff and fold into the whipped cream for a lighter and less rich topping. Pile the whipped cream on top or around the edge of the custard. Alternatively, pipe the cream over the top, using a star tube in a piping bag. Decorate with the almonds, crystallised fruits, ratafias and pistachio nuts.

# SUMMER PUDDING

*Serves 4–5*

about 6–8 thin slices white bread
1 lb/450 g raspberries
8 oz/225 g redcurrants
8 oz/225 g blackcurrants

2 tablespoons water
4 oz/100 g castor sugar
½ pint/3 dl double cream

Cut off the bread crusts. Lightly butter a 2-pint (1-litre) bowl or pudding basin. Line the bowl with the bread slices covering the bottom and sides of the bowl completely. Reserve a few slices for the top of the pudding.

Place the raspberries, redcurrants and blackcurrants in a large saucepan and add the water and sugar. Simmer over moderate heat until the fruit is soft. If desired, the seeds may be removed by sieving the cooked fruit at this stage. Spoon the fruit into the bread-lined bowl and cover with a layer of the remaining bread slices. Place a square of greaseproof paper over the top of the pudding, then a small saucer or plate and finally a weight to compress the contents of the bowl. Set aside overnight in a cool place.

Next day, remove the weight, saucer and the paper, loosen the pudding in the bowl with a spatula and turn out on to a deep plate. Whip half the cream and pile on top of the pudding or, with a star tube in a piping bag, pipe the cream in a decorative pattern. Serve the remaining cream separately.

# RATAFIAS

*Makes about 36*

3 oz/75 g ground almonds
1 egg white

3 drops ratafia or almond essence
3 oz/75 g castor sugar

Loosen any lumps in the ground almonds. Whisk the egg white until frothy but not stiff. Add the ratafia or almond essence, the sugar and two-thirds of the almonds. Stir gently until well blended, adding the remaining ground almonds as necessary to form a soft and slightly sticky mixture. Form the mixture into balls about ½ inch (1 cm) in diameter. Place on to very lightly buttered baking trays. Bake in a moderately hot oven (375°F, 190°C, Gas Mark 5) for about 6–7 minutes.

Cool for several minutes, then lift the ratafias from the trays with a spatula. Ratafias may be stored in a tightly covered container.

# BAKEWELL TART

*Serves 4–6*

**for the shortcrust pastry:**
8 oz/225 g plain flour
pinch salt
4 oz/110 g butter
about ¼ pint/1·5 dl cold water
**for the filling:**
3 oz/75 g butter
3 oz/75 g castor sugar
1 egg

1 oz/25 g plain flour
3 oz/75 g ground almonds
1 oz/25 g chopped mixed candied
    peel (optional)
1½ oz/40 g soft cake crumbs
2 tablespoons milk
3 tablespoons raspberry jam
sifted icing sugar for dusting

Prepare the pastry as for Mince Pies, page 53. Roll out the pastry to ¼ inch (5 mm) thick and line an 8-inch (20-cm) pie tin or shallow sponge cake tin.

To make the filling, cream the butter and sugar together in a mixing bowl until very soft and fluffy. Beat in the egg. Sift the flour and fold into the creamed mixture with the almonds, candied peel, cake crumbs and milk. Spread the jam over the bottom of the pastry case. Spoon the filling over the top of the jam and spread evenly with a knife. Bake in a moderately hot oven (375°F, 190°C, Gas Mark 5) for 40–50 minutes. Cool slightly, remove from the pie tin or sponge cake tin and dust lightly with the icing sugar.

*Apple cake*

# APPLE CAKE

*Serves 6–8*

12 oz/350 g self-raising flour
5 oz/150 g butter
6 oz/175 g castor sugar
2 medium-sized cooking apples
1 egg
1 oz/25 g demerara sugar

$\frac{1}{4}$ teaspoon ground cinnamon
1 tablespoon milk
**for the topping:**
1 oz/25 g castor sugar
pinch ground cinnamon

Sift the flour into a mixing bowl. Cut the butter into pieces and add. Rub the mixture lightly between the fingertips, allowing it to fall back into the bowl, until the butter is evenly distributed. Stir in the castor sugar. Peel, core and dice the apples. Whisk the egg. Blend the demerara sugar with the cinnamon and coat the apples with this mixture. Stir the apples into the flour mixture. Add the egg and milk and mix to a soft sticky dough which should be stiff enough to stand in peaks. Line an 8-inch (20-cm) round cake tin with buttered and lightly floured greaseproof paper. Spoon the dough into the tin, smooth flat on top and sprinkle with the sugar and cinnamon. Bake in a moderate oven (350°F, 180°C, Gas Mark 4) for about 1¼ hours, or until the cake is firm and golden brown. Lower the heat to 300°F (150°C, Gas Mark 2) after 50 minutes if the cake becomes too brown. Remove from the oven, cool slightly and turn out on to a wire rack. Serve while still warm with a hard cheese, such as Cheddar, or a pat of butter.

# EVE'S PUDDING

*Serves 4*

1½ lb/700 g cooking apples
¼ pint/1·5 dl water
2 oz/50 g sugar
**for the topping:**
2 oz/50 g butter

2 oz/50 g plain flour
generous ½ pint/3·5 dl milk
2–3 drops vanilla essence
3 eggs
1 oz/25 g castor sugar

Peel and slice the apples. Place in a saucepan, add the water and sugar and simmer gently until the apples are soft. Remove from the heat and put the apples into a 2-pint (1-litre) lightly greased pie dish.

For the topping, heat the butter in a large saucepan, stir in the flour and cook for 2 minutes. Stir in the milk with the vanilla essence and bring to the boil. Cook, stirring constantly, until thickened, and remove from the heat. Separate the eggs. Stir the sugar and egg yolks into the hot sauce and beat well. Whisk the egg whites until very stiff and fold into the sauce. Spoon the sauce over the apples and spread evenly. Bake in a moderately hot oven (375°F, 190°C, Gas Mark 5) for about 40 minutes. Serve immediately.

*Flummery*

# QUEEN OF PUDDINGS

*Serves 4–6*

| | |
|---|---|
| 4 tablespoons raspberry jam | 3 oz/75 g chopped candied lemon |
| 4 oz/100 g fine fresh breadcrumbs | peel |
| 1 pint/6 dl milk | **for the meringue:** |
| 1 oz/25 g butter | 3 egg whites |
| 3 egg yolks | 3 oz/75 g castor sugar |
| 1 oz/25 g castor sugar | 4 glacé cherries |
| 1 teaspoon grated lemon rind | small piece angelica |

Spread half the jam on the bottom of a 2-pint (1-litre) pie dish. Put the breadcrumbs into a mixing bowl. Heat the milk and butter together in a saucepan until hot, but not boiling. Whisk the egg yolks with the sugar and stir in the hot milk. Strain the mixture into the breadcrumbs and stir in the grated lemon rind and candied lemon peel. Let stand for 10–15 minutes. Pour the thickened mixture into the pie dish and bake in a moderate oven (325°F, 160°C, Gas Mark 3) for 45 minutes–1 hour, or until just firm to the touch. Spread the remaining jam on top of the pudding.

To make the meringue, whisk the egg whites until very stiff and beat in half the sugar. Fold in the remaining sugar very gently using a metal spoon. Spread the meringue over the pudding and decorate with the cherries and angelica. Replace in the oven for 15–20 minutes, or until the meringue is golden on the peaks. Serve hot.

# LEMON SORBET

*Serves 4*

| | |
|---|---|
| 2 large or 3 medium-sized lemons | 1 teaspoon powdered gelatine |
| ½ pint/3 dl water | 2 egg whites |
| 4 oz/100 g castor sugar | |

Thinly pare the rind from the lemons, without including any of the white inner skin. Put the lemon rind and water into a saucepan, cover tightly and simmer gently for about 8 minutes. Remove from the heat and add the sugar and gelatine while the liquid is still hot. Stir until both have dissolved. Meanwhile, squeeze the lemons and pour the juice into a mixing bowl. Strain the gelatine mixture on to the lemon juice. Stir to blend, then pour into a freezing tray or other container and freeze until slightly thickened. Whisk the egg whites until very stiff, then fold into the partially frozen lemon mixture. Taste and add a little extra sugar if too sour. Freeze until firm and store until required.

Serve the sorbet in stemmed glasses with frosted rims. To prepare the frosting, lightly whisk 1 egg white with a fork–the mixture should not be frothy. Pour into a saucer or shallow plate. Dip the rim of each glass first into the egg white then into castor sugar. Chill the glasses. Remove the sorbet from the freezer, let stand for a few minutes then spoon into the glasses.

*Note:* If freezing sorbets in a home freezer, the mixture may be put into the empty lemon cases and frozen in these, then wrapped in polythene for storage. If freezing more slowly in an ordinary domestic refrigerator, the lemon case hinders freezing and therefore there is a tendency for the egg whites to separate. It is better to freeze the mixture in ice trays and pack into the lemon cases when frozen if you wish to serve the sorbet in this way.

# FLUMMERY

*Serves 6*

| | |
|---|---|
| ½ pint/3 dl single cream | 4 oz/100 g blanched almonds, |
| 1 stick cinnamon, about 2 | finely chopped |
| inches/5 cm | 2 teaspoons gelatine |
| 2 teaspoons orange flower water | 2 tablespoons brandy |
| or 2 teaspoons grated orange | ¼ pint/1·5 dl sweet white wine |
| rind | ½ pint/3 dl double cream |
| 4 oz/100 g castor sugar | 2 oz/50 g whole blanched |
| (see recipe) | almonds |

Put the single cream, cinnamon stick and orange flower water into a saucepan and heat almost to the boiling point. Stir in half the sugar and the chopped almonds. Remove the pan from the heat.

Mix the gelatine with the brandy in a small heat-resistant bowl and place in a pan of very hot water until the gelatine dissolves. Gradually stir the gelatine into the cream mixture. Strain the mixture through a fine sieve, then add the remaining sugar and the wine. Flummery should have a sharp flavour; therefore the quantity of sugar may be reduced, if desired. Allow the cream mixture to cool until just beginning to thicken. Whip the double cream until stiff enough to stand in peaks and fold into the cream mixture. Pile into individual glasses or a shallow glass bowl. Decorate with the whole blanched almonds which may be lightly toasted, if preferred.

# GINGER CAKE

*Makes 1 8-inch (20-cm) cake*

| | |
|---|---|
| 8 oz/225 g plain flour | 1 egg yolk |
| 1 teaspoon ground ginger | 3 tablespoons sieved apricot jam |
| ¼ teaspoon baking powder | **for the meringue:** |
| 4 oz/110 g butter | 2 egg whites |
| 4 oz/110 g castor sugar | 4 oz/110 g castor sugar |

Sift the flour, ginger and baking powder into a mixing bowl. Cut the butter into pieces and add. Rub the mixture lightly between the fingertips, allowing it to fall back into the bowl. When the butter is evenly distributed and the mixture is like fine breadcrumbs, stir in the sugar. Add the egg yolk and knead to a stiff dough. Press the dough into an 8-inch (20-cm) round shallow cake tin or pie tin. Alternatively, shape into a circle directly on a baking tray. Prick the surface with a fine skewer to prevent the mixture from rising. Bake in a moderately hot oven (400°F, 200°C, Gas Mark 6) for about 20 minutes, or until golden brown. Cool slightly, then spread with the jam.

Whisk the egg whites until very stiff. Gradually whisk in half the sugar. Fold in the remaining sugar, using a metal spoon. Pile the meringue over the cake base or pipe it, using a star tube in a piping bag. Return the cake to a very cool oven (250°F, 130°C, Gas Mark ½) for 1 hour, or until the meringue is crisp and golden brown. Cool and serve.

# JUNKET

*Serves 3–4*

| | |
|---|---|
| 1 pint/6 dl milk | scant ½ pint/2·5 double cream |
| 3 teaspoons sugar | grated nutmeg |
| 2 teaspoons rennet | |

Pour the milk into a saucepan and place over moderate heat until barely lukewarm. Remove from the heat and stir in the sugar and rennet. Pour into individual serving dishes or into one large serving dish, and let stand at room temperature for several hours. Do not disturb the junket or put into the refrigerator until it has set. Top with whipped cream and grated nutmeg or serve with fresh fruit.

# ECCLES CAKES

*Makes 12–15*

| **for the flaky pastry:** | 3 oz/75 g sultanas |
|---|---|
| 8 oz/225 g plain flour | 3 oz/75 g currants |
| pinch salt | 3 oz/75 g chopped mixed candied |
| 6 oz/170 g butter or 4 oz/110 g | peel |
| butter and 2 oz/60 g cooking | 3 tablespoons lemon juice |
| fat | 1 teaspoon grated lemon rind |
| about ¼ pint/1·5 dl cold water | ¼ teaspoon mixed spice |
| **for the filling:** | **for glazing:** |
| 3 oz/75 g butter | 2 tablespoons milk |
| 3 oz/75 g castor or soft brown | 1 oz/25 g castor sugar |
| sugar | |

Prepare the flaky pastry as for Steak and Kidney Pie, page 40. It is important to allow the pastry to rest between rollings, particularly after the final rolling, as for Eccles cakes the pastry is thinly rolled.

To make the filling, cream the butter and sugar together in a mixing bowl. Add the sultanas, currants, candied peel, lemon juice, lemon rind and mixed spice and mix thoroughly.

Roll out the pastry to ⅛ inch (3 mm) thick. Cut into 3½-inch (8·5-cm) circles. Place a little of the filling in the centre of each circle. Brush the edge of the pastry with water, gather the outside edge over the filling and press together at the top to seal firmly. Turn each cake over so the sealed edge is underneath. Roll gently on top with a rolling pin to flatten and form a circle about 3 inches (7·5 cm) in diameter. Make 2 or 3 splits on top of each cake and lift on to a baking tray. Brush with milk and sprinkle very lightly with the sugar. Bake in a hot oven (425°F, 220°C, Gas Mark 7) for about 20 minutes, or until the pastry is well risen and golden brown. Lower the heat for the final 5–8 minutes, if the cakes are becoming too brown. Serve cold with tea or coffee.

*Note:* In Shropshire, similar cakes are filled with butter blended with granulated sugar, currants, chopped mixed candied peel and fresh mint. Banbury cakes contain finely crushed biscuit crumbs flavoured with a little rum and are generally made in an oval shape.

# GINGERBREAD

*Makes 1 9-inch (23-cm) cake*

| | |
|---|---|
| 12 oz/350 g plain flour | 6 oz/175 g butter |
| 1½ teaspoons bicarbonate of soda | 8 oz/225 g black treacle |
| 1 teaspoon mixed spice | 3 oz/75 g golden syrup |
| 2 teaspoons ground ginger | ¼ pint/1·5 dl water |
| 3 oz/75 g castor or soft brown sugar | 2 eggs |
| | 3 tablespoons milk |

Sift the flour, bicarbonate of soda, mixed spice and ginger into a mixing bowl. Add the sugar and make a well in the centre. Melt the butter with the black treacle and golden syrup in a heavy saucepan over moderate heat. Cool slightly, pour into the dry ingredients and beat well. Pour the water into the same pan, bring to the boil and stir to loosen any treacle left in the pan.

Add the eggs and milk to the mixture and beat well. Then add the hot water from the pan and beat again. Pour the mixture into a greased and lined 9-inch (23-cm) round or square cake tin. Bake in a cool oven (300°F, 150°C, Gas Mark 2) for about 1–1¼ hours. Do not open the oven door until the last 5 minutes as the gingerbread will sink in the middle if subjected to a sudden draught.

Press gently in the centre of the gingerbread and if no impression remains the gingerbread is done. Place the tin on a wire rack and let stand until almost cool, since gingerbread breaks easily when warm. Turn out and remove the paper lining immediately. When cold, wrap in greaseproof paper or foil and store in a tightly covered container for at least 1 week before eating.

# WELSH CAKES

*Makes about 16 cakes*

| | |
|---|---|
| 8 oz/225 g plain flour | 4 oz/110 g currants |
| 2 teaspoons baking powder | 1 egg |
| pinch salt | about 2 teaspoons milk |
| 4 oz/110 g butter or margarine | castor sugar for dusting |
| 3 oz/75 g castor sugar | |

Sift the flour and salt into a mixing bowl. Cut the butter into pieces and add. Rub the mixture lightly between the fingertips, allowing it to fall back into the bowl. When the butter is evenly distributed and the mixture is like fine breadcrumbs, stir in the sugar and currants. Add the egg and enough milk to make a soft dough. Turn the dough out on to a floured board, knead lightly and roll out to ¼ inch (5 mm) thick. Cut the dough into small triangles or into 2½-inch (6-cm) circles using a floured round cutter.

Lightly grease a griddle or a heavy frying pan with cooking fat and heat very slowly for about 20 minutes before using. Test the temperature of the griddle by sprinkling a little flour on the surface. If the flour turns golden brown in 1 minute the griddle is the correct temperature; if it takes more than 1 minute, allow the griddle to heat a little longer. If the flour browns very quickly, lower the heat and allow the griddle to cool before cooking the cakes. Cook the cakes for about 3 minutes on each side, or until firm and golden brown. Place on a wire rack, sprinkle with sugar and set aside to cool slightly. Serve freshly baked.

*Note:* Welsh cakes should be crisp and sugary on the outside and light inside. They should be eaten freshly baked, but if any are left over they may be reheated for a few moments in the oven or on the griddle. They will become crisp and fresh-tasting again.

# OATCAKES

*Makes 8–12 oatcakes*

| | |
|---|---|
| 1 oz/25 g plain flour | 1 oz/25 g melted clarified dripping or butter |
| pinch salt | |
| pinch bicarbonate of soda | about ¼ pint/1·5 dl milk |
| pinch cream of tartar | (see recipe) |
| 7 oz/200 g fine oatmeal | |

Sift the flour, salt, bicarbonate of soda and cream of tartar into a mixing bowl. Add the oatmeal and make a well in the centre. Slightly cool the melted clarified dripping or butter and pour into the well with enough of the milk to form a soft mixture. Sprinkle the pastry board with a little extra oatmeal. Divide the dough into two or three portions and knead thoroughly on the board. Roll each portion into a large circle about ¼ inch (5 mm) thick. Cut each circle into quarters and place on lightly greased baking trays. Bake in a moderate oven (325°F, 160°C, Gas Mark 3) for about 20–30 minutes, or until the edges are crisp and beginning to curl. Cool on the baking trays, remove and store in an airtight container. Serve with butter and cheese or butter and jam.

# SCOTCH PANCAKES

*Makes 12–18 pancakes*

| | |
|---|---|
| 4 oz/100 g plain flour | 1 oz/25 g castor sugar |
| 2 teaspoons baking powder | 1 egg |
| 1 teaspoon cream of tartar | ¼ pint/1·5 dl milk |
| pinch salt | 1 oz/25 g butter |

Sift the flour, baking powder, cream of tartar and salt into a mixing bowl. Add the sugar and make a well in the centre. Whisk the egg and milk together, pour into the well and mix to a smooth batter with a wooden spoon. Melt the butter and stir into the batter. The butter is not essential but helps to keep the pancakes moist. Grease and heat a griddle or a large, heavy frying pan. To test if the correct temperature has been reached, drop a teaspoonful of the batter on the hot surface. The underside should turn golden brown within 1 minute. Drop tablespoonfuls of the batter on to the hot griddle. Cook until the surface of the pancakes is covered with bubbles, then turn over and cook for half a minute, or until brown.

When the first batch is ready, remove the pancakes from the griddle or pan and wrap them in a clean tea towel to prevent them from drying and curling at the edges as they cool. Continue until all the pancakes are cooked and serve spread with butter and jam or honey.

*Oatcakes; Scotch pancakes*

60

61

# SCANDINAVIAN

Lennart Thölén and Ejler Jørgensen

*Photography by John Lee*

As is inevitable with two countries so similar in culture, climate and geography, there is little difference between Norwegian and Swedish cooking. Many of the national dishes are claimed by both countries to be their own. In Norway, the cold table – *koldt bord* – is a culinary institution of the same kind and of the same importance as the Swedish *smörgåsbord*.

The Norwegian housewife has always been proud of her stockpot; full-bodied, nourishing soups are something of a mainstay in Norwegian home economy. The main feature of Norwegian cooking, however, is fish in all its forms. Norway's long Atlantic seaboard, deep fjords, rivers and mountain streams, ensure abundant supplies of fish and shellfish. If one particular fish is to be singled out as typical of the Norwegian cuisine it is the cod. Nowhere in the world is it so delicious and prepared so devotedly as in Norway. Notable too are the country's fish puddings and mousses, which literally melt in the mouth. Fish balls, one of the earliest of all fish products to be prepared commercially, are of Norwegian origin and continue to be one of the country's favourite dishes.

*Husmanskost*, country fare, is the everyday cooking of Sweden and the foundation of the Swedish cuisine. Swedish dishes are suited to a relatively severe climate and are usually substantial, sustaining and nutritious. The Sunday roast is veal, though pork has a time-honoured place in Swedish cooking, often being prepared with prunes and apples.

As in all the Scandinavian countries, fish plays an important role in catering. Special mention should perhaps be made of the herring, the most popular and the most abundant fish, served from south to north in a great number of guises. Game is plentiful in the vast forests of Sweden, and the traditional recipes are ancient and rich in variations.

Among the herbs and spices used, dill is pre-eminent. It is perhaps the most characteristically Swedish of all seasonings and may be traced as a green thread woven through the fabric of the Swedish cuisine, enhancing the flavour of meat, fish, sauces and stews.

Denmark, although a small country, retains a distinctive character which sets it apart from the rest of Scandinavia. Until a century ago, Denmark had a very unproductive agriculture. A poor soil which was unsuitable for growing cereal crops made the Danes turn to livestock so that now Denmark is a major exporter of meat and dairy produce. It is only natural that Danish cooking should make great use of cream and butter to enrich sauces, soups and desserts.

Another important source of food is the sea and Danish fish dishes are unusual and delicious. Smoked, fresh and pickled herring and mackerel always appear in some guise on the cold table. There are also excellent fresh-water fish such as pike and salmon which are often cooked in cream or served with a rich butter sauce.

The Danish cuisine is renowned for its *smørrebrød*, or open sandwiches, but it is probably in the area of baking that the Danes excel. Above all others, the pastries most associated with Denmark are undoubtedly the *wienerbrød*, known throughout the rest of the world simply as Danish pastries. Ideal for serving when friends drop in, these delicate, buttery pastries represent the best of Denmark's renowned hospitality and cooking.

# HERRING SALAD MOULD

*Serves 6*

| | |
|---|---|
| 1 salted herring | freshly ground white pepper |
| 4 medium-sized potatoes | **for the garnish:** |
| 4 medium-sized pickled beetroot | 2 hard-boiled eggs |
| 1 pickled cucumber | 1 small pickled beetroot |
| 1 large cooking apple | **for the dressing:** |
| 2 tablespoons finely chopped onion | generous ¼ pint/ 2 dl double cream |
| 8 oz/225 g cooked meat, finely chopped | 1 teaspoon dry mustard |
| pickled beetroot juice (see recipe) | pickled beetroot juice (see recipe) |

Gut the herring and rinse under cold running water. Fillet the fish, discarding the skin and bones. (See Planked Lake Superior Whitefish, page 14.) Soak overnight in plenty of cold water to remove the excess salt. Drain well. Peel the potatoes and boil until tender. Drain and set aside until cold. Dice the herring, potatoes, beetroot and pickled cucumber and place in a large bowl. Peel, core and dice the apple. Add the apple, onion and meat to the bowl. Mix thoroughly. Sprinkle with pickled beetroot juice and pepper to taste. Pack the salad into a mould and place in the refrigerator, or in a cold place, for several hours.

To prepare the garnish, finely chop the egg yolks and whites separately. Finely chop the beetroot. Unmould the salad on to the centre of a serving plate and garnish with concentric circles of chopped beetroot and egg.

To make the dressing, lightly whisk the cream and then stir in the mustard. Add pickled beetroot juice to taste. Serve with the salad.

# DANISH LIVER PÂTÉ

*Serves 6*

| | |
|---|---|
| 8 oz/225 g chicken livers | 1 egg |
| 8 oz/225 g pig's liver | **for the sauce:** |
| 8 oz/225 g pork or bacon fat | 1 oz/25 g butter |
| 6 anchovy fillets | 1 oz/25 g plain flour |
| 1 teaspoon finely ground black pepper | ¾ pint/4·5 dl milk |
| ¼ teaspoon nutmeg | ¼ pint/1·5 dl port or Madeira |

Finely mince the chicken livers, pig's liver and pork fat. Add the anchovies, pepper, nutmeg and egg. Mix thoroughly.

To make the sauce, melt the butter in a small saucepan. Remove from the heat and stir in the flour. Add the milk gradually, mixing thoroughly after each addition. Bring to the boil over moderate heat, stirring constantly until the mixture thickens. Remove from the heat and stir in the port or Madeira.

Stir the sauce into the liver mixture and blend thoroughly. Pour into a loaf tin or mould about 9 by 5 inches (23 by 13 cm). Bake in a moderate oven (350°F, 180°C, Gas Mark 4) for 1½–2 hours, or until set.

When cooked, remove from the oven and set aside to cool. Turn out of the tin and cut into thick slices. Serve with toast.

# SUNNY EYE

*Serves 1*

| | |
|---|---|
| 1 egg yolk | 1 tablespoon chopped onion |
| 5 anchovy fillets | 1 tablespoon chopped pickled |
| 1 tablespoon capers | beetroot |

Place the yolk in an eggcup. Lay a small plate on top and invert both the eggcup and the plate carefully so none of the yolk escapes. Leave the eggcup in place.

Chop the anchovy fillets and arrange with the capers, onion and beetroot in concentric circles around the rim of the eggcup. (The beetroot should form the outer ring.) Remove the eggcup just before serving. Mix the egg yolk with the other ingredients at the table. Serve as an appetiser.

# JANSSON'S TEMPTATION

*Serves 4*

| | |
|---|---|
| 8 Swedish anchovies or 1 (2-oz/ | 1 oz/25 g butter |
| 56-g) can anchovy fillets | freshly ground white pepper |
| 2 medium-sized onions | ½ pint/3 dl single cream |
| 3 large potatoes | |

If using Swedish anchovies, gut and fillet them and discard the bones. If using canned anchovy fillets, soak them in milk or water for 10–15 minutes to remove the excess salt and then drain. Peel and slice the onions. Peel the potatoes and cut into ¼- by 2-inch (5-mm by 5-cm) strips. Melt half the butter in a frying pan over moderate heat. Add the onions and sauté until soft but not browned.

Arrange the anchovy fillets, potatoes and onions in layers in a well-buttered casserole, beginning and ending with a layer of potatoes. Season each layer with pepper. Pour half the cream on top. Cover the casserole tightly with the lid, or aluminium foil, and bake in a moderately hot oven (400°F, 200°C, Gas Mark 6) for about 30 minutes. Remove the lid or foil. Pour the remaining cream over the top and dot the surface with the remaining butter. Bake for 25 minutes, or until the potatoes are tender. Serve hot from the casserole.

# CUCUMBER SALAD

*Serves 4*

| | |
|---|---|
| 1 large cucumber | 2 tablespoons castor sugar |
| 2 teaspoons salt | white pepper |
| 6 tablespoons distilled white | 1 tablespoon chopped parsley |
| vinegar | |

The cucumber may be peeled or not, according to taste. If not, simply rinse under cold running water and pat dry. Slice the cucumber very thinly into a shallow dish. Sprinkle with the salt and lightly press by covering with a plate and placing a weight on top. Set aside for 1 hour, then pour away all the juices that have collected.

Mix together the vinegar, sugar and white pepper to taste. Pour over the pressed cucumber slices and allow to stand for 1 hour. Sprinkle with chopped parsley and serve.

# GLASSBLOWER'S HERRING

*Serves 8*

| | |
|---|---|
| 2 salted herring | 1 medium-sized carrot |
| 5 tablespoons distilled white | 3 thin slices fresh horseradish root |
| vinegar | 2 thin slices fresh root ginger |
| ¼ pint/1·5 dl water | 2 teaspoons mustard seeds |
| 6 oz/175 g castor sugar | 2 bay leaves |
| 1 medium-sized onion | |

Gut the fish but leave the skins and backbones intact. Soak in water overnight to remove the excess salt.

Place the vinegar, water and sugar in a saucepan and bring slowly to the boil. Remove from the heat and set aside until cold. Meanwhile, rinse the fish under cold running water and pat dry with a muslin fish cloth or kitchen paper. Cut the fish into 1-inch (2·5-cm) pieces. Peel and thinly slice the onion and carrot.

Arrange layers of the fish, onion, carrot, horseradish, ginger, mustard seeds and bay leaves in a glass jar and add the vinegar solution. Place the jar in the refrigerator, or in a cold place, for several days. Serve directly from the jar as an appetiser, or include on the *smörgåsbord*.

# MARINATED HERRING

*Serves 4*

| | |
|---|---|
| 4 fresh herring | 8 cloves |
| 1 tablespoon salt | 2 bay leaves |
| 1 pint/6 dl distilled white vinegar | 1 teaspoon saltpetre |
| 4 shallots | 1 oz/25 g castor sugar |
| ½ teaspoon whole allspice | onion rings for garnish |
| ½ teaspoon white peppercorns | |

Gut the herring. Discard the heads and remove the backbones. Rinse the fish thoroughly under cold running water and pat dry with a cloth or kitchen paper. Place in a shallow dish and sprinkle lightly with the salt. Cover with half the vinegar and set aside to marinate overnight.

Peel and finely chop the shallots. Drain the vinegar from the herring and pat dry. Place the fish in layers in an earthenware container and sprinkle each layer with the chopped shallots and the allspice, peppercorns, cloves, bay leaves, saltpetre and sugar. Cover the herring with the remaining vinegar and set aside for 2–3 hours.

Before serving, drain the herring, cut into strips 1 inch (2·5 cm) wide and garnish with onion rings.

It can undoubtedly be a stimulating experience to be confronted by the magnificence of a large *smörgåsbord*, the Swedish word for the famous Scandinavian cold table. It developed at a time when people liked to eat copiously and well, and to take their time about it. Now it is revived in all its splendour only at Christmas time and during the tourist season in large hotels and restaurants, but on a modified scale it is a very enjoyable way of entertaining.

Accompaniments for the *smörgåsbord* may be set out on the main table or on a side table. Have as many varieties of bread as possible, both crisp and fresh. The fresh should be sliced but covered up until the last minute to prevent it drying out. Make sure there is plenty of butter placed around the table and, to be very Danish, homemade drippings made from pork, goose or duck, or a mixture of the three. There should be a good selection of pickles and pickled vegetables as well as jams and jellies for those who prefer sweet accompaniments with strong cheese. The final extras are salt and pepper, preferably in mills, mustards, oil and vinegar and mayonnaise. The drinks normally served with a *smörgåsbord* are ice-cold *schnapps* and cold beer, but a light wine, red, white or rosé, is equally appropriate.

Start with fish dishes, how many varieties depending on the number of guests. A typical table would include two or three different marinated herring dishes, smoked fish, shrimp and a selection of canned fish with small dishes of garnishes such as capers, chopped onions and onion rings. Follow with cold, sliced meats, colourfully garnished, liver pâté, egg dishes and various salads, some with mayonnaise and others with oil and vinegar. Finally, bring in the cheeses. Four or five varieties would be a suitable number, a mild one, a strong one and two or three cream cheeses. Serve with various breads and a selection of fresh fruit.

from left to right:
top row: *Sunny eye; herring salad mould (see page 63)*
second row: *Swedish steak and onions; dill-cured salmon; country-cured ham; glassblower's herring*
third row: *Swedish meat balls (see page 72); Jansson's temptation; vanilla cream (see page 82); cucumber salad*
bottom row: *Danish liver pâté (see page 63); marinated herring*

# DILL-CURED SALMON

*Serves 8*

| | |
|---|---|
| 1 middle cut of salmon about 2¼ lb/1 kg | 10 white peppercorns, crushed |
| 2 oz/50 g salt | **for the garnish:** |
| 2 oz/50 g castor sugar | 2 lemons, cut in wedges |
| 1 large bunch dill | 4 sprigs dill |

Scale the salmon but do not rinse. Place the salmon on end and cut in half vertically through the backbone. Remove and discard the backbone and all the small bones, but leave the skin on. Mix together the salt and sugar and rub the fleshy sides with the mixture.

Place one half of the salmon on a plate skin-side down. Sprinkle with half the dill and all the peppercorns. Place the other half of the salmon on top, skin-side up, with the thick part lying on top of the thin part of the other half. Cover with the remaining dill. Put a weighted plate or heavy chopping board on top. Place in the refrigerator, or in a dark cold place, for 24 hours.

When ready to serve, discard the dill and peppercorns from the salmon and slice the flesh thinly, discarding the skin. If using as a *smörgåsbord* dish, arrange the slices in rolls and garnish with the lemon wedges and dill. Alternatively, the slices may be arranged on a serving dish and the salmon served accompanied by boiled potatoes and dill mayonnaise (see page 76).

# MEADOW SOUP

*Serves 4*

| | |
|---|---|
| 1 medium-sized carrot | 1 teaspoon salt |
| 1 parsnip | 1 tablespoon plain flour |
| 1 leek | generous ¾ pint/5 dl milk |
| 1 small cauliflower | salt and white pepper |
| 1 small piece celeriac | 1 tablespoon chopped parsley |
| generous ¾ pint/5 dl water | |

Peel the carrot and parsnip and cut into thin strips. Trim and thoroughly wash the leek and slice thinly. Break the cauliflower into florets and rinse under cold running water. Cut the celeriac into strips. Place the water and salt in a large saucepan and bring to the boil. Add the carrot, parsnip cauliflower and celeriac. Simmer over moderate heat for 10–12 minutes. Add the leek and continue simmering until all the vegetables are tender.

Blend the flour with a little of the milk and stir into the soup. Bring to the boil and simmer for 3–4 minutes, stirring constantly. Add the remaining milk and reheat the soup until boiling. Season with salt and pepper to taste. Pour into a heated soup tureen and sprinkle with the parsley. Serve with buttered crisp rye bread topped with slices of cheese.

# TRONDHEIM SWEET SOUP

*Serves 6*

| | |
|---|---|
| 1¾ pints/1 litre water | 1 tablespoon lemon juice |
| 3 oz/75 g barley | 1 tablespoon plain flour |
| scant ½ pint/2·5 dl raspberry juice | ¼ pint/1·5 dl milk |
| 3 oz/75 g raisins | 5 tablespoons soured cream |
| 3 oz/75 g stoned cooked prunes | 5 tablespoons double cream |
| 1 oz/25 g castor sugar | |

Bring the water and barley to the boil in a large saucepan over moderate heat. Lower the heat, cover the pan tightly and simmer for 2 hours. Add the raspberry juice, raisins, prunes, sugar and lemon juice. Blend the flour with the milk and beat into the soup. Simmer for 10 minutes.

Whisk the soured cream and pour into a soup tureen. Add the soup, stirring vigorously. Whip the double cream until stiff. Serve the soup hot or cold with the whipped cream as an accompaniment.

*Meadow Soup*

# YELLOW PEA SOUP WITH PORK

*Serves 4*

| | |
|---|---|
| 1 lb/450 g yellow split peas (see note) | **for cooking:** |
| | 3½ pints/2 litres water |
| **for soaking:** | 1 medium-sized onion |
| 3½ pints/2 litres water | 1 lb/450 g salted shoulder of pork |
| 2 tablespoons salt | 1 teaspoon dried marjoram |
| | ¼ teaspoon ground ginger |

Place the peas in a large bowl with the water and the salt and soak overnight. Drain the peas and place in a large saucepan. Add the fresh water for cooking and bring to the boil over high heat (see note).

Peel the onion, leaving it whole. Add the onion, pork, marjoram and ginger to the saucepan. Cover the pan, lower the heat and simmer the soup for 1–2 hours, or until the peas are tender. Remove and discard the onion. Lift out the pork, carve it into thin slices and keep hot. Serve the soup first and then serve the pork with mustard as a second course.

*Note:* In Denmark whole yellow peas are normally used. If these are used, remove the skins with a perforated spoon as they float to the surface when the peas are first brought to the boil.

# WHITE CABBAGE SOUP WITH MEAT BALLS

*Serves 4*

| **for the soup:** | **for the meat balls:** |
|---|---|
| 1 white cabbage, about 1¾ lb/800 g | 2 tablespoons dried white breadcrumbs |
| 1 oz/25 g butter | generous ¼ pint/2 dl water |
| 2 teaspoons syrup or sugar | 8 oz/225 g lean veal, minced |
| generous 2½ pints/1·5 litres beef or ham stock | 8 oz/225 g lean pork, minced |
| 5 whole allspice | 2 egg yolks |
| 5 white peppercorns | 1 teaspoon salt |
| salt | ¼ teaspoon white pepper |

To make the soup, remove and discard the coarse outer leaves and centre core of the cabbage and shred coarsely. Melt the butter in a large saucepan over high heat. Add the cabbage and syrup and sauté until the cabbage is golden brown, stirring constantly. Add the stock, allspice and peppercorns. Cover tightly and simmer for about 30 minutes, or until the cabbage is tender. Season with salt to taste.

To make the meat balls, place the breadcrumbs in a bowl with the water and soak for 2–3 minutes. Add the veal, pork, egg yolks, salt and pepper. Work the mixture until it is smooth, then shape into walnut-sized balls. Place these in the soup towards the end of the cooking time and simmer for 5 minutes. Transfer to a heated soup tureen and serve.

# ELDERBERRY SOUP

*Serves 8–10*

| | |
|---|---|
| 2¼ lb/1 kg elderberries | 5¼ pints/generous 3 litres water |
| 4 stalks rhubarb (optional) | 4 cooking apples |
| 2 teaspoons grated lemon rind | castor sugar (see recipe) |
| 6 tablespoons lemon juice | 2 oz/50 g cornflour |

Holding the thick portion of each elderberry stalk, strip the berries off with the tines of a fork. Rinse thoroughly under cold running water. Trim and rinse the rhubarb and cut into small pieces. Place the elderberries, rhubarb, lemon rind, lemon juice and water in a large saucepan. Bring to the boil over moderate heat then lower the heat and simmer for 25–30 minutes. Strain through a sieve, reserving the liquid but discarding the fruit.

Peel, core and quarter the apples and place in a second saucepan. Pour in enough water to cover partially and add sugar to taste. Simmer over moderate heat until tender but still whole. Drain the apples (reserving the juice) and place in a soup tureen. Keep hot.

Pour the reserved apple juice and elderberry liquid into a large saucepan and bring to the boil over moderate heat. Blend the cornflour with enough cold water to make a smooth thin paste. Pour into the hot soup, stirring vigorously. Continue stirring until the soup comes to the boil. Pour the soup over the apples in the soup tureen and serve immediately. Alternatively, in the summer this soup is delicious served cold with a spoonful of thick cream for each serving.

# CHERVIL SOUP

*Serves 6*

| | |
|---|---|
| 12 new carrots | 6 eggs |
| 4½ pints/2·5 litres beef stock | salt and pepper |
| 3 oz/75 g unsalted butter | 5 tablespoons finely chopped fresh chervil |
| 3 oz/75 g plain flour | |

Scrape the carrots, rinse under cold running water and slice. Pour about a quarter of the stock into a saucepan and bring to the boil over moderate heat. Add the carrots. Lower the heat and simmer for 25–30 minutes.

Meanwhile, melt the butter in a large saucepan and stir in the flour. Remove the pan from the heat and add the remaining stock gradually, mixing thoroughly after each addition. Bring to the boil over moderate heat, stirring constantly until the mixture thickens. Add the carrots with the stock in which they were cooked. Simmer for 25–30 minutes. Meanwhile, poach the eggs.

Season the soup with salt and pepper to taste and add the chervil. Place an egg in each soup bowl and add the soup. Serve immediately.

# GRILLED SALMON WITH BÉARNAISE SAUCE

*Serves 6*

| | |
|---|---|
| 1 middle cut of salmon, about 2¼ lb/1 kg | 2 teaspoons chopped fresh tarragon |
| 1 teaspoon coarse salt | 2 teaspoons chopped fresh chervil |
| 1 tablespoon olive oil | 1 sprig thyme |
| 2 lb/1 kg fresh asparagus | 1 bay leaf |
| 1 lb/450 g fresh spinach | salt and pepper |
| 2 oz/50 g unsalted butter | 2 tablespoons white wine vinegar |
| 1 red sweet pepper | 2 tablespoons dry white wine |
| 1 tablespoon chopped parsley | 3 egg yolks |
| 3 lemons, cut in half | 1 teaspoon cold water |
| **for the sauce:** | 8 oz/225 g melted butter |
| 1 teaspoon finely chopped shallot | 1 teaspoon lemon juice |

Rinse the salmon under cold running water. Dry well with a cloth. Rub the salmon inside and out with coarse salt. Cut into 6 cutlets. Brush both sides of each cutlet with olive oil.

Cut off the woody fibrous base from each asparagus spear and lightly scrape any coarse skin from the lower half of the stalk. Rinse the asparagus under cold running water. Cook in lightly salted boiling water until tender. Drain well.

Meanwhile, to make the sauce, place the shallot, half the tarragon and chervil, the thyme, bay leaf, salt and pepper to taste, vinegar and wine in a small heavy saucepan. Bring to the boil, then simmer until reduced by half. Mix the egg yolks with the water and add to the reduced mixture. Whisk constantly over very low heat until the mixture begins to thicken. Pour in the butter a little at a time, whisking constantly until the mixture becomes very thick. Whisk in the lemon juice. Remove from the heat and strain through a muslin cloth. Stir in the remaining tarragon and chervil. Keep hot in a double saucepan, or in a bowl over a saucepan of boiling water.

Grill the salmon cutlets under moderate heat for 5–6 minutes on each side. Meanwhile, remove the stalks and rinse the spinach thoroughly under cold running water. Melt the butter in a frying pan, add the spinach, cover and cook over low heat for 5–10 minutes, stirring frequently.

Remove the seeds from the red pepper and slice the flesh very thinly.

Transfer the cooked fish to a heated serving dish and garnish with the asparagus, sautéed spinach, red pepper, parsley and lemon halves. Serve with the *béarnaise* sauce and French bread. A dry white wine or champagne is excellent with this dish.

# HERRING BALLS WITH CURRANT SAUCE

*Serves 4*

| | |
|---|---|
| 1 large salted herring | 1 oz/25 g butter |
| 3 medium-sized potatoes | **for the sauce:** |
| 1 medium-sized onion | 2 tablespoons currants |
| 6 oz/175 g leftover cooked meat | ½ pint/3 dl water |
| 1 egg | 1½ oz/40 g butter |
| 1 teaspoon potato flour | 2 tablespoons plain flour |
| ¼ teaspoon white pepper | 5 tablespoons vegetable stock |
| 2 tablespoons water | 1 tablespoon syrup or sugar |
| 3 tablespoons fine toasted breadcrumbs | 1 tablespoon white wine vinegar |
| | salt |

Gut the herring and rinse under cold running water. Fillet the fish, discarding the skin and bones. (See Planked Lake Superior Whitefish, page 14.) Soak overnight in plenty of cold water to remove the excess salt. Peel the potatoes and boil until tender. Peel the onion. Mince the fish with the potatoes, onion and meat. Add the egg, potato flour and pepper. Mix well, then stir in the water.

Shape the mixture into 1½-inch (3·5-cm) balls and flatten these slightly. Coat with the breadcrumbs. Heat the butter in a frying pan over moderate heat. Add the herring balls and sauté for 2–3 minutes on each side, or until golden brown. Remove from the pan and keep hot in a serving dish.

To make the sauce, clean and rinse the currants. Place in a saucepan with the water and simmer over moderate heat for 8–10 minutes, or until tender. Strain off the cooking liquid and reserve. Melt two-thirds of the butter in a small saucepan and stir in the flour. Gradually add the cooking liquid and the stock. Bring to the boil, stirring constantly until the mixture thickens. Simmer the sauce for 10 minutes. Add the syrup, vinegar and salt to taste. Bring the sauce back to the boil. Add the currants and stir in the remaining butter. Serve hot with the herring balls.

*Grilled salmon with béarnaise sauce*

69

# FRIED HERRING WITH BROWN BUTTER SAUCE

*Serves 4*

4 large herring
seasoned flour for coating
1 beaten egg
fine fresh breadcrumbs for coating
2 oz/50 g unsalted butter

**for the sauce:**
4 oz/100 g unsalted butter
2 tablespoons distilled white vinegar
1 lemon, quartered

Scrape the fish carefully to remove the scales. Discard the heads, tails and fins. Gut the herring and rinse under cold running water. Dry inside and out with a clean cloth or kitchen paper. Coat each fish with the flour, egg and breadcrumbs. Alternatively, coat with flour only.

Melt the butter in a heavy frying pan over moderate heat. Fry the herring for 4–5 minutes on each side. Hold the fish closed by pressing them lightly with a spatula during the first few minutes of frying, otherwise they tend to open up. Remove the fish from the pan, drain on kitchen paper and keep hot in a serving dish.

To make the sauce, cook the butter in a heavy saucepan over moderate heat until the frothing stops and it is well browned. Remove the pan from the heat immediately and stir in the vinegar. Pour the hot sauce over the fish. Garnish with the lemon and serve immediately.

# FAEROESE COD BALLS WITH CURRY SAUCE

*Serves 6*

2 lb/1 kg cod fillets
1 medium-sized onion
2 oz/50 g melted butter
2 oz/50 g plain flour
2 egg yolks
4 egg whites
salt and pepper
**for the curry sauce:**
3–4 shallots
1–2 cloves garlic

1 small banana
1 lb/450 g cooking apples
2 oz/50 g butter
3 tablespoons curry powder
1 tablespoon lemon juice
dash Tabasco sauce
¼ pint/1·5 dl double cream
2 tablespoons tomato purée
1 teaspoon mango chutney
salt and pepper

Discard the skin and any bones from the fish and rinse the fish under cold water. Mince the flesh or blend in a liquidiser. Peel and finely chop the onion and add to the fish with the butter, flour, egg yolks and egg whites. Season with salt and pepper. Mix thoroughly and shape into 12 large balls about the size of small dessert apples. Simmer in lightly salted boiling water for 10–12 minutes. When the cod balls are cooked they will rise to the surface. Remove from the pan with a perforated spoon and place in a heated serving dish.

To make the curry sauce, peel and finely chop the shallots and garlic. Sieve the banana. Peel, core and quarter the apples and cover with cold water until required. Melt the butter in a saucepan over moderate heat. Add the shallots, garlic and curry powder. Fry gently for 10 minutes. Drain the apple slices and add to the curry mixture. Add the mashed banana. Cook for 10–15 minutes over low heat until the apples are reduced to a pulp. Add a little water if the mixture begins to stick to the pan. Stir in the lemon juice, Tabasco sauce, cream, tomato purée and chutney. Add salt and pepper to

taste and continue cooking until the mixture is reduced by about one-fifth. The sauce should be fairly thick. Serve hot with the cod balls. Boiled potatoes should accompany this dish.

# CRAB SANDWICH

*Serves 4*

4 thin slices white bread
2 oz/50 g butter
7½ oz/about 200 g canned crab meat
1 egg

3 tablespoons mayonnaise
1 tablespoon chopped fresh dill or 2 teaspoons dried dill weed

Cut off the crusts from the bread. Spread each slice of bread with butter. Discarding any hard membrane, spread the crab meat on the buttered slices. Separate the egg yolk from the white. Mix the yolk with the mayonnaise and dill. Whisk the white until stiff peaks are formed, then fold into the mayonnaise mixture. Spread the egg mixture over the crab. Place the slices on a baking tray and bake in a hot oven (450°F, 230°C, Gas Mark 8) for 10 minutes. Serve as an appetiser, or with a green salad as a light supper dish.

# BORNHOLM HERRING OMELETTE

*Serves 6*

6 smoked herring fillets
4 large tomatoes
1 large onion
6 eggs
5 tablespoons milk

2 teaspoons plain flour
4 oz/100 g butter
salt and pepper
2 teaspoons chopped fresh chives

Cut the fish into small pieces. Slice the tomatoes. Peel and chop the onion. Whisk together the eggs, milk and flour.

Heat the butter in a large frying pan over moderate heat. Pour in the egg mixture. When the egg is partly set, sprinkle with the pieces of fish and the onion. Place the tomato slices on top and sprinkle with salt and pepper to taste. Continue cooking until the egg is almost set. Sprinkle with the chopped chives and serve immediately from the pan.

*Fried herring with brown butter sauce;*
*Bornholm herring omelette*

# BAKED PIKE WITH MOREL SAUCE

*Serves 4*

| | |
|---|---|
| 1 pike, about 2¼ lb/1 kg | 1 oz/25 g butter |
| 1 tablespoon salt | 1 tablespoon plain flour |
| 1 beaten egg | scant ¾ pint/4 dl double cream |
| 2 tablespoons coarse toasted breadcrumbs | salt and white pepper |
| ½ oz/15 g butter | 1 tablespoon medium dry sherry |
| ¼ pint/1·5 dl water | **for the garnish:** |
| ¼ pint/1·5 dl double cream | 1 lemon, thinly sliced |
| **for the sauce:** | 4–5 sprigs parsley |
| 1 oz/25 g dried morels or dried mushrooms, soaked and drained | |

Scale and gut the fish. Leave the head on but remove the fins. Rinse thoroughly under cold running water and dry with a muslin fish cloth or kitchen paper. Rub the fish with the salt and place it, spine-side uppermost, in a well-buttered casserole. Brush with the egg and sprinkle with the breadcrumbs. Dot with pats of the butter.

Bake in a hot oven (425°F, 220°C, Gas Mark 7) for 10 minutes. Add the water, pouring it along the side of the dish and not directly over the fish. Bake for 40 minutes, or until the fish is almost tender. Add the cream and bake for 5 minutes.

Meanwhile, to make the sauce, place the morels in a saucepan and add enough water to cover them completely. Bring to the boil over high heat. Lower the heat and simmer for 2–3 minutes. Remove the pan from the heat and discard the water. Coarsely chop the morels. Melt the butter in a frying pan over moderate heat. Add the morels and sauté for 2–3 minutes. Sprinkle in the flour, then slowly add the cream, stirring constantly. Lower the heat and simmer the sauce gently for 20 minutes. Season with salt and pepper to taste and add the sherry.

Garnish the pike with slices of lemon and parsley. Serve with the morel sauce and boiled potatoes.

# HARE WITH JUNIPER BERRIES

*Serves 5*

| | |
|---|---|
| 1 hare, drawn and skinned | 3 tablespoons lemon juice |
| 1 medium-sized onion | 5 juniper berries, crushed |
| 2 medium-sized carrots | few sprigs parsley |
| 4 oz/100 g butter | ½ bay leaf |
| ½ pint/3 dl beef stock | 2 tablespoons plain flour |
| generous ⅓ pint/2 dl dry red wine | salt and white pepper |

Joint the hare into 10 equal-sized pieces. Rinse thoroughly under cold running water, then dry with a cloth or kitchen paper. Peel and chop the onion and carrots. Heat half the butter in a heavy saucepan over moderate heat until pale golden brown. Add the hare and sauté with the onion and carrots until well browned. Add the stock, wine, lemon juice, juniper berries, parsley and bay leaf. Bring to the boil, then lower the heat and cover the pan tightly. Simmer for 1½–2 hours, or until tender.

Blend the remaining butter and flour to form a soft paste.

Stir into the pan juices and simmer for 3–4 minutes. Season with salt and pepper to taste. Transfer to a heated serving dish and serve the hare with boiled potatoes and rowanberry or redcurrant jelly.

# SWEDISH MEAT BALLS

*Serves 4*

| | |
|---|---|
| 1½ oz/40 g fine toasted breadcrumbs | 4 oz/100 g lean pork, minced |
| generous ⅓ pint/2 dl water | 1 egg |
| ½ medium-sized onion | salt and freshly ground black pepper |
| 2 oz/50 g butter | 1 tablespoon plain flour |
| 8 oz/225 g lean beaf, minced | generous ⅓ pint/2 dl beef stock |
| 4 oz/100 g lean veal, minced | |

Soak the breadcrumbs in the water for a few minutes. Drain and place in a bowl. Peel and finely chop the onion. Melt a quarter of the butter in a frying pan over moderate heat and sauté the onion until lightly browned. Add the onion, beef, veal, pork and egg to the breadcrumbs. Beat the mixture vigorously with a wooden spoon until smooth. Season with salt and pepper. Moisten the fingertips slightly and shape the mixture into walnut-sized balls. Place on a dampened chopping board.

Heat the remaining butter in a frying pan over low heat. Add the meat balls and fry slowly for about 10 minutes, shaking the pan occasionally so they maintain their round shape and are evenly browned. Sprinkle them with the flour, then pour the stock over. Cover the pan and simmer for 4–5 minutes. Serve with boiled or mashed potatoes, cranberry sauce and cucumber slices sprinkled with salt.

# MOCK CHICKEN

*Serves 6*

| | |
|---|---|
| 6 veal escalopes, about 8 oz/225 g each | **for the gravy:** |
| salt and pepper | 1 oz/25 g butter |
| 6 rashers streaky bacon | 1 oz/25 g plain flour |
| 3 tablespoons chopped parsley | veal stock (see recipe) |
| 2 oz/50 g butter | ¼ pint/1·5 single cream |
| 5 tablespoons tomato purée | salt and pepper |
| ¾ pint/4·5 dl water | gravy browning (optional) |

Pound each veal escalope with a meat mallet until about ¼ inch (5 mm) thick. Sprinkle with salt and pepper. Flatten the bacon rashers with a spatula and place one on each escalope. Sprinkle with chopped parsley and roll up, completely enclosing the bacon and parsley. Secure each roll with a wooden cocktail stick or fine string.

Cook the butter in a heavy saucepan over moderate heat until the frothing stops and it is pale golden brown. Add the veal rolls and fry until lightly browned. Add the tomato purée and the water blended together. This should completely cover the veal. If necessary, add more water. Simmer for 25–30 minutes, or until the meat is tender.

Take the pan off the heat and remove the rolls. Transfer to a heated serving dish and carefully remove the cocktail sticks or string. Reserve the stock for the gravy.

To make the gravy, melt the butter in a small saucepan over moderate heat. Remove from the heat and stir in the flour. Add the reserved stock gradually, mixing well after each addition. Return to low heat and bring slowly to the simmering point, stirring constantly until the mixture thickens. Stir in the cream. Reheat, but do not boil. Season to taste with salt and pepper and add a little gravy browning, if wished. Strain the gravy and serve with the mock chicken, accompanied by boiled potatoes and cucumber salad (see page 64).

# CHICKEN IN HORSERADISH SAUCE

*Serves 6*

| | |
|---|---|
| 1 boiling chicken, about 4½ lb/2 kg | 2 oz/50 g plain flour |
| 2 teaspoons salt | ¾ pint/5 dl single cream |
| 8 oz/225 g celeriac | 3 tablespoons grated fresh |
| 2 medium-sized carrots | horseradish root |
| 2 medium-sized onions | sugar and salt to taste |
| 2 leeks | 1 tablespoon finely chopped |
| **for the sauce:** | parsley |
| 2 oz/50 g butter | |

Place the chicken in a large saucepan and cover with water. Add the salt. Peel and thickly slice the celeriac, carrots and onions. Trim the leeks and rinse thoroughly under cold running water. Place the prepared vegetables in the pan with the chicken and bring to the boil over moderate heat. Lower the heat and simmer the chicken for about 2 hours, or until tender. Remove the chicken from the pan and cut into large pieces, discarding any skin and bone. Keep hot in a serving dish.

Meanwhile, melt the butter in a saucepan over moderate heat. Stir in the flour and cook the mixture for about 1 minute. Remove from the heat and add the cream a little at a time, mixing thoroughly after each addition. Stir in the grated horseradish and return to moderate heat. Stir constantly over low heat until the mixture thickens. Do not boil. Remove from the heat and add sugar and salt to taste. Pour the hot sauce over the chicken, sprinkle with the chopped parsley and serve immediately with puff pastry triangles.

*Chicken in horseradish sauce*

# MARINATED POT ROAST

*Serves 6*

| | |
|---|---|
| 3½ lb/1·5 kg silverside or topside of beef | 2 bay leaves |
| **for the marinade:** | **for cooking:** |
| 1¾ pints/1 litre beer | 4 oz/100 g pork fat |
| 5 tablespoons distilled malt vinegar | 1 tablespoon salt |
| | 1 oz/25 g butter |
| 3 oz/75 g castor sugar | generous ½ pint/4 dl beef stock |
| 1 medium-sized onion | **for the sauce:** |
| 1 medium-sized carrot | generous ¼ pint/2 dl marinade |
| 5 white peppercorns | (see recipe) |
| 5 whole allspice | 2 tablespoons plain flour |
| 5 whole cloves | 5 tablespoons double cream |
| 5 juniper berries, crushed | salt and white pepper |

Wipe the beef with a damp cloth or kitchen paper. Pour the beer and vinegar into a large stoneware crock or china bowl. Add the sugar and stir. Peel and slice the onion and carrot. Add the onion, carrot, peppercorns, allspice, cloves, juniper berries and bay leaves to the crock. Put the beef into the marinade, making sure it is well covered by the liquid. Set the crock aside for 5–6 days in a cold place, turning the meat occasionally.

Remove the meat, rinse quickly under cold running water and dry thoroughly. Reserve the marinade. Cut the pork fat into narrow strips. Lard the beef with the pork fat, using a larding needle; alternatively, pierce the meat with a sharp knife and insert the strips of fat. Rub the salt into the meat. Melt the butter in a heavy saucepan. Add the meat and sauté until thoroughly browned. Heat the stock separately and add to the meat. Cover the pan tightly and bring to the boil over moderate heat. Lower the heat and simmer for about 2 hours, or until the beef is tender.

Take the pan off the heat. Remove the beef and keep hot. Pour a generous ¼ pint (2 dl) of the reserved marinade into the meat juices in the pan. Blend the flour with the cream and add to the pan. Place over moderate heat and bring to the boil, stirring constantly until the mixture thickens. Simmer for 2–3 minutes. Season with salt and pepper to taste. Serve the beef with the sauce, mashed potatoes, lingonberry preserve or cranberry sauce and pickled cucumbers.

# STUFFED PORK FILLETS

*Serves 4–6*

| | |
|---|---|
| 2 pork fillets, about 1 lb/450 g each | 1½ oz/40 g butter |
| 1–2 cooking apples | ½ pint/3 dl water |
| 8 prunes, soaked overnight | 2 tablespoons tomato purée |
| salt and pepper | ¼ pint/1·5 dl single cream |

Trim the pork fillets and remove any skin or sinew. Using a sharp knife, cut each fillet lengthwise but only halfway through. Open out and beat gently with a rolling pin to flatten them slightly. Peel, core and slice the apples and stone the prunes. Arrange the apple slices and prunes down the centre of each piece of meat. Season with salt and pepper. Close the fillets again and tie tightly with fine string to hold the shape.

Melt the butter in a heavy frying pan. Add the meat and brown it thoroughly. Pour in the water and tomato purée and bring just to the boil. Cover and simmer gently for 20–30 minutes. Add the cream. Season with salt and pepper and simmer gently for a further 10–15 minutes, or until the meat is tender.

Lift the fillets from the pan, slice crosswise and arrange neatly on a serving dish. Pour the sauce from the pan into a hot sauceboat. Serve the meat with the sauce, boiled potatoes and sweet red cabbage (see page 76).

# WILD DUCK IN CREAM SAUCE

*Serves 6*

| | |
|---|---|
| 3 wild ducks | juice of 1 lemon |
| milk (see recipe) | salt and pepper |
| 12 oz/350 g butter | **for the garnish:** |
| generous 2½ pints/1·25 litres double cream | 3 dessert apples |
| 3 tablespoons redcurrant jelly | 3 tablespoons rowanberry or cranberry jelly |
| 2 teaspoons crumbled Roquefort or Danish blue cheese | |

Clean the wild ducks and rinse them thoroughly under cold running water. Place in a large bowl and cover with milk. Set aside for 12 hours. (This minimises the fishy taste.) Remove the ducks from the milk and dry thoroughly.

Heat the butter in a large heavy frying pan and sauté the ducks until well browned. Place the ducks in a casserole and add the cream and the redcurrant jelly. Cover and cook in a moderate oven (325°F, 160°C, Gas Mark 3) for 1–1½ hours, or until the ducks are tender. To test the ducks, pinch the drumsticks; if the flesh feels soft this indicates that it is cooked sufficiently. It is important that each drumstick is tested.

Lift the ducks out of the casserole. Cut each one in half and place on a heated serving dish. Cover and keep hot while completing the sauce.

Skim the fat from the sauce in which the ducks were cooked. Pour the sauce into a saucepan, place over moderate heat and reduce by about half.

While the sauce is reducing, peel, core and halve the apples. Simmer in water to cover for about 5 minutes, or until tender but still whole. Drain well and place a spoonful of rowanberry jelly on each half.

Stir the cheese and lemon juice into the sauce. Season to taste with salt and pepper. Pour some of the sauce over the ducks and serve the remainder in a sauceboat. Garnish the ducks with the halved apples and serve immediately with caramelised potatoes (see page 76).

*Stuffed pork fillets*

# FRICASSEE OF VEAL WITH DILL SAUCE

*Serves 4*

2–2½ lb/1–1·25 kg boned leg of
   veal
2 teaspoons salt for each
   1¾ pints/1 litre water
1 small onion
5 white peppercorns
½ bay leaf
**for the sauce:**
1 oz/25 g butter
2 tablespoons plain flour

scant ¾ pint/4 dl veal stock (see
   recipe)
2 tablespoons chopped fresh dill
   or 1 tablespoon dried dill weed
1 tablespoon white wine vinegar
2 teaspoons castor sugar
¼ teaspoon salt
1 egg yolk
few sprigs dill

Trim the veal and wipe with a cloth or kitchen paper. Place in a saucepan with enough water to cover the meat completely. Add the salt. Bring to the boil over high heat and then skim. Peel and slice the onion and add to the veal with the peppercorns and bay leaf. Simmer for 1¼–1½ hours, or until the veal is tender.

Remove the veal from the pan and cut into 1½-inch (3·5-cm) cubes. Place on a heated serving dish and keep hot. Reserve the stock for the sauce.

To make the dill sauce, melt the butter in a small saucepan over moderate heat. Stir in the flour, then gradually stir in the reserved stock. Bring to the boil, stirring constantly until the mixture thickens. Add the chopped dill, vinegar, sugar and salt. Remove the pan from the heat and beat in the egg yolk. Pour the sauce into a sauceboat. Garnish the veal with the sprigs of dill and serve with the sauce and boiled potatoes or boiled rice.

# BAKED BACON PANCAKE

*Serves 4*

2 eggs
1 pint/6 dl milk
6 oz/175 g plain flour
½ teaspoon salt

12 oz/350 g lean smoked bacon,
   in 1 piece
1 tablespoon vegetable oil

Whisk the eggs with a quarter of the milk. Place the flour and salt in a bowl. Stir in the eggs and remaining milk and beat until smooth. Set the batter aside for 10 minutes.

Cut the bacon into ¼-inch (5-mm) cubes. Heat the oil in a 9-by 7-inch (23- by 18-cm) roasting tin and fry the bacon until crisp. Pour the batter over the bacon and bake in a hot oven (425°F, 220°C, Gas Mark 7) for 30–40 minutes, or until browned. Cut into portions and serve with cranberry sauce and a green salad.

# DANISH HASH

*Serves 6*

1 lb/450 g leftover cooked meat
4 large onions
8 medium-sized potatoes
salt and pepper
8 oz/225 g butter

1 teaspoon curry powder
 (optional)
1 tablespoon paprika
1 tablespoon turmeric
6 eggs

Cut the meat into very small cubes of uniform size. Peel and coarsely chop the onions. Peel the potatoes, cut into small cubes and sprinkle with salt. Divide the butter into 3 portions and heat one portion in a heavy frying pan over moderate heat. Add the meat and fry for about 10 minutes, or until golden brown. Season to taste with salt and pepper. Remove and keep hot.

Add the second portion of butter to the pan. Fry the onions with the curry powder, paprika, turmeric and salt and pepper to taste, for 10–15 minutes or until soft and golden brown. Remove and add to the meat.

Add the remaining butter to the pan. Fry the potatoes until golden brown. Add the meat and onions to the potatoes in the pan, mix well and season with salt and pepper to taste. Arrange on a large warm serving dish.

Fry the eggs and place on top of the hash. Serve immediately.

# CARAMELISED POTATOES

*Serves 4*

1½ lb/700 g even-sized new
 potatoes

6 oz/150 g castor sugar
3 oz/75 g butter

Cook the potatoes in their skins in boiling salted water for 10–15 minutes, or until tender. Drain and peel the potatoes, then rinse in cold water.

Place the sugar in a frying pan over low heat. Stir occasionally until the sugar has melted and turned to a golden caramel. Add the butter to the pan. When melted, add the potatoes. Continue to fry, shaking the pan gently until the potatoes are completely coated with the caramel and are golden brown. Serve immediately. Caramelised potatoes are particularly suitable for serving with roast pork, roast duck and roast goose.

# SWEET RED CABBAGE

*Serves 6*

1 red cabbage, about 2 lb/1 kg
2 oz/50 g butter
2 tablespoons castor sugar
5 tablespoons vinegar

scant ½ pint/2·5 dl redcurrant juice
 or 3 tablespoons redcurrant
 jelly dissolved in ¼ pint/2 dl hot
 water
salt

Discard the coarse outer leaves of the cabbage. Quarter it and cut away the hard centre core. Finely shred the cabbage and place in a large saucepan with the butter, sugar, vinegar, redcurrant juice and salt to taste. Bring to the simmering point over moderate heat, then lower the heat and cover the pan with a tight-fitting lid. Cook the cabbage for about

1 hour, or until tender. During the last 15 minutes, stir the cabbage constantly. Add more vinegar, sugar or salt to taste. Serve hot.

# DILL MAYONNAISE

*Serves 8*

1 tablespoon French mustard
1 tablespoon Swedish or sweet
 mustard
1 tablespoon castor sugar

2 tablespoons white wine vinegar
generous ¼ pint/2 dl vegetable oil
salt and white pepper
4 tablespoons finely chopped dill

Mix the mustards together in a small bowl. Add the sugar and vinegar and stir to form a paste. Add the oil drop by drop, whisking well after each addition. Season with salt and pepper to taste and stir in the dill. Serve as an accompaniment to dill-cured salmon (see page 65).

# NORRLAND POTATO DUMPLINGS

*Serves 6*

6 large potatoes
4 oz/100 g barley meal
5 oz/150 g plain flour

1 medium-sized onion
1¼ lb/600 g cooked salted pork

Peel, rinse and coarsely grate the potatoes. Twist the grated potato in a cloth to squeeze out the water. Place in a bowl with the barley meal and the flour and stir to form a soft mixture. Peel and finely chop the onion. Finely chop the pork. Mix the onion and pork together.

Shape the potato mixture into dumplings about the size of an apple and make a hollow in each one with the thumb. Press a little of the pork mixture into each hollow and seal the opening so the filling is completely enclosed. Place the dumplings in a large saucepan half filled with lightly salted boiling water. Simmer gently for 30–35 minutes, or until they float to the surface. Remove with a perforated spoon. Drain well and serve with melted butter and lingonberry preserve or cranberry sauce.

*Danish hash*

76

Denmark's national speciality is *smørrebrød*, colourful, appetising open sandwiches. They are invariably eaten for lunch, but their attractive appearance and the ease and speed with which they can be prepared make them an excellent and unusual choice for an informal supper party.

Two or three open sandwiches are sufficient for each person. Arrange them on large trays or wooden boards and allow guests to help themselves using a broad server rather like a cake slice. In Denmark it is customary to serve the open sandwiches made with fish first, and then the meat, poultry and cheese varieties. Supply each guest with a knife and fork with which to eat the sandwiches and serve tiny glasses of ice-cold Danish *schnapps* with the fish, followed by tall, cool glasses of Danish lager with the remainder of the meal.

A small version of an open sandwich is called a *snitter*. They are triangles of bread garnished in the same way as the open sandwich and are often served in the evenings with tea or beer, either for home entertainment or at a restaurant after the theatre.

The bread chosen for open sandwiches should be fresh with a good crust, and close-textured to take the weight of the toppings. Brown bread goes well with ham, liver pâté or egg, whereas white bread makes a suitable base for shrimp, chicken or beef. When strong-flavoured toppings are used, such as salami, marinated herring or Danish blue cheese, the traditional Danish rye bread should be used.

Danish Open Sandwiches
top: *Liver pâté with mushrooms and bacon; ham with Italian salad; egg and tomato*
centre: *Liver pâté with cucumber and pickled beetroot; Danish blue cheese and radish; marinated herring and onion; caviar with egg; shrimp and lemon*
bottom: *Ham with scrambled egg; salami and onion*

# ITALIAN SALAD

*Serves 4*

| | |
|---|---|
| 1 large beetroot, cooked | **for the mayonnaise:** |
| 1 large potato, cooked | 2 egg yolks |
| 2 medium-sized carrots, cooked | salt and pepper |
| 2 thick slices celeriac, cooked | scant ½ pint/2·5 dl olive oil |
| 1 dessert apple | 1½ tablespoons distilled vinegar |
| 1 pickled cucumber | 2 teaspoons tarragon vinegar |

Using a whisk, or a small wooden spoon, mix the egg yolks with salt and pepper to taste in a small bowl. Add the oil a drop at a time, whipping thoroughly after each addition. Continue until all the oil has been added and the mixture has become thick and smooth. Stir in the vinegars.

Dice the beetroot, potato, carrots, celeriac, apple and pickled cucumber and place in a serving dish. Coat the diced vegetables very thickly with the mayonnaise.

# GRATED CARROT AND APPLE SALAD

*Serves 4*
1 lb/450 g carrots
1 lb/450 g dessert apples
juice of 1–2 lemons
sugar to taste

Scrape or peel the carrots as necessary. Peel the apples. Grate the apples and carrots finely and mix with the lemon juice. Add sugar to taste. Serve in a glass bowl.

# LIVER PÂTÉ WITH MUSHROOMS AND BACON

2–3 slices Danish liver pâté (see page 63)
buttered bread
few slices mushrooms, sautéed in butter
1 rasher bacon, crisply fried
1 small lettuce leaf

Cut the liver pâté into thick slices and arrange these overlapping on the buttered bread. Heap a few slices of sautéed mushrooms in the centre. Arrange the rasher of fried bacon across the top and tuck the lettuce leaf into one side.

# HAM WITH ITALIAN SALAD

2–3 thin slices cooked ham
buttered bread
1 crisp lettuce leaf
1 tablespoon Italian salad (see preceding page)
1 wedge tomato

Fold each slice of ham loosely in half and arrange slightly overlapping on the buttered bread. Place the lettuce leaf in the centre and spoon in the Italian salad. Place the tomato wedge on top.

# EGG AND TOMATO

4 slices tomato
4 slices hard-boiled egg
buttered bread
mustard and cress or chopped chives

Arrange the slices of egg and tomato alternately in 2 rows of 4 on the buttered bread. Garnish with mustard and cress or chopped chives in the centre.

# SCRAMBLED EGG FOR OPEN SANDWICHES

4 eggs
½ pint/3 dl milk

1 teaspoon salt
pinch white pepper

Break the eggs into a bowl and add the milk and seasoning. Whisk lightly to mix the ingredients. Pour into a greased 1-quart (1-litre) baking dish and place the dish in a larger baking or roasting tin filled to a depth of 1 inch (2·5 cm) with cold water. Bake in a cool oven (300°F, 150°C, Gas Mark 2) for about 1 hour, or until the mixture is set firm. Remove from the heat and allow to cool, preferably overnight. Cut into strips and use as required.

# LIVER PÂTÉ WITH CUCUMBER AND PICKLED BEETROOT

1½ oz/40 g Danish liver pâté (see page 63)
buttered bread

1 slice fresh cucumber
1 slice pickled beetroot
1 small lettuce leaf

Spread the liver pâté generously on the buttered bread. Make a cut from the edge to the centre of the cucumber and beetroot slices. Place them together and bend each half in opposite directions to make a twist. Arrange on top of the pâté, off centre, and tuck the lettuce leaf into one side.

# MARINATED HERRING AND ONION

1 marinated herring fillet (see page 64)

buttered rye bread
3–4 onion rings

Cut the herring fillet into 1-inch (2·5-cm) pieces. Arrange neatly on the buttered bread and top with overlapping rings of onion.

# DANISH BLUE CHEESE AND RADISH

2 slices Danish blue cheese
buttered rye bread

1 radish

Cut the cheese slices about ¼ inch (5 mm) thick and arrange overlapping on the buttered rye bread. Garnish with the washed radish cut in thin slices or with a radish rose. To make the rose, cut the radish in sections down from the top, leaving a part uncut at the bottom end to hold the radish together. Place in iced water until the radish opens out like a rose. Drain and use as a garnish.

# CAVIAR WITH EGG

1 oz/25 g Danish caviar
buttered bread

1 raw egg yolk

Spread the caviar generously over the buttered bread. Make a slight hollow in the centre and gently tip in the egg yolk.

# HAM WITH SCRAMBLED EGG

2–3 thin slices cooked ham
buttered bread
1 strip scrambled egg (see above)

1 teaspoon chopped chives
1 wedge tomato

Fold each slice of ham to give height to the sandwich and arrange attractively over the buttered bread. Place the strip of scrambled egg across the top and sprinkle with the chives. Garnish with the tomato wedge on one side.

# SHRIMP AND LEMON

1 crisp lettuce leaf
buttered bread

2 oz/50 g peeled shrimps
1 slice lemon

Press the lettuce leaf on to the well-buttered bread. Neatly pile the shrimps on to the lettuce leaf. Cut the lemon slice halfway through, bend the ends in opposite directions to make a twist, and place on top.

# SALAMI AND ONION

3 thin slices Danish salami
buttered rye bread

4 raw onion rings
sprig parsley

Arrange the slices of salami overlapping each other on the buttered bread. Snip 3 of the onion rings with scissors and arrange them over the salami, linking them through each other into the unbroken ring of onion. Garnish with a sprig of parsley.

# YEOMAN'S SNUFF

*Serves 4*

1 oz/25 g butter
3 oz/75 g fine fresh wholemeal
  breadcrumbs
½ pint/3 dl double cream

1 teaspoon vanilla sugar
  (see note)
2½ oz/65 g plain chocolate
5 tablespoons strawberry jam

Melt the butter in a heavy frying pan over moderate heat. Add the breadcrumbs and sauté until crisp and browned. Remove from the pan and set aside until cool.

Whisk the cream with the vanilla sugar until stiff. Grate the chocolate. Arrange layers of breadcrumbs, jam, chocolate and cream in a glass bowl. Finish with a layer of cream and sprinkle a little grated chocolate on top.

*Note:* Vanilla sugar may be bought from continental delicatessens or alternatively prepared by placing a vanilla pod in a jar of sugar until the flavour is absorbed.

# EGG CHEESE

*Serves 6*

5¼ pints/3 litres milk
6 eggs
2 teaspoons acetic acid or vinegar

¼ teaspoon salt
1½ oz/40 g castor sugar

Pour three-quarters of the milk into a saucepan. Whisk the eggs with the remaining milk, the acetic acid and the salt. Add to the milk in the pan. Stir constantly over very low heat until the mixture curdles. (It should not be allowed to boil.) Remove the pan from the heat, cover tightly and set aside for about 10 minutes until the curds separate from the whey.

Remove the curds with a perforated spoon and place in layers in an egg-cheese mould (a special pan with small holes in it). Alternatively, spoon the curds into a sieve lined with muslin and placed over a bowl. Sprinkle a little of the sugar on each layer.

Put the egg cheese in the refrigerator, or in a cold place, for several hours. When all the whey has drained off, unmould the egg cheese and serve with raspberry jam.

*Yeoman's snuff*

# VANILLA CREAM

*Serves 6*

1 oz/25 g gelatine
¼ pint/1·5 dl water
4 egg yolks
3 oz/75 g castor sugar

1 pint/6 dl milk
½ teaspoon vanilla essence
½ pint/3 dl double cream

Blend the gelatine with the water in a small bowl. Stand the bowl in hot water until the gelatine has completely dissolved.

Whisk the egg yolks with the sugar in a large bowl. Bring the milk to the boil. Remove from the heat and add to the egg mixture, whisking vigorously. Return to the saucepan and bring almost to the boil, whisking constantly. Remove from the heat and stir in the dissolved gelatine. Add the vanilla essence. Set aside until cold, stirring frequently.

Whip the cream until thick and stir into the cold egg mixture. Pour into a 3-pint (1·5-litre) mould and leave in a cool place to set. Turn out and serve when required.

# COUNTRY GIRLS IN VEILS

*Serves 4*

4½ oz/125 g butter
14 oz/400 g rye breadcrumbs
4½ oz/125 g castor sugar
about 1 lb/450 g apple purée

about 4 oz/100 g strawberry jam
  or redcurrant jelly
scant ¾ pint/4 dl double cream

Melt the butter in a large heavy saucepan over moderate heat until the frothing stops. Add the breadcrumbs and the sugar and cook gently for 5–10 minutes, stirring frequently. The crumbs will absorb all the butter and become crisp. Spread half the crumbs in the bottom of a glass serving dish. Cover with the apple purée and a layer of jam. Cover with the remaining crumbs. Whip the cream until thick and spread over the top layer of crumbs. Decorate with the remaining jam and serve cold.

# RICE AND ALMOND MOULD

*Serves 8*

generous 2½ pints/1·5 litres milk
8 oz/225 g short-grain rice
1 teaspoon salt
5 oz/150 g castor sugar
1 vanilla pod
½ oz/15 g gelatine
1 tablespoon icing sugar, sifted
1¼ pints/7·5 dl double cream

5 oz/150 g blanched almonds,
  flaked
**for the raspberry purée:**
10 oz/275 g castor sugar
1 pint/6 dl water
1 lb/450 g raspberries
2 tablespoons kirsch

Heat the milk in a saucepan until boiling and add the rice, salt, sugar and vanilla pod. Pour into a casserole and cover tightly. Cook in a moderately hot oven (400°F, 200°C, Gas Mark 6) for 30–40 minutes, or until the rice is tender. Remove the vanilla pod.

Meanwhile, dissolve the gelatine in 3 tablespoons hot water. Rinse a 4-pint (2·25-litre) mould with cold water and dust lightly with the icing sugar. Stir the dissolved gelatine into the rice and allow the mixture to cool. Lightly whip the cream and fold into the rice with the almonds. Pour into the prepared mould and set aside in a cold place until set.

Meanwhile, to prepare the raspberry purée, dissolve the sugar in the water over low heat. Add the raspberries and simmer gently for a few minutes, or until the raspberries are reduced to a purée. Sieve the purée to remove the pips. Pour into a bowl and set aside to cool, then stir in the kirsch and chill until ready to serve.

Serve the rice and almond mould with the raspberry purée, both well chilled.

*Note:* This dessert is served on Christmas Eve if the traditional rice pudding has not been served as a first course. A bowl of it is always put aside for the *nisse* – a mischievous elf who is part of the Christmas festivities.

# NORWEGIAN RHUBARB COMPOTE

*Serves 4–6*

1½ lb/700 g rhubarb
5 tablespoons water
8 oz/225 g castor sugar
1 tablespoon potato flour
**for the custard:**
2 eggs
1 oz/25 g castor sugar

scant ½ pint/2·5 dl milk
2 teaspoons vanilla sugar (see
  Yeoman's Snuff, preceding page)
**for the decoration:**
10 cooked prunes
10 blanched almonds

Trim and rinse the rhubarb. Cut it into 2-inch (5-cm) pieces. Bring the water and sugar to the boil over moderate heat. Add the rhubarb. Lower the heat and simmer for about 5 minutes, or until the rhubarb is still whole and barely tender. Remove it with a perforated spoon and place in a serving dish. Leave the syrup in the pan, but remove from the heat. Blend the potato flour with a little water and stir into the syrup. Return the pan to the heat. Bring to the boil and simmer for 3 minutes, or until thickened, stirring constantly. Pour the syrup over the rhubarb and mix well. Set aside to cool.

To make the custard, whisk the eggs and sugar together in a bowl until the mixture thickens and becomes pale yellow in colour. Scald the milk and whisk it vigorously into the egg mixture. Pour the custard into a saucepan and stir constantly over low heat until it thickens. Remove the pan from the heat and add the vanilla sugar. Stir until the custard is cold and pour it over the rhubarb. Stone the prunes and place an almond inside each one. Decorate the rhubarb custard with the stuffed prunes. Serve cold.

*Strawberry gateau*

# STRAWBERRY GATEAU

*Makes 1 10-inch (26-cm) gateau*

**for the sponge layers:**
3 eggs
3 oz/75 g castor sugar
3 oz/75 g plain flour
2 oz/50 g melted butter
**for the custard filling:**
¼ pint/1·5 dl milk
1 egg
2 teaspoons castor sugar
2 teaspoons cornflour

few drops vanilla essence
**for the fruit filling:**
8 oz/225 g strawberries
2 macaroons, crushed
2 tablespoons sherry
**for the decoration:**
½ pint/3 dl double cream
3 walnuts, finely chopped, or
   whole strawberries (see recipe)

First prepare the cake layers. Whisk the eggs and sugar together until light and foamy. Carefully fold in half the flour, then the melted butter and lastly the remaining flour. Divide the mixture equally between 2 greased 10-inch (26-cm) sandwich tins. Bake in the centre of a moderately hot oven (400°F, 200°C, Gas Mark 6) for 20–25 minutes, or until the sponge layers are evenly risen and golden brown. Remove and cool on a wire rack. When completely cold, cut each sponge across in half to make 4 sponge layers altogether.

For the custard filling, bring the milk to the boil in a saucepan. Meanwhile, mix the egg, sugar, cornflour and vanilla essence together in a bowl. Gradually whisk the boiling milk into the egg mixture. Blend well and return the custard to the saucepan. Replace over the heat and bring back to the boil, stirring all the time. Simmer for 2 minutes, then draw off the heat and set aside to cool.

To make the fruit filling, hull and wipe the strawberries.

Place the first sponge layer on a serving plate. Sprinkle with the macaroons and then with the sherry. Cover with half the strawberries. Place the second sponge layer on top and spread with the cooled custard. Place the third layer on top and cover with the remaining strawberries. Finally, top the cake with the last sponge layer.

To decorate, lightly whip the cream and spread over the top and sides of the gateau. Sprinkle with the chopped walnuts or decorate with the whole strawberries. Chill before serving.

# SMÅLÄNDSK CHEESECAKE

*Serves 4–5*

5¼ pints/3 litres milk
1 oz/25 g plain flour
2 teaspoons rennet
2 eggs

scant ½ pint/2·5 dl double cream
1 oz/25 g blanched almonds,
   chopped
1½ oz/40 g castor sugar

Heat the milk to 95°F (35°C). Pour into a large bowl and beat in the flour and rennet. Stir until the mixture thickens, then set aside until it separates into curds and whey. Stir a few times so the whey rises to the surface. Strain the mixture and discard the whey.

Pour the curds into a bowl. Lightly whisk the eggs. Add to the curds with the cream, almonds and sugar. Pour into a buttered mould or ovenproof dish and place in a pan half-filled with water. Bake in a moderate oven (350°F, 180°C, Gas Mark 4) for 1 hour. Allow the cheesecake to cool in the mould. Turn out and serve with whipped cream and strawberry jam.

# DANISH FRUIT DESSERT

*Serves 6*

| | |
|---|---|
| 2¼ lb/1 kg redcurrants and raspberries (see note) | 2 oz/50 g sago flour or 1 oz/25 g cornflour |
| 1¾ pints/1 litre water | 1 vanilla pod |
| 9 oz/250 g castor sugar | castor sugar (see recipe) |
| | 2 tablespoons chopped almonds |

Prepare the fruit according to kind and place in a large saucepan with the water. Simmer over moderate heat for 15–20 minutes, or until the fruit is very soft. Press through a sieve and return to the pan. Add the sugar and stir until dissolved. Blend the sago flour or cornflour with a little water to make a smooth, thin paste. Stir this into the fruit purée. Bring to the boil over moderate heat, stirring constantly until the mixture thickens. Remove from the heat and add the vanilla pod. Cool, remove the vanilla pod and pour into large glass dishes. Sprinkle with sugar (to prevent a skin forming) and chopped almonds. Serve with ice-cold double cream.

*Note:* Other fruit combinations which are equally good are: redcurrants and blackcurrants; redcurrants and cherries; redcurrants, raspberries and strawberries.

# CREAM PUDDING

*Serves 4*

| | |
|---|---|
| 3 tablespoons water | ½ vanilla pod |
| ½ oz/15 g gelatine | ¼ pint/1·5 dl double cream |
| 3 eggs | **for the caramel sauce:** |
| 2 oz/50 g castor sugar | 3 oz/75 g castor sugar |
| generous ¾ pint/5 dl milk or single cream | 4 tablespoons water |
| | ¼ pint/1·5 dl double cream |

Measure the water into a small saucepan and sprinkle in the gelatine. Stir over low heat until the gelatine has dissolved (but do not allow to boil). Draw off the heat. Separate the eggs, placing the yolks together in one bowl and the whites in a second larger bowl. Add the sugar to the yolks and whisk together until thick and light in colour. Pour the milk or cream into a saucepan. Add the vanilla pod and bring to the boil. Draw off the heat and remove the vanilla pod, then whisk the hot milk into the egg yolks and sugar. Blend well and return the mixture to the pan. Heat gently, stirring constantly until the custard begins to thicken, but do not allow to boil. Draw off the heat, stir in the gelatine and set aside until the mixture is cool and beginning to set.

Lightly whip the cream and stiffly whisk the egg whites. Fold both into the mixture and pour into a 2-pint (1-litre) ring mould previously rinsed out with cold water. Set aside in a cool place until set firm.

For the caramel sauce, heat the sugar gently in a dry saucepan, stirring occasionally, until the sugar has melted and turned to a caramel. Add the water (take care at this stage as the mixture will boil furiously with the addition of the cold liquid). Continue to stir over the heat until the mixture has formed a smooth, thin, caramel liquid. Draw off the heat and set aside until quite cold. Lightly whip the cream and fold into the caramel liquid.

Unmould the cream pudding, pour over the caramel sauce and serve.

# PANCAKE GATEAU

*Serves 4*

| | |
|---|---|
| **for the pancakes:** | butter for frying |
| 2 eggs | **for the filling:** |
| 1 pint/6 dl milk | sugar-coated berries or jam or apple purée |
| 6 oz/175 g plain flour | |
| 1 teaspoon castor sugar | **for the meringue:** |
| ¼ teaspoon salt | 3 egg whites |
| 2 tablespoons melted butter | 2 oz/50 g castor sugar |

Whisk the eggs with half the milk. Beat in the flour, sugar and salt, and finally, the remaining milk. Stir in the melted butter just before cooking the pancakes.

Heat a pancake pan, or a small frying pan, and add a pat of butter. Pour in a little batter and tilt the pan so the batter spreads to cover the bottom. Fry until golden brown on one side, then very carefully turn the pancake over and fry until golden brown on the other side. Turn the pancake out, and repeat the procedure until all the batter is used. The mixture will make 10–12 thin pancakes. Stack the pancakes on a round, heated, ovenproof serving dish, spreading a little of the chosen filling between the layers.

To make the meringue, whisk the egg whites until stiff. Continue whisking for a little longer, then carefully fold in the sugar. Spread the meringue over the top and sides of the pancake gateau. Bake in a moderate oven (350°F, 180°C, Gas Mark 4) for about 10 minutes, or until the meringue is slightly crisp and golden brown. Serve with whipped cream.

# CREAM CONES

*Makes 16 cones*

| | |
|---|---|
| 1½ oz/40 g castor sugar | **for the filling:** |
| 1 egg | ¼ pint/1·5 dl double cream |
| 1½ oz/40 g plain flour | redcurrant jelly or raspberry jam (see recipe) |
| ½ teaspoon vanilla essence | |
| 1 teaspoon water | |

Whisk the sugar and egg in a bowl until light and creamy. Gently fold in the flour, vanilla essence and water. Blend well.

Grease several baking trays and flour lightly. Using a tablespoon, spread the mixture thinly on the baking trays in oval shapes about 4 by 2½ inches (10 by 6 cm). Spread only 3 or 4 portions of the mixture on each tray at a time. If necessary bake them in batches. Bake in a hot oven (425°F, 220°C, Gas Mark 7) for about 5 minutes, or until lightly browned. Keeping the remainder warm, remove one baked oval from the tray using a spatula. Shape into a cone using the palms of the hands and place in a clean bottle neck or narrow tumbler so it keeps its shape. Remove when cool and firm. Repeat until all the ovals have been made into cones.

Just before serving, whip the cream until stiff and spoon or pipe into the cones. Decorate each one with a teaspoon of jam or jelly. Arrange attractively side by side on a plate, or stand up in a bowl filled with sugar to hold them steady.

Unfilled cones may be stored for several weeks in an airtight container.

*Cream cones*

# POPPY SEED ROLLS

*Makes about 12 rolls*

| | |
|---|---|
| 8 oz/225 g plain flour | 1 oz/25 g fresh yeast |
| ½ teaspoon salt | or ½ oz/15 g dried yeast |
| 1 teaspoon castor sugar | 3 tablespoons milk |
| 7 oz/200 g butter | poppy seeds for coating |
| 2 eggs | |

Sift the flour and salt into a large bowl. Add the sugar. Cut 4 oz (110 g) of the butter into small pieces and rub into the dry ingredients. Make a well in the centre and crack into it one of the eggs.

Blend the fresh yeast with the cold milk. If using dried yeast, warm the milk, sprinkle in the dried yeast and set aside for 10 minutes until frothy. Add the yeast mixture to the centre of the flour and mix all the ingredients together to make a dough. Knead the dough well and set aside to rest in a cool place for 10 minutes.

On a lightly-floured working surface, roll the dough out to a rectangle about 8 inches (20 cm) wide and 24 inches (62 cm) long. Brush the surface of the dough with cold water and cover with the remaining butter, thinly sliced. Fold the dough in three from left to right to make one strip of dough about 24 inches (62 cm) long and 2½ inches (6 cm) wide. Turn this around so the longest side is horizontal. Cut into 2-inch (5-cm) wide strips. Arrange on a baking tray, cover with oiled polythene and leave to rise in a warm place for about 30 minutes.

Whisk the remaining egg. Brush the surface of each roll with beaten egg and sprinkle lavishly with poppy seeds. Bake in a hot oven (425°F, 220°C, Gas Mark 7) for 12–15 minutes. Slice through and spread with butter. Serve warm.

# HAAKON COOKIES

*Makes 80*

| | |
|---|---|
| 9 oz/250 g plain flour | 1 vanilla pod |
| 7 oz/200 g butter | granulated sugar for coating |
| 3 oz/75 g icing sugar, sifted | |

Sift the flour into a large mixing bowl. Cut the butter into pieces and rub lightly into the flour using the fingertips. Add the sugar and the seeds from the vanilla pod. Gather the mixture together to make a dough and turn out on a lightly floured working surface. Knead lightly. Divide the mixture in half and roll each piece into a sausage about 1½ inches (3·5 cm) thick and about 10 inches (26 cm) long. Roll each sausage in granulated sugar and place in the refrigerator or a cold place for about 1–2 hours, or until firm. Cut each portion of dough into thin slices about ¼ inch (5 mm) thick and place on a greased baking tray. Bake in a moderately hot oven (400°F, 200°C, Gas Mark 6) for 10–15 minutes. Cool on a wire rack and store in an airtight container.

# DANISH PASTRY DOUGH

*Makes 2 lb/1 kg dough*

| | |
|---|---|
| 1 oz/25 g fresh yeast | 12 oz/350 g butter |
|   or ½ oz/15 g dried yeast | 1 egg |
| 1 oz/25 g castor sugar | pinch ground cardamom |
| ½ teaspoon salt | 12 oz/350 g plain flour |
| ¼ pint/1·5 dl cold milk | |

Dissolve the yeast, sugar and salt in the milk in a large bowl. If using dried yeast the milk should be hand hot and the mixture should be set aside for 15 minutes until it becomes frothy. Soften about one-eighth of the butter and beat it with the egg and cardamom. Add to the yeast mixture and blend well. Add the flour and mix thoroughly to a fairly soft dough. Knead the dough for 1–2 minutes on a lightly floured surface. Cover and set aside to rest for 10 minutes.

Soften the remaining butter and reshape into a slab about 4 by 8 inches (10 by 20 cm). Roll the rested dough into a square about 10 by 10 inches (26 by 26 cm). Place the slab of butter lengthwise in the centre of the dough. Fold the uncovered sides of the dough over the butter, overlapping a little down the centre. Press the edges of the dough lightly together, completely enclosing the butter. Roll out carefully into a rectangle about 18 by 6 inches (46 by 15 cm). Fold the bottom third of the dough up and the top third down, making a square about 6 by 6 inches (15 by 15 cm). Give the pastry a half turn to the right and roll again into a rectangle. The dough should be rolled and folded 3 times in this way. If the dough becomes sticky or elastic, cover and set aside to rest in a cool place for 15–20 minutes between each rolling and folding.

Before using the dough, it should be covered and rested for at least 30 minutes.

*Using the Danish pastry dough*

In most cases two or more variations of Danish pastries are prepared at one baking. The fillings and toppings in each of the following recipes are sufficient for 1 lb (450 g) Danish pastry which is half the basic quantity of dough. With the prepared basic recipe for 2 lb (1 kg) of Danish pastry, any two of the following variations can be prepared.

# ENVELOPES

*Makes 18–24*

| | |
|---|---|
| 1 lb/450 g Danish pastry dough | **for baking:** |
| **for the filling:** | 1 beaten egg |
| 3 oz/75 g butter | 2 oz/50 g almonds, chopped |
| 3 oz/75 g castor sugar | **for the decoration:** |
| vanilla essence (see recipe) | 2 teaspoons hot water |
| | 4 oz/100 g icing sugar |
| | 3 tablespoons raspberry jam |

Make the dough following the instructions above, and use half the dough to make this recipe.

To make the filling, cream the butter and sugar together until soft and fluffy. Beat in vanilla essence to taste.

Roll the dough into an oblong about ⅛ inch (3 mm) thick. Cut the dough into squares 3 by 3 inches (7·5 by 7·5 cm). Place 1 level teaspoonful of the filling in the centre of each square. Draw the 4 corners of the dough together and press

firmly on to the filling so the join will not open during the baking. Place the envelopes on a baking tray and set aside in a warm place to rise for 15–20 minutes. Brush with the beaten egg and sprinkle with the chopped almonds. Bake in a hot oven (450°F, 230°C, Gas Mark 8) for 15 minutes.

Meanwhile, add the hot water to the icing sugar and blend to a smooth, fairly thick glacé icing. When the pastries are baked, decorate when still warm with a teaspoonful of jam in the centre of each and spread with a little icing. Then remove from the baking tray and cool on a wire rack.

# CREAM BALLS

*Makes about 12*

| | |
|---|---|
| 1 lb/450 g Danish pastry dough | 2 egg yolks |
| **for the confectioners' custard:** | 1–2 tablespoons castor sugar |
| ¼ pint/1·5 dl single cream | **for the decoration:** |
| 1 oz/25 g castor sugar | melted butter and vanilla sugar |
| ¼ vanilla pod |   (see recipe) |
| ½ oz/15 g cornflour | |

Make the dough following the instructions above, and use half the dough to make this recipe.

To make the confectioners' custard, pour the cream into a small heavy saucepan. Add half the sugar and the vanilla pod. Place over moderate heat until hot, but not boiling. Remove from the heat. Meanwhile, mix the cornflour with the remaining sugar in a small bowl. Stir in the egg yolks and 5 tablespoons of the hot cream. Pour this mixture into the remaining hot cream and bring to the boil over moderate heat, stirring constantly until the mixture thickens. Remove the vanilla pod. Pour the confectioners' custard into a bowl and sprinkle with sugar to prevent a skin forming. Set aside until cold.

Roll the dough into an oblong about ⅛ inch (3 mm) thick. Cut the dough into squares 4 by 4 inches (10 by 10 cm). Place 2 tablespoons of the confectioners' custard in the centre of each square and draw the edges of the dough together to enclose the filling completely. Arrange on a baking tray with the joins underneath and set aside in a warm place to rise for 15–20 minutes. Bake in a hot oven (450°F, 230°C, Gas Mark 8) for 10 minutes.

To decorate the cream balls, brush with melted butter and then dip into vanilla sugar while still hot. Cool on a wire rack.

*Danish pastries – envelopes and combs*

# SNAILS

*Makes 18–24*

1 lb/450 g Danish pastry dough
**for the filling:**
2 oz/50 g butter
2 oz/50 g castor sugar
vanilla essence (see recipe)
**for baking:**
2 oz/50 g chopped mixed candied
    peel

1 oz/25 g cinnamon
1 beaten egg
2 oz/50 g almonds, blanched and
    slivered
**for the icing:**
2 teaspoons hot water
4 oz/100 g icing sugar

Make the dough following the instructions on the preceding page, and use half the dough to make this recipe.

To make the filling, cream the butter and sugar together until soft and fluffy. Beat in vanilla essence to taste.

Roll the dough into an oblong about $\frac{1}{8}$ inch (3 mm) thick. Spread the filling over the dough and sprinkle with the candied peel and the cinnamon. Roll the dough into a sausage shape and cut into slices $\frac{1}{2}$–$\frac{3}{4}$ inch (1–1·5 cm) thick. Place well spaced out on a baking tray, pressing each one down quite firmly in the centre. Set aside in a warm place to rise for 15–20 minutes. Brush with the beaten egg and sprinkle with the almonds. Bake in a hot oven (450°F, 230°C, Gas Mark 8) for 10 minutes.

Meanwhile, add the hot water to the icing sugar and blend to a smooth, fairly thick, glacé icing. When the pastries are baked, spread each with a little icing while still hot. Then remove from the baking tray and cool on a wire rack.

# COMBS

*Makes 18–24*

1 lb/450 g Danish pastry dough
**for the almond paste:**
2 oz/50 g ground almonds
1 oz/25 g castor sugar
1 oz/25 g icing sugar, sifted
2 teaspoons lightly beaten egg
1 drop almond essence

3 oz/75 g butter
vanilla essence (see recipe)
**for baking:**
1 beaten egg
2 oz/50 g vanilla sugar (see
    Yeoman's Snuff, page 81)

Make the dough following the instructions on the preceding page, and use half the dough to make this recipe.

To make the almond paste, place the almonds, castor sugar and icing sugar in a bowl. Stir and then add the 2 teaspoons of egg and the almond essence. Mix to a smooth paste. If the mixture is dry and crumbly, add a little more egg. Blend the butter with the almond mixture to make a soft paste. Add vanilla essence to taste.

Roll the dough into an oblong about $\frac{1}{8}$ inch (3 mm) thick. Cut into long strips about 3 inches (7·5 cm) wide. Spread each strip thinly with the almond paste.

Fold the strips lengthwise and cut into 3-inch (7·5-cm) pieces. Make 5 cuts, $\frac{1}{2}$ inch (1 cm) long and about $\frac{1}{2}$ inch (1 cm) apart, on the folded edge on each piece to produce a comb shape. Place on a baking tray and set aside in a warm place to rise for 15–20 minutes. Brush with the egg and sprinkle with the vanilla sugar. Bake in a hot oven (450°F, 230°C, Gas Mark 8) for 10 minutes.

Remove from the baking tray while still hot and cool on a wire rack.

# GERMAN

Arne Krüger

*Photography by Arne Krüger and John Miller*

Two distinct phases can be seen in the German cuisine. Before the Napoleonic wars in the early nineteenth century, German cooking was mainly determined by the seasonal availability of fruit, vegetables and meat, which were prepared according to local customs. The ingenuity of the people, who had to provide nourishing meals from the coarser cuts of meat and the more common vegetables, combined with the culinary skill exercised in the palaces of ruling princes and on the great estates, helped to develop a great variety of regional dishes, based on such foods as were readily available in the area. Where the country was covered by extensive forests and game was plentiful, game dishes were a prominent feature on menus. In regions dominated by lakes and rivers, or in those bordering on the sea, an endless variety of fish dishes could be found. And in the more luxuriant areas, where cattle breeding and agriculture were the main means of support, the food showed a tendency to be excessively rich with cream being used in the preparation of most dishes.

When Napoleon's armies marched over Europe, terms and methods derived from the French cuisine were gradually assimilated by the Germans. However, new trends were not always accepted without resistance and it often took a long time for a 'foreign' dish to be incorporated into the local menus. Eventually, many of the new dishes became adjusted to such an extent that they barely resembled the original version.

New developments came about by the end of the last century, when modern means of transport and of storing and preserving food opened up new possibilities. New varieties of fruit and vegetables became generally available, with the result that German cooking was tremendously enriched and began to make a name for itself.

The German cuisine is strongly regional in character. In recent years there has been a revival of interest in traditional cooking, as can be seen by the many restaurants specialising in country fare which have appeared in the larger towns.

Delicious seafood comes from the coast of northern Germany – mussels, eels, sole, herring – providing heartwarming stews and soups. Westphalia is renowned for its pumpernickel, the dark rye bread which is so delicious with the smoked hams and cheeses and strongly flavoured sausages from the same area. Freshwater fish, in particular carp, pike and trout, come from the rivers and lakes of Franconia, the region of the Main, Neckar and Rhine rivers. Carp is traditionally served for Christmas Eve dinner in Germany, and many recipes for its preparation have been handed down over the generations.

Dumplings and sausages are popular everywhere and each region has its own special way of making them, varying the seasoning according to the herbs available. A favourite dish in Thuringia, sweet and sour lentils with black pudding, incorporates another national culinary feature, the mixing of sweet flavours with sour ones. Perhaps the most well-known of these dishes is *sauerbraten* – marinated beef in sultana sauce.

Finally, mention must also be made of the superb cakes and rich tarts, filled with fruit, nuts and chocolate, for which Germany is justly renowned.

# BLACK FOREST HUNTER'S BREAKFAST

*Serves 4*

| | |
|---|---|
| 6 medium-sized potatoes | 4 tablespoons oil |
| 4 oz/100 g button mushrooms | salt and pepper |
| 8 oz/225 g leftover cooked game, such as venison | 4 eggs |

Bake the potatoes in their jackets in a moderately hot oven (400°F, 200°C, Gas Mark 6) for 1 hour, or until tender. Set aside to cool. Peel the potatoes and cut into slices. Wash and slice the mushrooms. Cut the game into small cubes.

Heat the oil in a large frying pan over moderate heat. Add the potatoes, mushrooms and game. Cover the pan and allow the mixture to heat through. Season with salt and pepper. Whisk the eggs and pour over the potato mixture. Cook very gently until the eggs are just set. Cut the omelette into portions and serve with a lettuce salad.

# ONION TART

*Serves 4–6*

| for the pastry: | for the filling: |
|---|---|
| 1 oz/25 g fresh yeast or ½ oz/15 g dried yeast | 2 lb/1 kg onions |
| 6–8 tablespoons lukewarm milk (see recipe) | 1½ oz/40 g butter |
| pinch sugar | 3–4 eggs |
| 8 oz/225 g plain flour | 1 (5-oz/141-g) carton soured cream |
| 2 oz/50 g melted butter | 1½ oz/40 g plain flour |
| 1 egg yolk | ½ teaspoon salt |
| ½ teaspoon salt | 1 teaspoon caraway seeds |
| | 4 oz/100 g fat bacon |

To make the dough, crumble the yeast into the lukewarm milk, add the sugar and stir until dissolved. If using dried yeast, stir the sugar into the lukewarm milk and sprinkle in the yeast. Let the mixture stand for 10 minutes, until it is frothy. Mix 3–4 tablespoons of the flour into the yeast mixture. Cover and set aside in a warm place for 15 minutes.

Sift the remaining flour into a bowl and add the yeast mixture, cooled melted butter, egg yolk and salt. Beat with a wooden spoon until the dough is bubbly and, if necessary, add a little more milk. Knead well with floured hands until the dough leaves the hands and the side of the bowl clean. Cover the bowl with a damp cloth, making sure the cloth does not touch the dough, and put in a warm place until the dough has doubled in bulk.

To make the filling, peel and finely slice the onions. Melt the butter in a large frying pan and sauté the onions over low heat until soft. Remove the pan from the heat. Mix together the eggs, soured cream and flour until smooth. Stir this mixture into the onions. Add the salt and caraway seeds. Roll out the dough and line a 9-inch (23-cm) flan tin. Pour in the filling and smooth the top with a spatula. Cut the bacon into small pieces and sprinkle over the top. Bake the tart in a moderately hot oven (400°F, 200°C, Gas Mark 6) for 30–45 minutes until set and golden brown. Serve hot from the oven, warm or cooled, but never straight from the refrigerator.

# VINEYARD SNAILS

*Serves 4*

24 canned snails, with shells
1 medium-sized onion
1 clove garlic
1 oz/25 g smoked streaky bacon
2 oz/50 g butter
4 tablespoons chopped fresh
    parsley

2 tablespoons chopped fresh
    chives
½ teaspoon sugar
salt
2 tablespoons fine fresh
    breadcrumbs

Drain the snails and reserve the liquid. Wash and dry the shells. Peel and finely chop the onion and garlic. Chop the bacon finely. Soften the butter in a small saucepan for a few moments over moderate heat. Remove the pan from the heat and stir in the onion, garlic, bacon, parsley, chives, sugar, salt and breadcrumbs. Mix until creamy.

Place 1 snail in each shell. Add 1 teaspoon of the reserved juice and sufficient amount of the butter mixture to fill the opening. Place the snails in snail plates or, if these are not available, sprinkle a thick layer of coarse salt, about 3 inches (7·5 cm) deep, in the bottom of an ovenproof dish and arrange the snails, open end uppermost, on the salt. Place the snail plate or dish in the centre of a cool oven (300°F, 150°C, Gas Mark 2) and cook for 15–20 minutes. Serve hot, with crusty white bread and a dry white wine.

# POTATO SOUP WITH SMOKED MEAT

*Serves 4*

4 medium-sized potatoes
bunch flavouring vegetables (fresh
    parsley, celery leaves and leek)
1¾ pints/1 litre beef stock
½ teaspoon salt
¼ teaspoon pepper
4 oz/100 g streaky bacon, in 1
    piece
4 medium-sized onions

6 oz/175 g *Hamburger
Rauchfleisch* (smoked meat) or
    smoked cooked ham
4 tablespoons chopped fresh
    parsley
4 tablespoons chopped fresh
    chives
2 tablespoons chopped fresh
    chervil

Peel the potatoes and cut into cubes. Wash and chop the parsley and celery leaves. Trim the leek, wash thoroughly and chop. Place the vegetables in a saucepan and add the stock. Bring to the boil over high heat, then reduce the heat and simmer, partially covered, for 15–20 minutes, or until the potatoes are cooked. Remove the pan from the heat and press the liquid and vegetables through a sieve. Season with the salt and pepper and keep hot.

Removing any rind, cut the bacon into small cubes. Peel and chop the onions and cut the smoked meat or ham into small strips. Lightly sauté the bacon in a large frying pan for 4–5 minutes. Add the onions and sauté for a few minutes. Add the smoked meat or ham and continue cooking, stirring frequently, until the mixture becomes lightly browned. Spoon the sautéed ingredients on top of the hot soup, garnish with the chopped herbs and serve immediately.

# BROTH WITH LIVER DUMPLINGS

*Serves 4*

4 oz/100 g ox liver
1 medium-sized onion
1 clove garlic (optional)
2 oz/50 g plain flour
2 eggs
generous ¼ pint/2 dl milk

salt and pepper
2–3 sprigs parsley
2 teaspoons grated lemon rind
pinch dried marjoram
1¾ pints/1 litre clear, strong broth

Mince or finely chop the liver. Peel and chop the onion and garlic. Beat together the flour, eggs and milk in a bowl. Season with salt and pepper. Chop the parsley. Add the liver, onion, garlic, parsley, lemon rind and marjoram to the egg mixture, and thoroughly mix the ingredients. Drop half teaspoonfuls of the mixture into a saucepan of rapidly boiling salted water. Add only a few at a time to maintain a rolling boil. Remove the floating dumplings with a perforated spoon as soon as they rise to the surface. Keep them hot in a heated soup tureen. Heat the broth. Pour it over the dumplings and serve immediately.

# MEAT AND VEGETABLE SOUP WITH SPÄTZLE

*Serves 3–4*

1¼ lb/600 g stewing beef
3 pints/1·5 litres water
1 teaspoon salt
2 large carrots
¼ celeriac
2 medium-sized onions
1 leek
4 medium-sized potatoes

1 teaspoon mixed pickling spice
1 teaspoon salt
¼ teaspoon pepper
¼ teaspoon grated nutmeg
8 oz/225 g *Spätzle* (see page 107)
1 oz/25 g butter
7–8 sprigs parsley

Cut the meat into large cubes and place in a large saucepan with the water and salt. Bring to the boil over high heat, then lower the heat and simmer for 40 minutes. Meanwhile, peel and chop the carrots, celeriac and one of the onions. Trim, wash and chop the leek. Peel and dice the potatoes. Add the chopped vegetables to the meat in the pan, with the pickling spices, salt, pepper and nutmeg, and cook with the meat for the last 15 minutes.

Using half quantities of the ingredients, prepare the *Spätzle* according to the recipe on page 107 and put them into a pan filled with plenty of boiling salted water. Simmer for 12 minutes, then drain in a sieve and keep hot. Peel and finely chop the remaining onion. Melt the butter in a saucepan, add the onion and sauté until golden brown. Add the *Spätzle* and mix thoroughly. Chop the parsley. Arrange the meat and vegetables on a heated serving plate, top with the *Spätzle* mixture and sprinkle with the parsley. Serve immediately.

*Vineyard snails*

*Württemberg soup with pancake strips*

# PALATINE ONION SOUP

*Serves 4*

| | |
|---|---|
| 3 small onions | 1 tablespoon plain flour |
| 1 oz/25 g butter | 1¾ pints/1 litre beef stock |
| 1 teaspoon concentrated tomato | 1 egg yolk (optional) |
|    purée | 2 tablespoons double cream |
| ¼ teaspoon paprika |    (optional) |

Peel and slice the onions. Melt the butter in a saucepan and sauté the onions until golden brown. Stir in the tomato purée and paprika and simmer over low heat for 3–4 minutes. Stir in the flour and add the stock gradually, stirring to blend the ingredients. Bring to the boil, stirring constantly, then lower the heat and simmer gently for 15–20 minutes. Remove from the heat. The soup may be thickened with an egg yolk and cream, in which case blend the yolk and cream in a small mixing bowl, add a few tablespoons of the hot soup to the egg mixture and blend well. Slowly pour the mixture into the soup, stirring constantly. Serve immediately with fried croutons.

# WÜRTTEMBERG SOUP WITH PANCAKE STRIPS

*Serves 4*

| | |
|---|---|
| 1 egg | small bunch fresh chives |
| pinch salt | 1 oz/25 g butter |
| pinch grated nutmeg | 1¾ pints/1 litre clear, strong beef |
| 2 oz/50 g plain flour |    broth |
| 6 tablespoons water | |

Blend the egg, salt and nutmeg together in a bowl. Using a wooden spoon, stir in the flour and water alternately. Mix thoroughly after each addition to make a thin batter. Chop the chives and add half to the batter. Melt a little of the butter over moderate heat in a large, heavy frying pan. Pour about half the batter into the centre of the pan, then tilt the pan in all directions until the batter covers the bottom, making an almost transparent pancake. Cook, turning the pancake once, until it is a deep golden colour on both sides. Keep the pancake hot and repeat the process, making 2 large pancakes. Cut the pancakes into very thin strips. Heat the broth, add the pancake strips and the remaining chives and serve.

# PIKE WITH LEMON AND SOURED CREAM SAUCE

*Serves 6*

| | |
|---|---|
| 1 pike, about 2½–3½ lb/ 1·25–1·5 kg | 4 (5-oz/141-g) cartons soured cream |
| 1 teaspoon salt | 1 tablespoon lemon juice |
| ½ teaspoon pepper | 1 teaspoon grated lemon rind |
| 8 oz/225 g fat bacon | 1 teaspoon castor sugar |
| 4 oz/100 g cooking fat | salt and pepper |
| 2 tablespoons plain flour | 1 tablespoon coarsely chopped |
| scant ½ pint/1·5 dl cold water | lemon balm (optional) |

Gut the pike, leaving the fish whole. Wash inside and out and remove all membranes and traces of blood. Remove the scales with the back of a knife or a special scaling knife and then rinse under cold water and dry with kitchen paper. Mix together the salt and pepper and rub the inside of the pike with this seasoning. Cut the bacon into thin strips and, using a larding needle, thread the strips through the flesh of the pike at right angles to the backbone. Melt the cooking fat in a roasting tin. Put the fish into the hot fat, spine-side uppermost, place the tin in the centre of a moderately hot oven (400°F, 200°C, Gas Mark 6) and cook for about 40 minutes. Baste the fish during the cooking. The fish is cooked when the fins on the back come away easily.

Lift the pike carefully from the tin, place on a heated serving dish, spine-side uppermost, and keep hot. Add the flour to the residue in the roasting tin and mix over low heat to a smooth paste. Add the cold water and mix until well blended. Add the soured cream, lemon juice, grated lemon rind and sugar. Heat, stirring constantly, until the sauce has thickened. Adjust the seasoning with salt and pepper to taste. Add the lemon balm and serve the sauce separately in a sauceboat. Serve the fish with potatoes boiled in their skins and a fresh green salad.

# FRISIAN MUSSEL STEW

*Serves 5–6*

| | |
|---|---|
| 2 quarts/about 2 litres fresh mussels | 4 oz/100 g butter |
| 2 leeks | generous ¼ pint/2 dl white wine |
| 1 medium-sized onion | ½ teaspoon salt |
| 1 green sweet pepper | ¼ teaspoon pepper |
| | 1 teaspoon grated lemon rind |

Mussels must be alive before cooking. Discard any that are not tightly closed or do not close when sharply tapped. Scrub the shells in plenty of cold water, using a hard brush. Remove the beards, rinse the mussels under cold running water and set aside while preparing the other ingredients.

Discard the coarse outer leaves of the leeks and cut the leeks in half lengthwise. Wash thoroughly and shred finely. Peel and chop the onion. Remove the seeds from the sweet pepper and chop the flesh. Melt the butter in a large saucepan over moderate heat. Add the leeks and sauté lightly

for 3–4 minutes. Add the wine, onion, sweet pepper, salt, pepper and lemon rind. Put the mussels into the pan, cover with a tightly fitting lid and raise the heat. Cook for 7–8 minutes, during which time the mussels will open. Discard any that have not opened. Pour the stew into a heated tureen or into 5 or 6 heated plates. Serve with dark rye bread and butter.

# CARP IN SOURED CREAM SAUCE

*Serves 4*

| | |
|---|---|
| 1 carp, about 4 lb/1·75 kg | 1 oz/25 g fine fresh breadcrumbs |
| salt and pepper | 2 oz/50 g firm butter |
| 1 medium-sized onion | 2 oz/50 g melted butter |
| 3 tablespoons lemon juice | few sprigs parsley |
| 1 (5-oz/141-g) carton soured cream | 1 tablespoon capers (optional) |

Trim, gut and scale the carp. Wash thoroughly, inside and out, removing all the dark membrane and traces of blood. Sprinkle with salt and pepper. Peel and finely chop the onion and sprinkle over the bottom of a buttered casserole. Place the carp on the bed of onion. Sprinkle with the lemon juice, pour over the soured cream and sprinkle with the bread-crumbs. Cut the butter into cubes and dot over the top. Pour over the melted butter. Bake in the centre of a moderately hot oven (375°F, 190°C, Gas Mark 5) for 30 minutes. Meanwhile, chop the parsley. Serve the fish hot, garnished with the parsley, and capers if used, and accompanied by creamed potatoes.

# FRIED PLAICE WITH ANCHOVY SAUCE

*Serves 4*

| | |
|---|---|
| 4 plaice, about 8–12 oz/ 225–350 g each | 1½ oz/40 g cooking fat |
| ½ teaspoon salt | 1 oz/25 g butter |
| 1½ tablespoons lemon juice | ½ teaspoon anchovy paste |
| 2 oz/50 g plain flour | 1 lemon |
| rind of a smoked ham or 1½ tablespoons bacon dripping | 2 tablespoons chopped fresh parsley |

Trim and gut the fish, but leave whole. Rinse under cold running water and dry thoroughly. Rub the fish with the salt and lemon juice, then coat with the flour and set aside for about 20–30 minutes, so the flour forms a fairly hard crust.

Scrape the fat off the back of the ham rind. Melt this or the bacon dripping in a frying pan with the cooking fat – this gives the fish its typical smoky taste. When the fat is very hot, put the fish into the pan one at a time, with the dark skin downwards. Lower the heat slightly and fry the fish for 4–5 minutes on each side. Remove the fish from the pan, drain on kitchen paper and keep hot on a serving dish. After the last fish has been fried, stir the butter and anchovy paste into the residue in the pan to make a thin sauce. Meanwhile, slice the lemon. Pour the sauce over the fish, garnish with the parsley and the lemon slices and serve with potato salad.

# STEWED EEL IN DILL SAUCE

*Serves 4*

| | |
|---|---|
| 1 large eel or 2 small eels, about 2–2¼ lb/1 kg | 6 tablespoons vinegar |
| salt (see recipe) | **for the sauce:** |
| bunch flavouring vegetables (carrot, celery and leek) | 2 leeks |
| | 2 oz/50 g butter |
| 1¾ pints/1 litre water | 2 tablespoons plain flour |
| 1 bay leaf | ¾ pint/4·5 dl eel stock (see recipe) |
| 6 whole allspice | bunch fresh dill |
| 6 white peppercorns | ½ teaspoon salt |
| 1 teaspoon salt | ¼ teaspoon pepper |
| 2 slices lemon | 3 tablespoons single cream |

Clean the eel and discard the head. Rub the skin liberally with salt to remove the slippery surface and wash well under cold running water. Drain, chop into 1-inch (2·5-cm) pieces and place in a saucepan. Peel and dice the carrot. Wash and chop the celery. Wash and chop the leek, discarding the coarse outer leaves. Place the vegetables in a second saucepan. Add the water, bay leaf, allspice, peppercorns, salt and lemon slices. Place over high heat and bring to the boil, then lower the heat and simmer for 10–15 minutes. Heat the vinegar until hot but not boiling. Pour over the eel and let stand for 10 minutes. Strain the liquid from the vegetables over the eel and vinegar, discarding the vegetables. Place the pan over moderate heat and bring just to the simmering point. Simmer for 2 minutes, then strain off the stock and reserve. Place the eel in a covered dish and keep hot.

To make the dill sauce, wash and chop only the white parts of the leeks, discarding the outer leaves. Melt the butter in a saucepan and sauté the leeks until tender. Remove from the heat and stir in the flour. Add the reserved stock gradually, stirring well after each addition. Chop half the dill and reserve the remainder. Season the sauce with the salt and pepper and stir in the chopped dill. Return to the heat and bring to the boil, stirring constantly until the mixture thickens. Stir in the cream. Pour the sauce over the eel and garnish with the reserved dill.

# PICKLED HERRING WITH BEANS

*Serves 4*

| | |
|---|---|
| 1½ lb/700 g fresh French beans | 2 oz/50 g bacon or fat pork |
| 1 medium-sized onion | 8 pickled herring fillets, about 1 lb/450 g |
| 4 tablespoons water | |
| 2 oz/50 g butter | 4 tablespoons chopped fresh parsley |
| sprig fresh savory | |
| 1 tablespoon flour | 1 tomato, quartered |

Rinse the beans and break into 1-inch (2·5-cm) pieces. Peel and finely chop the onion. Place the beans and onion in a saucepan with the water, butter and savory. Bring to the boil over moderate heat then lower the heat and simmer, uncovered, for 15 minutes. Sprinkle the flour evenly over the beans, using a small sieve or sprinkling by hand. Mix well and simmer the beans for a further 10 minutes. Remove and discard the savory.

Cut the bacon or fat pork into very small cubes or chop finely. Place in a heavy saucepan and sauté over moderate heat until the fat runs. Pour into a heated sauceboat.

Meanwhile, rinse the herring fillets under cold water and dry well. Serve the herring chilled, or on crushed ice, garnished with the parsley and tomato. Serve the beans and the bacon sauce separately.

Potatoes, boiled in their jackets, make a good accompaniment, with *schnapps* or light beer to drink.

*Pickled herring with beans*

# STEWED VEAL WITH PRUNES

*Serves 4–6*

| | |
|---|---|
| 1–1¼ lb/450–600 g lean veal or fillet of veal | 1 tablespoon plain flour |
| 1 medium-sized onion | scant ½ pint/2·5 dl white wine |
| 1½–2 oz/40–50 g butter | scant ½ pint/2·5 dl water |
| water (see recipe) | 4 oz/100 g tenderised prunes (see note) |
| ½ teaspoon salt | 1 teaspoon lemon juice |
| pinch pepper | ½ teaspoon sugar |

Cut the veal into large cubes. Peel and chop the onion. Melt the butter in a large saucepan, add the onion and the veal cubes and sauté over low heat until golden brown. Simmer until the juices from the onion and meat have been absorbed. Then add 6–7 tablespoons of water and continue simmering until the water has been absorbed. Repeat this procedure once or twice more until the onions are very soft but not burned. Add the salt, pepper and flour. Stir until well blended. Add the wine and the water, stirring constantly, and bring to the boil. Lower the heat and simmer for 30 minutes.

Meanwhile, wash the prunes and remove the stones. Add the prunes to the saucepan and cook for a further 10 minutes. Adjust the seasoning, if necessary. Add the lemon juice and sugar. Serve with boiled potatoes or noodles and a green salad.

*Note:* If tenderised prunes are not available, substitute ordinary prunes which have been soaked for 2–3 hours or overnight.

# DÜSSELDORF CHOPS

*Serves 4*

| | |
|---|---|
| 4 veal neck cutlets | pinch pepper |
| 4 shallots | ½ oz/15 g melted butter |
| 6 mushrooms | 1 egg yolk |
| 4 oz/100 g fat pork | 3 oz/75 g fine fresh breadcrumbs |
| 2 truffles (optional) | 2 oz/50 g butter |
| few sprigs parsley | 4 slices lemon |
| ½ teaspoon salt | |

Bone the cutlets and remove any sinews from the meat. Peel the shallots and cook in boiling salted water for 5–10 minutes until tender, then drain. Wash and dry the mushrooms. Finely chop or mince the veal, shallots, mushrooms, fat pork, truffles, if used, and parsley. Mix the ingredients together thoroughly. Shape the mixture into 4 chops. Sprinkle with salt and pepper, cover and set aside for 1 hour.

About 30 minutes before serving the chops, mix the melted butter with the egg yolk. Coat each chop first with the egg mixture and then with the breadcrumbs. Melt the 2 oz (50 g) of butter in a heavy frying pan. Add the chops and sauté slowly until golden brown on both sides. Arrange the chops on a heated serving dish and garnish with the lemon slices. Serve with cauliflower and creamed potatoes.

# SAUTÉED VEAL

*Serves 4*

| | |
|---|---|
| 1 lb/450 g boned leg of veal | ¼ teaspoon salt |
| 2 tomatoes | pinch paprika (optional) |
| 2 oz/50 g butter | 1 (4½-oz/127-g) carton yoghurt |
| 1 tablespoon plain flour | pinch sugar |
| 6 tablespoons hot water | |

Cut the veal into very thin slices. Peel and chop the tomatoes. Heat the butter in a large frying pan over high heat and sauté the meat until golden brown, stirring constantly. Lower the heat to moderate and sprinkle the flour over the meat. Stir in the tomatoes, hot water, salt, paprika, yoghurt and sugar. Bring to the boil, stirring constantly, and cook for 3–4 minutes. Pour into a heated serving dish and serve immediately with rice, bread or mashed potatoes, and a green salad.

# LEG OF VEAL WITH SOURED CREAM SAUCE

*Serves 4*

| | |
|---|---|
| 2 lb/1 kg leg of veal | 1 medium-sized onion |
| scant ½ pint/2·5 dl vinegar | 1 medium-sized carrot |
| scant ½ pint/2·5 dl water | salt and pepper |
| 1 bay leaf | 2 (5-oz/141-g) cartons soured cream |
| 2 cloves | 1 tablespoon plain flour |
| 4 whole peppercorns | 1 teaspoon castor sugar |
| 2 oz/50 g smoked fat bacon | |

Wipe the meat with a damp cloth. Prepare the marinade by mixing together the vinegar, water, bay leaf, cloves and peppercorns. Place the meat in a china or earthenware bowl and pour the marinade over. Cover and leave to pickle in the mixture for 2–3 days, turning frequently. Lift the meat out of the marinade and dry well. Reserve the marinade.

Cut the bacon into thin strips and lard the meat with it, using a larding needle, or push the bacon strips into small slits cut in the meat with a sharp knife. Peel and slice the onion and carrot and place with the meat in a roasting tin.

Sprinkle with salt and pepper and pour in half the marinade. Place the tin in the centre of a moderately hot oven (400°F, 200°C, Gas Mark 6) and roast for 1–1½ hours. Spoon over a little of the soured cream, at about 15-minute intervals, during the roasting. Remove the meat from the oven and keep hot in a covered dish. Strain the liquid from the roasting tin through a sieve into a small saucepan. Blend the flour and sugar with a little water to form a smooth paste and stir into the strained liquid. Add the remaining soured cream. Place the pan over moderate heat and bring slowly to the simmering point, stirring constantly until the mixture thickens. Slice the meat and serve on a heated plate. Serve the sauce separately.

# VEAL AND MUSHROOM SOUFFLÉ

*Serves 4*

| | |
|---|---|
| 1 medium-sized cauliflower | ¼ pint/1·5 dl cauliflower |
| 1¼ pints/7·5 dl water | stock (see recipe) |
| 1 teaspoon salt | 2 eggs |
| 8 oz/225 g button mushrooms | few sprigs parsley |
| 1 lb/450 g leftover roast veal | 6 tablespoons milk or soured |
| 2 oz/50 g butter | cream |
| 1 oz/25 g plain flour | pinch pepper |
| | 2 oz/50 g hard cheese, grated |

Break the cauliflower into florets and wash thoroughly. Discard the leaves and stalk. Put the water and salt into a saucepan and bring to the boil. Add the cauliflower and cook until almost tender. Drain well and reserve ¼ pint (1·5 dl) of the stock. Wash and slice the mushrooms. Cut the cooked veal into small cubes.

Melt three-quarters of the butter in a saucepan, add the mushrooms and sauté over moderate heat until soft. Stir in the flour and then add the reserved cauliflower stock gradually, mixing thoroughly after each addition. Stir until the mixture thickens, then remove from the heat and cool slightly. Butter a 3-pint (1·5-litre) soufflé dish and place the cauliflower and meat in the bottom. Separate the eggs and chop the parsley. Stir the milk or soured cream, egg yolks, pepper and parsley into the cooled mushroom sauce. Whisk the egg whites until stiff and fold into the mushroom mixture. Pour into the prepared soufflé dish. Sprinkle with the grated cheese and top with the remaining butter, cut into small pieces. Bake in the centre of a moderately hot oven (375°F, 190°C, Gas Mark 5) for 30 minutes. Reduce the heat to 350°F (180°C, Gas Mark 4) and bake for a further 20–30 minutes, or until the soufflé is well risen and lightly browned. When baked, the centre should still be slightly creamy. Serve immediately.

# OX TONGUE WITH SULTANA SAUCE

*Serves 4*

| | |
|---|---|
| 1 fresh ox tongue, about | 1½ oz/40 g butter |
| 4½ lb/2 kg | 2 tablespoons plain flour |
| bunch flavouring vegetables | ¾–1¼ pints/5–7·5 dl stock from the |
| (carrot, celery and leek) | tongue (see recipe) |
| 1 medium-sized onion | 2 tablespoons wine vinegar |
| 2 teaspoons salt | 2 tablespoons concentrated |
| 6 peppercorns | tomato purée |
| **for the sauce:** | 1 tablespoon castor sugar |
| 5 oz/150 g sultanas | salt and pepper |

Rinse the tongue under cold running water and place in a large saucepan. Peel and chop the carrot. Wash and chop the celery. Wash and chop the leek, discarding the coarse outer leaves. Peel and chop the onion. Add the carrot, celery, leek, onion, salt and peppercorns to the tongue. Add cold water to cover, place the pan over high heat and bring to the boil. Lower the heat and simmer gently, partially covered, for 4½–5 hours. If necessary, add more water during the cooking to keep the tongue covered. When cooked, remove the tongue from the pan and rinse under cold water. Peel off the skin and remove the bones and gristle from the back of the tongue. Set aside until required. Strain the stock and reserve the amount required for the sauce. Discard the vegetables.

To make the sauce, soak the sultanas in cold water for 3–4 hours. Drain and place in a saucepan. Add just enough fresh water to cover. Bring to the boiling point over moderate heat and simmer for 10–15 minutes, or until the sultanas are tender. Melt the butter in another saucepan, stir in the flour and cook over moderately high heat, stirring constantly until the mixture browns. Remove from the heat. Add the reserved stock gradually, mixing well after each addition. Return the pan to moderate heat and bring to the boil, stirring constantly until the mixture thickens. Add the sultanas, vinegar, tomato purée, sugar and salt and pepper to taste and cook for a further 3–4 minutes. Slice the tongue thinly and heat the slices in the sauce for about 3–4 minutes. Transfer to a heated dish and serve immediately.

# CURLY KALE WITH SAUSAGE

*Serves 4*

| | |
|---|---|
| 2½–3 lb/1·25–1·5 kg curly kale | 1 large onion |
| 4 oz/100 g smoked fat bacon, in | 1 large potato |
| 1 piece | salt and pepper |
| 3 tablespoons cooking oil | pinch grated nutmeg |
| 3 pints/1·5 litres water | 1 beef stock cube |
| 1¼ lb/600 g cooking *Mettwurst* | |
| (see note) | |

Strip the leaves of the curly kale from the stalks and wash thoroughly in cold water. Place in a saucepan of boiling salted water. Bring back to the boil, then drain and rinse with cold water. Dice the bacon. Heat the oil in a large saucepan, add the bacon and sauté lightly until golden brown. Add the kale and water. Place the saucepan over moderate heat and bring to the boil. Lower the heat, cover the pan and simmer for 1½ hours.

Place the *Mettwurst* on top of the kale. Add a little more water, if necessary, but there must not be too much liquid. Simmer for 20 minutes. Peel and grate the onion and potato. Lift out the sausage and keep hot. Stir the kale well and add the onion, potato, salt and pepper to taste, nutmeg and the beef stock cube. Simmer for 10 minutes. Drain off any excess liquid and arrange the kale and the sausage on a heated shallow serving dish. Serve accompanied by roast potatoes.

*Note: Mettwurst* is a coarse sausage which is made in several varieties. It may be mild or strong, soft or fairly firm, smoked or unsmoked. Available in most continental delicatessen shops.

*Curly kale with sausage*

96

# SPICED PORK CHOPS

*Serves 4*

| | |
|---|---|
| 4 small pork chops | 3–4 peppercorns |
| 1 tablespoon caraway seeds | 3–4 juniper berries |
| 1 medium-sized onion | salt and pepper |
| 2–3 tablespoons water | 1 tablespoon plain flour |

Lightly beat the pork chops with a mallet to flatten them and rub with the caraway seeds. Peel and finely chop the onion. Heat the water in a frying pan. Add the chops, onion, peppercorns and juniper berries. Sprinkle with salt and pepper and simmer the chops, partially covered, over moderate heat for 20–30 minutes, or until tender. Remove the pan from the heat. Arrange the chops on a heated plate, cover and keep hot.

Add 3–4 extra tablespoons water to the juices in the pan and bring to the boil. Blend the flour to a smooth paste with a little cold water. Stir the paste into the pan juices and mix well. Place over moderate heat and bring to the boil, stirring constantly. Adjust the seasoning and pour the sauce over the chops. Serve with cooked shredded white cabbage sprinkled with melted pork dripping.

# BAVARIAN PORK OR VEAL KNUCKLES

*Serves 4*

| | |
|---|---|
| 2 large knuckles of pork or veal | 1 medium-sized carrot |
| 1 teaspoon salt | scant ½ pint/2·5 dl light ale |
| 1 teaspoon paprika | 1 bay leaf |
| ½ teaspoon pepper | ½ teaspoon caraway seeds |
| 2 oz/50 g cooking fat | scant ½ pint/2·5 dl water |
| 2 medium-sized onions | 1 tablespoon cornflour |

Wash the knuckles and dry them with a cloth. Rub the meat all over with the salt, paprika and pepper. Heat the cooking fat in a heavy roasting tin or flameproof casserole over moderate heat and brown the knuckles for 15 minutes, turning frequently. It is important that they should be browned evenly all over, but not burned.

Peel and chop the onions and carrot and add to the roasting tin or casserole with the meat. Add all but 3 or 4 tablespoons of the light ale, the bay leaf and the caraway seeds. Place the tin in a moderately hot oven (400°F, 200°C, Gas Mark 6) and cook for 45–50 minutes. After 10 minutes, baste with the juices in the tin.

Transfer the knuckles to a grill pan. Place the pan under moderate heat and baste with the remaining ale until the skin on the knuckles becomes crisp and tender.

To make the sauce, blend the water with the cornflour and stir into the remaining juices in the roasting tin. Cook over moderate heat, stirring constantly, until the sauce thickens. If necessary, adjust the seasoning. Strain through a sieve into a heated sauceboat. Make incisions in the knuckles before serving, loosening the sinews so the meat can easily be removed from the bone. Serve with the sauce, boiled potatoes, a mixed salad and beer.

*Sweet and sour lentils with black pudding*

# SAUERKRAUT WITH PORK

*Serves 4*

| | |
|---|---|
| 1 oz/25 g lard or goose fat | 1 lb/450 g smoked bacon, in |
| 1 onion | 1 piece, soaked overnight |
| 1¼ lb/600 g sauerkraut | 4 small pork chops |
| ¼ pint/1·5 dl dry white wine | 8 medium-sized potatoes |
| 1 cooking apple, peeled and sliced | 3 tablespoons kirsch |
| 10 juniper berries, crushed | 8 frankfurter sausages |
| 1¼ pints/7·5 dl chicken stock | |

Use a flameproof casserole or a large heavy saucepan. Melt the lard or goose fat in the casserole. Peel and chop the onion, add it to the fat and brown it. Stir in the sauerkraut over high heat and add the white wine, apple and juniper berries. Stir in the stock, cover and cook very slowly for 3 hours.

Add the soaked bacon and the pork chops. Cover and cook for 30 minutes. Meanwhile, wash and scrub the potatoes, but do not peel them. Cook for 15–20 minutes in boiling water. Add the kirsch to the sauerkraut and cook for a further 10 minutes. Prick the frankfurters with a fork, so they do not burst, and put them into a saucepan of boiling water. Keep the heat low and warm the frankfurters through. Remove the bacon from the casserole and slice it. Spoon the sauerkraut into the middle of a large, heated serving dish. Lay the pork chops, bacon and frankfurters on top and surround with the potatoes. Serve with a well cooled white wine.

# SWEET AND SOUR LENTILS WITH BLACK PUDDING

*Serves 4*

| | |
|---|---|
| 8 oz/225 g brown lentils | 2 tablespoons plain flour |
| bunch flavouring vegetables | 3 tablespoons wine vinegar |
| (celery, carrot, onion and leek) | ½ teaspoon salt |
| 4 oz/100 g fat pork or smoked fat | pinch pepper |
| bacon | 1 lb/450 g *Blutwurst* (black |
| 2 medium-sized onions | pudding) |

Pick over the lentils. Wash well and soak overnight in plenty of cold water. The next day bring them to the boil very slowly in the water in which they were soaked. Wash the celery, peel the carrot and onion and wash the leek, discarding the coarse outer leaves. Chop the vegetables, add to the lentils and continue to simmer over low heat for about 1½ hours.

Cut the fat pork or smoked bacon into cubes and sauté briefly in a separate saucepan. Peel and slice the onions, add to the pan and sauté quickly, until lightly browned. Stir in the flour and continue cooking until the mixture is well browned. Stir in the vinegar, salt and pepper. Mix thoroughly and add to the lentils. Cook for 5–10 minutes, or until well blended. Add the black pudding and simmer, very slowly to prevent the sausage from bursting, for a further 10–15 minutes. Remove the black pudding, split it open and scoop out the filling on to a heated serving plate. Pour the lentil mixture into a heated serving dish. Serve immediately.

# BAYREUTH STUFFED CABBAGE

*Serves 4*

| | |
|---|---|
| 1 white cabbage, about 1 lb/450 g | 2 (5-oz/141-g) cartons soured |
| 3 medium-sized onions | cream |
| 4 tablespoons oil | 1 lb/450 g cooked beef and pork, |
| 1 teaspoon salt | minced |
| pinch pepper | 2 oz/50 g smoked bacon or fat |
| small piece bay leaf | pork, thinly sliced |
| 2–3 cloves | |

Wash the cabbage. Remove the centre core with a sharp knife and discard it. Peel off 4 of the large outer leaves. Blanch these in hot water, rinse in cold water and set aside. Finely shred the remaining cabbage. Peel and chop the onions. Heat the oil in a frying pan and sauté the onions until soft. Add the shredded cabbage, salt, pepper, bay leaf and cloves and simmer over low heat for 10 minutes. Remove the pan from the heat and mix the cabbage mixture with the soured cream and minced meat. Adjust the seasoning if necessary.

Butter a casserole and line it with 2 of the blanched cabbage leaves. Arrange the meat and cabbage mixture on top. Cover with the remaining cabbage leaves. Arrange the bacon slices on top and bake in a moderately hot oven (375°F, 190°C, Gas Mark 5) for 30–35 minutes. Serve hot.

# HUNTER'S MEAT LOAF

*Serves 4–6*

| | |
|---|---|
| 2 hard-boiled eggs | pinch dried marjoram |
| 2 stale crusty bread rolls | 1 large onion |
| 8–12 oz/225–350 g lean stewing | 2–3 sprigs parsley |
| beef | 4 oz/100 g fat bacon |
| 8–12 oz/225–350 g lean pork or | 3 tablespoons plain flour (see |
| pork fillet | recipe) |
| 1 egg | 2 oz/50 g cooking fat |
| ½ teaspoon salt | 6 tablespoons water |
| pinch pepper | 1 (4½-oz/127-g) carton yoghurt |
| 2 teaspoons grated lemon rind | |

Shell the hard-boiled eggs. Soak the rolls in a little cold water for 2–3 minutes, then squeeze out the excess water. Mince together the beef and pork. Whisk the egg. Mix the soaked bread with the minced meat and add the beaten egg, salt, pepper, lemon rind and marjoram. Peel and finely chop the onion. Chop the parsley. Dice the bacon and sauté lightly in a frying pan for 2–3 minutes. Add the onion and parsley and sauté for a further 2–3 minutes. Remove from the heat, add to the meat mixture and mix well. Shape the meat mixture into a large loaf, placing the hard-boiled eggs in the centre. The eggs should be completely enclosed. Dust the meat loaf lightly with half the flour and set aside for about 30 minutes.

Melt the cooking fat in a wide saucepan or flameproof casserole over moderate heat. Place the meat loaf in the hot fat and sauté until brown on all sides. Add the remaining flour to the hot fat and stir in the water. Cover the pan and simmer gently over low heat. If using a casserole, cover it and place in the centre of a moderate oven (350°F, 180°C, Gas Mark 4). Cook the meat loaf for 45 minutes–1 hour. Add a

little more water during the cooking, if necessary. Lift the meat loaf from the liquid and place on a heated serving plate. Add the yoghurt to the liquid remaining in the pan and stir until the sauce is well blended and hot. Pour the sauce into a sauceboat and serve with the meat loaf.

# SILESIAN HEAVEN

*Serves 4*

| | |
|---|---|
| 8 oz/225 g dried apple rings | 3 tablespoons water |
| 8 oz/225 g dried pear slices | 1½ tablespoons plain flour |
| 8 oz/225 g dried prunes | pinch salt (optional) |
| 1¼ lb/600 g smoked streaky bacon, | 1 tablespoon lemon juice |
| in 1 piece | ½ oz/15 g castor sugar |

Soak the dried apples and pears overnight, then drain. Soak the prunes in cold water to cover for about 1 hour. Place the bacon in a saucepan and barely cover with cold water. Bring to the boil over moderate heat, cover the pan, reduce the heat and simmer for 1 hour. Add the drained apples and pears, the prunes and the water in which the prunes were soaked. Simmer for a further 30 minutes. Mix the water and flour to form a smooth paste and stir into the liquid in the pan. Continue stirring until the liquid thickens. Taste and add salt if necessary (the dish will have absorbed some salt from the bacon). Stir in the lemon juice and sugar. Serve with Silesian potato dumplings (see page 105).

# WESTPHALIAN STEW

*Serves 4*

| | |
|---|---|
| 1 lb/450 g streaky bacon, in | 4 medium-sized potatoes |
| 1 piece | 8 oz/225 g pears |
| 8 oz/225 g shelled broad beans | 8 oz/225 g cooking apples |
| 1½ lb/700 g French beans | salt and pepper |
| 4 medium-sized carrots | |

Place the bacon in a saucepan and cover with cold water. Bring to the boil and simmer gently for about 30 minutes, or until the bacon is tender. Place the broad beans in a second saucepan and just cover with cold water. Bring to the boil and simmer for 10–15 minutes, or until just tender.

Meanwhile, lift the cooked bacon from the liquid and keep hot. Reserve the bacon liquid. When the beans are almost cooked, strain off the water and replace it with the reserved bacon liquid.

Clean and slice the French beans. Peel and dice the carrots and potatoes. Peel and slice the pears and apples. Add the French beans, carrots and potatoes to the broad beans and simmer gently without stirring until the vegetables are tender. Add the pears and apples and simmer for a further 15 minutes, or until the fruit is just tender. If necessary, the stew may be thickened with 1 tablespoon of flour blended with a little cold water. Stir in gently and bring to the boil. Season with salt and pepper to taste. Cut the bacon into cubes and add to the stew. Heat the stew through and serve in a heated dish.

*Bayreuth stuffed cabbage*

# HEAVEN AND EARTH

*Serves 6–8*

2 lb/1 kg large potatoes
2 teaspoons salt
2 lb/1 kg cooking apples
4 oz/100 g castor sugar
2 large onions

4 oz/100 g lean bacon
pepper
1 lb/450 g *Blutwurst* (black
  pudding)
1 oz/25 g butter

Peel the potatoes, cut into thick slices and place in a large saucepan. Add the salt and cover the potatoes with water. Cook over moderate heat for 15–20 minutes, or until the potatoes are tender. Meanwhile, peel, core and quarter the apples. Place in a second saucepan, add the sugar and cover with water. Simmer very gently until the apples are tender.

When the potatoes are tender, drain off and discard one-third of the water, leaving the remaining water and the potatoes in the pan. Mash the cooked potatoes very thoroughly, then beat with a rotary beater or hand whisk until very smooth. Add the apples, including the liquid in which they were cooked, and stir well. Place the pan over low heat and simmer gently.

Peel and finely slice the onions and dice the bacon. Sauté both together in a saucepan until browned. Add to the potatoes and apples and season to taste. Cut the black pudding into 2 or 3 pieces and cut each piece in half lengthwise. Melt the butter in a frying pan, place the black pudding, cut side down, in the butter and fry quickly. Serve the apple and potato mixture in a heated tureen garnished with the fried black pudding.

# OXTAIL WITH HORSERADISH SAUCE

*Serves 4*

1¼ lb/600 g oxtail
2 medium-sized carrots
½ small celeriac
1 leek
1 teaspoon salt
3 pints/1·5 litres water
5 medium-sized potatoes

**for the horseradish sauce:**
3 slices white bread
4 tablespoons milk
4 tablespoons double cream
4 tablespoons grated horseradish
pinch salt
½ teaspoon castor sugar
2 teaspoons lemon juice

Rinse the oxtail joints thoroughly in cold water. Peel and coarsely chop the carrots and celeriac. Trim, wash and slice the leek. Put the meat into a large saucepan with the water. Place over high heat and bring to the boil, removing the scum with a metal spoon as it rises to the surface. Reduce the heat, add the salt, carrots, celeriac and leek, and simmer, partially covered, for 1½ hours. After about 1 hour, peel the potatoes and cut into cubes. Add the potatoes to the meat for the remainder of the cooking time.

To make the sauce, trim the crusts from the bread and discard. Cut the bread into small cubes. Heat the milk and cream in a saucepan until just simmering. Remove the pan from the heat, add the bread, horseradish, salt, sugar and lemon juice and beat until fairly smooth. Pour the sauce into a heated sauceboat. Serve the meat in a heated dish with the vegetable broth and horseradish sauce separately.

# BEEF IN BEER SAUCE

*Serves 4*

1 medium-sized onion
1 medium-sized carrot
scant ½ pint/2·5 dl dark sweet malt beer or stout
1 teaspoon salt
1 bay leaf
12 white peppercorns
1 teaspoon sugar
1¼ lb/600 g brisket of beef
1 oz/25 g butter
1 tablespoon plain flour

Peel and slice the onion and carrot and place in a saucepan with the beer, salt, bay leaf, peppercorns and sugar, and sufficient water to cover the meat to be cooked. Place the pan over high heat and bring to the boil. Add the meat, reduce the heat and simmer, partially covered, for about 2 hours, or until the meat is tender. Turn the meat over from time to time during the cooking.

Lift the beef from the pan and keep hot. Strain the cooking liquid and reserve. Discard the vegetables. Melt the butter in a saucepan. Stir in the flour and cook gently until the mixture is golden brown. Add the reserved liquid, a little at a time, stirring well after each addition. Place the pan over moderate heat and bring to the boil, stirring constantly until the mixture thickens. Adjust the seasoning, if necessary.

Carve the meat into slices and arrange on a large heated serving dish. Pour half the beer sauce over the beef and serve the remaining sauce separately. Serve with pickled beetroot and boiled potatoes accompanied by malt beer or a mixture of equal quantities of malt beer and a sparkling white wine.

# SAUERBRATEN (MARINATED BEEF)

*Serves 4*

2 oz/50 g smoked bacon
2 lb/1 kg topside of beef
**for the marinade:**
1 large onion
1–2 carrots
1 celeriac
½ beef stock cube
¾ pint/4·5 dl water
scant ½ pint/2·5 dl wine vinegar
1 bay leaf
3–4 juniper berries
3–4 cloves
3–4 peppercorns
**for cooking the beef:**
salt and pepper
2 oz/50 g cooking fat
6 tablespoons water
1 tablespoon plain flour or cornflour
1 tablespoon blanched chopped almonds
1½ oz/40 g sultanas
salt and pepper
little dry white wine
pinch sugar
3 tablespoons soured cream
lemon juice (see recipe)

Cut the bacon into thin strips and lard the beef with it, using a larding needle. Alternatively, make cuts in the meat with a sharp knife and insert the strips into the cuts. To prepare the marinade, peel and chop the onion, carrot and celeriac. Place the vegetables in a saucepan with the ½ beef stock cube, water, vinegar, bay leaf, juniper berries, cloves and peppercorns and bring to the boil. Simmer gently for 3–4 minutes, then set aside to cool. Place the meat in a stone crock, cover with the marinade and marinate for 3 days, during which time the meat must be turned occasionally.

Remove the meat and reserve the marinade. Dry the meat with a cloth or kitchen paper and rub with salt and pepper. Melt the cooking fat in a heavy saucepan, add the meat and brown on all sides. Add the water and an equal quantity of the marinade, cover the pan and simmer over low heat for 1¼ hours. Lift out the meat and keep hot. Add 4–5 tablespoons cold water to the liquid remaining in the pan and bring to the boil. Blend the flour or cornflour with a little cold water to a smooth paste and stir into the boiling liquid. Add the almonds and sultanas and season with salt and pepper to taste. Add white wine to taste, the sugar and soured cream. Taste the sauce, and if preferred add a few drops of lemon juice. Pour into a hot sauceboat. Serve the meat in one piece and carve at the table. Serve the sauce separately.

# BOILED BEEF WITH FRANKFURT GREEN SAUCE

*Serves 4*

1½ lb/700 g brisket of beef
bunch flavouring vegetables (onion, carrot, leek, celery stick and leaves and parsley sprigs)
2 lb/1 kg potatoes
1 teaspoon salt
**for the sauce:**
4 eggs
3 tablespoons oil
2 (5-oz/141-g) cartons soured cream
2 tablespoons wine vinegar
½ teaspoon salt
pinch pepper
½ teaspoon sugar
3 oz/75 g chopped fresh herbs (parsley, chives, chervil, sorrel, tarragon, borage and dill)
pinch dry mustard (optional)

Rinse the beef under cold running water and place in a large saucepan. Cover with cold water, place the pan over high heat and bring to the boil. Reduce the heat and simmer, partially covered, for 1 hour. Peel and chop the onion and carrot. Wash and chop the leek, celery stick and leaves and the parsley sprigs. Peel the potatoes and cut into large pieces. Add these vegetables with the salt to the meat in the pan and simmer for 20–30 minutes, or until the potatoes are well done.

Meanwhile, prepare the sauce. Boil the eggs for 5–7 minutes; they should be slightly soft in the centre. Cool in cold water and shell. Separate the yolks from the whites and chop the whites finely. Mash the yolks in a bowl, using a wooden spoon. Add the oil, a drop at a time, beating until the mixture is smooth and thick. Stir in the soured cream, vinegar, salt, pepper, sugar, chopped herbs and egg whites. A pinch of dry mustard may also be added. Cover the bowl and set aside for 30 minutes or until required. Lift the meat from the pan, carve into slices and arrange on a heated serving plate. Serve the vegetables separately with some of the strained cooking liquid. Serve the sauce in a sauceboat.

*Sauerbraten (marinated beef)*

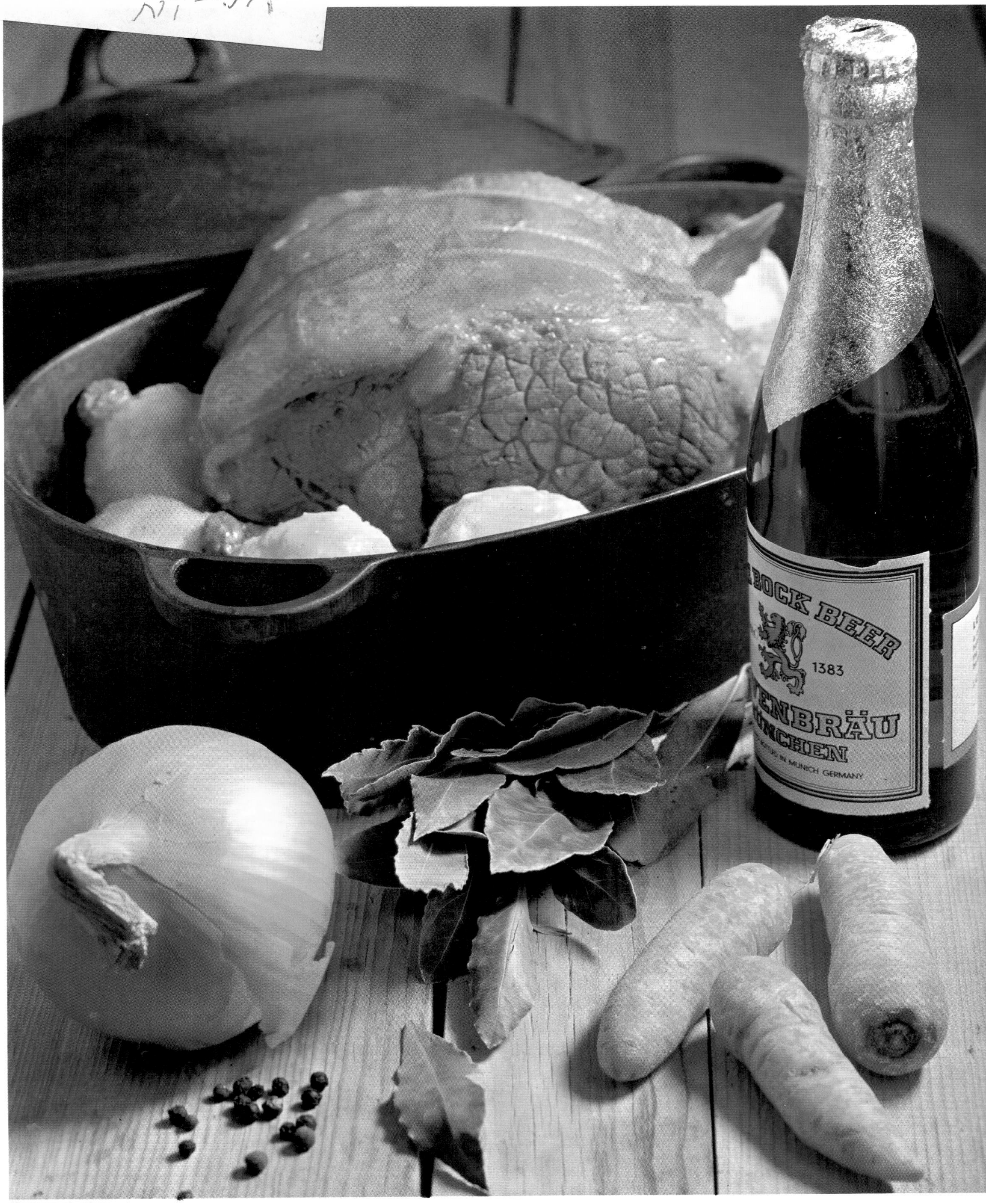
BOCK BEER
1383

# JELLIED GOOSE

*Serves 4*

| | |
|---|---|
| ½ goose, about 3–5 lb/1·5–2·25 kg | 1½ teaspoons salt |
| 3 medium-sized carrots | 3–4 peppercorns |
| 1 large onion | 1 bay leaf |
| ½ celeriac | 1 oz/25 g gelatine |
| 1 leek | 1 tablespoon castor sugar |
| 1 parsley root or bunch parsley | 2 tablespoons vinegar |
| stalks | salt and pepper |
| 3 pints/1·5 litres water | |

Wash and dry the meat and chop into small pieces. Peel and chop the carrots, onion and celeriac. Trim, wash and chop the leek. Scrape and chop the parsley root (if using parsley stalks, wash and chop). Put the water and salt into a large saucepan, place over high heat and bring to the boil. Add the pieces of goose, with the carrots, onion, celeriac, leek, parsley root or stalks, peppercorns and bay leaf. Lower the heat, cover and simmer for 1 hour, or until the meat is cooked. Remove from the heat and set aside to cool.

When lukewarm, remove the pieces of goose and place in a glass dish. Strain the liquid and reserve. Discard the vegetables. Mix the gelatine and sugar with a little of the liquid in a small saucepan. Stir over low heat until the gelatine is dissolved and add the mixture, with the vinegar, to the remaining reserved liquid. Adjust the seasoning, if necessary, with salt and pepper to taste. Set aside until cold and beginning to set, then pour over the goose pieces and chill until set into a firm jelly. Serve with fried potatoes.

# HARE IN YOGHURT AND SOURED CREAM

*Serves 4*

| | |
|---|---|
| saddle and hind legs of 1 hare | *bouquet garni* (see recipe) |
| 4 oz/100 g fat bacon | 6 tablespoons red wine |
| salt and pepper | 1 (4½-oz/127-g) carton yoghurt |
| 1 medium-sized onion | 1 (5-oz/141-g) carton soured |
| 1 medium-sized carrot | cream |
| 2 oz/50 g butter | 6 tablespoons stock or water |

Remove all sinews and skin from the hare, as they tend to harden during cooking. Rinse and dry the pieces thoroughly. Cut the bacon into thin strips. Using a larding needle, insert the strips in the flesh of the hare, or make small slits with the point of a knife and insert the strips. Sprinkle the pieces with salt and pepper. Peel and slice the onion and carrot. Melt the butter in a roasting tin and add the hare, onion, carrot, *bouquet garni* (1 bay leaf, 3 sprigs parsley and 1 sprig thyme, tied together) and wine. Pour over the yoghurt and soured cream. Place the tin in the centre of a moderately hot oven (375°F, 190°C, Gas Mark 5) and roast for 1½–2 hours, basting frequently. Lift the hare from the tin and cut into slices. Keep hot in a covered dish while preparing the sauce.

To make the sauce, add the stock or water to the liquid remaining in the roasting tin and bring to the boil. Stir until well blended. Strain the sauce over the hare and serve with Thuringian potato dumplings (see page 106) and cranberry sauce.

# CALF'S LIVER WITH APPLE RINGS

*Serves 4*

| | |
|---|---|
| 2 lb/1 kg potatoes | 4 oz/100 g butter |
| 1 lb/450 g calf's liver | 2 cooking apples |
| 2 tablespoons plain flour | 2 medium-sized onions |
| ½ teaspoon salt | generous ¼ pint/2 dl water |
| ¼ teaspoon white pepper | |

Peel the potatoes and cook in boiling salted water until tender. Mash and keep warm. Meanwhile, cut the liver into 8 slices. Season the flour with the salt and pepper and coat the liver. Melt half the butter in a large heavy frying pan and sauté the liver for about 5 minutes, turning the slices frequently; the insides should still be pink. Spoon the mashed potato on to a heated serving dish. Remove the liver from the pan and place on the bed of mashed potato. Cover the dish and keep hot.

Peel and core the apples and cut into thick rings. Heat the remaining butter in a second frying pan and gently sauté the apple rings for about 2–3 minutes on each side, or until tender and golden brown. Remove from the pan, place on top of the liver and keep hot.

Meanwhile, peel the onions and slice into rings. Add to the butter remaining in the pan and sauté until pale golden brown. Drain and arrange the onions on top of the liver with the apples. Add half the water to the residue in each of the frying pans, heat until boiling and then blend the contents of the two pans together to make a gravy. Strain the gravy over the dish and serve immediately.

# WHITE CABBAGE SALAD

*Serves 4*

| | |
|---|---|
| 1 small firm white cabbage | pinch pepper |
| 1 teaspoon salt | 1–2 tablespoons soured cream or |
| 3 tablespoons oil | yoghurt (optional) |
| 2 tablespoons vinegar | |

Wash the cabbage. Remove the centre core with a sharp knife and discard. Grate the cabbage very finely. If the cabbage is old or tough, pour boiling water over it and let stand for 2 minutes, then drain and rinse with cold water. Sprinkle with half the salt and pound with a mallet or a rolling pin until the cabbage is limp and slightly soft. The salt will make the juices run.

Prepare a salad dressing with the oil, vinegar, remaining salt and the pepper. Shake or stir vigorously. Mix the dressing into the cabbage and add the soured cream or yoghurt, if liked. Mix again and let the salad stand, covered, for 1–2 hours before serving with roast pork, sausages or veal knuckles (see page 98).

# BAKED NOODLES WITH HAM AND CHEESE

*Serves 4*

8 oz/225 g noodles, macaroni or spaghetti
6 oz/175 g cooked ham, in 1 piece
small bunch chives
4 oz/100 g hard cheese, grated
2 eggs
½ teaspoon salt
2 (5-oz/141-g) cartons soured cream or yoghurt
1 oz/25 g butter
1 tablespoon fine dried breadcrumbs

Cook the noodles in plenty of salted water for 10–12 minutes, or until just tender. Drain well in a colander. Cut the ham into small cubes. Chop the chives. Butter a 2-pint (1-litre) casserole. Put a third of the noodles in the bottom of the casserole. Sprinkle with half the ham, half the chives and a third of the grated cheese. Add another layer of noodles. Top with the remaining ham and chives and a third of the grated cheese and finish with a layer of noodles.

Whisk together the eggs, salt and soured cream or yoghurt and pour the mixture evenly over the noodles. Sprinkle the remaining cheese over the top.

Cut the butter into small pieces and dot over the cheese. Sprinkle with the breadcrumbs. Bake in a moderately hot oven (375°F, 190°C, Gas Mark 5) for 40 minutes. Serve with a fresh green salad.

*Silesian potato dumplings*

# SILESIAN POTATO DUMPLINGS

*Serves 4*

2 lb/1 kg potatoes
1 oz/25 g plain flour
1 oz/25 g semolina
½ teaspoon salt
pinch grated nutmeg
4 oz/100 g white bread
2 oz/50 g butter

If possible, cook the potatoes the day before. Scrub, but do not peel, the potatoes and place them in a saucepan of boiling water. Simmer gently for 15–25 minutes until just soft. Drain and let stand overnight.

Peel the potatoes and mash or grate them. Place in a bowl and mix in the flour, semolina, salt and nutmeg to form a smooth dough. With floured fingers, shape the mixture into 8 large dumplings and set aside on a floured surface.

Cut the bread into cubes. Melt the butter in a heavy saucepan and gently sauté the cubes until pale golden brown. Drain. Ease the dumplings open and press about 4 sautéed cubes into the centre of each dumpling. Seal up the opening, completely enclosing the cubes. Fill a large saucepan three-quarters full with salted water. Bring the water to the boil, add the dumplings, then reduce the heat and simmer for 20 minutes. Remove the dumplings with a perforated spoon and drain on a plate before serving. Serve hot with Silesian Heaven (see page 100) or with a casserole such as *Sauerbraten* (see page 102).

# THURINGIAN POTATO DUMPLINGS

*Serves 4*

9 medium-sized potatoes

2 slices rye bread

2 oz/50 g butter

Peel the potatoes and grate two-thirds of them. Place the grated potatoes in a linen bag or a sieve and squeeze out as much moisture as possible, so they are quite dry. Reserve the liquid. Place the grated potato in a large bowl, spreading out the shreds by hand. Let the liquid stand for a little while, pour off the water very carefully and add the residue at the bottom of the bowl (the potato starch) to the grated potatoes.

Meanwhile, cook the remaining potatoes in boiling salted water until tender. Drain, leaving 4–6 tablespoons of water in the pan. Mash the potatoes and cook over moderate heat, stirring constantly, until the mixture is fairly thick. Take care when the mixture comes to the boil as it may splash. Pour the boiling potatoes quickly over the grated raw potatoes and mix together to form a smooth dumpling paste.

Cut the bread into small cubes. Melt the butter in a frying pan, add the bread cubes and sauté until browned. Drain. With hands rinsed in cold water, shape the potato mixture into 8 dumplings. Press 3 or 4 bread cubes into the centre of each dumpling and seal the opening.

Bring plenty of well-salted water to the boil and drop the dumplings in. Lower the heat, half cover the saucepan and let the dumplings poach. When they rise to the surface they are ready. Lift the dumplings out with a perforated spoon and serve at once with a stew or casserole.

# DRESDEN DUMPLINGS

*Serves 4*

2 oz/50 g butter

6 tablespoons stock or milk

pinch salt, pepper and nutmeg (see recipe)

3 oz/75 g plain flour

2 eggs

**to cook the dumplings:**

3 pints/1·5 litres clear broth or stock

Heat the butter and stock or milk in a saucepan. If milk is used, add salt, pepper and nutmeg. Remove the pan from the heat. Cool a little of the stock and stir into the flour. Stir the paste into the hot stock. Return the pan to the heat and cook, stirring constantly, until the mixture leaves the sides of the pan clean. Remove from the heat and cool slightly. Add the eggs, one at a time, mixing well after each addition, until the mixture is shiny and fairly stiff. Cover the pan and set aside until cold.

To cook the dumplings, boil the broth or stock. Drop teaspoonfuls of the dumpling mixture into the boiling broth. Cover the pan and let the dumplings poach over moderate heat until they rise to the surface. Serve the dumplings with the soup or, drained, with roast meat.

*Cheese noodles*

106

# FRANCONIAN DUMPLINGS

*Serves 4*

| | |
|---|---|
| 4 stale crusty bread rolls | 3 eggs |
| 2 oz/50 g butter | 2 teaspoons salt |
| 1 lb/450 g plain flour | scant ½ pint/2·5 dl water or milk |

Cut the rolls into large cubes. Heat the butter in a frying pan and sauté the bread cubes until lightly browned. Mix the flour with the eggs, salt and water or milk in a bowl to form a soft dough. Stir the bread cubes into the dough and let stand for 1 hour. With wet hands, form the mixture into 8 dumplings.

Drop the dumplings into a large saucepan of boiling salted water. Bring to the boil, keeping the lid on the pan. Lower the heat and simmer, partially covered, for 20–25 minutes. Serve hot with a meat stew or with roast meat.

# CARAWAY SEED DUMPLINGS

*Serves 4*

| | |
|---|---|
| 8 stale crusty bread rolls | ½ teaspoon salt |
| 1 teaspoon caraway seeds | scant ½ pint/2·5 dl lukewarm milk |
| 1 medium-sized onion | 2 eggs |
| 1 oz/25 g butter | |

Cut the rolls into thick slices and place in a mixing bowl. Crush the caraway seeds and peel and slice the onion. Heat the butter in a frying pan, add the onion and sauté lightly until soft. Cover the sliced bread with the onion, sprinkle with the salt and add the lukewarm milk. Cover the bowl with a plate and let stand for 5 minutes until the milk has been completely absorbed and the rolls are soft. Add the crushed caraway seeds and the eggs and mix thoroughly.

Using a wet tablespoon, scoop out a portion of the mixture and lower the spoon with the dumpling into a saucepan of boiling salted water. Once the dumpling is in the boiling water, it will slip off the spoon. Continue until all the mixture is used, making about 16 dumplings. Lower the heat and simmer the dumplings gently for 15–20 minutes. Remove from the water with a perforated spoon and drain on a plate before serving with a roast or casserole.

# CHEESE NOODLES

*Serves 4*

| | |
|---|---|
| 14 oz/400 g plain flour | 4 oz/100 g hard cheese, grated |
| ½ teaspoon salt | 2 oz/50 g melted butter |
| 3 eggs | 3 tablespoons hot beef stock |
| 6 tablespoons water | |

Sift the flour and salt into a bowl and make a well in the centre. Add the eggs and water and beat with a wooden spoon until all the liquid has been absorbed. Knead the dough in a bowl until smooth. Roll out on a floured board to ⅛ inch (3 mm) thick and cut into fine strips to make noodles. Drop the noodles, a few at a time, into boiling salted water. When they rise to the surface, remove them from the water with a perforated spoon.

Place a layer of noodles in a heated serving dish and sprinkle with a little of the grated cheese. Repeat until all the noodles have been used up. Finish with a layer of noodles. Pour the melted butter and the beef stock over the noodles just before serving. Garnish with any remaining cheese. Serve with a green salad or tomato salad.

# SPÄTZLE

*Serves 4–6*

| | |
|---|---|
| 1 lb/450 g plain flour | 2 eggs |
| 1 teaspoon salt | scant ½ pint/2·5 dl water |

Sift the flour and salt into a bowl and make a well in the centre. Add the eggs and mix together. Stir in the water gradually, beating well after each addition. Beat the mixture to make a well-aerated, soft dough. Dip a pastry board in cold water. Spread a spoonful of dough on it and then hold the board at a slant over a pan of lightly salted boiling water. Using a spatula, scrape thin strips, about ¼ inch (5 mm) wide, into the water. When the noodles rise to the surface, remove with a perforated spoon. Dip briefly into hot water to remove the excess starch. Drain the *Spätzle* in a sieve and keep warm in a covered dish until all the dough has been used.

# POTATO NOODLES

*Serves 6*

| | |
|---|---|
| 8 medium-sized potatoes | 10 oz/275 g plain flour |
| 1 egg | 2 oz/50 g butter |
| 1 teaspoon salt | 2 tablespoons dried breadcrumbs |
| pinch grated nutmeg | |

Scrub the potatoes but do not peel them. Place in a large saucepan and cover with cold salted water. Bring to the boil and cook for 20–25 minutes, or until tender. Drain, skin and mash the potatoes. Add the egg, salt, nutmeg and flour, and mix together to make a fairly firm dough. If necessary, add a little more flour.

Lightly flour a pastry board. Divide the dough into 4 portions and make up long rolls of the mixture, about ½ inch (1 cm) thick. Cut into 1-inch (2·5-cm) pieces. Shape each piece into a thin roll, about 2 inches (5 cm) long. Drop the noodles into lightly salted boiling water in a wide, but not too shallow, saucepan. Simmer gently until they rise to the surface, then remove with a perforated spoon and drain in a sieve. Melt the butter in a frying pan, fry the breadcrumbs until golden brown and sprinkle over the noodles. Serve with sauerkraut.

# COTTAGE CHEESE FINGERS

*Serves 4–6*

6 medium-sized potatoes
1 egg
8 oz/225 g cottage cheese
pinch salt
pinch grated nutmeg
2 teaspoons grated lemon rind

4 oz/100 g currants
plain flour (see recipe)
oil or cooking fat for deep-frying
1 teaspoon castor sugar
¼ teaspoon ground cinnamon

If possible, cook the potatoes the day before. Scrub, but do not peel, the potatoes. Put into a saucepan of boiling salted water and cook over moderate heat for about 20 minutes, or until just soft. Drain and let stand overnight.

Peel the potatoes and grate or press through a sieve into a bowl. Whisk the egg and add with the cottage cheese, salt, nutmeg, lemon rind and currants to the grated potatoes. Mix thoroughly, working in as much flour as the mixture will absorb. With well-floured hands roll into small finger or croquette shapes. Deep-fry in hot oil or cooking fat until golden brown. Drain on kitchen paper. Mix the sugar with the cinnamon, sprinkle over the cheese fingers and serve hot with a fruit sauce, such as plum (see below).

# PLUM SAUCE

*Makes about 1 pint (6 dl)*

1 lb/450 g plums
2 oz/50 g castor sugar
pinch ground cinnamon

½ oz/15 g butter
1 tablespoon cornflour
6 tablespoons water

Remove and discard the stones from the plums, using a sharp knife, and put the fruit into a saucepan. Add the sugar and cinnamon and enough water to barely cover the fruit. Bring to the boil over high heat, then lower the heat and simmer for 10–15 minutes, or until the fruit is tender. Remove from the heat and stir in the butter. Blend the cornflour with the water and stir into the cooked fruit. Return to the heat and bring to the boil, stirring constantly. Serve the sauce hot.

# DIPLOMAT PUDDING

*Serves 4–6*

6 stale crusty bread rolls
generous ½ pint/3·5 dl milk
2 oz/50 g blanched almonds
4 eggs
5 oz/150 g butter
5 oz/150 g castor sugar
vanilla essence or grated lemon
  rind

few drops rum essence
2 oz/50 g currants
2 oz/50 g sultanas
2 tablespoons cornflour
2 tablespoons fine fresh white
  breadcrumbs

Cut the rolls into cubes and place in a bowl. Bring the milk to the boil and pour over the rolls. Cover and let stand for 30 minutes. Chop the almonds and separate the eggs. Cream the butter with the sugar and egg yolks until the mixture is soft. Stir in the vanilla essence or grated lemon rind to taste and the rum essence. Beat the softened bread until smooth and add the almonds, currants, sultanas and cornflour. Add the fruit mixture to the butter mixture and beat thoroughly. Whisk the egg whites until stiff and fold into the mixture.

Grease a 3-pint (1·5-litre) heat-resistant bowl or pudding basin and sprinkle the inside with the breadcrumbs. Spoon the mixture into the bowl and cover with a lid or buttered greaseproof paper. Place the bowl in a saucepan, pour in boiling water to reach halfway up the sides of the bowl, cover the pan and steam for about 1½ hours. Replenish with boiling water when necessary. Serve hot with vanilla sauce (see below).

# VANILLA SAUCE

*Serves 4–6*

¾ pint/4·5 dl milk
2 oz/50 g castor sugar
2 tablespoons cornflour
2 tablespoons cold water

1 tablespoon vanilla sugar (see
  note)
2 egg yolks
3 tablespoons advocat liqueur

Bring the milk to the boil over low heat. Add the castor sugar, stir to dissolve and remove the saucepan from the heat. Measure the cornflour into a bowl and blend with the water. Stir in the vanilla sugar or the additional sugar and vanilla essence. Stir the cornflour mixture into the hot milk and return the pan to the heat. Bring to the boil again, stirring constantly, and remove from the heat.

Place the egg yolks in a bowl. Stir the liqueur into the yolks, with 3 tablespoons of the hot sauce. Blend well and then stir into the hot sauce. Beat thoroughly, set aside to cool and chill in the refrigerator before serving.

*Note:* If vanilla sugar is not available, substitute castor sugar to which has been added a few drops of vanilla essence.

# RED FRUIT DESSERT

*Serves 6*

10 oz/275 g redcurrants
10 oz/275 g fresh or frozen
  raspberries
scant ½ pint/2·5 dl water
about 8 oz/225 g castor sugar

2 tablespoons cornflour
4 tablespoons water
generous ¼ pint/2 dl double cream
  (optional)

Wash the redcurrants and remove the stalks. Pick over the raspberries or defrost them if frozen. Place the redcurrants and raspberries in a large heavy saucepan and add the water. Bring to the simmering point over low heat and cook for 10 minutes. Press the fruit through a sieve into a second pan. Add the sugar, bring to the boil and remove from the heat.

Blend the cornflour with the water and stir into the hot fruit mixture. Return to the heat and bring to the boil, stirring constantly. Remove the pan from the heat and set aside to cool. Pour into serving glasses. Chill thoroughly and serve with fresh cream. If preferred, the dessert may be decorated with whipped cream.

*Red fruit dessert*

# BAVARIAN CREAM STRUDEL

*Serves 4*

**for the pastry:**
8 oz/225 g plain flour
pinch salt
6 tablespoons lukewarm water
1 oz/25 g melted butter
1 egg
**for the filling:**
1½ oz/40 g butter

1 oz/25 g fine fresh breadcrumbs
1–2 (5-oz/141-g) cartons
   soured cream
4 oz/100 g sultanas
scant ½ pint/2·5 dl milk
1 tablespoon castor sugar
sifted icing sugar (see recipe)

To make the pastry, sift the flour and salt on to a pastry board and make a small well in the centre. Gradually add the lukewarm water, melted butter and egg. Drawing the flour from around the sides, work the ingredients to a smooth, close-textured dough. Knead the dough thoroughly until small air bubbles appear on the surface. Set aside, cover with a warm cloth and let stand for 30 minutes.

Divide the dough into 3 equal portions. Prepare each portion of the dough in turn. Roll out the pieces of dough on a cloth lightly dusted with flour, until they are the thickness of the back of a knife. Then, using your fingertips and working from the edges, pull out the dough until it is transparent. You should be able to see through it but the dough should not tear. To make the filling, melt two-thirds of the butter in a frying pan over moderate heat, add the breadcrumbs and sauté until crisp and golden brown. Spread the soured cream evenly over each piece of dough. Sprinkle with the sultanas and sautéed breadcrumbs. Lift the cloth under each strudel in front and roll up, completely enclosing the filling. Bring the milk to the boil, add the sugar and the remaining butter. Pour the milk mixture into a large roasting tin or ovenproof dish and arrange the strudels in the tin, side by side. Place the tin in the centre of a moderately hot oven (400°F, 200°C, Gas Mark 6) for about 40 minutes, until the milk has been absorbed and the strudels are pale golden brown. Transfer the strudels to a dish and serve at once, dusted with icing sugar.

# RICE DUMPLINGS IN WHITE WINE SAUCE

*Serves 4*

**for the dumplings:**
5 oz/150 g short-grain rice
generous ¾ pint/5 dl milk
4 oz/100 g butter
pinch salt
little grated lemon rind or
   vanilla essence
2 oz/50 g crystallised lemon peel
3 oz/75 g castor sugar

4 eggs
4 oz/100 g sultanas
1 oz/25 g plain flour
1 oz/25 g fine dried breadcrumbs
oil or cooking fat for deep-frying
**for the sauce:**
generous ¾ pint/5 dl white wine
1 oz/25 g castor sugar
small strip lemon rind

Wash the rice several times in lukewarm water. Cook the rice slowly in the milk with the butter, salt and grated lemon rind or vanilla essence for about 15 minutes, or until tender. Finely shred the crystallised lemon peel. Separate 1 of the eggs. Mix together in a bowl, the sugar and 2 whole eggs plus 1 egg yolk.

When cooked, drain the rice and add to the bowl with the crystallised lemon peel, sultanas and flour. Mix well and form the mixture into small dumplings. Whisk together the remaining egg and the egg white. Dip the dumplings first into the egg mixture, then into the breadcrumbs. Deep-fry in hot oil until pale golden brown and drain thoroughly on kitchen paper. Place the dumplings in a heated dish and keep hot. To make the sauce, heat the wine with the sugar and the strip of lemon rind until hot but not boiling. Strain and pour over the dumplings. Serve immediately.

# GOOSEBERRY TART

*Serves 6–8*

**for the pastry:**
5 oz/150 g butter
1–2 tablespoons ground hazelnuts
   or toasted breadcrumbs
8 oz/225 g plain flour
1 teaspoon baking powder
pinch salt
4 oz/100 g castor sugar
pinch ground cinnamon

1 tablespoon milk or water
2 egg yolks
**for the filling:**
1–1½ lb/450–700 g firm
   gooseberries
6 tablespoons water
8 oz/225 g castor sugar
1 tablespoon dried breadcrumbs
2 egg whites

To make the pastry, cut the butter into small cubes and place in the refrigerator or a cold place for 10 minutes. Butter a 9- or 10-inch (23- or 26-cm) flan tin and sprinkle with the hazelnuts or breadcrumbs. Sift the flour, baking powder and salt on to a pastry board and make a well in the centre. Place the sugar, cinnamon, milk or water and egg yolks in the well and distribute the cubes of butter evenly over the flour. First mix together the sugar, cinnamon, milk and egg yolks, then gradually draw in the butter and flour from around the sides. Mix to a smooth dough and let stand in the refrigerator or a cold place for 5 minutes. Roll out the pastry and line the prepared flan tin, pressing the pastry carefully over the bottom and around the sides up to the height of 1 inch (2·5 cm). Bake in a moderately hot oven (400°F, 200°C, Gas Mark 6) for 20–25 minutes, or until the pastry is golden brown. Set aside to cool.

Meanwhile, prepare the filling. Top and tail the gooseberries, wash thoroughly and place in a heavy saucepan. Add the water and half the sugar. Bring to the boil over moderate heat. Lower the heat and simmer very gently for 5–10 minutes, until the fruit is just tender but still whole. Drain the berries in a sieve and reserve the juice (see note). Sprinkle the breadcrumbs into the cooled pastry case and arrange the gooseberries on top. Whisk the egg whites in a bowl until stiff. Slowly whisk in half of the remaining sugar until the mixture stands up in peaks. Using a metal spoon, fold in the remaining sugar. Put the meringue into a piping bag with a large tube and pipe in a crisscross pattern over the gooseberries. Bake the tart in a hot oven (425°F, 220°C, Gas Mark 7) for 3–4 minutes until the meringue is very lightly browned. Serve warm or cold.

*Note:* The reserved gooseberry juice may be thickened with 1 teaspoon arrowroot or 2½ teaspoons cornflour for each ½ pint (3 dl) of juice, and poured over the fruit.

*Plum tart with almonds*

# PEARS IN BATTER

*Serves 4*

2 lb/1 kg very ripe pears
¾ pint/4·5 dl water
1 tablespoon castor sugar
3 tablespoons lemon juice
2 oz/50 g margarine or
    cooking fat

**for the batter:**

8 oz/225 g plain flour
1 teaspoon baking powder
4 oz/100 g castor sugar
1 teaspoon vanilla sugar or few
    drops vanilla essence
2 eggs
½ pint/3 dl milk

Peel, halve and core the pears. Rinse under cold running water and place in a heavy saucepan. Add the water, sugar and lemon juice. Bring to the boil over moderate heat, lower the heat and simmer gently for 10 minutes. Drain the pears in a sieve. The juice may be reserved for a sauce (see note).

Grease a 3-pint (1·5-litre) baking dish with the margarine. Arrange the pears closely together in the dish, rounded side up. Set aside while preparing the batter.

To make the batter, sift together the flour, baking powder, sugar and vanilla sugar into a mixing bowl. Add the eggs and milk. Beat until the mixture is smooth, making a fairly thick batter. Pour the batter over the pears and smooth the top with a knife. Place the dish in the centre of a moderate oven (350°F, 180°C, Gas Mark 4) and bake for 1–1¼ hours until the batter is firm, golden brown and well risen. Serve hot or cold as a dessert.

*Note:* The reserved pear juice may be thickened with 1 teaspoon cornflour blended with 2–3 teaspoons cold water. The sauce should be served separately, warm or chilled.

# PLUM TART WITH ALMONDS

*Serves 6*

6 oz/175 g butter
8 oz/225 g plain flour
1 teaspoon baking powder
4 oz/100 g castor sugar
pinch salt
2 teaspoons grated lemon rind
1 egg or 2 egg yolks

**for the filling:**

3 tablespoons biscuit crumbs
2 lb/1 kg firm purple plums
2 oz/50 g castor sugar
1 teaspoon ground cinnamon
4 oz/100 g blanched almonds,
    flaked

To make the pastry, cut the butter into small cubes and place in the refrigerator for 10 minutes. Butter a 9- or 10-inch (23- or 26-cm) flan tin. Sift the flour and baking powder on to a pastry board and make a well in the centre. Place the sugar, salt, grated lemon rind and egg or egg yolks in the well. Distribute the cubes of butter evenly over the flour. First mix together the sugar, salt, lemon rind and egg, then gradually draw in the butter and flour from around the sides. Mix to a smooth dough and let stand in a cool place for at least 30 minutes. Roll out the pastry thinly and line the prepared flan tin. To make the filling, sprinkle the biscuit crumbs over the bottom of the pastry case. Halve and stone the plums. Arrange in circles in the pastry case and sprinkle with the sugar and cinnamon. Sprinkle the almonds over the plums. Place the flan tin in the top of a moderately hot oven (400°F, 200°C, Gas Mark 6) and bake for 20 minutes. Lower the heat to 350°F (180°C, Gas Mark 4) and bake for a further 15 minutes. Serve hot or cold.

# BLACK FOREST CHERRY TORTE

*Makes 1 9-inch (23-cm) cake*

**for the cake:**
4 oz/100 g plain flour
4 oz/100 g cornflour
1 teaspoon baking powder
2 tablespoons cocoa
5 eggs
8 oz/225 g castor sugar

**for the filling:**
1½ lb/700 g Morello or sour
  cherries

¼ pint/1·5 dl water
5 oz/150 g castor sugar
6 tablespoons kirsch
1 teaspoon powdered gelatine
¾ pint/4·5 dl double cream
castor sugar (see recipe)
4 oz/100 g blanched almonds,
  chopped
1 oz/25 g plain chocolate, grated

If possible, make the cake about 24 hours before it is needed. Sift together the flour, cornflour, baking powder and cocoa. Grease and line a 9-inch (23-cm) round cake tin. Whisk together the eggs and sugar in a mixing bowl over a saucepan of hot water until the mixture is thick and warm. Remove the mixing bowl from the water and continue to whisk until the mixture is cold. Gently but thoroughly fold in the sifted dry ingredients, using a metal spoon. Pour the mixture into the prepared cake tin and bake in a moderately hot oven (375°F, 190°C, Gas Mark 5) for 35–40 minutes. Turn out and cool on a wire rack.

Cut the cake into 3 equal layers. Stone the cherries. Heat together 6 tablespoons of the water and the sugar in a small saucepan over low heat until the sugar has dissolved, then boil until the mixture is thick and syrupy. Remove the pan from the heat and add half the kirsch. While still warm, sprinkle over the cake layers.

To make the filling, dissolve the gelatine in the remaining 2 tablespoons of water in a small bowl over a saucepan of hot water. Set aside until cool but not set. Whip the cream until stiff and gently stir in the remaining kirsch and the cooled, dissolved gelatine. Sprinkle in sugar to taste.

Place one cake layer on a cake plate. Spread with a thin layer of the cream filling and arrange the stoned cherries on top, reserving a few for decorating. Cover with a second layer of cake. Spread this thinly with cream filling and cover with the third layer of cake. Spread most of the remaining cream filling over the top and sides of the cake. Coat the sides of the cake with the chopped almonds. Decorate the cake with the remaining cream filling, using a piping bag and a fluted tube. Sprinkle with the grated chocolate and top with the remaining cherries.

Store in the refrigerator and serve chilled.

# STUTTGART CHERRY CAKE

*Makes 1 9-inch (23-cm) cake*

5 eggs
5 oz/150 g castor sugar
1 teaspoon grated lemon rind
1 teaspoon ground cloves
1 teaspoon ground cinnamon
4 oz/100 g ground almonds

4 oz/100 g dark rye breadcrumbs
1 tablespoon arak or rum
1 lb/450 g stoned black cherries
  or canned stoned sweet cherries
1 oz/25 g sifted icing sugar

Separate the eggs. Whisk together the sugar and egg yolks until foamy. Stir in the lemon rind, cloves, cinnamon and ground almonds. Sprinkle the arak or rum over the crumbs, then add the crumbs to the mixture. Whisk the egg whites until stiff and fold carefully into the mixture.

Pour the mixture into a well-buttered 9-inch (23-cm) deep cake tin. Arrange the cherries on top. Bake in the centre of a moderate oven (350°F, 180°C, Gas Mark 5) for about 50 minutes. Set aside until cool, then remove the cake from the cake tin. Dust with the icing sugar and serve.

*Black Forest cherry torte*

# RUM YEAST CAKE WITH SULTANAS

*Makes 1 9-inch (23-cm) cake*

| | |
|---|---|
| 1 oz/25 g fresh yeast or ½ oz/15 g dried yeast | 4 eggs |
| ⅓ pint/3 dl lukewarm milk | 7 oz/200 g butter |
| 1 lb/450 g plain flour | 7 oz/200 g castor sugar |
| 2 teaspoons grated lemon rind | 5 oz/150 g sultanas |
| 3 tablespoons lemon juice | 2 oz/50 g ground almonds |
| pinch salt | 2 tablespoons rum |
| | 4 oz/100 g sifted icing sugar |

Dissolve the fresh yeast in the milk in a large bowl. If using dried yeast, stir the yeast into the milk and set aside for 10 minutes. Add half the flour and the grated lemon rind, lemon juice and salt. Cover the bowl with a cloth and leave to rise in a warm place for 20 minutes.

Place the eggs, in their shells, in warm water for 2–3 minutes. (They will then be warmer and a better cake texture will be achieved.) Cream the butter until soft and gradually beat in the eggs and sugar. Beat the remaining flour into the yeast mixture and combine with the butter mixture. Mix in the sultanas, almonds and rum with a wooden spoon and beat until the mixture is well aerated. Butter a 3-pint (1·5-litre) *Kugelhopf* tin or a 9-inch (23-cm) tube tin and pour in the mixture. The tin must be only half full. Smooth the mixture and sprinkle lightly with flour. Cover the tin with a cloth and leave in a warm place until the mixture has risen to the rim. Bake in a moderately hot oven (400°F, 200°C, Gas Mark 6) for 30 minutes. Reduce the heat to 350°F (180°C, Gas Mark 4) and cook for a further 30–40 minutes. Let the cake cool in the tin for 2 hours and then turn out on to a round plate. Dust with the icing sugar to give a snowy appearance.

# REDCURRANT CAKE, COUNTRY STYLE

*Serves 8–10*

| | |
|---|---|
| 1 lb/450 g plain flour | 8 oz/225 g semolina |
| pinch salt | 2 teaspoons grated lemon rind |
| 1 oz/25 g fresh yeast or ½ oz/15 g dried yeast | 1¾ pints/1 litre milk |
| 1 teaspoon castor sugar | 1 lb/450 g fresh redcurrants, stripped from the stalks |
| scant ½ pint/2·5 dl lukewarm milk | **for the topping:** |
| 4 oz/100 g melted butter | 3 (5-oz/141-g) cartons soured cream |
| 2 teaspoons grated lemon rind | 1 oz/25 g castor sugar |
| **for the filling:** | 2 oz/50 g plain flour |
| 1½ oz/40 g castor sugar | |
| pinch vanilla sugar or 1 drop vanilla essence | |

Sift the flour and salt into a bowl and make a well in the centre. Mix the yeast with the sugar and milk and pour into the well in the flour. Sprinkle a little of the flour over the yeast mixture and set aside until frothy. Add the melted butter and lemon rind. Mix all the ingredients together to form a soft dough. Knead well on a floured board until the dough becomes smooth and elastic. Place the dough in a bowl, cover with a cloth and leave to rise in a warm place until doubled in bulk.

To make the filling, place the sugar, vanilla sugar or essence, semolina and lemon rind in a large, heavy saucepan. Stir in the milk, half at a time. Place the pan over moderate heat and bring the mixture slowly to the boil, stirring constantly with a wooden spoon until the mixture becomes smooth and fairly thick. Remove the pan from the heat, cover with a piece of greaseproof paper to prevent a skin from forming on top and set aside to cool.

Knock back the dough and roll out to a rectangle, about 12 by 9 inches (30 by 23 cm). Place the dough on a greased and floured baking tray, cover with a cloth and let rise for 5–10 minutes only. Spread the filling over the slightly risen dough to within about 1½ inches (3·5 cm) of the edge. Cover with the redcurrants.

To make the topping, mix the soured cream with the sugar and flour and pour the mixture over the redcurrants. Place the baking tray in the centre of a moderately hot oven (375°F, 190°C, Gas Mark 5) and bake for 35–40 minutes, or until the filling has set and the dough is golden brown. Serve hot or cold.

# CHOCOLATE HONEY CAKE

*Makes about 36 2-inch (5-cm) squares*

| | |
|---|---|
| 8 oz/225 g honey | **for the icing:** |
| 8 oz/225 g castor sugar | 2 oz/50 g plain chocolate |
| 2 oz/50 g butter | 1½ tablespoons cocoa |
| 6 tablespoons beer | 4 oz/100 g icing sugar |
| 1 egg | about 2 tablespoons hot water |
| 3 teaspoons allspice | 1 oz/25 g butter |
| 12 oz/350 g plain flour | 4 tablespoons apricot jam |
| 2 teaspoons baking powder | 1–2 oz/25–50 g blanched almonds, halved |
| 1 tablespoon rum | |
| 4 oz/100 g ground almonds | |

Combine the honey, sugar, butter and beer in a large saucepan. Heat gently, stirring until the mixture is blended, then remove from the heat and set aside to cool. Add the egg and beat into the honey mixture with the allspice. Sift in the flour and baking powder, a little at a time, mixing thoroughly after each addition. Stir in the rum and almonds. Spread the mixture in a lightly greased Swiss roll tin, about 15½ by 10½ inches (40 by 27 cm), and smooth the surface with a spatula. Bake in the centre of a moderately hot oven (375°F, 190°C, Gas Mark 5) for 25–30 minutes, or until firm. Turn out and ice while the cake is still warm.

To make the icing, melt the chocolate in a double saucepan or in a small bowl over a saucepan of simmering water, then remove from the heat. Sift the cocoa with the icing sugar and stir into the melted chocolate. Gradually stir in the hot water until the icing is thick enough to coat the back of a spoon. Stir in the butter very gently.

First spread the warm cake with the apricot jam and then cover with the chocolate icing. Leave to set for 5 minutes, then cut the cake into squares while still slightly warm. Place half an almond in the centre of each square. Serve immediately, or allow the cake to cool completely and store in an airtight container until required.

# EBERSWALDE FRIED RINGS

*Makes about 24 rings*

generous ¾ pint//5 dl milk
4 oz/100 g butter
3 tablespoons castor sugar
1 teaspoon grated lemon rind
pinch salt

14 oz/400 g plain flour
8 eggs
oil or cooking fat for deep-frying
sifted icing sugar (see recipe)

Put the milk, butter, sugar, lemon rind and salt into a large saucepan. Bring to the boil and remove the pan from the heat. Add the flour and beat with a wooden spoon until smooth. Return the pan to the heat and beat until the mixture leaves the sides and bottom of the saucepan clean. Remove from the heat again and allow to cool until the pan is only slightly warm to the touch. Stir in the eggs, one at a time, and beat until the mixture is smooth and shiny. Place the mixture in a piping bag fitted with a large star tube.

Heat the oil or cooking fat for deep-frying in a wide saucepan, but do not let it get very hot. Cut a circle of greaseproof paper or aluminium foil, ½ inch (1 cm) smaller than the inside of the pan, and dip this into the warmed oil. Remove the paper at once and lay it on a plate. Pipe the mixture in small rings on to the paper. Heat the oil to 375°F (190°C) and slip the round of paper carefully into the hot oil, holding on to the edge with a pair of kitchen tongs, so the rings slip off the paper. Fry the rings on each side until golden brown. Use the same piece of paper again for the next batch of rings. Drain each batch well and dust with icing sugar. Serve warm.

# CHRISTMAS BREAD

*Makes 1 large loaf*

7 oz/200 g sultanas
7 oz/200 g currants
9 oz/250 g castor sugar
2 tablespoons rum (optional)
4 oz/100 g fresh yeast or 2 oz/50 g
  dried yeast
¾ pint/4·5 lukewarm milk
2¼ lb/1 kg plain flour
1 teaspoon salt
13 oz/375 g butter
pinch grated nutmeg

pinch ground ginger
grated rind of 1 lemon and 1
  orange
1 tablespoon plain flour
7 oz/200 g blanched almonds,
  slivered
4 oz/100 g chopped candied citron
  peel
3 oz/75 g butter
sifted icing sugar (see recipe)

Place the sultanas and currants in a bowl. Sprinkle the fruit with 3 tablespoons of the sugar and the rum, if used. Cover the bowl and let stand for 24 hours.

Stir the fresh or dried yeast into the lukewarm milk. Sift the flour and salt into a bowl and make a well in the centre. Pour the yeast mixture into the well and stir a little of the surrounding flour into the liquid. Cover with a cloth and let stand in a warm place for about 30 minutes. Measure the butter and let stand at room temperature.

Sprinkle the remaining sugar, the nutmeg, ginger and grated lemon and orange rind over the flour. Mix the dry ingredients into the yeast mixture and beat in the softened, but not melted, butter. Knead the dough well on a floured board until no longer sticky. Place in a bowl, cover with a cloth and let stand in a warm place for several hours until

doubled in bulk. Sprinkle the sultanas and currants with the 1 tablespoon of flour and knead into the dough on a floured board with the almonds and candied peel. Shape the dough into an oval. Cover with a cloth and let rise on the board, in a warm place, for 30 minutes.

Using a rolling pin, make a deep depression lengthwise along the centre of the oval and fold one half down over the other. Place the dough on a warm, baking tray lined with buttered greaseproof paper. Once more cover the dough with a cloth and let rise for a further 30 minutes. Bake in the centre of a moderately hot oven (375°F, 190°C, Gas Mark 5) for 1 hour. Remove from the oven and, while still warm, spread liberally with the butter. Then coat thickly with the icing sugar.

*Note:* Since Christmas bread matures and improves in flavour on keeping, it is advisable to make it at least 1 month before it is required, and keep in an airtight tin or wrap in aluminium foil.

# ULM SWEET BREAD

*Makes 2 loaves*

½ pint/3 dl double cream
½ pint/3 dl milk
2 oz/50 g fresh yeast or 1 oz/25 g
  dried yeast
1 teaspoon castor sugar
2¼ lb/1 kg plain flour
4 oz/100 g chopped candied
  orange peel

4 oz/100 g chopped candied
  lemon peel
4½ oz/125 g castor sugar
2 teaspoons grated lemon rind
1 tablespoon aniseed
1 tablespoon ground cardamom
4 tablespoons rose water
2 teaspoons salt
1 egg for glazing

Gently heat together the cream and milk until lukewarm. In a bowl, blend the fresh yeast with the teaspoon of sugar and the warmed liquid. If using dried yeast, stir the yeast and sugar into the milk and set aside for 10 minutes. Beat about a quarter of the flour into the yeast mixture. Cover the bowl with a damp cloth and let the mixture stand in a warm place until frothy. Sift the remaining flour into a large bowl and add the orange and lemon peel, sugar, grated lemon rind, aniseed, cardamom, rose water and salt. Stir the yeast mixture into the dry ingredients and blend together.

Knead the dough thoroughly on a floured board until the aniseed begins to fall out of the dough. Divide the dough into 2 pieces. Shape the pieces into oblongs and place on a floured baking tray. Cover the loaves lightly with a cloth and put in a warm place to rise for 1–2 hours, or until almost doubled in bulk.

Whisk the egg and brush over the loaves. With a sharp knife, make several lengthwise cuts along the top of each loaf. Place the baking tray in the centre of a hot oven (425°F, 220°C, Gas Mark 7) and bake for 15 minutes. Reduce the heat to 375°F (190°C, Gas Mark 5) and bake for 20–30 minutes. Cool the loaves on wire racks. Serve, thinly sliced, with tea, coffee or hot chocolate.

*Eberswalde fried rings*

# FRENCH

Monique Guillaume

*Photography by Christian Délu*

The provinces of France have all jealously guarded their culinary secrets. Their dishes are naturally based on food which is readily available locally.

The salt-meadow sheep and superior cattle of Normandy and Brittany are well known. The region produces excellent butter and cream – many recipes combine the bland taste of cream with the tart taste of the local cider apples. The big fishing fleets provide the rest of France with a delicious variety of seafood. Freshwater fish are also plentiful.

Fish, however, is not the only speciality of the region. Brittany is also the kitchen garden of France. Because of the mild climate the vegetables are ready earlier in the season than similar produce from other regions. The fruit is of equally good quality, especially the apples and the famous Plougastel strawberries.

The cooking of Normandy and Brittany, although good and wholesome, is plain. Rich sauces are to be found in the other provinces, especially in the wine-growing regions such as Dauphiné-Savoy, Burgundy, Bordeaux, Alsace-Lorraine, Languedoc, Provence. From Provence come liqueurs perfumed with the herbs which are also used extensively in the local dishes – garlic, rosemary, basil, fennel, wild thyme and even lavender – and another factor common to the cooking of Provence is the fragrant, greenish golden oil pressed from locally grown olives. This is the oil used in the famous garlic mayonnaise, aïoli. Garlic and olive oil are also basic ingredients for the dishes of the Pyrenees, together with sweet red and green peppers.

In Languedoc, however, the olives are usually eaten in their natural state or preserved in salt. Pâtés are a speciality – hare, rabbit, mutton – prepared from recipes dating back a thousand years. Toulouse Carcassone and Castelnaudary each claim the best recipe for the famous cassoulet.

The Massif Central comprises three regions: Bourbonnais, a pleasant country of gentle hills and valleys, full of fruit and vegetable gardens and lakes well stocked with carp and pike; Limousin, a vast parkland where cattle graze and acres of cherry orchards surround the châteaux; and Auvergne, a mountainous land of swift-flowing rivers and forests where wild boar still roam. With all these natural resources the cooking of the Massif Central is excellent. Picanchâgne is a traditional pear cake from the Bourbonnais region; clafouti, a cherry cake from Limousin; milliard, a black cherry pudding from the Auvergne.

It is in the wine-growing province of Burgundy that one finds the famous escargots. One of the best soft fruits of this region is the blackcurrant, from which cassis liqueur is distilled and an excellent ice cream can be made.

In Alsace-Lorraine, the traditions of cooking have been preserved more valiantly than anywhere else in France. Lorraine is particularly noted for its quiche, as Alsace is for its onion tart, and game served with fruit sauce, such as the delicious venison with blueberry sauce, is special to this area.

Not to be forgotten are the various cheeses from all over France. They are world-renowned; Camembert, Brie, Port-Salut, Roquefort, Tome au raisin, Boursin are but a few of the best known.

# QUICHE LORRAINE

*Serves 4*

| for the pastry: | for the filling: |
|---|---|
| 8 oz/225 g plain flour | 8 oz/225 g bacon, thinly sliced |
| 4 oz/110 g butter (see recipe) | 2 whole eggs |
| 4 tablespoons cold water | 3 egg yolks |
| pinch salt | ¼ pint/1·5 dl double cream |
| | freshly ground pepper |

Make the pastry as for Mince Pies, page 53. (In Lorraine, unsalted butter is used. If you use salted butter, do not add salt to the pastry.) Shape the dough into a ball and let stand for 1 hour, covered with a cloth.

Roll out the pastry thinly on a floured board, or on a table covered with a floured cloth, shaping it into a circle. Grease a 9-inch (23-cm) *quiche* or flan dish and line it with pastry. Trim the edges with your fingertips. Then press all around the inside of the rim with the tines of a fork. Prick the bottom of the tart at regular intervals, so that it is dotted with tiny holes. Arrange the bacon slices, trimmed if necessary, over the bottom. Bake in a moderately hot oven (400°F, 200°C, Gas Mark 6) for 10 minutes. Remove from the oven and set aside. Whisk the eggs, egg yolks and cream together. It is not necessary to add salt as the bacon is already salty, but add pepper lavishly from a mill. Pour the mixture over the bacon and return the *quiche* to the oven for 30 minutes. Serve hot as a first course at a special dinner or as the main course of a light meal.

# KIDNEYS IN WHITE WINE

*Serves 4*

| | |
|---|---|
| 4 oz/100 g mushrooms | 1 teaspoon French mustard |
| 4 oz/100 g butter | generous ¼ pint/2 dl dry white |
| 1 shallot | wine |
| 1 clove garlic | 3 white peppercorns, pounded |
| few sprigs parsley | 1 tablespoon plain flour |
| 4 lambs' kidneys | pinch salt |

Cut off the ends of the mushroom stalks. Wash and dry the mushrooms and thinly slice lengthwise. Heat a quarter of the butter in a small saucepan. Peel and chop the shallot. Peel and crush the garlic. Chop the parsley. Add the parsley, shallot, garlic and mushrooms to the butter in the pan. Sauté for a few moments over high heat, then cover and cook for 5 minutes over moderate heat. Remove the pan from the heat.

Remove the fine skin and cores from the kidneys and slice the kidneys thinly. Heat the remainder of the butter in a frying pan and, when hot, add the kidneys. Cook for 3 minutes, turning occasionally.

While the kidneys are cooking, mix the mustard with the white wine and pepper. Sprinkle the kidneys with flour, stir, add the seasoned white wine and then the mushroom mixture. Cook for a further 3 minutes over gentle heat to thicken the sauce. Serve the kidneys in sauce on slices of buttered toast or on bread fried in butter. If you want to serve them as a main dish, use twice the amount of kidneys and surround with rice.

Serve accompanied by the same dry white wine as was used to prepare the sauce.

# CHEESE PASTRY RING

*Serves 6*

| | |
|---|---|
| 4 oz/100 g Gruyère cheese | 4 oz/100 g plain flour |
| scant ½ pint/2·5 dl milk | pinch grated nutmeg |
| generous pinch salt | 4 eggs |
| 4 oz/100 g butter | |

Cut the Gruyère cheese into small, very thin slices and set aside until required. Pour the milk into a saucepan and add the salt and butter. Bring slowly to the boil, stirring constantly. When the liquid boils, immediately add the flour and stir briskly with a wooden spoon. Continue to cook over low heat for a few minutes, beating well until the mixture has thickened. Remove the pan from the heat and beat for a little longer. Then add the nutmeg and 3 of the eggs, one by one, beating constantly after each addition. Add the cheese slices to the mixture. Thoroughly grease and flour a baking tray. Spoon the dough on to it in the shape of a ring. Whisk the remaining egg and glaze the pastry ring. Bake in the centre of a moderately hot oven (400°F, 200°C, Gas Mark 6) for about 20 minutes. Cut the baked pastry ring into slices and serve hot as a first course, accompanied by a dry white wine.

# POTTED HARE

*Serves 8*

| | |
|---|---|
| 1 saddle of hare | pinch dried thyme |
| few sprigs parsley | 5 juniper berries |
| 8 oz/225 g lean veal, minced | about 8 oz/225 g pork fat |
| 6 oz/175 g sausage meat | 5 tablespoons cognac or gin |
| salt and pepper | |

Bone the hare and chop the flesh. Chop the parsley and mix with the minced veal, the sausage meat and the hare. Sprinkle lightly with salt and pepper. Add the thyme. Pound the juniper berries and add. Mix well. Cut the pork fat into 8 strips. Line the bottom and sides of a large earthenware casserole with 6 strips. Place the chopped mixture on top. Press well with the palm of the hand. Sprinkle with cognac or gin and place the 2 remaining strips of pork fat on top. Cover the casserole. In order to hermetically seal it, wrap a dampened, floured cloth around the lid. Cook in a cool oven (300°F, 150°C, Gas Mark 2) for 4 hours. Serve very cold with a green salad. The dish should be accompanied by a good red wine such as a burgundy.

*Note:* If you have to keep the potted hare longer than a few days, cover the surface of the *terrine* with a thick layer of melted lard and store in a cool place.

# PIPÉRADE

*Serves 2*

| | |
|---|---|
| 3 green sweet peppers | 3 tablespoons oil |
| ½ small chilli (optional) | 4 eggs |
| 1 medium-sized onion | salt |
| 2 cloves garlic | 2 oz/50 g goose or bacon fat |
| few sprigs parsley | 4 slices Parma ham or lean |
| 4 tomatoes | trimmed bacon |

Trim the peppers and chilli and remove the seeds. Slice the flesh into small strips. Peel and chop the onion and garlic. Place all together in a large bowl, chop the parsley and sprinkle it over. Scald the tomatoes in boiling water for 1 minute. Drain, peel and remove the seeds. Chop the flesh and add to the pepper mixture.

Heat the oil in a small saucepan, add the vegetables and sauté gently over low heat for 5 minutes, stirring occasionally. Meanwhile, whisk the eggs with a little salt. Heat the goose or bacon fat in a frying pan. Pour the beaten eggs into the pan, as for an omelette. Allow them to just set over high heat, then immediately pour the pepper mixture on top. Lower the heat and stir briskly with a wooden spoon, as if scrambling eggs but more quickly. Cook for less than 1 minute. The eggs must be cooked but still moist. Transfer to a heated dish. Lightly fry the ham or bacon slices, arrange on top of the *pipérade* and serve immediately.

# DUCK PÂTÉ

*Serves 6–8*

| | |
|---|---|
| 1 duckling, about 2½ lb/1·25 kg | 1½ lb/700 g lean pork, minced |
| 1 oz/25 g butter | generous pinch dried sage |
| salt and pepper | 8 oz/225 g smoked ham (such as |
| pinch ground nutmeg | Parma), sliced |
| about 12 oz/350 g pork fat | 5 tablespoons orange liqueur |
| few sprigs parsley | (cointreau or curaçao) or cognac |
| 1 egg | |

Rub the duckling with butter and roast it in a very hot oven (475°F, 240°C, Gas Mark 9) for about 30 minutes. Slice the meat, which should still be rosy. Set aside the *aiguillettes* (the flesh from the breast). Bone, skin and mince the rest. Sprinkle with salt, pepper and nutmeg. Cut the pork fat into strips. Chop the parsley and whisk the egg. Line the bottom and sides of an earthenware dish or bowl with half of the pork fat strips. Add the minced duckling flesh and minced pork, chopped parsley, sage and beaten egg, and then the sliced smoked ham and the *aiguillettes* in alternate layers. Sprinkle with the liqueur or cognac. Cover with the remainder of the pork fat strips. Cook in a moderately hot oven (400°F, 200°C, Gas Mark 6) for 15 minutes, then lower the heat to 250°F (120°C, Gas Mark ½) and cook for 3½ hours. Serve the pâté cold in the earthenware dish, accompanied by French bread or coarse wholewheat bread and a full-bodied wine.

*Pipérade*

# CRAB FLAMBÉ

*Serves 6*

| | |
|---|---|
| 1 large crab | salt and pepper |
| few sprigs parsley | scant ½ pint/2·5 dl tomato juice |
| 6 tablespoons dark rum or whisky | |

If you buy a live crab, plunge it into a very large pot of boiling water with some white wine and herbs, such as thyme, bay leaf and parsley. Cook for 10–15 minutes for a 2½-lb (1·25-kg) crab, or according to size. Let cool before removing the flesh from the shell. Prepare the crab as for Scalloped Crabs, page 35. Chop the parsley.

Warm the crab meat and the rum in a frying pan over a low heat. Remove the pan from the heat and flambé. While the rum burns, shake the pan gently so that the flames spread all over the contents. When the flames have died down, add salt and pepper, the chopped parsley and the tomato juice. Bring to the boil. Serve at once, with rice if you wish to make it a substantial main dish or just as it is for a first course.

# SNAILS IN RED WINE

*Serves 4*

| | |
|---|---|
| about 40 canned snails, without shells | 2 oz/50 g bacon |
| | 2 oz/50 g lard |
| sprig dried thyme | 1 tablespoon plain flour |
| 2 cloves garlic | generous ¼ pint/2 dl red wine |
| 4 shallots | 4 slices white toasting bread |
| small bunch parsley | salt and pepper |

Wash and drain the snails and sprinkle with thyme. Peel the garlic and shallots and chop with the parsley. Dice the bacon. Heat the lard in a frying pan and lightly sauté the shallots, garlic and parsley. Add the diced bacon. As soon as the mixture is golden brown, sprinkle with flour and stir briskly. Add the red wine gradually, stirring well, then lower the heat, cover and cook gently. Toast the bread, arrange on a heated serving plate and keep warm. Add the snails to the sauce, stir and season. Cook gently for 3 minutes and pour the snails in sauce over the toast.

# COQUILLES SAINT-JACQUES

*Serves 6*

| | |
|---|---|
| 16 scallops | salt and pepper |
| 2 shallots | generous ¼ pint/2 dl dry white wine |
| few sprigs parsley | |
| 1 oz/25 g butter | |

For this recipe use scallops which have been shelled. Slice the white part of the scallop across into 2 or 3 pieces. Peel and chop the shallots and chop the parsley. Melt the butter in a frying pan. Add the shallots and the parsley. Sauté for a few moments and then add the scallops. If using fresh scallops, add the coral. Cook over high heat for a few minutes, turning the pieces over until they are a light golden brown. Season with salt and quite a lot of pepper. Remove the pan from the heat and spoon the scallops into a warm serving dish. Pour the wine into the pan and bring quickly to the boil. Pour over the scallops and serve.

# MARSEILLES BOUILLABAISSE

*Serves 8*

| | |
|---|---|
| 4 lb/1·75 kg fresh fish, as varied as possible (whiting, red mullet, hake, sea bass, mackerel, etc.) | 1 wineglass white wine (optional) |
| | bunch parsley |
| | few sprigs fresh green fennel |
| 12 Dublin Bay prawns or 1 lobster | sprig fresh wild savory (optional) |
| | 4 tomatoes |
| 3½ pints/2 litres water | 16 slices French bread |
| 3 cloves garlic | **for the sauce:** |
| 1 large onion | 1 clove garlic |
| 3 shallots | 1 small red chilli |
| generous ¼ pint/2 dl olive oil | 1 slice cooked potato |
| salt and pepper | livers of 3 fish (from the red mullet, if possible) |
| 1 teaspoon saffron strands | |

Cut the biggest fish into large pieces. Leave the little ones whole, but gut them. Set aside the livers of the red mullet for the sauce. Bring the water to the boil in a large saucepan. Toss in the prawns or the lobster. Cook for 7 minutes, then remove from the water. Reserve this water, covered.

Shell the prawns or if using lobster, prepare as for Lobster à l'Américaine, page 124, and cut into pieces. Peel the garlic, onion and shallots and chop roughly. Heat the oil in a large saucepan and add the vegetables with the salt, pepper and saffron strands. Sauté lightly over high heat. Add the liquid in which the shellfish were cooked, the wine if used, the herbs and tomatoes. Remove the tomatoes after 1 minute, rinse in cold water, peel and remove the seeds. Replace the tomatoes in the soup. Cook over very low heat until the liquid boils. Add the shellfish and large pieces of fish to the pan. Cook over high heat for 8 minutes. Add the small fish. Lower the heat and simmer for 7 minutes.

Meanwhile, prepare the sauce. Peel the garlic. Pound the red chilli (some cooks prefer to soak it for 6 hours in cold water beforehand) with the garlic, potato and fish livers. Thin down this paste with some of the liquid from the fish soup. Pour the sauce into a heated sauceboat.

Line a soup tureen with slices of bread (according to tradition, these should be dried in the oven, not toasted). Remove the shellfish and fish with a perforated spoon and arrange on a heated dish. Pour the soup liquid on the slices of bread. Both dishes should be eaten together accompanied by the sauce.

*Marseilles bouillabaisse*

# BACON SOUP

*Serves 6*

3½ pints/2 litres water
2 onions
3 shallots
2 leeks
1 green cabbage
1-lb/450-g piece of bacon (collar or hock), soaked overnight
1 stick celery
sprig parsley
14 oz/400 g dried haricot beans (see recipe)
pepper
12 slices French bread

Measure the water into a saucepan. Peel the onions and shallots, but leave whole. Trim, wash and chop the leeks. Discarding the outer leaves, cut the cabbage into quarters. Add the bacon to the water in the pan with the prepared vegetables, celery, parsley and dried beans. (If the beans are very dry, soak according to the directions on the packet.) Season with pepper, cover and bring to the boil. Lower the heat and simmer gently for 3 hours. Remove the bacon and cut into slices. Keep warm on a heated serving dish. Remove the vegetables and keep warm in a separate dish.

Toast the slices of bread and place them in the bottom of a soup tureen. Strain over the soup liquid. Serve the vegetables and the bacon slices separately.

# FISH SOUP WITH AÏOLI

*Serves 4*

2 lb/1 kg fresh fish, any variety
3 pints/1·5 litres water
1 large onion
4 cloves
2 cloves garlic
1 piece dried or fresh orange rind
few sprigs thyme
3 bay leaves
salt and pepper
1 teaspoon saffron strands or ¼ teaspoon saffron powder
*aïoli* (see page 137)
12 slices French bread

Wash and gut the fish. Cut the larger ones into pieces. Measure the water into a large saucepan. Peel the onion and stick it with the cloves. Peel the garlic. Add both to the pan with the orange rind, thyme and bay leaves. Bring to the boil and add the salt, pepper and saffron. Simmer for 1 minute. Add the fish and simmer for 12 minutes, without a lid. Pour the *aïoli* into a large bowl and very slowly strain the fish stock over it, stirring well. Arrange the slices of bread in a soup tureen and pour over the soup. Serve the fish separately.

*Note:* This recipe, like many others, varies according to the place where it is made. Sometimes the bread is left out and the soup is poured over the fish. In this case, select large fish and cut into slices.

# FRENCH ONION SOUP

*Serves 4*

3 large onions
2 oz/50 g butter
2 tablespoons plain flour
3 pints/1·5 dl beef stock (see recipe)
12 slices French bread
8 oz/225 g Gruyère cheese, grated

Peel the onions and either finely chop or grate. Melt the butter in a large saucepan. Add the onions and sauté until soft and transparent, but not brown. Sprinkle with flour and cook over low heat for 1 minute, stirring briskly with a wooden spoon. Gradually pour in the stock – made with a beef stock cube, if necessary – stirring constantly. Bring to the boil, then lower the heat until the soup is just simmering and cook for 30 minutes. Toast the slices of bread and serve with the soup. Serve the grated cheese separately.

# POACHED EGGS WITH CHEESE AND WINE

*Serves 4*

few sprigs parsley
1 oz/25 g butter
6 oz/175 g Gruyère cheese, grated
5 tablespoons dry white wine

pinch pepper
pinch ground nutmeg
4 eggs

Chop the parsley. Melt the butter in a gratin dish or shallow flameproof casserole. Add the Gruyère cheese and the white wine. Heat gently, stirring constantly until the cheese melts. Add the pepper, nutmeg and chopped parsley. Cook for a moment, then gently break the eggs into the dish. When almost cooked, put the gratin dish under the grill for 1 minute. Serve in the dish, accompanied by a white wine.

# CARP WITH WHITE WINE, TOMATOES AND MUSHROOMS

*Serves 4*

1 carp, about 2 lb/1 kg
¼ pint/1·5 dl olive oil
salt and pepper
scented fresh herbs, such as
   thyme, savory, fennel and basil

½ bottle dry white wine
3 tomatoes
3 large mushrooms
½ oz/15 g cornflour
1 oz/25 g butter

Skin and gut the carp. Wash under cold running water and pat dry. Place the fish in a shallow baking dish. Sprinkle with olive oil, season with salt and pepper and add the herbs. Put the dish in a cool oven (300°F, 150°C, Gas Mark 2). Allow a carp weighing 2 lb (1 kg) to cook for 45 minutes.

Scald the tomatoes for 1 minute in boiling water, peel, remove the seeds and cut the flesh into pieces. Trim, dry and thinly slice the mushrooms. As soon as the carp begins to turn brown or becomes crisp (after about 20–30 minutes), pour over the white wine and surround the fish with the tomatoes and mushrooms. Continue to cook very slowly. When the fish is cooked, the liquid will have reduced a little. When ready to serve, place the carp on a heated serving dish and pour the liquid into a small saucepan. Blend the cornflour with the butter to make a *beurre manié*, and add it in pieces to the sauce over low heat. Stir constantly, until the sauce is well blended and thickened. Pour over the carp and serve.

# TROUT BAKED IN FOIL

*Serves 4*

4 small trout
4 sprigs fresh or dried thyme
juice of 1 lemon

1½ oz/40 g butter
4 thin slices Parma ham

Gut the trout, wash carefully and pat dry. Place a sprig of thyme inside each one. Sprinkle each trout with a little lemon juice. Grease 4 sheets of foil with the butter. Wrap each trout in a slice of ham. Place each fish in a sheet of the foil, greased side to the inside, and completely enclose the fish. Arrange the foil-wrapped fish in a baking dish and bake in a moderately hot oven (400°F, 200°C, Gas Mark 6) for 10 minutes. Then lower the heat to 350°F (180°C, Gas Mark 4) for a further 10 minutes. Serve the trout in their foil packages–each guest will open his own on his plate.

*Poached eggs with cheese and wine*

*Salade rhodanienne*

# LOBSTER À L'AMÉRICAINE

*Serves 3–4*

| | |
|---|---|
| 1 lobster, about 2 lb/1 kg | ¼ pint/1·5 dl fish stock (made by |
| 4 tablespoons oil | cooking the heads and bones of |
| salt and pepper | fish with thyme and bay leaf in |
| 2 tablespoons cognac | generous ¾ pint/5 dl water for |
| generous ¼ pint/2 dl dry white | 30 minutes, or until the liquid is |
| wine | reduced) |
| 2 shallots | generous pinch cayenne pepper |
| 1 clove garlic | 3 tomatoes |
| 1 tablespoon meat stock | few sprigs chervil and tarragon |
| | 7 oz/200 g butter |
| | 1 lemon |

Drop the live lobster into warm water and bring to the boil. Remove from the heat. Place the lobster on a board, back uppermost, and using a sharp knife split it in half along its entire length. Press the two halves open and remove the gills, the stomach sac in the head and the dark intestinal vein which runs down the tail. The green creamy liver in the head and the coral of the female lobster should be retained. Cut the lobster up, dividing the tail into 4 pieces and splitting the

claws into 2 pieces. Heat the oil in a flameproof casserole and add all the lobster pieces except the head. Season with salt and pepper and cook over high heat until the lobster pieces turn very red. Pour off some of the hot fat. Sprinkle with cognac and white wine. Lower the heat and warm for a moment. Remove the casserole from the stove and flambé. Set aside.

Peel and chop the shallots, peel and crush the garlic, strain the fish stock, and scald, peel and chop the tomatoes, removing the seeds. Place the casserole over the heat once again and add the shallots, garlic, meat stock, fish stock, cayenne pepper and tomatoes. Cover and cook in a moderate oven (350°F, 180°C, Gas Mark 4) for 10–15 minutes. While the lobster is cooking, chop the chervil and tarragon very finely and blend with the butter. Remove the lobster from the oven. Take out the pieces and remove all the meat from the shell (or you can serve the meat in the shell). Place on a heated serving plate. Strain the sauce. Then add the herb butter in small pieces and stir until the butter is melted and the sauce well bound together. Pour the sauce over the lobster and sprinkle with lemon juice.

*Note:* This dish from Brittany is sometimes called Lobster *à l'amoricaine*. The origin of the name is endlessly disputed.

124

# SALADE RHODANIENNE

*Serves 4*

| | |
|---|---|
| 3 large potatoes | 4 oz/100 g Gruyère cheese |
| scant ½ pint/2·5 dl dry white wine | 4 anchovy fillets in oil |
| salt and pepper | few sprigs fresh chervil |
| ½ bunch watercress | 4 oz/100 g green olives, stoned |
| 8 oz/225 g garlic sausage (*saucisson* | if preferred |
| or *salami*) | 3 tablespoons olive oil |
| 8 oz/225 g smoked ham | 1 tablespoon vinegar |

Peel the potatoes, halve them and place in a saucepan of boiling water. Bring to the boil again, then lower the heat and cook for 10 minutes, or until the potatoes are just tender. Drain, cool a little and cut into thick slices. Place in a salad bowl, sprinkle with the white wine and season with salt and pepper.

Wash and trim the watercress. Dice the sausage, ham and Gruyère cheese. Cut the anchovy fillets into small pieces. Chop the chervil. Add the watercress, sausage, ham, cheese, anchovy fillets and olives to the potatoes in the bowl. Sprinkle with the oil and vinegar and then the chervil, and serve.

# SALADE DE MORLAIX

*Serves 4*

| | |
|---|---|
| 1 small or ½ large cauliflower | generous ¼ pint/2 dl dry white wine |
| salt | 8 anchovy fillets in oil |
| white pepper | 3 tablespoons capers in vinegar |

Cut away the stalk from the cauliflower, remove any part which is brown or bruised and divide the cauliflower into florets. Cook in lightly salted boiling water for about 5 minutes or until the cauliflower is just tender but still crisp. Drain and place in a salad bowl. While still warm, add a little pepper and sprinkle with white wine. Cut the anchovy fillets into small pieces and add with the capers. Allow to cool completely before serving.

*Note:* Nasturtium flowers make a colourful garnish when in season. Not only are they decorative, but they also have a slightly peppery taste which gourmets find very delicate.

# SALADE AU ROQUEFORT

*Serves 4*

| | |
|---|---|
| ½–1 head curly endive | 6 tablespoons double cream |
| 1 clove garlic | juice of 1 lemon |
| 4 oz/100 g shelled walnuts | 4 tablespoons walnut oil or |
| 6 oz/175 g Roquefort cheese | groundnut oil |

Wash the endive, strip off the leaves by hand, one by one (break large leaves in half) and drain well. Peel the garlic and rub the inside of a salad bowl with it. Chop the walnuts and sprinkle them into the salad bowl, add the Roquefort cheese and blend together. Gradually mix in the cream and the lemon juice. Then add the oil and mix thoroughly with a wooden spoon. Add the endive and mix until thoroughly coated in the salad dressing.

# SALADE NIÇOISE

*Serves 4*

| | |
|---|---|
| 8 small or 6 large tomatoes | 20 black olives, stoned |
| 1 green sweet pepper | 4 tablespoons olive oil |
| 1 (7-oz/198-g) can tuna fish, | 1 tablespoon wine vinegar |
| drained | 1 teaspoon French mustard |
| 8 anchovy fillets in oil | pepper |
| 12 red radishes (optional) | |

Scald the tomatoes in boiling water for 1 minute, drain and peel. Quarter, remove the seeds and place the quarters in a salad bowl. Trim the pepper and remove the stalk and seeds. Slice the flesh into thin strips and grill quickly to improve the flavour. Break the tuna fish into large pieces. Cut the anchovy fillets in half. Wash and peel the radishes, leaving on the small tops. Add the tuna, anchovy fillets, radishes and olives to the tomatoes in the salad bowl. Mix the oil, vinegar, mustard and pepper in a small jar. Shake vigorously and pour the dressing over the salad.

# GAME SALAD

*Serves 4*

| | |
|---|---|
| 2 roasted partridges, cold | juice of 1 lemon |
| 1 shallot | 6 anchovy fillets in oil |
| 4 tablespoons olive oil or, ideally, | 6 gherkins |
| walnut oil | 1 tablespoon capers in vinegar |
| 1 tablespoon tarragon vinegar | 1 lettuce heart |
| 1 teaspoon French mustard | few sprigs tarragon (optional) |
| salt and pepper | few sprigs parsley |
| 6 small mushrooms | |

Carve the birds, removing the skin and bones. Cut the flesh into fairly large pieces. Peel and finely chop the shallot and mix with the oil, tarragon vinegar, mustard, salt and pepper. Pour the dressing into a salad bowl. Add the meat and stir well so that it is lightly coated with the dressing. Wipe the mushrooms and trim the ends (it is better not to wash them). Sprinkle with the lemon juice and add to the salad bowl. Cut the anchovy fillets into pieces and finely slice the gherkins. Add these and the capers to the salad. Wash and dry the lettuce – use only the freshest leaves in the centre. Place these leaves in a circle on a flat dish. Spoon the salad into the centre. Chop the tarragon and parsley and sprinkle over the salad.

# BOEUF BOURGUIGNON

*Serves 4*

| | |
|---|---|
| 2 lb/1 kg braising beef | sprig thyme |
| 1 shallot | 2 bay leaves |
| 1 tablespoon oil | 1 teaspoon sugar |
| 1 oz/25 g butter | salt and pepper |
| ½ bottle red wine | few sprigs parsley |
| (preferably burgundy) | 4 oz/100 g small mushrooms |
| ½ pint/3 dl beef stock (see recipe) | 4 oz/100 g streaky bacon |
| 1 onion | 1 tablespoon cornflour |
| 2 cloves | 2 tablespoons water |

Cut the beef into large cubes and remove all the fat. Peel and chop the shallot. Heat the oil and butter in a saucepan and add the pieces of meat and the shallot. Sauté gently. Gradually add the wine and the stock – make this with a beef stock cube, if necessary. Peel the onion and stick it with the cloves. Add the onion, thyme and bay leaves. Stir in the sugar and season with pepper and only a little salt, as the stock is salty. Cover and simmer for 1½ hours over low heat. Chop the parsley. Trim, wash and dry the mushrooms.

Before serving, dice the bacon and sauté it gently in a frying pan until the fat runs. Add the chopped parsley and mushrooms to the bacon and cook for a few moments. Add this mixture to the beef in the saucepan. Moisten the cornflour with the 2 tablespoons water and stir the paste into the saucepan. Bring to the boil, stirring briskly. Serve immediately with boiled potatoes and the same wine as was used to make the sauce.

# INDIVIDUALLY COOKED STEAKS

*Serves 4*

| | |
|---|---|
| 1 onion | 1 large veal bone, chopped in |
| 3 cloves | half, or the carcass of a chicken |
| 1 leek | 5 peppercorns |
| 1 stick celery | *bouquet garni* (see recipe) |
| 4 medium-sized carrots | 3½ pints/2 litres water |
| 1 turnip | 2 lb/1 kg beef fillet, cut into 4 |
| 2 teaspoons salt | thick slices |

Peel the onion and stick it with the cloves. Trim, wash and slice the leek. Trim and wash the celery and cut the stick in half. Peel the carrots and turnip and cut into pieces. To make the stock, place all the vegetables, the salt, veal bone or chicken carcass, peppercorns and *bouquet garni* (3 bay leaves, 3 sprigs parsley, 1 sprig thyme, tied together) in a large saucepan with the water, and bring to the boil. If possible, cook the stock in an earthenware pot with an asbestos mat underneath for protection. As soon as the water boils, skim, lower the heat, cover and cook gently for 1–2 hours. Then strain the stock and reheat to boiling point.

Trim the meat. Tie each piece up like a package and make a long loop of string. Hang the steaks from the handle of a wooden spoon. Place the spoon across the top of the pot so that the steaks are suspended in the boiling stock. For rare beef, simmer for 25 minutes; for well-done beef, 30 minutes or longer. Remove the meat and serve with mustard, pickles, coarse salt in little dishes and baked potatoes.

# ENTRECÔTE STEAKS IN BERCY SAUCE

*Serves 4*

| | |
|---|---|
| 4 entrecôte steaks | ¾ pint/4·5 dl dry white wine |
| salt and pepper | sprig fresh or pinch dried thyme |
| 1½ oz/40 g butter | 1 bay leaf |
| **for the sauce:** | salt and pepper |
| 1 medium-sized carrot | 1 teaspoon sugar |
| 1 shallot | 2 oz/50 g butter |

Begin by making the sauce. Scrape the carrot and slice it into thin rounds. Peel and finely chop the shallot. Measure the wine into a small saucepan and add the carrot, shallot, thyme, bay leaf, salt and pepper to taste and sugar. Simmer until the wine is reduced by half. Meanwhile, season the steaks and cook them quickly in hot butter in a frying pan, rare or well done, according to taste.

When the wine is reduced, remove the sauce from the heat. Strain it and return to the pan. Cut the butter into small pieces and stir into the sauce with a whisk.

Place the steaks on a heated serving dish, cover with the sauce and serve immediately.

# CASSEROLE OF TRIPE WITH CIDER AND CALVADOS

*Serves 8*

| | |
|---|---|
| 3½ lb/1·5 kg dressed tripe | 2 bay leaves |
| 8 medium-sized carrots | 1 calf's foot |
| 4 leeks | salt and pepper |
| 4 large onions | scant ½ pint/2·5 dl calvados (apple |
| 3 cloves | brandy) |
| few sprigs parsley | about 1¾ pints/1 litre dry cider |
| sprig thyme | |

Wash the tripe carefully in cold water. Drain and cut into 2-inch (5-cm) strips. Clean and peel the vegetables and cut into thin slices. Save one onion, which should be peeled but left whole and stuck with cloves. Line a large earthenware casserole with the sliced vegetables. Place the strips of tripe on top. Add the herbs, the calf's foot, salt and pepper to taste, the calvados and enough cider to cover. Put on the lid and encase it with a dampened, floured cloth to minimise evaporation. Cook in a very cool oven (250°F, 120°C, Gas Mark ¼) for 10 hours. Discard the calf's foot and the onion stuck with cloves and serve with boiled potatoes, macaroni or rice.

*Note:* This casserole may be cooked in a pressure cooker instead of an earthenware casserole. Reduce the cooking time to 2¾ hours.

*Individually cooked steaks*

# CASSOULET

*Serves 8*

| | |
|---|---|
| 2 lb/1 kg haricot beans | salt and pepper |
| 1 medium-sized carrot | 1 large onion |
| 1 large onion | 3 cloves garlic |
| 4 cloves | 5 tomatoes |
| 12 oz/350 g breast of salt pork | scant ½ pint/2·5 dl stock |
| 8 oz/225 g fresh pork rind | *bouquet garni* (see recipe) |
| *bouquet garni* (see recipe) | **for the garnish:** |
| 2 oz/50 g goose fat, lard or bacon fat | 10 oz/275 g Toulouse garlic sausage or well seasoned cooked sausage |
| 4 cloves garlic | 2 large pieces preserved goose (optional) |
| **for the meat:** | 4 oz/100 g toasted breadcrumbs |
| 1 lb/450 g boned shoulder of lamb (approximately ½ shoulder, boned) | 3 oz/75 g goose fat, lard or bacon fat |
| 1 lb/450 g boned loin of pork | |
| 2 oz/50 g goose fat, lard or bacon fat | |

Soak the beans in a bowl of cold water for 3 hours or overnight. Drain. Put the beans into an earthenware pot separated from the heat by an asbestos mat, or into a large saucepan. Peel the carrot and stick the onion with the cloves. Add the whole breast of salt pork, pork rind, carrot, onion, *bouquet garni* (3 bay leaves, 3 sprigs parsley, 1 sprig thyme, tied together) and the fat. Add water to just cover the beans. Peel the garlic and add it. Cover and bring to the boil. Lower the heat and simmer gently, so the beans do not burst. Cook for 2½ hours, stirring gently from time to time and adding a little more water, if necessary.

Meanwhile, brown the shoulder of lamb and loin of pork in the goose fat in a large frying pan. Transfer the meat to a large saucepan and set aside the frying pan for browning the sausage later. Season the meat with salt and pepper. Chop the onion and peel and crush the garlic. Add both to the pan containing the meat. Scald the tomatoes for 1 minute in boiling water, drain and peel. Remove the seeds, chop the tomatoes and add to the pan. Moisten with stock, using a stock cube if necessary. Add a little water and the *bouquet garni* (3 bay leaves, 3 sprigs parsley, 1 sprig thyme, tied together) and simmer for the same length of time as the beans.

Cut the sausage into large slices and brown in the pan which was set aside. Remove and discard the piece of salt pork and pork rind from the beans. Cut the meat into pieces. Place the meat and the beans in a large, deep casserole in alternate layers. Finish with a layer of the preserved goose (if used) and the sausage slices, pushing them down a little into the beans. Sprinkle with breadcrumbs. Add the remaining fat, cut into small pieces. Place the casserole in a large roasting tin half filled with hot water. Cook in a cool oven (300°F, 150°C, Gas Mark 2) for at least 45 minutes. Serve very hot in the casserole.

*Cassoulet*

# LEG OF LAMB À LA CASSETTE

*Serves 6*

| | |
|---|---|
| 1 leg of lamb, about 4 lb/1·75 kg | scant ½ pint/2·5 dl water |
| 4 cloves garlic | salt and pepper |
| 6 oz/175 g bacon, in 1 piece | 1 bay leaf |
| 2 oz/50 g butter | sprig parsley |
| 4 large potatoes | sprig thyme |

Ask the butcher to cut the knuckle off the leg, or else fold it back, so that the meat can be placed in a deep casserole.

Make a deep incision in the lamb near the knuckle and slide in the garlic cloves. (Peel them or not, according to whether you want a strong or mild garlic taste.) Cube a small piece of the bacon and slice the remainder thinly. Then make six other incisions all over the leg and insert the bacon cubes. Grease the casserole with a little of the butter. Peel the potatoes and slice thinly. Lay the slices in the bottom of the buttered casserole with the sliced bacon. Pour over the water. Season with salt and pepper and add the bay leaf. Place the lamb on top of the potatoes. Chop the parsley. Sprinkle with a few thyme leaves and the parsley. Dot the rest of the butter over the lamb. Cook uncovered in a moderately hot oven (400°F, 200°C, Gas Mark 6) for 1½ hours; allow 25 minutes per lb (per half kilo) for fairly well cooked meat. The water should be completely absorbed by the potatoes, and the lamb and the potatoes should be golden brown.

# CALF'S SWEETBREADS WITH MUSHROOMS

*Serves 6*

| | |
|---|---|
| 3 pairs calf's sweetbreads | 2 tablespoons plain flour |
| 4 oz/100 g button mushrooms | ¼ pint/1·5 dl dry white wine |
| few sprigs parsley | salt and pepper |
| 1 oz/25 g butter | 6 tablespoons double cream |

The sweetbreads must be very white with no traces of blood. Soak in an earthenware bowl filled with cold water for 2 hours, changing the water 4 or 5 times. Place the sweetbreads in a saucepan, cover with cold water, bring to the boil and simmer for 2–3 minutes. Plunge into cold water, drain and cool. Dry carefully, remove any membrane and cut into thin slices.

Wash and dry the mushrooms. If small, leave whole; otherwise slice lengthwise. Chop the parsley. Sauté the mushrooms and the parsley lightly in the butter for about 3 minutes. Add the sweetbreads, shaking the pan frequently. Sprinkle with flour, stirring gently, and add the white wine and salt and pepper to taste. Cook for 5 minutes, then add the cream, stirring thoroughly. Bring to the boil and cook for 2 minutes. Serve on a heated plate accompanied by the same white wine as is used in the dish.

*Note:* In restaurants this dish is often garnished with tiny crescents of puff pastry.

# POULE-AU-POT HENRI IV

*Serves 8*

| | |
|---|---|
| 1 chicken, about 4 lb/1·75 kg | 1 large onion |
| **for the stuffing:** | 3 cloves |
| 1 oz/25 g butter | 1 leek |
| 1 chicken liver | 1 stick celery |
| 9 oz/250 g breadcrumbs | 4 medium-sized carrots |
| 2 eggs | 4 turnips |
| 8 oz/225 g Parma ham or lean | salt |
|   bacon | 4 peppercorns |
| salt and pepper | sprig thyme |
| 1 clove garlic | 3 bay leaves |
| few sprigs parsley | 1¾ pints/1 litre chicken stock |
| 3 tablespoons cognac | 8 oz/225 g long-grain rice |
| **for the stock pot:** | |
| 4½ pints/2·5 litres water | |

First prepare the stuffing for the chicken. Melt the butter in a frying pan, add the chicken liver and brown it. Place the liver in a mixing bowl and mash with the breadcrumbs. Whisk the eggs. Finely chop the ham and add to the bowl with the beaten eggs, salt and pepper. Peel the garlic and chop with the parsley. Add to the mixture. Finally, add the cognac, mix well and stuff the chicken with the mixture. Sew up the opening with strong white thread.

Heat the water in a large earthenware pot, protected from the heat by an asbestos mat. Peel the onion and stick it with the cloves. Trim and wash the leek and the celery. Peel the carrots and turnips. Cut up the vegetables and add to the pot with the salt, peppercorns, thyme and bay leaves. Bring to the boil and add the chicken. Simmer for 1½ hours.

About 20 minutes before cooking time is completed, heat the stock for cooking the rice in a saucepan. When boiling, sprinkle in the rice, washed if necessary, and boil rapidly for 15–20 minutes. Drain the rice and spoon into the centre of a large serving dish.

Discard the onion stuck with cloves and the herbs. Place the vegetables from the pot around the rice. Serve the chicken separately. Check the seasoning and serve the soup from the pot in individual bowls at the same time or to start the meal.

*Note:* The soup, just as it is, is quite greasy. An alternative is to reserve it for another meal. If put into a refrigerator or left in a cool place overnight, the fat will rise to the surface and can then be easily removed.

# SAUTÉED CHICKEN WITH COGNAC

*Serves 4*

| | |
|---|---|
| 2 shallots | 1 chicken, about 3½ lb/1·5 kg, cut |
| few sprigs parsley |   into 8 pieces |
| 4 oz/100 g small mushrooms | generous ¼ pint/2 dl dry white |
| 4 oz/100 g bacon |   wine |
| few sprigs chervil and tarragon | 5 tablespoons cognac |
| 2 oz/50 g butter | generous ¼ pint/2 dl tomato juice |
| 1 tablespoon oil | salt and pepper |

Peel and chop the shallots and chop the parsley. Trim, wash and dry the mushrooms. Dice the bacon. Chop the chervil

and tarragon. Heat the butter and oil together in a large, heavy frying pan. Add the parsley and the shallots and sauté gently until golden brown. Add the pieces of chicken and sauté over high heat, turning until slightly browned. Add the white wine, a tablespoon at a time, to prevent the chicken from sticking. Lower the heat and cover. After about 30 minutes, when the chicken is brown and tender, remove the pan from the heat, warm the cognac, add to the pan and flambé. When the flames have died down, cover and continue to cook gently for a few minutes. Add the mushrooms and cook quickly for 3 minutes. Add the bacon and tomato juice. Cook over a high heat until the liquid is reduced. Season with pepper. Taste before adding salt. Transfer to a heated serving dish, sprinkle with the chopped chervil and tarragon and serve with boiled potatoes or plain boiled rice and green beans.

# CHICKEN EN CROÛTE

*Serves 4*

| | |
|---|---|
| 1 chicken, about 2 lb/1 kg | 2 tablespoons cognac or brandy |
| **for the stuffing:** | salt and pepper |
| 4 oz/100 g bacon | **for the shortcrust pastry:** |
| few sprigs parsley | 8 oz/225 g plain flour |
| sprig thyme | 4 oz/110 g butter |
| 1 egg | 4 tablespoons water |
| 5 oz/150 g white breadcrumbs | pinch salt |
| 3 tablespoons milk | 1 egg for glazing |

Wipe the chicken. Chop the bacon, parsley and thyme. Whisk the egg. Soak the breadcrumbs in the milk, beaten egg and brandy. Season with the salt and pepper and stir in the bacon and herbs. Mix well and pack the stuffing inside the bird. Sew up the opening with strong white thread.

Make the pastry as for Mince Pies, page 53. Place on a floured board, or on a floured cloth on a table, and roll out thinly to a circle large enough to completely enclose the chicken.

Place the chicken, on its side, on one half of the pastry, with the breastbone towards the centre of the circle. Moisten the edge of the circle. Fold over the second half of the pastry to enclose the chicken. Seal the pastry where it joins along the backbone of the bird. Turn the bird breast side up and seal the ends.

Place on a greased baking tray and brush the pastry with beaten egg. Bake in a moderately hot oven (400°F, 200°C, Gas Mark 6) for 30 minutes. Lower the heat, cover with foil and cook for a further 30 minutes at 350°F (180°C, Gas Mark 4). To serve, cut away both leg joints. Then carve the chicken, cutting through both pastry and chicken flesh. Serve with a watercress salad.

*Poule-au-pot Henri IV*

# DUCKLING WITH GREEN OLIVE STUFFING

*Serves 4*

1 young duckling, about 3½ lb/
   1·5 kg

**for the stuffing:**
4 oz/100 g stoned green olives
3 Toulouse sausages or other well
   seasoned cooked sausages
5 cloves garlic (or to taste)

3 oz/75 g butter
1 duckling liver
4 slices white bread
generous ¼ pint/2 dl dry white
   wine
salt and pepper

Wipe the duckling and prepare the stuffing. Add the olives to a saucepan of boiling salted water and simmer for 5 minutes to soften them. Then drain. Remove the skins from the sausages and slice the sausages into rounds or cut into pieces. Peel and crush the garlic. Mix the olives, sausage and garlic together. Heat a third of the butter in a frying pan, add the duckling liver and brown on both sides. Remove the liver from the pan, mash and add to the stuffing.

Stuff the duckling with the mixture and sew up the opening with strong white thread. Roast on a spit (an electric rotisserie gives excellent results) or place the duckling on a rack in a lightly greased roasting tin and roast in a moderate oven (350°F, 180°C, Gas Mark 4), basting occasionally. Cook for about 45 minutes on the electric rotisserie, or 1 hour in the oven.

Towards the end of the cooking time, dice the bread. Heat the remaining butter in a frying pan and brown the bread, turning occasionally. Lightly season the cooked duckling and cut into portions. Arrange them on the sautéed bread on a hot serving dish, with the stuffing on the top. Pour off the fat from the roasting tin (or tin underneath the spit) but save most of the meat dripping. Add the wine, stir with a fork and pour the mixture into a saucepan. Season with salt and pepper. Bring almost to the boil and pour the sauce over the duckling.

# STUFFED PARTRIDGES FLAMBÉ

*Serves 2*

8 juniper berries
2 partridges
8 oz/225 g foie gras mousse or
   pâté

salt and pepper
scant ½ pint/3 dl marc or gin
2 oz/50 g butter

Crush the juniper berries. Stuff the partridges with a mixture of foie gras mousse or pâté, crushed juniper berries, a seasoning of salt and pepper and 2 tablespoons of the marc or gin. Roast on a spit for about 20 minutes, basting with the butter. Alternatively, roast in a moderately hot oven (400°F, 200°C, Gas Mark 6) for 20–30 minutes. When ready to serve, place the partridges on a hot serving dish, warm the remaining marc or gin, pour it over the birds and flambé. Serve the birds surrounded by soufflé potatoes (see page 136).

# PARTRIDGE PIE

*Serves 6*

**for the puff pastry:**
1 lb/450 g plain flour
scant ¾ pint/4 dl very cold
   water
generous pinch salt
14 oz/400 g butter, firm but not
   too hard
**for the pie filling:**
2 partridges
1 oz/25 g butter
few sprigs parsley

few sprigs chervil
sprig dried thyme
2 eggs
1 lb/450 g veal, minced
salt and pepper
pinch mixed spices
5 tablespoons dry white wine
6 oz/175 g streaky bacon
3 tablespoons calvados or cognac
1 egg for glazing

To make the pastry, sift the flour in a heap on a floured board or a floured cloth placed on the kitchen table, and make a well in the centre. Into this well pour the very cold water and the salt. (The importance of using really cold water cannot be stressed enough – it makes all the difference.) Knead lightly with the fingertips, form the pastry into a ball and let 'rest' for 30 minutes in the refrigerator.

Roll the pastry into a large circle. Scatter small pieces of butter (firm, but not straight from the refrigerator) in the middle of this circle and then fold the pastry to enclose the butter, as if making a parcel. Sprinkle with flour and roll out very lightly into a long, narrow rectangle. The pieces of butter will stick out. Fold the rectangle 3 times. Turn it a quarter of the way around. Roll out again into a long,

narrow rectangle, sprinkle with flour and again fold it 3 times. Let rest for 20 minutes. Do the same thing again; that is, roll the pastry into a long, narrow rectangle and fold it 3 times, twice-running, turning the pastry a quarter of the way around each time after folding. Let rest again for 20 minutes. Begin the process again. This is called giving 6 turns to the pastry; in other words, rolling it twice, 3 times.

Rub the birds with butter. Roast in a moderately hot oven (400°F, 200°C, Gas Mark 6) or on a spit for 25 minutes, basting occasionally. Then joint, bone and skin the birds. Chop the parsley and chervil and crumble the thyme. Whisk the 2 eggs. Mix the minced veal with salt and pepper, the parsley, chervil, thyme, spices, beaten eggs and wine.

Roll out the pastry and divide into 2 parts, one larger than the other. Line the bottom of a buttered 9-inch (23-cm) flan tin with the larger piece. Remove the bacon rind and finely dice the bacon. Place half on the pastry. Cover with half the prepared stuffing. Put pieces of boned partridge on top. Cover with the remainder of the stuffing, then the remainder of the bacon. Finally, put on the pastry lid, pressing the edges together with the fingertips. Make a small round hole in the centre to allow the steam to escape during cooking. Pour the calvados through this opening. Brush with beaten egg. Cook in a moderately hot oven (400°F, 200°C, Gas Mark 6) for 1 hour. Serve hot.

To serve the pie cold, pour a little melted jellied stock, preferably made with partridge bones, through the opening in the pastry lid.

*Stuffed partridges flambé*

# STUFFED ROAST PHEASANT

*Serves 4*

| | |
|---|---|
| 3 chicken livers | salt and pepper |
| 2 oz/50 g butter | 1 hen pheasant |
| 1 small fresh *petit-suisse* cheese | 4 slices white bread |
| few sprigs chives and parsley, chopped | generous ½ pint/3·5 dl double cream |

Brown the chicken livers in half the butter. Then mash and mix with the cheese, the chopped herbs and a seasoning of salt and pepper. Stuff the bird with this mixture. Sew up the opening in the pheasant with strong white thread, dot the bird with butter and season lightly with salt and pepper. Roast in a moderately hot oven (400°F, 200°C, Gas Mark 6) for about 30 minutes.

A few minutes before the pheasant has finished cooking, toast the bread. Remove the bird and turn off the oven. Then carve the pheasant into slices and lay these out on a flat serving dish, with the toast in the middle. Cover the toast with the stuffing. Return the dish to the warm oven. Pour the cream into the roasting tin and season lightly with salt and pepper. Heat quickly, stirring constantly, but do not allow the liquid to boil. Pour over the pheasant and serve immediately.

# VENISON WITH BLUEBERRY SAUCE

*Serves 4*

| | |
|---|---|
| 1½ lb/700 g boned loin of venison | 3 shallots |
| 1 bottle dry white wine | few sprigs parsley |
| 10 juniper berries | 2 oz/50 g butter |
| 4 carrots | 1 tablespoon groundnut oil |
| 1 onion | **for the blueberry sauce:** |
| 6 cloves | 10 oz/275 g fresh or frozen |
| 1 teaspoon sugar | blueberries |
| salt | 6 oz/175 g sugar |
| 6 peppercorns | 4 tablespoons water |
| 2 bay leaves | 1 tablespoon cornflour |
| 6–8 rashers streaky bacon | |

The venison should be rolled as for roasting and tied up. It is best to marinate it the day before. Put the meat into a large bowl and pour over the wine. Crush the juniper berries and peel and slice the carrots. Peel the onion and stick it with the cloves. Add the juniper berries, carrots, onion, sugar, a little salt, whole peppercorns and bay leaves to the marinade.

Let stand for at least 2–3 hours, or overnight if possible. Then strain the marinade. Wipe the venison thoroughly and cover with the bacon rashers, holding the bacon in place with cocktail sticks. Peel and chop the shallots and chop the parsley. Melt the butter and oil in a large saucepan, add the onions and parsley and sauté gently for a few minutes. Add the meat and gradually pour over the strained marinade until it half covers the meat. Bring to the boil, then lower the heat, cover and cook gently for 1 hour.

Meanwhile, put the blueberries, sugar and water into a second saucepan. Cook for a few minutes over high heat. Lower the heat, cover and simmer gently for 15 minutes. Watch carefully, but do not stir too much to avoid breaking the fruit.

When ready to serve, put the venison on a heated serving dish and remove the bacon. Strain the blueberries, reserving the juice, and place around the venison. Add the reserved blueberry juice to the juices from the venison, moisten the cornflour with a little water and stir into the combined juices over moderate heat. Bring to the boil, stirring constantly, and pour into a heated sauceboat.

# WILD BOAR WITH RED WINE

*Serves 4*

| | |
|---|---|
| 2 lb/1 kg wild boar or pork, in 1 | salt and pepper |
| piece | 1 lemon |
| 12 juniper berries | 1 oz/25 g butter |
| 1 bottle red wine | 3 tablespoons oil |
| 1 onion | 4 shallots |
| 4 cloves | 1 teaspoon sugar |
| 1 clove garlic | 5 tablespoons cognac |
| few sprigs parsley | 1 slice rye bread |
| 3 bay leaves | 1 tablespoon vinegar |
| sprig thyme | |

If you use tender young wild boar, it is not necessary to marinate it the day before: 1 hour is enough. Otherwise,

prepare the meat the day before. Roll up the meat into a roast and tie together if necessary. Crush 3 of the juniper berries and rub the meat with them. Place the meat in a bowl and cover with the wine. Peel the onion and stick it with the cloves. Peel the garlic and add to the bowl with the onion, parsley, bay leaves, thyme, salt and pepper and a little rind from the lemon. Marinate overnight.

Remove the meat from the marinade. Heat the butter and oil in a large saucepan. Chop the shallots and add to the pan, then add the meat. Sauté gently, turning several times. As soon as the meat is lightly golden brown, pour over the unstrained marinade. Add the sugar and remaining juniper berries. Cover and cook very gently for 3 hours. Remove the cooked meat from the pan and strain the liquid. Replace the meat in the pan, warm the cognac and pour over. Flambé, keeping the dish away from the heat. Add the strained liquid, reheat and cook for 10 minutes.

Trim the crusts from the rye bread and cut the bread into small pieces. Sprinkle with vinegar and add to the sauce around the meat. Stir and let the sauce cook for a minute to thicken. Serve the meat coated with a little of the sauce, with the remainder in a heated sauceboat. This dish is often served with a purée of chestnuts, potatoes or lentils, and sometimes with all three. The same wine that was used in making the sauce should be served with it.

# RATATOUILLE

*Serves 6*

| | |
|---|---|
| 1 lb/450 g aubergines | few sprigs parsley |
| 1 lb/450 g courgettes | 4 tablespoons olive oil |
| 1½ lb/700 g tomatoes | sprig thyme |
| 3 sweet peppers, different colours | 1 bay leaf |
| if possible | 1 teaspoon sugar |
| 3 shallots | salt and pepper |
| 2 cloves garlic | |

Cut the aubergines into pieces and soak in heavily salted water for 30 minutes. Drain, rinse in cold water and drain again. Cut the courgettes into pieces. Scald the tomatoes in boiling water for 1 minute and drain immediately. Peel, cut in half and remove the seeds. Trim the sweet peppers, remove the seeds and chop the flesh. Peel and chop the shallots and garlic and chop the parsley. Heat the oil in a large heavy saucepan and sauté the shallots, garlic and parsley. Add the thyme, bay leaf, remaining prepared vegetables, sugar and seasoning. Cook over high heat for 5 minutes, cover and lower the heat. Cook for 20 minutes, stirring from time to time and, if necessary, adding enough water to keep the mixture moist. Serve hot or cold.

*Note: Ratatouille* is equally tasty when prepared in advance and reheated when required.

*Ratatouille*

*Potatoes à la lyonnaise*

## POTATOES À LA LYONNAISE

*Serves 4*

| | |
|---|---|
| 4 large potatoes | 1 tablespoon oil |
| 2 large onions | few sprigs parsley |
| 3 oz/75 g butter | salt and pepper |

Wash and scrub the potatoes and bake in a moderately hot oven (400°F, 200°C, Gas Mark 6) for about 30 minutes. They should be tender, but not completely cooked. Peel and cut into thick slices. Peel and finely chop the onions. Heat the butter and oil in a frying pan and gently brown the slices of potato and onion. Sprinkle with parsley, season with salt and pepper and serve very hot.

## SOUFFLÉ POTATOES

*Serves 6*

| | |
|---|---|
| 4 large old potatoes | salt and pepper |
| oil for deep-frying | |

Peel the potatoes and slice into rounds, about ⅛ inch (3 mm) thick. Dry well – this is important. Heat the oil in a deep frying pan to very hot, 360°F (182°C) on a cooking thermometer. (Another guide is to add a small cube of bread to the oil; it should turn golden brown within half a minute.) Add the potatoes, a few at a time, and cook over high heat until golden brown. Remove from the oil and cool. Reheat the oil to 400°F (204°C) and fry the potatoes a second time until swollen and golden brown. Remove from the oil and drain on kitchen paper. Place the potatoes in a heated serving dish. Season and serve at once.

*Note:* Soufflé potatoes are usually served with game or grilled meats. If they are to accompany a dish with a sauce, serve on small plates to avoid soaking with sauce.

## POTATOES À LA DAUPHINOISE

*Serves 4*

| | |
|---|---|
| 3 large potatoes | salt and grated nutmeg |
| 1 clove garlic | ½ pint/3 dl double cream |
| 3 oz/75 g butter | (see note) |

Peel and wash the potatoes. Cut into very thin slices and dry well with a cloth. Peel the clove of garlic and rub it around the inside of a baking dish. Butter the dish well, using a third of the butter, and arrange the potato slices inside in layers, seasoning each layer with salt. Sprinkle the top lightly with nutmeg and pour over the cream. Dot the remaining butter over the surface. Bake in a hot oven (425°F, 220°C, Gas Mark 7) for 10 minutes. Then lower the heat to 350°F (180°C, Gas Mark 4) and cook for 1 hour. This dish is excellent served with a roast.

*Note:* Potatoes *à la dauphinoise* may also be made with milk in place of the cream, or with half milk and half cream.

# AÏOLI (GARLIC MAYONNAISE)

*Makes approximately ½ pint (3 dl)*

| | |
|---|---|
| 1 oz/25 g (or 2 small heads) garlic | ½ pint/3 dl olive oil |
| 2 egg yolks | juice of 1 lemon |
| pinch salt | 1 teaspoon cold water |

Peel the garlic and pound it, if possible in a mortar. Add the egg yolks and mix slowly. Add the salt. Then begin to pour in the olive oil, almost drop by drop, as for mayonnaise. When it thickens, add the oil more quickly. Finish by mixing in the lemon juice and then the water.

To prepare in a liquidiser, place the peeled and roughly chopped garlic in the liquidiser with the egg yolks, salt and lemon juice. Cover and blend at low speed for a few moments. Remove the centre cap in the liquidiser lid and slowly pour in the oil. When the mixture has thickened and all the oil is added, add the water and switch off.

# ARTICHOKE MOUSSELINE

*Serves 4*

| | |
|---|---|
| 4 lb/1·75 kg (about 8 medium-sized) artichokes | 2 oz/50 g butter |
| | salt and pepper |
| 2 tablespoons double cream | |

For the purée, you should use only the hearts of the artichokes. Do not discard the remainder: when the heart is removed, keep the tender leaves and boil them in water. Use the strained stock for soups.

Cover the artichoke hearts with boiling water and simmer with the lid on for about 35 minutes. Drain and press through a sieve to make a purée. Beat in the cream, butter and seasoning. Alternatively, blend the hearts to a smooth purée in a liquidiser. Then add the remaining ingredients to make a smooth sauce. Just before serving, reheat in a double saucepan or a *bain marie* (a pan placed in a large roasting tin filled with boiling water) or in a heavy saucepan over very low heat. Serve with roast veal, pigeons or chicken.

# FRESH PEAS IN CREAM SAUCE

*Serves 6*

| | |
|---|---|
| 3 lb/1·5 kg shelled fresh peas | 1 teaspoon sugar |
| 2 oz/50 g butter | pinch salt |
| 1 lettuce | 4 tablespoons double cream |
| few sprigs parsley | 2 egg yolks |
| 5 tablespoons water | |

Rinse the peas. Melt the butter in a heavy saucepan and add the peas. Sauté over high heat for a few minutes, constantly shaking the pan. Wash the lettuce and cut into quarters. Add the lettuce quarters, the parsley and the water to the pan. To keep the temperature low in the traditional manner, cover the pan with a soup dish filled with cold water. As the water in the soup dish becomes hot, replace it with cold water. Cook the peas very slowly for 1 hour, adding a little extra water if necessary. Add the sugar and salt and continue to simmer gently. Meanwhile, blend the cream and egg yolks together in a bowl. Add to the peas and reheat, stirring all the time, but do not boil. Remove the parsley and serve at once.

*Potatoes à la dauphinoise*

# PEACHES IN BRANDY

*Makes about 6 lb (2·75 kg)*

24 ripe peaches
1 lb/450 g granulated sugar
generous ¾ pint/5 dl water
8 cloves

stick cinnamon, broken into
  small pieces
1¾ pints/1 litre brandy

Prick the peaches in two or three places with a long needle. Place in a large saucepan of boiling water. Leave for a minute and then remove with a perforated spoon. Rinse the peaches under cold running water. Peel and let dry. Cut the peaches in half and place in sterilized jars, filling the jars not more than three-quarters full.

Dissolve the sugar in the water and bring to the boil. Cook for 3 minutes. Pour the syrup over the peaches and add the cloves and the cinnamon. Let cool completely before covering with the brandy. Seal the jars and leave for 1 month before serving. Delicious after a meal, these peaches can also be used to enhance sweet dishes, ice cream, fruit salads and flans.

# STRAWBERRY TART

*Serves 6–8*

**for the sablé pastry:**
8 oz/225 g plain flour
2 egg yolks
4 oz/110 g butter
½ teaspoon salt
2 tablespoons water
2 oz/50 g icing sugar
**for the pastry cream:**
4 oz/100 g icing sugar
2 egg yolks

2 oz/50 g plain flour
scant ½ pint/2·5 dl lukewarm milk
½ vanilla pod or few drops vanilla
  essence
small pinch salt
1 oz/25 g butter
**for the filling:**
1½ lb/700 g strawberries
6 oz/175 g redcurrant or
  raspberry jelly

Remove the butter from the refrigerator 1 hour before you begin. Sift the flour into a bowl and make a well in the centre. Add the egg yolks, slightly softened butter, salt, water and sugar. Mix very quickly, rubbing between the fingertips to make a dough. Form the dough into a ball. Let rest in a cool place for 20 minutes. Roll out the pastry on a floured board, or on a table covered with a floured cloth. Line a 9-inch (23-cm) greased flan dish with the pastry. To prevent the centre from rising, prick with a fork, line carefully with foil or greaseproof paper and fill with dried beans. Bake in a moderately hot oven (400°F, 200°C, Gas Mark 6) for 25 minutes. Cool for 10 minutes before removing beans and foil.

In the meantime, prepare the pastry cream. Mix the icing sugar and the egg yolks together in a saucepan. Add the flour and stir thoroughly. Add the milk gradually, stirring constantly. Then add the vanilla pod or vanilla essence and the salt. Place the pan over low heat and bring to the boil, stirring constantly with a wooden spoon until the mixture has thickened. Remove from the heat. Lift out the vanilla pod, if used, and add the butter, stirring vigorously. Let the mixture cool until lukewarm. Pour the cream into the cooked pastry case, smoothing it with a spatula. Then wash and hull the strawberries and arrange on top. Melt the redcurrant jelly in a small saucepan over low heat. Spoon over the strawberries. Serve the strawberry tart cold.

# VANILLA CREAM PIE

*Serves 6*

**for the puff pastry:**
8 oz/225 g plain flour
generous ¼ pint/2 dl very cold
   water
pinch salt
7 oz/200 g butter, firm but not
   too hard
milk for glazing
**for the pastry cream:**
scant ½ pint/2·5 dl milk

½ vanilla pod or 2–3 drops vanilla
   essence
grated rind of 1 orange
4 oz/100 g castor sugar
1 oz/25 g plain flour
3 egg yolks
pinch salt
1 oz/25 g butter
**for the topping:**
2 oz/50 g castor sugar

Make the pastry as for Partridge Pie, page 132. Grease an 8-
or 9-inch (20- or 23-cm) flan dish and line with puff pastry.
Prick the pastry with a fork, so it rises evenly. Brush the
edges with milk and bake in a moderately hot oven (400°F,
200°C, Gas Mark 6) for 12 minutes.

   Meanwhile, prepare the pastry cream. Heat the milk with
the vanilla pod or essence and a little grated orange rind. Mix
the sugar and flour together in a saucepan. Add the egg yolks
and gradually stir in the hot milk mixture. Cook over low
heat for about 5 minutes, stirring constantly with a spoon or
a whisk until the mixture thickens. Remove the pan from the
heat and take out the vanilla pod, if used. Cut the butter into
small pieces and stir it in. Pour this thick cream mixture into
the pastry case. Sprinkle with the remaining sugar. Grill
quickly until the sugar melts and caramelises. Serve warm.

# APPLE TART

*Serves 6–8*

**for the pastry:**
8 oz/225 g plain flour
2 tablespoons water
pinch salt
2 oz/50 g icing sugar
4 oz/110 g butter
2 egg yolks

**for the filling:**
2 lb/1 kg eating apples
juice of ½ lemon
2 oz/50 g castor sugar
pinch ground cinnamon
8 oz/225 g apricot jam
2 tablespoons water

Sift the flour into a bowl and make a well in the centre.
Place the water, salt, sugar, butter, cut into small pieces, and
egg yolks in the well. Mix together thoroughly with the flour,
rubbing between the fingertips to make a dough. Form the
pastry into a ball. Roll out on a floured board, or on a table
covered with a floured cloth. Avoid handling it too much as
this pastry is very fragile. Line a greased 10-inch (26-cm) flan
tin with it.

   Peel, quarter and core the apples. Cut into thin slices and
sprinkle with the lemon juice. Arrange them, overlapping,
in the pastry case. Sprinkle with the sugar and cinnamon.
Bake in a moderately hot oven (400°F, 200°C, Gas Mark 6)
for 30 minutes. Remove the tart from the oven. Sieve the
apricot jam and combine with the water in a small saucepan.
Warm through over low heat, then pour evenly over the
surface of the tart to form a glaze.

*Peaches in brandy*

*Blackcurrant ice cream*

# CRÊPES SUZETTE

*Serves 4*

| 4 oz/100 g plain flour | 4 small oranges or tangerines |
| 2 eggs | 2 oz/50 g butter |
| ¼ pint/1·5 dl water | cooking fat (see recipe) |
| ¼ pint/1·5 dl light ale or beer | 4 oz/100 g icing sugar |
| pinch salt | 8 teaspoons curaçao or cointreau |

**for the orange butter:**
20 sugar cubes

For the batter, sift the flour into a bowl and make a well in the centre. Add the eggs, water, ale and salt. Mix in the centre of the bowl, gradually drawing in the flour from the sides. When the ingredients are blended, beat to a smooth batter. (The batter can also be prepared in a liquidiser. In this case, place the eggs, water and salt in the liquidiser. Add the flour and then the ale. Cover and blend for a few seconds at high speed.) Let the batter stand for 30 minutes to make it lighter.

Meanwhile, prepare the orange butter. Rub the sugar cubes over the unpeeled fruit to absorb the oil in the rind. Then crush the cubes thoroughly and mix into the slightly softened butter. Add a little orange juice to taste.

Heat a small frying pan and, when hot, lightly grease with a piece of cooking fat. Pour a little of the batter into the pan. Make a pancake, toss it then discard it, for the first one is never successful. Rub the pan again with cooking fat,

reheat and pour about 2 tablespoons of batter into the pan. Tip the pan so that the batter spreads thinly over the surface. As soon as the edges turn golden brown and bubbles start to burst and form little holes on the surface, turn the pancake over. Cook for a moment. Spread each pancake with a little of the orange butter, fold in half twice and place in a hot flat dish. When all the pancakes are made and filled, dredge them with icing sugar. Warm the curaçao and pour over. Flambé and serve.

# BLACKCURRANT ICE CREAM

*Serves 6*

| 1 lb/450 g blackcurrants | juice of ½ lemon |
| 7 oz/200 g icing sugar | ½ pint/3 dl double cream |

Crush the blackcurrants in a sieve – preferably a conical sieve – and retain the juice. Blend the juice with the sifted icing sugar and the lemon juice. Whip the cream until thick, then fold into the blackcurrant mixture. Pour the mixture into a large ice tray and freeze for about 2 hours, or until firm. The ice cream is sometimes served with additional fresh cream, whipped up with sugar. Serve with sweet white wine or champagne.

# BRETON PANCAKES

*Serves 8*

| | |
|---|---|
| 4 eggs | 8 oz/225 g buckwheat flour |
| pinch salt | (see note) |
| 5 tablespoons dark rum | scant ½ pint/2·5 dl water |
| 1½ tablespoons oil | lard or bacon fat |
| ¼ pint/1·5 dl light ale | |

Whisk the eggs in a large bowl with the salt, rum and oil. Gradually add the ale and the flour, stirring constantly with a wooden spoon. Cover with a cloth and let stand in a warm place for at least 1 hour. Then stir in the water.

Heat a small frying pan (ideally, one kept especially for pancakes) and rub with a piece of lard or bacon fat. Pour a little of the batter in the pan and tip it so that the batter spreads all over the bottom. As soon as the pancake is covered with little golden holes, turn it over. Cook a moment longer, then slide on to a plate. In Brittany, the first pancake is given to the birds for luck.

Grease the pan again and cook a second pancake in the same way. Pile them on top of each other on a heated dish, dusting them lightly with sugar. Breton women often use two pans at once to save time. Serve the pancakes with melted butter, honey or jam.

*Note:* Buckwheat flour is available from most health food shops.

# BLACK CHERRY PUDDING

*Serves 4*

| | |
|---|---|
| 1 lb/450 g black cherries | 3 tablespoons castor sugar |
| 3 oz/75 g butter | pinch salt |
| 10 oz/275 g plain flour | 5 tablespoons water |
| 3 eggs | |

Stone the cherries. Grease a 12-inch (30-cm) round cake tin or a 9-inch (23-cm) loaf tin, using a third of the butter, and place half the cherries in the bottom. Sift the flour into a bowl and make a well in the centre. Place the eggs, sugar, salt and water in the well. Stir, drawing the mixture together, then beat to a smooth batter. Pour the batter into the tin, spread it evenly and cover with the rest of the cherries. Dot the surface with the remaining butter. Bake in a moderately hot oven (400°F, 200°C, Gas Mark 6) for about 30 minutes. Allow the pudding to cool before removing it from the tin.

# BAKED CHESTNUT PUDDING

*Serves 4*

| | |
|---|---|
| 1½ lb/700 g fresh chestnuts or | 7 oz/200 g castor sugar |
| 1 lb/450 g canned whole | 4 eggs, separated |
| chestnuts | pinch salt |
| salt | 2 oz/50 g icing sugar |
| 4 oz/100 g butter | |
| ½ vanilla pod or 2–3 drops vanilla | |
| essence | |
| scant ½ pint/2·5 dl milk | |

If using fresh chestnuts, slash them and cook for 15 minutes in boiling salted water. Strain and remove the shells and skins. Return the chestnuts to the saucepan, cover again with boiling water and simmer for 30 minutes, or until tender. If using canned chestnuts, simply drain and rinse them.

Press the chestnuts through a sieve or food mill to make a purée. Cut the butter into small pieces, add it and mix well. Add the vanilla pod or essence to the milk and bring to the boil in a saucepan. Discard the pod, if used, and pour the hot milk slowly over the chestnut mixture, stirring it in gradually. Mix in the sugar and egg yolks. Whisk the egg whites with a pinch of salt until stiff. Fold into the mixture.

Thoroughly grease a medium-sized soufflé dish and pour in the mixture. Cook in a moderate oven (350°F, 180°C, Gas Mark 4) for 30 minutes. Chill the pudding completely before unmoulding, and then sprinkle with icing sugar. Serve as it is, or cover with vanilla-flavoured whipped cream.

# ALSACE HONEY BISCUITS

*Makes about 48*

| | |
|---|---|
| 7 oz/200 g plain flour | 3 oz/75 g ground almonds |
| 4 oz/100 g castor sugar | 3 tablespoons milk |
| ½ teaspoon baking powder | 1 teaspoon ground cinnamon |
| 3 oz/75 g butter, softened | 5 tablespoons thick honey |

Sift the flour into a mixing bowl and add the sugar and baking powder. Mix with a wooden spoon. Add the butter and rub it into the mixture, using the fingertips. Add the ground almonds and the milk and knead again until the dough is smooth. Roll out on a floured board and cut into a variety of shapes – hearts, stars, diamonds, etc. Place the biscuits on a greased baking tray. Sprinkle cinnamon on each biscuit and put a little honey in the centre. Bake in a moderately hot oven (400°F, 200°C, Gas Mark 6) for 12 minutes. Serve with white wine, coffee or kirsch.

# MADELEINES

*Makes about 24*

| | |
|---|---|
| 4 oz/100 g castor sugar | 4 oz/100 g butter |
| 4 eggs | few drops vanilla essence or 1 |
| pinch salt (see recipe) | tablespoon orange flower water |
| 4 oz/100 g plain flour | |

Put the sugar in a bowl. Separate the eggs and whisk the whites with the salt until stiff. (Include salt only if unsalted butter is used in the recipe.) Add the whites to the sugar and mix well. Add the egg yolks and mix again. Then add the flour, a little at a time, stirring constantly. Melt the butter and stir it in, with the vanilla essence or orange flower water. Beat with a fork or whisk until the mixture has thickened. (Alternatively, use an electric mixer at slow speed.)

Grease little shell-shaped tins and pour in the mixture to completely fill the tins. Bake in a moderately hot oven (400°F, 200°C, Gas Mark 6) for 15–20 minutes, until the cakes are golden brown. Remove the Madeleines from the oven and cool in the tins.

# PEAR CAKE

*Makes 1 9-inch (23-cm) cake*

9 oz/250 g plain flour
4 oz/100 g icing sugar
1 tablespoon baking powder
¼ pint/1·5 dl groundnut or corn oil
¼ pint/1·5 dl sweet white wine
3 eggs
small pinch salt

6–8 small pears
**for the glaze:**
5 oz/150 g granulated sugar
¾ pint/4·5 dl water
pinch ground cinnamon
2 tablespoons cherry jam

Grease an 8- or 9-inch (20- or 23-cm) round cake tin and line the sides and bottom with buttered greaseproof paper.

Sift the flour into a bowl and make a well in the centre. Sift the sugar into the well, add the baking powder and then the oil and white wine. Mix everything together with a wooden spoon, drawing in the flour from the sides of the bowl. Separate the eggs. Add the egg yolks to the mixture and mix again until quite smooth. Whisk the egg whites with a pinch of salt until stiff. Fold into the mixture quickly but thoroughly. The mixture must be creamy. Turn into the prepared tin. Bake in the centre of a moderately hot oven (400°F, 200°C, Gas Mark 6) for 15 minutes. Then reduce the heat to 350°F (180°C, Gas Mark 4) and bake for a further 20–25 minutes. The cake is cooked as soon as the warmed blade of a knife, pushed into the centre, comes out clean. The surface of the cake must be golden brown. Let cool completely before turning out.

Meanwhile, put the sugar for the glaze into a saucepan with the water and bring to the boil. Add the whole pears, washed but unpeeled. Add a pinch of cinnamon and the cherry jam to add colour. Cook over medium heat for 15 minutes or until the pears are soft. Let cool and drain on kitchen paper. Set the pears upright on the cake, cutting off their bases so they will stand easily.

# HONEY SPICE CAKE

*Serves 8–12*

1 lb/450 g thick honey
1 lb/450 g rye flour
pinch salt
pinch ground ginger
pinch ground cinnamon
4 cloves, crushed
3 tablespoons milk

2 eggs
½ teaspoon bicarbonate of soda
**for the icing:**
4 oz/100 g icing sugar
1 tablespoon lemon juice or kirsch
crystallised fruits for decoration

Warm the honey in a saucepan over very low heat, stirring constantly with a wooden spoon. Measure the flour into an earthenware bowl, and make a well in the centre. Add the honey, salt and spices. Mix and knead to a rough dough. Cover the dough with greaseproof paper or polythene to prevent drying. Let stand at room temperature for 24 hours.

Warm the milk. Meanwhile, lightly whisk the eggs. Dissolve the bicarbonate of soda in the warm milk, then whisk in the eggs. Add the mixture to the dough and mix well. Knead thoroughly for at least 10 minutes. The dough should be quite stiff and rough in texture. Spoon the dough into a well greased loaf tin. Bake in a moderate oven (325°F, 160°C, Gas Mark 3) for 1 hour 20 minutes, or until a skewer inserted into the cake comes out clean. Cool before removing.

Mix the icing sugar with lemon juice or kirsch and stir well. Spread the mixture over the surface of the spice cake with a spatula and decorate with pieces of crystallised fruit.

# RASPBERRY RING CAKE

*Serves 6*

2 eggs
7 oz/200 g castor sugar
grated rind of ¼ orange
generous ¼ pint/2 dl sweet white wine
5 tablespoons groundnut oil

8 oz/225 g plain flour
2 teaspoons baking powder
**for the filling:**
8 oz/225 g raspberries
4 oz/100 g castor sugar
generous ¼ pint/2 dl double cream

Whisk the eggs with the sugar and add the grated orange rind. Whisk again until the mixture is frothy. Pour the wine and oil into the egg mixture and mix well. Sift the flour and add. Mix again and finally stir in the baking powder. Grease a ring mould, about 9 inches (23 cm) in diameter, and pour in the mixture. Bake in the centre of a moderately hot oven (375°F, 190°C, Gas Mark 5) for 35 minutes, or until the cake is risen and brown. Let the cake cool completely before removing from the mould. Place the raspberries in the centre of the cake. Dust with the sugar and cover with the cream – whipped, if desired.

# PRUNE CAKE

*Serves 6*

8 oz/225 g tenderised prunes
7 oz/200 g plain flour
7 oz/200 g castor sugar
1 teaspoon baking powder

pinch salt
pinch grated nutmeg
2 oz/50 g butter, softened
½ pint/3 dl milk

This cake is best made with really fresh tenderised prunes. Otherwise, soak the prunes for a few hours in either cold tea or port wine, then drain well. Remove the stones and cut the prunes into small pieces. Sift the flour into a bowl and add the prunes. Then add the sugar, baking powder, salt and nutmeg. Mix by hand. Turn the pieces of prune over and over until well coated. Add the softened butter and mix again. Heat the milk to lukewarm and stir in, a little at a time. Grease a 9-inch (23-cm) round cake tin and pour in the mixture. Bake in a moderately hot oven (375°F, 190°C, Gas Mark 5) for about 30 minutes. As soon as the top is golden brown, the cake is cooked. Serve warm or cold.

*Honey spice cake*

# SPANISH

Maruja Callaved

*Photography by Christian Délu*

Spanish cooking forms an integral part of the history of Spain and was gradually evolved during the successive foreign invasions suffered by the Iberian peninsula.

The Phoenicians brought with them the seeds of the olive trees. The Romans introduced new ingredients to Spanish cooking, among which garlic was the most important. The Arabs brought spices, bitter lemons and oranges and sweet essences to flavour their confectionery. They taught the Spaniards to make *churros* (batter rings deep-fried in oil), *freixuelos* (honey fritters), sugared and candied almonds, almond paste and nougat. The unification of Spain in 1492 put an end to the long period of foreign occupation.

This amalgam of contributions from other lands and the traditional cooking of the early inhabitants of the Iberian peninsula is the foundation of traditional Spanish cooking.

Fish is a fundamental part of the diet all along the Spanish coastline, although the methods of cooking vary according to the region. In the north, fish is usually prepared with a sauce or garnish, as in such dishes as *marmitako* (fish stew with vegetables), and hake in green sauce, whereas in the south fried fish is more popular. Shellfish is the speciality of Galicia and a few places along the eastern and southern coasts. The inland areas of the north support large herds of cattle and have a large output of agricultural products. Typical local dishes are hashes, stews and beef-steaks. The rivers abound in fresh-water fish and the north is famous for its charcoal-grilled trout.

The eastern coast, on the Mediterranean, not only has abundant fish, but also produces rice, vegetables, fruit and almonds. All these products place the Mediterranean style of cooking among the richest and most varied in Spain. The best-known and probably the finest dish of this region is *paella*.

Southern Spain, with its stretches of tropical vegetation, is the warmest part of the country, where olives, soft fruits, grapes and almonds grow in profusion and where large numbers of cattle and pigs are raised. The dishes of the south are simple and light, and the meals basically consist of fried foods, salads and *gazpacho* (a refreshing, cold vegetable soup).

The central and western parts of the mainland are inland regions which support a large livestock population and produce a high percentage of the country's cereals and wine. Solid, down-to-earth dishes based on these products are typical of these areas.

The gastronomic traditions of Spain are highlighted by a series of carnivals and events held throughout the year. These include the festivals celebrating the grape harvest in September and others that mark the seasons for river fishing and hunting, particularly boar-hunting; the time for sausage-making in winter; the fruit harvest and resultant jam-making in the autumn; nougat-making at Christmas, and so on. These are all legacies of a popular and traditional nature and at these times the people keep certain customs in cooking, although the modern way of life is threatening to obliterate them.

Vineyards are cultivated in almost every region of Spain. Many excellent Spanish wines could be mentioned, but the 'king of wines' is sherry, which ranges in colour from topaz to mahogany and is a fortified wine with an unequalled bouquet.

# OCTOPUS WITH GARLIC AND PAPRIKA DRESSING

*Serves 6*

| | |
|---|---|
| 2¼ lb/1 kg octopus or cuttlefish | salt |
| 2 cloves garlic | ¼ pint/1·5 dl olive oil |
| 2 teaspoons paprika | |

Discard the ink sac, the intestines and the transparent spinal bone from the octopus or cuttlefish. Rinse very thoroughly under cold running water, place on a flat surface and pound with a mallet to tenderise and soften the flesh.

Place the octopus in a large saucepan and add enough water to cover. Bring to the boil, then lower the heat, cover tightly and simmer for 1–1½ hours.

Meanwhile, peel and finely chop the garlic. Combine the garlic, paprika, salt and oil to make the dressing. Drain the fish thoroughly and cut into small pieces. Transfer to a serving dish and sprinkle with the prepared dressing.

# SHELLFISH OMELETTE

*Serves 4*

| | |
|---|---|
| **for the tomato sauce:** | 10 fresh mussels |
| 1 lb/450 g tomatoes | 8 eggs |
| 5 tablespoons olive oil | 2 tablespoons milk |
| ¼ teaspoon salt | 2 teaspoons salt |
| **for the omelette:** | 1–2 tablespoons olive oil |
| 20 fresh or frozen scampi | 2 teaspoons chopped parsley |
| 5 fresh or frozen Dublin Bay prawns | |

To make the tomato sauce, peel and finely chop the tomatoes. Heat the oil in a heavy saucepan and sauté the tomatoes for 10–15 minutes, stirring frequently, until reduced to a pulp. Remove from the heat and press the tomatoes through a sieve to make a fairly thick sauce. Season with salt.

To make the omelette, if using fresh, uncooked scampi and prawns, rinse thoroughly under cold running water, plunge into lightly salted boiling water and boil for 7 minutes. Drain well and set aside to cool. Scrub the mussels thoroughly under cold running water and remove the beards. Place in a saucepan and add just enough water to cover the bottom of the pan. Cover the pan tightly and steam the mussels over moderate heat for about 5 minutes, or until they open. Discard any that do not open. Remove the mussels from their shells and place in a bowl. Peel and devein the scampi and prawns, cut into small pieces and place in a bowl with the mussels. Lightly whisk together the eggs, milk and salt in a large bowl. Stir in the prepared shellfish.

Heat the oil in a large omelette pan or frying pan over moderate heat. Pour in the egg mixture and tilt the pan gently so the egg runs almost to the rim. When the omelette begins to set, lift the edges with a spatula to allow the uncooked egg to run underneath. When the omelette has a high rounded edge but is still slightly soft in the centre, place a lightly greased plate over the pan and invert the omelette on to it. Slide it back into the pan so the browned side is on top. Cook for a further 2–3 minutes, shaking the pan gently. Remove from the heat and garnish with the chopped parsley. Serve immediately with the reheated tomato sauce.

# TUNA FISH OMELETTE

*Serves 4*

| | |
|---|---|
| **for the tomato sauce:** | ¼ pint/1·5 dl milk |
| 1 lb/450 g tomatoes | 2 oz/50 g butter |
| 5 tablespoons olive oil | 4 oz/100 g canned tuna fish |
| ¼ teaspoon salt | 6 eggs |
| **for the omelette:** | 1½ teaspoons salt |
| 2 medium-sized potatoes, cooked | 1 tablespoon chopped parsley |
| 6 tablespoons cooked chopped spinach | |

Prepare the tomato sauce as for Shellfish Omelette on the preceding page. Press the potato and spinach through a sieve to make a purée. Stir in the milk and half the butter and heat gently until hot. Cut the tuna fish into small pieces and add half to the prepared tomato sauce. Heat gently until hot. Whisk the eggs and add the salt, parsley and remaining tuna fish.

Heat the remaining butter in an omelette pan or heavy frying pan. Add the egg mixture and cook until the omelette is almost set. Place the spinach mixture along the centre of the omelette and fold each side towards the middle, completely enclosing the filling. Transfer to a heated serving dish, cover with the tomato sauce and serve immediately.

# SCAMPI WITH WHITE RUM

*Serves 4*

| | |
|---|---|
| 1 small onion | generous ¼ pint/2 dl water |
| 1 tomato | ¼–scant ½ pint/1·5–2·5 dl white rum |
| 5 tablespoons olive oil | |
| ½ teaspoon paprika | 20 fresh or frozen scampi, peeled and deveined |
| ½ oz/15 g plain flour | |
| 2 teaspoons salt | 3 tablespoons anisette |

Peel and finely chop the onion and tomato. Heat the oil in a frying pan and sauté the onion until lightly browned. Add the tomato and paprika and sauté for 1 minute. Stir in the flour and salt. Add the water gradually, stirring well after each addition. Bring to the boil, stirring constantly until the mixture thickens. Stir in the rum and simmer for 2–3 minutes. Add the scampi and simmer for 5 minutes. Add the anisette and simmer for 5–10 minutes. Remove the pan from the heat and serve.

# MARINATED TROUT

*Serves 4*

| | |
|---|---|
| 4 small trout | 2 sprigs parsley |
| 6 cloves garlic | 1 teaspoon salt |
| 5 tablespoons olive oil | generous pinch white pepper |
| 2 tablespoons vinegar | 1 teaspoon paprika |

Gut the trout and cut off the fins, tails and heads. Rinse under cold running water and pat dry with kitchen paper. Cut each trout into 3 pieces. Peel and chop the garlic.

Place the trout pieces in a saucepan and add the garlic, olive oil, vinegar, parsley, salt, white pepper and paprika. Bring to the boil over high heat, then lower the heat and simmer for 10 minutes. Transfer the trout to a heated serving dish and pour over the juices from the pan. Serve immediately as an appetiser or set aside until cold.

# BONITO A LA PLANCHA

*Serves 6*

| | |
|---|---|
| 3½ lb/1·5 kg bonito or tuna fish | 1½ tablespoons lemon juice |
| 2 teaspoons salt | 1 lb/450 g small mushrooms |
| 4 cloves garlic | 5 tablespoons olive oil |
| 3 sprigs parsley | |

Cut the fish into slices 1½ inches (3·5 cm) thick. Sprinkle with the salt. Peel 2 cloves of the garlic, place in a mortar with the parsley and pound until smooth. Add the lemon juice. Brush the fish slices with the garlic and lemon mixture.

Traditionally the fish is cooked on a *plancha* (see note), but alternatively it may be cooked in a greased heavy frying pan. Cook the slices for 5–6 minutes on each side. Brush with the remaining lemon mixture during the cooking.

Meanwhile, rinse the mushrooms thoroughly under cold running water and simmer in lightly salted boiling water for 5–6 minutes. Drain well. Peel and chop the remaining garlic. Heat the oil in a small saucepan and sauté the garlic for 2–3 minutes. Add the mushrooms and sauté for 5–6 minutes. Drain on kitchen paper.

Arrange the fish slices on a heated serving dish, garnish with the mushrooms and serve as an appetiser.

*Note:* A *plancha* is a thick iron plate, heated from below, similar to a griddle. Bonito, like tuna fish, is very suitable for cooking *a la plancha* because it contains a high quantity of fat.

# RICE AND VEGETABLE MOULD

*Serves 4*

| | |
|---|---|
| 8 oz/225 g Brussels sprouts | 2 eggs |
| 2 medium-sized carrots | ¾ pint/4·5 dl water |
| 1½ lb/700 g fresh peas | 1 bay leaf |
| 8 oz/225 g French beans | 1 teaspoon salt |
| 2 cloves garlic | 8 oz/225 g long-grain rice |
| 5 tablespoons olive oil | |

Discard the coarse outer leaves of the Brussels sprouts and trim the stalks. Cut the sprouts into small pieces. Peel and coarsely chop the carrots. Shell the peas. Trim and coarsely chop the beans. Peel the garlic. Cook the Brussels sprouts, carrots, peas and beans separately in lightly salted boiling water until just tender. Drain well.

Heat half the oil in a frying pan. Sauté the cloves of garlic for 2–3 minutes, then remove and discard them. Sauté the cooked vegetables in the flavoured oil for about 5 minutes. Lightly whisk the eggs and stir into the vegetables. Cook for 3–4 minutes, or until the egg sets. Remove from the heat and set aside to cool.

Pour the water into a saucepan and add the remaining oil, the bay leaf and the salt. Bring to the boil. Add the rice, lower the heat and simmer for 12–15 minutes, or until the rice is

*La Mancha soup*

tender and all the water has been absorbed. Remove from the heat and set aside to cool.

Lightly brush the inside of a 3-pint (1·5-litre) mould with oil. Place a layer of rice in the bottom followed by a layer of the vegetable mixture. Repeat twice and finish with the layer of rice. Press the top firmly, then turn the mixture out of the mould on to a plate and serve with mayonnaise.

# LA MANCHA SOUP

*Serves 6*

| | |
|---|---|
| 4 cloves garlic | 2 oz/50 g plain flour |
| 6 slices bread | ½ teaspoon paprika |
| 8 oz/225 g lean bacon, in 1 piece | ¼ teaspoon pepper |
| 4 oz/100 g *serrano* ham (see note) | 2 teaspoons salt |
| 4 oz/100 g *chorizo* (see note) | 3 pints/1·75 litres water |
| 5 tablespoons olive oil | |

Peel and halve the garlic cloves. Cut the bread, bacon, ham and *chorizo* into ½-inch (1-cm) cubes. Heat the oil in a saucepan and sauté the garlic cloves until they begin to brown. Add the bacon, ham and *chorizo* and sauté for about 5 minutes. Remove with a perforated spoon and drain on kitchen paper. Add the bread cubes and sauté until crisp and golden brown. Remove with a perforated spoon and drain on kitchen paper.

Add the flour, paprika, pepper and salt to the oil remaining in the pan and cook for 5 minutes, stirring constantly. Add the water gradually, stirring well after each addition. Bring to the boil and boil for 15 minutes, stirring constantly. Add the bread cubes, garlic, bacon, ham and *chorizo*. Boil for a further 5 minutes and then serve in deep soup bowls.

*Note:* Serrano ham is a lightly salted ham for which York ham is a good substitute. *Chorizo* is a highly spiced pork sausage containing saffron and garlic.

# GAZPACHO

*Serves 6*

| | |
|---|---|
| 2 cloves garlic | 3 thick slices bread |
| pinch cumin | 5 tablespoons olive oil |
| 2 lb/1 kg tomatoes | 3 teaspoons salt |
| 2 medium-sized onions | 6 tablespoons vinegar |
| ½ large cucumber | 2 pints/generous litre water |
| 2 large green sweet peppers | |

Peel the garlic and pound to a paste with the cumin in a mortar. Peel and coarsely chop the tomatoes, onions and cucumber. Remove the seeds from the peppers and chop the flesh. Soak the bread in cold water for about 30 seconds, then squeeze out the excess moisture.

Place three-quarters of the tomatoes, onions, cucumber and peppers in a liquidiser with the garlic paste, bread and oil and reduce to a purée. Pour into a bowl, stir in the salt, vinegar and water and chill thoroughly. (Alternatively, three-quarters of the vegetables may be very finely chopped, then mixed with the bread, garlic paste, oil, salt, vinegar and water and chilled well.) Very finely chop the remaining vegetables and place separately in small bowls as accompaniments to the soup. Serve the *gazpacho*, very cold, in deep soup bowls or cups.

# COLD RABBIT SOUP

*Serves 6*

2¼ lb/1 kg rabbit, with liver

**for the marinade:**

2 tablespoons olive oil

5 tablespoons vinegar

3 teaspoons salt

1 sprig fresh marjoram or
  ½ teaspoon dried marjoram

**for the soup:**

3 oz/75 g fine fresh breadcrumbs

3 cloves garlic

4 hard-boiled eggs

generous ¼ pint/2 dl olive oil

1 tablespoon vinegar

1¾ pints/1 litre water

salt

Rinse the rabbit under cold running water, dry well with kitchen paper and cut into 2-inch (5-cm) pieces. Reserve the liver until required.

To prepare the marinade, pour the oil and vinegar into a bowl and add the salt and marjoram. Mix well and add the rabbit pieces. Turn the pieces over several times until well coated with the marinade. Set aside to marinate for 24 hours.

To make the soup, transfer the rabbit pieces and the marinade to a roasting tin and add the rabbit liver. Roast in a moderate oven (350°F, 180°C, Gas Mark 4) for 30–40 minutes. Remove from the oven and set aside to cool. Reserve the liver. Strip the meat off the bones and set aside until required. Reserve the marinade but discard the bones. Soak the breadcrumbs for 1 minute in cold water. Squeeze to remove the excess moisture and place the crumbs in a mortar. Peel the garlic and place in the mortar. Separate the egg yolks from the whites and use the whites for another recipe if required. Add the egg yolks to the mortar with the rabbit liver. Pound the breadcrumbs, garlic, egg yolks and liver together until reduced to a paste. Add the olive oil gradually, mixing well after each addition. Pour into a large bowl and stir in the vinegar, water and salt to taste. Add the strips of rabbit meat and the marinade and mix well. Set aside in a cold place until well chilled. Serve in deep soup bowls or cups.

# CREAM OF BEAN SOUP

*Serves 6*

1 lb/450 g dried red beans

½ head garlic

2 medium-sized carrots

1 medium-sized onion

1 leek

1 bay leaf

1¾ pints/1 litre milk

2 oz/50 g butter

pinch nutmeg

2 hard-boiled eggs or sautéed
  croutons for garnishing

Soak the beans in plenty of cold water for 24 hours. Drain before using. Peel the garlic, carrots and onion. Trim the leek and rinse thoroughly under cold running water.

Place the beans, garlic, carrots, onion, leek and bay leaf in a saucepan. Add enough water to cover. Bring to the boil over high heat, then lower the heat, cover tightly and simmer for 2½–3 hours, or until the beans are very soft. Drain well and discard the liquid. Press the beans through a fine sieve to make a very thick purée, and return the purée to the pan. Add the milk, butter and nutmeg and stir thoroughly until well blended. Chop the eggs if used. Reheat the soup and pour into individual soup bowls. Garnish with the chopped eggs or croutons and serve.

# GARLIC SOUP WITH EGGS

*Serves 4*

5 cloves garlic

8 oz/225 g crusty bread

5 tablespoons olive oil

1 teaspoon paprika

2 teaspoons salt

1¾ pints/1 litre boiling water

4 eggs

Peel 4 cloves of the garlic and slice thinly. Cut the bread into 1-inch (2·5-cm) cubes. Heat the oil in a frying pan and sauté the sliced garlic until well browned. Add the bread cubes and sauté over low heat for 3–5 minutes, or until the garlic and bread are very brown. Remove the pan from the heat before the garlic burns. Add the paprika and transfer the contents of the pan to a flameproof casserole. Add the salt and boiling water. Break the eggs into the soup, taking care to keep them whole. Place the casserole over moderate heat and poach the eggs until they are just set. Peel and chop the remaining clove of garlic and sprinkle over the soup. Serve in the casserole.

# RICE AND CRAB SOUP

*Serves 6*

1 lb/450 g *centello* (spider crab) or
  crab meat

1 medium-sized onion

8 oz/225 g tomatoes

5 tablespoons oil

½ teaspoon paprika

2 teaspoons salt

3 pints/1·5 litres boiling water

2 cloves garlic

1 sprig parsley

3 saffron strands

8 oz/225 g long-grain rice

Cut the *centello* or crab meat into ½-inch (1-cm) pieces. Peel and finely chop the onion and tomatoes. Heat the oil in a saucepan and sauté the crab meat until lightly browned. Add the onion and sauté for 5 minutes. Add the tomatoes, paprika, salt and water. Cover and simmer for 45 minutes.

Meanwhile, peel the garlic and pound in a mortar with the parsley. Add the saffron and 2 tablespoons of the simmering stock. Add the rice and the garlic mixture to the saucepan and simmer for 20 minutes. Turn off the heat. Adjust the seasoning if necessary and then leave to rest on the hot stove for 3 minutes. Pour into a soup tureen and serve.

*Salt cod with chilli and tomato sauce*

# SALT COD WITH CHILLI AND TOMATO SAUCE

*Serves 6*

2¼ lb/1 kg dried salt cod
1 lb/450 g tomatoes
2 cloves garlic
plain flour for coating
generous ¼ pint/2 dl olive oil

6 chillies
½ oz/15 g castor sugar
1 oz/25 g blanched almonds
generous ¼ pint/2 dl water
salt

Rinse the dried salt cod under cold running water. Place in a large bowl and cover with water. Set aside for at least 24 hours, changing the water frequently to extract the excess salt.

Peel and chop the tomatoes. Peel the garlic. Drain and rinse the cod. Cut into 2½-inch (6-cm) pieces and coat with flour. Heat the oil in a frying pan and sauté the cod pieces until lightly browned. Drain well and place in a shallow ovenproof dish. Sauté the chillies and the garlic for 2–3 minutes in the oil remaining in the pan, remove with a perforated spoon, drain and set aside. Sauté the tomatoes in the same pan until reduced to a pulp. Stir in the sugar and remove from the heat. Pound the garlic and almonds to a paste in a mortar. Stir in the water. Add to the tomato pulp with the chillies and salt to taste. Pour the tomato mixture over the fish and bake in a moderate oven (350°F, 180°C, Gas Mark 4) for 20 minutes. Serve in the ovenproof dish.

# SALT COD CASSEROLE WITH SWEET PEPPERS

*Serves 6*

2¼ lb/1 kg dried salt cod
  (see note)
8 red sweet peppers
2¼ lb/1 kg onions

2 cloves garlic
5 tablespoons olive oil
1 teaspoon paprika

Rinse the dried salt cod under cold running water. Place in a bowl and cover with cold water. Set aside for at least 24 hours, changing the water frequently.

Remove the seeds from the peppers and cut the flesh into thin rings. Peel the onions and garlic and cut into thin rings. Drain the cod and place in a large saucepan with enough water to cover. Bring to the simmering point over moderate heat. Remove from the heat, drain, remove the bones and cut the fish into small pieces.

Heat the oil in a frying pan and sauté the peppers very gently until soft but not brown. Remove the peppers from the pan and set aside until required. Add the onions and garlic to the oil remaining in the pan and sauté until soft but not brown. Remove the pan from the heat.

Place the cod, peppers and onion and garlic mixture in alternate layers in a casserole. Sprinkle each layer of onion with a little paprika. Cover the casserole and bake in a moderate oven (350°F, 180°C, Gas Mark 4) for about 20 minutes, or until the cod is tender. Serve in the casserole.

*Note:* Use only the thicker, fleshier portions of the cod.

# SEA BREAM IN TOMATO AND WINE SAUCE

*Serves 6*

1 sea bream, about 3½ lb/1·5 kg
2 teaspoons salt
1 tablespoon chopped parsley
2 oz/50 g plain flour
1 large onion
2 cloves garlic
8 oz/225 g tomatoes

1 medium-sized carrot
2 sticks celery
5 tablespoons olive oil
1 tablespoon sugar
5 tablespoons water
5 tablespoons dry white wine

Gut the fish and cut off the head, tail and fins. Scrape the fish very carefully to remove the scales. Rinse under cold running water and dry with kitchen paper. Cut the fish into slices about 2 inches (5 cm) thick. Sprinkle the slices lightly with salt and chopped parsley and coat with the flour. Peel and finely chop the onion, garlic and tomatoes. Peel and grate the carrot. Finely chop the celery.

Heat the oil in a frying pan and fry the fish for 5 minutes on each side. Remove from the pan and place in a flameproof casserole or saucepan. Sauté the onion, garlic, carrot and celery in the oil remaining in the pan for 10–15 minutes, or until soft and lightly browned. Add the tomatoes, sugar and water and simmer for about 10 minutes. Press the mixture through a sieve into a bowl. Stir in the wine and pour the sauce over the fish. Simmer for a further 5 minutes.

Transfer the fish to a heated serving plate and pour the sauce over. Serve with boiled potatoes.

# HAKE IN GREEN SAUCE

*Serves 6*

1 hake head
generous ¼ pint/2 dl water
6 hake cutlets, about
   6 oz/175 g each
plain flour for coating
1 medium-sized onion

5 tablespoons olive oil
2 tablespoons chopped parsley
5 tablespoons dry white wine
1 teaspoon salt
pinch pepper

Place the hake head in a saucepan with the water, bring to the boil and simmer for 10 minutes. Remove and discard the hake head and set the stock aside to cool. Coat the hake cutlets with flour. Peel and chop the onion.

Heat the oil in a flameproof casserole and sauté the onion until it begins to brown. Place the hake cutlets and the parsley in the casserole and sauté gently until the hake is well browned on both sides, turning the casserole constantly in a circular motion (see note). Add the white wine, the reserved fish stock, salt and pepper. Lower the heat and simmer gently for 15–20 minutes, still rotating the casserole at frequent intervals. Serve the hake very hot, preferably in the casserole.

*Note:* This is a classic Basque dish and the secret of its success lies in the preparation. The casserole must be gently revolved so the hake exudes its gelatine which thickens the sauce.

*Sea bream in tomato and wine sauce*

# HAKE WITH STUFFED TOMATOES

*Serves 6*

| | |
|---|---|
| generous ¼ pint/2 dl olive oil | 6 large tomatoes |
| 4 oz/100 g fine fresh breadcrumbs | 2 oz/50 g cheese, grated |
| 5 tablespoons milk | 2 oz/50 g butter |
| 2 oz/50 g pickled or canned tuna fish | 6 slices hake, about 6 oz/175 g each |
| 1 teaspoon chopped parsley | 2 oz/50 g plain flour |
| 1 teaspoon salt | 2 lemons, sliced |
| pinch pepper | |

Heat 2 tablespoons of the oil in a frying pan and sauté the breadcrumbs until crisp and golden brown. Drain on kitchen paper and place in a bowl. Add the milk and set aside for 5 minutes. Add the tuna fish, parsley, salt and pepper and mix well.

Halve the tomatoes and scoop out the pulp and seeds which may be used as required in another dish. Press the breadcrumb mixture into the halved tomatoes. Place in an ovenproof dish, sprinkle with the cheese and place a knob of butter on each tomato half. Bake in a moderately hot oven (375°F, 190°C, Gas Mark 5) for 15–20 minutes.

Meanwhile, coat the hake slices with flour. Heat the remaining oil in a frying pan and fry the hake slices for 4–5 minutes on each side, or until the flesh is tender and white and the outside golden brown. Place the fish on a heated serving plate. Arrange 2 tomato halves on each slice. Garnish the fish with the lemon slices and serve hot with sautéed potatoes.

# JUGGED HAKE

*Serves 4*

| | |
|---|---|
| 1 lb/450 g hake | skin of 1 onion |
| 1 teaspoon salt | 2 oz/50 g fine fresh breadcrumbs |
| pinch pepper | 5 tablespoons water |
| 2 cloves garlic | 3 tablespoons dry white wine |
| 3–4 sprigs parsley | 2 hard-boiled eggs or |
| ¼ teaspoon paprika | 2 canned red pimentos |
| 5 tablespoons olive oil | for garnishing |

Cut the fish into 4 slices and season with the salt and pepper. Finely chop the garlic and parsley. Place the fish in a shallow ovenproof dish and sprinkle with the garlic, parsley and paprika.

Heat the oil in a small saucepan and sauté the onion skin for 3–4 minutes. Discard the onion skin and pour the flavoured oil over the fish. Set aside to marinate for about 4 hours. Sprinkle the breadcrumbs over the fish and pour over the water and wine. Bake in a moderately hot oven (375°F, 190°C, Gas Mark 5) for 20 minutes.

To garnish the dish, either very finely chop the hard-boiled eggs and sprinkle them over the surface, or cut the pimentos into thin strips and arrange on the top.

# FISH IN ROMESCO SAUCE

*Serves 4*

| | |
|---|---|
| 2¼ lb/1 kg halibut, turbot or hake | scant ½ pint/2·5 dl olive oil |
| **for the romesco sauce:** | 3 cloves garlic |
| 1 red sweet pepper | 2 oz/50 g ground almonds |
| 1 chilli | 1 bay leaf, crushed |
| 1 thick slice bread | 6 tablespoons water |

Cut the fish into 4 pieces. Remove the seeds and chop the red sweet pepper and the chilli. Cut off and discard the crusts from the bread. Cut the bread into ½-inch (1-cm) cubes. Heat the oil in a frying pan and sauté the red pepper, chilli and bread cubes for 5–10 minutes.

Meanwhile, peel the garlic and place in a mortar with the ground almonds and bay leaf. Pound with a pestle until well blended. Add the red pepper, chilli and bread cubes and continue pounding until reduced to a paste. Stir in the water.

Heat the oil remaining in the pan and add the pounded mixture. Cover and simmer for 2 minutes. Add the fish, replace the lid and cook for 15–20 minutes, or until the flesh of the fish is tender and white. Transfer to a heated serving dish and serve.

# BASQUE PAELLA

*Serves 6*

| | |
|---|---|
| 1 lb/450 g white fish (cod or haddock) | ¼ pint/1·5 dl olive oil |
| 1 lb/450 g squid | 4 oz/100 g fresh or frozen prawns, peeled and deveined |
| 8 oz/225 g cooked cockles or mussels | 6 fresh or frozen scampi, peeled and deveined |
| 1 medium-sized onion | 1 pint/6 dl water |
| 4 oz/100 g tomatoes | 10 oz/275 g long-grain rice |
| 1 clove garlic | 4 oz/100 g fresh or frozen shelled peas |
| 1 green or red sweet pepper | 2 teaspoons salt |
| 1 sprig parsley | |
| few saffron strands | |

Gut the fish, wash and cut into pieces. Clean the squid, remove and discard the ink sacs and intestines and cut into pieces. Rinse the cockles or mussels under cold running water. Peel and finely chop the onion and tomatoes. Peel the garlic. Remove the seeds from the sweet pepper and finely chop the flesh. Pound the garlic, parsley and saffron together in a mortar.

Heat the oil in a *paella* pan, or in a large frying pan, and sauté the onion and sweet pepper until lightly browned. Add the tomatoes and sauté for 2 minutes. Add the fish and squid and cook for a further 5 minutes. Add the prawns, scampi and cockles, and cook for a further 5 minutes. Add the garlic, parsley, the saffron mixture and the water and bring to the boil. Add the rice, peas and salt, cover tightly and cook for 5 minutes over high heat. Lower the heat and simmer gently for 15 minutes, or until the rice is just cooked. Remove from the heat and set aside for 5 minutes before serving.

# SOLE FILLETS WITH MUSHROOM AND PRAWN SAUCE

*Serves 4*

| | |
|---|---|
| 2 sole, about 1¼ lb/600 g each | generous ¾ pint/5 dl water |
| 2 oz/50 g melted butter | 1 medium-sized onion |
| 1 teaspoon salt | 2 medium-sized carrots |
| **for the sauce:** | 4 oz/100 g fresh or frozen prawns, |
| 2 quarts/2·25 litres mussels |    peeled and deveined |
| 8 oz/225 g button mushrooms | 5 tablespoons dry white wine |
| 5 oz/150 g butter | 1 oz/25 g plain flour |
| 1 slice lemon | 2 egg yolks |
| salt | 2–3 sprigs parsley |

Skin the fish and fillet each one into 4 pieces (see note). Reserve the skin and bones. Brush the fillets well with the melted butter and sprinkle with the salt. Place in a buttered, shallow ovenproof dish and bake in a moderately hot oven (375°F, 190°C, Gas Mark 5) for 20–25 minutes, or until the fish is tender and white.

To prepare the sauce, scrub the mussels under cold running water and remove the beards. Place in a large saucepan and add enough water to cover the bottom of the pan. Cover with a tightly fitting lid, place over moderate heat and steam the mussels for 5–10 minutes, or until the shells open. Discard any that do not open. Take the mussels out of the shells and set aside until required. Discard the shells. Rinse the mushrooms under cold running water, drain and slice thinly. Place in a saucepan with enough water to cover and add half the butter, the lemon slice and a pinch of salt. Bring to the boil over moderate heat, then lower the heat and simmer the mushrooms for 5–10 minutes, or until tender. Drain well, discard the lemon slice and set the mushrooms aside until required.

Place the reserved fish skins and bones in a saucepan and add the water. Bring to the boil over moderate heat, then reduce the heat and simmer for 5–10 minutes. Strain the fish stock through a sieve into a clean saucepan and discard the skin and bones. Peel and finely chop the onion and carrots. Add both to the fish stock with the mussels, mushrooms, prawns, white wine and a pinch of salt. Place over moderate heat and bring to the boil. Lower the heat and boil gently for 20 minutes.

Meanwhile, melt the remaining butter in a saucepan and stir in the flour. Cook gently for 2–3 minutes, stirring constantly. Remove from the heat. Blend the egg yolks with a little of the fish stock and gradually add to the flour and butter mixture, stirring thoroughly after each addition. Pour into the fish stock and bring to the boil, stirring constantly until the stock thickens, making a thick sauce. Lower the heat and simmer for 5 minutes. Spoon the sauce over the sole fillets, garnish with the parsley and serve.

*Note:* To fillet the fish, lay it on a board, dark skin uppermost, and cut off the fins. Cut down the backbone from head to tail. Then make a semi-circular cut, just below the head, through half the thickness of the fish. With short sharp strokes separate the left fillet from the backbone. Cut away above the tail. Repeat with the right fillet, turn the fish over and remove the fillets on the other side.

*Sole fillets with mushroom and prawn sauce*

# RICE MOULD WITH SQUID

*Serves 6*

| | |
|---|---|
| 2¼ lb/1 kg squid | 1 tablespoon chopped parsley |
| 1 large onion | **for the rice mould:** |
| 5 tablespoons olive oil | 1 small onion |
| ¼ pint/1·5 dl dry white wine | 3 tablespoons olive oil |
| 5 tablespoons water | 1 bay leaf |
| 1 tablespoon fine fresh | 1 lb/450 g long-grain rice |
|   breadcrumbs | 2 teaspoons salt |
| 3 teaspoons salt | 1¼ pints/7·5 dl water |

Remove the ink sacs from the squid and set aside until required. Discard the intestines and bones. Cut the squid into thick rings. Peel and chop the onion. Heat the oil in a frying pan and sauté the onion until soft and lightly browned. Add the squid and sauté for 5 minutes. Pound the reserved ink sacs in a mortar. Add to the squid with the wine, water, breadcrumbs, salt and parsley. Bring to the boil, then lower the heat and simmer for 10–15 minutes.

To prepare the rice mould, peel and chop the onion. Heat the oil and bay leaf in a saucepan and sauté the onion until lightly browned. Add the rice, salt and water. Bring to the boil, then lower the heat and simmer, uncovered, for 20 minutes. The rice should be dry and fluffy at the end of the cooking time. Press the rice into a buttered 9-inch (23-cm) ring mould. Set aside for 2–3 minutes, then turn out on to a plate. Spoon the squid and the sauce into the centre of the rice mould. Serve hot.

# STUFFED SQUID

*Serves 4*

| | |
|---|---|
| 2¼ lb/1 kg small squid | 1 tablespoon chopped parsley |
| 1 medium-sized onion | 1 tablespoon concentrated tomato |
| 1 clove garlic |   purée |
| 3 medium-sized tomatoes | 1 oz/25 g fine fresh breadcrumbs |
| 2 hard-boiled eggs | plain flour for coating |
| ¼ pint/1·5 dl olive oil | 5 tablespoons dry white wine |

Remove the ink sacs from the squid and set aside until required. Discard the intestines and bones. Cut off the tentacles and chop coarsely. Peel and chop the onion, garlic and tomatoes. Shell and chop the eggs.

Heat one-third of the oil in a frying pan and sauté half the onion, the garlic and the parsley for 5 minutes. Add the chopped squid and sauté for a further 5 minutes. Remove from the heat and mix in the chopped egg, tomato purée and breadcrumbs. Stuff the squid with this mixture and close the openings with cocktail sticks. Coat with flour.

Heat the remaining oil in a frying pan and sauté the squid for 15 minutes. Transfer to a casserole. Add the remaining onion and the tomatoes to the hot oil in the pan and sauté for 5 minutes. Stir in the white wine and pour the mixture over the squid. Bake in a moderate oven (350°F, 180°C, Gas Mark 4) for 30–40 minutes. Strain the ink through a sieve and add to the squid. Bake for a further 5 minutes. Serve hot with fried croutons.

*Breaded sardines*

# SARDINE PIE

*Serves 4*

| **for the pastry:** | 2 medium-sized onions |
| 4 oz/100 g cornflour | 8 oz/225 g tomatoes |
| 6 oz/175 g plain flour | 4 canned red pimentos |
| 4 oz/100 g lard | 4 tablespoons olive oil |
| 1 egg | 1 tablespoon chopped parsley |
| about 5 tablespoons water | ½ teaspoon salt |
| **for the filling:** | **for the glaze:** |
| 1 lb/450 g fresh sardines | 1 egg |
| 1 oz/25 g plain flour | |

To make the pastry, sift the cornflour and flour into a mixing bowl. Cut the lard into small pieces and add. Using the fingertips, rub the lard into the dry ingredients until evenly distributed. Make a well in the centre and add the egg and the water. Mix to a soft dough and knead lightly until smooth. Cover and set aside for 30 minutes.

Meanwhile, make the filling. Gut the sardines, cut off the heads and scrape the fish gently to remove the scales. Rinse under cold running water, dry well with kitchen paper and coat with flour. Peel and chop the onions and tomatoes.

Drain the canned pimentos. Heat half the oil in a frying pan and fry the sardines for 2–3 minutes on each side. Drain well on kitchen paper. Heat the remaining oil in the pan and sauté the onions, tomatoes, pimentos and parsley for about 5–10 minutes, or until the onions are soft but not brown. Remove from the heat and stir in the salt. Mix the sardines with the sautéed mixture and set aside to cool.

Divide the dough in half. Roll out one half into a 9-inch (23-cm) circle and place on a well-buttered baking tray. Spread the fish mixture over the circle to within 1 inch (2·5 cm) of the edge. Brush the edge of the pastry with water. Roll out the remaining dough into a circle slightly larger than the base and place over the fish filling. Press the edges of the pie firmly together, completely enclosing the filling. Flute the edges of the pastry and make a small hole in the top to allow the steam to escape during cooking. Whisk the egg and brush over the pie to glaze the surface. Bake in a moderately hot oven (400°F, 200°C, Gas Mark 6) for 30–40 minutes, or until golden brown. Serve hot or cold and cut into slices at the table.

# BREADED SARDINES

*Serves 4*

| | |
|---|---|
| 2¼ lb/1 kg fresh sardines | 2–3 oz/50–75 g fine fresh |
| 2 cloves garlic | breadcrumbs |
| 1 tablespoon chopped parsley | generous ¼ pint/2 dl olive oil |
| | 2 lemons, sliced |

Scrape the sardines to remove the scales and then gut them. Cut off the heads and remove the backbones. Peel and chop the garlic. Mix together the garlic, parsley and breadcrumbs.

Brush the sardines with some of the olive oil and then coat with the breadcrumb mixture. Pour the remaining oil into an ovenproof dish and arrange the sardines in the dish. Bake in a moderate oven (350°F, 180°C, Gas Mark 4) for 15–20 minutes, or until the sardines are cooked and the breadcrumbs are crisp. Garnish the sardines with the lemon slices and serve hot.

# TUNA FISH WITH TOMATOES

*Serves 6*

| | |
|---|---|
| 6 fresh tuna steaks, about 6–8 oz/ 175–225 g each | 2 tablespoons chopped parsley |
| 3 medium-sized onions | 3 teaspoons salt |
| 2 cloves garlic | 1 teaspoon castor sugar |
| 2¼ lb/1 kg tomatoes | 1 sprig fresh peppermint or ¼ teaspoon dried peppermint |

Wipe the tuna steaks with a damp cloth. Peel and chop the onions, garlic and tomatoes.

Heat the oil in a flameproof casserole or a deep frying pan and sauté the tuna steaks for about 5 minutes on each side, or until golden brown. Drain on kitchen paper. Sauté the onion and garlic in the oil remaining in the casserole or frying pan until lightly browned. Return the tuna steaks to the casserole and reheat for 2 minutes. Add the tomatoes, parsley, salt, sugar and peppermint, cover tightly and cook over very low heat for 20–30 minutes. Draw the pan to the side of the heat and let stand for about 15 minutes before serving.

# MARINATED BONITO WITH MIXED VEGETABLES

*Serves 6*

| | |
|---|---|
| 2 lb/1 kg bonito or tuna fish | scant ½ pint/2·5 dl white wine |
| 1 small onion | 2 lb/1 kg fresh peas |
| 2 medium-sized carrots | 1 small cauliflower |
| 2 cloves garlic | plain flour for coating |
| 6 black peppercorns | oil for shallow-frying |
| 2 tablespoons olive oil | 6 thick slices bread |
| 2 tablespoons vinegar | 3 oz/75 g butter |
| 1 lb/450 g shallots | |

Cut the fish into 6 slices and place in a bowl. Peel and chop the onion, carrots and garlic and sprinkle over the fish. Add the peppercorns, oil and vinegar, and set aside to marinate for 24 hours.

Peel the shallots and place in a saucepan with the white wine. Bring to the boil over moderate heat, then lower the heat, cover the pan tightly and simmer for 20–25 minutes, or until tender. Shell the peas and cook in lightly salted boiling water for 8–10 minutes, or until tender. Break the cauliflower into florets and rinse well under cold running water. Cook in lightly salted boiling water for about 10 minutes, or until tender.

Meanwhile, remove the slices of fish from the marinade and coat them with flour. Sauté in hot oil for about 4–5 minutes on each side, until cooked and golden brown. Drain on kitchen paper and keep hot. Fry the slices of bread in the same pan until crisp and golden brown. Drain well and place in the centre of a large heated serving dish. Arrange the slices of fish around the bread.

Drain the shallots, peas and cauliflower. Toss the peas in half the butter and the cauliflower in the remainder. Spoon the vegetables over the fried bread and serve.

# FISH AND VEGETABLE STEW

*Serves 6*

| | |
|---|---|
| 2 lb/1 kg bonito or tuna fish | 5 tablespoons olive oil |
| 1 leek | 4 oz/100 g tomatoes |
| 1 medium-sized carrot | 2 tablespoons dried sweet pepper flakes |
| 4 sticks celery | 2¼ lb/1 kg potatoes |
| 2 teaspoons salt | 2 sprigs mint |
| 2 pints/generous litre water | pinch paprika |
| 1 clove garlic | 5 tablespoons dry white wine |
| 1 medium-sized onion | |
| 1 green sweet pepper | |

Rinse the fish under cold running water. Dry with kitchen paper and cut into 2-inch (5-cm) pieces. Trim the leek and rinse under cold running water. Peel the carrot. Place the leek, carrot and celery in a large saucepan. Add the salt and water and bring to the boil over high heat. Lower the heat, cover and simmer for 15–20 minutes. Strain and reserve the stock, discarding the vegetables.

Meanwhile, peel and chop the garlic and onion. Remove the seeds from the sweet pepper and chop the flesh. Heat half the oil in a frying pan and sauté the garlic, onion and sweet pepper for about 10 minutes, or until soft. Remove from the heat and set aside until required. Peel and chop the tomatoes. Heat the remaining oil in a flameproof casserole or a large saucepan and add the tomatoes, pepper flakes and the sautéed vegetables. Sauté gently for 10 minutes, stirring frequently, to make a thick tomato sauce.

Peel the potatoes and cut into thick slices. Place the fish in the casserole, submerging the pieces in the sauce, and cover with the potato slices. Add the mint, paprika, white wine and reserved stock, covering the potatoes completely. Bring to the boil, then lower the heat and simmer for 30 minutes. Serve hot in the casserole.

# PEASANT'S SALAD WITH VINEGAR DRESSING

*Serves 4*

| | for the vinegar dressing: |
|---|---|
| 1 red sweet pepper | 3 canned red pimentos |
| 2 hard-boiled eggs | 2 hard-boiled eggs |
| 1 medium-sized onion | 2 tablespoons olive oil |
| 8 oz/225 g tomatoes | 5 tablespoons wine vinegar |
| 8 oz/225 g cooked French beans | 2 tablespoons finely chopped onion |
| 8 oz/225 g canned tuna fish | |
| 4 oz/100 g black olives | 1 oz/25 g capers |
| 4 cooked artichoke hearts | 1 tablespoon chopped parsley |
| 8 oz/225 g cooked asparagus | salt |

Bake the pepper in a moderately hot oven (400°F, 200°C, Gas Mark 6) for 10–15 minutes, or until the skin is charred. Peel the pepper, remove the seeds and cut into rings. Shell the eggs and cut into slices. Peel and thinly slice the onion and tomatoes. Cut the French beans into 1½-inch (3·5-cm) lengths. In a large bowl, mix together the pepper, eggs, onion, tomatoes, beans, tuna fish, olives, artichoke hearts and asparagus.

To make the vinegar dressing, finely chop the canned pimentos. Separate the egg whites from the yolks. Chop the egg whites and add to the salad. Pound the yolks to a paste. Mix together the oil and the vinegar and add to the egg yolks very gradually, beating well after each addition, until the mixture thickens slightly. Stir in the pimentos, chopped onion, capers, parsley and salt to taste.

Pour the vinegar dressing over the salad and serve.

# SUMMER SALAD

*Serves 4*

| | |
|---|---|
| 2 large beetroot | ¼ teaspoon freshly ground white pepper |
| 2 large potatoes | |
| 8 oz/225 g dried salt cod | 2 tablespoons vinegar |
| 4 oz/100 g shallots | ¼ pint/1·5 dl olive oil |
| 1 clove garlic | 5 tablespoons water |
| 2 medium-sized tomatoes | 4 hard-boiled eggs |
| 1 tablespoon chopped parsley | 4 oz/100 g black olives |

Rinse the beetroot and potatoes thoroughly under cold running water. Cook the beetroot in boiling water for about 1 hour, or until tender. Drain and peel. Cook the potatoes in boiling water for about 20–25 minutes. Drain and peel. Slice the beetroot and potatoes into rounds about ¼–½ inch (5 mm–1 cm) thick and place in a deep salad bowl.

Place the cod in a roasting tin and bake in a moderately hot oven (400°F, 200°C, Gas Mark 6) for 15–20 minutes. When the cod is cool enough to handle, remove the bones. Flake the fish and place in a bowl under cold running water to remove the salt.

Meanwhile, peel and finely chop the shallots and garlic. Peel and chop the tomatoes. Mix together the shallots, garlic, tomatoes, parsley, pepper, vinegar, oil and water and beat well. Shell and slice the eggs.

Drain the cod thoroughly, place in the bowl with the beetroot and potatoes and sprinkle with the tomato mixture. Toss lightly. Garnish the salad with slices of egg and the black olives. Serve well chilled.

# LAMB'S PLUCK WITH EGGS

*Serves 4*

| | |
|---|---|
| 1–2 lambs' plucks (liver, heart and lungs), about 1 lb/450 g | ½ oz/15 g plain flour |
| | scant ½ pint/2·5 dl dry white wine |
| 1 medium-sized onion | 1 teaspoon salt |
| 3 cloves garlic | pinch pepper |
| ¼ pint/1·5 dl olive oil | pinch nutmeg |
| 1 sprig parsley | 8 eggs |
| 1 bay leaf | |

Cut away any gristle and membrane from the lambs' plucks and dice finely. Peel and chop the onion and garlic.

Heat the oil in a frying pan and sauté the onion, garlic, parsley and bay leaf until the onion is soft but not brown. Remove from the pan and drain on kitchen paper. Sauté the lambs' plucks in the oil remaining in the pan until lightly browned and tender. Stir in the flour. Add the wine, salt, pepper and nutmeg and simmer for 5 minutes. Stir in the onion, garlic and parsley. Discard the bay leaf. Transfer the mixture to a shallow ovenproof dish. Lightly whisk the eggs and pour over the lambs' plucks. Bake in a moderately hot oven (375°F, 190°C, Gas Mark 5) for 6–10 minutes, or until the egg has set. Serve immediately.

# CASSEROLE OF LAMBS' TONGUES

*Serves 6*

| | |
|---|---|
| 6 lambs' tongues | 1 leek |
| 3 teaspoons salt | 1 stick celery |
| 6 oz/175 g vegetable marrow | 3 sprigs parsley |
| 1 small onion | 1 sprig thyme |
| 2 cloves garlic | 5 tablespoons olive oil |
| 1 large carrot | 5 tablespoons white wine |
| 2 medium-sized tomatoes | 2 oz/50 g melted lard |
| 1 medium-sized potato | 2 oz/50 g fine fresh breadcrumbs |

Rinse the lambs' tongues thoroughly under cold running water and place in a saucepan. Add 1 teaspoon of the salt and enough water to cover. Bring to the boil over moderate heat, then lower the heat, cover tightly and simmer for about 1½ hours, or until tender.

Meanwhile, peel the marrow, onion, garlic, carrot, tomatoes and potato and slice thinly. Trim the leek, rinse thoroughly under cold running water and slice into rings. Chop the celery. Place all the prepared vegetables in a large flameproof casserole or saucepan with the parsley and the remaining salt.

Drain the tongues and, while still warm, remove the skins. Place the tongues on top of the vegetables and sprinkle with the oil. Sauté very gently over moderate heat, stirring the ingredients occasionally, until the tongues are lightly browned on all sides and the vegetables are almost tender. Add the white wine, cover and simmer for 20 minutes.

Remove the tongues from the casserole or saucepan and drain well. Brush with the melted lard and coat with the breadcrumbs. Place in a roasting tin and cook in a very hot oven (425°F, 240°C, Gas Mark 9) for 5 minutes.

Place the tongues in the centre of a heated serving dish. Drain the vegetables, place around the edge as a garnish and serve.

# MADRID COCIDO

*Serves 6*

| | |
|---|---|
| 8 oz/225 g chick peas | 1–2 teaspoons salt |
| 3½ pints/2 litres water | 3 medium-sized potatoes |
| 1 lb/450 g brisket of beef | 1 large cabbage, about 2 lb/1 kg |
| 4 oz/100 g lean bacon, in 1 piece | 6 oz/150 g *chorizo* or garlic |
| 1 small boiling chicken, about |    sausage |
|    1–2 lb/450 g–1 kg | 1 *butifarra* (black pudding) |
| 1 onion | 2 tablespoons olive oil |
| 1 leek | 8 oz/225 g fine egg noodles |
| 1 carrot | |

Cover the chick peas with cold water and set aside to soak overnight. Drain well. Pour the water into a large saucepan, place over high heat and bring to the boil. Add the chick peas, beef, bacon and chicken. Bring back to the boil and skim the surface.

Meanwhile, peel the onion. Trim the leek and wash thoroughly under cold running water. Peel the carrot and cut into slices. Add the onion, leek, carrot and salt to the pan. Cover tightly, lower the heat and simmer for 3 hours.

While the *cocido* is cooking, peel and cut the potatoes into even-sized pieces. Set aside in cold water to cover. Discard the coarse outer leaves of the cabbage, cut in half and cut away the hard centre core. Shred the cabbage and wash well in salted water.

About 20 minutes before the end of the cooking time, add the potatoes to the *cocido*. In a separate saucepan, cook the cabbage, *chorizo* and *butifarra* in boiling salted water for 15 minutes, or until the cabbage is tender. Using a perforated spoon, lift out the sausages and keep hot. Drain the cabbage and return it to the pan with the olive oil. Reheat gently when required.

Draw the cooked *cocido* off the heat, remove the beef, bacon and chicken and, using a perforated spoon, lift out the chick peas and vegetables. Add the fine egg noodles to the hot stock, replace the pan over the heat and simmer for a further 10 minutes. Cut the sausages, beef, bacon and chicken into slices.

Place a mound of the cooked chick peas in the centre of a large serving dish. Arrange the sausage, meat and chicken slices around the edge of the dish. Pile the cooked vegetables at each end. Keep hot. Serve the reheated cabbage separately.

Pour the hot stock and noodles into a soup tureen and serve as the first course followed by the dish of meats and vegetables and the cabbage as the main course.

*Some ingredients for a typical cocido (boiled dinner)*

# COUNTRY LAMB STEW

*Serves 8–10*

| | |
|---|---|
| 4 lb/1·75 kg boned lamb, cut from the shoulder or leg | 3½ pints/2 litres water |
| 6 cloves garlic | 1 lamb's liver |
| ½ pint/3 dl olive oil | 2 oz/50 g fine fresh breadcrumbs |
| 4 teaspoons salt | 1 chilli |
| ½ teaspoon pepper | 5 tablespoons water |
| | 2 tablespoons wine vinegar |

Chop the lamb into 2½-inch (6-cm) pieces. Peel and chop the garlic. Heat three-quarters of the oil in a large casserole or saucepan. Add the lamb and garlic and sauté for about 15 minutes, or until golden brown. Sprinkle with the salt and pepper and add the 3½ pints (2 litres) water. Bring to the boil, then lower the heat, cover tightly and simmer the lamb for about 30–40 minutes, or until tender.

Meanwhile, thickly slice the liver. Heat the remaining oil in a frying pan and fry the liver until lightly browned but still soft in the centre. Remove from the pan and drain well on kitchen paper. Sauté the breadcrumbs in the oil remaining in the pan until very lightly browned. Remove from the pan and drain on kitchen paper.

Remove the seeds from the chilli and chop the flesh very finely. Pound the liver, breadcrumbs and chilli in a mortar until reduced to a paste. Add the 5 tablespoons water and the wine vinegar and stir the mixture into the simmering lamb about 5–10 minutes before the end of the cooking time. Transfer to a heated serving dish and serve.

# CASSEROLED VEAL CUTLETS WITH WINE

*Serves 6*

| | |
|---|---|
| 6 veal neck cutlets, about 6 oz/175 g each | 2 large potatoes |
| 2 teaspoons salt | 5 tablespoons olive oil |
| 2 oz/50 g plain flour | ¼ pint/1·5 dl dry white wine |
| 2¼ lb/1 kg shallots | 4 tablespoons water |
| | 1 tablespoon chopped parsley |

Season the cutlets with salt and coat with flour. Peel the shallots and potatoes. Cut the potatoes into strips similar in size to the shallots. Cover the potatoes with cold water until required.

Heat the oil in a frying pan and sauté the cutlets for about 5 minutes on each side, or until well browned. Transfer to a casserole and add the white wine and water. Cover and place in a moderately hot oven (375°F, 190°C, Gas Mark 5) for 15 minutes.

Meanwhile, drain and dry the potatoes. Sauté the shallots and potatoes in the oil remaining in the pan for 5–10 minutes, or until browned on all sides. Add to the casserole and cook for a further 15–20 minutes, or until the meat, shallots and potatoes are tender.

Sprinkle with the chopped parsley and serve in the casserole.

*Veal and ham rolls with orange sauce*

# VEAL AND HAM ROLLS WITH ORANGE SAUCE

*Serves 4*

| | |
|---|---|
| 4 veal escalopes, about 4 oz/ 100 g each | 6 tablespoons milk |
| 4 slices *serrano* or York ham, about 2 oz/50 g each | 1 oz/25 g butter |
| 1 teaspoon salt | pinch nutmeg |
| ¼ teaspoon pepper | thinly pared rind of ½ orange |
| 1 beaten egg | **for the sauce:** |
| 2 oz/50 g fine dried breadcrumbs | 1 small onion |
| 5 tablespoons olive oil | 2 teaspoons cornflour |
| 2 lb/1 kg potatoes | 6 tablespoons fresh orange juice |
| | ½ teaspoon grated orange rind |
| | 5 tablespoons dry sherry |

If the veal escalopes are too thick to roll up, flatten them with a meat mallet. They should be the same size as the slices of ham. Place one slice of ham on each veal escalope. Roll up with the veal on the outside and secure with cocktail sticks. Sprinkle with salt and pepper and coat with the beaten egg and the breadcrumbs.

Heat the oil in a frying pan and sauté the veal rolls for 10–15 minutes, or until tender and golden brown. Drain on kitchen paper, place in  heated serving dish and keep hot.

Peel the potatoes and cut into small pieces. Cook in lightly salted boiling water until tender. Drain well and mash very thoroughly with the milk, butter and nutmeg.

While the potatoes are cooking, prepare the sauce. Peel and finely chop the onion. Reheat the oil remaining in the pan and sauté the onion until lightly browned. Stir in the cornflour and cook for 1 minute. Add the orange juice, grated orange rind and sherry, a little at a time, stirring thoroughly after each addition. Bring to the boil, stirring constantly, and simmer very gently for 5–10 minutes.

Pour the orange sauce over the veal and ham rolls, garnish with the mashed potato and the pared orange rind and serve.

# HAM WITH MÁLAGA SAUCE

*Serves 4*

| | |
|---|---|
| 3 oz/75 g butter | 4 slices *serrano* or York ham, about 4 oz/100 g each |
| generous ¼ pint/2 dl Málaga wine or port | |

Melt the butter in a heavy frying pan. Add the wine and simmer gently for 10 minutes. Place the slices of *serrano* ham in the pan and simmer for 8–10 minutes, or until the wine has reduced to about a quarter of the original quantity. Transfer to a heated serving dish and serve immediately with sautéed potatoes as an accompaniment.

*Note:* Málaga wine is strong and sweet, similar to the wine of Oporto. It combines with the ham to make a dish with a unique, sophisticated taste.

*The following three recipes may be adapted and varied according to ingredients available.* Morcilla *may be substituted for* butifarra, *salt pork for bacon, etc.*

# ASTURIAN FABADA

*Serves 6*

| | |
|---|---|
| 1 lb/450 g haricot beans | 1 *chorizo* or garlic sausage |
| 4 oz/100 g salt pork, in 1 piece | 2 *morcillas* (see note) |
| generous 2½ pints/1·5 litres water | 4 oz/100 g back bacon, in 1 piece |
| 10 saffron strands or ¼ teaspoon ground saffron | 4 oz/100 g *serrano* or York ham |
| | salt |

Soak the beans overnight in plenty of cold water. Soak the piece of salt pork separately for about 1 hour in cold water. Drain the beans and pork well before using.

Place the beans and salt pork in a flameproof casserole and add the water to completely cover the beans. Place over moderate heat and bring to the boil. Lower the heat immediately and simmer gently for about 1 hour.

Meanwhile, if using saffron strands, pound them to a powder in a mortar. When the beans have been cooking for 1 hour, add the *chorizo, morcillas*, bacon, *serrano* ham and saffron. Do not cover the casserole. Cook very gently for 2–3 hours without stirring. The beans should absorb all the liquid and be tender, but unbroken.

Just before the end of the cooking sprinkle lightly with salt to taste and serve from the casserole.

*Note:* Morcilla is a pork sausage made with blood similar to a black pudding.

# SAUSAGE AND BEAN CASSEROLE

*Serves 4*

| | |
|---|---|
| 4½ lb/2 kg broad beans | 2 teaspoons salt |
| 4 oz/100 g streaky bacon | 5 tablespoons dry white wine |
| 1 medium-sized onion | 4 oz/100 g *butifarra* (black pudding) |
| 3 cloves garlic | |
| 1 large tomato | 1 tablespoon chopped parsley |
| 1 oz/25 g lard | 1 bay leaf |
| 3–4 sprigs mint | |

Shell the beans. Cut the bacon into small pieces. Peel and chop the onion, garlic and tomato. Heat the lard in a large saucepan and fry the bacon for 3–4 minutes. Add the onion and sauté until lightly browned. Add the tomato, mint sprigs, salt and beans and sauté for 10 minutes, stirring frequently. Add the wine, the whole *butifarra*, garlic, parsley and bay leaf. Cover tightly and simmer for about 15 minutes, or until the beans are tender. Transfer to a heated dish and serve.

*Sausage and bean casserole*

# SIMMERED PORK AND BEANS

*Serves 4*

| | |
|---|---|
| 1 lb/450 g haricot beans | 4 oz/100 g back bacon, in 1 piece |
| 2 medium-sized onions | 4 oz/100 g bacon hock |
| 1 head garlic | 2 teaspoons salt |
| 4 oz/100 g pig's cheek | 3 saffron strands |
| 1 pig's trotter | |

Soak the beans overnight in plenty of cold water. Drain before using. Peel the onions and cut into quarters. Peel the garlic.

Place the beans in a large saucepan with the onion, garlic, pig's cheek, pig's trotter, back bacon, bacon hock, salt and saffron. Add enough water to completely cover the ingredients. Place over moderate heat and bring to the boil. Lower the heat, cover tightly and simmer for 2½–3 hours, or until the beans are very soft and the liquid has almost completely evaporated. Do not stir during the cooking as this will break the beans. Serve hot.

# MINCED PORK PIE

*Serves 6*

| **for the pastry:** | **for the filling:** |
|---|---|
| 1 lb/450 g plain flour | 1 medium-sized onion |
| 1 teaspoon salt | 4 oz/100 g ham |
| 5 tablespoons olive oil | 2 oz/50 g lard |
| 5 tablespoons dry white wine | 14 oz/400 g lean pork, minced |
| generous pinch cinnamon | 2 eggs |
| 5 tablespoons milk | **for the glaze:** |
| 1 oz/25 g castor sugar | 1 beaten egg |

To make the dough, sift the flour and salt into a mixing bowl and make a well in the centre. Mix together the olive oil, wine, cinnamon, milk and sugar and pour into the flour. Mix to a fairly firm dough and knead well until smooth. Cover with a damp cloth and set aside for about 1 hour.

To make the filling, peel and chop the onion. Chop the ham. Melt the lard in a frying pan over moderate heat and sauté the onion until soft and lightly brown. Add the ham and the minced pork and sauté gently for about 15–20 minutes, or until tender. Whisk the eggs and stir them into the meat mixture. Continue stirring until the egg sets, then remove from the heat immediately.

Divide the dough in half. Roll out one half into a 10-inch (26-cm) circle and place on a well-buttered baking tray. Spread the prepared meat filling over the circle to within 1 inch (2·5 cm) of the edge. Brush the edge of the pastry with water. Roll out the remaining dough into a circle slightly larger than the base and place over the meat filling. Press the edges of the pastry firmly together, completely enclosing the filling. Flute the edge of the pie and make a small hole in the top to allow the steam to escape during cooking. Brush well with the beaten egg to glaze the surface. Bake in a moderately hot oven (375°F, 190°C, Gas Mark 5) for 30–40 minutes, or until golden brown. Serve hot or cold, cut into slices.

# VALENCIA PAELLA

*Serves 6*

| | |
|---|---|
| 1 chicken, about 3 lb/1·5 kg | 1¾ pints/1 litre water |
| 3 teaspoons salt | 1 teaspoon paprika |
| 2 lb/1 kg fresh peas | 3 saffron strands |
| 8 oz/225 g French beans | 12 cooked snails |
| 1 clove garlic | 1 lb/450 g long-grain rice |
| 1 medium-sized tomato | 1 lemon, cut in wedges |
| 5 tablespoons olive oil | |

Cut the chicken into 14 or 16 pieces and sprinkle with the salt. Shell the peas. Trim the beans and cut into 2½-inch (6-cm) pieces. Peel and finely chop the garlic and tomato. Heat the oil in a *paella* pan or in a large heavy frying pan. Sauté the chicken pieces for 5 minutes, then add the garlic and tomato and sauté for 2 minutes. Add the peas and beans and sauté for 2 minutes. Add the water and paprika and bring to the boil. Add the saffron strands and the snails. Lower the heat and simmer for 20 minutes. Add enough boiling water to replace the amount that has evaporated. Raise the heat until the water is boiling rapidly and then stir in the rice. Boil for 2 minutes, then lower the heat and simmer gently for about 12–15 minutes, or until the rice is tender and dry. Remove from the heat, but leave on the hot stove for 5 minutes. Garnish with the wedges of lemon and serve from the *paella* pan.

# SAUTÉED CHICKEN WITH SWEET PEPPERS AND TOMATOES

*Serves 6*

| | |
|---|---|
| 1 chicken, about 3½ lb/1·5 kg | 8 oz/225 g *serrano* or York ham |
| 1 medium-sized onion | generous ¼ pint/2 dl olive oil |
| 2 cloves garlic | 3 teaspoons salt |
| 2¼ lb/1 kg red sweet peppers | 1 sprig parsley |
| 2¼ lb/1 kg tomatoes | |

Divide the chicken into 6 portions. Peel and finely chop the onion and garlic. Halve the peppers, remove the seeds and cut each pepper into 4 or 6 pieces. Peel and chop the tomatoes. Chop the ham.

Heat the oil in a flameproof casserole or saucepan. Sauté the chicken portions until well browned. Add the onion and half the garlic. Sauté until the onion is well browned and soft. Add the peppers and ham and sauté for 5 minutes. Add the tomatoes and salt. Cover tightly and cook very gently for 20–25 minutes, or until the chicken is tender.

Pound the remaining garlic with the parsley in a mortar and then mix in 1 tablespoon cold water. Stir this mixture into the casserole 10 minutes before the end of the cooking time.

Transfer to a heated serving dish and serve.

# FRIED CHICKEN WITH MELON SALAD

*Serves 6*

| | |
|---|---|
| 1 chicken, about 3 lb/1·5 kg | 1 lb/450 g eating apples |
| salt | 4 oz/100 g shelled walnut halves |
| 6 cloves garlic | 1 teaspoon finely grated lemon |
| ¼ pint/1·5 dl olive oil | rind |
| **for the salad:** | 5 tablespoons olive oil |
| 1 lb/450 g melon, approximately | salt |
| ½ small honeydew | |

Divide the chicken into joints and remove the flesh from the bones. Cut the flesh into 1½-inch (3·5-cm) pieces and sprinkle with salt. Discard the bones. Peel the garlic and cut each clove in half lengthwise.

Heat the oil in a frying pan and sauté the chicken for about 5 minutes. Add the garlic and sauté the chicken for a further 5–10 minutes, or until tender and golden brown. Drain well on kitchen paper and set aside to cool.

Meanwhile, peel the melon, remove the seeds and cut into pieces. Place in a deep salad bowl. Peel, core and slice the apples and add to the melon with the walnut halves, lemon rind and olive oil. Season with salt and toss lightly. Chill well. Arrange the chicken on a serving dish and serve with the melon salad.

# WILD DUCK WITH FRIED VEGETABLES

*Serves 6*

| | |
|---|---|
| 1 wild duck, about 3½ lb/1·5 kg | **for the vegetables:** |
| 2 teaspoons salt | 1 lb/450 g aubergines |
| 4 oz/100 g *serrano* or York ham | 1 egg |
| 2 oz/50 g lard | 2 oz/50 g plain flour |
| 3 tablespoons brandy | generous ¼ pint/2 dl olive oil |
| 5 tablespoons dry white wine | 6 cooked artichoke hearts |
| | 2 large potatoes |

Wipe the duck with a damp cloth and sprinkle with the salt. Finely chop the ham. Heat the lard in a flameproof casserole or large saucepan and sauté the duck until lightly browned on all sides. Add the ham and sauté until the duck is well browned, then pour in the brandy and simmer for 5 minutes. Add the wine, cover tightly and simmer gently for 1–1¼ hours, or until the duck is tender.

Meanwhile, to prepare the vegetables, wipe the aubergines with a damp cloth and cut into rounds ½–1 inch (1–2·5 cm) thick. Whisk the egg, stir in the flour and coat the aubergines with the batter. Heat half the oil in a frying pan and sauté the aubergines for 3–4 minutes on each side, or until tender and golden brown. Drain and keep hot. Coat the artichoke hearts in the same way and sauté for about 5 minutes, or until golden brown. Drain and keep hot. Peel the potatoes and cut into ½-inch (1-cm) cubes. Heat the remaining oil in the pan and sauté the potatoes until tender, crisp and well browned. Drain well.

Transfer the duck to a heated serving dish and pour over any juices remaining in the casserole. Surround with the aubergines, artichokes and potatoes and serve.

# PIGEONS WITH BACON

*Serves 6*

| | |
|---|---|
| 6 tender pigeons | 6 rashers back bacon |
| 1 lb/450 g shallots | generous ¼ pint/2 dl olive oil |
| 2 medium-sized carrots | generous ¼ pint/2 dl water |
| 1 lb/450 g tomatoes | 1 tablespoon vinegar |
| 2¼ lb/1 kg small new potatoes | |

Rinse the pigeons under cold running water and dry well with kitchen paper. Peel the shallots. Peel the carrots and cut into rounds. Peel and chop the tomatoes. Scrape the potatoes and cover with cold water until required. Line the bottom of a casserole with the bacon rashers.

Heat the oil in a frying pan and sauté the pigeons for 5 minutes, or until lightly browned. Place in the casserole with the shallots, carrots and the drained potatoes. Pour the oil remaining in the pan into the casserole. Cover tightly and cook in a moderate oven (350°F, 180°C, Gas Mark 4) for 40 minutes. Add the tomatoes, water and vinegar and cook for a further 40–50 minutes, or until the pigeons are tender. Serve hot in the casserole.

# QUAIL IN BRANDY SAUCE

*Serves 4*

| | |
|---|---|
| 8 quail | 1½ oz/40 g lard |
| 1 medium-sized carrot | 2 teaspoons chopped parsley |
| 2 cloves garlic | 2 teaspoons salt |
| 4 oz/100 g *serrano* or York ham | ¼ pint/1·5 dl brandy |
| 2 tablespoons olive oil | |

Wipe the quail with a damp cloth and place in a flameproof casserole or large saucepan. Peel and chop the carrot and garlic. Chop the ham. Add the oil, lard, carrot, garlic, ham, parsley and salt to the casserole. Place over moderate heat for 5 minutes. Add the brandy and enough water to cover the quail completely, cover tightly and simmer for about 15–20 minutes, or until the quail are tender and the liquid is reduced by half.

Lift the quail from the casserole and arrange in a heated serving dish, pour over the sauce remaining in the casserole and serve.

*Fried chicken with melon salad*

# SPICED WILD RABBIT STEW

*Serves 6–8*

| | |
|---|---|
| 1 rabbit, about 4½ lb/2 kg | 2 large onions |
| scant ½ pint/2·5 dl olive oil | 1 head garlic |
| generous ¾ pint/5 dl white wine | 6 oz/175 g *chorizo* or garlic |
| 2 chillies | sausage |
| 3 teaspoons salt | 4½ lb/2 kg potatoes |
| 1 sprig thyme | 2 bay leaves |
| 3½ lb/1·5 kg fresh peas or | 1 tablespoon chopped parsley |
| 1 lb/450 g frozen peas | 2–3 pints/1–1·5 litres water |
| 1 lb/450g fresh asparagus | 6 young, tender globe artichokes |

Rinse the rabbit under cold running water and pat dry with kitchen paper. Cut into small portions.

Heat the olive oil in a large cast-iron saucepan or heavy-based saucepan and sauté the rabbit pieces until lightly browned. Add the white wine, chillies, salt and thyme and bring to the boil. Lower the heat, cover the pan tightly and simmer the rabbit for 1 hour.

Meanwhile, shell the beans and peas. Cut off the woody fibrous base from each asparagus spear and lightly scrape any coarse skin from the lower half of the stalk. Cook the peas and asparagus separately in lightly salted boiling water until tender. Drain and set aside until required. Peel and chop the onions. Peel the garlic. Cut the *chorizo* sausage into thick rounds. Peel the potatoes and cut into 2-inch (5-cm) cubes. Add the potatoes, onions, garlic, *chorizo*, bay leaves and chopped parsley to the rabbit and simmer gently for 15 minutes, or until the potatoes are partially cooked.

Meanwhile, cut the tips off the artichoke leaves and cut off the stalks. Cut the artichokes in half and remove the chokes. Add the artichoke halves to the ingredients in the pan with the beans and the water, which should be sufficient to cover the ingredients. Bring to the boil, then lower the heat and simmer, partly covered, for about 20 minutes, or until the artichokes are almost tender. Add the pre-cooked peas and asparagus and heat through for a further 10 minutes. Remove from the heat, transfer to a heated serving dish and serve.

# HARE IN CHOCOLATE SAUCE

*Serves 4*

| | |
|---|---|
| 1 small hare or about 2¼ lb/1 kg | 12 oz/350 g shallots |
| hare pieces | generous ¼ pint/2 dl olive oil |
| 4 cloves garlic | 3 large tomatoes |
| 2 small onions | 5 tablespoons dry white wine |
| 2 medium-sized carrots | 1 oz/25 g pine nuts |
| 1 bay leaf | 1½ oz/40 g unsweetened cooking |
| 5 tablespoons red wine | chocolate, grated |

Divide the hare into 8 pieces and place in a bowl. Peel 2 cloves of the garlic. Peel and thinly slice 1 onion and the carrots. Add the onion, carrots, peeled garlic, bay leaf and red wine to the hare pieces. Set aside to marinate for 24 hours.

Peel the shallots and cook in lightly salted boiling water

for 15 minutes. Drain and set aside until required. Heat the oil in a frying pan. Remove the hare from the marinade and sauté the pieces in the hot oil for about 10 minutes, or until well browned. Remove from the pan and place in a casserole.

Peel and chop the tomatoes. Peel and slice the remaining onion and garlic and sauté in the oil remaining in the pan until lightly browned. Add the tomatoes and sauté until reduced to a pulp. Stir in the white wine and cooked shallots and pour the mixture over the hare. Pound the pine nuts in a mortar and sprinkle the nuts and the grated chocolate over the hare. Cover and cook in a moderately hot oven (375°F, 190°C, Gas Mark 5) for 1–1¼ hours, or until the hare is tender. Transfer to a heated serving dish and serve.

# PARTRIDGES IN SALMOREJO SAUCE

*Serves 4*

| | |
|---|---|
| 4 partridges | 2 fresh red sweet peppers or |
| 1 medium-sized onion | canned red pimentos |
| 1 bay leaf | 8 hard-boiled eggs |
| 3 teaspoons salt | 5 tablespoons olive oil |
| 3½ pints/2 litres water | pinch pepper |
| **for the salmorejo sauce:** | 1 tablespoon vinegar |
| 1¼ pints/7·5 dl stock (see recipe) | |

Rinse the partridges under cold running water, drain and place in a large saucepan. Peel the onion and add to the pan with the bay leaf, salt and water. Place over high heat and bring to the boil. Lower the heat, cover tightly and simmer for about 45 minutes–1 hour, or until tender. Remove the partridges from the pan with a perforated spoon and set aside to cool. Reserve the 1¼ pints (7·5 dl) stock.

If using fresh sweet peppers, place in a hot oven (425°F, 220°C, Gas Mark 7) for about 15 minutes, or until the skins are charred. Peel the peppers, remove the seeds and shred the flesh finely. If using canned pimentos, drain and shred finely.

Separate the egg yolks from the whites. Finely chop the whites. Pound the yolks in a bowl. Add the olive oil gradually, beating well after each addition. Add the pepper, vinegar, egg whites, sweet peppers or pimentos and the reserved stock and mix the sauce thoroughly.

Divide each partridge into four and place in a deep casserole. Pour the sauce over the partridges and set aside for 1 hour so the flavours in the sauce are absorbed by the partridge flesh. Serve cold.

# STUFFED ONIONS

*Serves 4*

| | |
|---|---|
| 1 clove garlic | 3 teaspoons lemon juice |
| 12 oz/350 g lean pork, minced | 8 large Spanish onions |
| 1 teaspoon salt | 3 oz/75 g fine fresh breadcrumbs |
| ¼ teaspoon pepper | plain flour for coating |
| pinch cinnamon | ¼ pint/1·5 dl olive oil |
| 2 teaspoons finely chopped | 1 oz/25 g plain flour |
|   parsley | 2 tablespoons dry white wine |
| 1 egg | generous ¼ pint/2 dl water |
| 2 tablespoons milk | |

Peel and finely chop the garlic. Place the pork in a bowl, add the garlic, salt, pepper, cinnamon, parsley, egg, milk and lemon juice and mix together thoroughly. Set aside for about 30 minutes.

Peel the onions and cut a thin slice off the top of each one. Scoop out the inside of each onion and set aside, leaving only the 2 outer layers completely intact. Fill the onions with the prepared meat mixture and press the breadcrumbs on top. Roll the onions in flour to coat thoroughly.

Heat the oil in a heavy frying pan over low heat and fry the stuffed onions very gently for about 20 minutes, or until golden brown. Baste frequently. Remove the onions carefully and drain on kitchen paper. Place in a shallow casserole.

Finely chop the reserved onion and sauté in the oil remaining in the pan until lightly browned and soft. Stir in the flour and cook for about 30 seconds. Remove from the heat and gradually stir in the wine and water, mixing well after each addition. Bring to the boil over moderate heat, stirring constantly until the mixture thickens. Spoon the mixture over the stuffed onions. Bake the onions in a moderate oven (325°F, 160°C, Gas Mark 3) for about 1 hour, or until tender. Serve hot.

# SAUTÉED VEGETABLES WITH SCRAMBLED EGGS

*Serves 4*

| | |
|---|---|
| 1 green sweet pepper | 1 large potato |
| 8 oz/225 g courgettes | 5 tablespoons olive oil |
| 8 oz/225 g aubergines | 2 teaspoons salt |
| 1 medium-sized onion | 6 eggs |
| 1 lb/450 g tomatoes | |

Halve the pepper, remove the seeds and chop the flesh. Cut the courgettes and aubergines into ½-inch (1-cm) rounds. Peel and chop the onion and tomatoes. Peel the potato and cut into ½-inch (1-cm) rounds.

Heat the oil in a heavy frying pan. Add the pepper, courgettes, aubergines, onion, potato and salt. Sauté the vegetables for 10–15 minutes, or until lightly browned. Add the tomatoes and cook the mixture very gently for a further 15–20 minutes, or until all the vegetables are soft.

Whisk the eggs and pour into the vegetable mixture. Stir very gently until the egg begins to thicken; it should not be allowed to set on the bottom of the pan. Serve immediately with fresh, crusty bread.

*Spiced wild rabbit stew*

# FLAMBÉED CARAMEL CUSTARDS

*Serves 6*

**for the caramel:**
2 oz/50 g granulated sugar
2 tablespoons water

**for the custard:**
3 eggs
5 oz/150 g castor sugar

¾ pint/4·5 dl milk
generous pinch cinnamon
thinly pared rind of 1 lemon
generous ¼ pint/2 dl rum or
   brandy

To make the caramel, place the sugar and water in a small heavy saucepan. Place over low heat until the sugar dissolves, then raise the heat to moderate and boil the syrup until it begins to turn golden brown. Remove from the heat immediately and pour a little into 6 ramekins or individual moulds.

To make the custard, lightly whisk together the eggs and sugar in a bowl. Pour the milk into a saucepan and add the cinnamon and lemon rind. Place over moderate heat until simmering. Remove from the heat and stir into the egg mixture. Discard the lemon rind and pour an equal quantity of the custard into each ramekin. Place the ramekins in a large saucepan and add enough water to come about two-thirds of the way up the sides of the ramekins. Bring to the boil over moderate heat. Lower the heat, cover the pan tightly and cook the custards for 10–15 minutes, or until set. Alternatively, place the ramekins in a deep roasting tin and add the water. Bake in a cool oven (300°F, 150°C, Gas Mark 2) for about 1 hour, or until set.

While still hot, turn out the custards on to a serving dish. Heat the rum or brandy in a ladle or small saucepan over an open flame until simmering. Tilt the container and allow the flame to ignite the rum or brandy. Burn for about 10 seconds and then pour over the custards. Spoon the flaming rum or brandy over the custards until the flames are extinguished. Serve immediately.

# TURRON (ALMOND BRITTLE)

*Makes 2¼ lb (1 kg)*

1 tablespoon water
½ teaspoon lemon juice
1 lb/450 g castor sugar

1 lb/450 g blanched almonds
4 oz/100 g miniature sweets

Put the water, lemon juice and sugar into a heavy saucepan. Place over low heat until the sugar has completely dissolved. Raise the heat to moderate and boil the syrup until it becomes golden brown. Remove from the heat immediately and stir in the almonds. Pour the mixture on to a well-greased marble slab or baking tray and decorate with the miniature sweets. Set aside until cold. Break into small pieces for serving. *Turron* can be stored in an airtight container or glass jar.

*Flambéed caramel custards*

# BAKED APPLES WITH SHERRY

*Serves 6*

| | |
|---|---|
| 6 large cooking apples | 5 tablespoons medium sweet |
| 2 hard-boiled eggs | sherry |
| 1 teaspoon anisette | 4 oz/100 g castor sugar |
| | 1 oz/25 g melted butter |

Rinse the apples under cold running water. Remove the cores, taking care not to cut too deeply into the flesh.

Separate the egg yolks from the whites and reserve the whites for another dish. Pound the yolks to a paste. Add the anisette and mix well. Add the sherry gradually, mixing well after each addition. Stir in the sugar and the melted butter. Stand the apples in a shallow baking dish and spoon some of the mixture into the centre of each one. Bake in a hot oven (425°F, 220°C, Gas Mark 7) for about 30–40 minutes, or until tender. If the skins of the apples become too brown before they are cooked, lower the heat after 30 minutes to 375°F (190°C, Gas Mark 5) and bake for an extra 10–15 minutes. Serve hot or cold.

# EGG AND SUGAR SWEETS

*Makes about 18*

| | |
|---|---|
| 12 egg yolks | 1 piece cinnamon stick, about |
| 3 tablespoons water | 1 inch/2·5 cm long |
| 8 oz/225 g castor sugar | 2 oz/50 g castor sugar for coating |
| thinly pared rind of 1 lemon | |

Whisk the egg yolks and strain through a sieve into a bowl. Pour the water into a heavy saucepan. Add the sugar, lemon rind and cinnamon. Place over low heat until the sugar has completely dissolved and a thin syrup has formed. Raise the heat and simmer, stirring constantly, until the syrup begins to thicken and form threads. To test, dip a spoon into the hot syrup, then touch the syrup coating quickly with a knife blade. Small threads should draw out as the knife is lifted away. Remove from the heat and discard the lemon rind and the cinnamon stick. Pour the egg yolks into the syrup in a continuous stream, whisking constantly. Return the pan to low heat and cook very gently, still stirring constantly, until the mixture forms a thick paste in the centre of the pan. This takes about 5 minutes.

Spread the mixture on to a plate or a wooden board and set aside until cool enough to handle. Sprinkle with half the sugar and divide into small pieces. Roll each piece into a ball about 1 inch (2·5 cm) in diameter. Toss the balls in the remaining sugar and place in paper or foil sweet cases. Serve freshly made or store in an airtight container until required.

# ORANGE OMELETTE

*Serves 1*

| | |
|---|---|
| 2 eggs | castor sugar for sprinkling |
| ½ oz/15 g castor sugar | pinch cinnamon |
| pinch salt | 2 tablespoons rum |
| ½ oz/15 g butter | 2 tablespoons brandy |
| 2 oz/50 g orange marmalade | |

Whisk the eggs with the sugar and salt. Melt the butter in an omelette pan or frying pan over moderate heat. Pour the egg into the pan and cook gently until the egg sets. Spoon the marmalade over the centre of the omelette, fold in half and transfer to a heated plate.

Sprinkle the sugar and cinnamon over the omelette and with a red-hot poker burn a crisscross pattern in the sugar. Warm the rum and brandy, pour over the omelette and flambé at the table. Serve immediately the flames are extinguished.

# ICED MILK DESSERT

*Serves 6*

| | |
|---|---|
| 1 lemon | 8 oz/225 g castor sugar |
| 1¾ pints/1 litre milk | 3 egg whites |
| 1 stick cinnamon | ground cinnamon |

Thinly pare the rind from the lemon and place it in a saucepan with the milk, cinnamon stick and three-quarters of the sugar. Bring to the boil over moderate heat, then set aside until cold. Discard the lemon rind and the cinnamon stick.

Whisk the egg whites until stiff and then whisk in the remaining sugar. Fold the egg white mixture into the cold milk and pour into 6 individual glasses. Place in the freezing compartment of the refrigerator until beginning to set, then sprinkle with ground cinnamon and serve.

# FILLED SPONGE FINGERS

*Makes 24*

| | |
|---|---|
| **for the sponge fingers:** | 4 oz/100 g castor sugar |
| 4 eggs | 6 egg yolks |
| 4½ oz/125 g castor sugar | **for the syrup:** |
| 4½ oz/125 g plain flour | ¼ pint/2 dl water |
| **for the filling:** | 3–4 drops lemon essence |
| 5 tablespoons water | 10 oz/275 g castor sugar |

Whisk together the eggs and sugar in a bowl over simmering water until thick and creamy. Add the flour and fold in very carefully, using a metal spoon. Using a piping bag with a large fluted tube, pipe 3-inch (7·5-cm) lengths of the mixture on to a baking tray lined with buttered greaseproof paper.

*Orange omelette*

Bake in a cool oven (300°F, 150°C, Gas Mark 2) for 20–25 minutes, or until crisp and lightly browned. Leave the sponge fingers on the baking tray until cool, then remove from the greaseproof paper and place on a wire rack until cold.

To make the filling, place the water and sugar in a heavy saucepan. Heat gently until the sugar has completely dissolved. Raise the heat and boil the syrup until it thickens very slightly and begins to form threads. Remove from the heat and cool for about 5 minutes. Whisk the egg yolks and pour into the syrup in a thin continuous stream, whisking constantly. Return the pan to low heat and cook the mixture until it becomes thick and smooth. While the filling is still warm, spread the mixture over the bottom of each sponge finger and sandwich them together in pairs.

To make the syrup, place the water, lemon essence and sugar in a heavy saucepan. Heat gently until the sugar has dissolved. Raise the heat and boil the syrup until it becomes slightly thick. Remove from the heat and set aside to cool. Dip the filled sponge fingers in the syrup and place on a wire rack until cold. Serve freshly made or store in an airtight container lined with greaseproof paper.

# SWEET WINE CAKES

*Makes 8–12*

6 eggs
3 oz/75 g castor sugar
¼ teaspoon grated lemon rind
8 oz/225 g plain flour

**for the syrup:**
6 tablespoons water
10 oz/275 g castor sugar
pinch cinnamon
5 tablespoons sweet white wine

Separate the egg whites from the egg yolks. Place the egg yolks, sugar and lemon rind in a mixing bowl and whisk well until thick and creamy. Sift the flour and fold into the egg yolk mixture with a metal spoon. Whisk the egg whites until stiff and fold into the mixture. Pour into a large greased and lined Swiss roll tin and bake in a moderately hot oven (400°F, 200°C, Gas Mark 6) for 20–25 minutes, or until well risen and golden brown. When slightly cool, turn out of the tin and cut into 8 to 12 pieces.

Meanwhile, to make the syrup, heat the water, sugar and cinnamon in a small heavy saucepan over low heat until the sugar has completely dissolved. Raise the heat and boil the syrup until it becomes thick. Remove from the heat, stir in the wine and set aside to cool.

Place the pieces of cake on a tray and pour the syrup over. Sprinkle with cinnamon and set aside for about 3 hours before serving so the cakes are thoroughly saturated with the syrup. Serve when freshly made as a dessert or store in an airtight container lined with greaseproof paper.

*Filled sponge fingers*

# HOLY WEEK FRIED CAKES

*Makes about 36*

3 eggs
5 tablespoons olive oil
5 tablespoons milk
2 tablespoons brandy
1 oz/25 g castor sugar

about 1 lb/450 g plain flour
oil for deep-frying
4 oz/100 g castor sugar for
   dusting

Whisk together the eggs, olive oil, milk, brandy and sugar in a mixing bowl. Add the flour gradually, beating well after each addition. When the mixture becomes firm, knead in enough flour to make a firm smooth dough. Knead the dough lightly on a floured surface and roll out to ⅛ inch (3 mm) thick. Cut into 3-inch (7·5-cm) squares or 4- by 2-inch (10- by 5-cm) rectangles.

Deep-fry in hot oil for about 1 minute, or until well risen and golden brown. Drain well on kitchen paper, and, while still warm, sprinkle with sugar. Serve freshly made.

# FRIED LEMON PASTRIES

*Makes about 60*

½ oz/15 g fresh yeast or ¼ oz/7 g
   dried yeast
1 tablespoon warm water
3 eggs
1 teaspoon grated lemon rind
5 tablespoons olive oil

8 oz/225 g castor sugar
2–3 drops oil of lemon or lemon
   essence
14 oz/400 g plain flour
oil for deep-frying
castor sugar for coating

If using fresh yeast, blend the yeast with the warm water in a large bowl. If using dried yeast, add 1 teaspoon of the sugar to the water, sprinkle in the dried yeast and set aside for 10 minutes until frothy. Add the eggs and whisk until slightly frothy. Add the lemon rind, olive oil, sugar and oil of lemon or lemon essence. Whisk the mixture until it becomes thick and creamy. Sift the flour gently into the egg mixture and fold in carefully with a metal spoon.

Drop small teaspoons of the mixture into hot oil and fry until crisp and golden brown. Drain well on kitchen paper and toss in sugar. Serve freshly made or store in an airtight container until required.

# ALMOND CAKE

*Serves 10*

12 eggs
1 lb/450 g castor sugar
pinch cinnamon
1 teaspoon grated lemon rind

1 lb/450 g ground almonds
2 oz/50 g fine biscuit crumbs
castor sugar for dusting

Separate the egg yolks from the whites. Place the yolks in a bowl with the sugar and whisk until thick and creamy. Stir in the cinnamon, lemon rind and ground almonds. Whisk the egg whites until stiff and carefully stir into the almond mixture, using a metal spoon.

Grease a 10-inch (26-cm) square cake tin and coat with the biscuit crumbs. Spoon the prepared batter into the tin. Bake in a moderate oven (350°F, 180°C, Gas Mark 4) for 1 hour,

or until firm and golden brown. While still warm, turn the cake out on to a wire rack and set aside to cool. Sprinkle with the sugar and cut into slices for serving.

# ALMOND BISCUITS

*Makes 30–36*

8 oz/225 g lard
6 oz/175 g castor sugar
1 egg
½ teaspoon grated lemon rind

generous pinch cinnamon
about 1 lb/450 g plain flour
4 oz/100 g ground almonds
1 oz/25 g icing sugar

Cream the lard with the sugar in a mixing bowl until soft and creamy. Whisk the egg and gradually beat it into the creamed mixture with the grated lemon rind and the cinnamon. Knead in the flour gradually, forming a fairly soft dough. Knead in the ground almonds. Roll the dough out on a lightly floured surface to about ½ inch (1 cm) thick. Cut into circles with a 2-inch (5-cm) cutter and place on a baking tray. Bake in a moderate oven (325°F, 160°C, Gas Mark 3) for 25–30 minutes, or until golden brown.

While still warm, lightly dust the biscuits with the icing sugar and place on a wire rack to cool. Serve freshly baked or store in an airtight container until required.

# ANISE BISCUITS

*Makes 16–18*

1 egg
6 tablespoons olive oil
3 oz/75 g castor sugar
1 tablespoon anisette

5 tablespoons dry white wine
½ teaspoon grated lemon rind
about 12 oz/350 g plain flour

Place the egg, oil, sugar, anisette, wine and lemon rind in a bowl. Whisk vigorously for 5 minutes until frothy and well blended. Gradually add the flour, stirring well after each addition until the mixture becomes a soft dough. Continue adding the flour, which should be kneaded in until the dough becomes smooth and fairly firm. It should not be sticky.

Roll the dough out on a lightly floured surface to about ¼ inch (5 mm) thick. Cut into circles with a 2½-inch (6-cm) cutter and place on a baking tray. Bake in a moderate oven (325°F, 160°C, Gas Mark 3) for 20–30 minutes, or until crisp and golden brown. Cool on a wire rack and serve freshly baked or store in an airtight container until required.

*Almond cake*

170

# ITALIAN

Luigi Veronelli

*Photography by Eric Carter*

Until quite recently, Italy was like a crazy paving of independent states. Although unification was finally achieved in 1861, the last century has failed to eradicate deep and basic differences between the Italian provinces, far greater than between provinces in most other countries of the world. But it is precisely because it rests on a dozen distinct traditions that the Italian cuisine is among the finest in the world. The concept of an *Italian* restaurant is as puzzling to the Italians as a *continental* restaurant is to continentals, but they would know what to expect in a restaurant offering Neapolitan, Genoese or Florentine specialities.

The stereotype of an Italian meal as understood outside Italy would lay heavy stress on spaghetti, olive oil and tomatoes. But spaghetti is only one of the many varieties of pasta prepared in innumerable ways – in broth, with shellfish, stuffed with meat and cheese. Nor is the pasta family, with all its ramifications, the only source of carbohydrate on the Italian table. In the northern provinces its place is usurped by rice, often served as a *risotto*, and corn meal pudding (*polenta*) which is served with almost everything and can be boiled, fried, grilled or baked. It can be eaten with butter and cheese and is the natural accompaniment to salt cod (*baccalà*). Bread is a staple food throughout the country.

As for olive oil, Italy produces great quantities of wonderful, fruity oil, basic to much of the cooking in the southernmost areas and the far north. But great quantities of good butter are used also. The Milanese cuisine is almost entirely dependent on it. In and around Rome, pork lard (*strutto*) is used.

Soup is rarely served with a meal that includes pasta or rice. Thick vegetable-and-pasta soups such as *minestrone* are really meals in themselves. Many Italian soups are thickened at the table with grated cheese.

Octopus, squid and cuttlefish are eaten by the million. Red mullet, anchovies and sardines, scampi and lobster, oysters and sea-urchins, fresh from the ocean, are a revelation to any palate.

Popular desserts include pastries and, of course, rich ice cream made of natural ingredients. And the cheeses, made of milk from cows, goats, ewes and buffalo, are varied and mouth-watering: Parmesan, the blue-veined Stracchino and Gorgonzola, Bel Paese, Fontina from Piedmont – the list is endless.

The islands of Sicily and Sardinia, with their own culinary contributions, should not be forgotten. Pasta, in fact, is said to have originated in Sicily in the thirteenth century. Macaroni with sardines and fennel is a famous Sicilian dish. Sicily has no great indigenous meat dishes. Sardinia has two, which are really rival ways of cooking a suckling pig.

Both islands have superb fish recipes and many good vegetable dishes. Oranges and lemons grow abundantly in Sicily and form the fruity basis of many ice creams. A favourite Sicilian dessert is Sicilian pastry horns, filled with sweetened Ricotta cheese mixed with pistachio nuts and candied peel. Among Sicilian wines the best known must be Marsala, a rich brown sweet wine used in the preparation of *zabaione*.

These recipes are designed to be within the scope of any non-Italian kitchen, and whether cooked at home or eaten abroad, these Italian dishes should provide great pleasure.

# TRUFFLE FONDUE

*Serves 4*

| | |
|---|---|
| ¼ pint/1·5 dl milk | 1 oz/25 g butter |
| 10 oz/275 g Fontina or Gruyère cheese, thinly sliced | 1 large Alba truffle, thinly sliced |
| pinch salt | 4 slices toast |
| 3 egg yolks | |

Place 4 ramekins in the oven to warm. Pour half the milk into the top of a double saucepan or into a pudding basin, then add the cheese and salt. Place over hot, but not boiling, water and stir vigorously until the cheese begins to melt and absorb the milk. Continue heating and stirring until the cheese has completely melted and the mixture is soft and creamy. Remove the double saucepan from the heat immediately, since prolonged heating makes the cheese stringy.

Meanwhile, heat the remaining milk in a small saucepan until warm, remove from the heat, add the egg yolks and stir until blended. Gradually add the egg mixture to the melted cheese, mixing thoroughly after each addition. Add the butter and beat until the mixture is smooth and glossy. Trim the crusts from the toast and cut each slice into 4 triangles. Arrange in the heated ramekins and pour the *fondue* over the toast. Garnish with the truffle and serve immediately.

# SKEWERED SCAMPI WITH BRANDY SAUCE

*Serves 6*

| | |
|---|---|
| 24 large fresh or frozen uncooked scampi | **for the sauce:** |
| | 2 cloves garlic |
| 18 bay leaves | 6 anchovy fillets |
| salt and freshly ground black pepper | 3 oz/75 g butter |
| | 4 tablespoons brandy |
| 1 tablespoon olive oil | few drops *Duca d'Urbino* sauce or Worcestershire sauce |
| | 1 tablespoon French mustard |
| | 2 teaspoons lemon juice |

Using 6 skewers, thread 4 scampi on to each skewer alternating with the bay leaves. Season with the salt and pepper and sprinkle with the olive oil. Grease a roasting tin with the oil and place the skewers in it. Cook in a moderately hot oven (375°F, 190°C, Gas Mark 5) for 15 minutes, or until tender and golden brown, brushing occasionally with the pan juices and a little more olive oil, if necessary.

Meanwhile, make the sauce. Peel and crush the garlic. Pound the anchovy fillets with two-thirds of the butter to make a paste. Heat the remaining butter in a frying pan over moderate heat, add the garlic and sauté until lightly browned. Add the brandy and *Duca d'Urbino* sauce and reduce by half over high heat. Add the anchovy paste, mustard and lemon juice. Pour the sauce on to an oval heated serving dish and arrange the skewers of scampi on top. Serve very hot.

# MARINATED EEL

*Serves 6*

| | |
|---|---|
| 2 lb cleaned eel | salt |
| 3 cloves garlic | ¼ fresh chili, chopped, or |
| all-purpose flour for coating | ½ teaspoon dried chili powder |
| olive oil for deep-frying | 1½ cups red wine vinegar |
| ¼ teaspoon oregano | |

Rinse the eel under cold running water, dry well and cut into 2-inch pieces. Peel 1 clove of the garlic and cut in half. Rub the eel with the cut sides of the garlic and coat with flour.

Peel and slice the remaining garlic. Heat the olive oil until very hot, add the eel and sauté until brown. Drain well and place in an earthenware bowl, in layers, seasoning each layer with the garlic, oregano, salt and chili. Pour the vinegar into a saucepan and reduce by one-third over high heat. Remove the pan from the heat, mix in 3 tablespoons of the frying olive oil and pour over the eel. Set aside and marinate for at least 24 hours, but preferably 2–3 days to allow the maximum flavor to develop, before using.

# SNAILS WITH TOMATO AND ANCHOVY SAUCE

*Serves 6*

| | |
|---|---|
| 36 canned snails, with shells | 4–5 tablespoons olive oil |
| 6 anchovy fillets | 1 teaspoon chopped parsley |
| ¼ cup milk | ½ chili |
| 1 lb tomatoes | 1 tablespoon chopped mint leaves |
| 3 cloves garlic | salt |

Drain the snails, wash and dry the shells and replace the snails. Set aside until required.

To make the sauce, soak the anchovy fillets in the milk for about 10 minutes to remove the excess salt, then drain. Peel the tomatoes and press through a sieve. Peel and crush the garlic. Heat the olive oil in a flameproof casserole or a saucepan over moderate heat. Add the anchovy fillets, garlic, parsley and the tomato purée. Remove the seeds from the chili, chop the flesh and add to the casserole with the mint leaves. Season with salt to taste. Simmer the sauce for 30 minutes, stirring occasionally. Add the snails in their shells and simmer in the sauce for 2–3 minutes. Serve in the casserole.

*Marinated eel*

174

# PEPERONATA

*Serves 6*

| | |
|---|---|
| 1 large onion | 1½ lb/700 g tomatoes |
| 2–3 cloves garlic | 6 tablespoons olive oil |
| 2 lb/1 kg red or green sweet peppers | 6 small bay leaves |
| | salt and pepper |

Peel and coarsely chop the onion. Peel and slice the garlic. Discard the seeds from the sweet peppers and chop the flesh. Peel the tomatoes. Heat the olive oil in a saucepan over moderate heat. Add the onion, garlic and bay leaves and sauté until golden brown. Add the sweet peppers and season with salt and pepper. Cook over high heat for about 10 minutes, stirring constantly. Add the tomatoes, lower the heat and simmer gently for a further 15 minutes. Pour into a heated serving dish and serve as an appetiser.

*Note:* This dish may be reheated and therefore can be prepared in advance when entertaining.

# CREAMED SALT COD

*Serves 6*

| | |
|---|---|
| 1¼ lb/600 g dried salt cod | 3 tablespoons olive oil |
| 3 cloves garlic | pinch ground cinnamon |
| 1–1½ pints/6–9 dl milk | salt and pepper |

Soak the fish for 24 hours in plenty of cold water, changing the water frequently. Drain, rinse under cold running water and dry with a cloth or kitchen paper. Discard any skin and bones and thinly slice the fish. Peel the garlic and rub over the inside of a flameproof casserole or a large saucepan.

Place the fish in the casserole and add enough of the milk to cover. Simmer over moderate heat until the mixture begins to darken in colour. While the fish cooks, break it into small pieces with a wooden spoon. Heat the remaining milk and gradually stir it into the casserole with the olive oil to obtain a soft purée. It may not be necessary to use all the milk. Season with the cinnamon and salt and pepper to taste. Serve hot with warm slices of *polenta* (see page 197).

*Peperonata*

# MINESTRONE ALLA MILANESE

*Serves 6*

2 oz/50 g *borlotti* beans (see note) or haricot beans
4 oz/100 g lean, mild cured bacon, in 1 piece
1 medium-sized potato
1 large carrot
1 medium-sized aubergine
12 oz/350 g fresh peas or 1 (4-oz/113-g) packet frozen peas
8 oz/225 g tomatoes
½ small onion
1 leek
1 small celery heart
4 oz/100 g butter
*bouquet garni* (see recipe)
salt and freshly ground black pepper
3½ pints/2 litres chicken stock
8 oz/225 g long-grain rice
1 clove garlic
4 oz/100 g Parmesan cheese, grated

Soak the beans in cold water for 24 hours. Drain well and cook in lightly salted boiling water for about 1 hour, or until tender. Drain before using. Simmer the bacon in boiling water for 15–20 minutes. Drain well and cut into ¼-inch (5-mm) cubes.

Peel and dice the potato, carrot and aubergine. Shell the peas, if using fresh ones. Peel the tomatoes. Peel and chop the onion. Cut off the green part of the leek and trim away the root. Rinse the white part very thoroughly under cold running water and chop coarsely. Trim and thinly slice the celery heart. Heat one-third of the butter in a saucepan over moderate heat and add the bacon, onion, leek and the *bouquet garni* (few sprigs parsley, 1 sprig rosemary, ½ bay leaf, tied together). Cook together over moderate heat for 3–4 minutes, remove the herbs, add the tomatoes and season with salt and pepper to taste. Simmer gently.

Heat the remaining butter in a second saucepan over high heat and sauté the beans, potato, carrot, aubergine, peas and celery over moderate heat for 5–8 minutes. Add to the tomato mixture, simmer together for 2–3 minutes then pour in the stock. Simmer over moderate heat until the vegetables are tender. Increase the heat and, when the stock boils, add the rice and simmer for about 15 minutes, or until *al dente* (cooked but still firm). Peel and chop the garlic. A few moments before removing the soup from the heat, add the garlic. Pour into a heated soup tureen and serve with the cheese as an accompaniment.

*Note: Borlotti* beans are the speckled red and white variety.

# BROAD BEAN MINESTRONE

*Serves 6*

3 lb/1·5 kg broad beans
1 small onion
1 small carrot
½ stick celery
4 oz/100 g butter
3 pints/1·5 litres water
4 teaspoons salt

**for the pasta:**
5 eggs
1 tablespoon olive oil
1 lb/450 g plain flour
1 teaspoon salt
4 oz/100 g Pecorino or Parmesan cheese, grated

Shell the beans. Peel and chop the onion and carrot. Chop the celery. Heat the butter in a saucepan over moderate heat, add the onion, carrot and celery and sauté until browned. Add the beans and the water. Season with salt and bring to the boil. Lower the heat and simmer the beans for 30–40 minutes, or until soft and very tender.

To make the pasta, lightly whisk together the eggs and olive oil in a small bowl. Sift the flour and salt on to a marble slab or into a mixing bowl and make a well in the centre. Pour in the eggs and oil, mix to a firm, smooth dough and knead well. Wrap in a damp cloth and set aside for about 30 minutes.

Roll the dough on a floured surface into sheets, about 8 inches (20 cm) wide, 12 inches (30 cm) long and 1/16 inch (1·5 mm) thick. Fold each sheet in half lengthwise, then in half lengthwise again several times. Cut the roll into ¼-inch (5-mm) ribbon noodles. Unfold the noodles, arrange them on a lightly floured surface and allow to dry for about 30 minutes.

Bring the soup to the boil and add the egg noodles. Cook for 7–8 minutes, or until the noodles are *al dente* (cooked but still firm). Pour the soup into a tureen and serve with the cheese as an accompaniment.

# TOMATO AND PASTA SOUP

*Serves 6*

3 cloves garlic
1 medium-sized tomato
10 oz/275 g *bavette* (see note)
3 tablespoons olive oil
3 oz/75 g ham or bacon fat, minced
1¾ pints/1 litre cold water
salt and freshly ground black pepper
2 tablespoons finely chopped basil
4 oz/100 g Pecorino or Parmesan cheese, grated

Peel and chop the garlic. Peel and slice the tomato. Break the *bavette* into 1- to 1½-inch (2·5- to 3·5-cm) pieces. Heat the olive oil in a saucepan over moderate heat, add the garlic and ham fat and sauté until lightly browned. Add the slices of tomato, stir for a few minutes and then add the water. Season with salt and pepper and bring to the boil. Add the *bavette* and cook for 10–12 minutes, or until *al dente* (cooked but still firm). Remove the pan from the heat and add the basil and 2 tablespoons of the cheese. Serve hot with the remaining cheese as an accompaniment.

*Note: Bavette* are rods of pasta, each with a central groove, like a pencil split longitudinally with the lead removed.

*Broad bean minestrone*

176

# CHEESE-STUFFED CAPPELLETTI IN BROTH

*Serves 6*

**for the pasta:**
4 eggs
2 teaspoons olive oil
12 oz/350 g plain flour
¾ teaspoon salt

**for the filling:**
6 oz/175 g Ricotta cheese or half
  Ricotta cheese and half Cacio
  cheese

5 oz/150 g Parmesan cheese,
  grated
1 egg
1 egg yolk
¼ teaspoon grated lemon rind
pinch mixed dried herbs
salt
4½ pints/2·5 litres beef or chicken
  broth

To make the pasta, lightly whisk together the eggs and olive oil in a small bowl. Sift the flour and salt on to a marble slab or into a mixing bowl and make a well in the centre. Pour in the eggs and oil. Mix to a smooth dough and knead well. Wrap in a damp cloth and set aside for about 30 minutes.

To make the filling, mix together the Ricotta cheese, one-third of the Parmesan cheese, the egg, egg yolk, lemon rind and herbs. Season with salt to taste. Roll the mixture into balls about the size of a small walnut and place on a floured surface until required.

Knead the dough lightly and roll out into sheets, ¹⁄₁₆ inch (1·5 mm) thick. Using a 2-inch (5-cm) floured cutter, cut out circles of dough. Alternatively, cut 2-inch (5-cm) squares, using a floured sharp knife. Place one ball of filling in the centre of each piece of dough. Fold in half and firmly press the edges together to form the *cappelletti*. Press the leftover dough into a ball and repeat the process until all the pasta and filling are used. Bring the broth to the boil. Add the *cappelletti* and simmer for 5–10 minutes, or until they rise to the surface. Serve immediately in heated soup dishes with the remaining cheese as an accompaniment.

*Note:* Cappelletti means 'little hats' and these ravioli appear throughout northern Italy with a variety of fillings.

# RICE AND CHICKEN LIVER SOUP

*Serves 6*

generous 3½ pints/2 litres chicken
  stock
6 oz/175 g chicken livers
8 oz/225 g long-grain rice

1 tablespoon chopped parsley
4 oz/100 g Parmesan cheese,
  grated

Bring the stock to the boil in a large saucepan. Clean the chicken livers and chop coarsely. Pour 3 tablespoons of the boiling stock over the livers to scald them. Add the rice to the pan and simmer for about 15 minutes, or until *al dente* (cooked but still firm). Add the chicken livers with the stock in which they were scalded and the parsley. Simmer for 2–3 minutes, then serve in heated soup bowls, sprinkled with the cheese.

*Cheese-stuffed cappelletti in broth*

# MUSSEL HOT-POT

*Serves 6*

| | |
|---|---|
| 3 pints/1·5 litres mussels | 4 medium-sized potatoes |
| 2 tablespoons olive oil | 4 oz/100 g bacon fat, minced |
| ¼ teaspoon freshly ground black pepper | 3½ pints/2 litres cold water |
| | salt |
| 1 small onion | 12 oz/350 g long-grain rice |
| 1 clove garlic | |

Scrub the mussels very thoroughly under running water. Remove the beards. Heat half the olive oil in a saucepan over moderate heat. Add the mussels and pepper and sauté until the mussels open. Shake the pan frequently to prevent the mussels from sticking. Drain in a colander over a large bowl and cool. Discard any mussels that have not opened. Strain and reserve the liquid. Remove and discard the mussel shells. Set the mussels aside until required.

Peel and finely chop the onion and garlic. Peel and slice the potatoes. Heat the bacon fat and the remaining olive oil in a flameproof casserole or a saucepan over low heat. Add the onion and garlic and sauté until lightly browned. Add the water and the potatoes, season with salt and bring to the boil. After 10 minutes, add the rice and cook over high heat for about 15 minutes. Add the mussels and the reserved liquid 2–3 minutes before the end of the cooking time. Pour into a heated serving dish and serve immediately.

# ANCHOVY OMELETTE

*Serves 6*

| | |
|---|---|
| 6 anchovy fillets | 3 generous tablespoons olive oil |
| 3 tablespoons milk | 1 small chilli |
| 1 tablespoon chopped parsley | salt |
| 1 clove garlic | 10 eggs |
| 12 oz/350 g tomatoes | pepper |

Soak the anchovies in the milk for about 10 minutes to remove the excess salt. Drain and pound to a paste with the parsley. Peel and crush the garlic. Peel and chop the tomatoes. Heat one-third of the olive oil in a frying pan over moderate heat, add the garlic and sauté until lightly browned. Discard the garlic and add the anchovy mixture to the pan, then add the tomatoes and chilli and season with a little salt. Continue cooking for 8 minutes, pour the mixture into a bowl and let stand until cool.

Discard the chilli. Whisk the eggs well and stir into the cooled anchovy mixture. Season with salt and pepper. Heat half the remaining oil in the pan over moderate heat and pour in the egg mixture. Stir for a few seconds until the bottom of the omelette is golden brown. Continue cooking for 1–2 minutes until the mixture begins to set. Remove the pan from the heat and invert the omelette on to a large round plate. Heat the remaining oil in the pan and slide the omelette into the pan with the browned side up. Cook until golden brown, then slide the omelette on to a heated serving plate and serve immediately.

# SARDINES WITH CAPER AND OLIVE STUFFING

*Serves 6*

24 large fresh sardines
1 large clove garlic
2 oz/50 g stoned black olives
2 oz/50 g capers
6 tablespoons finely chopped parsley
1½ oz/40 g fine fresh breadcrumbs
salt and pepper
olive oil (see recipe)

Cut off the heads and tails of the fish, gut them and remove the backbones. Rinse thoroughly under cold running water and dry well with a cloth or kitchen paper. Place skin-side down on a flat surface. Peel and chop the garlic. Coarsely chop the olives and capers. Mix the garlic, olives, capers, parsley, breadcrumbs and salt and pepper together in a bowl. Add enough olive oil to bind the mixture together.

Spread a little of the mixture on the flesh, fold the fish over the filling and place in a greased casserole. Lightly sprinkle with olive oil, season with a little more salt and cook in a moderately hot oven (400°F, 200°C, Gas Mark 6) for about 20 minutes. Serve hot or cold.

# BAKED SEA BASS

*Serves 6*

1 sea bass, about 3 lb/1·5 kg
salt and pepper
2 oz/50 g butter
1 tablespoon olive oil
1 medium-sized onion
2 lemons

Scale and gut the bass. Rinse under cold running water and dry with a cloth or kitchen paper. Make a diagonal slit on each side of the fish to help the heat to penetrate while cooking. Season with salt and pepper. Place the fish in a casserole with the butter and olive oil. Peel and slice the onion and arrange over the fish. Bake in a moderately hot oven (375°F, 190°C, Gas Mark 5) for 45–50 minutes, or until the flesh of the fish is firm and white. During cooking, baste occasionally with the juices in the casserole.

Carefully remove the fish from the casserole and place on a heated serving plate. Slice the lemons and arrange around the fish. Strain the juices left in the casserole, pour a little over the fish and serve immediately.

*Sardines with caper and olive stuffing*

# OCTOPUS IN SPICY TOMATO SAUCE

*Serves 6*

2 rock octopus, 1 lb/450 g each
6 oz/175 g tomatoes
salt
1 chilli

1 tablespoon chopped parsley
6 tablespoons olive oil
1 lemon

Clean and skin each octopus. Remove the eyes, mouth (beak) and the small bladder. Rinse well under cold running water and pound lightly with a meat mallet to tenderise. Place the octopus in a large flameproof casserole. Peel and slice the tomatoes and place on top. Add the salt, chilli, parsley and olive oil. Place greaseproof paper over the top of the casserole, secure with string and cover tightly. Simmer over low heat for about 2 hours.

Remove the casserole from the heat and set aside for 2–3 minutes. Remove the greaseproof paper and the chilli. Cut the lemon into wedges. Cut the octopus into pieces in the casserole and garnish with the lemon. This dish is excellent served either hot or cold.

# RICE AND SHELLFISH SALAD

*Serves 6*

1 pint/6 dl clams
1 pint/6 dl mussels
1 pint/6 dl cockles
3 tablespoons dry white wine
4 oz/100 g fresh or frozen
  uncooked scampi
1 lb/450 g long-grain rice

3 hard-boiled eggs
about 3 tablespoons olive oil
pinch saffron powder
few drops *Duca d'Urbino* sauce or
  Worcestershire sauce
salt and pepper
1 tablespoon chopped parsley

Scrub the clams, mussels and cockles and rinse well under cold running water. Place in a large saucepan with the wine. Cover tightly and cook over high heat. Shake the saucepan gently until the shellfish open. Drain and set aside to cool. Remove the fish from their shells and discard the shells. Peel the scampi and simmer in lightly salted boiling water for 4–5 minutes. Drain well and dice. Cook the rice in plenty of lightly salted boiling water for about 15 minutes, or until *al dente* (cooked but still firm). Drain and set aside to cool.

Pound the eggs to a paste, using a pestle and mortar or a liquidiser. Add the oil gradually, beating constantly. Add the saffron powder and *Duca d'Urbino* sauce. Season with salt and pepper to taste. Mix the rice with the shellfish, place in a glass dish and cover with the sauce. Sprinkle with the parsley. Toss the salad at the table just before serving.

# BAKED STUFFED SQUID

*Serves 6*

3 lb/1·5 kg fairly large squid
2 cloves garlic
1 tablespoon chopped parsley
½ oz/15 g fine fresh breadcrumbs

2 tablespoons olive oil
salt and pepper
3 tablespoons dry white wine

To clean the squid, carefully remove the transparent bone, the small bladder containing the black ink and the pouch containing the yellow coloured deposit. Rinse the squid thoroughly in plenty of cold water and pat dry with a cloth or kitchen paper. Remove the tentacles and chop coarsely. Peel and finely chop the garlic. Mix together the squid tentacles, garlic, parsley, breadcrumbs, half the olive oil and salt and pepper. Fill the body of each squid with the stuffing.

Sew up the body or secure with wooden cocktail sticks to completely enclose the filling. Place the stuffed squid in a greased casserole and sprinkle with the remaining olive oil, a little salt and pepper and the wine. Place the casserole in a moderately hot oven (375°F, 190°C, Gas Mark 5) and bake for 45–50 minutes, or until tender. Remove the thread or cocktail sticks and serve.

# CUTTLEFISH AND HARICOT BEAN SALAD

*Serves 6*

1 lb/450 g haricot beans
2¼ lb/1 kg cuttlefish or squid
1 large onion
1 large carrot
1 stick celery
1¾ pints/1 litre water
salt and pepper

**for the dressing:**
4 tablespoons olive oil
3 tablespoons lemon juice
2–3 tablespoons cuttlefish stock
  (see recipe)
salt
6 hard-boiled eggs

Soak the beans overnight in plenty of cold water. Drain and cook in plenty of lightly salted boiling water for about 45–50 minutes, or until tender. Drain well and set aside until required.

Meanwhile, clean the cuttlefish or squid (see Baked Stuffed Squid, above), rinse under cold running water and slice quite thickly. Peel the onion and carrot and place in a large saucepan with the celery, water and salt and pepper. Place the pan over moderate heat and bring to the boil. Lower the heat and simmer for 5 minutes. Add the cuttlefish and simmer for about 1 hour, or until the fish is tender. Drain and set aside to cool. Discard the vegetables but reserve the required amount of stock for the dressing.

To make the dressing, mix together the olive oil, lemon juice and cuttlefish stock. Season with salt to taste. Shell the hard-boiled eggs and cut into quarters. Place the beans and cuttlefish in a salad bowl and pour over the dressing. Garnish with the eggs. Mix together at the table before serving.

# TOMATO AND ANCHOVY PIZZA

*Serves 6*

| for the pasta: | for the topping: |
|---|---|
| 1 oz/25 g fresh yeast or ½ oz/15 g dried yeast | 12 anchovy fillets |
| ½ pint/3 dl lukewarm water | 3 tablespoons milk |
| 1 lb/450 g plain flour | 12 oz/350 g tomatoes |
| 1 teaspoon salt | 2 cloves garlic |
| 1 tablespoon olive oil | 3 oz/75 g lard |
| | ½ teaspoon dried oregano |
| | salt and pepper |

To make the pasta, dissolve the yeast in the water. Sift the flour and salt on to a marble slab or into a mixing bowl and make a well in the centre. Pour in the yeast mixture and the olive oil. Gradually knead the flour into the liquid to make a smooth, soft dough. Form into a ball and put into a floured bowl. Cover and let stand in a warm place for 1½–2 hours, or until doubled in bulk.

To make the topping, soak the anchovy fillets in the milk for 10–15 minutes to remove the excess salt. Drain before using. Peel and slice the tomatoes and garlic. Sprinkle the table with a little flour and knead the risen dough for 2–3 minutes. Roll out the dough to ⅛ inch (3 mm) thick. Cut into 6 circles, each 6 inches (15 cm) in diameter. Melt the lard and brush a little over each circle. Arrange the anchovy fillets, tomatoes and garlic over the surface. Sprinkle with the oregano and the remaining melted lard and season with the salt and pepper. Place on a baking tray and bake in a hot oven (450°F, 230°C, Gas Mark 8) for about 15–20 minutes. Serve hot.

# MACARONI WITH SARDINES AND FENNEL

*Serves 6*

| | |
|---|---|
| 4 oz/100 g anchovy fillets | 4 tablespoons water |
| ¼ pint/1·5 dl milk | small pinch saffron powder |
| 1 lb/450 g fresh sardines | salt and pepper |
| 3 cloves garlic | 1 tablespoon chopped parsley |
| ¼ onion | 1½ oz/40 g sultanas |
| 1 fennel, about 12 oz/350 g | 1½ oz/40 g pine nut kernels |
| 4 tablespoons olive oil | 1¾ lb/800 g macaroni |

Soak the anchovy fillets in the milk for 10–15 minutes to remove the excess salt, then drain. Cut off the heads and tails of the sardines, gut them and remove the backbones. Rinse thoroughly under cold running water and dry well with a cloth or kitchen paper.

Peel the garlic. Peel and finely chop the onion. Trim and wash the fennel and cut into 8 pieces. Heat half the olive oil in a saucepan over moderate heat and add 2 cloves of the garlic, the water, saffron and 1 piece of fennel. Season with salt and pepper. Sauté together until golden brown, then add the sardines and cook for 2–3 minutes. Remove the pan from the heat and set aside until required. Discard the garlic.

Place the remaining fennel in a second saucepan with boiling salted water, simmer for 15 minutes, drain, chop and set aside. Reserve the cooking water.

Pound the anchovies to a paste with the parsley. Place the remaining olive oil in a saucepan over moderate heat, add the remaining clove of garlic with the onion and sauté until brown. Add the fennel, the anchovy mixture diluted with 6 tablespoons of the cooking water from the fennel, the sultanas and the pine nut kernels. Simmer over moderate heat for 2–3 minutes.

Place the remaining cooking water from the fennel in a third saucepan and bring to the boil. Add the macaroni and enough lightly salted boiling water to cover. Simmer until the macaroni is *al dente* (cooked but still firm), adding more boiling water if necessary. Drain well and place the macaroni in layers in a heated casserole, alternating with layers of the sardine mixture and the anchovy mixture, and beginning and ending with a layer of macaroni. Cook in a moderate oven (350°F, 180°C, Gas Mark 4) for 20 minutes. Serve very hot.

# SPAGHETTI WITH CHEESE AND BACON

*Serves 6*

| | |
|---|---|
| 1¼ lb/600 g spaghetti | 1 oz/25 g lard |
| 1 small onion | ¼ chilli |
| 1 clove garlic | pinch salt |
| 8 oz/225 g bacon rashers | 4 oz/100g Pecorino or Parmesan cheese, grated |
| 2 tablespoons olive oil | |

Cook the spaghetti in plenty of salted boiling water for about 10–12 minutes, or until *al dente* (cooked but still firm). Drain, turn into a deep heated serving dish and keep hot. Meanwhile, peel and chop the onion and garlic and cut the bacon into ¼-inch (5-mm) pieces.

Heat the olive oil with the lard in a frying pan over moderate heat and add the bacon and chilli. When the bacon begins to brown, remove it from the pan and set aside. Add the onion, garlic and salt to the pan, stir together and remove from the heat when lightly coloured. Discard the chilli and add the bacon. Sprinkle the spaghetti with the bacon mixture and the cheese. Mix at the table and serve.

# FETTUCCINE WITH RICOTTA CHEESE

*Serves 6*

| for the pasta: | for the topping: |
|---|---|
| 5 eggs | 12 oz/350 g Ricotta cheese |
| 1 tablespoon olive oil | 3–4 tablespoons olive oil |
| 1 lb/450 g plain flour | salt and freshly ground pepper |
| 1 teaspoon salt | |

To make the pasta, lightly whisk together the eggs and olive oil in a small bowl. Sift the flour and salt on to a marble slab or into a mixing bowl and make a well in the centre. Pour in the eggs and the oil, mix to a firm, smooth dough and knead well. Wrap in a damp cloth and set aside for about 30 minutes.

Roll out the dough on a floured surface into sheets, about

8 inches (20 cm) wide, 12 inches (30 cm) long and $\frac{1}{16}$ inch (1·5 mm) thick. Fold each sheet in half lengthwise, then in half lengthwise again, several times. Cut the roll into $\frac{1}{4}$-inch (5-mm) ribbon noodles. Unfold the noodles, arrange on a floured surface and allow to dry for about 30 minutes. Place the noodles in a large saucepan half filled with lightly salted boiling water and simmer for about 8 minutes, or until *al dente* (cooked but still firm). Drain and place on a heated serving plate. Reserve the cooking water.

Press the Ricotta cheese through a sieve over the noodles and sprinkle with olive oil, salt and pepper and, if necessary, a little of the water in which the noodles were cooked, to help melt and blend the cheese. Mix together and serve.

# POTATO GNOCCHI WITH MEAT SAUCE

*Serves 6*

| | |
|---|---|
| 8 large potatoes | 4 oz/100 g butter |
| about 1 lb/450 g plain flour | 6 oz/175 g Parmesan cheese, |
| 2 teaspoons salt | grated |
| generous $\frac{3}{4}$ pint/5 dl meat sauce | |
| (see page 198) | |

Scrub the potatoes under cold running water and boil in lightly salted water to cover until barely tender. Drain, peel and press through a sieve on to a marble slab or into a mixing bowl. While still warm, make a well in the centre and add the flour and salt. Mix to form a soft dough, adding a little more flour if necessary. Knead lightly until smooth. Divide the dough into pieces and, with floured hands, form into long rolls, about 1 inch (2·5 cm) in diameter. Cut the rolls into 1½-inch (3·5-cm) pieces and make a lengthwise groove on either side of each piece by pressing between the index and second fingers. Arrange the *gnocchi* on a lightly floured surface, making sure they do not touch. Set aside for 10–15 minutes to dry.

Place a few *gnocchi* at a time in a large saucepan half filled with lightly salted boiling water. As soon as they come to the surface, remove them with a perforated spoon, drain well and place on a large heated serving dish. Heat the meat sauce and pour half of it over the *gnocchi*. Dot the surface with pieces of butter and sprinkle with one-third of the cheese. Serve very hot, accompanied by the remaining sauce and cheese.

*Tomato and anchovy pizza*

*Pansôti with walnut sauce*

# PANSÔTI WITH WALNUT SAUCE

*Serves 6*

**for the filling:**
2 oz/50 g lamb's brains
2 oz/50g lamb's sweetbreads
12 oz/350 g spinach
8 oz/225 g beetroot leaves
8 oz/225 g fresh borage
8 oz/225 g watercress
2½ oz/70 g butter
6 oz/175 g Ricotta cheese
2 eggs
1 clove garlic
pinch ground nutmeg
salt

**for the pasta:**
4 eggs
2 tablespoons warm water
1½ lb/700 g plain flour
1 teaspoon salt
1 beaten egg

**for the sauce:**
1 clove garlic
4 oz/100 g shelled walnuts
2 oz/50 g pine nut kernels
about ¼ pint/1·5 dl olive oil
4 oz/100 g Parmesan cheese,
    grated

To make the filling, soak the brains and sweetbreads in cold water for 1 hour. Blanch in boiling water, drain well and remove any skin, blood vessels and coarse tissue. Rinse the spinach, beetroot leaves, borage and watercress under cold running water. Remove any tough stalks and veins and shred all the leaves. Cook the leaves in lightly salted boiling water until tender. Drain thoroughly and press through a sieve into a large bowl. Heat the butter in a frying pan over moderate heat and sauté the brains and sweetbreads for 5–6 minutes, stirring frequently. Press through a sieve into the bowl with the sieved greens.

Sieve the Ricotta cheese, whisk the eggs, peel and crush the garlic and stir them all into the brain mixture. Add the nutmeg and season with salt to taste. Mix to a stiff paste. With floured hands, roll the paste into small balls, about the size of a walnut, and set aside while making the pasta.

To make the pasta, lightly whisk together the eggs and water in a small bowl. Sift the flour and salt on to a marble slab or into a mixing bowl and make a well in the centre. Pour in the eggs and water, mix to a firm smooth dough and knead well. Wrap the dough in a damp cloth and set aside for about 30 minutes.

Roll the dough into 2 sheets, about $\frac{1}{16}$ inch (1·5 mm) thick, and brush the first sheet with beaten egg. Place the balls of filling about 2 inches (5 cm) apart on the first sheet of dough. Cover with the second sheet and press firmly between the rounds of filling to seal together the two layers. Using a fluted pastry wheel or a sharp knife, cut the *pansôti* into 2-inch (5-cm) squares. Place on a floured surface until required.

To make the sauce, peel the garlic and crush with the walnuts and pine nut kernels. Press the mixture through a sieve into a bowl. Add the olive oil, drop by drop, beating constantly as if making a mayonnaise, until a thick coating mixture is formed. Add more oil, if necessary. Place a few *pansôti* at a time in a large saucepan half filled with lightly salted boiling water. Simmer for about 15 minutes. Remove with a perforated spoon and drain well. Place in a heated serving dish, sprinkle with the Parmesan cheese and cover with walnut sauce. Mix well and place in a moderately hot oven (400°F, 200°C, Gas Mark 6) for 3–4 minutes. Serve immediately.

*Note: Pansôti* are small squares of ravioli. The literal translation of *pansôti* is 'pot-bellied', implying that the ravioli should be well filled.

# LASAGNE VERDE WITH MEAT SAUCE

*Serves 6*

8 oz/225 g spinach
2 eggs
1 tablespoon olive oil
1 lb/450 g plain flour
1 teaspoon salt
¾ pint/4·5 dl meat sauce (see page 198)

generous ¼ pint/2 dl white sauce
6 oz/175 g Parmesan cheese,
    grated
4–6 oz/100–175 g melted butter
1 truffle (optional)

Rinse the spinach under cold running water and drain well. Cook in a very little boiling salted water for 10 minutes. Drain thoroughly. Chop finely, press through a sieve and set aside until cold. Lightly whisk together the eggs and olive oil in a small bowl. Sift the flour and salt on to a marble slab or into a mixing bowl and make a well in the centre. Pour in the eggs and olive oil and add the spinach. Mix to a smooth firm dough and knead well until the mixture is evenly coloured. Wrap in a damp cloth and set aside for about 30 minutes.

Roll the dough into 3 sheets, about $\frac{1}{16}$ inch (1·5 mm) thick, and cut into 3-inch (7·5-cm) squares. Cook 6 to 8 of the squares at a time in a shallow saucepan half filled with lightly salted boiling water for 3–4 minutes. Remove with a perforated spoon, drain well and set aside to cool on a damp cloth. Butter a 2-quart (2-litre) casserole and arrange the pasta in layers, covering each layer with 5 tablespoons of the meat sauce and a little white sauce, grated cheese and butter. Sprinkle the top with cheese and butter only. Bake in a moderate oven (350°F, 180°C, Gas Mark 4) for 20–30 minutes, or until the surface is well browned. Slice the truffle. Garnish with the truffle and serve with any remaining cheese.

# TAGLIATELLE WITH PESTO

*Serves 6*

5 eggs
1 tablespoon olive oil
1 lb/450 g plain flour
1 teaspoon salt

12 oz/350 g potatoes
2 oz/50 g Pecorino Sardo or
    Parmesan cheese, grated
*pesto* (see page 198)

Make the pasta as for Fettuccine, page 182. Wrap in a damp cloth and set aside for about 30 minutes.

Roll the dough into sheets, about $\frac{1}{16}$ inch (1·5 mm) thick. Fold each sheet in half lengthwise, then fold in half lengthwise again, several times. With a sharp knife, cut the dough into noodles, 1 inch (2·5 cm) wide. Unfold the noodles and place on a floured surface. Cover with a lightly floured cloth and set aside for 10–15 minutes, or until required.

Peel and thickly slice the potatoes and simmer in lightly salted boiling water until almost cooked. Add the noodles and continue simmering until *al dente* (cooked but still firm). Drain the noodles and potatoes and reserve 2 tablespoons of the liquid. Place the noodles and potatoes on an oval heated serving dish, sprinkle with the cheese and the reserved cooking liquid and mix lightly. Pour the *pesto* over and bring to the table. Mix together until the potatoes and noodles are well coated and serve.

# GENOESE GNOCCHI WITH PESTO

*Serves 6*

| | |
|---|---|
| 4½ lb/2 kg potatoes | 1 oz/25 g butter |
| about 12 oz/350 g plain flour | 1 teaspoon salt |
| 1 tablespoon Pecorino or Parmesan cheese, grated | 4 egg yolks (optional) |
| 2 tablespoons fine fresh breadcrumbs | *pesto* (see page 198) |

Scrub the potatoes under cold running water and boil in lightly salted water to cover until barely tender. Meanwhile, mix together the flour, cheese, breadcrumbs, butter and salt. Drain and peel the potatoes and press through a sieve on to a marble slab or into a mixing bowl.

While the potato is still warm, make a well in the centre and add the flour mixture and egg yolks. Mix to a soft dough, adding a little more flour if necessary. Mix lightly, handling the dough as little as possible. Divide the dough into pieces and, with floured hands, form into long rolls, about 1 inch (2·5 cm) in diameter. Cut the rolls into 1½-inch (3·5-cm) pieces and make a lengthwise groove on either side of each piece by pressing between the index and second fingers. Arrange on a lightly floured surface, making sure they do not touch. Set aside for 10–15 minutes to dry.

Place a few of the *gnocchi* at a time into a large saucepan half filled with lightly salted boiling water. As they come to the surface, remove with a perforated spoon, drain well and place on a large heated serving plate. Heat the *pesto* diluted with 2 tablespoons of the cooking liquid from the *gnocchi*. Pour over the *gnocchi*, mix and serve.

# BEEF-STUFFED PASTA WITH HERB BUTTER

*Serves 6*

| | |
|---|---|
| **for the pasta:** | 1 tablespoon Parmesan cheese, grated |
| 5 eggs | |
| 1 tablespoon melted butter | pinch ground nutmeg |
| 1 lb/450 g plain flour | salt and pepper |
| 1 teaspoon salt | 1–2 eggs |
| **for the filling:** | **for serving:** |
| 1 oz/25 g butter | 6 oz/175 g butter |
| 2 cloves garlic | fresh sage leaves, chopped (see recipe) |
| 1 tablespoon chopped parsley | |
| 8 oz/225 g beef, minced | 4 oz/100 g Parmesan cheese, grated |
| 2 tablespoons fine fresh breadcrumbs | |

To make the pasta, lightly beat the eggs and butter in a small bowl. Sift the flour and salt on to a marble slab or into a mixing bowl and make a well in the centre. Pour in the egg mixture, mix to a firm dough and knead well. Wrap in a damp cloth and set aside for about 30 minutes.

To make the filling, heat the butter in a frying pan over moderate heat. Peel and finely chop the garlic. Add the garlic and parsley and sauté until they begin to brown, then add the beef and sauté for about 10 minutes, stirring frequently. Remove the pan from the heat, add the breadcrumbs and

cheese and set aside in a bowl to cool. Season with the nutmeg and salt and pepper to taste and blend to a paste with the eggs.

Roll out the dough into sheets, about $\frac{1}{16}$ inch (1·5 mm) thick, on a lightly floured surface. Cut 3½-inch (9-cm) squares of dough and put 1 tablespoon of the filling on half of each square. Brush the edges of the square with the water. Fold the uncovered half of the square over the filling and press the edges together to completely enclose the filling. Place on a lightly floured tray until required.

Cook the pasta squares, a few at a time, in a large saucepan half filled with lightly salted boiling water for about 5 minutes. Remove with a perforated spoon as they come to the surface. Drain well and place on a heated serving dish. Heat the butter until golden brown, sprinkle in chopped sage leaves to taste and pour over the pasta. Sprinkle with the cheese and serve.

# BONE MARROW-STUFFED PASTA

*Serves 6*

| | |
|---|---|
| **for the pasta:** | salt and pepper |
| 5 eggs | pinch ground nutmeg |
| 1 tablespoon olive oil | 2 egg yolks |
| 1 lb/450 g plain flour | 1–2 tablespoons beef stock |
| 1 teaspoon salt | |
| **for the filling:** | 1 beaten egg |
| 10 oz/275 g dried breadcrumbs | **for serving:** |
| 6 oz/175 g Parmesan cheese, grated | 6 oz/175 g melted butter |
| 4 oz/100g melted bone marrow | 4 oz/100 g Parmesan cheese, grated |

Make the pasta as for Fettuccine, page 182. Wrap in a damp cloth and set aside for about 30 minutes.

To make the filling, mix together the breadcrumbs, cheese, bone marrow, salt and pepper and nutmeg. Add the egg yolks and mix to a soft dough, adding the stock if necessary. Roll the dough into two thin sheets, about $\frac{1}{16}$ inch (1·5 mm) thick. Brush the surface of the first sheet of pasta with beaten egg and, using a piping bag and a ½-inch (1-cm) tube, pipe small amounts of filling on to the sheet about 2 inches (5 cm) apart. Cover with the second sheet of pasta, brush with the egg and seal the layers together by pressing the spaces between the filling with the fingertips. Cut into squares, using a pastry wheel or a sharp knife, and place on a lightly floured board until required.

Cook the pasta squares, a few at a time, in a large saucepan half filled with lightly salted boiling water, for 8–10 minutes, or until they rise to the surface. Remove with a perforated spoon and drain well.

Heat the butter in a saucepan over moderate heat until lightly browned. Arrange the pasta squares in layers in an ovenproof serving dish alternating with the butter and half the cheese. Heat through in a moderate oven (350°F, 180°C, Gas Mark 4) for about 15 minutes. Serve with the remaining cheese.

*Noodles in hare sauce*

# NOODLES IN HARE SAUCE

*Serves 6*

| | |
|---|---|
| 3 lb/1·5 kg hare pieces | 1 lb/450 g plain flour |
| **for the marinade:** | 1 teaspoon salt |
| ½ small onion | **for the sauce:** |
| ½ stick celery | ½ onion |
| 1 bay leaf | ½ carrot |
| generous ¾ pint/5 dl full-bodied | 2 rashers very lean bacon |
| red wine | 1 tablespoon olive oil |
| 2 peppercorns | salt |
| **for the pasta:** | pinch ground nutmeg |
| 4 eggs | chicken stock (see recipe) |
| 1 tablespoon olive oil | 2 oz/50 g butter |

Rinse the hare pieces under cold running water and dry with a cloth or kitchen paper.

To make the marinade, peel the onion, slice the celery and crumble the bay leaf. Place in a bowl with the wine and peppercorns. Add the hare and set aside to marinate for several hours, turning occasionally.

Make the pasta as for Fettuccine, page 182. Wrap in a damp cloth and set aside for about 30 minutes.

Roll the dough on a floured surface to about $\frac{1}{16}$ inch (1·5 mm) thick. With a sharp knife, cut the dough into noodles about ¼ inch (5 mm) wide. Set aside on a floured surface to dry until required.

To make the sauce, peel and chop the onion and carrot. Chop the bacon. Heat the oil in a frying pan over moderate heat, add the onion, carrot and bacon and sauté until lightly browned. Drain the pieces of hare, season with salt and nutmeg, add to the pan and sauté until browned. Lower the heat and cook gently for about 1 hour, or until tender, occasionally adding 1 tablespoon of the marinade and 1 tablespoon of the stock to form a thin sauce. Remove the pieces of hare and strain the sauce through a fine sieve. Keep both hot.

Place the noodles in a large saucepan half filled with lightly salted boiling water. Simmer for 8–12 minutes, or until *al dente* (cooked but still firm). Drain and pour into a deep heated serving dish. Cover with the sauce and place small pieces of the butter on the surface. Bring to the table and mix thoroughly before serving.

Serve the hare as a separate course accompanied by seasonal vegetables.

# MIXED BOILED MEATS WITH GREEN SAUCE

*Serves 8*

8 oz/225 g *cotechino* sausage (see note)
1 lb/450 g lean bacon, in 1 piece (optional)
1 capon, about 4 lb/1·75 kg
2 lb/1 kg lamb, best end of neck
1 veal hock
8 oz/225 g Italian pork sausage
1 small carrot
2 sticks celery
2 cloves
1 onion
coarse salt
green sauce (see page 198)

Prick the *cotechino* and place in a very large saucepan with the bacon, if used. Add just enough water to cover and bring to the boil over moderate heat. Lower the heat and simmer the meats for about 1 hour. Add the capon, lamb, veal and sausage and enough water to cover completely. Bring to the boil and skim the surface of the liquid. Peel the carrot, wash the celery and add to the pan. Stick the cloves into the onion and add to the pan with the salt. Cover the pan and simmer for 1½–2 hours. Remove the different meats when tender, drain and keep hot.

Meanwhile, make the green sauce following the instructions on page 198, and pour into a sauceboat. Serve the cooked meats as hot as possible on a wooden meat platter, with pickles, radishes, grated fresh horseradish root, a variety of seasonal green vegetables, boiled potatoes and *mostarda*, an Italian relish of candied fruits in a spicy mustard syrup.

*Note:* Cotechino is a large, round pork sausage, highly spiced and seasoned with garlic.

# FRICASSÉE OF LAMB

*Serves 6*

2 lb/1 kg boned leg or shoulder of lamb
1 very small onion
2 tablespoons olive oil
2 oz/50 g lean and fat ham, minced
pinch ground nutmeg
salt and pepper
generous ¼ pint/2 dl dry white wine
½ oz/15 g plain flour
2 cloves garlic
few sprigs parsley
4 egg yolks
2 tablespoons lemon juice

Cut the lamb into 1½-inch (3·5-cm) cubes. Peel and chop the onion. Heat the olive oil in a flameproof casserole or a saucepan over moderate heat. Add the lamb, onion, ham, nutmeg and salt and pepper and stir constantly. When the meat begins to brown, add the wine and reduce it to 1 tablespoon. Sprinkle in the flour and mix thoroughly. Stir in enough water barely to cover the lamb. Simmer over low heat for 50 minutes–1 hour, or until the lamb is tender. During the cooking add a few tablespoons of water to prevent the meat from sticking, if necessary.

Peel the garlic and chop with the parsley. Stir in the garlic and parsley 2–3 minutes before the end of the cooking time. Remove the casserole from the heat. Lightly whisk the egg yolks with the lemon juice, blend into the liquid in the casserole and replace over the heat until the mixture is hot and the sauce thickens (see note). Remove the casserole from the heat immediately, pour the fricassée into a deep heated serving dish and serve.

*Note:* Special care should be taken to prevent the fricassée from reaching the boiling point since the egg will curdle and ruin the appearance and smooth texture of the sauce.

# ITALIAN LAMB STEW

*Serves 6*

2 lb/1 kg shoulder or neck fillet of lamb
½ small carrot
½ onion
1 clove garlic
1 stick celery
1 tablespoon olive oil
4 oz/100 g bacon fat, minced
¼ pint/1·5 dl dry white wine
generous ¼ pint/2 dl tomato sauce (see page 197)
generous ¼ pint/2 dl water
salt
¼ teaspoon chilli powder
3 medium-sized potatoes

Cut the lamb into 1½-inch (3·5-cm) cubes. Peel and finely chop the carrot, onion and garlic. Finely chop the celery. Heat the olive oil in a flameproof casserole or a saucepan over high heat, add the lamb and sauté until browned. Remove the lamb and set aside until required.

Add the bacon fat, carrot, onion, garlic and celery to the casserole. Sauté until browned, then pour in the wine and reduce to 3 tablespoons over high heat. Add the tomato sauce diluted with the water, season lightly with salt and chilli powder and simmer gently over moderate heat for 15 minutes. Return the lamb to the casserole and simmer for a further 20–30 minutes, stirring frequently, until the lamb is tender. Meanwhile, peel the potatoes and cut into small pieces. Place in a saucepan, cover with water, bring to the boil and simmer until three-quarters cooked. Drain well and add to the lamb about 10 minutes before the end of the cooking time.

# STEAK WITH TOMATO AND GARLIC SAUCE

*Serves 4*

2 medium-sized tomatoes
3 cloves garlic
2 tablespoons olive oil
4 porterhouse steaks, ¾ inch/1·5 cm thick
salt and pepper
pinch oregano

Peel and slice the tomatoes. Peel and crush the garlic. Heat the olive oil in a heavy frying pan over high heat. Add the steaks and sauté on each side until well browned, then lower the heat and cook for a further 2–3 minutes. Remove the steaks from the pan and place on a heated plate, sprinkle with salt and pepper and keep hot.

Add the garlic to the same pan and sauté over moderate heat until lightly browned. Add the tomatoes and oregano, season with salt and simmer for about 8 minutes, stirring frequently. Return the steaks and any juices that have drained from them to the pan and simmer for 3–4 minutes. Place the steaks on heated plates, pour a little of the sauce over each and serve.

*Italian lamb stew*

# VEAL WITH HAM AND SAGE IN WHITE WINE

*Serves 6*

| | |
|---|---|
| 12 thin veal escalopes | 12 thin slices Parma ham |
| salt and freshly ground black | plain flour for coating |
| pepper | 4 oz/100 g butter |
| 12 fresh sage leaves | 5 tablespoons dry white wine |

Flatten the veal with a meat mallet or a wooden rolling pin. Season with the salt and pepper, then place 1 sage leaf and 1 slice of ham on each piece of veal. Roll the veal, or fold in half, and secure with a wooden cocktail stick. Coat lightly with flour.

Heat three-quarters of the butter in a frying pan over moderate heat and fry the veal until evenly browned and tender. Remove the cocktail sticks, place the veal on a heated serving plate and keep hot.

Pour the wine into the pan and reduce to 1 tablespoon over high heat. Loosen the residue on the bottom of the pan and stir in the remaining butter. Simmer for a few seconds, then pour over the veal rolls and serve.

# STUFFED VEAL

*Serves 6*

| | |
|---|---|
| 2 lb/1 kg boned breast of veal | 1½ oz/40 g Parmesan cheese, |
| **for the stuffing:** | grated |
| 4 oz/100 g lamb's or calf's | 8 oz/225 g shelled peas or roughly |
| sweetbreads | chopped beetroot leaves |
| ½ lemon | 2 oz/50 g pistachio nuts |
| 8 oz/225 g white bread | 4 eggs |
| scant ½ pint/2·5 dl milk | pinch ground nutmeg |
| 1 lb/450 g pork fillet or fillet of | salt and pepper |
| veal, minced | **for cooking the veal:** |
| 4 oz/100 g bacon fat, minced | 1 medium-sized onion |
| 2 tablespoons chopped fresh | 1 small carrot |
| marjoram or 3 teaspoons dried | ½ bay leaf |
| marjoram | 2 peppercorns |
| | salt |

Cut a slit at one end of the veal, insert a long sharp knife through the slit and cut the inside of the veal, making a 'pocket' to hold the stuffing. Set aside until required.

To make the stuffing, soak the sweetbreads in cold water for 1 hour. Drain well and dry with a cloth or kitchen paper. Rub the surface of the sweetbreads with the cut side of the lemon, then replace in cold water and soak for about 30 minutes, or until they become very white. Drain the sweetbreads and rinse under cold running water. Dry thoroughly and cut into ¼-inch (5-mm) cubes. Cut off the bread crusts. Soak the bread in the milk, then squeeze out the excess moisture. Place the sweetbreads, bread, pork fillet, bacon fat, marjoram, cheese, peas, pistachio nuts, eggs, nutmeg and salt and pepper in a bowl. Mix to form a paste.

Press the stuffing into the 'pocket' in the veal and sew up the opening with white thread. Loosely tie the veal with thin string so that it maintains its shape when cooking. Place in a flameproof casserole or large saucepan and cover with plenty of cold water.

Peel and slice the onion and carrot and add to the casserole. Add the bay leaf, peppercorns and salt. Place over moderate heat and bring to the boil. Lower the heat and simmer, partially covered, for 2 hours, or until the veal is tender.

Remove the veal from the liquid and place on a firm flat surface (reserve the liquid for soup stock, if desired). Place a wooden board on top of the veal and press the meat, using heavy weights, for about 2 hours. Serve cold.

# VEAL WITH TUNA FISH SAUCE

*Serves 6*

| | |
|---|---|
| 8 anchovy fillets | **for the sauce:** |
| 3 tablespoons milk | 1 (7-oz/198-g) can tuna fish |
| 1 medium-sized onion | 2 anchovy fillets |
| 2 medium-sized carrots | 3 tablespoons veal stock |
| 6 gherkins | (see recipe) |
| 1 stick celery | 4 egg yolks |
| ½ lemon | ¾ pint/4·5 dl olive oil |
| 1 boned and rolled breast of veal, | 3 tablespoons lemon juice |
| about 2¼ lb/1 kg | salt |
| ¼ pint/1·5 dl dry white wine | **for the garnish:** |
| 3 tablespoons olive oil | 2 tablespoons capers |
| ½ pint/3 dl cold water | 3 pickled onions |

Soak the anchovy fillets in the milk for 10–15 minutes to remove the excess salt. Drain and discard the milk. Peel and slice the onion and one of the carrots. Peel the remaining carrot and cut into thick strips. Cut the gherkins in half lengthwise. Slice the celery. Thinly pare the rind from the lemon and squeeze the lemon to extract the juice.

Using a sharp knife, make small incisions in the veal and insert the anchovy fillets. Tie the strips of carrot and the gherkins on to the veal with thin string. Place the veal in a flameproof casserole or large saucepan with the sliced onion, carrot and celery. Add the lemon rind, lemon juice, wine, olive oil and water. Cover the casserole and simmer over moderate heat for about 2 hours, or until tender. Remove the casserole from the heat, take out the veal and remove the string. Place the veal in a bowl. Discard all the vegetables in the casserole, strain the stock over the veal and set aside to cool. When cold, pour the stock into a small saucepan and boil rapidly over high heat until reduced to about 4 tablespoons. Remove from the heat and set aside until required.

To make the sauce, drain the tuna fish and pound with the anchovy fillets to form a paste. Dilute the paste with 3 tablespoons of the reserved veal stock and press through a fine sieve. Place the egg yolks in a mixing bowl or liquidiser. Add the olive oil drop by drop, beating constantly until a thick mayonnaise is formed. Add the lemon juice and gradually stir in the tuna fish paste. The sauce should be of a thick pouring consistency. If it is too thick, add the remaining veal stock. Season with salt to taste.

Thinly slice the veal and place on a serving dish. Coat with some of the tuna fish sauce and garnish with the capers and the pickled onions. Serve cold, accompanied by the remaining sauce.

# OSSOBUCO ALLA MILANESE

*Serves 6*

| | |
|---|---|
| 2 veal hocks, cut into 6 pieces | small strip thinly peeled lemon rind |
| plain flour for coating | rind |
| 1 small onion | 4 oz/100 g butter |
| 2 cloves garlic | salt and pepper |
| 1 medium-sized carrot | ¼ pint/1·5 dl dry white wine |
| 2 ripe tomatoes | about 2–3 tablespoons vegetable stock |
| 1 stick celery | stock |
| few sprigs marjoram | grated rind of ½ lemon |
| | *risotto alla milanese* (see page 196) |

Wipe the pieces of veal with a damp cloth or kitchen paper and coat with flour. Peel and finely chop the onion, 1 clove of garlic, the carrot and tomatoes. Finely chop the celery, marjoram and strip of lemon rind. Melt three-quarters of the butter in a large saucepan over high heat, add the pieces of veal and sauté until browned. Add the onion, garlic, carrot, celery, marjoram and strip of lemon rind and season with salt and pepper. When the mixture is lightly browned, add the wine and simmer until reduced to 1 tablespoon. Add the

tomatoes and the stock. Lower the heat, cover the pan tightly and simmer for 1 hour or more, adding a little additional stock, if necessary, to prevent the sauce from sticking.

Meanwhile, prepare the *risotto alla milanese* following the instructions on page 196. Peel and chop the remaining clove of garlic. Add the garlic, grated lemon rind and remaining butter to the veal. Stir and simmer for 2–3 minutes over moderate heat. Arrange the veal in a crown shape on a round heated serving dish and cover with the sauce. Serve with the *risotto alla milanese*.

*Veal with tuna fish sauce*

# SKEWERED MEATS WITH POLENTA

*Serves 6*

| | |
|---|---|
| 6 chicken livers | 1½ lb/700 g fillet of veal |
| salt and pepper | 6 sage leaves |
| 4 oz/100 g butter | 6 slices cold *polenta* (see page 197) |
| 1 lb/450 g lean bacon | 2 tablespoons olive oil |
| 4 oz/100 g calf's sweetbreads | |

Cut each chicken liver in half. Season with salt and pepper. Heat half the butter in a frying pan, add the livers and sauté until firm but still soft in the centre. Drain and cool. Cut the bacon into 24 pieces, each about ½ inch by 2 inches (1 by 5 cm). Simmer the bacon in boiling water for 5 minutes. Drain and dry well on kitchen paper. Remove and discard any membrane from the sweetbreads. Cut the sweetbreads into 6 slices and each slice into quarters. Cut the fillet of veal into 24 pieces.

Thread the liver, bacon, sweetbreads and veal alternately on to 6 skewers, adding 1 sage leaf to each skewer. Season with salt and pepper and arrange on a baking tray greased with the remaining butter. Cook in a moderately hot oven (400°F, 200°C, Gas Mark 6) for 15–20 minutes.

Meanwhile, sauté the *polenta* slices in the oil until golden brown and arrange on a heated serving plate. Place the skewers of meat on top and serve.

# SWEETBREADS IN MUSHROOM AND MEAT SAUCE

*Serves 6*

| | |
|---|---|
| 1 lb/450 g lamb's sweetbreads | salt and pepper |
| 1 lb/450 g fresh mushrooms | 5 tablespoons Marsala |
| 4 oz/100 g butter | ¼ pint/1·5 dl meat sauce (see page 198) |
| 1 tablespoon finely chopped onion | |

Soak the sweetbreads in cold water for 30 minutes. Drain and rinse. Place in a saucepan and cover with cold water. Bring to the boil over moderate heat. Boil for 1 minute, then drain and rinse again under cold running water. Discard any skin and coarse tissue and dry the sweetbreads thoroughly with a cloth or kitchen paper. Rinse the mushrooms under cold running water and slice thickly.

Heat three-quarters of the butter in a frying pan over moderate heat. Add the sweetbreads, onion and salt and pepper and sauté until golden brown. Remove the contents of the pan, drain and keep hot. Add the mushrooms and a pinch of salt to the pan, sauté over moderate heat until soft, remove, drain and keep hot with the sweetbreads.

Pour the Marsala into the juices remaining in the pan and reduce by half over high heat. Stir in the meat sauce and simmer to reduce and thicken. Stir in the sweetbreads, onion and mushrooms and add the remaining butter. Cook for a few seconds before serving in a heated serving dish.

# OXTAIL IN WINE SAUCE

*Serves 6*

| | |
|---|---|
| 3–4 lb/1·5–1·75 kg oxtail | ½ teaspoon chopped fresh marjoram or ¼ teaspoon dried marjoram |
| 1 small carrot | |
| 1 leek | |
| 5 pints/3 litres cold water | generous ¼ pint/2 dl dry white wine |
| 2–3 teaspoons coarse salt | |
| 1 stick celery | pinch ground nutmeg |
| ½ bay leaf | salt and pepper |
| 1 small onion | 3 lb/1·5 kg celery hearts |
| 2 lb/1 kg tomatoes | pinch ground cinnamon |
| 4 oz/100 g gammon | 1 tablespoon pine nut kernels |
| 2 tablespoons olive oil | 1 tablespoon sultanas |

Cut the oxtail into 1½-inch (3·5-cm) pieces and soak for 1 hour in cold water, or let stand for 30 minutes under slowly running water. Place in a large saucepan with plenty of cold water and bring to the boil. Simmer for about 10 minutes, drain well and dry with a cloth or kitchen paper. Peel the carrot. Trim the leek and wash thoroughly. Trim and wash

the celery. Return the oxtail to the pan and add the measured cold water and the salt. Place over high heat and bring to the boil. Lower the heat and skim carefully. Add the carrot, leek, celery and bay leaf and simmer gently for 3 hours.

Remove the oxtail, drain and dry with a cloth or kitchen paper. Discard the vegetables and bay leaf and reserve the stock. Peel and finely chop the onion. Peel and chop the tomatoes and press through a sieve. Mince the gammon. Heat the olive oil in a saucepan over moderate heat, add the gammon, onion and marjoram and sauté until lightly browned. Add the oxtail. Simmer for 2–3 minutes, then pour in the wine and reduce to 1 tablespoon. Stir in the tomatoes, season with the nutmeg and salt and pepper and continue cooking for about 1 hour, or until the meat comes away from the bone. If the sauce begins to thicken too much, add a little of the reserved oxtail stock.

Meanwhile, cook the celery hearts in lightly salted boiling water until barely tender. Drain and add to the oxtail with the cinnamon about 10 minutes before the end of the cooking time. Just before serving, stir in the pine nut kernels and sultanas. Pour into a deep heated serving dish and serve.

*Easter pie*

# EASTER PIE

Serves 6

| | |
|---|---|
| 2 lb/1 kg plain flour | 12 oz/350 g Ricotta cheese |
| 1½ teaspoons salt | ½ oz/15 g plain flour |
| 1 tablespoon olive oil | 3 tablespoons single cream |
| 1 pint/6 dl water | salt and freshly ground black |
| **for the filling:** | pepper |
| 4 oz/100 g young, small-veined | 2 tablespoons olive oil |
| beetroot leaves or very young | 6 eggs |
| artichokes | 2 oz/50 g melted butter |
| 2 oz/50 g Parmesan cheese, grated | |
| 1½ teaspoons chopped fresh | |
| marjoram and parsley or 1 | |
| teaspoon dried marjoram and | |
| parsley | |

Sift the flour and salt on to a marble slab or into a mixing bowl and make a well in the centre. Pour in the olive oil and water and mix to a very soft dough. Knead well and divide into 20 pieces. Place the pieces on a floured cloth and cover with a damp cloth.

Rinse the beetroot leaves under cold running water. Drain well and shred finely. Cook in lightly salted boiling water for 8–10 minutes. Drain the beetroot leaves, squeeze to remove the excess moisture and spread on a large plate. Sprinkle with half the Parmesan cheese and the marjoram and parsley. If using artichokes, discard the coarse outer leaves, clean the remaining leaves thoroughly, cut into fine strips and cook in lightly salted boiling water. Drain well and continue as above.

Blend the Ricotta cheese with the remaining flour and press through a sieve into a bowl. Add the cream and the salt and pepper. Roll out 10 pieces of the dough into very thin round sheets, each about 14 inches (36 cm) in diameter. Place in layers in a greased 12-inch (30-cm) deep cake tin, loose-bottomed if possible, brushing each layer except the last with olive oil. Carefully press them firmly against the bottom and sides of the tin. Spread the beetroot leaves evenly over the top layer of dough. Sprinkle with olive oil and cover with the Ricotta mixture. With the back of a spoon, make 6 hollows in the cheese mixture and carefully crack 1 egg into each one, without breaking the yolks. Pour a little of the melted butter over each egg. Season with salt and pepper to taste and sprinkle with the remaining Parmesan cheese.

Roll out the remaining pieces of dough to the same size as the previous pieces. Place in layers over the mixture, brushing each one with oil. Trim the surplus dough overlapping the edge of the tin. Make a braid with these trimmings and place it around the edge of the pie. Brush the surface of the dough with oil and lightly prick with a fork, without breaking the egg yolks, to allow the steam to escape during cooking. Bake in a moderately hot oven (375°F, 190°C, Gas Mark 5) for 50 minutes–1 hour. Serve hot or cold.

# STUFFED CAPON

*Serves 6*

| | |
|---|---|
| 1 capon, about 4 lb/1·75 kg | 2–3 tablespoons chicken stock |
| salt and pepper | cold water (see recipe) |
| 4 oz/100 g Stravecchio cheese | 1 small carrot |
|    (matured Parmesan), grated | 1 small onion |
| 3 oz/75 g butter | 1 clove |
| 2 eggs | 1 stick celery |
| 3 oz/75 g fine fresh breadcrumbs | |

Using a sharp knife, remove the breast bone from the capon. Season the cavity of the capon with salt and pepper. Mix together the cheese, butter, eggs, breadcrumbs and salt and pepper to taste, adding enough stock to make a soft stuffing. Stuff the bird, sew up the opening and truss the bird with fine string. Place in a flameproof casserole or a large saucepan and cover with lightly salted cold water. Bring to the boil over moderate heat and skim the surface carefully.

Meanwhile, peel the carrot and onion. Stick the clove into the onion and add with the carrot and the celery to the casserole. Lower the heat, cover tightly and simmer for about 1½ hours, or until the capon is tender.

Remove the capon, drain well and remove the string. Carve and arrange on a heated serving plate. Surround with boiled seasonal vegetables or vegetables fried in butter. Serve with green sauce (see page 198).


# STEWED GOOSE

*Serves 6*

| | |
|---|---|
| 1 goose, about 6 lb/2·75 kg | vegetable stock (see recipe) |
| salt and pepper | ¼ pint/1·5 dl tomato sauce (see |
| 1 large onion |    page 197) |
| 1 large carrot | pinch mixed spice |
| 1 clove garlic | 4 oz/100 g bacon |
| 4 oz/100 g goose fat | 1 lb/450 g *luganeghe* or pure pork |
| 4 tablespoons dry red wine |    sausage |
| ½ oz/15 g plain flour | |

Cut the goose into pieces and season with salt and pepper. Peel and thinly slice the onion and carrot. Peel and crush the garlic. Heat half the goose fat in a saucepan. Add the goose, onion and carrot and sauté until browned. Add the wine and reduce it over moderate heat until evaporated almost completely, then sprinkle in the flour, a little at a time. Cook until golden brown, stirring constantly. Pour in enough stock to cover the goose completely. Add the garlic, tomato sauce and mixed spice. Bring to the boil, cover tightly and simmer for about 1½ hours, or until tender.

Meanwhile, dice the bacon and cut the sausage into 2-inch (5-cm) pieces. Heat the remaining goose fat in a second saucepan, add the bacon and sausage and sauté for 5–10 minutes.

Drain the goose, place in a clean saucepan and add the sautéed bacon and sausage. Strain the sauce over the goose through a fine sieve, place over low heat and bring to the boil. Cover the pan tightly and simmer for 1 hour. Serve very hot.

*Stuffed capon; green sauce (see page 198)*


# ROAST WOODCOCK

*Serves 2*

| | |
|---|---|
| 1 woodcock, hung but not | 1½ teaspoons chopped bacon fat |
|    dressed | 1 teaspoon brandy |
| salt and pepper | 4 tablespoons chicken stock |
| 3–4 thin slices bacon fat | 1 teaspoon butter |
| 4 oz/100 g butter | 1 teaspoon lemon juice |
| 2 slices bread | |

Pluck the woodcock and remove and discard the feet, eyes and gizzard, but do not draw the bird. Singe, then wipe thoroughly with a clean cloth or kitchen paper. Truss the legs together. Bend the head towards the tail and push the long beak like a skewer through the nearest leg, the body, then the second leg, to hold the bird in position. Season with salt and pepper. Wrap the woodcock in the bacon fat and secure with fine string. Melt half the butter in a saucepan over high heat, add the woodcock and sauté until brown. Lower the heat and continue cooking for about 20 minutes.

Meanwhile, melt the remaining butter in a frying pan over moderate heat. Cut off the bread crusts and sauté the bread until golden brown on each side. Remove from the pan and drain.

Remove the woodcock from the saucepan, discard the string and slices of bacon fat, cut the bird in half lengthwise and scoop the intestines into a bowl. Add the chopped bacon fat, brandy and salt and pepper. Blend thoroughly with a fork and spread the mixture on the sautéed bread slices. Place in a moderately hot oven (400°F, 200°C, Gas Mark 6) for 2 minutes to set the mixture.

Add the stock to the juices remaining in the saucepan and reduce to 3 tablespoons over moderate heat. Remove the pan from the heat and add the butter and the lemon juice. Place the bread slices on 2 heated plates with half a woodcock on each. Pour over the gravy and serve.


# SPIT-ROASTED WOOD PIGEONS WITH OLIVES AND WINE

*Serves 6*

| | |
|---|---|
| 3 wood pigeons | 3 tablespoons dry white wine |
| 12 green olives, stoned | 3 tablespoons lemon juice |
| 2–3 fresh or dried sage leaves, | salt and pepper |
|    chopped | fried croutons |
| 4 tablespoons olive oil | |

Clean, wash and dry the pigeons. Pound the olives with a pestle in a mortar or with a wooden rolling pin in a bowl. Add the sage to the olives with the olive oil, wine, lemon juice and salt and pepper. Thread the pigeons on to a spit rod and brush with the olive mixture, reserving a little for basting. Place over wood embers and charcoal or in a rôtisserie with a pan beneath to collect the juices. Cook for about 1 hour, brushing the pigeons occasionally with the remaining olive mixture.

Cut the pigeons in half lengthwise and arrange on a heated serving plate. Pour the juices from the drippings pan over them and garnish with fried croutons. Serve immediately.

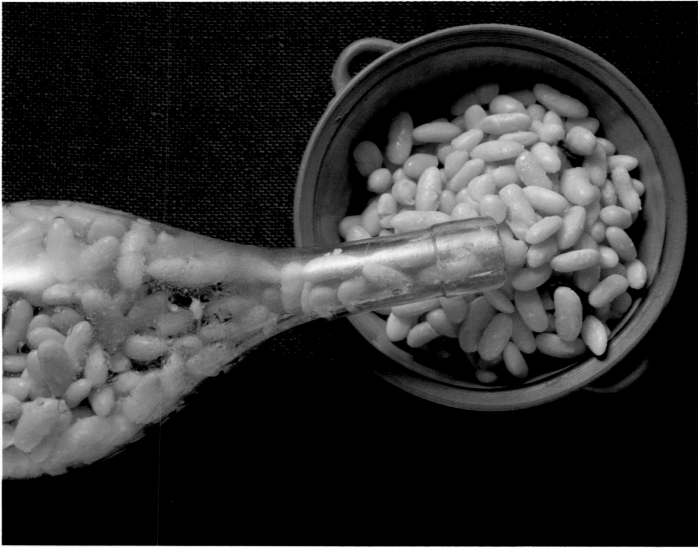

*Beans in a flask*

# RISOTTO ALLA MILANESE

*Serves 6*

| | |
|---|---|
| ¼ onion | salt |
| 8 oz/225 g butter | pinch saffron powder |
| 1 oz/25 g bone marrow | about 1¾ pints/1 litre vegetable |
| pinch pepper | stock |
| ¼ pint/1·5 dl dry white wine | 4 oz/100 g Parmesan cheese, |
| 1 lb/450 g long-grain rice | grated |

Finely chop the onion. Melt about one-third of the butter in a saucepan over low heat and add the onion, bone marrow and pepper. Sauté the onion until soft, but not browned, then add the wine and reduce by half. Add the rice and salt and cook for 2–3 minutes, stirring constantly. Add the saffron powder and stock and bring to the boil, still stirring. Simmer for about 15 minutes, stirring constantly and adding a little additional hot stock, if necessary, to prevent the rice from sticking to the pan. Remove the pan from the heat when the rice is *al dente* (cooked but still firm). Add the remaining butter and 2–3 tablespoons of the cheese. Set aside for 2–3 minutes in a warm place, then transfer to a heated serving dish. Serve with the remaining cheese.

# BEANS IN A FLASK

*Serves 6*

| | |
|---|---|
| 12 oz/350 g dried *toscanelli* beans | 5 tablespoons olive oil |
| or haricot beans | few fresh or dried sage leaves |
| 2 cloves garlic | salt and freshly ground pepper |

Clean the beans and soak in plenty of cold water for at least 12 hours. Drain and place in a chianti flask from which the straw has been removed. The flask should be about three-quarters full so that the beans can swell. Peel and crush the garlic. Add the garlic, olive oil and sage and cover with water. Plug the flask loosely with straw or cotton wool so the steam can escape during cooking and help the beans absorb the oil.

Place the flask over the glowing embers of a charcoal fire or in a moderately hot oven (375°F, 190°C, Gas Mark 5) and cook for 3 hours. Pour the beans into a heated serving bowl and season with a little more olive oil and salt and pepper to taste. Serve hot.

# POLENTA (CORN MEAL PUDDING)

*Serves 6*

1¾ pints/1 litre water
1 teaspoon salt

12 oz/350 g yellow corn meal
2–3 tablespoons boiling water

Boil the water with the salt in a large heavy saucepan. Sprinkle in one-third of the corn meal, a little at a time. Using a wooden spoon, stir the mixture constantly. As the mixture thickens, add the 2–3 tablespoons boiling water. After 15 minutes, sprinkle in another third of the corn meal, stirring constantly. Gradually add the remaining corn meal and continue stirring until the mixture is well blended. The *polenta* is perfectly cooked when it comes away easily from the side of the pan. This takes 30–45 minutes, but to make the corn meal easier to digest, and to remove its slightly bitter taste, it is advisable to extend the cooking period to at least 1 hour, stirring frequently.

The *polenta* may be eaten very hot with various sauces and garnishes, or cold, sliced in the classic way using strong fine thread or cheese wire rather than a knife, and served with butter and freshly grated Parmesan cheese. It may also be cut into thick slices and fried. Sliced cold *polenta* is a good substitute for bread, especially with a beef stew.

# POLENTA WITH SALAMI AND TOMATO SAUCE

*Serves 6*

*polenta* (see preceding recipe)
1 lb/450 g *codeghì* salami (see note)
2 rashers streaky bacon
1½ lb/700 g tomatoes

6 oz/175 g butter
pinch ground nutmeg
salt and pepper
6 oz/175 g Parmesan cheese, grated

Prepare the *polenta* following the instructions in the preceding recipe. Turn it out of the saucepan on to a slightly dampened marble slab and, using the flat side of a knife dipped frequently in boiling water, spread it out to ½ inch (1 cm) thick. Let stand until cold. Slice the *codeghì*. Chop the bacon rashers. Peel the tomatoes and press through a sieve into a small bowl. Melt two-thirds of the butter in a frying pan over moderate heat. Add the *codeghì* and the bacon and sauté until well browned. Add the tomatoes and season with the nutmeg and salt and pepper to taste. Cook over moderate heat for about 1 hour, adding 2–3 tablespoons of water if the sauce becomes too thick.

Grease a 1½-quart (1·5-litre) casserole or pie dish with half the remaining butter and line with 2 or 3 layers of sliced *polenta*, laid crisscross, sprinkling each layer with a few tablespoons of sauce and cheese, leaving half the cheese for serving. Dot the remaining butter in small pieces on the surface. Cook in a moderately hot oven (400°F, 200°C, Gas Mark 6) until golden brown. Serve with the remaining cheese.

*Note:* Codeghì is salami with a high percentage of lean meat.

# BOLOGNESE SAUCE

*Makes approximately 1 pint (6 dl)*

½ small onion
½ small carrot
1 small clove garlic
1 small stick celery
3 dried mushrooms, soaked and drained, or 3 fresh mushrooms
1 oz/25 g butter
2 tablespoons olive oil

2 oz/50 g lean and fat ham or lean bacon, chopped
8 oz/225 g beef, coarsely minced
5 tablespoons dry red wine
sprig parsley
sprig marjoram
salt and pepper
2 teaspoons plain flour
8 oz/225 g tomatoes

Peel and chop the onion, carrot and garlic. Chop the celery and mushrooms. Melt the butter in a frying pan over moderate heat, add the onion, carrot, garlic and celery and sauté until lightly browned. Remove the pan from the heat and set aside.

Heat the olive oil in a saucepan over moderate heat, add the ham and sauté until lightly browned. Add the onion mixture, mushrooms and beef. Cook for 10–15 minutes over moderate heat, then pour the wine over the ingredients. Chop the parsley and marjoram together, add to the pan and season with salt and pepper.

When the wine is almost completely reduced, remove the pan from the heat and stir in the flour. Mix thoroughly, then return to the heat and cook the mixture very gently for 10–15 minutes, stirring constantly. Peel and chop the tomatoes and add to the sauce. Add 1 tablespoon of water occasionally to prevent the sauce from sticking. Remove the pan from the heat as soon as the sauce is well blended and slightly thickened. Use as required.

# TOMATO SAUCE

*Makes approximately 1 pint (6 dl)*

2 lb/1 kg tomatoes
1 medium-sized onion
1 small carrot
1 stick celery
1 clove garlic
2 oz/50 g lard
2 oz/50 g ham or bacon fat, finely minced

few sprigs parsley
few sprigs marjoram
1 clove
paprika
¼ pint/1·5 dl dry white wine
salt

Peel and slice the tomatoes, onion and carrot. Wash and slice the celery. Peel and crush the garlic. Heat the lard and ham fat in a saucepan over moderate heat, add the garlic and sauté until lightly browned. Add the onion, carrot, celery, parsley, marjoram, clove and paprika to taste. Stir together until lightly browned, then pour in the wine and reduce almost completely. Add the tomatoes and season with salt. Cover the pan tightly and simmer over moderate heat for about 1 hour, stirring occasionally. Add a little hot water occasionally, if necessary, to prevent the sauce from becoming too thick. Remove the pan from the heat and strain through a fine sieve. Use as required.

# GREEN SAUCE

*Makes approximately ½ pint (3 dl)*

1 large bunch parsley
2–3 anchovy fillets
3–4 pickled onions
1 small potato, cooked
1 clove garlic

1 tablespoon chopped onion
pinch salt
5 tablespoons olive oil
1 tablespoon vinegar

Remove the parsley leaves from the stalks and place with the anchovy fillets, pickled onions and cold potato in a mortar or a mixing bowl. Peel the garlic and chop finely. Add with the onion and salt to the mortar. Pound the ingredients with a pestle or wooden rolling pin to form a soft paste. Place the mixture in a bowl and gradually add the oil, drop by drop, beating well after each addition until it resembles thick mayonnaise. Stir in the vinegar. Serve with cold fish and egg dishes and with salads.

# MEAT SAUCE

*Makes approximately 1¼ pints (7·5 dl)*

4 oz/100 g pork or ham rind
4 oz/100 g lean bacon, in 1 piece
1 lb/450 g topside of beef
2 teaspoons salt
¼ teaspoon pepper
2 medium-sized carrots
1 medium-sized onion
1 clove garlic
1 stick celery

1½ oz/40 g ham or gammon, minced
3 dried mushrooms, soaked and drained, or 3 fresh mushrooms
1 clove
*bouquet garni* (see recipe)
4 tablespoons dry red wine
1 large tomato
1 oz/25 g plain flour
1½ pints/9 dl hot water

Simmer the pork rind in boiling water for 5 minutes. Drain well and chop coarsely. Cut the bacon into ½-inch (1-cm) cubes. Make small incisions in the beef and press a cube of bacon into each incision. Sprinkle the beef with the salt and pepper. Peel and slice the carrots, onion and garlic. Clean and chop the celery.

Place the pork rind and ham in a flameproof casserole. Sauté very gently over low heat until the fat on the rind begins to melt. Place the beef in the casserole with the carrots, onion, garlic, celery, mushrooms and clove. Increase the heat to moderate and sauté the ingredients until the beef begins to brown. Add the *bouquet garni* (1 bay leaf, 1 sprig thyme, 1 sprig marjoram, tied together) and the wine. Increase the heat to high and boil rapidly until the wine is almost completely reduced. Peel and chop the tomato. Remove the casserole from the heat and stir in the flour. Return to moderate heat and simmer for 2–3 minutes, stirring constantly. Stir in the tomato and the water and bring to the boil. Cover tightly and cook in a cool oven (300°F, 150°C, Gas Mark 2) for 4 hours.

Remove the beef from the casserole and use in another dish. Remove the *bouquet garni* and press the sauce through a sieve into a saucepan. Simmer gently over moderate heat until reduced to a consistency thick enough to coat the back of a spoon. Adjust the seasoning and skim the surface to remove any fat. Pour the sauce into a bowl and set aside to cool. Use as required. This meat sauce will keep for several days in the refrigerator.

# HOT GARLIC AND ANCHOVY SAUCE

*Serves 6*

5 cloves garlic
½ pint/3 dl milk
4 oz/100 g anchovy fillets

scant ½ pint/2·5 dl olive oil
2 oz/50 g butter

Peel and finely chop the garlic and soak in half the milk for 2 hours. Soak the anchovy fillets in the remaining milk for 10–15 minutes to remove the excess salt.

Drain the garlic. Drain the anchovy fillets and pound to form a paste. Heat the olive oil and butter in a small saucepan over very low heat, add the anchovy paste and mix well. Add the garlic and continue cooking very gently for 20 minutes, stirring occasionally. Pour the sauce into a chafing dish, place over low heat and serve as a dip with raw vegetables such as celery, carrots, fennel stems, cauliflower florets and radishes.

# PESTO (BASIL, GARLIC AND CHEESE SAUCE)

*Serves 6*

1 large bunch fresh basil
few spinach leaves (optional)
few sprigs parsley (optional)
few sprigs marjoram (optional)
3 cloves garlic
pinch coarse salt

3–4 oz/75–100 g Pecorino Sardo or Parmesan cheese, grated
5 tablespoons olive oil
1–2 tablespoons liquid (see recipe)

Remove the stalks and thoroughly clean the basil in a cloth without washing. Clean the spinach, parsley and marjoram, if used, in a similar manner. Peel the garlic. Place the basil, spinach, parsley, marjoram, garlic and the salt in a large mortar or a bowl. Pound the mixture carefully, stirring occasionally, until reduced to a smooth pulp. Add the cheese and pound to a well-blended paste.

Add the oil drop by drop, beating constantly, as if making a mayonnaise. Blend liquid into the paste until smooth (preferably use water in which pasta has been cooked or, alternatively, cold water).

*Note:* If *pesto* is made in a large quantity, it may be poured into jars, covered with a layer of olive oil and stored for use as required.

*Sicilian pastry horns*

# SICILIAN PASTRY HORNS

*Serves 6*

**for the pastry:**
12 oz/350 g plain flour
pinch salt
¼ pint/1·5 dl plus 3 tablespoons
  Marsala
pinch sugar
olive oil for deep-frying

**for the filling:**
1 oz/25 g pistachio nuts
1 oz/25 g chopped mixed candied
  peel
1 lb/450 g Ricotta cheese
8 oz/225 g castor sugar
**for the decoration:**
sifted icing sugar

Sift the flour and salt on to a marble slab or into a mixing bowl and make a well in the centre. Pour in the Marsala, add the sugar and mix to a firm dough. Knead lightly until smooth, cover with a damp cloth and set aside for about 2 hours.

Roll the pastry into sheets, about ⅛ inch (3 mm) thick, and cut into 4-inch (10-cm) squares. Roll each square around a cream horn tin or a metal cone-shaped mould about 4 inches (10 cm) long, and set aside for about 30 minutes.

Heat the olive oil in a deep saucepan and add the pastry covered tins. Remove them when the pastry is golden brown and drain well. Place on a cloth to cool slightly. Slide the pastry horns carefully off the tins and let stand until cold.

To make the filling, finely chop the pistachio nuts and the candied peel. Blend thoroughly with the cheese and the sugar. Place the filling in a piping bag with a large plain tube. Fill the pastry horns and dust with icing sugar.

# ZABAIONE

*Serves 4*

4 egg yolks
4 oz/100 g castor sugar
1 tablespoon cold water

6 tablespoons sweet white wine or
  Marsala

Stir together the egg yolks, sugar and cold water in the top of a double saucepan or in a large pudding basin over simmering water. When the mixture is smooth and slightly thickened, pour in the wine gradually. Whisk vigorously until thick and foamy.

Remove the double saucepan from the heat and continue whisking for a few moments off the heat. Pour into 4 large serving glasses and serve immediately.

# ZUPPA INGLESE (TRIFLE)

*Serves 6*

sponge cake (see below)
3 tablespoons Alkermes liqueur (see note) or fruit or flower liqueur
3 tablespoons rum
1 tablespoon cold water
**for the custard:**
generous ¾ pint/5 dl milk
3 oz/75 g castor sugar
2 oz/50 g plain flour

3 egg yolks
1 tablespoon finely chopped mixed candied peel
**for the meringue:**
3 egg whites
4 oz/100 g castor sugar
**for the decoration:**
strips candied orange peel
castor sugar for dusting

Make the sponge cake following the instructions given below, cut into thin pieces and place on two plates. Sprinkle the Alkermes over the cake on one plate, and the rum, diluted with the water, over the remaining cake. Set aside for 20–30 minutes.

To make the custard, scald the milk in a small saucepan. Mix the sugar and flour together in a second saucepan. Lightly whisk the egg yolks and blend into the sugar mixture. Gradually stir in the hot milk. Place over low heat and cook for about 5 minutes, or until the mixture thickens, stirring constantly with a wooden spoon or whisk. It should be a thick pouring consistency. Spread 3 tablespoons of the custard on a round ovenproof serving plate, about 12 inches (30 cm) in diameter. Arrange the cake soaked in Alkermes on top. Add the candied peel to the remaining custard, stir and spoon over the cake. Arrange the sponge slices soaked in rum on top in a dome shape.

To make the meringue, whisk the egg whites until stiff and fold in the sugar. Spread the meringue smoothly over the surface of the trifle with a spatula. Decorate with the orange peel and lightly dust with sugar. Bake in a moderate oven (325°F, 160°C, Gas Mark 3) for about 15 minutes, or until the meringue is lightly coloured. Remove from the oven and set aside to cool before serving.

*Note:* Alkermes is a cordial or liqueur flavoured with various herbs and spices mixed with sugar.

# SPONGE CAKE

*Serves 6*

8 oz/225 g castor sugar
6 eggs
pinch salt
4 oz/100 g plain flour

3 oz/75 g potato flour or cornflour
1 oz/25 g melted butter

Place the sugar, eggs and salt in a bowl, preferably copper, over a saucepan of simmering water. Whisk lightly until the mixture begins to thicken, then remove from the heat and continue to whisk until the mixture is very thick and almost white in colour. Sift the flour with the potato flour, then sift it into the egg mixture and fold in very gently, using a metal spoon. Fold in the butter.

Pour the mixture into 2 lined, buttered and floured 9-inch (23-cm) sandwich tins and bake in a moderate oven (350°F, 180°C, Gas Mark 4) for 35–40 minutes. Let stand in the tins to cool for 5 minutes, then turn on to a rack and set aside to cool completely. Use as required.

# ST. JOSEPH'S SUGAR PUFFS

*Serves 6*

3 oz/75 g butter
pinch salt
scant ½ pint/2·5 dl cold water
6 oz/175 g plain flour
4 eggs
2 egg yolks

1 teaspoon sugar
2 teaspoons grated lemon rind
olive oil and lard for deep-frying
vanilla sugar for dusting (see Yeoman's Snuff, page 81)

Place the butter and salt in a saucepan and add the water. Bring to the boil over moderate heat, then remove from the heat and add the flour all at once. Blend together thoroughly with a wooden spoon, replace over the heat and stir until the paste comes away from the side of the pan to form a ball. Remove from the heat, allow to cool very slightly and then beat in the eggs and egg yolks one at a time, beating thoroughly after each addition.

When tiny bubbles appear, add the sugar and lemon rind and mix until thoroughly blended. Form into a ball, remove from the pan, wrap in a cloth and let stand in a cool place for about 30 minutes.

Roll pieces of the dough into walnut-sized balls. Heat the olive oil and lard in a large saucepan over moderate heat and drop in a few of the balls. The puffs will turn over automatically in the hot oil. When they begin to swell, increase the heat. Fry for about 5–10 minutes, or until golden brown. Remove and drain. Let the oil cool slightly, then repeat the procedure with a few more balls. Dust with vanilla sugar and serve very hot on a plate lined with a paper napkin.

# CRISP FLORENTINE PASTRIES

*Serves 6*

12 oz/350 g plain flour
2 oz/50 g butter
3 eggs
pinch sugar

pinch salt
oil for deep-frying
vanilla sugar for dusting (see Yeoman's Snuff, page 81)

Sift the flour on to a marble or wooden surface or into a mixing bowl and make a well in the centre. Cream the butter until soft, then place the butter, eggs, sugar and the salt in the well, mix to a dough and knead until all the flour has been absorbed. Continue kneading until the pastry is smooth and firm. Wrap in a lightly floured cloth and set aside in a cool place for about 1 hour.

Place the dough on a floured surface and cut into 2 or 3 pieces. Roll each piece into a sheet, about ⅛ inch (3 mm) thick, and cut into circles, rectangles and strips.

Heat the oil in a deep saucepan until very hot and fry the pastries, a few at a time, until golden brown. Drain well and sprinkle with vanilla sugar. Serve on a plate lined with a paper napkin.

*Crisp Florentine pastries*

# EASTERN MEDITERRANEAN

Bulent Rauf

*Photography by John Lee*

The Byzantine-Ottoman, or Eastern Mediterranean, cuisine ranks among the most famous in the world. The area termed 'Eastern Mediterranean' comprises the geographic crescent of land that lies on the eastern shores of the Mediterranean, from Greece, east through Turkey and south to Lebanon. Further south is Israel which has a *kosher* cuisine. Since this is quite a different type of cooking, it has its own section in this book. Then comes Egypt which, again, falls under the influence of Eastern Mediterranean cooking.

Vegetables have a place to themselves as in no other cuisine. They constitute dishes in their own right, not as a mere side dish or garnish for meat and fish. The variety and taste are exceptional: they are considered to be at their best when still very young and tender. Most vegetables are cooked *mijote* (cooked very slowly in a covered container) with a plate, fitting loosely into the cooking pot, placed upside down on the vegetables before the lid is put on.

Istanbul, the focal point for Eastern Mediterranean cooking, is renowned for its vegetables and fish. The fish spawn in the Black Sea and the young ones are caught as they swim down the Bosporus on their way to the Mediterranean. Their taste is superb.

The Turkish province of Ismir is a region rich in mineral resources and the fertile soil yields many important crops such as chestnuts, olives, raisins, figs, sesame, wheat, barley and beans. Ismir is famous for its seedless raisins and delicious dried figs. When fresh, the green grapes from which the raisins are made are small, extremely thin-skinned and brown speckled. The figs are also small and some of them are left to ripen on the tree until they are entirely sun-soaked, half dried and the taste is concentrated.

The soft fruits of the Lebanon are among the best in the world. The queen of all apricots grows in the region around the city of Baalbek. It is a white, translucent fruit, with the stone visible through the flesh if held up to the light. These apricots do not travel well and consequently are never exported. Superb cherries are grown in the village of Hammana, and the purple plums from the sun-drenched slopes of the Lebanon Mountains are probably unequalled in size and juiciness.

Egypt, because of its climate, can produce three annual crops of each vegetable, and with such an abundance it was natural that the Egyptians should have favoured the Eastern Mediterranean methods of preparing and cooking vegetables, since these are among the finest in the world. One dish that is so utterly 'ancient Egypt' it cannot be prepared elsewhere is *faseekh*. This is a fish which has to be cured buried in sun-soaked sands. When it is unearthed after 40–50 days' burial, its smell and taste are quite distinctive!

Greece has developed a style of cooking which is peculiar to its more limited natural resources. Lack of pasture land, and as a result, of butter, has resulted in a greater use of oil and a strong dependence on the sea for food. Fish is the staple diet along the coasts.

Yet, with all its differences, Greek cooking remains a part of the rich and extensive school of Eastern Mediterranean cooking which links the Balkan States with Asia, the Black Sea with the Aegean, and reaches from the eastern shores of the Mediterranean down to the northern tip of Africa.

# AUBERGINE IN TAHINA SAUCE

*Serves 4*

| | |
|---|---|
| 2 large aubergines | cold water (see recipe) |
| few drops lemon juice | 1½ tablespoons lemon juice |
| salt and pepper | salt and pepper |
| 1 teaspoon chopped fresh parsley | 1 teaspoon olive oil |
| **for the sauce:** | |
| 2 tablespoons *tahina* (sesame paste, see note) | |

Rinse the aubergines under cold running water. Place in a moderately hot oven (400°F, 200°C, Gas Mark 6) for 15–20 minutes, or until the skins are charred and the aubergines are limp. Remove from the oven and, when cool enough to handle, cut in half lengthwise and remove the pulpy flesh. Discard the skins. Mash the flesh in a bowl with a few drops of lemon juice, salt and pepper to taste and the parsley.

To make the sauce, mix the *tahina* in a bowl with enough cold water to give a soft, creamy consistency. Stir in the lemon juice, a little salt and pepper to taste and the olive oil. Mix the aubergine into the *tahina* sauce and serve cold.

*Note:* Prepare the *tahina* as for *Houmous v' tehina*, page 246. It may also be purchased in an oriental food store or in a health food shop.

# CRACKED WHEAT PILAV

*Serves 6*

| | |
|---|---|
| 8 oz/225 g cracked wheat | salt and pepper |
| 8 oz/225 g lamb, cut from the leg | 1 Italian red pepper pod |
| 1 large onion | (see note) |
| 2 oz/50 g butter | |

Wash the cracked wheat in a sieve under cold running water and soak in cold water for 1 hour. Cut the lamb into 1-inch (2·5-cm) cubes. Peel and finely chop the onion. Melt the butter in a saucepan over moderate heat and sauté the onion until golden brown. Add the lamb and cook until it begins to brown. Add salt and pepper to taste and just enough water to cover the meat. Tightly cover the pan and boil the meat rapidly for 15 minutes. Reduce the heat to a minimum and simmer for a further 30–35 minutes, or until all the liquid has been absorbed.

Drain the cracked wheat and add to the meat with the red pepper pod. Cook very slowly, adding warm water at frequent intervals, until the cracked wheat bursts and all the liquid has been absorbed. This takes about 20–30 minutes.

Heap the *pilav* in a mound on a heated serving dish and place the red pepper pod on top. Serve the hot *pilav*, without accompaniment, to begin a meal.

*Note:* The Italian species of long, red pepper pods, less hot than chilli pepper but more aromatic, is largely used in this region. A small dried red chilli may be substituted.

# SOUR LEEKS

*Serves 4*

| | |
|---|---|
| 12 large leeks | 1 teaspoon sugar |
| 3 tablespoons olive oil | salt and pepper |
| 1 tablespoon vinegar | 1 teaspoon chopped fresh parsley |

Cut off the green upper part of the leeks and about ¼ inch (5 mm) from the root end. Reserve the tender green leaves for another dish. Cut the white part of the leeks in half lengthwise and rinse thoroughly under cold running water to remove any sand. Slice the leeks lengthwise very finely.

Heat the oil in a heavy saucepan over high heat, add the sliced leeks and sauté until golden brown, stirring constantly. Lower the heat, add just enough water to cover the leeks and stir in the vinegar, sugar and salt and pepper to taste. Simmer over fairly low heat for 30 minutes. Place the leeks in a serving dish and set aside until cold. Serve sprinkled with the parsley.

# CUCUMBER IN YOGHURT

*Serves 4*

| | |
|---|---|
| ½ large cucumber | 4 (4½-oz/127-g) cartons natural |
| 1 teaspoon finely chopped fresh | yoghurt |
| mint | salt and pepper |
| | olive oil |

Peel and finely chop the cucumber, place in a bowl and add half the mint. Whip the yoghurt with salt and pepper to taste and mix with the cucumber. Adjust the seasoning, if necessary, and trickle olive oil over the surface. Sprinkle with the remaining mint and serve well chilled with a bowl of olives and brown bread.

# YOGHURT SOUP

*Serves 4*

| | |
|---|---|
| 2 oz/50 g plain flour | salt and pepper |
| cold water (see recipe) | ½ teaspoon paprika |
| 1½ pints/9 dl meat broth | 2 teaspoons chopped fresh mint |
| 2 (4½-oz/127-g) cartons natural | |
| yoghurt | |

Blend the flour with a little cold water to form a smooth soft paste. Pour the broth into a large saucepan and bring to the boil. Remove the pan from the heat and stir in the flour and water paste. Return the pan to the heat and bring back to the boil, stirring constantly until the liquid thickens. Remove the pan from the heat.

Beat the yoghurt with salt and pepper to taste, most of the paprika and the mint. Stir the mixture into the thickened broth. Serve in a heated soup tureen with a sprinkling of the remaining paprika. A spoonful of yoghurt may also be added to each bowl.

# FRIED MUSSELS

*Serves 4–6*

| | |
|---|---|
| 2 pints/generous litre mussels | 4 oz/100 g plain flour |
| ¼ pint/1·5 dl water | ¼ pint/1·5 dl pale ale |
| **for the batter:** | oil for deep-frying |
| 2 eggs | 1 lemon, sliced |
| salt and pepper | few sprigs parsley |

Discarding any that are open, scrub the mussels well under cold water and remove the beards. Place the mussels in a large saucepan and add the water. Tightly cover the pan and place over high heat for 8–10 minutes, or until the mussels open. Remove the pan from the heat and, when cool enough to handle, remove each mussel from its shell. Discard the shells and any unopened mussels and set the mussels aside until required.

To make the batter, whisk the eggs until frothy. Add the salt and pepper to taste. Sift the flour into a bowl and add the beaten eggs gradually, beating thoroughly after each addition, until the mixture is smooth. Beat in the pale ale. Let the batter stand for 40 minutes. Heat the oil in a deep saucepan. Dip each mussel into the batter and deep-fry until crisp and golden brown. Drain on kitchen paper. Serve the hot mussels garnished with the lemon slices and parsley.

# FISH SOUP WITH TOMATOES

*Serves 4*

| | |
|---|---|
| 1½ lb/700 g cod, haddock, halibut | 1 fish head |
| or turbot | 3–4 large sprigs fresh parsley |
| 1 teaspoon salt | 3 pints/1·75 litres water |
| 2 large onions | salt and pepper |
| 2 medium-sized carrots | 6 tablespoons olive oil |
| 4 medium-sized tomatoes | 2 oz/50 g short-grain rice |
| 2 sticks celery | |

Discard the bones and skin from the fish. Rinse the flesh under cold running water and then cut into 2-inch (5-cm) pieces. Sprinkle the fish pieces with the salt and drain in a colander. Peel and thinly slice the onions and carrots. Peel the tomatoes. Chop the celery. Place the vegetables in a large saucepan with the fish head and parsley sprigs. Add the water and salt and pepper to taste. Place the pan over moderate heat, bring to the boil, then lower the heat and simmer for 45 minutes. Remove the fish head and parsley sprigs. Add the pieces of fish to the simmering stock and poach for 20–25 minutes, or until the fish is cooked but still firm.

Remove the fish from the pan and keep hot in a covered dish. Gently stir the olive oil into the soup and add the rice. Increase the heat to moderate and cook for 30 minutes, or until the rice is tender. The liquid will reduce in quantity during this cooking time. Replace the fish in the soup. Reheat gently and serve hot.

*Fish soup with tomatoes*

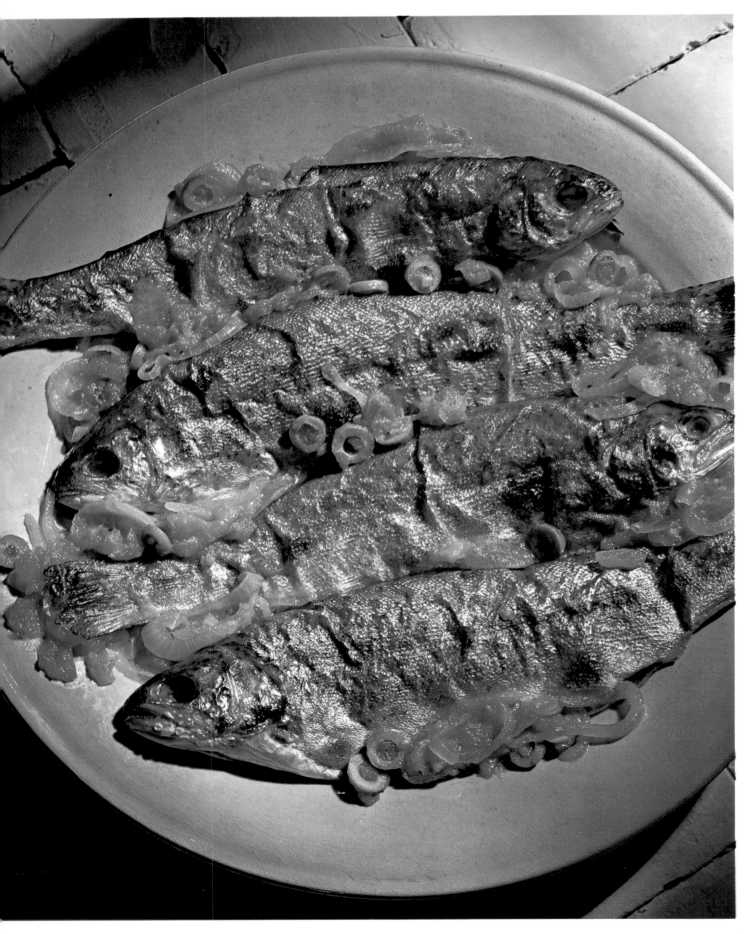

# GREEK EASTER SOUP

*Serves 8*

3 lb/1·5 kg lamb's tripe, kidneys, liver and heart
2 oz/50 g plain flour
scant ½ pint/2·5 dl cold water
3 pints/1·5 litres lukewarm water
6 spring onions
2 oz/50 g butter
2 tablespoons chopped fresh parsley
2 tablespoons chopped fresh dill
4 oz/100 g short-grain rice
**for the avgolemono:**
2 egg yolks
2 tablespoons lemon juice
6 tablespoons soup (see recipe)
2 tablespoons milk

Clean the tripe thoroughly and rinse under cold running water. Discard any membrane and gristly parts from the kidney, liver and heart. Rinse the meat thoroughly under cold running water and drain for 2–3 minutes. Boil the tripe in salted water for 10 minutes, then drain and discard the liquid. When cool, cut the tripe into very small pieces and place in a large saucepan. Blend the flour to a very soft, smooth paste with the cold water and pour the paste over the tripe. Add the lukewarm water and bring to the boil over moderate heat, stirring constantly, until the liquid thickens slightly. Partially cover the pan, lower the heat and simmer gently for 20 minutes.

Cut the kidney, liver and heart into fairly small pieces, and boil in salted water to cover for 5–10 minutes. Drain off and discard the liquid. When cool, cut the meat into very small pieces. Chop the spring onions.

Melt the butter in a frying pan over moderate heat. Add the kidney, liver, heart, spring onions, parsley and dill, and sauté the ingredients for 5–10 minutes, stirring frequently. Add the mixture to the simmering tripe and continue to simmer for 20–25 minutes, or until the offal is tender. Strain the liquid into a third saucepan and keep the offal warm. Add the rice to the strained liquid and bring to the boil over moderate heat. Tightly cover the pan and continue to boil for 30 minutes, or until the rice is cooked. Remove the pan from the heat.

To make the *avgolemono*, whisk the egg yolks and lemon juice in a small bowl. Gradually add the 6 tablespoons of soup, stirring constantly. Pour the egg yolk mixture back into the hot soup, add the offal and, if necessary, reheat the soup to the simmering point, but do not boil. Just before serving, add the milk.

*Note:* The Eastern Mediterranean sauce made from egg yolks and lemon juice is called *avgolemono* in Greece and *terbiye* in Turkey. It is blended with either soup or stock according to the individual recipe.

# GRILLED FISH WITH OLIVES

*Serves 4*

4 trout, mackerel or herring
**for the sauce:**
1 medium-sized onion
5 medium-sized tomatoes
12 stuffed green olives
4 tablespoons olive oil
3 tablespoons pale ale
salt and pepper
1 lemon, quartered
few sprigs parsley

Gut the fish and discard the fins and eyes. Rinse under cold running water and drain in a colander until required.

To make the sauce, peel and thinly slice the onion and the tomatoes. Slice the olives. Heat three-quarters of the oil in a frying pan over moderate heat and sauté the onion until golden brown. Add the tomatoes, olives, ale and salt and pepper to taste. Lower the heat and simmer very gently for 20–30 minutes, stirring frequently.

Meanwhile, brush the prepared fish with the remaining oil and grill under moderate heat for 5–6 minutes on each side, or until the flesh becomes firm and white. Place the fish on a heated serving dish and spoon the sauce over and around them. Garnish with the lemon quarters and the parsley.

# ALEXANDRIAN BAKED FISH

*Serves 4*

4 mackerel, trout or herring
salt and pepper
4 large onions
8 medium-sized tomatoes
1 tablespoon chopped fresh basil or 2 teaspoons dried basil
3 tablespoons olive oil

Gut the fish and discard the heads. Place the opened underside of each fish on a board and press firmly along the backbone to loosen the flesh from the bone. Turn the fish over and ease out the backbone. Rinse the fish under cold running water and dry with a cloth or kitchen paper. Sprinkle with salt and pepper to taste.

Peel and thinly slice the onions and tomatoes. Place half the onion and tomato slices in the bottom of a roasting tin or casserole and sprinkle with half the basil. Place the fish on top, cover with the remaining onion and tomato slices and sprinkle with the remaining basil and salt and pepper to taste. Sprinkle the olive oil over the top and bake the fish in a moderate oven (325°F, 160°C, Gas Mark 3) for 40–45 minutes, or until the fish is firm and white and the onions are soft.

Place the fish on a heated serving dish, arrange the onions and tomatoes over and around it, and serve hot with boiled potatoes.

*Grilled fish with olives*

# COLD POACHED SEA BASS

*Serves 4*

1 sea bass, about 3 lb/1·5 kg
**for the broth:**
1 medium-sized onion
1 large carrot
small bunch celery leaves

4 bay leaves
salt and pepper
1½ tablespoons lemon juice
small strip lemon rind
2 pints/generous litre water

Gut the fish and wash under cold running water. Set aside while preparing the broth. Peel the onion and leave whole. Peel and thickly slice the carrot and place both in a large saucepan, with the celery leaves, bay leaves, salt and pepper to taste, lemon juice, lemon rind and water. Place the pan over high heat and bring to the boil. Lower the heat and simmer for about 25–30 minutes, or until the onion and carrot are cooked. Strain through a sieve and reserve the liquid, carrot and bay leaves. Discard the remaining ingredients.

Place the fish in the saucepan, if necessary cutting it in half. Add the reserved broth and poach slowly for 20–30 minutes, or until the flesh is firm and can be removed easily from the bones. Carefully lift the fish out of the stock. Remove the skin and bones and arrange the fish in a long shallow china serving dish. Garnish with the reserved carrot and bay leaves. Return the skin and bones to the pan and boil the broth rapidly until reduced to about one-third of the original quantity. Strain the liquid through a sieve and pour over the fish. Leave overnight in a cold place, preferably in the refrigerator, until well chilled. Serve cold in the serving dish, with boiled potatoes and lemon wedges as accompaniments.

# SWORDFISH KEBAB

*Serves 4*

**for the marinade:**
1 onion
2 dried bay leaves
2 tablespoons olive oil

**for the kebab:**
1½ lb/700 g swordfish steaks or
  middle cut of salmon
32 bay leaves
1 lemon, quartered

To make the marinade, peel and chop the onion, crush the bay leaves and mix both with the olive oil.

To make the kebabs, carefully remove the skin and bones from the fish. Cut the fish into 1-inch (2·5-cm) cubes. Place about 8 fish cubes and 8 bay leaves alternately on each of 4 skewers, pushing the fish to the centre of the skewer. Place the skewers in the marinade for 1 hour. If preferred, the kebabs may be cooked immediately instead of being marinated beforehand.

Cook the kebabs on each side for 3–4 minutes over a charcoal grill, or under a hot electric or gas grill. If an electric or gas grill is used, the kebabs must be well marinated so that they are soaked in oil. Serve the kebabs hot, garnished with the lemon quarters.

# FISH WITH GARLIC SAUCE

*Serves 4*

**for the sauce:**
1 large potato
4 cloves garlic, peeled
1 teaspoon salt
4 oz/100 g ground almonds
6 tablespoons olive oil
3 tablespoons vinegar
4 tablespoons water

lemon juice (see recipe)
**for the fish:**
4 steaks of cod, haddock, halibut
  or turbot, about 4–6 oz/
  100–175 g each
salt and pepper
plain flour for coating
oil for deep-frying

To make the garlic sauce, peel and quarter the potato and cook in lightly salted water to cover until tender. Drain and set aside. Pound the garlic and salt in a mortar or bowl until it is a smooth paste. Add the almonds and potato and continue pounding until a smooth paste is formed. Add the olive oil very gradually, beating well after each addition. Stir in the vinegar and water and mix thoroughly. The mixture should be the consistency of thick mayonnaise. If necessary, add lemon juice until the correct consistency is achieved.

Wipe the fish with a damp cloth or kitchen paper. Sprinkle with salt and pepper to taste and coat the pieces with flour. Deep-fry in hot oil until crisp and golden brown. Drain on kitchen paper. Serve hot with the garlic sauce.

Note: When less garlic is used, this is an excellent sauce to accompany vegetables.

# WHITEBAIT BIRDS

*Serves 4*

1 lb/450 g whitebait or sprats
3 oz/75 g plain flour
6 tablespoons olive oil

salt and pepper
bunch parsley
1 lemon, quartered

Wash the whitebait under cold running water. Drain well. Put the flour into a large paper bag and toss the whitebait in the flour until the fish are well coated. Place the floured fish on a tray or a large plate. Take 4 or 5 whitebait at a time and press the heads together, the bodies radiating out like the spokes of a wheel or the wing of a bird. Heat the oil in a shallow pan over moderate heat and fry the whitebait 'birds' until crisp and brown. Drain on kitchen paper and sprinkle with salt and pepper to taste. Arrange the 'birds' on a heated flat plate and keep warm. Sauté the parsley in the oil until crisp and arrange around the fish like a nest. Garnish with the lemon quarters and serve hot.

*Whitebait birds*

left: *baklava* (see page 228); right: *stuffed vegetables* (see page 220);
in the background: *skewered lamb fillets*

# STUFFED MACKEREL

*Serves 4*

4 mackerel

**for the stuffing:**

4 small onions

6 tablespoons olive oil

2 tablespoons finely chopped fresh
  parsley

1 oz/25 g currants

4 teaspoons chopped fresh dill or
  2 teaspoons dried dill weed

1 teaspoon cinnamon

salt and pepper

½ oz/15 g pine nut kernels

6 tablespoons water

plain flour for coating

1 lemon, sliced

Remove the fins from the mackerel without breaking the skin. With a sharp knife or scissors, make a cut along the underside of the fish to within about 1 inch (2·5 cm) of the head and tail. Gut the fish. Snip the backbone at each end from the inside and very gently ease out the bone, removing as little of the flesh as possible. To help loosen the backbone, carefully press lightly along the bone on the outside of the fish, without breaking the skin. Wash the fish inside and out and dry with kitchen paper. Set aside until required.

To make the stuffing, peel and finely chop the onions. Heat half the oil in a large frying pan, add the onions and sauté gently until soft. Add the parsley, currants, dill or dried dill weed, cinnamon, salt and pepper and pine nut kernels. Sauté for a further 5–10 minutes, stirring frequently until the mixture begins to brown. Add the water and simmer for a further 5–10 minutes until all the liquid has evaporated. Remove the pan from the heat and cool slightly. Spoon the stuffing into the fish and loosely sew up the openings with thread, or insert several small skewers and lace closed. Coat the fish with flour.

Heat the remaining oil in the frying pan over very moderate heat and cook the mackerel for about 8–10 minutes on each side. Remove from the pan, drain on kitchen paper and remove the thread or skewers. Serve the fish hot or cold, garnished with the lemon slices.

*Note:* Traditionally mackerel are gutted and boned through the gills, leaving the fish whole and free from knife cuts. The backbone is snapped at the head and tail end without breaking the skin. The fish is then rolled gently but firmly between the palms of the hands, after which the backbone is removed through the gills.

# IRONMONGERS' SALAD

*Serves 4*

4 large ripe tomatoes
2 long green sweet peppers
1 large onion
salt
1 tablespoon water
freshly ground black pepper
½ teaspoon finely chopped fresh
  parsley

½ teaspoon finely chopped fresh
  mint
1½ tablespoons lemon juice
1 teaspoon vinegar
1–2 tablespoons olive oil
8–10 black olives

Peel the tomatoes and scoop out the seeds into a fine sieve placed over a bowl. Discard the seeds and reserve the juice. Trim the peppers, remove the seeds and cut the flesh into rings. Peel the onion and cut in half lengthwise. Slice each half lengthwise into very thin slices. Place the onion in a wire sieve and sprinkle liberally with salt. Press the onion and salt together until the salt has dissolved and the juice runs from the onion. Rinse the onion thoroughly under cold running water and set aside to drain.

Put half a teaspoon of salt in a salad bowl, add the water and stir well to dissolve the salt. Add the reserved tomato juice, pepper, parsley, mint, lemon juice and vinegar. Mix well and add the olive oil. The oil should be sufficient to completely cover the surface of the liquid already in the bowl. Add the tomatoes, green peppers, onion and olives and mix the ingredients. Let stand for about 30 minutes before serving.

# SKEWERED LAMB FILLETS

*Serves 4*

1 large onion
4 fillets of lamb, about 1–1½ lb/
  450–700 g (see note)

2 tablespoons olive oil
salt and pepper
small bunch parsley

Peel and thinly slice the onion. Place in a bowl with the lamb. Add the olive oil and salt and pepper to taste. Turn the lamb over several times until the meat is well coated with oil and seasonings. Marinate overnight.

Thread each piece of meat on to a skewer in the shape of an S. Cook over a charcoal grill, or under a moderately hot electric or gas grill, for about 10–12 minutes. Turn the skewers frequently so that the lamb is evenly cooked. Serve on a bed of parsley with rice.

*Note:* The lamb for this dish is usually cut from the narrow flat end of the neck fillet. Each piece of lamb should be no longer than 5–6 inches (13–15 cm). If neck fillets are not available, thin, tapering fillets cut from the leg are a suitable alternative.

# ONION SALAD

*Serves 4*

3–4 large Spanish onions
4 tablespoons salt
1 teaspoon tarragon or other
  vinegar
1½ tablespoons lemon juice

1½ teaspoons cold water
salt and pepper
3 tablespoons olive oil
1 tablespoon coarsely chopped
  fresh parsley

Peel the onions and cut in half. Place cut side down on a chopping board and slice lengthwise very thinly. Place the sliced onions in a large wire sieve and sprinkle with the salt. Press the onions and salt together until all the salt has dissolved, then rinse the onions thoroughly under cold running water. Drain well.

Mix together the vinegar, lemon juice and water in a salad bowl and season with salt and pepper to taste. Whisk in the olive oil gradually. Add the onion slices and parsley and mix thoroughly before serving.

# LAMB SMOTHERED IN AUBERGINE

*Serves 4*

1½ lb/700 g lamb, cut from the leg
  or shoulder
4 aubergines
salt
2 large onions
2 oz/50 g butter

pepper
1 teaspoon chopped fresh parsley
scant ½ pint/2·5 dl water
6 tablespoons olive oil
1 large tomato

Cut the lamb into 3-inch (7·5-cm) pieces. Discard the stalks from the aubergines and slice the aubergines lengthwise into the same number of slices as there are pieces of lamb. Sprinkle the slices very lightly with salt and set aside until required. Peel and coarsely chop the onions. Melt the butter in a saucepan over moderate heat and sauté the onions until golden brown. Add the pieces of meat and sauté until browned, turning frequently. Add salt and pepper to taste, the parsley and the water. Cover the pan and simmer for 35–40 minutes. Remove from the heat and let stand until cool.

Rinse the aubergine slices under cold running water and dry thoroughly with a cloth or kitchen paper. Heat the oil in a frying pan over moderate heat and sauté the aubergines until lightly browned on both sides. Drain well on kitchen paper.

Remove the meat from the saucepan, wrap one slice of aubergine around each piece of lamb and place the wrapped pieces in a flameproof casserole. Pour over the liquid remaining in the saucepan.

Thinly slice the tomato, cut the slices in half and garnish each wrapped piece of lamb with one half slice. Cover the casserole, place over moderate heat and simmer for 30–40 minutes. Serve hot in the casserole. Alternatively, transfer to a heated serving dish, being careful to disturb the aubergines as little as possible, and pour over the sauce.

# LITTLE DOMES

*Serves 4*

8 oz/225 g lamb, cut from
   the leg
¼ teaspoon dried thyme
¼ teaspoon dried marjoram
8 oz/225 g cracked wheat
1 large onion

2 oz/50 g butter
1 teaspoon pine nut kernels
salt and pepper
oil for deep-frying
few sprigs parsley

Finely mince the lamb and pound it very thoroughly to a smooth pulp in a mortar or a bowl with one end of a wooden rolling pin. Remove any sinews or gristle. Add half the thyme and marjoram, continue pounding for 1–2 minutes and then set aside until the mixture is required. Pound the cracked wheat in the same way to a fine gritty consistency. Set aside until required.

Peel and finely chop the onion. Heat the butter in a frying pan over moderate heat. Add the onion, sauté until soft, and when the onion is just beginning to brown, add the pine nut kernels. Continue to sauté until both the onion and nuts are well browned. Remove the pan from the heat, stir in the remaining thyme and marjoram and add salt and pepper to taste. Set aside until required.

Mix together the lamb and cracked wheat and squeeze the mixture together with the hands until the ingredients are thoroughly mixed. Divide into 24 small portions. Shape each one into a ball and make a hollow in the centre. Place a little less than 1 teaspoon of the onion and nut mixture into the hollow. Seal up the opening, completely enclosing the filling, and shape into a dome. Continue until the meat and onion mixtures are used. Heat the oil in a deep saucepan and deep-fry the domes. Drain the domes on kitchen paper, arrange on a serving dish and garnish with sprigs of parsley. Serve either hot or cold.

# İSKENDER'S KEBAB

*Serves 4*

1 lb/450 g lamb, cut from the leg
1 onion
2 tablespoons olive oil
salt and pepper

1 *pide* (see note)
4 (4½-oz/127-g) cartons natural
   yoghurt
2 oz/50 g butter

Cut the lamb into 1-inch (2·5-cm) cubes. Peel and thinly slice the onion. Place the lamb and onion in a bowl and add the olive oil and salt and pepper to taste. Mix thoroughly and set aside to marinate overnight.

Cut the *pide* into small cubes and place in 4 heat-resistant soup bowls. Place in a warm oven while preparing the kebabs. Whip the yoghurt with salt and pepper to taste and set aside to come to room temperature. Thread the marinated lamb on to 4 skewers and cook over a charcoal grill or under a hot electric or gas grill for 5–6 minutes, turning the skewers frequently to brown the lamb evenly. Melt the butter until it sizzles.

When the kebabs are cooked, slide the meat off the skewers on to the warmed *pide*. Cover with the whipped yoghurt and pour a little hot butter over each serving. Serve immediately.

*Note:* Pide in Turkey is a special flat bread which is traditionally present on every table during the fasting month of Ramadan. It is very much like the Syrian bread, though whiter, larger and with quilt-like markings. If *pide* cannot be obtained, a Syrian bread, plain baked *pizza* dough (see page 182) or *pita* bread (see page 245) may be substituted.

# BEEF STEW WITH QUINCES

*Serves 6*

1½ lb/700 g lean braising steak
1 medium-sized onion
4 oz/100 g butter
½ pint/3 dl hot water

salt and pepper
1½ lb/700 g quinces
2 teaspoons sugar

Cut the beef into small cubes. Peel and chop the onion. Melt the butter in a saucepan over moderate heat. Add the onion and sauté until transparent and soft. Add the beef and continue to sauté, stirring frequently, until the meat is well browned. Add the hot water and salt and pepper to taste, and bring slowly to the boil.

Meanwhile, peel, core and thickly slice the quinces. Place the quinces on top of the beef, sprinkle with the sugar and cook for 30–40 minutes, or until the beef and the quinces are tender. Transfer to a heated serving dish and serve immediately.

# TRAY KIBBA (MEAT LOAF)

*Serves 4*

8 oz/225 g lean lamb, finely
   minced
8 oz/225 g cracked wheat
salt and pepper
**for the filling:**
1 large onion

4 oz/100 g butter
1 teaspoon fresh thyme
   or ½ teaspoon dried thyme
1 teaspoon pine nut kernels

Pound the lamb to a fine pulp in a mortar or in a bowl with one end of a wooden rolling pin. Remove any sinews or gristle. Pound the cracked wheat in the same way to a fine gritty consistency. Mix the lamb and wheat together and add salt and pepper to taste. Set aside until required.

To prepare the filling, peel and finely chop the onion. Melt half the butter in a small saucepan over moderate heat. Add the onion and sauté until soft and golden brown. Remove the pan from the heat and stir in the thyme and pine nut kernels.

Spread half the lamb mixture in a small roasting tin. Cover with the filling, then spread the remaining lamb mixture over the filling. Cut the remaining butter into small cubes and place on top. Bake in a moderately hot oven (375°F, 190°C, Gas Mark 5) for 40 minutes. Cut the *kibba* into squares in the tin and serve hot as a main dish with a green salad or vegetables.

*İskender's kebab*

# LAMB WITH OKRA

*Serves 4*

1½–2 lb/700–900 g lamb, cut from the leg
2 large onions
1 lb/450 g fresh okra or 2 (13-oz/369-g) cans okra
1½ tablespoons lemon juice
2 oz/50 g butter

1 teaspoon chopped fresh parsley
1½ teaspoons chopped fresh marjoram or 1 teaspoon dried marjoram
salt and pepper
scant ½ pint/2·5 dl water

Cut the lamb into 3-inch (7·5-cm) pieces. Peel and thickly slice the onions. If using fresh okra, wash them and trim the stalks, shaping the ends into cones and taking care not to cut through the flesh. Cover with water and add the lemon juice to prevent the okra from discolouring.

Melt the butter in a saucepan over moderate heat. Add the onions and sauté gently until soft but not browned. Add the pieces of lamb, increase the heat slightly and sauté the lamb with the onions until the meat is lightly browned. Add the parsley, marjoram, salt and pepper to taste and the water. Tightly cover the pan and cook for 30 minutes. Add the okra, replace the lid and cook for a further 20 minutes. Check the amount of liquid in the pan 10 minutes before the end of the cooking time. If there is a lot, remove the lid and allow the liquid to evaporate. Serve in a heated serving dish.

# LAMB'S LIVER IN SHARP SAUCE

*Serves 4*

1 lb/450 g lamb's liver
1½ oz/40 g plain flour
½ teaspoon salt
pinch pepper
6 tablespoons olive oil

2 tablespoons vinegar
¼ pint/1·5 dl water
1 teaspoon tomato purée
pinch fresh or dried rosemary
salt and pepper

Cut the liver into slices, about ½ inch (1 cm) thick, and remove any membrane or skin. Mix a third of the flour with the salt and pepper. Coat the slices of liver with the seasoned flour. Heat half the oil in a frying pan over moderate heat and sauté the liver slices until browned on both sides. Remove from the pan and place in a fairly deep serving dish.

Add the remaining oil to the oil and residue in the pan. Stir in the remaining flour and cook over moderate heat, stirring constantly, until the mixture is golden brown. Gradually stir in the vinegar to form a smooth paste. Add the water, tomato purée and rosemary and mix well. Bring to the simmering point, adjust the seasoning, if necessary, and simmer for about 5 minutes. Pour the sauce over the liver, making sure that the liver is completely covered. Set aside until cold. Serve with a fresh green salad.

*Paper-wrapped lamb*

## PAPER-WRAPPED LAMB

*Serves 4*

1 lb/450 g fillets of lamb, cut from the neck or leg
1 medium-sized onion
1 oz/25 g butter
¼ teaspoon chopped fresh thyme or ¼ teaspoon dried thyme
½ teaspoon chopped fresh marjoram or ¼ teaspoon dried marjoram
½ teaspoon chopped fresh basil or ¼ teaspoon dried basil
½ teaspoon chopped fresh rosemary or ¼ teaspoon dried rosemary
½ teaspoon chopped fresh parsley or ¼ teaspoon dried parsley
½ teaspoon chopped fresh dill or ¼ teaspoon dried dill weed
½ dried bay leaf, crushed
salt and pepper

Cut the meat into 1-inch (2·5-cm) cubes. Peel and slice the onion very thinly. Spread equal amounts of butter on to the centre of 4 12-inch (30-cm) squares of brown paper or aluminium foil. Place equal quantities of meat, onion and herbs on each square. Sprinkle with salt and pepper to taste. Fold the paper or foil around the filling like an envelope and twist the ends firmly together, completely enclosing the filling. Cook the parcels in the centre of a moderately hot oven (375°F, 190°C, Gas Mark 5) for 1–1¼ hours.

Serve the *kebabí* unopened, accompanied by courgettes or white *pilav* (see page 220).

## KEFTEDES IN SAUCE

*Serves 4*

2 cloves garlic
4 slices bread
1 lb/450 g lean lamb, minced
½ teaspoon dried marjoram
2 eggs
2 tablespoons plain flour
½ teaspoon salt
pinch pepper
**for the sauce:**
1 medium-sized onion
1 oz/25 g butter
½ oz/15 g plain flour
1 tablespoon tomato purée
¾ pint/4·5 dl water
salt and pepper
pinch sugar
1 teaspoon chopped fresh parsley
½ teaspoon dried marjoram

Peel and crush the garlic. Cut off the crusts from the bread and discard them. Soak the bread in a little cold water for 2 minutes. Squeeze out as much water as possible. Place the lamb in a bowl. Add the bread, garlic, marjoram and eggs, and mix thoroughly to a fairly stiff paste. Roll the mixture into finger shapes, about 1 inch (2·5 cm) thick and 3 inches (7·5 cm) long. Mix the flour with the salt and pepper. Coat the meat fingers well with the seasoned flour and set aside until required.

To make the sauce, peel and finely chop the onion. Melt the butter in a saucepan over moderate heat and sauté the onion until golden brown. Stir in the flour and continue

214

cooking for 1–2 minutes. Stir in the tomato purée. Add the water gradually, mixing thoroughly after each addition. Add the salt and pepper to taste, sugar, parsley and marjoram, and bring the sauce to the boil, stirring constantly. Lower the heat to a minimum and simmer the sauce for 5 minutes.

Place the meat fingers, one by one, into the sauce, and simmer for 10–12 minutes. Transfer the meat fingers and sauce to a heated serving dish and serve hot with white *pilav* (see page 220).

# CEPHALONIAN MEAT PIE

*Serves 4–6*

**for the filling:**
1 lb/450 g lamb, cut from the leg
1 large potato
1 large onion
2 cloves garlic
4 medium-sized tomatoes
1½ oz/40 g short-grain rice
¼ teaspoon grated orange rind
2 oz/50 g hard cheese, grated
1 tablespoon chopped fresh parsley
1 teaspoon chopped fresh mint

1 oz/25 g melted butter
1 tablespoon olive oil
2 hard-boiled eggs
6 tablespoons vegetable stock
**for the shortcrust pastry:**
1 lb/450 g plain flour
pinch salt
8 oz/225 g margarine or cooking fat
4–6 tablespoons water
1 tablespoon melted butter for glazing

Cut the lamb into ½-inch (1-cm) cubes. Peel and finely dice the potato. Peel and finely chop the onion and garlic. Peel and chop the tomatoes, removing the seeds. Mix together the lamb, potato, onion, garlic, tomatoes, rice, orange rind, cheese, parsley, mint, butter and oil in a large bowl. Prepare the pastry as for Mince Pies, page 53.

Roll out half the pastry on a floured board into a circle, ¼ inch (5 mm) thick and about 1½ inches (3·5 cm) larger than a 9-inch (23-cm) pie tin. Line the pie tin with the pastry and place the filling in the centre. Shell and slice the hard-boiled eggs and place the slices on top of the filling. Moisten the edges of the pastry with a little of the stock and pour the remainder over the filling. Roll out the remaining pastry into a circle, slightly larger than the pie tin, and place it over the pie filling. Press the layers of pastry firmly together and trim off any excess pastry. Brush the top with the melted butter and bake in a moderately hot oven (375°F, 190°C, Gas Mark 5) for 1–1¼ hours.

# HARICOT BEANS WITH LAMB

*Serves 4–6*

8 oz/225 g haricot beans (see note)
8 oz/225 g lamb, cut from the leg
3 large onions

3 oz/75 g butter
salt and pepper
pinch sugar

Soak the beans overnight in plenty of cold water. Drain and put in a saucepan with just enough fresh water to cover. Place the pan over high heat and bring to the boil. Lower the heat to moderate and continue boiling the beans for 30 minutes, or until half cooked. Drain well.

Meanwhile, cut the lamb into 2-inch (5-cm) pieces. Peel and coarsely chop the onions. Melt the butter in a saucepan over moderate heat, add the onions and sauté until soft and golden brown. Add the lamb and cook until it is browned. Add the beans, salt and pepper to taste, sugar and enough water to cover. Cover tightly and simmer for 1½ hours. If the lamb is not tender after this time, add a little warm water, replace the lid and continue to simmer for a further 30 minutes, stirring occasionally. Place in a heated serving dish and serve hot with white *pilav* (see page 220).

*Note:* Canned beans may be substituted for dried beans in this recipe, in which case the lamb should be previously cooked. The simmering time will need to be reduced accordingly.

# MEAT BALLS WITH TERBIYE

*Serves 4*

2 oz/50 g short-grain rice
1 lb/450 g lean lamb or beef, minced
salt and pepper
plain flour (see recipe)

1 pint/6 dl beef stock
**for the terbiye:**
2 egg yolks
2 tablespoons lemon juice

Cook the rice in lightly salted boiling water for 10 minutes. Drain and cool. Place the rice and meat in a bowl. Season with salt and pepper. Knead and squeeze the ingredients to make a soft paste. Roll into 1½-inch (3·5-cm) balls with floured hands. Measure the beef stock into a saucepan and bring to the boil over high heat. Drop the meat balls into the stock, reduce the heat and simmer until they rise to the surface. Remove the meat balls with a perforated spoon and keep hot in a heated covered serving dish.

Raise the heat and rapidly boil the stock until it is reduced to about half the original quantity. Remove the pan from the heat and make the *terbiye* as for Greek Easter Soup, page 207. Stir the *terbiye* into the remaining hot stock and, if necessary, reheat to simmering point, but do not boil. Pour the *terbiye* over the meat balls and serve immediately with boiled potatoes.

# LAMB WITH PRUNES AND ALMONDS

*Serves 6*

| | |
|---|---|
| 1 lb/450 g stoned prunes | ½ oz/15 g plain flour |
| 2½ lb/1·25 kg boned lamb, cut from the leg or shoulder | vegetable stock or water (see recipe) |
| 1 large onion | salt and pepper |
| 3 tablespoons lemon juice | 8 oz/225 g blanched almonds |
| 2 oz/50 g butter | 1 oz/25 g castor sugar |

Soak the prunes overnight in plenty of cold water. Cut the lamb into ½-inch (1-cm) cubes. Peel and thinly slice the onion. Mix the lamb, onion and half the lemon juice in a large bowl and marinate for at least 1 hour.

Remove the lamb from the marinade and dry with a cloth or kitchen paper. Heat the butter in a saucepan over moderate heat. Add the lamb and sauté gently for 5 minutes. Stir in the flour and continue cooking until the lamb and flour become lightly browned. Stir in enough stock or water to cover the meat completely. Add salt and pepper to taste. Bring to the boil, stirring constantly. When the mixture thickens, reduce the heat and simmer, partially covered, for 45 minutes.

Drain the prunes and add with the almonds to the meat in the pan. Continue to simmer for about 20–30 minutes, or until the prunes are cooked. Stir in the sugar and the remaining lemon juice, increase the heat and bring to the boiling point. Pour into a heated serving dish and serve immediately.


# CIRCASSIAN CHICKEN

*Serves 4*

| | |
|---|---|
| 1 chicken, about 3 lb/1·5 kg | ½ pint/3 dl chicken broth (see recipe) |
| 1 large onion | 1 lb/450 g ground walnuts |
| 1 large carrot | 1 small red chilli or 1 Italian red pepper pod |
| 1 large bay leaf | salt and pepper |
| 1 teaspoon salt | |

Wipe the chicken inside and out with a damp cloth or kitchen paper. Peel the onion and carrot. Place the chicken, onion, carrot, bay leaf and salt in a large saucepan. Add enough water to barely cover the chicken. Bring to the boil over high heat. Lower the heat and simmer the chicken for about 1½ hours, or until tender.

Meanwhile, place in a mortar the walnuts, red pepper and a seasoning of salt and pepper, and pound to a very fine paste. Take portions of the paste and place these in a clean fine cloth. Twist the ends in opposite directions and squeeze the paste to extract the oil from the walnuts. It is essential to do this, otherwise the texture of the dish may be too heavy. Retain the oil, which will be tinted with the red colour from the chilli, in a bowl and reserve the walnut paste.

When the chicken is cooked, remove the pan from the heat. Lift out the chicken, strain the broth and reserve the required amount to make the sauce. When the chicken is cool enough to handle, remove the skin and separate the chicken into joints. Discard the breastbone, the backbone and any other small bones except those in the wings and legs.

Blend the walnut paste with sufficient of the reserved chicken broth to make a thick sauce, adding the broth a little at a time. Pour the sauce over the chicken pieces. Pour over the red oil from the walnuts. Traditionally this dish is served on a platter surrounded with a border of boiled short-grain rice.

*Note:* A stainless steel knife should be used for cutting through the chicken since the combination of the chicken juices and the walnut oil causes discoloration.


# ELBASAN CHICKEN SOUFFLÉ

*Serves 4*

| | |
|---|---|
| 1 chicken, about 3 lb/1·5 kg | 2 oz/50 g butter |
| 1 medium-sized carrot | 1 oz/25 g plain flour |
| 1 medium-sized onion | 2 eggs |
| 1 clove | 1 (4½-oz/127-g) carton natural yoghurt |
| 1 bay leaf | salt and pepper |
| 1 teaspoon salt | |
| ¼ pint/1·5 dl chicken broth (see recipe) | |

Wipe the chicken inside and out with a damp cloth or kitchen paper. Place in a saucepan and add just enough water to cover. Peel the carrot and onion and add to the pan with the clove, bay leaf and salt. Bring to the boil then lower the heat and simmer the chicken for about 1½ hours, or until tender. Remove the chicken from the broth and set aside to drain and cool. Strain the broth and discard the vegetables, clove and bay leaf. Reserve the amount of chicken broth required in the recipe.

Butter a 2-pint (1-litre) soufflé dish or casserole. Cut the chicken into pieces. Remove the breast from the ribs and discard the bones. Place the pieces in the prepared dish and keep warm.

Melt the butter in a saucepan, stir in the flour and cook for 2–3 minutes. Remove the pan from the heat and add the chicken broth gradually, stirring well after each addition. Return the pan to moderate heat and bring the liquid to the boil, stirring constantly until the sauce is smooth and thick. Remove the pan from the heat. Separate the eggs. Whisk a few tablespoons of the hot sauce into the egg yolks. Add the yoghurt and salt and pepper to taste and whisk the mixture thoroughly. Stir the egg yolk mixture into the sauce in the pan. Stiffly whisk the egg whites, fold them into the sauce and pour the mixture over the chicken. Place the dish in a moderately hot oven (375°F, 190°C, Gas Mark 5) for 30–35 minutes until the soufflé is well risen and golden brown. Serve immediately.

# CHICK PEA AND CHICKEN CASSEROLE

*Serves 6*

1 cup chick peas
1 chicken, about 3 lb
8 oz shallots
¼ cup butter
1 teaspoon chopped fresh parsley
¼ teaspoon dried thyme

½ teaspoon chopped fresh rosemary or ¼ teaspoon dried rosemary
dash sugar
salt and pepper

Soak the chick peas overnight in plenty of cold water. Drain well, remove the membranes and split the peas before using. Cut the chicken into 6 portions and discard the carcass. Peel the shallots and leave whole.

Melt the butter in a flameproof casserole over moderate heat and add the shallots and chicken. Sauté until the shallots just begin to soften. Add the drained chick peas, parsley, thyme, rosemary, sugar, salt and pepper to taste and just enough water to cover the ingredients. Cover the casserole and cook in a preheated moderately hot oven (400°) for 50 minutes–1 hour. Check the water from time to time, adding a little more if necessary. Serve hot.

# PIGEONS WITH OLIVES

*Serves 4*

4 plump young pigeons
  or 6 squabs
¼ cup butter
1 bay leaf
salt and pepper

about 1¼ cups red wine
12 green olives
1 teaspoon all-purpose flour
1 teaspoon soft butter

Clean the pigeons, rinse under cold running water and dry with a cloth or absorbent paper. Cut each pigeon in half. Melt the butter in a heavy saucepan over low heat and sauté the pigeons until evenly browned. Add the bay leaf, salt and pepper to taste and enough red wine to cover the pigeons. Place the pan over moderate heat and bring to a boil. Reduce the heat and simmer very slowly, partially covered, for 1–1½ hours, or until the pigeons are tender.

Place the olives in a colander, rinse with boiling water and add to the pigeons for the last 2–3 minutes of cooking time. Blend the flour to a smooth paste with the soft butter and a little of the stock from the pan. Stir the paste into the wine stock and simmer for a further 10 minutes. Remove the pigeons and olives from the pan and arrange in a fairly deep serving dish. Strain the sauce, pour it over the pigeons and serve hot with boiled potatoes.

*Lamb with prunes and almonds*

# QUAIL LOAF

*Serves 6*

| | |
|---|---|
| 1 round crusty white loaf, about 8 inches/20 cm in diameter | salt and pepper |
| 4 oz/100 g butter | 1 large onion |
| 6 plump quail | 6 tomatoes |
| | 3 large aubergines |

Cut a circular lid from the top of the loaf. Remove the soft bread from the inside. This may be set aside and used as required. Spread the inside of the loaf and lid very generously with half the butter. Open the quail along the back and remove the backbone, ribs and breastbone. Rinse the quail under cold running water, dry well with a cloth or kitchen paper and sprinkle with salt and pepper to taste. Peel the onion and slice thinly into rings. Thinly slice the tomatoes and aubergines.

Fill the inside of the loaf with alternate layers of tomato, aubergine, quail and onion rings. Sprinkle lightly with salt and pepper to taste between the layers. Repeat until all the ingredients have been used, finishing with a layer of tomato. Cover with the lid and spread the outside of the loaf with the remaining butter. Wrap the bread tightly in a large sheet of aluminium foil. Bake in a moderate oven (350°F, 180°C, Gas Mark 4) for about 2½ hours. Remove the foil and place the quail loaf on a decorative serving plate. Cut it into wedges for serving.

*Note:* The oven temperature must be steady so that the slow penetration of heat is constant. If in doubt, prolong the cooking time for another 30 minutes, or increase the heat to 400°F (200°C, Gas Mark 6) for the last 20 minutes of the cooking time.

# LAMB'S LIVER PILAV

*Serves 4*

| | |
|---|---|
| 4 oz/100 g lamb's liver | 1 tablespoon chopped fresh parsley |
| 2 oz/50 g butter | ½ teaspoon cinnamon |
| 1 teaspoon pine nut kernels | salt and pepper |
| 1 teaspoon currants | 8 oz/225 g long-grain rice |
| 1 tablespoon chopped fresh dill or 2 teaspoons dried dill weed | generous ¾ pint/5 dl water |

Wash the liver under cold running water and dry with a cloth or kitchen paper. Cut it into ¼-inch (5-mm) cubes. Melt the butter in a medium-sized saucepan over moderate heat and sauté the liver until it just begins to brown. Add the pine nut kernels and continue cooking, stirring frequently, for 4–5 minutes. Add the currants, dill, parsley, cinnamon, salt and pepper to taste and the rice. Continue to cook following the instructions on the next page for white *pilav*.

This *pilav* may also be served with lamb, roasted or cooked on the spit, or used as a stuffing for roast lamb.

*Pigeons with olives (see page 217); quail loaf*

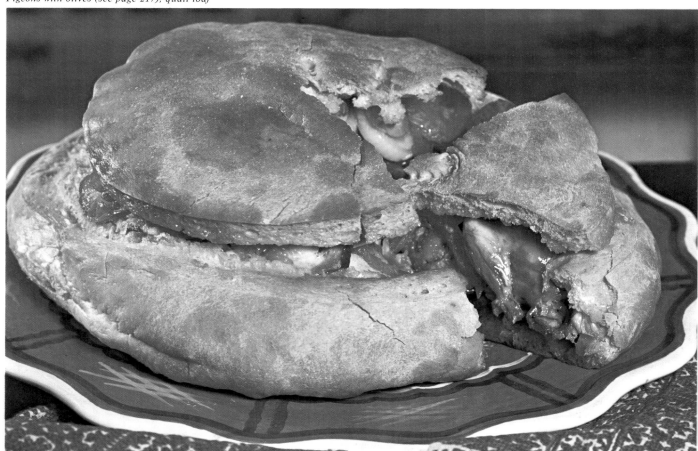

# WHITE PILAV

*Serves 6*

4 oz/100 g butter
1 lb/450 g long-grain rice

1½–2 pints/about 1 litre water
salt and pepper

Heat the butter in a large heavy saucepan. Stir in the rice and cook gently until most of the grains become opaque. Remove the pan from the heat and gradually stir in the water. After each addition, push the spoon across the bottom of the pan from the near side towards the opposite side. When enough water has been added, the rice will form a peak just above the surface of the liquid, about three-quarters of the way across the pan. Add salt and pepper to taste.

Place the pan over high heat and bring to the boil. Lower the heat, tightly cover the pan and cook for 25 minutes. Stir the rice gently with a wooden spoon, starting from the edges and heaping the rice into a cone in the centre. Replace the lid and leave the pan over low heat for a further 5 minutes. Remove from the heat, uncover and let the rice stand for 3 minutes. Use the rice as required or serve by itself, heaped into a cone shape, on a heated plate. If white *pilav* is served on its own, a bowl of natural yoghurt should accompany it, and the yoghurt may be spooned over the *pilav*.

### Variations

*Red pilav:* This variation of *pilav* is usually eaten un-accompanied or occasionally with meat. It is never mixed with other ingredients or served with yoghurt. Proceed as above, but before adding the water, add 2–3 tablespoons tomato purée. Add the water and continue as above.

*Pilav with barley vermicelli:* Proceed as above, but before adding the rice to the butter, sauté 1 oz (25 g) barley-shaped vermicelli or fine noodles in the butter until dark brown. Add the rice and continue as above.

*Pilav with thyme:* Proceed as above, but before adding the water, add 2 teaspoons chopped fresh thyme or 1 teaspoon dried thyme. Add the water and continue as above.

# AUBERGINE BÖREĞI

*Serves 4*

4 aubergines (see note)
1–2 teaspoons salt
3 oz/75 g curd or cottage cheese
¼ teaspoon finely chopped fresh
    mint
¼ teaspoon finely chopped fresh
    parsley

salt and pepper
2 eggs
1 tablespoon cold water
6 tablespoons olive oil
plain flour (see recipe)
few sprigs parsley

Pare the aubergines lengthwise at intervals of ¾ inch (1·5 cm), to give a striped effect. Cut them crosswise into slices, about 1½ inches (3·5 cm) thick. Place the slices on a large plate or wooden board and sprinkle with the salt. Let stand for 15–20 minutes then rinse under cold running water and dry thoroughly with a cloth or kitchen paper. Using a sharp pointed knife, make a horizontal incision, about 1½ inches (3·5 cm) long, in the side of each slice of aubergine. Move the knife in both directions, making a pouch or a pocket inside the slice. Be careful not to cut the outside except where the knife enters.

Mix together the cheese, mint, parsley and salt and pepper to taste, and carefully press about 1 teaspoon of the mixture into the pouch in each slice. Whisk the eggs with the cold water.

Heat the oil in a heavy shallow frying pan over moderate heat. Coat the aubergine slices with flour, then dip them into the beaten egg. Place immediately in the hot oil and sauté on each side until golden brown. (The egg should run off the aubergine slices when they are first placed in the pan, forming thin threads all round each slice.) Remove from the pan and drain on kitchen paper. Garnish with parsley and serve hot.

*Note:* Usually the round, flat type of aubergines are used for this dish, but long ones may be substituted, making smaller sized *böreği*.

# STUFFED VEGETABLES

*Serves 6*

6 small aubergines
6 courgettes, not less than 1 inch/
    2·5 cm thick
6 green sweet peppers
6 medium-sized tomatoes
**for the stuffing:**
3–4 large onions
scant ½ pint/2·5 dl olive oil
1 oz/25 g pine nut kernels
1 oz/25 g currants
3 tablespoons chopped fresh dill
    or 2 tablespoons dried dill weed

1½ teaspoons finely chopped fresh
    mint
2 tablespoons finely chopped fresh
    parsley
1 tablespoon cinnamon
salt and pepper
8 oz/225 g long-grain rice
1½ tablespoons lemon juice
½ pint/3 dl water
3 lemons
few sprigs parsley

Cut off the stalks of the aubergines with a sharp knife. Using a teaspoon, hollow out the inside without piercing the skin, leaving a shell with a ¼-inch (5-mm) thick wall around the sides and the base. Prepare the courgettes in the same way. Cut off and reserve the tops of the green peppers. Scoop out and discard both the seeds and the coarse white portions. Cut a lid from the top of each tomato without detaching it and scoop out the seeds and centre pulp. Press the pulp through a wire sieve, reserve the juice and discard the seeds.

To make the stuffing, peel and coarsely chop the onions. Heat about three-quarters of the oil in a large saucepan over moderate heat. Add the onions and sauté them, stirring frequently, until soft and golden brown. Add the pine nut kernels and sauté for 3–4 minutes, then add the currants, dill, mint, parsley, cinnamon, salt and pepper to taste and the rice. Continue cooking, stirring frequently, until the rice becomes opaque. Stir in the reserved tomato juice, the lemon juice and the water. Simmer gently for about 10 minutes, or until the water has been absorbed. It is not necessary, however, for the rice to be completely cooked at this stage.

Remove the pan from the heat and lightly pack the mixture into the prepared vegetables, starting with the peppers, then the aubergines, courgettes, and lastly the tomatoes. Stand the stuffed vegetables, open ends uppermost, in a large saucepan, with the peppers in the centre. Replace the lids on the peppers. Add the remaining oil and enough water to come half-way up the tomatoes. Place a small plate upside down in the pan so that it rests on the vegetables. Cover the pan, place it over moderate heat and

*Aubergine böreği*

simmer for 1 hour. Remove the lid and plate and leave the vegetables in the pan until cold.

Thinly slice 2 of the lemons. Using two spoons, carefully remove the stuffed vegetables from the pan and arrange on a shallow serving dish. Pour over the juice remaining in the pan and garnish with sprigs of parsley and lemon slices. Let stand in a cool place until the following day. Cut the remaining lemon into wedges and serve with the stuffed vegetables.

*Note:* Cabbage and vine leaves may also be stuffed and cooked in a similar way to the above vegetables. Before stuffing they should be blanched in boiling water for 5–10 minutes until they are pliable. Remove any thick veins and stalks. When cooking, line the bottom of the saucepan with several whole cabbage or vine leaves to prevent the stuffed leaves from sticking to the bottom of the pan.

# FRIED ARTICHOKES

*Serves 4*

| | |
|---|---|
| 4 globe artichokes | ½ teaspoon salt |
| 1 lemon | 1 tablespoon olive oil |
| **for the batter:** | 6 tablespoons water |
| 1 egg | oil for deep-frying |
| 4 oz/100 g plain flour | |

Wash each artichoke and discard the coarse outer leaves and the soft inner leaves. Discard the hairy choke and retain only the heart. Cut the lemon in half. Cut each heart into quarters and rub these with one of the lemon halves. Place the artichoke hearts in a bowl and add cold water to cover. Squeeze the juice from the remaining lemon half and add it to the water. Set the bowl aside while making the batter.

Whisk the egg thoroughly in a small bowl. Sift the flour and salt into a large bowl and add the olive oil very gradually, beating well with a wooden spoon after each addition. Add the water gradually and beat until the batter is quite smooth. Stir in the beaten egg.

Drain the artichokes in a colander or sieve and dry them with a cloth or kitchen paper. Heat the oil in a deep saucepan. Coat each artichoke quarter with the batter and deep-fry until crisp and golden brown. Drain on kitchen paper and serve hot with grilled meat.

*Note:* The lemon and water prevents the artichokes from discolouring and also gives a slightly sour flavour to counteract the heaviness of the oil.

221

*Buttered spinach with yoghurt*

# STUFFED VINE LEAVES WITH CALF'S FOOT

*Serves 6*

1 calf's foot
2 medium-sized onions
3 celery leaves, about
   3 inches/7·5 cm long
1 sprig fresh dill
2 bay leaves
salt and pepper

**for the stuffed vine leaves:**

12–14 oz/350–400 g fresh or
   canned vine leaves
1 large onion
4 oz/100 g butter

1 lb/450 g lean lamb, finely
   minced
4–5 oz/100–150 g long-grain rice
1 tablespoon finely chopped fresh
   parsley
1 tablespoon finely chopped fresh
   mint
1 tablespoon finely chopped fresh
   dill
salt and pepper
1½ tablespoons lemon juice

Wash the calf's foot and rinse it well under cold running water. Peel the onions and leave whole. Place the calf's foot and onions in a large saucepan. Add the celery leaves, dill, bay leaves, salt and pepper to taste and cold water to cover. Bring to the boil over moderate heat. Lower the heat and simmer, partially covered, for about 2 hours. Remove the calf's foot from the pan and set aside to cool. Strain, reserve the stock and discard the onions and herbs.

If using fresh vine leaves, rinse well under cold running water and blanch in boiling water for 5–10 minutes, until soft and pliable. Drain well. Preserved leaves should be rinsed thoroughly with boiling water and drained well.

Peel and finely chop the onion. Melt the butter in a saucepan over low heat and sauté the onion until soft and transparent, but not browned. Add the lamb, rice, parsley, mint, dill, salt and pepper to taste and the lemon juice. Mix the ingredients thoroughly and remove the pan from the heat.

Line the bottom and sides of a large heavy saucepan with several vine leaves. Place the remaining vine leaves, dull side uppermost, on a flat working surface. Place a teaspoon of the rice mixture on each leaf. Roll up the leaf, tucking in the ends and completely enclosing the filling to make a neat roll, about 1½ inches (3·5 cm) long and 1 inch (2·5 cm) thick. Place the stuffed vine leaves very close together in the pan, starting around the outside and working towards the centre. Make several layers, if necessary. Thinly slice the meat from the calf's foot and sprinkle the slices over the stuffed vine leaves. Cover with the stock from the calf's foot and place a small plate over the leaves and meat. Tightly cover the pan and simmer over low heat for 1–1¼ hours. Drain off the stock and arrange the stuffed vine leaves on a plate. Serve hot with natural yoghurt.

# BUTTERED SPINACH WITH YOGHURT

*Serves 4*

2 lb/1 kg fresh spinach
1 large onion
2 oz/50 g butter
salt and pepper

1 (15½-oz/440-g) carton natural
    yoghurt
salt and pepper

Wash the spinach thoroughly under cold running water. Discard the thick stalks. Tear the spinach into shreds and drain it in a colander. Peel and finely chop the onion.

Melt the butter in a saucepan over moderate heat. Add the onion and sauté until transparent but not browned, stirring occasionally. Add the spinach, a little at a time, stirring constantly. Add salt and pepper to taste and cook gently until all the liquid has evaporated and the spinach is dark green. Place the spinach in a serving dish and make a well in the centre. Beat the yoghurt with a little salt and pepper to taste and pour into the well. Serve immediately.

# ARTICHOKES IN OLIVE OIL

*Serves 4*

4 artichokes (see note)
1 lemon
8 oz/225 g broad beans
2 large potatoes
4 oz/100 g shallots
3 tablespoons olive oil

salt and pepper
1 tablespoon chopped fresh dill or
    2 teaspoons dried dill weed
½ teaspoon chopped fresh parsley
few sprigs parsley

Peel off and discard the coarse outer leaves of the artichokes until you reach the soft, blue-tinted inner leaves. Cut the artichokes horizontally with a sharp knife. Remove and discard the soft leaves and the choke (the hairy core in the centre.) This will leave a semicircle with the stalk as a handle. Trim the stalk of each artichoke until it is flat-sided and about ¼ inch (5 mm) square. Cut the lemon in half. Rub the artichokes with one half of the lemon and squeeze the juice from the remaining half into a bowl of water. Add the prepared artichokes and set aside to soak until required. Shell the beans. Peel the potatoes and cut into quarters lengthwise. Peel the shallots and leave whole.

Heat the olive oil in a saucepan over moderate heat. Add the shallots and sauté until almost soft, but not browned. Add the beans, salt and pepper to taste, dill, chopped parsley and enough water to just cover the vegetables. Simmer very gently for about 5 minutes, or until the shallots are fully cooked. Drain the artichokes, add to the vegetables in the pan and simmer for 20 minutes, adding more water if necessary. Add the potatoes and simmer for a further 20 minutes, or until all the vegetables are tender. Remove the pan from the heat and set aside to cool.

Stand the artichokes, stalks uppermost, on a china dish. Spoon the other vegetables and the juice around them. Garnish with the parsley sprigs and serve cold.

*Note:* Great care should be taken to choose artichokes that are large and fully grown, yet still young enough to be tender. Their stalks should be about 2 inches (5 cm) long.

# COURGETTES WITH MINT

*Serves 4*

6 large courgettes
2 large onions
2 oz/50 g butter

2 teaspoons chopped fresh mint
salt and pepper
½ teaspoon sugar

Rinse the courgettes under cold running water and dry thoroughly with a cloth or kitchen paper. Scrape the courgettes, removing only the outer green skin, and cut crosswise into slices. Peel the onions and slice thinly into rings.

Melt the butter in a saucepan over moderate heat and add the courgettes, onion, mint, salt and pepper to taste and the sugar. Tightly cover the pan and cook gently for about 40 minutes.

Shake the pan from time to time and check that the ingredients are not sticking to the bottom. If necessary, add 1–2 tablespoons of cold water. When cooked, the ingredients should be tender, with just a suggestion of juice. Serve hot.

# EGYPTIAN BROWN BEANS

*Serves 4*

8 oz/225 g dried brown Egyptian
    beans
1 medium-sized onion

1 pint/6 dl water
½ teaspoon salt
butter or olive oil (see recipe)

Soak the beans overnight in plenty of cold water. Drain well before using. Peel the onion and leave whole. Place in a saucepan with the drained beans, water and salt. Bring to the boil over high heat. Lower the heat, tightly cover the pan and simmer for 2 hours, or until the beans are very soft and the liquid is thick. Discard the onion.

Serve hot with butter or cold with olive oil. The butter or oil is usually added by each diner, according to taste.

# COTTAGE CHEESE BÖREĞI AND COURGETTE BÖREĞI

*Makes 36 of each filling*

**for the pastry (see note):**
1 lb/450 g plain flour
1 teaspoon baking powder
1 teaspoon salt in ½ pint/3 dl lukewarm water
**for the first filling:**
4 oz/100 g cottage or curd cheese
1 teaspoon finely chopped fresh parsley
1 teaspoon finely chopped fresh mint
salt and pepper
**for the second filling:**
6 oz/175 g courgettes
1 teaspoon chopped fresh mint
salt and pepper
**for frying:**
1 oz/25 g butter

To prepare the pastry, sift together the flour and baking powder. Place about three-quarters of the flour mixture on a pastry board, reserving the remainder. Make a well in the centre and gradually add the salted water, working the flour and salted water together to make a smooth elastic dough. Knead the dough on the board for 15–20 minutes. Wrap the dough in a cloth or greaseproof paper and set aside in a cool place for about 1 hour.

Sprinkle the remaining flour over a board. Cut the dough in half. Roll out each half until it is paper-thin and almost transparent. Use it immediately, or, if the dough is to be stored, cut it into strips, about 4 by 12 inches (10 by 30 cm), and pile the strips, one on top of the other, with a thin coating of flour between to prevent them from sticking together. Wrap in a cloth, foil or greaseproof paper.

To make the first filling, mix together the cottage cheese, parsley, mint and salt and pepper to taste in a small bowl. To make the second filling, wash the courgettes and cut off the stalks. Chop the courgettes coarsely and cook in boiling salted water for about 10 minutes, or until just tender. Drain well. Stir in the mint and salt and pepper to taste, and set aside until the mixture is cool.

To make the *muska* (triangular) *böreği*, cut half the amount of pastry into strips, 6 by 2 inches (15 by 5 cm). Place a teaspoon of the cheese on the pastry and fold (see photograph). Tuck in the remaining flap. Repeat until all the pastry and filling have been used.

To make the *cigara* (cigar-shaped) *böreği*, cut the pastry into strips, 6 by 2 inches (15 by 5 cm). Place a teaspoon of the courgette on the pastry and fold the shorter sides over the filling (see photograph). Roll the pastry around the filling, making *cigara böreği* of about 4 inches (10 cm) long. Repeat until all the pastry and filling have been used.

Heat the butter in a frying pan. Shallow-fry the *böreği*, a few at a time, until golden brown all over. Drain on kitchen paper and serve hot with *raki*, the Turkish national drink, or as an accompaniment to cocktails.

*Note:* Yufka pastry may be bought already prepared in Greek and Cypriot food shops under the name of *phylo* pastry.

# GREEK EASTER BREAD

*Serves 8–10*

1 tablespoon aniseed
5 tablespoons water
2 oz/50 g fresh yeast or 1 oz/25 g dried yeast
6 tablespoons lukewarm milk
1½ lb/700 g plain flour
½ teaspoon salt
1½ teaspoons grated orange rind
4 eggs
6 oz/175 g melted butter
8 oz/225 g castor sugar
1 egg yolk
3 oz/75 g blanched almonds, chopped

Simmer the aniseed in the water for 5 minutes. Strain through a sieve, reserve the liquid and discard the seeds. Place the yeast in a small bowl and add the lukewarm milk, a little at a time, stirring well after each addition until the mixture is smooth. Let stand for about 5 minutes, or until the mixture is frothy. Add 2 oz (50 g) of the flour and mix to a smooth batter. Cover the bowl with a cloth and let stand in a warm place until large bubbles begin to form on the surface of the batter. Meanwhile, sift the remaining flour and the salt into a large bowl. Make a well in the centre and add the aniseed water, yeast mixture, orange rind, eggs, melted butter and sugar. Mix thoroughly and knead to a smooth dough. Cover the bowl with a damp cloth and let stand in a warm place for 2–3 hours, or until the dough has doubled in bulk.

Turn the dough on to a well-floured board, and knead until smooth and elastic. Cut the dough into 3 portions and roll each portion into a rope about 12 inches (30 cm) long. Braid the three ropes together to make one large loaf. Tuck the ends under to prevent the braids from coming undone as the dough rises. Place on a greased baking tray and cover lightly with a damp cloth. Let stand in a warm place until the dough has doubled in bulk. Whisk the egg yolk with a little cold water and brush it over the dough, just before baking. Sprinkle with the chopped almonds and bake in a moderately hot oven (400°F, 200°C, Gas Mark 6) for 30–35 minutes, or until firm and golden brown. Cool the loaf on a wire rack.

*Note:* This delicious bread is sent to friends at Easter, surrounded by Easter eggs, dyed red. These eggs are often buried in the dough before the bread is baked.

# GROUND ALMOND, LEMON AND CREAM DESSERT

*Serves 4*

½ pint/3 dl double cream
2 teaspoons grated lemon rind
1 oz/25 g ground almonds
3 tablespoons lemon juice
2 oz/50 g castor sugar
4 small pieces crystallised lemon peel

Measure the cream into a bowl and add the lemon rind, ground almonds, lemon juice and sugar. Whisk until the mixture is thick and light. Pour the mixture into 4 serving glasses and decorate each one with a piece of crystallised lemon peel. Chill for several hours before serving.

*Cottage cheese böreği and courgette böreği*

# VIZIER'S FINGERS

*Serves 4*

4 oz/100 g semolina
scant ½ pint/2·5 dl milk
1 egg
4 oz/100 g castor sugar
scant ½ pint/2·5 dl water

1½ tablespoons lemon juice
few drops almond essence
2 oz/50 g butter
rose water (optional)

Place the semolina in a saucepan and stir in the milk. Place the pan over moderate heat and bring to the boil, stirring constantly until the mixture becomes very stiff. Remove the pan from the heat and beat in the egg. Turn out the mixture on to a buttered plate or foil and let stand until cool.

Meanwhile, put the sugar, water and lemon juice into a heavy saucepan over low heat. Stir until the sugar dissolves, add the almond essence, and bring the liquid to the boil. Continue boiling until a thick syrup is formed. At this stage, the syrup will begin to turn to a pale golden brown and the pan should be removed from the heat immediately. Set aside in a warm place until the syrup is required.

Shape the cooled semolina mixture into finger shapes about 2½ inches (6 cm) long. Melt the butter in a heavy frying pan and sauté the fingers until browned on both sides. A lighter band should be visible on either side along the length of each finger. Remove from the pan and drain on kitchen paper. Arrange on a serving dish and pour over the warm syrup. Alternatively, a few drops of rose water may be sprinkled over the fingers, just before pouring over the warm syrup. Serve cold.


# ALI'S MOTHER

*Serves 4–6*

**for the layered pastry:**
8 oz/225 g plain flour
1 teaspoon salt
¼ pint/1·5 dl water
4 oz/110 g butter

**for the sweetened milk:**
½ pint/3 dl milk
2 oz/50 g castor sugar
2 teaspoons cinnamon

To make the pastry, sift the flour and salt into a bowl. Add the water and mix to a soft dough. Knead the dough for 20 minutes on a lightly floured surface. Cover with a damp cloth and set aside for 1 hour. Knead for a further 20 minutes, cover again with the damp cloth and set aside overnight in the refrigerator or a cold place.

The next day, shape the dough into a long rope, about 2 inches (5 cm) in diameter, and cut into 12 equal-sized portions. Roll all the portions of dough into 12 very thin circles of equal size, approximately 8 inches (20 cm) in diameter. Melt the butter in a heavy frying pan over fairly low heat and sauté each pastry circle separately until golden brown. Stack the circles in a shallow ovenproof baking dish.

To make the sweetened milk, heat the milk, sugar and cinnamon together until the sugar has dissolved, and then pour the mixture over the pastry. Bake in a moderately hot oven (400°F, 200°C, Gas Mark 6) for about 30 minutes, or until the top layer is golden brown. Cut into wedges and serve warm in the dish in which it was cooked.


# CHESTNUT BALLS

Serves 4–6

2 lb/1 kg chestnuts or 2 (15½-oz/440-g) cans unsweetened chestnut purée
½ pint/3 dl milk
1 stick cinnamon
6 oz/175 g castor sugar
2 oz/50 g glacé cherries, chopped

2 oz/50 g mixed chopped candied peel
2 eggs
4 oz/100 g fine dried breadcrumbs
oil for deep-frying
castor sugar for coating
ground cinnamon
single cream (optional)

If using fresh chestnuts, make a deep slit in the outer skin of each chestnut with a sharp knife. Place the chestnuts in a large saucepan and cover with water. Bring to the boil over moderate heat and simmer for 20 minutes. Drain the chestnuts into a colander and let stand until cool. Discard the outer and inner skins. Return the peeled chestnuts to the pan and add the milk, cinnamon stick and a quarter of the sugar. Simmer gently over low heat until all the liquid has been absorbed. Discard the cinnamon stick. Press the chestnuts through a wire sieve, making a thick purée. If using canned chestnut purée, follow the recipe from this stage.

Mix the remaining sugar with the chestnut purée. Add the glacé cherries and mixed candied peel and mix well. Roll the mixture into balls, about 1½ inches (3·5 cm) in diameter. Whisk the eggs. Coat the balls with egg, roll them in the breadcrumbs and deep-fry in hot oil until crisp and golden brown. Drain the balls on kitchen paper and roll them several times in a mixture of sugar and cinnamon. Serve hot with cream, or leave until cold and serve with coffee.


# PUMPKIN DESSERT

Serves 4

1 lb/450 g fresh pumpkin
1 tablespoon water
½ pint/3 dl pumpkin liquid (see recipe)

2 oz/50 g castor sugar
1½ tablespoons lemon juice
4 oz/100 g walnuts, finely chopped

Remove the seeds and the soft stringy pulp from the pumpkin flesh, but leave the pumpkin unpeeled. Cut it into 4 pieces, each piece about 2 by 3 inches (5 by 7·5 cm). Place the pumpkin pieces, skin side up, in a saucepan. Add the water and tightly cover the pan. Cook gently over very low heat until the pumpkin is tender. Drain off the juice that forms during cooking into a measuring cup, and add water to make the amount of liquid required. Add the sugar and lemon juice and pour the mixture into a small saucepan. Place the pan over low heat to dissolve the sugar, then increase the heat and boil the liquid rapidly until reduced to about half the original quantity.

Place the pumpkin in a serving dish, with the skin side underneath. Pour over the juice and sprinkle with chopped walnuts. Serve warm or cold.

*Chestnut balls*

226

# DOUGHNUTS IN SCENTED SYRUP

*Serves 6*

**for the dough:**
½ oz/15 g fresh yeast or
   ¼ oz/7 g dried yeast
1 teaspoon sugar
½ pint/3 dl lukewarm water
1 lb/450 g plain flour
½ pint/3 dl milk
**for the syrup:**
½ pint/3 dl water

2 tablespoons lemon juice
1½ lb/700 g castor sugar
2 tablespoons rose water
2 tablespoons orange flower water
oil for deep-frying
2–3 oz/50–75 g castor sugar for
   coating
ground cinnamon (optional)

If using fresh yeast, blend the yeast with the sugar and the water. If using dried yeast, set aside for 10–15 minutes, or until the liquid becomes frothy.

Sift the flour into a mixing bowl and make a well in the centre. Lightly whip the milk into the yeast mixture and pour the mixture into the flour. Beat well to form a very soft batter. Cover the bowl and set aside in a warm place for 1 hour. Beat well, cover the bowl again and set aside to rise again for a further hour. Repeat this process once or twice. Thorough beating at regular intervals helps to make the dough elastic and the doughnuts a perfectly round shape.

Meanwhile, to make the syrup, pour the water and lemon juice into a heavy saucepan and add the sugar. Bring to the boil over moderate heat, taking care that the sugar dissolves before the boiling point is reached. Lower the heat and simmer the liquid until the syrup is thick enough to coat the back of a spoon. Add the rose water and orange flower water and simmer for a further 2–3 minutes. Remove the pan from the heat and set aside until cold. The syrup should be well chilled when used.

Heat the oil in a heavy saucepan. Beat the dough well and, using a wet teaspoon or a cloth piping bag and large plain tube, drop small amounts of the batter into the hot oil. The doughnuts will rise to the surface quickly. Turn them over and fry them for a further 2–3 minutes, or until crisp and golden brown.

Drain the doughnuts well on kitchen paper and, while still hot, dip them into the syrup. Serve hot or cold, with a sprinkling of sugar. A little cinnamon may also be sprinkled over the sugar-coated doughnuts.

# FRESH PLUM COMPOTE

*Serves 4*

12 ripe plums
½ pint/3 dl water
4 oz/100 g castor sugar
1 tablespoon whole blanched
   almonds

1½ tablespoons lemon juice
cinnamon stick, about 1 inch/
   2·5 cm
4 cloves

The plums should be ripe but firm. Make a small slit in the side of each plum. Place the water, sugar, almonds, lemon juice, cinnamon stick and cloves in a small heavy saucepan. Bring to the boil over moderate heat, making sure that the sugar has dissolved before the liquid boils. Simmer until the liquid becomes slightly thick and syrupy. Add the plums and cook gently until the skins begin to curl up along the slits. Remove the pan from the heat and chill the compote well before serving.

# BAKLAVA

*Makes 12*

1 lb/450 g *yufka (phylo)* pastry
  (see Cottage Cheese Böreği,
  page 225)
12 oz/350 g blanched almonds
8 oz/225 g butter

**for the syrup:**
scant ¾ pint/4 dl water
2 teaspoons lemon juice
12 oz/350 g castor sugar
stick cinnamon, about 2 inches/
  5 cm

Prepare the *yufka* pastry, wrap and set aside in a cool place for 1 hour. Meanwhile, toast the almonds until lightly browned and chop coarsely. Melt the butter. Roll out the pastry until it is as thin as paper and cut into as many 9-inch (23-cm) squares as possible.

Using a little of the melted butter, grease a deep baking tray or meat tin, and place a square of pastry in the bottom. Brush the pastry layer with a little of the melted butter and sprinkle with chopped almonds. Cover with a second layer of pastry. Continue in this way until all the pastry and almonds and most of the butter have been used. Brush the top layer of pastry well with melted butter. With a sharp knife, mark the top of the *baklava* into 12 oblong pieces. Place the tray in a moderate oven (350°F, 180°C, Gas Mark 4) for approximately 45 minutes, or until the *baklava* is golden brown. Remove the tray from the oven and set aside until the *baklava* is cold.

Meanwhile, place the water, lemon juice, sugar and cinnamon stick in a small heavy saucepan. Heat slowly until the sugar has completely dissolved. Bring to the boil, lower the heat and simmer for 5 minutes.

Pour the hot syrup over the cold *baklava* and set aside until the syrup is cold. Cut along the marks that were made before baking and serve as required.

# HALVA

*Makes 16–20 portions*

4 oz/100 g butter
8 oz/225 g castor sugar
4 eggs
4 oz/100 g ground almonds
1 teaspoon cinnamon

8 oz/225 g semolina
**for the syrup:**
8 oz/225 g castor sugar
¼ pint/3 dl water
3 tablespoons lemon juice

Cream together the butter and sugar until the mixture is soft and creamy. Lightly whisk the eggs and beat them into the mixture with the ground almonds, cinnamon and semolina.

Line a large Swiss roll tin with greaseproof paper, allowing the paper to stand about 1 inch (2·5 cm) higher than the tin. Grease the paper lightly. Spread the mixture into the prepared tin. Bake in the centre of a moderate oven (350°F, 180°C, Gas Mark 4) for about 40 minutes. Remove the tin from the oven and prepare the syrup.

Measure the sugar and water into a saucepan. Stir over low heat until the sugar has dissolved. Add the lemon juice and bring to the boil. Simmer for 5 minutes until the syrup is dissolved slightly. Remove the pan from the heat, let it cool a little then pour the hot syrup over the *halva*. Leave to soak until the *halva* is cool. Cut into squares to serve.

# TURKISH DELIGHT

*Makes 1½ lb/700 g*

generous ¼ pint/2 dl water
3 tablespoons orange juice
3 tablespoons lemon juice
1½ lb/700 g castor sugar

1 oz/25 g gelatine
3 oz/75 g cornflour
3–4 drops colouring (optional)
icing sugar (see recipe)

Combine the water, the orange and lemon juice and the sugar in a heavy saucepan. Bring to the boil over low heat, taking care that the sugar has dissolved before the boiling point is reached. Lower the heat and boil the liquid very gently until it reaches a temperature of 230°F (110°C) on a sugar thermometer – the long thread stage. Meanwhile, dissolve the gelatine in a little hot water. Blend the cornflour with enough cold water to make a thin paste and add the paste to the hot syrup, stirring constantly. Stir in the gelatine and boil the mixture until clear, stirring occasionally. Add the colouring, if used, and pour the mixture into an 8-inch (20-cm) square cake tin. Set aside for at least 24 hours.

Loosen the Turkish delight in the tin and turn out on to a thick layer of icing sugar. Sprinkle the top with icing sugar and cut into 1-inch (2·5-cm) squares with a sharp knife. Coat each square with icing sugar immediately. Serve as required.

*Note:* Alternatively, rose water may be substituted for the orange and lemon juice.

# STUFFED APRICOT MERINGUE

*Serves 6*

9 fresh ripe apricots or peaches
1 tablespoon lemon juice
8 oz/225 g soft brown sugar
4 oz/100 g pine nut kernels
8 oz/225 g ground almonds

2 tablespoons rose water
**for the meringue:**
4 egg whites
3 oz/75 g castor sugar

Wash and halve the apricots and remove the stones. Place the apricots in a saucepan with the lemon juice. Simmer gently over low heat until some of the fruit juice has been extracted from the fruit. Add half the sugar and continue to simmer for about 15 minutes, or until the apricots are tender. Remove the pan from the heat and set aside to cool.

Finely chop the pine nut kernels. Mix together half the ground almonds, the remaining sugar and the pine nut kernels in a bowl. Add the rose water, blending the mixture to a soft paste. Drain the apricots and reserve the syrup. Place teaspoons of the mixture in the centre of each of the apricot halves. Arrange the filled apricots in a well-buttered baking dish. Pour the syrup over and sprinkle with the remainder of the ground almonds. Whisk the egg whites until stiff, add the sugar and whisk again until the mixture is glossy. Spoon the meringue over the apricots, taking care that the meringue completely covers the apricots and is spread to the sides of the dish. Bake in a cool oven (300°F, 150°C, Gas Mark 2) for about 30 minutes, or until the meringue is golden brown and firm. Serve immediately with whipped cream.

*Turkish delight*

# JEWISH

## Molly Lyons Bar-David

*Photography by John Miller*

Jewish cooking has evolved from the adoption of culinary ideas from many nations, altered to keep within the traditional laws.

The laws of *kosher* cooking may have had their origins in hygiene as well as moral teachings. The ritually permitted meats are classified as *kosher* (clean). Animals must have cloven hooves and chew the cud. Beef, lamb and meat from the goat and deer families come within this category. The slaughtering must be done ritually and the animal carefully checked to make certain there is no infection. The meat is then salted and soaked to comply with the injunction against consuming blood. Liver must be salted and then grilled to extract the blood. If poultry flesh is grilled it does not require salting or soaking. It is also one of the traditional practices of Jewish religious life not to mix meat and dairy products.

Fish with fins and scales are the only permitted variety; shellfish are forbidden. Birds of prey, scavengers and all winged creeping creatures are not allowed in Jewish cooking. Poultry may not be cooked in milk or cream, as dressed veal or lamb could be mistaken for poultry.

These rules, then, have formed the core of all Jewish cookery throughout the ages and throughout the world. Cooking has been made easier today by the introduction of new *kosher* products, such as butter-tasting margarine which can be eaten with meat, *pareve* which is a non-meat and non-dairy vegetarian milk or cream product and *kosher* gelatines and aspics made of vegetable colloids.

Many Biblical and symbolic foods have retained their importance in Jewish cooking. Chief among these, perhaps, are the many breads using the Biblical grains of wheat, barley, spelt (rye) and millet. The symbolic *challah* loaves vary in shape depending on the festival. The Sabbath loaves are braided. The Rosh Hashana loaves are circular symbolising happiness all the year round. Cakes using olive oil and honey recorded in the Bible are still made, and unleavened wafers 'anointed with oil' result in very rich biscuits akin to Western shortbread.

Salted herring and other fish are popular in most Jewish communities since, until recent times, fish had to be salted or sun-dried or smoked to make it saleable throughout Israel. Today, fresh or frozen fish is more readily available. The use of fat is still high on the list of Jewish cooking in the Middle East, stemming from Biblical days when it was used in feasts. Its popularity is dwindling today in other Jewish communities because of the modern approach to diet. The vegetables listed in the Bible are the most-used in Israel, and the fruits, from the date to the grape, are symbolically served at many festivals. Unusual flavourings are still outstanding. Cassia is frequently used in baking. Cinnamon even goes into meat, lamb and poultry dishes. Mint is popular in local salads and coriander is still used to symbolise the ancient *manna* flavour. Dill and mustard – wild herbs in Israel – appear in many main dishes, and capers, which also grow wild, are invariably used in salads.

The Biblical foods are still a part of the Jewish cuisine because of ancient lore and prolific native crops, but there are many other dishes for the various festivals which have evolved from the Jewish communities throughout the world.

# CHOPPED LIVER

*Serves 6*

| | |
|---|---|
| 4 eggs | ¾ teaspoon salt |
| 1 lb/450 g chicken or ox liver | pinch pepper |
| 3 onions | 1 tomato |
| 3 tablespoons chicken fat | lettuce leaves (see recipe) |

Hard-boil the eggs, shell, cut in halves and separate the yolks and whites. Dip the liver in salted iced water and then grill until cooked according to taste. Peel and chop the onions. Melt the chicken fat in a frying pan and sauté the onions until tender but not browned. Remove from the pan. Put the liver, onions and egg yolks through a mincer and mix together. Add the salt and pepper and any fat left in the pan after cooking the onions and mix well. Chop the egg whites and slice the tomato.

Wash and dry several lettuce leaves and either arrange on a serving dish or on individual plates. Place the liver mixture on the lettuce leaves and serve garnished with the egg whites and sliced tomato.

# CHOPPED HERRING

*Serves 6*

| | |
|---|---|
| 2 salted herrings | ¼ teaspoon freshly ground black |
| 2 eggs | pepper |
| 1 slice white bread | 1½ tablespoons oil |
| 1 onion | 2 tablespoons wine vinegar |
| 1 eating apple | few spring onions |
| 1 teaspoon sugar | few black olives |
| pinch celery salt, mace or ground allspice (optional) | |

Soak the herrings overnight in cold water. Drain and pat dry. Gut the fish and remove the skin and bones. Hard-boil the eggs and shell them. Soak the bread for a few minutes in cold water and squeeze out the excess moisture. Peel and quarter the onion. Peel, quarter and core the apple.

Put the fish, eggs, bread, onion and apple through a mincer. Add the sugar, celery salt, pepper, oil and vinegar and mix well. Wash and trim the spring onions. Serve the chopped herrings garnished with the spring onions and black olives.

# FENNEL WITH OLIVES AND CAPERS

*Serves 6*

| | |
|---|---|
| 2 large or 3 small fennel bulbs | 1 tablespoon chopped green |
| 12 black olives | fennel tops |
| 12 green olives | 2 tablespoons olive oil |
| 1 heaped tablespoon pickled capers | salt |

Wash, trim and drain the fennel and cut into thin slices across the grain. Arrange the slices on a serving dish and garnish with the black and green olives (stoned, if preferred). Sprinkle with the pickled capers and the chopped fennel tops. Pour over the olive oil and sprinkle with salt to taste.

# AVOCADO MOULDS

*Serves 6*

½ oz/15 g gelatine
1½ tablespoons lemon juice
6 tablespoons hot water
scant ½ pint /2·5 dl fruit juice
    (apple, cider, pineapple or
    citrus juices)
2 avocados
2–3 spring onion tops
1 tablespoon finely chopped fresh
    herbs (mint, parsley or dill)

2 drops hot sauce (Worcestershire
    or Tabasco) or ¼ teaspoon
    prepared mustard
½ teaspoon salt
¼ pint/1·5 dl mayonnaise
for the garnish:
lettuce leaves
tomato slices
few black olives (optional)

Mix the gelatine and lemon juice with the hot water in a bowl. Set the bowl in a pan of boiling water and stir until the gelatine is dissolved. Remove the bowl from the heat. Add the fruit juice and stir well. Set aside until the mixture begins to thicken, stirring occasionally. At this stage, peel the avocados, remove the stones and mash the flesh to a pulp.

Chop the spring onion tops. Add the chopped herbs and onion tops, hot sauce, salt and mayonnaise to the avocado pulp, and beat together until well blended. Stir in the slightly thickened fruit juice and pour the mixture into 6 individual moulds or 1 large mould. Chill for several hours until firm.

To unmould, dip the moulds in warm, but not hot water. Loosen the edges with a sharp knife. Place a plate over each mould and quickly invert. Shake gently and slowly lift off the mould. Slide each mould carefully on to a bed of lettuce and garnish each with a slice of tomato. If desired, add black olives as an additional garnish.

*Note:* If using 1 large mould, an alternative method of unmoulding is to place a serving plate over the mould, invert and press a warm, dampened cloth around the mould, shaking gently to loosen the contents. Repeat several times with a fresh warm cloth if necessary.

# CARROT-FILLED AVOCADOS

*Serves 6*

3 oranges
juice of ½ lemon
5–6 medium-sized carrots
8 oz/225 g pineapple cubes
    (fresh or canned)

pinch ground ginger or cloves
salt
sugar (see recipe)
2 avocados

Add the juice from 2 of the oranges to the lemon juice. Peel the carrots, grate coarsely and soak in the orange and lemon juice for about 2 hours. Peel the remaining orange and remove the white skin. Cut the flesh into small cubes, taking care to remove any pips. Mix the carrot mixture with the orange and pineapple cubes; add the spice and salt and sugar to taste. Drain off the excess juices and reserve.

Cut the avocados lengthwise into three sections and discard the stones. Rub the avocado flesh lightly with lemon juice to prevent discoloration. Fill each portion with the drained carrot mixture. Alternatively, remove the skins from the avocados using a sharp knife. Cut the flesh into thin slices and sprinkle with lemon juice. Place the carrot mixture in a serving dish and arrange the avocado slices around the outside.

Sprinkle the avocados with some of the reserved fruit juice before serving.

*Note:* If the avocados require ripening before they are used, set them aside in a dark place for several days, until the flesh is slightly soft. If the avocado flesh is prepared in advance, placing the stones in the bowl with the slices will also act as a deterrent to discoloration.

# CHICKEN COCKTAIL

*Serves 6*

| for the cocktail: | for the sauce: |
|---|---|
| 2 cooked chicken breasts, about 8 oz/225 g | ½ pint/3 dl mayonnaise |
| 3 canned pineapple rings | 6 tablespoons tomato ketchup |
| 2 oranges | 1 tablespoon tomato purée |
| 1 small grapefruit | 1 teaspoon grated horseradish |
| 6 oz/175 g cooked cherries | 1 tablespoon brandy |

Dice the chicken and pineapple rings. Peel the oranges and grapefruit, removing as much of the white inner skin as possible, and cut into cubes. Discard the pips. Stone the cherries. Mix together the prepared chicken, pineapple, oranges, grapefruit and cherries and divide equally into 6 glasses.

To make the sauce, place the mayonnaise, tomato ketchup, tomato purée, grated horseradish and brandy in a bowl and mix thoroughly. Spoon over the chicken and fruit mixture. Chill well before serving.

# HARD ROE WITH SMOKED SALMON

*Serves 6*

8 oz/225 g hard fish roe
scant ½ pint/2·5 dl oil (see recipe)
salt and pepper
2 slices white bread

6 tablespoons lemon juice
lettuce leaves
6 thin slices smoked salmon

Put the raw roe into a bowl. Cover with oil and refrigerate for about 24 hours.

Remove the membrane from the roe. Replace the roe in the oil and beat until soft. Add salt and pepper to taste. Soak the bread in water for 2–3 minutes and squeeze well to remove the excess moisture before crumbling and adding to the roe.

Beat the mixture well to blend the ingredients together. Add the lemon juice slowly and continue to beat. If the mixture does not emulsify sufficiently (the consistency should be like mayonnaise), beat in more oil. Serve on lettuce leaves and garnish with smoked salmon slices.

*Note: Ikre* (fish eggs) is basically a Rumanian Jewish appetiser, just as *lox* (smoked salmon) is an American Jewish speciality. *Lox* is often eaten for breakfast with cream cheese and *bagels* (small doughnut-shaped rolls).

*Carrot-filled avocados*

# ISRAELI FRESH FRUIT SOUP

*Serves 6*

| | |
|---|---|
| 2 eating apples | ½ lemon |
| 6 bananas | scant ½ pint/2·5 dl grapefruit juice |
| 1 lb/450 g fresh or frozen strawberries | 6 tablespoons clear honey |
| 12 oz/350 g fresh or canned loquats | **for decorating:** |
| | sprigs of fresh mint |
| 1¾ pints/1 litre orange juice | 6 strawberries |
| | whipped cream (optional) |

Peel, quarter and core the apples. Peel and slice the bananas. Place all the fruits in a liquidiser with a little of the orange juice and reduce to a purée. Squeeze the lemon and add the juice to the liquidiser with the remaining orange juice, the grapefruit juice and honey. Place in the refrigerator and chill well.

Pour the fruit soup into 6 bowls and decorate each one with sprigs of mint, whole or sliced strawberries and a little whipped cream.

*Note:* A mixture of dried fruits may be used when fresh fruit is not readily available. Other fruit flavours which blend nicely in this soup are quince, apricot, mulberry, fig, cherry, grape, guava, melon, peach, pear and plum.

# BORSCHT

*Serves 6*

| | |
|---|---|
| 4 beetroot | ½ bay leaf (optional) |
| 1 lb/450 g stewing beef | 3 peppercorns |
| 4 tomatoes | 5 tablespoons vinegar |
| 3½ pints/2 litres water | 2 tablespoons sugar |
| 2–3 large cabbage leaves | 6 small potatoes |
| 2 teaspoons salt | 2 egg yolks (optional) |

Cook the beetroot in boiling water to cover for about 30 minutes. Rinse under cold running water, drain and cool. Remove the skins and grate the beetroot into a large saucepan. Cut the beef into 3 or 4 large pieces. Peel and chop the tomatoes. Place the beef and tomatoes in the pan and add the water.

Coarsely shred the cabbage leaves and add to the pan with the salt, bay leaf, peppercorns, vinegar and sugar. Place over high heat and bring to the boil. Lower the heat, cover the pan and simmer gently for about 1½ hours, or until the beef is tender.

Remove the beef and reserve for another dish. Peel the potatoes and drop them into the soup. Continue simmering until the potatoes are tender but still firm. Take the soup off the heat and mix 2–3 tablespoons of the soup with the egg yolks, if used. Stir this mixture back into the soup and serve

*Yemenite Rosh Hashana soup*

234

without reheating. Serve the soup with a potato in each soup bowl. Borscht may also be served chilled.

*Note:* There are several ways to garnish this soup. Slices of hard-boiled egg may be added or a little chopped dill sprinkled in the centre of each bowl. Alternatively, crush or finely chop half a cucumber and a few spring onions with a small amount of salt. Add 1 teaspoon of the cucumber mixture to each bowl of soup.

# YEMENITE ROSH HASHANA SOUP

*Serves 6*

| | |
|---|---|
| 1 oxtail or 2½ lb/1·25 kg beef bones | 2 teaspoons salt |
| 2 onions | 1 teaspoon curry powder |
| 4 leeks | pinch chilli powder |
| 3½ pints/2 litres water | pinch ground coriander |
| 2 cloves garlic | pinch ground cumin |
| 6 tablespoons tomato purée | pinch ground cardamom |

Chop the oxtail or beef bones into pieces of a manageable size. Peel and chop the onions and wash, trim and chop the leeks. Place all these ingredients in a large saucepan with the water. Bring to the boil. Lower the heat and simmer, partly covered, for 2½ hours. Remove the oxtail or beef bones from the soup. Peel and crush the garlic and add to the soup with the tomato purée, salt and all the spices, and cook for a further 5 minutes. Serve the soup poured over *pita* bread (see page 245) or with croutons.

# ATONEMENT SOUP WITH KREPLACH (STUFFED DUMPLINGS)

*Serves 6*

| | |
|---|---|
| 1 chicken or chicken pieces, about 3 lb/1·5 kg | salt |
| 1 carrot | 4 pints/2·25 litres water |
| 1 celeriac or head of celery | **for the kreplach:** |
| 1 parsley root or small bunch fresh parsley sprigs | 4 oz/100 g plain flour |
| 1 onion | salt and pepper |
| 1 kohlrabi or turnip | 1 egg |
| 1 small sweet potato | 2 teaspoons water |
| 4 whole allspice or pinch ground allspice | 1 small onion |
| | 2 tablespoons oil |
| | 4 oz/100 g cooked beef, minced |

To make the soup, cut the chicken into 6 portions. Peel or scrape the carrot, celeriac and parsley root (or chop the parsley sprigs). Peel the onion, kohlrabi or turnip and sweet potato. Chop the vegetables coarsely. Place the chicken, vegetables, allspice and water in a large saucepan, season to taste and simmer until the chicken is tender, about 2 hours.

Meanwhile, make the *kreplach*. Sift the flour with a pinch of salt into a bowl. Whisk together the egg and water. Add to the flour and salt and knead lightly. Roll out thinly and cut into 2-inch (5-cm) squares. Peel and chop the onion and

sauté in the oil. Add the beef and mix well. Season to taste. Put a spoonful of this mixture on each square of dough. Dampen the edges with water, fold into triangles and pinch the edges together.

Fasten together two corners of each triangle to make heart-shaped pockets.

Remove the chicken and vegetables, strain the broth but do not remove the surface fat. Reserve the chicken for another meal and return the broth to the pan. Bring to the boil, add the *kreplach* and simmer for 20 minutes before serving.

# CHICKEN BROTH WITH MATZO-MEAL DUMPLINGS

*Serves 6*

| **for the broth:** | 5 pints/3 litres water |
|---|---|
| 2 onions | **for the dumplings:** |
| 1 celeriac | 2 eggs |
| 1 carrot | 5 oz/150 g fine matzo meal |
| 1 boiling chicken (including the neck, feet and gizzard) | 6 tablespoons water or broth |
| 1 chicken stock cube (optional) | 1 teaspoon salt |
| 2 teaspoons salt | pinch ground nutmeg, allspice or ginger |
| pepper | 3 tablespoons oil |

To make the broth, peel and chop the onions, celeriac and carrot. Place the vegetables, the chicken, chicken stock cube (if used), salt, pepper to taste and the water in a large saucepan and simmer over low heat for about 1½–2 hours, or until the chicken is tender. Strain off the broth and keep hot. The surface fat may be left on for this traditional soup. Reserve the chicken and vegetables for another meal.

To make the dumplings, whisk the eggs well and mix in the matzo meal, water or broth, salt, nutmeg, allspice or ginger and the oil. Set aside for at least 4 hours before cooking. Roll into balls with moistened hands and drop gently into boiling water or the boiling broth. Simmer for 30 minutes. Serve in the hot broth.

# GALILEAN FISH – SEPHARDIC STYLE

*Serves 6*

| | |
|---|---|
| 1 large fish, about 3 lb/1·5 kg (St. Peter's or other fish – see note) | 4 tomatoes |
| | ½ lemon |
| salt and pepper | pinch powdered saffron or |
| 3 onions | safflower |
| 1 clove garlic | 2 tablespoons pine nut kernels |
| 5 tablespoons olive oil | white wine (see recipe) |
| 6 sprigs fresh parsley | |

Gut the fish, wash and pat dry and place in a greased casserole. Season with salt and pepper to taste. Peel and finely chop the onions and garlic and lightly sauté in half the oil in a frying pan. Chop the parsley. Remove the onions and garlic from the pan and mix with the parsley.

Chop the tomatoes and cook lightly in the remaining oil. Squeeze the juice from the half lemon and mix with the powdered saffron or safflower.

Cover the fish with the onions, garlic, tomato and parsley, and sprinkle with the lemon juice mixture and pine nut kernels. Add sufficient water to reach halfway up the fish. Bake in a moderately hot oven (375°F, 190°C, Gas Mark 5) for 35–40 minutes. Pour a little white wine over the fish, if desired, and bake for a further 5 minutes. Serve hot.

*Note:* St. Peter's fish thrives only in the Sea of Galilee. It is very popular whether grilled, roasted and served with *tehina* (sesame seed) sauce or prepared in this Sephardic way. Carp or bass make an excellent substitute.

# GEFILTE FISH

*Serves 6–8*

| | |
|---|---|
| 1 whole carp or other freshwater fish, about 4 lb/1·75 kg | 2 eggs |
| **for the stuffing:** | slice of *challah* or other white bread, about 1 inch/2·5 cm thick |
| 1 large onion | |
| 1 small carrot or piece of celeriac | **for the base:** |
| 2 teaspoons salt | 2 large carrots |
| ½ teaspoon pepper | 2 large onions |
| 1 tablespoon sugar | 1 parsnip or piece of celeriac |

Leaving the head attached to the skin, carefully remove the skin from the fish and reserve. Fillet the fish, discarding the bones (see Planked Lake Superior Whitefish, page 14).

To make the stuffing, peel the onion and carrot or celeriac and chop finely. Mince the fillets of fish and mix with the prepared vegetables. Add the salt, pepper, sugar and eggs. Soak the bread in a little water. Then squeeze dry and mix into the stuffing. Pack the stuffing into the fish skin and head to reshape the fish. Then sew up the opening.

Peel and slice the carrots, onions and parsnip or celeriac for the base. Place in a large oval pan or flameproof casserole and put the fish on top. Add water to cover the fish. Cover the pan and bring to the boil over high heat. Lower the heat and continue to simmer for 2 hours, or transfer to a moderate oven (325°F, 160°C, Gas Mark 3) and cook for the same length of time. When cooked, lift the fish out on to a serving plate. Reserve the vegetables.

Boil the cooking liquid until reduced to about half and

strain over the fish. Set aside to cool and set. Garnish with some of the reserved carrot slices and serve with the remaining vegetables.

*Note:* Alternatively, the stuffing mixture may be formed into balls using slightly moistened hands. Place the balls, and the fish skin and head to provide additional flavouring, on top of the vegetable base. Proceed as above, but reduce the simmering time to 1 hour. Discard the fish skin and head at the end of the cooking time.

# SWEET CARP

*Serves 6*

| | |
|---|---|
| 2 large onions | 3 oz/75 g gingernut crumbs |
| 2 lb/1 kg carp | 3 tablespoons white wine |
| 1 teaspoon salt | 2 oz/50 g brown sugar |
| 1½ tablespoons vinegar | 2 tablespoons seedless raisins |
| 1 tablespoon sugar | juice of 1 lemon |

Peel and finely slice the onions and place in a large frying pan. Cut the carp into thick slices and arrange the pieces on top of the onions. Add the salt, vinegar and enough water to barely cover the fish. Simmer, uncovered, over low heat for 20–25 minutes, or until the fish is just cooked. Transfer the fish and onions to a serving dish and retain a scant ½ pint (2·5 dl) of the liquid.

Mix the fish liquid with the crumbs, white wine, brown sugar and raisins. Add the lemon juice. Bring to the boil, stirring constantly, and pour over the fish. Serve hot, or leave in a cool place to set and serve cold.

# PICKLED SOLE

*Serves 6*

| | |
|---|---|
| 2½ lb/1·25 kg filleted sole | scant ½ pint/2·5 dl mild vinegar |
| oil for deep-frying | 1 teaspoon salt |
| 1 lemon | 6 tablespoons water |
| 1½ tablespoons curry powder (optional) | 3 bay leaves |
| 1 tablespoon oil (optional) | 6 black peppercorns |
| 2 cloves garlic | 4 whole allspice |
| | 2 tablespoons sugar |

Cut the fish into 12 pieces and deep-fry in very hot oil. Drain well and, when cool, arrange in a serving dish. Thinly slice the lemon and put half a lemon slice on each piece of fish.

If using curry powder, place in a saucepan with the 1 tablespoon of oil and heat gently until bubbling. Remove from the heat. Peel and crush the garlic and add to the pan with the vinegar, salt, water, bay leaves, peppercorns, whole allspice and sugar. Bring to the boil over moderate heat. Remove from the heat and, when cold, pour over the fish. Marinate the fish for 2 days in the refrigerator. It keeps very well for up to 1 week.

*Pickled sole*

*Orange, onion and olive salad*

# MINT-FLAVOURED SALAD

*Serves 8*

| | |
|---|---|
| 5 tomatoes | small bunch fresh mint |
| 2 small cucumbers | 1 tablespoon pickled capers |
| 4 red radishes | 4 tablespoons olive oil |
| 1 green sweet pepper | 2 tablespoons lemon juice |
| 1 red sweet pepper | salt and pepper |
| 4 spring onions | **for the garnish:** |
| 1 clove garlic | few mint leaves |
| 1 small mild chilli | 8 black olives |
| 2 sprigs fresh parsley | |

This salad will be most attractive if the vegetables are diced into cubes of the same size. Wash and dice the tomatoes. Dice the cucumbers, peeling them first if preferred. Trim, wash and dice the radishes. Trim the sweet peppers, remove the seeds and dice. Trim, peel and chop the spring onions. Peel and very finely chop the garlic. Trim the chilli, remove the seeds and chop very finely. Remove the stalks from the parsley and mint and chop the leaves.

Place the olive oil, lemon juice, salt and pepper in a small jar and shake it vigorously to combine the ingredients. Alternatively, use a liquidiser. Pour the salad dressing over the vegetables and toss well. Garnish the salad with the mint leaves and the olives.

# ORANGE, ONION AND OLIVE SALAD

*Serves 6*

| | |
|---|---|
| 4 oranges | olive oil (see recipe) |
| 2 onions | lemon juice (see recipe) |
| 18 black olives | |

Peel and thinly slice the oranges and onions. Remove the stones from the olives, if desired. Arrange the orange slices on a serving dish with the onions on top. Garnish with the olives. Sprinkle with olive oil and lemon juice to taste. Serve as an appetiser or a garnish.

# RADISH CRACKLING SALAD

*Serves 6*

| | |
|---|---|
| 1 medium-sized onion | 6 oz/175 g black or red radishes |
| 2 tablespoons chicken fat or oil | salt and pepper |
| 3 large poultry cracklings (see recipe) | 3 small red radishes for garnishing |

Peel and finely chop the onion and sauté in the chicken fat or oil until golden. Remove from the saucepan and drain. Chop the cracklings (crisply fried poultry skins). Coarsely grate the black or red radishes and mix with the onion and cracklings. Add salt and pepper to taste.

Before serving, garnish the salad with the remaining red radishes cut into thin slices or 'roses'.

*Note:* To make radish 'roses', see Danish Blue Cheese and Radish open sandwich, page 80.

# FRUITED CABBAGE SALAD

*Serves 6–8*

| | |
|---|---|
| 1 kohlrabi or turnip | 3 celery sticks |
| 2 shallots or 6 spring onions | 4 oz/100 g pineapple cubes |
| 1 green sweet pepper | mayonnaise or any other salad |
| 1 grapefruit or pomelo | dressing |
| 3 oz/75 g hazelnuts (see recipe) | salt |
| ½ medium-sized red cabbage | |

Peel the outer layer from the kohlrabi or turnip and grate the flesh coarsely. Peel and chop the shallots or spring onions. Trim the pepper, remove the seeds and shred the flesh finely. Remove the peel and white inner skin from the grapefruit or pomelo and cut the flesh into cubes. Chop the hazelnuts coarsely. (Other nuts may be used, if preferred. If walnuts are used, add just before serving to avoid any discoloration of the salad.) Shred the red cabbage. Mix together all the prepared vegetables, fruits and nuts and add mayonnaise or salad dressing and salt to taste. Arrange on lettuce or cabbage leaves, or in a hollowed-out cabbage.

# MARINATED BEAN AND PEPPER SALAD

*Serves 6*

| | |
|---|---|
| 1 lb/450 g fresh yellow string beans (see note) | 1½ tablespoons lemon juice |
| ½ pint/3 dl water | 2 tablespoons oil |
| 3 tablespoons vinegar | pinch garlic salt |
| 2 green sweet peppers | pinch pepper |
| 1 red sweet pepper | pinch paprika |
| 1 small spring onion | ½ teaspoon salt |
| 1 teaspoon chopped fresh dill or chopped fresh parsley | 1 tablespoon honey |
| | lettuce leaves or tomato slices |

Remove the strings from the beans and cut the beans into 1-inch (2·5-cm) pieces. Place in a saucepan and add the water and vinegar. Bring to the boil, lower the heat and simmer for about 15 minutes.

While the beans are cooking, trim and remove the seeds from the peppers, and grill under high heat until the skins blister. Remove the charred skins under cold water. Cut the peppers into thin strips and simmer with the beans for the last 2–3 minutes. Chop the spring onion. Drain the liquid from the beans and peppers and mix them with the spring onion, dill or parsley, lemon juice, oil, seasonings and honey. Set aside until cold. Serve garnished with lettuce leaves or sliced tomatoes.

*Note:* If yellow string beans are not available, French beans may be substituted.

# BAKED BRISKET OF BEEF

*Serves 6*

| | |
|---|---|
| 2 tablespoons plain flour | 1 small celeriac |
| 1 teaspoon salt | 1 parsnip |
| pinch black pepper | 1 clove garlic |
| pinch paprika | 1 bay leaf |
| 1 tablespoon brown sugar | 4 whole allspice |
| 3 lb/1·5 kg brisket of beef | 6 peppercorns |
| 3 onions | 6 tablespoons water |
| 2 carrots | |

Mix together the flour, salt, pepper, paprika and sugar. Rub the meat with this mixture. Peel and chop the onions, carrots, celeriac, parsnip and garlic and place in a casserole with the meat on top. Add the bay leaf, spices and water. Place the casserole, uncovered, in a moderately hot oven (400°F, 200°C, Gas Mark 6) for 10 minutes. Lower the heat to 350°F (180°C, Gas Mark 4) and continue cooking for about 1½–2 hours, or until the meat is tender. Baste the meat during cooking with the liquid in the casserole. About 20 minutes before the end of cooking, turn the meat over to brown evenly. Serve hot.

# CHOLENT WITH DRIED FRUITS

*Serves 6*

| | |
|---|---|
| 1 lb/450 g yellow turnips or carrots | 1 tablespoon salt |
| 2 large potatoes | ½ teaspoon pepper |
| 2 lb/1 kg brisket of beef | 4 tablespoons honey |
| 1 lb/450 g prunes | juice of 1 lemon |

Peel the turnips or carrots and the potatoes and cut into even-sized pieces. Place the meat in a heavy saucepan with the prepared vegetables and prunes. Combine the salt, pepper, honey and lemon juice and pour over the meat and vegetables. Add enough water to cover. Place over moderate heat and bring to the boil. Lower the heat, cover the pan and simmer for at least 3 hours. Traditionally, *cholent* is cooked over very low heat or in a very cool oven (225°F, 110°C, Gas Mark ¼) overnight. Most of the sauce evaporates or is absorbed during cooking. Transfer to a serving dish and serve hot.

# KNAIDEL (DUMPLING)

*Serves 6*

| | |
|---|---|
| 6 oz/175 g self-raising flour | 3 oz/75 g chopped suet |
| 1½ tablespoons semolina | 1 egg |
| salt and pepper | 4 tablespoons water |
| pinch ground nutmeg | |

Mix the flour, semolina, seasonings and chopped suet in a bowl. Whisk the egg well, then whisk in the water and mix into the dry ingredients. Knead lightly on a floured board and form into a ball. Add to the *cholent* (see above) when the liquid is boiling. Cook for at least 1 hour, or as long as you cook the *cholent*.

# KISHKE (STUFFED BEEF DERMA)

*Serves 6*

| | |
|---|---|
| beef sausage casing (intestines), 18 inches/45 cm if thin, 12 inches/30 cm if thick | 6 oz/175 g plain flour, sifted |
| | 1 teaspoon salt |
| 2 oz/50 g suet (see recipe) | ¼ teaspoon pepper |
| 2 large onions | liquid to cover (see recipe) |

Remove most of the suet from the outside of the casing and chop. Measure the amount required for the recipe and reserve the rest for another dish. Thoroughly clean the inside of the casing. Peel and grate the onions. Mix the grated onion with the suet, flour, salt and pepper.

Sew up one end of the casing and push the sewn end down the centre of the casing to form a bag. Start filling the bag with the stuffing, pushing the sewn end through so the shiny inside becomes the outside. Do not fill the casing more than two-thirds full to allow for expansion. Sew the end closed.

Cook with a *cholent* or with a pot roast, or on a bed of sliced onions in a flameproof casserole. Cover with liquid (stock, gravy or water) which will be absorbed by the filling. Cook over low heat for 2 hours or in a very cool oven (225°F, 110°C, Gas Mark ¼) overnight.

# STUFFED ARTICHOKE HEARTS

*Serves 6*

| | |
|---|---|
| 6 large globe artichokes or 12 small artichokes | 2 tablespoons breadcrumbs |
| | salt and pepper |
| 1 tablespoon vinegar | 2 eggs |
| 1 teaspoon salt | plain flour for coating |
| 8 oz/225 g beef, minced | oil for deep-frying |
| 1½ tablespoons pine nut kernels (optional) | ½ chicken stock cube (optional) |
| | juice of 1 lemon (see recipe) |

Wash the artichokes thoroughly and cut off the stalks. Place the artichokes in a saucepan with the vinegar, salt and enough water to cover. Bring to the boil and cook for about 30 minutes, or until tender, when a leaf may be easily removed. Lift the artichokes from the pan and drain them upside down for a few minutes. Remove the leaves and reserve for soup or stock. Discard the hairy choke from each artichoke, leaving the hearts intact. Mix the beef, nuts and breadcrumbs and season with salt and pepper according to taste. Pack the mixture into the centre of the artichoke hearts. Whisk the eggs. Dip the filled hearts into the beaten egg. Coat with flour. Dip again into the beaten egg. Deep-fry in hot oil for 3–4 minutes to seal the filling. Drain and place the artichokes in a saucepan, meat side uppermost. Add enough water to partially cover and add the chicken stock cube and lemon juice. If preferred, add more lemon juice for a sharp flavour. Simmer over low heat for about 1 hour. Drain well and serve hot or cold as a side dish or appetiser.

*Note:* The large artichokes may be cooked in a pressure cooker for 15 minutes at 15 lb or the small ones for 8 minutes at 15 lb rather than boiling them. Cool the pressure cooker under cold running water, remove the artichokes, drain and continue as above.

# MEAT-FILLED QUINCES

*Serves 6*

6 large quinces
1 small onion
1½ tablespoons oil
1 lb/450 g beef, minced
1 teaspoon salt
pinch ground allspice, pepper or
  cinnamon

4 tablespoons vinegar
6 tablespoons black or red cherry
  jam or 4 oz/100 g granulated
  sugar and 1 tablespoon rose
  water

Peel the quinces, slice off the pointed ends and scoop out and discard the core. With a small teaspoon remove the insides of the quinces, leaving them hollow. Take care not to break the sides or bases. Peel and chop the onion and lightly sauté in the oil. Then add the meat and sauté until browned. Add the salt and spices. Pack the mixture into the quinces. Place the filled quinces in a casserole or roasting tin and half cover with water. Cook in a moderately hot oven (400°F, 200°C, Gas Mark 6) for about 1½ hours, or until tender. Baste frequently during cooking and add more water, if necessary. About 30 minutes before the end of cooking, mix the vinegar with the jam (or sugar and rose water) and pour a little over each filled quince. Serve hot.

# STUFFED CABBAGE ROLLS

*Serves 6*

12 large cabbage leaves
2 onions
1 celeriac or 2–3 parsnips
2 lb/1 kg beef, minced
3 oz/75 g long-grain rice
1 egg
salt and pepper
pinch ground nutmeg

1 clove garlic
3 tablespoons oil
6 oz/175 g tomato purée
2 tablespoons seedless raisins
  (optional)
3 tablespoons wine vinegar
3 oz/75 g brown sugar
6 tablespoons rosé or white wine

Blanch the cabbage leaves in boiling water for 4–5 minutes to make them pliable. Peel and chop the onions and peel and grate the celeriac or parsnips. Mix with the minced beef, rice, egg, salt and pepper to taste and nutmeg. Place an equal quantity of the mixture into the centre of each cabbage leaf. Fold over and tuck in the edges. Roll up the filled leaves, completely enclosing the stuffing. Place in a casserole. Peel and crush the garlic, mix together with the oil, tomato purée, raisins, wine vinegar, sugar and wine and pour over the stuffed cabbage leaves. Add a small quantity of water, if necessary, to cover the rolls. Cook, uncovered, in a hot oven (425°F, 220°C, Gas Mark 7) for 30 minutes.

Lower the heat to 350°F (180°C, Gas Mark 4) and cook for about a further 30 minutes, by which time most of the liquid will have been absorbed. Serve hot.

*Meat-filled quinces*

# ROLLED VEAL WITH CHICKEN LIVERS

*Serves 6–8*

4 lb/1·75 kg boned best end
   neck or breast of veal
2 lb/1 kg courgettes
6 chicken livers
6 eggs
1½ tablespoons olive oil
pinch chilli powder
pinch garlic salt
pinch sweet basil
salt and pepper
4 oz/100 g margarine
6 tablespoons water or *Sharir*
   (sherry) wine

Beat the veal with a meat mallet to flatten it and to make it easier to roll. It should measure about 12 by 18 inches (30 by 45 cm). Trim and wash the courgettes and slice into thin circles. Grill the chicken livers and thickly slice them. Whisk the eggs. Heat the olive oil in a saucepan, add the eggs and stir over low heat to scramble. Remove from the heat. Spread the scrambled eggs on the veal and cover with the sliced chicken livers and sliced courgettes. Sprinkle on the chilli powder, garlic salt, sweet basil and salt and pepper to taste. Roll up the meat, completely enclosing the filling. Secure with string or skewers.

Put the rolled veal into a large saucepan with the margarine and the water or *Sharir*. Use as little liquid as possible. Place the pan over medium heat and bring to the simmering point. Cover the pan and simmer the meat for 1¼–1½ hours until tender. Turn the meat over occasionally and if necessary replenish the liquid by adding extra water or *Sharir* from time to time. When cooked, cut the meat into slices and serve hot or cold.

# MOCK VENISON

*Serves 6*

scant ½ pint/2·5 dl water
scant ½ pint/2·5 dl wine vinegar
2 teaspoons sugar
6 peppercorns
1 tablespoon salt
1 teaspoon caraway seeds
2 bay leaves
1 clove garlic
2 onions
3 lb/1·5 kg boned loin or boned
   shoulder of lamb
1 tablespoon oil (optional)
6 tablespoons sweet red wine
2 tablespoons plum jam

Place the water, vinegar, sugar, peppercorns, salt, caraway seeds and bay leaves in a saucepan. Bring to the boil. Remove from the heat and set aside until cold. Peel and chop the garlic and onions and add to the cooled liquid. Pour this liquid over the lamb and marinate for 24 hours, turning the lamb over occasionally.

Remove the meat from the marinade and wipe dry with kitchen paper. If the meat is lean, brush with the oil. Place in a roasting tin and roast in a hot oven (450°F, 230°C, Gas Mark 8) for 30 minutes, or until browned.

Meanwhile, strain the marinade. Discard the spices, onions and garlic. Combine the liquid with the wine and jam and pour over the browned meat. Return the tin to the oven, lower the temperature to 300°F (150°C, Gas Mark 2) and cook for a further 1½ hours, basting from time to time.

When cooked, the meat may be sliced and served hot with any remaining liquid, or drained and left until cold.

# BOKHARIAN RICE

*Serves 4*

6 cooked chicken drumsticks or
   grilled chicken livers
4 oz/100 g chicken fat
2 large onions
2 medium-sized carrots
small bunch fresh parsley
6 oz/175 g long-grain rice
2 tablespoons seedless raisins
   (optional)
1 teaspoon turmeric
1 teaspoon salt
pinch pepper

If using chicken drumsticks, remove the meat from the bone and cut into small pieces. Alternatively, slice the grilled chicken livers. Place the pieces of chicken or chicken livers in a flameproof casserole.

Slowly melt the chicken fat in a saucepan with 1 tablespoon of hot water. Peel and chop the onions. Peel and grate the carrots. Add the onions and carrots to the melted fat and sauté until soft but not browned. Drain and add to the casserole. Remove the coarse stalks and chop the parsley. Sprinkle over the meat mixture. Mix the rice with the raisins (if used), turmeric, salt and pepper and sprinkle over the vegetables. Add any remaining melted fat and water (the level must be 1 inch (2·5 cm) above the top of the rice).

Bring the rice to the boil. Cover the casserole and cook in a moderate oven (350°F, 180°C, Gas Mark 4) for about 30 minutes, or until the rice is tender and all the liquid has been absorbed. Transfer to a heated serving dish and serve immediately.

# LAMB WITH LEMON

*Serves 6*

6 tablespoons cooking oil
scant ¼ pint/2·5 dl water
2 tablespoons rosé or white wine
pinch powdered saffron
pinch cinnamon
pinch rosemary (optional)
salt and pepper
6 lamb chops, about 8 oz/
   225 g each
1 lemon

Place the oil, water, wine, saffron, cinnamon, rosemary (if used) and salt and pepper according to taste in a saucepan. Bring to the boil and then remove from the heat. Place the lamb chops in a flameproof casserole. Thinly slice the lemon and place one slice on each lamb chop. Pour over the hot liquid. Cover the casserole and place over low heat. Simmer for about 1 hour. Serve hot or cold.

# MINCED COLD TURKEY BREAST

*Serves 6*

| | |
|---|---|
| 1 raw turkey breast (with skin but no bone) | pinch ground nutmeg |
| 4 oz/100 g margarine | 3 eggs |
| 4 oz/100 g sweet potatoes, cooked | salt and pepper |
| 2 oz/50 g fine fresh breadcrumbs | 1½ pints/9 dl chicken stock |

Place the turkey breast flat on a working surface, skin side down. Leaving a thin layer, carefully remove most of the flesh from the skin. Melt the margarine. Mince the turkey flesh and mix with the margarine, sweet potatoes, breadcrumbs, nutmeg and eggs. Season with salt and pepper to taste and beat well until thoroughly mixed. Place the stuffing in the centre of the turkey skin, draw the edges of the skin together and sew up securely. Do not over-fill or the skin will burst during cooking. As an extra precaution, puncture the skin in several places with a needle. Place the stuffed turkey breast in a saucepan with the stock and bring to the boil. Lower the heat to a minimum and simmer very gently for 1½ hours. Remove from the stock and cool before serving. The broth may be reserved for soup.

# MATHILDE ALKILAY'S CHICKEN

*Serves 5*

| | |
|---|---|
| 1 chicken or chicken pieces, about 3 lb/1·5 kg | 1 pint/6 dl dry white wine |
| 3 tablespoons cooking oil | 1 teaspoon salt |
| 3 tomatoes | 4 bay leaves |
| 7 small cloves garlic | 5 black peppercorns |
| ½ head celery | pinch ginger |
| 4 celery leaves | 12 green olives |
| 5 tablespoons cognac | 2 oranges |

Joint the chicken if using a whole bird. Heat the oil in a large frying pan over moderate heat, add the chicken pieces and sauté until evenly browned on all sides. Peel and chop the tomatoes and 2 cloves of the garlic and add to the pan. Cover and cook over low heat for 30 minutes.

Peel and chop the remaining garlic. Chop the celery and leaves and add to the pan with the garlic, cognac, wine, salt, bay leaves, peppercorns, ginger and olives. Cover and cook over low heat for a further 30 minutes, or until the chicken is tender.

Slice the whole oranges thinly without removing the rind. Discard the pips. When the chicken is tender, add the orange slices to the pan and heat in the liquid with the chicken pieces for 2–3 minutes before serving.

*Minced cold turkey breast*

*Duck with sweet rice filling*

# CHICKEN WITH ORANGE SAUCE AND STUFFED DATES

*Serves 6*

| | |
|---|---|
| 1 young chicken, about 5 lb/ 2·25 kg | 1 tablespoon lemon juice |
| ½ chicken stock cube or ¼ teaspoon monosodium glutamate | 1 tablespoon prepared mustard |
| | **for the stuffed dates:** |
| salt and pepper | 12 dates |
| 2 oz/50 g margarine | 2 tablespoons cooked minced meat |
| rind of 1 orange | pinch ground nutmeg |
| 1¼ pints/7·5 dl orange juice | salt |
| 2 tablespoons honey or 4 tablespoons soft brown sugar | 2 tablespoons curaçao (optional) |
| | 1 tablespoon cornflour |
| | 2 tablespoons cold water |

Rub the chicken inside and out with the chicken stock cube or monosodium glutamate and season with salt and pepper according to taste. Melt the margarine and brush the chicken with it. Finely shred the orange rind. Place the chicken in a roasting tin with the orange juice, shredded rind, honey or sugar, lemon juice and mustard. Cover to prevent the chicken from browning too quickly. Cook in a moderate oven (350°F, 180°C, Gas Mark 4) for 30 minutes. Uncover and continue cooking for a further 1¾ hours, or until tender. Baste from time to time with the juices in the tin.

Stone the dates. Season the minced meat with the nutmeg and salt. Stuff a little into each date. About 20 minutes before the chicken is cooked, drop the stuffed dates into the tin.

When the chicken is cooked, remove to a heated platter and surround with the dates. Stir the curaçao, if used, and the cornflour blended with the cold water into the pan. Simmer until the sauce thickens and serve separately.

# DUCK WITH SWEET RICE FILLING

*Serves 6*

| | |
|---|---|
| 1 duck, about 5 lb/2·25 kg | 4 oz/100 g long-grain rice |
| 1 chicken stock cube or ½ teaspoon monosodium glutamate | ¾ pint/4·5 dl orange juice |
| | 1 large onion |
| salt and pepper | 1 cooking apple |
| 2 oz/50 g margarine (see recipe) | grated rind of ½ lemon |
| **for the stuffing:** | 2 oz/50 g seedless raisins |
| 2 tablespoons oil | 2 tablespoons castor sugar |
| | pinch nutmeg |

Rub the duck inside and out with the crushed stock cube or monosodium glutamate and season with salt and pepper to taste. If the duck is lean, melt the margarine and brush the duck with it.

To make the stuffing, heat the oil in a saucepan and sauté the rice until it just begins to colour. Add the orange juice and bring to the boil. Cover tightly and cook over low heat for about 15 minutes, until the rice is tender and all the liquid has been absorbed. Remove from the heat.

Peel and chop the onion. Peel, core and chop the apple. Mix the cooked rice with the onion, apple, lemon rind, raisins, sugar and nutmeg. Season to taste. Stuff the duck with this mixture and sew up each end or secure with small skewers. Place on a wire rack in a roasting tin. Cook in a moderate oven (325°F, 160°C, Gas Mark 3) for about 2 hours, until the duck is tender and golden brown. Baste from time to time during cooking with the excess fat in the tin. Serve hot.

# PITA (PANCAKE BREAD)

*Makes 18*

1 oz/25 g fresh yeast or ½ oz/15 g
  dried yeast
1 teaspoon sugar
½ pint/3 dl lukewarm water

3 tablespoons cooking oil
1 lb/450 g plain flour
1 teaspoon salt

Measure the yeast and sugar into a mixing bowl, pour over the lukewarm water and stir until the yeast and sugar have dissolved. Add the oil. Stir in the flour and the salt and mix together until well blended. Knead until smooth and then divide the dough into 18 portions. Shape each portion into a ball. Roll out each ball on a floured board until the dough is about ⅛ inch (3 mm) thick. Lightly cover the *pita* with a cloth and set aside in a warm place to rise for 30 minutes, or until doubled in bulk. Roll out each piece once more, lightly cover with the cloth and let rise a second time for 30 minutes, or until doubled in bulk. Transfer the *pita* to a lightly floured baking tray. Bake in a hot oven (450°F, 230°C, Gas Mark 8) until they puff, about 4–5 minutes. Cool on a wire rack.

The hollow *pita* may be cut horizontally and filled with *felafel* (see below), relishes or salad, or dipped into *houmous v'tehina* (see page 246) or other pastes.

# FELAFEL (CHICK PEA BALLS)

*Serves 6–8*

8 oz/225 g chick peas
2 oz/50 g cracked wheat
¼ teaspoon bicarbonate of soda
2 cloves garlic
1 teaspoon salt
¾ oz/29 g plain flour

1 egg
½ teaspoon ground coriander
½ teaspoon ground cumin
pinch turmeric
pinch chilli powder
oil for deep-frying

Soak the chick peas and cracked wheat in plenty of water, to which the bicarbonate of soda has been added, for about 8 hours. Rinse well and drain. Peel and finely chop the garlic. Grind the chick peas and cracked wheat and place in a mixing bowl. Add the garlic, salt, flour, egg and spices, and mix well. Shape portions of the mixture into small balls about the size of a walnut.

Heat the oil in a deep saucepan until very hot. Place the balls, a few at a time, into a frying basket and lower into the oil. Fry until golden brown. Drain and serve hot. If necessary these may be reheated without spoiling.

*Note:* Besides being a favourite appetiser, *felafel* is often used as a filling for *pita* (see below) and garnished with *schoog* or *tehina* (see page 246).

*Pita bread with felafel*

# HOUMOUS V'TEHINA (CHICK PEA AND SESAME PASTE)

*Serves 6–8*

**for the houmous:**
1 lb/450 g chick peas
3 cloves garlic
juice of 1 large lemon
salt and pepper
cayenne pepper

**for the tehina:**
juice of 2 lemons
6 oz/175 g sesame seeds
scant ½ pint/2·5 dl water
2 cloves garlic

1 teaspoon salt
pinch cayenne pepper

**for the garnish:**
2 tablespoons olive oil
chick peas (see recipe)
few olives
red and green sweet pepper slices
  or pickled chillies
few sprigs fresh parsley
pinch paprika or cayenne pepper

To make the *houmous*, soak the chick peas overnight. Cook in boiling water to cover until the skins come off. Save a few for the garnish and make a purée with the remainder in a liquidiser while still hot. Peel and crush the garlic. Stir into the purée with the lemon juice. If the consistency is too stiff, add a little boiling water until it resembles a thick mayonnaise. Add salt, pepper and cayenne pepper to taste.

To make the *tehina*, place all the ingredients in a liquidiser and blend to a purée, or pound to a paste in a mortar. Mix together the *houmous* and *tehina*. Place on a flat plate. Pour the olive oil on top and swirl around to make circular grooves. Garnish the centre with the reserved whole chick peas, olives, sweet green pepper slices or chillies. Finely chop the parsley and add a sprinkling of parsley and paprika or cayenne pepper.

*Note: Tehina* may be used separately as a salad dressing, as a cocktail dip, as a topping for *felafels* and in *pitas* (see page 245). It will keep for several months in an airtight container stored in the refrigerator.

# SCHOOG (FIERY YEMENITE SAUCE)

*Serves 6–8*

4–6 large ripe tomatoes
3 cloves garlic
3 small hot chillies
4 tablespoons chopped fresh
  coriander or pinch ground
  coriander

2 cardamom seeds or pinch
  ground cardamom
2 teaspoons ground cumin
1 teaspoon salt

Peel the tomatoes, halve them and remove the seeds. Peel the garlic. Remove the stalks and seeds from the chillies. Put the tomatoes, garlic and chillies through a mincer, or briefly into a liquidiser. Place the minced tomatoes, garlic and chillies in a saucepan with the coriander, cardamom, cumin and salt. Bring slowly to the boil, then remove from the heat. Cool and mix with *tehina* or *houmous v'tehina* (see above) to tone down the sauce according to taste before serving as a dip or garnish.

# POTATO KUGEL (PUDDING)

*Serves 6*

8 medium-sized potatoes
1 celeriac or large parsnip or
  2–3 carrots
1 large onion
2 tablespoons chicken fat

1–2 sprigs fresh parsley
3 cracklings (see recipe)
6 eggs
1 teaspoon salt
pinch pepper

Peel the potatoes and cook in lightly salted boiling water until tender. Drain and mash. Peel and finely grate the celeriac or alternative vegetable. Peel and chop the onion and lightly sauté in the chicken fat until tender. Chop the parsley. Mix the potato with the celeriac, onion and parsley. Chop the cracklings (crisply fried chicken skins). Separate the egg yolks from the whites. Add the yolks with the salt, pepper and cracklings to the potato mixture, and beat thoroughly.

Whisk the egg whites until stiff and fold into the potato mixture. Pour into a greased casserole and bake in a moderate oven (350°F, 180°C, Gas Mark 4) for about 30 minutes, or until golden brown. Serve hot.

# POTATO LATKES (PANCAKES)

*Serves 6–8*

6 medium-sized potatoes
½ teaspoon bicarbonate of soda
1 onion
1 egg
pinch ground nutmeg or allspice

pinch pepper
1 teaspoon salt
3 tablespoons plain flour
oil for frying

Peel and finely grate the potatoes and immediately mix with the bicarbonate of soda. Peel and grate the onion. Squeeze the potatoes to remove any excess liquid. Whisk the egg lightly and mix with the onion, potato, nutmeg or allspice, pepper, salt and flour. Heat a small quantity of oil in a frying pan. Drop a large spoonful of the potato mixture into the hot oil. Flatten with the back of the spoon. Cook until crisp and golden brown, turn with a spatula and brown the other side. Drain and keep hot. Continue until all the mixture has been used. Alternatively, prepare in advance and reheat when required. Serve with apple sauce or apple chutney.

*Note:* These pancakes are thin and crisp. If thicker pancakes are preferred, do not flatten the potato mixture with the back of a spoon.

# BAKED MANGOLD TURNOVERS

*Makes 20*

**for the pastry:**
12 oz/350 g plain flour
1 teaspoon salt
8 oz/225 g margarine or butter
cold water (see recipe)
**for the filling:**
8 oz/225 g mangold leaves or
   spinach
4 sprigs fresh parsley

4 oz/100 g liver sausage, chopped,
   or 2 oz/50 g hard cheese, grated
3 egg yolks
salt and pepper
**for the topping:**
1 egg yolk
1 teaspoon water
3 oz/75 g sesame seeds

To make the pastry, sift the flour and salt into a bowl. Cut the margarine or butter into small pieces and add. Rub in the mixture lightly with the fingertips, lifting and allowing it to fall back into the bowl. When the margarine is evenly distributed and the mixture resembles fine breadcrumbs, add about 3 tablespoons water and mix to a firm dough. Knead lightly on a floured board and roll out to about ⅛ inch (3 mm) thick. Using a floured plain cutter, cut into 3-inch (7·5-cm) circles.

To make the filling, wash the mangold leaves or spinach thoroughly in cold water. Cook in a minimum amount of water over moderate heat until tender. Drain, squeeze out excess moisture and chop the greens. Remove the parsley stalks and chop the leaves. Add the liver sausage or cheese and the egg yolks to the chopped greens and mix well. Season with salt and pepper to taste. Place a generous spoonful of the mixture on each pastry circle. Dampen the edges of the pastry and fold the circles in half, completely enclosing the filling. Press the edges firmly together. For the topping, whisk the egg yolk with the water and brush over each pastry turnover. Sprinkle with the sesame seeds. Place on a well-greased baking tray in a moderately hot oven (375°F, 190°C, Gas Mark 5) and bake for about 25 minutes until golden brown. Serve hot or cold.

# POTATO KNISHES (PASTRIES)

*Serves 6*

**for the pastry:**
6 oz/175 g self-raising flour
pinch salt
2 oz/50 g cooking fat
1 egg
1 tablespoon cold water
**for the filling:**
2 large onions

3 tablespoons oil
12 oz/350 g cooked potatoes,
   mashed
1 egg
pinch ground nutmeg
salt and pepper
oil for glazing

To make the pastry, mix the flour and salt together in a bowl. Melt the cooking fat. Add the egg, water and cooking fat to the flour. Mix thoroughly, turn out and knead on a floured board until smooth. Roll out thinly. Cut into 3-inch (7·5-cm) circles.

For the filling, peel and chop the onions and sauté in the oil. Mix the onions and oil with the mashed potatoes. Add the egg, nutmeg and seasoning and mix well. Place a spoonful of the filling on each circle. Dampen the edges of

the pastry and pinch them together across the top of the filling. Brush with oil. If you want the pastry more flaky, chill for a few minutes and brush with more oil.

Place on a baking tray and bake in a moderately hot oven (400°F, 200°C, Gas Mark 6) for about 10 minutes. Reduce the heat to 375°F (190°C, Gas Mark 5) and bake for about 20 minutes more, or until golden. Serve hot or cold.

*Note:* An alternative way to prepare *knishes* is to make them look similar to slices of Swiss roll. Prepare the pastry as given above. Roll the dough as thinly as possible into a large rectangle, then brush with a little oil. Spread the filling over the pastry. Begin rolling from the long side, dampen a small strip at the opposite side and gently pinch the edge of pastry to seal it. Cut the roll into 1½-inch (3·5-cm) slices. Lightly oil a baking tray, place the slices on the tray and flatten slightly with the bottom of a glass or your fingers. Bake in a moderately hot oven (400°F, 200°C, Gas Mark 6) for about 10 minutes, then lower the heat to 375°F (190°C, Gas Mark 5) and bake for 20 minutes more, or until golden brown. Serve hot or cold.

# CARROT BAKE

*Serves 6–8*

3 medium-sized carrots
8 oz/225 g margarine
3 oz/75 g brown sugar
1 egg
1 tablespoon water

5 oz/150 g plain flour
½ teaspoon cinnamon
¼ teaspoon ground nutmeg
½ teaspoon salt
½ teaspoon bicarbonate of soda

Wash, peel and coarsely grate the carrots. Cream the margarine and sugar in a bowl until soft. Lightly whisk the egg and stir into the creamed mixture with the water. Mix well.

Sift together the flour, cinnamon, nutmeg, salt and bicarbonate of soda. Stir the sifted dry ingredients into the creamed mixture and beat well. Add the grated carrots and stir until the mixture is well blended. Spoon the mixture into a greased 8-inch (20-cm) ring mould. If this is not available, use a greased 7-inch (18-cm) cake tin. Bake in a moderate oven (350°F, 180°C, Gas Mark 4) for 1 hour. Turn out on to a serving dish and serve hot or cold.

# BROAD BEANS WITH DILL

*Serves 6*

1 lb/450 g young broad beans
1 large onion
1 clove garlic
3 tablespoons oil

3 sprigs fresh dill
salt and pepper
¼ pint/1·5 dl water

Remove the strings from the bean pods and slice the pods thinly, leaving the beans inside. Peel and finely chop the onion and garlic. Heat the oil in a heavy saucepan. Add the beans, onion and garlic and lightly sauté for 3–4 minutes. Chop the dill and add with salt and pepper to taste and the water. Place the pan over low heat. Cover and simmer for 15 minutes until the beans are tender. Drain off any excess liquid. Transfer the beans to a heated serving dish and serve hot.

*Carrot bake*

# SWEETENED CARROTS

*Serves 6*

| | |
|---|---|
| 6 medium-sized carrots | finely pared rind of 1 lemon |
| orange juice (see recipe) | ½ teaspoon salt |
| 6 tablespoons clear honey | pinch ground cinnamon, |
| 3 tablespoons brown sugar | ginger or cloves |
| 2 tablespoons oil or chicken fat | |

Peel and slice the carrots and place in a saucepan. Add enough orange juice to cover and cook for about 15 minutes over low heat. Add the honey, brown sugar, oil or chicken fat, pared lemon rind, salt and a pinch of cinnamon, ginger or cloves (only a subtle hint) and simmer for about 25 minutes, until the liquid has been absorbed and the carrots are highly glazed. Remove the lemon rind. Transfer the carrots to a heated dish and serve hot.

*Note:* The cooked carrots may be placed in a shallow flameproof casserole and grilled for a few minutes until golden brown before serving.

# ASPARAGUS WITH PISTACHIOS

*Serves 6*

| | |
|---|---|
| 2 lb/1 kg asparagus | 1 oz/25 g fine fresh breadcrumbs |
| 5 oz/150 g blanched pistachio | 3 oz/75 g margarine |
| nuts or blanched slivered | ¼ teaspoon salt |
| almonds (see note) | |

Wash the asparagus in cold water, lightly scrape the stalks with a knife and cut off the tough fibrous base. If the asparagus stalk is white, remove the outer fibrous skin from below the green tip to prevent a bitter flavour. Tie the asparagus spears in small bundles with white string or thread. Stand in a deep saucepan with the tips uppermost. Add enough salted water to come just below the tender tips. Cover the pan and simmer over low heat for 20–25 minutes, or until tender. Drain thoroughly and keep hot in a serving dish.

Lightly sauté the pistachio nuts or slivered almonds with the breadcrumbs in the margarine until golden brown. Add the salt. Serve the asparagus spears sprinkled with the browned nuts and breadcrumbs.

*Note:* Salted peanuts may be substituted for the pistachio nuts or almonds.

# BEETROOT WITH ORANGE

*Serves 6*

| | |
|---|---|
| 9 small fresh beetroot | ½ oz/15 g margarine |
| rind of 1 orange | 1 tablespoon lemon juice |
| 1 tablespoon cornflour | salt |
| scant ½ pint/2·5 dl orange juice | 1 teaspoon dried rosemary |

Cook the beetroot in boiling water to cover for about 45 minutes, or until tender. Meanwhile, finely grate the rind of the orange. Drain the beetroot, remove the skins and slice thinly. Blend the cornflour with the orange juice. Melt the margarine in a saucepan and add the lemon juice with the blended cornflour. Bring to the boil, stirring constantly, until thick and clear. Add the sliced beetroot, salt to taste, grated orange rind and rosemary, and cook gently for 3–4 minutes. Pour into a heated dish and serve hot.

# PEAS WITH MINT

*Serves 6*

| | |
|---|---|
| 2 lb/1 kg shelled peas | 3 sprigs fresh mint |
| 1 teaspoon dehydrated chicken | 3 sprigs fresh parsley |
| soup (optional) | ½ teaspoon salt |
| ½ teaspoon sugar | 1 tablespoon margarine |

Place the peas, dehydrated soup, sugar, mint, parsley and salt in a saucepan with enough boiling water to just cover. Place the saucepan over low heat, cover and simmer the peas for 10–15 minutes, or until tender. Remove the sprigs of mint and parsley. Drain off the liquid and toss the peas in the pan with the margarine. Transfer to a warmed serving dish and serve hot.

# LAYERED ONION MATZO BAKE

*Serves 6*

| | |
|---|---|
| 2 large potatoes | 6 tablespoons chopped green |
| 6 medium-sized onions | herbs (parsley, dill, etc.) |
| or leeks | 4 eggs |
| scant ½ pint/2·5 dl oil | salt and pepper |
| 4 matzos | |

Peel and cut the potatoes into small even-sized pieces. Cook in boiling, salted water to cover until tender. Drain well. Peel and slice the onions (or trim, wash and slice the leeks) and cook in boiling, salted water until just tender. Drain well. Heat the oil and pour into a casserole. Dip the matzos in water and place 2 in the bottom of the casserole. Cover with half the sliced onions. Mash the potatoes with the herbs and spread over the onions. Cover with the remaining onions. Place the 2 remaining matzos on top. Whisk the eggs, add salt and pepper to taste and pour over the matzos. Place the casserole in a moderately hot oven (400°F, 200°C, Gas Mark 6). After 10 minutes, reheat the remaining oil and pour over the top of the matzo bake. Cook for 30 minutes, remove from the oven and immediately pour off the excess oil before serving.

# LOKSHEN (SWEET NOODLE PUDDING) WITH APPLES

*Serves 6*

| | |
|---|---|
| 8 oz/225 g broad noodles (green, if available) | 4 oz/100 g margarine or butter (see recipe) |
| ¾ pint/4·5 dl milk or 2½ pints/1·25 litres water (see recipe) | 3 apples |
| 1 teaspoon salt | 3 oz/75 g sugar |
| 2 tablespoons oil | 3 oz/75 g chopped nuts |
| 3 eggs | 8 oz/225 g jam (blueberry or dark plum or grape) |

If served with a dairy meal, cook the noodles in the milk with the salt until the liquid is almost absorbed. For meat meals, bring the water to the boil, put in the noodles with the salt and cook until just tender. Drain and rinse, then drain again. Pour the oil over the noodles and mix well. Set aside about a third of the noodles to use as a lattice for the top.

Whisk the eggs and melt the margarine (or butter if the dish is to be served with a dairy meal). Mix the remainder of the noodles with the eggs and margarine or butter and place in a casserole. Peel and slice the apples thinly and mix with the sugar. Spread over the noodles in the casserole.

Mix the chopped nuts with the jam. Spread over the apples. Lattice the top with the reserved noodles so that the jam filling shows through. Bake in a moderately hot oven (375°F, 190°C, Gas Mark 5) for 35 minutes. Serve hot.

# COTTAGE CHEESE BLINTZES

*Serves 6*

| | |
|---|---|
| **for the batter:** | 1½ tablespoons castor sugar |
| 2 eggs | 2 oz/50 g seedless raisins (optional) |
| 1 oz/25 g butter | |
| pinch salt | pinch cinnamon |
| ¼ pint/1·5 dl milk | **for the topping:** |
| 3 oz/75 g plain flour | 2 (5-oz/141-g) cartons soured cream |
| cooking oil | |
| **for the filling:** | 4 tablespoons honey |
| 1 lb/450 g cottage cheese | cooked cherries or fresh strawberries (optional) |
| 1 egg | |

To make the batter, whisk the eggs lightly. Melt the butter. Add the butter, salt, milk and flour to the eggs and beat well. Heat a little oil in a small frying pan. Pour in 2 tablespoons of batter and swirl the pan around to distribute the batter. Cook over medium heat until the top is firm. Do not turn the pancake over while cooking. Pile each pancake, fried side up, on a cloth. Repeat until all the batter has been used.

For the filling, mix together the cottage cheese, egg, sugar, raisins (if used) and cinnamon. Spread a little of the mixture on to half of the fried side of each pancake. Fold the pancakes over the filling and then in half again to make into triangles. Fry in a little hot oil for 1 minute on each side, or until golden. Transfer to a serving dish.

For the topping, mix the soured cream with the honey and spread over the top. Decorate with the cherries or strawberries if desired. Serve slightly warm, allowing 2 per person.

*Layered onion matzo bake*

# COCONUT KISSES

*Makes about 24*

4 egg whites

8 oz/225 g icing sugar

8 oz/225 g desiccated coconut

Whisk the egg whites until stiff. Whisk the icing sugar into the egg whites a spoonful at a time. Fold in the coconut with a metal spoon. Drop heaped teaspoonfuls of the mixture on to a baking tray lined with greased and floured foil. Bake in a very cool oven (250°F, 130°C, Gas Mark ½) for 45 minutes, or until they begin to colour. Leave on the baking tray until cold.

# WINE FLUFF

*Serves 6*

1 oz/25 g gelatine

6 tablespoons cold water

generous ½ pint/4 dl sweet red wine

rind of 1 lemon or orange

2 teaspoons lemon juice

4 egg yolks

pinch salt

6 oz/175 g castor sugar

4 egg whites

desiccated coconut

Soak the gelatine in the cold water for a few minutes. Heat the wine with the lemon or orange rind and lemon juice, but do not boil. Discard the rind. Whisk the egg yolks with the salt and sugar until light in colour. Pour the wine mixture into the beaten egg yolks, then place the mixture in a double saucepan. Heat gently, stirring constantly, until the mixture is thick enough to coat the back of the spoon. Add the soaked gelatine and stir until dissolved. Remove from the heat and pour the mixture into a bowl.

Stand the bowl in cold water, or over ice, and continue stirring until the mixture begins to thicken. Whisk the egg whites until stiff and carefully fold into the wine mixture. Pour into 6 glasses and, when almost set, sprinkle with the coconut.

# NECTAR AND AMBROSIA

*Serves 6*

1 large orange

1 large grapefruit

2 tablespoons chopped crystallised citrus peel

4 tablespoons desiccated coconut

4 tablespoons clear honey mixed with 2 teaspoons rose water

6 dates

6 blanched almonds

6 red rose petals (optional)

Peel the orange and grapefruit and remove all the white inner skin. Cut each fruit horizontally into 6 slices. Place an orange slice and a grapefruit slice on each of 6 plates.

Heat the honey with the rose water in a small heavy saucepan and pour a little over the fruit slices on each plate. Sprinkle with the crystallised peel and coconut. Stone the dates and insert a blanched almond in each cavity. Place one date and one rose petal (if used) on each plate.

# CRYSTALLISED CITRUS PEEL

*Makes 1¼ lb (600 g)*

6 large oranges (see note)
1¼ lb/600 g granulated sugar

generous ½ pint/4 dl water
castor sugar for coating

Wash and dry the fruit and remove the peel in sections. Use the fruit for another purpose or for juice. Cut the sections of peel lengthwise into strips about ⅓ inch (8 mm) wide.

Place in a saucepan and cover with water. Bring to the boil over high heat and then drain. Repeat this process 6 times, using fresh water each time. Drain thoroughly. Add the sugar and water and place over very low heat until the sugar is dissolved. Increase the heat slightly and simmer until the syrup is absorbed. Dip each piece of citrus peel in sugar to coat and set aside on a tray for about 2 days to dry completely before storing in an airtight container. Serve as a confection or use as required for desserts.

*Note:* Although any kind of citrus fruit, such as lemon, lime, grapefruit or orange may be used, for this quantity of sugar and water the amount of peel should be equal to that of 6 large oranges (approximately 9½ oz/270 g).

# FRITTERS IN WINE SAUCE

*Serves 6*

**for the batter:**
6 tablespoons water
3 tablespoons oil
15 oz/425 g fine matzo meal
2 oz/50 g castor sugar
3 eggs
½ teaspoon salt
pinch cinnamon or grated rind of
  ½ lemon

**for the filling:**
2 oz/50 g chopped nuts
8 oz/225 g jam (any kind)
1½ tablespoons fine matzo meal
oil for deep-frying

**for the sauce:**
scant ½ pint/2·5 dl white wine
6 tablespoons clear honey
1½ tablespoons potato flour
1½ tablespoons water
2 egg yolks

To make the batter, heat together the water and oil until boiling. Mix the matzo meal and sugar in a bowl. Pour the water and oil over the matzo meal mixture and set aside until the liquid has been absorbed. Whisk the eggs well and add, with the salt and cinnamon or grated lemon rind, to the matzo meal mixture. Knead to a soft dough and form into 12 flat circles.

To make the filling, mix together the chopped nuts, jam and matzo meal. Place 1 teaspoon of the mixture in the centre of half the circles. Dampen the edges, cover with the remaining circles and pinch firmly together. Deep-fry in hot oil. Drain and keep warm.

To make the sauce, heat the wine and honey in a saucepan. Mix the potato flour with the water and stir into the hot wine and honey mixture. Bring slowly to the boil, stirring constantly until thick and clear. Whisk the egg yolks and add a little of the hot sauce to them. Stir the yolk mixture back into the remaining sauce. Serve with the fritters.

*Nectar and ambrosia*

# CHEESECAKE WITH FRUIT TOPPING

*Serves 6–8*

**for the crust:**
2 oz/50 g butter
5 oz/150 g biscuit crumbs
**for the filling:**
12 oz/350 g cottage cheese
2 (5-oz/141-g) cartons soured cream
4 oz/100 g castor sugar
2 eggs
1 teaspoon vanilla essence
½ oz/15 g plain flour
**for the topping:**
2 (5-oz/141-g) cartons soured cream
1½ tablespoons castor sugar
1 teaspoon vanilla essence
canned or fresh peach slices
fresh sugared strawberries

To make the crust, melt the butter and mix with the crumbs. Press the mixture into a 9-inch (23-cm) round loose-bottomed cake tin. Chill well.

For the filling, blend the cottage cheese, soured cream, sugar, eggs, vanilla and flour together and pour into the crust. Bake in a moderate oven (350°F, 180°C, Gas Mark 4) for 20 minutes. Remove from the oven and increase the heat to 450°F (230°C, Gas Mark 8). For the topping, mix together the soured cream, sugar and vanilla. Spoon on to the partially cooked cake. Place in the oven for 5 minutes, or until set. Remove from the oven and cool. Remove from the cake tin and decorate with the peach slices and strawberries.

# PASSOVER PIE

*Serves 6–8*

**for the crust:**
5 oz/150 g fine matzo meal
1½ tablespoons ground almonds
1 tablespoon castor sugar
2 oz/50 g margarine
**for the filling:**
6 bananas
1½ tablespoons lemon juice
8 oz/225 g cranberry sauce
**for the topping:**
2 egg whites
pinch salt
3 tablespoons castor sugar
3 tablespoons clear honey
grated rind of 1 lemon

To make the crust, place the matzo meal, ground almonds, sugar and margarine in a bowl and mix thoroughly. Press the mixture over the bottom and sides of a 7-inch (18-cm) flan dish and chill for 10 minutes. Bake in a moderately hot oven (400°F, 200°C, Gas Mark 6) for 10 minutes, until golden brown. Set aside to cool.

For the filling, peel the bananas and mash with the lemon juice. Beat in the cranberry sauce and pour the mixture into the prepared crust.

For the topping, whisk the egg whites with the salt until stiff. Whisk in the sugar, then the honey and finally the lemon rind. Spoon over the filling and serve.

*Cheesecake with fruit topping*

254

# MULLED WINE IN MELONS

*Serves 6*

2 tablespoons sugar
1 thin strip orange
  and/or lemon rind
cinnamon stick, about 1
  inch/2·5 cm
pinch ground allspice

2 whole cloves
6 tablespoons water
scant ½ pint/2·5 dl sweet red wine
3 small ogen or cantaloupe
  melons

In a heavy pan simmer the sugar, rind, cinnamon, allspice and cloves in the water for about 10 minutes. Add a little water if the syrup evaporates too much. Add the wine and heat but do not allow the mixture to boil. Meanwhile, cut the melons horizontally in half and carefully remove the seeds. Remove the rind and spices from the syrup.

In summer, the wine mixture should be cooled and chilled in the refrigerator and then spooned into the chilled melons. On cool days, the hot wine mixture may be spooned into the unchilled melon halves.

*Note:* The flesh of some of the larger varieties of melon, such as a watermelon, may be cut into balls and placed in serving bowls with the wine mixture. A combination of several types of melons is also delicious and very attractive.

# LAYERED FRUIT BAKE

*Serves 12–14*

**for the pastry:**
1 lb/450 g plain flour
2 oz/50 g ground almonds
7 oz/200 g castor sugar
8 oz/225 g cooking fat
  (see recipe)
1 egg
5 tablespoons water
**for the first filling:**
6 oz/175 g brown sugar

10 oz/275 g chopped dates
¼ pint/1·5 dl water
3 oz/75 g chopped nuts
4 oz/100 g biscuit crumbs
  (gingernuts, preferably)
**for the second filling:**
8 pears or apples
5 tablespoons castor sugar
3 oz/75 g seedless raisins

To make the pastry, mix together the flour, ground almonds and sugar in a bowl. Cut in the cooking fat (traditionally, chicken fat is used). Mix together the egg and water, add to the flour mixture and, using a knife, mix to a soft dough. Knead lightly on a floured board until smooth. Divide the pastry into 5 portions and roll each one into an 8-inch (20-cm) circle.

To make the first filling, gently heat the brown sugar, dates and water in a heavy saucepan until the sugar is dissolved. Beat in the nuts and biscuit crumbs and set aside to cool.

To make the second filling, peel, core and thinly slice the pears or apples. Mix with the sugar and raisins.

Place the pastry circles and both fillings in alternate layers in an 8-inch (20-cm) round cake tin, starting and finishing with a layer of pastry. Bake in a cool oven (300°F, 150°C, Gas Mark 2) for 2 hours. Leave in the tin for about 10 minutes before turning out. Serve either warm or cold.

*Note:* If you wish to bake a more shallow *fladen*, divide the pastry into 3 portions and roll each one into a 10-inch (26-cm) circle. Place one circle of pastry in the bottom of a 10-inch (26-cm) cake tin. Alternate the layers of filling with the remaining pastry circles, ending with a layer of pastry. Bake in a cool oven (300°F, 150°C, Gas Mark 2) for 1½ hours. Cool in the tin for 10 minutes before turning out. Serve warm or cold.

# APRICOT-MATZO PUDDING

*Serves 6*

3 lb/1·5 kg fresh apricots or
  2 large (1¼ lb/566-g) cans
  apricots
¾ pint/4·5 dl water and 10 oz/
  275 g granulated sugar or
  ¾ pint/4·5 dl syrup from the
  apricots (see recipe)

6 matzos
6 oz/175 g margarine
3 eggs
**for decoration:**
12 fresh cherries or strawberries
1½ tablespoons castor sugar

Halve the fresh apricots and remove the stones. Place in a saucepan with the water and sugar. Simmer gently over low heat for 2–3 minutes. Drain and retain the syrup. Alternatively, drain the syrup from the canned apricots (if these are used) and retain the amount required in the recipe. Dip the matzos into the syrup and place in alternate layers with the apricots in a greased casserole, finishing with a layer of apricots. Melt the margarine, whisk in the eggs and the remaining syrup and pour the mixture over the apricots and matzos.

Decorate with the fresh cherries or strawberries rolled in sugar. Bake in a cool oven (300°F, 150°C, Gas Mark 2) for 30 minutes, or until the egg mixture is fairly firm and golden brown. Serve warm or cold.

# POPPY SEED CAKE

*Makes 8–10 portions*

6 oz/175 g poppy seeds
6 oz/175 g margarine
7 oz/200 g castor sugar
3 egg yolks
1½ oz/40 g plain flour
1 oz/25 g cornflour
1½ tablespoons water

1½ tablespoons brandy
  or vermouth
3 egg whites
**for the topping:**
2 tablespoons dark plum jam
4 oz/100 g icing sugar

Grind the poppy seeds in a mortar or electric grinder. Cream the margarine and sugar together until soft. Beat in the egg yolks, one at a time. Add the poppy seeds to the mixture and beat well. Sift the flour with the cornflour. Mix the water with the brandy or vermouth. Fold the dry ingredients and liquid alternately into the creamed mixture.

Whisk the egg whites until stiff and fold into the mixture carefully. Pour into a greased and lined 9-inch (23-cm) sandwich tin. Bake in a moderate oven (350°F, 180°C, Gas Mark 4) for about 50 minutes–1 hour. Turn out on to a wire rack and cool. Serve the cake topped with the dark plum jam mixed with the icing sugar.

# SESAME SEED CANDY

*Makes about 36*

12 tablespoons clear honey
7 oz/200 g granulated sugar
6 tablespoons water
4 oz/100 g blanched,
    slivered almonds
10 oz/275 g sesame seeds

Boil the honey, sugar and water in a heavy saucepan until a little of the mixture dropped into a saucer of cold water forms a ball. Stir in the nuts and seeds and cook gently for about 5 minutes, or until the seeds are 'gilded'. Pour on to a wet board or marble slab and cut into diamond shaped pieces. When the candy has hardened it can be stored for a long time in an airtight container.

*Note:* Special care should be taken when making candy using honey. Make the candy on a dry day. Rainy or hot and humid weather is unsuitable since the honey absorbs moisture from the air and prevents the candy from hardening sufficiently. To prevent the pieces from sticking together, they may be individually wrapped in rice paper or cling film.

# MARZIPAN MORDECAI

*Makes about 18 biscuits*

8 oz/225 g margarine
4 oz/100 g castor sugar
8 oz/225 g ground almonds
10 oz/275 g plain flour
1 tablespoon lemon juice
1 tablespoon water
castor sugar for dusting

Cream the margarine with the sugar until soft. Mix together the ground almonds and flour and stir into the cream mixture. Add the lemon juice and water and mix to form a soft dough. If necessary, add a little more water. Knead on a floured board until smooth. Roll to ¼ inch (5 mm) thick and cut out with a 5-inch (13-cm) gingerbread-man cutter. Place on a baking tray and bake in a cool oven (300°F, 150°C, Gas Mark 2) for about 30–40 minutes. While still hot, sprinkle with the sugar. Cool on a wire rack until completely cold, then store in an airtight container.

# SPIRALLED PASTRIES

*Serves 6*

12 oz/350 g plain flour
pinch salt
1 egg
½ pint/3 dl water or milk
1½ tablespoons oil
oil for deep-frying
juice of 1 lemon
12 oz/350 g clear honey
pinch cinnamon

Mix the flour and salt together in a bowl. Whisk the egg and add with the water and the oil to the flour. Beat thoroughly until a thick batter is formed.

In a deep saucepan, heat the oil for deep-frying. Using a piping bag and a ¼-inch (5-mm) tube, pipe 2- to 3-inch (5- to 7·5-cm) lengths of the mixture into the hot oil. The mixture will automatically fall into uneven circular shapes. Do not try to fry too many at one time as the pastries cook very quickly. When the pastries are golden, remove from the oil and drain. Continue until all the mixture has been used.

Heat the lemon juice, honey and cinnamon in a saucepan until almost boiling. Remove the pan from the heat and drop the drained spiralled pastries into the syrup, a few at a time. Remove and drain on a wire rack with a plate underneath, so that the honey syrup may be collected, reheated and used again to coat the pastries.

# ROUND CHALLAH BREAD

*Makes 2 loaves*

½ pint/3 dl hot water
1 tablespoon salt
2 tablespoons castor sugar
2 tablespoons vegetable oil
2 oz/50 g fresh yeast, or 1 oz/25 g
    dried yeast
3 tablespoons lukewarm water
3 eggs
2 lb/900 g plain flour
2 oz/50 g seedless raisins
    (optional)
1 egg yolk
2 tablespoons poppy seeds

Mix the hot water with the salt, sugar and oil in a mixing bowl and set aside until lukewarm. Dissolve the yeast in the lukewarm water. Stir the yeast mixture into the mixing bowl. Whisk in the eggs. Mix the raisins with the flour and stir into the liquid. Mix well to a rough dough. Turn on to a lightly floured board and knead until smooth and elastic.

Replace the dough in the bowl, cover with a damp cloth and set aside in a warm place to rise for about 1 hour, or until doubled in bulk. Do not let the cloth touch the dough.

Divide the dough in half. Roll each half into a long rope, about 1 inch (2·5 cm) in diameter, and place on a baking tray in a circular cone shape. To do this, form the 'rope' of dough into a circle about 8 inches (20 cm) in diameter, and then fill the circle in, making each subsequent circle smaller and higher, until you have a cone shape. The loaf may be braided if preferred. Set aside for about 30 minutes, or until doubled in bulk.

Whisk the egg yolk and brush it on the dough. Sprinkle on the poppy seeds. Bake in a moderately hot oven (375°F, 190°C, Gas Mark 5) for about 1 hour. When cooked, cool on a wire rack.

*Note:* At every Jewish festival two sweet loaves, usually braided, are placed on the table for benediction. On *Rosh Hashana* and *Yom Kippur*, the loaves are decorated with a dove or a ladder, made from the dough, to represent the hope that prayers ascend heavenwards.

*Round challah bread; spiralled pastries*

# CHINESE

## Kenneth Lo

*Photography by John Miller*

In China, for over 20 centuries a Confucian country which practised ancestral worship and reverence for the old, eating was by far the most important form of social entertainment available. The pinnacle of lavishness in Chinese cooking and eating was reached in the Mandarin and inter-Mandarin banquets and entertainments, when the important government officials and bureaucrats entertained one another.

To make a comprehensive survey of ordinary Chinese cooking and eating as enjoyed by the average Chinese today, many sections of the Chinese culinary scene would have to be studied. One would need to look at the food prepared and sold by the restaurants (very different from many of the chop suey houses which have grown up in the West), by housewives, snack specialists, tea-houses, outdoor markets and finally street vendors, who sell food cooked on the spot and move from street corner to street corner all day and night.

Writing about Chinese cooking for the Western public, one is immediately aware of the need for clarification and explanation so that the reader may have a proper grasp of the form and concept of a Chinese meal, without which any attempt at Chinese cooking is bound to be unsuccessful. First of all, a Chinese meal is essentially a communal one, and for this reason the aim is not to produce a certain number of portions for a given number of people: a dish is simply produced for a table of diners, which may be any number from four to a dozen people. Dishes of food may be large or small, but how large or small is usually determined by the number of diners.

As a rule, there are a good many more dishes at a Chinese meal than at a corresponding Western one. For example, an ordinary Chinese dinner at home would consist of about four dishes, with one or two soups. The dishes are brought to the table at the same time, and the diners help themselves as they please. At a dinner party, there may be a dozen dishes or more, served in courses one after another with an interval of a few minutes between each. One could well have two or three soups, two or three fish or seafood dishes, several mixed quick-fried dishes, as many stews, casseroles and poultry dishes, two or three meats and several vegetables. This system gives an almost unlimited number of combinations when choosing and planning a Chinese menu. The scope of Chinese dishes is roughly divided into rice-accompanying dishes (*Fan Tsai*) – plain, home-cooked dishes; wine-accompanying dishes (*Ch'iu Tsai*) – quick-fried, highly seasoned, crispy-crunchy dishes; and 'big dishes' (*Ta Tsai*) – the larger casseroles and roasts. At a Chinese dinner, which invariably begins with some wine-accompanying dishes, rice is often not served at all, or else it is used for the purpose of 'settling the stomach'. Rice is usually served with those dishes which follow the 'big dishes'. The soups simply act as punctuations between the courses. There is no precise rule for the choice of ingredients, but the different divisions provide a framework on which the variation of texture, taste, flavour and substance may be built.

However, there are a few basic ingredients with which one has to get acquainted before attempting Chinese regional cooking – the glossary on the following page gives details of a few of them. You are advised to read this first and certainly before beginning to cook any of the recipes in this section.

# CHINESE COOKING METHODS

**Deep-frying:** The Chinese use a pan which slopes towards the centre, creating a well for the oil. The advantage of this pan is that when the food is pushed on to the sloping sides, the oil will drain off. In a Western kitchen, where the pan is equipped with a wire basket, deep-frying is much simpler. The ingredients are immersed in hot oil until pale golden in colour, then removed while the oil is reheated. They are then immersed again and cooked until crisp and golden on the outside and tender inside. If the ingredients are returned to the pan once, the method is known as double-frying; if returned twice it is called triple-frying.

The oil itself should be heated to different degrees. If cooking fish, kidneys or chicken, heat until it just begins to bubble; if cooking beef or pork, heat until the oil smokes.

**Steaming:** This method is used more frequently in Chinese cooking than in Western cooking, probably because either boiling or steaming rice produces large quantities of steam. This steam is utilised to cook other dishes by placing layers of steamers (which are basket-work trays) on top of the rice. When the rice is ready a whole series of dishes will also be ready at the same time. If a steamer is not available, an ovenproof dish or plate may be inverted in a large saucepan, which is filled with water until the bowl holding the food is a third underwater. The food to be steamed should be placed in an ovenproof bowl and set on top of the inverted plate. When the water boils, the steaming will start. In short-steaming, the bowl containing the food can be left open, as in the cooking of fish; in long-steaming (steaming over 30 minutes), the food is usually cooked covered. This can be done with a lid or by covering the top of the bowl with aluminium foil. The large saucepan should be covered tightly in both instances.

**Stir-frying (quick-frying):** The Chinese invented stir-frying (quick-frying), a cooking method similar to sautéing but needing only a few minutes of intense heat. The pan used for stir-frying is important – the thinner the metal, the faster it will conduct the heat. The process consists primarily of cooking one, or a number of foods, sliced into thin or matchstick-thin strips, in one or a few tablespoons of oil or fat. The ingredients in the pan are stirred with a metal spoon, spatula or a pair of bamboo chopsticks, while the ingredients cook. Seasonings and sauces are added and adjusted from time to time. Often the foods to be cooked together are stir-fried separately first, and then finally combined together in one big crescendo of cooking. This is sometimes necessary since the different foods combined in the dishes may require different lengths of cooking time. Another reason for separate cooking is the need to keep the flavours quite distinct until the final assembly. As a rule the oil used in stir-frying is corn oil or peanut oil; however, chicken fat is often employed in delicate cooking, for instance, to sauté vegetables. Although stir-frying may seem difficult at first, practice will make it increasingly easy.

*An average Chinese family meal usually consists of 4 or 5 dishes, with an accompaniment of rice, to be eaten by 4 or 5 persons. Extra dishes would be prepared for a party meal for more persons. The recipes in this section can be selected and combined according to taste, taking these servings as a guide.*

# GLOSSARY

*from left to right:*
Bean-curd; water chestnuts; dried tangerine (or orange) peel; red bean-curd cheese; fermented brown beans; dried Chinese mushrooms; winter bamboo shoots; wood-ears; fermented black beans; brown rock sugar; bamboo shoots; ginger root; lichees; lotus root; chillies; bêche-de-mer (sea cucumber); Chinese salted cabbage; bean sprouts; egg noodles; Chinese cabbage; Chinese ham; transparent pea-starch noodles; rice stick noodles; wheat-flour noodles.

### Bamboo Shoots
Probably eaten more for their crunchy texture than for their taste, which is extremely subtle. Winter bamboo shoots are somewhat more tender and smaller than ordinary bamboo shoots and are used by the Chinese for special dishes. Bamboo shoots are usually available canned, either whole or in large pieces. Rinse well with cold water before using.

### Bean-curd
Soya bean purée is set in cake form (about 3 inches/7·5 cm square and 1 inch/2·5 cm thick) to make bean-curd. It is an unusual soft spongy custard, creamy in colour and available either dried or fresh.

### Bean-curd Cheese, Red (Chinese Red Cheese)
A fermented derivative of bean-curd that has no Western equivalent in flavour. It may be bought canned in a red sauce. Mash the cubes before using.

### Bean Sprouts
The sprouts or shoots of Mung peas which are tiny whitish-green shoots, crunchy in texture. They should be cooked only briefly so that their crunchy quality is retained. They may be bought fresh, in cans, or in packages.

### Beans, Fermented Black (Black Bean Sauce)
These small, preserved soya beans are very salty and have a strong flavour. If unavailable, add extra salt to the recipe. They usually come dried and must be soaked and often mashed before using.

### Cabbage
*Chinese Celery Cabbage* (Chinese Lettuce): crisp vegetable resembling Cos, with firm, tightly packed vertical leaves which are pale yellow with a light green colour at the tips. As a substitute use young celery, Swiss chard or Savoy cabbage.
*Chinese Cabbage* (Chinese Chard): an extremely versatile and popular vegetable with long smooth whitish stalks and large dark-green crinkly leaves. It requires little cooking and has a delicate flavour.
*Chinese Salted Cabbage:* generally salted and dried in the sun. Sometimes hot pepper is added. Salted cabbage is used with meat as a flavouring agent. It must be soaked for 15 minutes in warm water, then rinsed in several changes of cold water.
*Mustard Cabbage:* similar in taste to broccoli, this dark-green vegetable has tightly packed scalloped leaves. It is similar in both size and texture to a small cabbage.

### Chillies
These small red peppers are extremely hot in taste (probably the hottest vegetable in existence). The white seeds inside are usually discarded. Chillies often come dried in which case they are even hotter. When dried chillies are fried in oil, they give it a red colour and impregnate the oil with their hotness. This chilli oil is used to cook meat and vegetables and is sometimes mixed with soya sauce to use as a dip at the table. Green and yellow chillies are occasionally available.

### Chinese Ham
The two best known hams in China are the *Yunnan* ham and the *Ching Hua* ham. They are usually available sliced in cans. A country-cured ham is a good substitute – the redder its colour the more similar it is to the Chinese variety.

### Chinese Noodles
Chinese noodles come in four varieties:
*Egg Noodles:* more yellow in colour than the following varieties, egg noodles are often precooked in 'pads' (like a small ball of wool but flattened). Precooked they require only a short period of simmering in boiling water to loosen up before they are stir-fried, cooked in sauce or added to soups.

260

*Rice Stick Noodles* (Rice-flour Noodles): usually whiter in colour than the wheat-flour noodles, these come in straight fine strands, about 8 inches (20 cm) in length. They are often cooked with wood-ears, mushrooms, meats or various seafoods such as oysters.

*Transparent Pea-starch Noodles:* made from ground Mung peas. Although the noodles are somewhat white and opaque when raw, they become transparent after a period of soaking or simmering in water. Soak in warm water for a few minutes before using to prevent absorbing excessive liquid from the prepared dish. Vermicelli may be substituted.

*Wheat-flour Noodles:* These noodles look like spaghetti and are made largely from the same ingredients. When cooked, they should be soft outside but still firm inside.

### Doilies for Peking Duck

Very similar in appearance to ordinary pancakes, except that they are thinner and feel drier, these are made without eggs and heated without the use of fat (see recipe, page 279). Very thin ordinary pancakes may be substituted.

### Dried Chinese Mushrooms

Fresh mushrooms are seldom used in Chinese cooking. The dried ones are brownish-black in colour and have a much stronger flavour and firmer texture than ordinary mushrooms. Clean them by rinsing in cold water, then soak in warm water for 20–30 minutes before using.

### Dried Tangerine or Orange Peel (Mandarin Orange Peel)

The dried peel of citrus fruits has a stronger flavour than fresh peel; therefore, it is used only in small quantities. If commercially unavailable, prepare it by drying fresh peel in a very cool oven (250°F, 130°C, Gas Mark ½) for 3 hours. Turn the heat off and let stand in the oven overnight. Dried peel is usually soaked for 30–45 minutes before using.

### Five-spice Powder

This very strong, fragrant mixed-spice powder consists of star anise, anise pepper, fennel, cloves and cinnamon. It is extremely pungent and should be used sparingly. Allspice may be used as a substitute.

### Ginger Root

It has a coarse yellow skin and is green inside with a white core. Scrape the root before using. Thin slices (about ⅛ inch/3 mm thick) are cut from the root as required. The unused portion may be wrapped in foil and stored for weeks in a cool, dry place or in the refrigerator.

### Ginger Water

Prepare ginger water by placing 1 tablespoon chopped fresh ginger root into a pan with 4 tablespoons of water. Simmer over low heat for 3 minutes, strain and use as required.

### Haisein Sauce or Hoisin Sauce (Red Vegetable Sauce)

Very similar in appearance to plum sauce – thick and viscous, brownish-red in colour, with a pungent sweet spiciness – this sauce is made from soya beans, garlic, chillies, sugar and vinegar.

### Lotus Leaves (Water Lily Leaves)

These come in large sheets, often more than 18 inches (45 cm) across. In Chinese cooking, they are frequently used for wrapping together various foods and flavouring ingredients before steaming them. Since lotus leaves are not easily obtainable in the West, large cabbage leaves may be used as a substitute.

### Monosodium Glutamate

This is a white, powdery substance, which enhances or accentuates the taste of foods. When increasing quantities of a recipe, the amount of the monosodium glutamate should remain unaltered. Used extensively in Japanese and Chinese cooking. Sold in jars and cans under a variety of brand names.

### Oyster Sauce

A thick greyish-brown liquid, this concentrate of oysters, soya sauce and brine is usually sold in bottles or cans. Used as a flavouring agent for cooking with meat, poultry and seafood.

### Plum Sauce

This is a thick amber-red sauce made from plums, apricots, sugar, chillies and vinegar. It is generally used as a table condiment for roast duck, pork and spare ribs. Available in jars and cans.

## Rock Sugar, Brown (Rock Candy)
The Chinese use large grains or lumps of crystallised sugar in cooking. Demerara sugar may be substituted.

## Secondary Broth
Bones are the only ingredients used in the preparation of secondary broth: chicken bones, fresh pork bones and smoked pork bones in the ratio of 2:2:1. Place the bones in a large saucepan and cover with cold water three times the depth of the bones. Bring to the boil, then reduce the heat immediately and skim the surface. Simmer for 4 hours, skimming hourly.

## Sesame Jam (Sesame Paste)
Also called *tehina* (see *Houmous v' tehina*, page 246). A good substitute may be obtained by adding 1 teaspoon of sesame oil to about 6–8 teaspoons of peanut butter.

## Sesame Oil
Sesame oil is used sparingly as a flavouring agent (usually less than 1 teaspoon at a time). It is made from toasted sesame seeds.

## Soya Jam (Soya Paste, Soya-bean Paste)
This thick, viscous, almost black paste is made from fermented soya beans. It is similar in flavour to soya sauce and may be interchanged with it. Soya jam is usually used where a thicker sauce is required – in the quick-frying of diced meat, for example. It may be obtained in cans or jars.

## Soya Sauce, Light- and Dark-coloured
This is a fermented sauce made from soya beans, wheat, yeast and salt. The sediment which forms is soya jam.

## Superior Broth
This broth is richer, purer and more concentrated than secondary broth. It calls for a maximum of meat and a minimum of liquid. Use a 2-lb (1-kg) chicken and 2 lb (1 kg) shoulder of pork to 4 pints (2·25 litres) water. Prepare as for secondary broth. Canned consommé may be substituted.

## Water Chestnuts
A root vegetable, round and somewhat flat in shape. They have a sweet, sugary juice and a crunchy texture. Only available in cans.

## Wine-sediment Paste
This is a thick paste, often maroon although it may be purple or cream-coloured. It is made from wine sediment and fermented rice. Wine-sediment paste is used in cooking meats, poultry and seafood, and especially snails.

## Wood-ears
These are a species of lichen. The type most often used in Chinese cooking is black in colour and dried. Before using the fungi, soak for about 1 hour and clean in several changes of water. Like bamboo shoots, they are used more for their texture (crunchy and slippery) than for their taste, which again is bland. Button mushrooms may be used as a substitute.

*Hot and sour soup*

# HOT AND SOUR SOUP

2 tablespoons cornflour
4 tablespoons water
2 tablespoons soya sauce
4 tablespoons vinegar
½ teaspoon black pepper
1 oz/25 g bean curd (optional)
1 egg
2 dried Chinese mushrooms
   soaked and drained

½ small chicken breast
1½ teaspoons lard
2 tablespoons chopped onion
1½ pints/9 dl meat broth
1 teaspoon monosodium
   glutamate (optional)
1 teaspoon sesame oil
½ teaspoon salt

Blend the cornflour with the water. Add the soya sauce, vinegar and pepper and mix together. Cut the bean curd into ¼-inch (5-mm) squares. Whisk the egg with a fork. Cut the mushrooms and chicken flesh into matchstick-thin strips.

Heat the lard in a saucepan. Add the onion and sauté for 2 minutes. Add the broth, then the bean curd, mushrooms and chicken. Bring to the boil and simmer for 15 minutes. Add the cornflour mixture and monosodium glutamate. Stir the soup until it begins to thicken; then, as the soup is swirling around in the pan, pour in the beaten egg along the tines of a fork steadily and slowly so that it separates into threads. Add the sesame oil and salt.

Give the soup an additional stir so that the 'egg-flower' (as the Chinese call it) will mix evenly with the rich brown soup. Pour into a heated tureen and serve immediately.

# CRISPY RAVIOLI SOUP WITH BAMBOO SHOOTS

**for the Hun Tun skin:**
6 oz/175 g plain flour
pinch salt
4 tablespoons boiling water
½ teaspoon lard
**for the filling:**
½ small onion
2 water chestnuts
1 teaspoon sesame oil
2 oz/50 g pork, finely minced
**for the soup:**
½ oz/15 g wood-ears, soaked for
   1 hour, or button mushrooms

1½ oz/40 g tender spring greens
2 tablespoons chopped leek
2 slices fresh root ginger
½ pint/3 dl water
1½ pints/9 dl superior broth
   (see page 262)
1½ tablespoons soya sauce
1½ oz/40 g bamboo shoots
½ teaspoon sesame oil
1 teaspoon monosodium
   glutamate (optional)
salt and pepper
vegetable oil for deep-frying

Prepare the *Hun Tun* skin as for Chinese swallow-skin ravioli (see Chinese Ravioli with Prawn-Pork Filling, page 281). After kneading, cut into 24 portions and roll each portion into a very thin dough.

For the filling, peel and chop the onion and chop the water chestnuts. Heat the sesame oil in a small frying pan and sauté the onion, water chestnuts and pork for 2 minutes. Remove from the heat and cool. Divide into 24 portions. Wrap a portion of filling in each dough skin.

For the soup, boil the wood-ears with the greens in water to cover for 5 minutes. Discard the water. Boil the leek and ginger in the ½ pint (3 dl) water for 10 minutes. Add the wood-ears, cabbage, one-third of the superior broth, the soya sauce and bamboo shoots to the leek and ginger. Simmer for 10 minutes.

Pour the soup into a large ovenproof tureen. Add the sesame oil, remaining superior broth, the monosodium glutamate and seasoning to taste.

Steam for 15 minutes. Simultaneously, deep-fry the ravioli in hot oil for 4 minutes, or until golden.

Place the fried ravioli at the bottom of a large, heated tureen and pour over the soup. Bring to the table quickly, while the crackling ravioli is 'singing' in the tureen.

# CHICKEN VELVET AND SWEET CORN SOUP

1 chicken breast
2 egg whites
1½ pints/9 dl chicken broth
1 (7-oz/198-g) can sweet corn
   kernels
1 tablespoon cornflour

3 tablespoons water
2 tablespoons fresh green peas
1 teaspoon salt
½ teaspoon monosodium
   glutamate (optional)
1 oz/25 g cooked ham

Finely chop the chicken flesh and mix thoroughly in a bowl with the egg whites. Bring the chicken broth to the boil in a saucepan. Add the sweet corn and then stir in the cornflour mixed with the water. When the contents reboil, stir in the chicken mixture. Stirring gently, add the peas, salt and monosodium glutamate. Simmer for 5–6 minutes over low heat. Chop the ham finely. Pour the soup into a heated tureen and garnish with the chopped ham before serving.

# CUCUMBER SOUP

1 lb/450 g pork bone
2 pints/generous litre water
1 large cucumber
vegetable oil for deep-frying
2 tablespoons dried shrimps

1 teaspoon salt
1 slice fresh root ginger
½ teaspoon monosodium
   glutamate (optional)

Boil the pork bone in the water for 15 minutes. Skim and continue to simmer for another 40 minutes. Cut the cucumber across into 3 sections. Deep-fry in very hot oil for 30 seconds. Drain the cucumber and add it to the pork bone broth. Add the dried shrimps, salt and ginger and simmer for 20 minutes. Add the monosodium glutamate.

Remove the pork bone. The soup should now be quite clear and the pieces of cucumber will appear like floating green logs. Pour into a heated soup tureen and serve.

*Fish-broth chrysanthemum hot pot*

# FISH-BROTH CHRYSANTHEMUM HOT POT

| | |
|---|---|
| 1½ oz/40 g transparent pea-starch noodles | 4 oz/100 g chicken livers |
| vegetable oil for deep-frying | 4 oz/100 g pig's liver |
| 1½ oz/40 g peanuts | fish bones, head and tail |
| ½ small Chinese celery cabbage heart | 2½ pints/1·25 litres chicken broth |
| 4 oz/100 g spinach | 3 slices fresh root ginger |
| 3 oz/75 g bean sprouts | few sprigs fresh parsley |
| ½ bunch watercress | 1½ teaspoons salt |
| 2 spring onions | 1 large chrysanthemum head |
| 8 oz/225 g fish fillets (sole, bream, carp, cod or halibut) | pepper |
| 1 large chicken breast | ½ oz/15 g lard |
| | ½ teaspoon monosodium glutamate (optional) |

Deep-fry the noodles in the hot oil just until they puff up. Then drain. Deep-fry the peanuts quickly until brown and crispy. Transfer the noodles and peanuts to 2 plates and place on the dining table. Wash and trim the cabbage, spinach, bean sprouts and watercress and place them neatly on 4 other plates on the dining table. Cut the spring onions into ½-inch (1-cm) lengths. Clean the fish and cut into very

thin slices 2 by 1½ inches (5 by 3·5 cm). Slice the chicken breast, chicken livers and pig's liver into bite-sized pieces.

Prepare a fish broth by boiling the fish bones, head and tail for 5 minutes in the chicken broth, with the spring onions, ginger, parsley and salt. Strain and reserve the broth.

Loosen and remove the petals of the chrysanthemum blossom and arrange on a small dish, imitating as nearly as possible the shape of the original bloom.

Heat the reserved broth and pour into the hot pot (see note), which is then placed in the centre of the table in front of the diners. Light the spirit stove and when the broth boils, drop in all the chrysanthemum petals. Add the fish, chicken and livers. When the contents boil, add the noodles, peanuts, cabbage and watercress, then the spinach and bean sprouts. Add pepper to taste, the lard and monosodium glutamate. When the contents reboil, wait for 25 seconds. Pick the various ingredients out of the pot with a pair of bamboo chopsticks and place in each diner's rice bowl.

The items from the pot may also be dipped in various mixes and dips such as salt-pepper, soya sauce-vinegar or haisein sauce, which are placed conveniently on the table. Not all the food needs to be cooked in the pot at the same time. Different quantities may be put in at various stages.

Although the chrysanthemum is the most common flower used in this form of hot pot, other flowers such as peach blossom may also be used (Peach Blossom hot pot).

*Note:* The Chrysanthemum hot pot is always fired with

methylated spirit, unlike the Peking hot pot, which is fired with charcoal in a hot pot-cum-stove, with a funnel running up the centre of the pot. The chrysanthemum type is more like a Swiss fondue set in that it is simply a brass or copper pot with a spirit stove burning underneath.

# GLISTENING CRYSTAL PRAWNS

1 lb/450 g cooked prawns, peeled and deveined
1 pint/6 dl salted water (use 1 tablespoon salt)
2 teaspoons cornflour
2 egg whites
2 tablespoons superior broth (see page 262)
½ teaspoon salt
1 oz/25 g lard

1 clove garlic
1 tablespoon chopped spring onion
½ tablespoon chopped fresh root ginger
**for the sauce mixture:**
1½ tablespoons cornflour
1 teaspoon monosodium glutamate (optional)
3 tablespoons water

Soak the prawns in the salted water and place in the refrigerator for 2 hours. Drain, rinse quickly and dry thoroughly. Mix the cornflour with the egg whites, broth and salt and stir in the prawns. Heat the lard in a frying pan until the fat begins to smoke. Add the prawns and scramble-fry for 30–40 seconds over high heat. Remove the prawns and set aside. Peel and crush the garlic.

Reheat the pan and add the garlic, spring onions and ginger. Sauté in the remaining lard for 10 seconds. Return the prawns to the pan. Stir, mix and scramble-fry for 10 seconds. Blend together the cornflour, monosodium gluta-

mate and water. Add to the pan and stir gently until the prawns take on a glistening, glossy look.

Serve immediately with quantities of rice.

# PORK-PRAWN LION'S HEAD WITH CRAB

1½ lb/700 g belly of pork
4 oz/100 g crab meat
2 tablespoons chopped onion
1 tablespoon chopped fresh root ginger
2 tablespoons dry sherry
2 tablespoons cornflour

1 teaspoon salt
4 lb/1·75 kg spring greens
1½ oz/40 g lard
2 oz/50 g cooked prawns, peeled and deveined
2 tablespoons chicken broth

Remove the pork skin and coarsely mince the flesh. Chop the crab meat. Add half the onion, half the ginger, the sherry, cornflour and salt to the pork and crab. Mix well and form into large balls. Discard any coarse outer leaves of the spring greens and chop off the stalks. Shred the greens. Heat two-thirds of the lard in a large saucepan. Fry the prawns for 1 minute. Then add the greens and fry for 3 minutes.

Heat the remaining lard and the broth in a large casserole. When the lard melts, line the bottom and sides of the dish with half the prawn mixture. Arrange the meat balls on top. Sprinkle with the remaining onion and ginger. Finally, spoon the remaining prawn mixture over the meat balls. Cover the dish and cook in a moderate oven (350°F, 180°C, Gas Mark 4) for 50 minutes.

Serve from the casserole. The host uses his chopsticks to remove the upper layer of prawns and greens.

*Glistening crystal prawns*

# FRIED FISH STRIPS TOSSED IN CELERY

1 lb/450 g fish fillets (bass, haddock, pike or cod)
1 teaspoon salt
1 egg
1½ tablespoons cornflour
1 small head celery
1 tablespoon light-coloured soya sauce
1 teaspoon sesame oil
½ teaspoon monosodium glutamate (optional)
1 oz/25 g cooked ham
vegetable oil for deep-frying

Cut the fish first into thin slices, then cut again into matchstick-thin strips about 2 inches (5 cm) long. Add the salt to the egg and whisk well. Coat the fish with this mixture and dredge with the cornflour. Wash the celery and cut into matchstick-thin strips. Plunge into boiling water for 30 seconds, then drain. Add the soya sauce, sesame oil and monosodium glutamate to the celery. Toss and mix well. Cut the ham into matchstick-thin strips.

Place the fish in a wire basket and spread the pieces out evenly with a pair of bamboo chopsticks. Lower into very hot oil and deep-fry for 3–4 minutes, after which time the strips of fish will float to the surface. Remove and drain them. Place the celery mixture in a large heated serving dish. Arrange the fried fish on top. Mix gently. Garnish with the ham. This dish may be accompanied by a chilli-soya dip (1 part chilli sauce to 6 parts soya sauce).

# DEEP-FRIED FISH IN RED WINE-SEDIMENT PASTE

2 lb/1 kg fish fillets (haddock, cod, halibut or bass)
1 teaspoon salt
3 tablespoons dry sherry
3 tablespoons red wine-sediment paste
2 spring onions
vegetable oil for deep-frying
1 tablespoon lard
1 tablespoon chopped fresh root ginger
1 tablespoon chopped onion
1 teaspoon sugar
1 teaspoon soya sauce
2 tablespoons chicken broth or superior broth (see page 262)
½ teaspoon monosodium glutamate (optional)

Cut the fish into thick pieces 2 inches by 1 inch by 1½ inches (5 by 2·5 by 3·5 cm). Rub with the salt and marinate in a mixture of half the sherry and half the red wine-sediment paste for 1 hour. Cut the spring onions into 1½-inch (3·5-cm) segments.

Heat the oil until very hot and deep-fry the fish for 3–4 minutes. Drain on kitchen paper then arrange the fish pieces on a large flat plate.

Heat the lard in a small frying pan. Add the ginger and onion and sauté over high heat for 1 minute. Add the remaining sherry, remaining wine-sediment paste, the sugar, soya sauce, broth and monosodium glutamate. Continue to stir-fry for 30 seconds. Pour the sauce over the fish and garnish with the spring onions.

# QUICK-FRIED SLICED FISH

8 oz/225 g fish fillets (sea bass, cod, haddock or sole)
1½ oz/40 g cornflour
1 pint/6 dl vegetable oil for semi-deep-frying
**for the sauce:**
1 tablespoon soya sauce
1 tablespoon sugar
1 tablespoon dry sherry
2 teaspoons vinegar
½ teaspoon monosodium glutamate (optional)
2 teaspoons cornflour
1 tablespoon water
1 oz/25 g lard
1 tablespoon chopped shallot
1 teaspoon chopped fresh root ginger

Slice the fillets into strips 1½ inches by ¾ inch by ¼ inch (3·5 cm by 1·5 cm by 5 mm). Dredge in the cornflour. Fry the pieces of fish in vegetable oil to cover in a large frying pan, adding each piece of fish separately (so they can be handled gently and do not stick to each other). The frying should be gentle, over low to medium heat, and the fish should be removed after 2 minutes. Drain and set aside while preparing the sauce.

Mix together in a bowl the soya sauce, sugar, sherry, vinegar, monosodium glutamate and cornflour blended with the water. Stir and mix well. Discard the oil in the pan and add the lard. When hot, add the shallot and ginger and fry for 30 seconds. Pour in the mixture from the bowl and stir until the sauce thickens. Return the slices of fish to the pan. Turn them over in the sauce a few times and then transfer to a heated dish. Serve immediately.

# SOFT-FRIED CRAB MEAT

1 lb/450 g crab meat
2 tablespoons chopped onion
3 tablespoons dry sherry
1 tablespoon cornflour
2 tablespoons water
1 oz/25 g pork fat
1½ oz/40 g lard
¼ teaspoon salt
1 tablespoon soya sauce
1½ teaspoons sugar
4 tablespoons chicken broth
1½ tablespoons ginger water

Mix the crab meat with half the onion and half the sherry. Blend the cornflour with the water. Cut the pork fat into small cubes. Heat two-thirds of the lard in a frying pan. Add the remaining onion and pork fat and sauté until golden. Add the crab meat mixture and stir-fry very gently without breaking it into pieces. After 30 seconds add the remaining sherry, salt, soya sauce, sugar, chicken broth and ginger water. Mix gently and simmer for 3 minutes. Add the cornflour mixture and remaining lard. When it boils, the dish is ready. The usual dips for this dish are mixtures of chopped root ginger with vinegar, or chopped garlic with vinegar.

*Quick-fried sliced fish*

# FRY-BRAISED FISH BALLS

2 lb/1 kg fish fillets (carp, cod, haddock, bass or halibut)
1 egg
1½ teaspoons salt
½ teaspoon monosodium glutamate (optional)
2 teaspoons sesame oil
pepper
2 tablespoons water
½ small green sweet pepper
3 water chestnuts

8 dried Chinese mushrooms, soaked and drained
2 cloves garlic
vegetable oil for deep-frying
3 tablespoons vegetable oil
1 oz/25 g bean sprouts
3 slices fresh root ginger
1 tablespoon chutney
3 tablespoons superior broth (see page 262)
½ oz/15 g cornflour

Clean the fish and mince the flesh. Whisk the egg and add to the fish with 1 teaspoon of the salt, the monosodium glutamate, half the sesame oil, pepper to taste and the water. Mix together thoroughly. Form into balls about ½ inch (1 cm) in diameter. Trim and thinly slice the green pepper and slice the water chestnuts. Discard the mushroom stalks. Peel and slice the garlic. Heat the oil and deep-fry the fish balls for 2 minutes. Drain and simmer in boiling water for 2 minutes. Drain and set aside.

Heat the 3 tablespoons oil in a large frying pan over high heat for 30 seconds. Add the remaining salt, the green pepper, water chestnuts, mushrooms, garlic, bean sprouts, ginger and chutney. Stir-fry quickly for 2 minutes. Add the fish balls and continue to stir-fry more slowly over lower heat for 1 minute. Add the broth and cornflour blended with a little water. Stir for 10 seconds and sprinkle with the remaining sesame oil. Transfer to a heated serving dish and serve immediately.

# SOYA-BRAISED FISH

1½ lb/700 g fish fillets (bream, bass, carp, halibut or cod)
1 teaspoon salt
4 spring onions
vegetable oil for deep-frying
1 oz/25 g lard
4 slices fresh root ginger

1 teaspoon coarsely chopped dried chilli
1 tablespoon soya sauce
2 tablespoons dry sherry
½ teaspoon monosodium glutamate (optional)
1 teaspoon sesame oil

Chop the fish into approximately 1-inch (2·5-cm) cubes. Rub evenly with the salt, using your fingers. Cut the spring onions into 1-inch (2·5-cm) long pieces. Heat the vegetable oil and deep-fry the fish for 2 minutes. Drain. Heat the lard in a frying pan and sauté the ginger and chilli for 30 seconds. Add the fish and turn it over in the lard a couple of times. Pour in the soya sauce and sherry. Turn the fish over several times and cover the pan. Simmer the contents over low heat for 3 minutes. Remove the lid and sprinkle the fish with the monosodium glutamate and sesame oil. Add the spring onions. Simmer for 1 minute and transfer to a heated serving dish. Because the gravy is sufficiently strong, no sauces or dips are required.

# GARNISHED STEAMED SOLE

2 soles, about 1 lb/450 g each
2 teaspoons salt
3 tablespoons dry sherry
2 tablespoons chicken broth
1½ teaspoons sugar
½ teaspoon monosodium glutamate (optional)
½ oz/15 g lard
**for the garnish:**
1 tablespoon diced pork fat

1½ teaspoons sugar
2 slices smoked ham
1 oz/25 g bamboo shoots
2 spring onions
12 small dried Chinese mushrooms, soaked and drained
8 slices fresh root ginger

Gut the fish, wash thoroughly and dry well. Rub both sides with the salt and half the sherry. Cut 3 slashes on each side of the soles, halfway through the flesh. Place them on an oval ovenproof dish. Heat the broth. Add the remaining sherry, the sugar, monosodium glutamate and lard and mix well. Sprinkle this mixture evenly over the fish. To make the garnish, pile the diced pork fat and sugar in the middle of each fish as a 'hub'. Cut the ham and bamboo shoots into thin 2-inch (5-cm) strips and cut the spring onions into 1-inch (2·5-cm) segments. Use the ham and bamboo shoots to form 2 lines at right angles to each other, meeting at the 'hub'. Put the spring onions, mushrooms and ginger in the spaces. Cover and steam over high heat for 20 minutes. Wipe the edge of the dish with a cloth and serve immediately.

# DOUBLE-FRIED EEL

3–4 lb/1·5–1·75 kg skinned eel
2 tablespoons sherry
vegetable oil for deep-frying
4 spring onions
2 tablespoons vegetable oil
1 tablespoon chopped fresh root ginger

2 tablespoons soya sauce
1 tablespoon sugar
¼ teaspoon five-spice powder or allspice
pepper

Blanch the eel in boiling water for 1 minute. Drain, dry and rub with half the sherry. Place in a wire basket and deep-fry in hot oil for 4 minutes. Drain, and cut the flesh of the eel neatly into 2- by 1-inch (5- by 2·5-cm) strips, discarding the head and tail. Cut the spring onions into 1-inch (2·5-cm) pieces.

Place the strips of eel in a wire basket and deep-fry again for 3 minutes, or until golden. (By this time there will probably be no more than 1 lb/450 g eel flesh left). Drain. Heat the 2 tablespoons oil in a frying pan. Add the remaining sherry, the spring onions, ginger, soya sauce, sugar and five-spice powder. Cook over high heat for 1 minute, stirring constantly. Add the eel strips. Baste and mix them with the sauce in the pan. Season with pepper to taste. Place on a heated dish and serve immediately.

# HOT-BRAISED SLICED BEEF

1 lb/450 g rump steak
1 egg
1 oz/25 g cornflour
1 teaspoon salt
1 small green or red sweet pepper
4 teaspoons coarsely chopped
  dried chillies
5 tablespoons vegetable oil
1 tablespoon fermented black
  beans, soaked for 1 hour
2 oz/50 g bamboo shoots

3 spring onions
1 tablespoon chopped onion
1 tablespoon chopped fresh root
  ginger
1 tablespoon sliced leek
¼ teaspoon black pepper
1 tablespoon dry sherry
2 tablespoons white wine
¼ pint/1·5 dl superior broth (see
  page 262)
1 teaspoon monosodium
  glutamate (optional)

Cut the beef into thin slices, 1½ inches by 1 inch (3·5 by 2·5 cm). Break the egg into a bowl. Add the cornflour and salt and blend to a smooth batter. Mix in the beef, using your fingers to coat the meat evenly with the batter.

Remove the seeds from the sweet pepper and chillies. Slice the sweet pepper into strips. Stir-fry in half the oil for 1½ minutes and set aside. Mash the fermented beans. Cut the bamboo shoots and spring onions into 1½-inch (3·5-cm) segments.

Heat the remaining oil in a large frying pan. Add the black beans, bamboo shoots, spring onions, onion, ginger, leek and pepper. Stir-fry slowly over medium heat for 2 minutes. Add the sherry and wine, and after 10 seconds add the broth and monosodium glutamate. Turn the heat to high. When the contents reboil, add the coated beef. After 30 seconds of stir-braising, transfer to a deep serving dish. Meanwhile, reheat the sweet pepper and chillies and pour them, with the oil, over the beef.

# SALTED BEEF WITH CABBAGE HEART

4 oz/100 g salted beef or pork
1½ lb/700 g cabbage or spring
  greens
2 tablespoons vegetable oil
4 tablespoons chicken broth

1 teaspoon salt
½ teaspoon monosodium
  glutamate (optional)
½ oz/15 g lard

Cut the meat into paper-thin slices, 1½ inches (3·5 cm) long and ½ inch (1 cm) wide. Discard the outer leaves of the cabbage and trim the stalk, leaving only the tender inside leaves. Cut these crisscross into 2-inch (5-cm) pieces.

Heat the oil in a frying pan over high heat. When very hot, add the cabbage and scramble-fry for 1½ minutes. Add the pork and broth. Sprinkle with the salt and monosodium glutamate. Stir-fry gently for 3 minutes. Add the lard and after a couple of stirs and tosses, transfer to a heated dish and serve.

# PINE-FLOWER MEAT SOUFFLÉ OMELETTE

6 eggs
1 oz/25 g plain flour
1 teaspoon salt
1 teaspoon monosodium
  glutamate (optional)
4 oz/100 g lean pork
2 spring onions
1 oz/25 g dried Chinese
  mushrooms, soaked and
  drained

1 oz/25 g bamboo shoots
1 teaspoon sugar
1 tablespoon soya sauce
¼ teaspoon five-spice powder or
  allspice (optional)
3 oz/75 g lard
2 tablespoons chopped fresh
  parsley
1 tablespoon dry sherry

Separate the egg whites from the yolks. Whisk the whites for 2 minutes or until nearly stiff. Fold in the yolks, salt and monosodium glutamate. Finely chop the pork and spring onions. Slice the mushrooms and bamboo shoots into matchstick-thin strips. Place the pork, spring onions, mushrooms, bamboo shoots, sugar, soya sauce and five-spice powder in a bowl. Mix well.

Heat 1 tablespoon of the lard in a small saucepan. Add the pork mixture and stir-fry for 3 minutes. Remove from the heat and set aside. Place half the remaining lard in a large frying pan over very low heat. When the lard has melted, add half the egg mixture, which will spread into a circle about 6 inches (15 cm) in diameter. When the egg has just started to set, gently put the cooked pork mixture into the centre.

After 1 minute of cooking over low heat, pour the remaining egg mixture over the filling. Heat the remaining lard in a small saucepan until very hot and pour it over the soft egg mixture. Sprinkle the parsley over the omelette, then pour over the sherry. Cook for 30 seconds without stirring. Gently lift one side of the omelette to drain away the lard. Use a large spatula to lift the omelette on to a heated serving plate.

# STEAMED BEEF IN RICE FLOUR

1¾ lb/800 g fillet or rump steak
1 tablespoon chopped fresh root
  ginger
5 tablespoons water
1½ tablespoons vegetable oil
1 tablespoon dry sherry
1½ tablespoons soya sauce
1 tablespoon fermented black
  beans, soaked for 1 hour

1½ teaspoons sugar
1 teaspoon chilli sauce
2 oz/50 g ground rice
crushed coriander seeds
bay leaves
chopped chives
fresh thyme

Cut the meat into pieces, 1½ inches by ¾ inch by ½ inch (3·5 by 1·5 by 1 cm). Prepare the ginger water by boiling the ginger in the water over low heat for 3 minutes; then strain. Place the meat in a bowl and add the ginger water, oil, sherry, soya sauce, black beans, sugar and chilli sauce. Work the mixture into the meat with your fingers. Finally, dry-fry the ground rice until it begins to turn brown. Coat the pieces of meat with the ground rice.

Divide the meat among 4 ovenproof bowls. To the first bowl, add a few coriander seeds, to the second, add a few bay leaves, to the third, a few chives, to the fourth, a little thyme. Place the bowls in a steamer, cover and steam for 30 minutes.

The beef in four flavours makes an excellent meal if served with rice and accompanied by a soup, a fish or egg dish and a vegetable dish.

# SLICED STEAK IN OYSTER SAUCE

8 oz/225 g rump or fillet steak
2 tablespoons dry sherry
1 tablespoon soya sauce
1 tablespoon cornflour
1 tablespoon water
4 tablespoons vegetable oil

1½ tablespoons oyster sauce
3 tablespoons superior broth (see
  page 262)
4–6 spring onions
3 slices fresh root ginger

Cut the meat across the grain into thin slices 1½ inches by 1 inch (3·5 by 2·5 cm). Place in a bowl with half the sherry, the soya sauce and half the cornflour blended with the water. Mix thoroughly. Add 1 tablespoon vegetable oil and work it into the meat with your fingers.

In another bowl, mix the remaining cornflour, the oyster sauce and broth. Cut the spring onions into 1-inch (2·5-cm) segments, using the white part only. Heat the remaining vegetable oil in a frying pan over high heat. When very hot, add the beef. Stir-fry for 30 seconds. Remove the beef and drain off the excess oil. Replace the pan over the heat and sauté the spring onions and ginger for 20 seconds.

Replace the beef in the pan and pour in the remaining sherry. Spread the beef evenly in the pan. Quickly pour in the oyster sauce mixture. Stir-scramble for about 8–10 seconds over high heat and transfer to a heated plate before serving.

*Steamed beef in rice flour*

271

# RED-SIMMERED KNUCKLE OF PORK

3–4 lb/1·5–1·75 kg knuckle of pork
3 pints/1·5 litres water
3 spring onions
6 tablespoons soya sauce
1½ oz/40 g sugar
6 tablespoons dry sherry
4 slices fresh root ginger
1 oz/25 g lard

Clean the knuckle of pork and slash the meat with a knife on either side to facilitate cooking. Place in a heavy saucepan and add the water. Bring to the boil and simmer for 10 minutes. Skim and simmer for another 15 minutes. Skim again; ladle out and discard one-third of the broth. Cut the spring onions into 1-inch (2·5-cm) segments. Add the spring onions, soya sauce, sugar, sherry, ginger and lard to the remaining broth. Cover and continue to simmer over low heat for 2 hours, uncovering once every 30 minutes to turn the knuckle over during cooking.

By the end of 2 hours, the liquid in the pan should have reduced to ¾ pint (4·5 dl). Reduce it again by half by increasing the heat for a few minutes. The gravy will have become rich brown and glossy. Remove the knuckle and place in a deep bowl. Pour the gravy over without any further thickening. Serve with plain cooked vegetables and rice.

# STEAMED RICE-PORK 'PEARLS'

8 oz/225 g short-grain rice
1¼ lb/600 g lean pork
12 oz/350 g pork fat
8 water chestnuts
2 teaspoons salt
¼ teaspoon pepper
1 teaspoon monosodium glutamate (optional)
3 eggs
1 tablespoon dry sherry
1½ tablespoons cornflour
5 tablespoons water
4 spring onions, chopped
2 teaspoons chopped fresh root ginger

Wash the rice 3 times and soak in cold water for 1 hour. Drain well and spread on a baking tray or sheet of greaseproof paper. Trim off any fat and mince the lean pork. Boil the pork fat in water for 5 minutes, drain and cut into pea-sized pieces. Cut the water chestnuts into pieces of the same size.

Place the pork in a bowl and add the salt, pepper, monosodium glutamate, eggs, sherry and cornflour blended with the water. Mix well. Then add the pork fat, spring onions, water chestnuts and ginger. Form the mixture into meat balls, ½ inch (1 cm) in diameter. Roll them in the rice to pick up a covering of grains. When well-covered, use your hands to press the rice more firmly into the meat balls.

Arrange the rice-covered meat balls in not more than 2 layers in a large ovenproof dish. Cover with foil and steam vigorously for 20 minutes.

*Steamed rice-pork 'pearls'*

# STEWED PORK WITH SHERRY AND GINGER

| | |
|---|---|
| 2 lb/1 kg belly or leg of pork | 1 tablespoon sugar |
| 1½ tablespoons vegetable oil | 1 teaspoon chopped fresh root |
| 1½ pints/9 dl water | ginger |
| 2 tablespoons dry sherry | 1 tablespoon chopped shallot |
| 2 tablespoons soya sauce | 1 tablespoon soya jam (optional) |

Cut the meat into 1- to 1½-inch (2·5–3·5-cm) cubes, preferably across the meat, fat and skin so that each piece will have all three. Heat the oil in a saucepan and sauté the meat for 4–5 minutes, or until it has turned white. Meanwhile, boil the water. Add the sherry, soya sauce, sugar, ginger, shallot and soya jam to the pan, and then pour in the boiling water. Boil for 2 minutes and skim the surface. Then lower the heat to a minimum, cover and simmer for 1½–1¾ hours. During the cooking, turn the meat over several times with a wooden spoon.

Transfer to a heated serving dish and serve with rice and plain cooked vegetables.

# SWEET AND SOUR PORK

| | |
|---|---|
| 1 lb/450 g belly of pork | for the sweet and sour sauce: |
| 1 teaspoon salt | 2 oz/50 g brown sugar |
| 2 tablespoons dry sherry | 2 tablespoons white vinegar |
| 2 tablespoons cornflour | 1 tablespoon tangerine (or |
| 1 egg | orange) juice |
| 1 green or red sweet pepper | 1 tablespoon tomato purée |
| 1 leek | 1 tablespoon soya sauce |
| ½ small onion | 1 tablespoon cornflour |
| 2 oz/50 g bamboo shoots | |
| generous ¼ pint/2 dl vegetable oil | |

Cut away the skin from the pork. Dice the flesh into ½-inch (1-cm) cubes. Add the salt and sherry and marinate for 30 minutes. Place the cornflour in a mixing bowl, make a well in the centre and break in the egg. Stir thoroughly to make a batter. Trim the pepper, remove the seeds and cut into thin strips. Cut the leek into ½-inch (1-cm) sections. Chop the onion and the bamboo shoots into slices ½ by ½ by ¼ inch (1 cm by 1 cm by 5 mm). For the sauce, mix together the brown sugar, vinegar, tangerine juice, tomato purée and soya sauce. Heat the mixture in a small saucepan until the sugar completely dissolves. Remove the pan from the heat.

Coat the pork in the batter. Heat the oil in a frying pan. Add the pork and stir-fry gently over high heat for 2½ minutes. Add the bamboo shoots and continue to stir-fry for 30 seconds. Remove the pork and bamboo shoots and set aside. Pour off the excess oil.

Replace the pan over the heat and add the pepper, leek and onion. Stir-fry for 1 minute. Add the cornflour to the sweet and sour sauce, blend well and pour it into the pan. Stir gently until the contents reboil. Then add the partially cooked pork and bamboo shoots. After a few quick stirs and scrambles, transfer to a heated serving plate and serve.

# RED-COOKED PORK WITH CHESTNUTS

| | |
|---|---|
| 2 lb/1 kg belly of pork | 2 tablespoons soya sauce |
| 1 small onion | ¾ pint/4·5 dl secondary broth |
| 1 lb/450 g chestnuts | (see page 262) |
| 2 tablespoons vegetable oil | 1 tablespoon sugar |
| 3 slices fresh root ginger | 2 tablespoons dry sherry |
| ½ teaspoon salt | |

Wash the pork in hot water and cut into 1-inch (2·5-cm) cubes so that each piece has lean and fat. Peel and quarter the onion. Slash the chestnuts and cook in boiling water for 20–25 minutes. Drain and remove the skins. Heat the oil in a heavy saucepan. Sauté the onion and ginger for 1 minute over medium heat. Add the pork and, raising the heat to high, stir-fry for 3 minutes. Add the salt and half the soya sauce. Stir-fry for 3 more minutes then pour in the broth. Bring to the boil, lower the heat to a minimum and simmer, covered, for 45 minutes, turning the meat over 3 or 4 times in the process.

Add the chestnuts, the remaining soya sauce, the sugar and sherry. Continue to slow-simmer for 30 minutes, mixing the chestnuts with the meat and turning the mixture over gently 3 or 4 times in the process. Serve with rice.

# AMOY PORK ESCALOPE

| | |
|---|---|
| 2 lb/1 kg belly of pork (with good | 6 radishes |
| proportion of lean to fat) | 2 teaspoons salt |
| 2 tablespoons soya sauce | 1 tablespoon sugar |
| 2 tablespoons dry sherry | 1 tablespoon vinegar |
| 2 bay leaves | 1 teaspoon sesame oil |
| 1 tablespoon brown rock sugar or | 2 duck or hen eggs |
| demerara sugar | 2½ oz/65 g breadcrumbs |
| 2 medium-sized carrots | vegetable oil for deep-frying |

Boil the pork in water to cover for 5 minutes. Drain and cut into thin slices containing both lean and fat. Place the pork in an ovenproof bowl and add the soya sauce, sherry, bay leaves and rock sugar. Marinate for 30 minutes. Place the bowl of marinated pork in a steamer. Cover and steam for 1 hour. Remove and cool in the refrigerator.

Coarsely grate the carrots and radishes into a colander, rub in the salt and let stand for 10 minutes. Rinse under cold water, drain and dry. Put the grated carrots and radishes in a bowl and mix in the sugar, vinegar and sesame oil.

When the pork is quite cold and solid, break the eggs into a bowl, whisk lightly and dip each piece of pork in the egg. Roll the pieces of pork in the breadcrumbs until completely covered. Heat the vegetable oil and deep-fry the pork in a wire basket (6 pieces at a time) for 3 minutes, or until golden. Cut each slice of pork into 3 pieces.

Arrange the grated radishes and carrots in a mound in the middle of a serving plate. Place the pieces of pork around and serve.

# PIG'S KIDNEYS IN SESAME JAM

4 pig's kidneys
1½ teaspoons salt
2 tablespoons dry sherry
2 oz/50 g sesame jam
1 teaspoon sugar

½ teaspoon monosodium glutamate (optional)
2 tablespoons water
1 lettuce

Remove the skins and discard the cores from the kidneys. Cut each one in half and cut again into paper-thin slices. Place in a bowl and marinate for 30 minutes in half the salt and the sherry.

Mix together the remaining salt, sesame jam, sugar, monosodium glutamate and water. Place the sliced kidneys with the marinade in a large frying pan and cover with boiling water. Separate the slices carefully. Simmer for 2–3 minutes. By this time the slices of kidney will curl up and should be just cooked.

Arrange the lettuce leaves on a large round serving plate. Place the sliced kidney on top of the lettuce and then pour the sesame jam mixture evenly over the kidney slices. Use prepared mustard as a dip.

# KUNG-PO HOT-FRIED KIDNEYS

12 oz/350 g pig's kidneys
1½ tablespoons cornflour
1 tablespoon water
1½ tablespoons dry sherry
½ teaspoon salt
1 tablespoon sugar
1 tablespoon vinegar
1 tablespoon soya sauce
½ teaspoon monosodium glutamate (optional)

2 tablespoons superior broth (see page 262)
3 spring onions
1 dried chilli
1 small leek
4–5 tablespoons vegetable oil
2 cloves garlic
3 slices fresh root ginger
¼ teaspoon chilli powder
pepper

Remove the skins and discard the cores from the kidneys. Cut each one in half. Slash with crisscross cuts ¼ inch (5 mm) apart and two-thirds through the kidney. Cut into 1- by ¾-inch (2·5- by 1·5-cm) pieces. Blend half the cornflour with the water, sherry and salt. Thoroughly coat the kidney pieces in this mixture. In a separate bowl, mix the sugar, vinegar, soya sauce, monosodium glutamate and broth. Set aside. Cut the spring onions into ½-inch (1-cm) pieces. Remove the seeds from the dried chilli. Cut the leek into ½-inch (1-cm) pieces.

Heat the oil in a frying pan until very hot. Add the kidney, spreading the pieces evenly, sauté for 4-5 minutes and then drain. Drain off the excess oil. In the same pan, sauté the dried chilli for 1 minute and discard. Crush the garlic, then stir-fry the spring onions, leek, garlic, ginger and chilli powder for 20 seconds. Add the kidney pieces and stir-fry for 10 seconds. Then gradually add the vinegar mixture to the pan. Stir-fry the kidneys gently for 15 seconds. Add pepper to taste and serve immediately.

# SPARE RIBS BRAISED IN FRUIT JUICE

2 lb/1 kg meaty pork spare ribs
2 tablespoons finely chopped leeks
1 teaspoon salt
2 teaspoons sugar
1½ tablespoons light-coloured soya sauce
½ teaspoon monosodium glutamate (optional)
1 tablespoon cornflour

3 tablespoons vegetable oil
2 tablespoons chopped onion
1 tablespoon apple juice
1 tablespoon orange juice
1 tablespoon tomato purée
4 tablespoons secondary broth (see page 262)
2 tablespoons dry sherry

Separate each rib and chop across the bone into 1-inch (2·5-cm) lengths or leave whole. Combine the leeks with the salt, sugar, soya sauce and monosodium glutamate in a bowl. Add the spare ribs and marinate for 30 minutes. Dust with cornflour and mix well.

Heat the oil in a frying pan, add the ribs and stir-fry gently for 25 minutes, or until golden. Drain off the excess oil and set the ribs aside.

Sauté the onion for 1 minute in the oil remaining in the pan. Add the spare ribs. Pour in the apple juice, orange juice, tomato purée, broth and sherry. Stir-fry for 1 minute. Cover the pan and cook for 5–6 minutes, or until the liquid has largely evaporated. Serve on a heated dish.

# SCRAMBLE-FRIED SLICED LAMB

8 oz/225 g leg of lamb
1 tablespoon cornflour
1 tablespoon water
10 spring onions
3 cloves garlic
4 tablespoons vegetable oil

1 tablespoon soya sauce
½ teaspoon salt
1 tablespoon dry sherry
½ teaspoon monosodium glutamate (optional)
1 teaspoon sesame oil

Cut the lamb across the grain into thin slices 2 inches by 1 inch (5 by 2·5 cm). Blend the cornflour with the water and mix evenly with the meat. Cut the spring onions diagonally into 2-inch (5-cm) segments (using the green parts as well as the white). Peel and crush the garlic.

Heat half the oil in a large frying pan over medium heat. When very hot, pour in the meat mixture and spread it evenly over the bottom of the pan. Stir-fry gently for 2 minutes. Remove the meat and set aside. Add the remaining oil to the pan and sauté the spring onions and garlic for 2 minutes. Return the lamb to the pan and add the soya sauce, salt, sherry and monosodium glutamate. Turn the heat to high and scramble-fry for 1 minute. Just before serving, add the sesame oil.

Since this is a mixed, scrambled dish, no garnishing is required. It should be carefully poured out on to a heated dish and served immediately.

# BEAN SPROUTS WITH SHREDDED PORK

4 oz/100 g lean pork
1 clove garlic
6 spring onions
2 tablespoons vegetable oil
1 tablespoon soya sauce

2 teaspoons sugar
1 tablespoon dry sherry
1½ lb/700 g bean sprouts
1 teaspoon salt

Cut the pork across the grain into matchstick-thin strips. Peel and crush the garlic and cut the spring onions into 1½-inch (3·5-cm) segments. Heat the oil in a large frying pan. Add the pork and sauté over high heat for 30 seconds. Add the soya sauce, sugar and sherry. Stir-fry for 1 minute. Remove the meat and set aside to drain.

Add the garlic and spring onions to the pan and stir-fry for 15 seconds. Add the bean sprouts and sprinkle with the salt. Stir-fry and scramble for 1 minute, keeping the pan over high heat. Replace the pork in the pan. After 1 minute of stir-frying, transfer to a heated dish and serve.

*Note:* Shredded meat dishes, when freshly and carefully served, rarely need any further garnish. The meat, sugar and soya sauce provide the necessary savouriness.

# YELLOW 'FLOWER' MEAT

4 eggs
½ teaspoon salt
4 oz/100 g lean pork
8 dried Chinese mushrooms, soaked and drained
3 spring onions
4 tablespoons vegetable oil
1 tablespoon soya sauce

2 tablespoons broth (superior or secondary, see page 262)
½ teaspoon monosodium glutamate (optional)
1 teaspoon sugar
1 tablespoon dry sherry
1 teaspoon sesame oil

Whisk the eggs in a bowl for a few seconds and add the salt. Shred the pork into matchstick-thin strips. Cut the mushrooms into thin strips or small pieces. Cut the spring onions into very thin slices. Heat half the oil in a frying pan and add the beaten egg. Lower the heat (so that none of the egg will burn) and just before the egg sets completely, scramble slightly, remove the egg from the pan, and set aside.

Add the remaining oil to the pan and place over high heat. Add the pork, mushrooms and spring onions. Sauté for 2 minutes, then add the soya sauce, broth, monosodium glutamate and sugar. Cook for a further 30–40 seconds. Add the scrambled egg, sherry and sesame oil. Stir gently to mix all the ingredients. Serve on a heated dish.

*Bean sprouts with shredded pork*

*Cannon-cracker chicken*

# CANNON-CRACKER CHICKEN

| | |
|---|---|
| 1 chicken breast | 1½ teaspoons chopped fresh root |
| 8 oz/225 g belly of pork (fat part | ginger |
| without skin) | 2 slices cooked ham |
| 1 tablespoon soya sauce | 1 bunch chives (see recipe) |
| ½ teaspoon salt | 2 eggs |
| 1½ teaspoons sugar | 1 tablespoon cornflour |
| 1 tablespoon chopped onion | vegetable oil for deep-frying |
| | 1 teaspoon sesame oil |

Cut the chicken into small thin slices. Cut the pork into thin slices about 3 by 2 inches (7·5 by 5 cm). Lay the slices of pork on a large plate or tray. Brush with the soya sauce and sprinkle with the salt, sugar, onion and ginger. Lay a piece of chicken on top of each piece of pork. Cut the ham into strips and place a strip in the centre of each piece of chicken. Roll up, wrapping the ham and chicken inside. Tie each roll securely with 2 of the chives (if unavailable, secure with a wooden cocktail stick).

Whisk the eggs and mix with the cornflour to make a thin batter. Dip each pork-chicken roll lightly into the batter. Deep-fry the rolls in hot oil for 5–6 minutes. Drain, remove the cocktail sticks if used, and arrange on a heated dish in an attractive pattern. Sprinkle with the sesame oil and serve. A suitable dip for this dish is a salt-pepper mix.

# SOOCHOW MELON CHICKEN

| | |
|---|---|
| 1 young chicken, about 1½ lb/700 g | 4 slices fresh root ginger |
| 2 pints/generous litre water | 1½ teaspoons salt |
| 1 oz/25 g cooked ham | 2 tablespoons dry sherry |
| 1½ oz/40 g bamboo shoots | 1 large honeydew melon |
| 8 dried Chinese mushrooms, | 1 teaspoon monosodium |
| soaked and drained | glutamate (optional) |

Boil the chicken in the water for 2 minutes. Remove the chicken and rinse in fresh water. Skim the broth. Thinly slice the ham and bamboo shoots, cut the mushrooms into strips and marinate in one-third of the broth with the ginger, salt and sherry. Return the chicken to the remaining broth. Place in a steamer, cover and steam for 1 hour.

Cut a lid off the melon and set aside. Carefully scoop out the melon, leaving the wall at least ½ inch (1 cm) thick. Reserve half the scooped-out melon.

Place the melon shell in a large bowl and fit the steamed chicken inside it, breast uppermost. Arrange the ham, bamboo shoots and mushrooms on the chicken. Slip pieces of the melon flesh down the sides around the chicken. Add the monosodium glutamate to the marinade and carefully pour this into the melon. Replace the lid of the melon and secure it with 3 wooden cocktail sticks. Place the bowl in a steamer, cover and steam for 20 minutes. Remove the bowl from the steamer and bring it to the table. Lift off the melon lid and serve the chicken from the melon shell.

# PEPPERED CHICKEN

1 chicken, about 2–2¼ lb/1 kg
6 spring onions
2 slices fresh root ginger
1 tablespoon soya sauce
1 tablespoon vinegar
1 teaspoon salt
1½ tablespoons sesame oil
2 teaspoons coarsely chopped
    dried red chillies

Plunge the chicken into boiling water to cover and simmer for 10 minutes. Chop into pieces about 1 by ½ inch (2·5 by 1 cm), including the bones. Arrange the pieces in a large ovenproof bowl, skin-side down. Cut the spring onions into ½-inch (1-cm) pieces. Add the spring onions and ginger to the chicken. Mix the soya sauce, vinegar and salt in a bowl.

Heat the sesame oil in a small frying pan and sauté the chillies in it for 2–3 minutes. Discard the chillies and pour the oil evenly over the chicken in the ovenproof bowl. Then pour the soya sauce mixture over the chicken. Place in a steamer, cover and steam for 30–35 minutes. Serve the chicken on a large heated serving dish.

# RED-BRAISED CHICKEN

1 chicken, about 3 lb/1·5 kg
2½ oz/65 g winter bamboo shoots
2 spring onions
1 oz/25 g lard
2 teaspoons chopped fresh root
    ginger
2 tablespoons red wine-sediment
    paste
1 tablespoon sugar
2 tablespoons light-coloured soya
    sauce
2 tablespoons dry sherry
scant ½ pint/2·5 dl chicken broth
1 teaspoon monosodium
    glutamate (optional)
2 teaspoons sesame oil

Chop the chicken into pieces 1 inch by 1½ inches (2·5 by 3·5 cm). Cut the bamboo shoots into similar-sized pieces and the white parts of the spring onions into 1-inch (2·5-cm) segments. Heat the lard in a large frying pan over high heat. Add the spring onions, ginger and red wine-sediment paste and stir-fry for 1 minute. Add the chicken pieces and bamboo shoots and continue to stir-fry for 1 minute. Add the sugar, soya sauce and sherry and continue stir-frying for 1 minute. Finally, pour in the broth. Bring to the boil and reduce the heat to low. Simmer for 35 minutes.

Lift the bamboo shoots out first and place in the bottom of a heated deep serving dish. Arrange the pieces of chicken on top. Strain the liquid from the pan and add the monosodium glutamate and sesame oil. Bring to the boil and pour over the chicken before serving.

# QUICK-FRIED CHICKEN

2 large chicken breasts
1 small red sweet pepper
2 oz/50 g bamboo shoots
1 spring onion
½ tablespoon coarsely chopped
    dried chillies
1 teaspoon salt
1 egg
1 tablespoon cornflour
3 tablespoons vegetable oil
1 oz/25 g lard
4 tablespoons chicken broth
1 tablespoon dry sherry
½ teaspoon monosodium
    glutamate (optional)
1 tablespoon light-coloured soya
    sauce
1 teaspoon sesame oil

Cut the chicken breasts into ¼-inch (5-mm) cubes. Trim the sweet pepper and remove the seeds. Cut the bamboo shoots and the sweet pepper into similar-sized pieces. Slice the spring onion into ¼-inch (5-mm) pieces.

Place the diced chicken in a bowl. Add the salt and rub it into the chicken. Break the egg into the bowl and mix well. Then blend in the cornflour. Heat the vegetable oil in a large frying pan. When quite hot, add the chicken and stir-fry for 1½ minutes. Remove the chicken and drain off any remaining oil. Add the lard to the pan. Stir-fry the bamboo shoots, sweet pepper, spring onion and chillies over high heat for 2 minutes. Mix the chicken broth with the sherry and add with the monosodium glutamate, soya sauce and sesame oil. Stir-fry gently for 30 seconds. Add the pieces of chicken and continue to stir-fry for another 30 seconds. Transfer to a heated dish and serve.

# STRANGE-FLAVOUR CHICKEN

6–8 chicken drumsticks (about
    1½ lb/700 g)
1 oz/25 g sesame seeds
1½ teaspoons sesame oil
1½ tablespoons soya sauce
2 teaspoons sugar
1 tablespoon vinegar
1 teaspoon chilli sauce
¼ teaspoon black pepper
6–8 spring onions

Cook the drumsticks in boiling water to cover for 20 minutes, allowing 5 minutes boiling and 15 minutes simmering time. Drain and cool for 10 minutes. Remove the bones from the drumsticks and slice each drumstick diagonally into 4 pieces.

Stir-fry the sesame seeds gently in a dry pan over very low heat until they are just turning golden and beginning to crackle. Place a third of these seeds in a dry bowl and pound the remaining two-thirds to a powder in a mortar, adding the sesame oil to make a sesame paste. Mix this paste with the soya sauce, sugar, vinegar, chilli sauce and pepper. Chop the white parts of the spring onions (reserving the green parts for another dish) and pile them in the centre of a heated serving dish. Arrange the pieces of chicken around the edge by overlapping them, skin-side out. Pour the sesame paste mixture evenly over the chicken and sprinkle the crispy, dry sesame seeds on top before serving.

# CANTONESE CRYSTAL CHICKEN

1 chicken, about 2–3 lb/1–1·5 kg
4 oz/100 g cooked ham
½ oz/15 g gelatine
1 teaspoon salt
1 teaspoon monosodium
  glutamate (optional)

3 tablespoons dry sherry
1½ pints/9 dl superior broth (see
  page 262)
red and green sweet peppers for
  garnishing

Clean the chicken thoroughly and dry. Place in a saucepan, cover with water, bring to the boil and simmer for 1 hour. Drain the chicken and, when cool, chop into 24 pieces. Cut the ham into similar sized pieces. Arrange the pieces of chicken and ham, interlaced in roof-tile fashion, in an oval dish.

Dissolve the gelatine in a little warm broth. Place the salt, monosodium glutamate, sherry, gelatine and broth in a saucepan and heat, stirring until the ingredients are well mixed. Cool for 15 minutes and then pour over the chicken. Place the dish in the refrigerator for 2 hours. After 2 hours, the jellied chicken and ham should have set. Turn out on to a plate. Trim the red and green sweet peppers, remove the seeds and cut into strips. Arrange around the jellied chicken as a colourful garnish.

# HOT DICED CHICKEN IN CHOPPED PEANUTS

3 large chicken breasts
1 tablespoon cornflour
1 egg
1½ oz/40 g peanuts
2 spring onions
1 tablespoon water
1½ teaspoons sugar

2 teaspoons vinegar
1½ teaspoons soya sauce
½ teaspoon salt
vegetable oil for deep-frying
4 teaspoons coarsely chopped
  dried chillies
1 oz/25 g lard

Dice the chicken. Mix in a bowl half the cornflour and the egg. Stir in the chicken. Chop the peanuts coarsely. Chop the spring onions into ½-inch (1-cm) segments and combine with the remainder of the cornflour blended with the water, sugar, vinegar, soya sauce and salt in a bowl. Deep-fry the diced chicken in the hot oil for 30 seconds. Drain and set aside. Discard the seeds from the chillies. Sauté in the lard for 30 seconds. Add the chicken and stir-fry for 10 seconds. Pour in the spring onion mixture and continue to stir-fry for 20 seconds. Sprinkle in the peanuts. After a few stirs, pour on to a heated serving dish.

*Cantonese crystal chicken*

# CANTONESE 'CRACKLING' CHICKEN

1 chicken, about 2–3 lb/1–1·5 kg
2 tablespoons honey
1 tablespoon cornflour
1 tablespoon soya sauce
vegetable oil for deep-frying

Clean the chicken thoroughly, then dip in boiling water for 2 seconds. Dry with a piece of cloth or kitchen paper. Dry for 5–6 hours (or overnight) in a cool, well-ventilated place.

Mix the honey, cornflour and soya sauce in a bowl. Rub the chicken with the mixture. Heat the oil for deep-frying and suspend the chicken over the pan in a wire basket. Baste it evenly with a long-handled ladle until golden all over. The total time required for cooking in this manner is about 30–40 minutes. When well-cooked, the skin of the chicken should be crispy.

Chop the chicken into 10 to 12 pieces and serve on a heated flat plate. Accompany with dips of plum sauce or haisein sauce.

# PEKING DUCK

1 duck, about 4–6 lb/1·75–2·75 kg
2 tablespoons sugar
1 tablespoon dry sherry
2 tablespoons water
pinch salt
30 doilies (see below)
15 spring onions or 1 cucumber

**for the garlic-vinegar dip:**
6 cloves garlic
6 tablespoons vinegar
**for the mustard-soya sauce dip:**
1 teaspoon dry mustard
2 tablespoons soya sauce
**for the chilli-soya sauce dip:**
1 tablespoon chilli sauce
3 tablespoons soya sauce

Clean the duck thoroughly and lower it momentarily into a pan of boiling water to scald. Dry immediately with kitchen paper and hang by the feet to dry overnight in a cool, airy place.

Mix together the sugar, sherry and water, adding the salt to help the sugar dissolve. Rub the outside of the duck with this sweetened water several hours before roasting. Hang to dry again. When dry, rub the duck a second time with the sweetened water.

Place the duck in a moderately hot oven (375°F, 190°C, Gas Mark 5) on a rack with a pan underneath to catch the drips. Roast for 20 minutes, then lower the temperature to 300°F (150°C, Gas Mark 2) for 1 hour. Finally, raise the temperature to 400°F (200°C, Gas Mark 6) for 20 minutes. The duck should then be well cooked and the skin very crispy.

While the duck is cooking, prepare the doilies according to the instructions given below, using double the quantities listed. Chop the spring onions into segments 2 inches (5 cm) long. If using the cucumber, peel and cut into thin strips about 2 inches (5 cm) long. For the garlic-vinegar dip, peel and crush the cloves of garlic and mix with the vinegar.

For the mustard-soya sauce dip, combine the dry mustard with the soya sauce.

For the chilli-soya sauce dip, combine the chilli sauce with the soya sauce. Plum sauce and haisein sauce are also traditionally served with the dish.

The duck is carved at the dining table. At the first carving, only the skin is sliced off. To eat, dip 1 or 2 pieces of the skin in a sauce and place in the middle of a doily. Top with a piece of spring onion or a strip of cucumber, fold over one end of the doily and roll up. Eat with the fingers while the duck skin is still crackling and warm.

Repeat the process until all the sliceable meat has been carved from the duck and each person has packed and eaten 3–6 doily rolls of duck skin and duck meat.

# DOILIES (THIN CAKES)

*Makes about 18*
6 oz/175 g plain flour
¼ pint/1·5 dl boiling water
2 tablespoons sesame oil

Place the flour in a bowl. Pour in the boiling water very slowly and gradually work to a warm dough. Knead gently for 1–2 minutes, then let stand for 10 minutes. Shape the dough into a roll 2 inches (5 cm) in diameter. Cut the roll into ½-inch (1-cm) thick slices. Brush one side of each slice with sesame oil and lay another slice on top of it with the oiled surfaces together like a sandwich. Roll the double piece out from the centre on a lightly floured working surface until it spreads out to a pancake with a diameter of about 5 inches (13 cm). Make as many pancakes as the dough allows. Heat a large, flat, heavy, ungreased frying pan or omelette pan over low heat. When quite hot, place a pancake in the pan. Rotate the pan above the heat every so often so the cooking is even. When the pancake starts to bubble, turn it over. After 2–3 minutes of heating on each side, pull each double piece of dough apart into separate slices. Fold each piece into a half circle on the side brushed with sesame oil. Pile the doilies on a plate and place in a steamer for 10 minutes. Bring to the table immediately for wrapping up pieces of duck.

# QUICK-FRIED RIBBON OF DUCK

12 oz/350 g cooked or smoked duck
2–3 sticks celery
1 small leek
1 red sweet pepper
2 teaspoons coarsely chopped dried chillies
2 cloves garlic
2 oz/50 g lard
1 tablespoon fermented black beans, soaked for 1 hour
1½ teaspoons sugar
1 tablespoon soya sauce
1 tablespoon vinegar

Slice the duck into matchstick-thin strips. Trim the celery and leek and cut into similar-sized strips. Remove the seeds from the red pepper and chillies. Cut the red pepper into thin strips. Peel and crush the garlic. Heat the lard in a frying pan. Sauté the chillies for 1 minute to flavour the lard then discard the chillies. Add the celery, leek, garlic, sweet pepper and black beans. Stir-fry over high heat for 1 minute. Add the duck, sugar and soya sauce. Continue to stir-fry for 1 minute. Finally, add the vinegar and stir-fry quickly for 10 seconds.

# CHINESE RAVIOLI WITH PRAWN-PORK FILLING

for the Chinese swallow-skin
  ravioli:
2 lb/900 g plain flour
½ teaspoon salt
1½ pints/9 dl boiling water
1 oz/25 g lard
for the filling:
8 oz/225 g cooked prawns, peeled
  and deveined
1 oz/25 g fat pork

2 oz/50 g lean pork
4 oz/100 g bamboo shoots
1 teaspoon salt
½ tablespoon soya sauce
1 tablespoon dry sherry
½ teaspoon dry mustard
½ tablespoon sesame oil
1 teaspoon sugar
pepper

To make the swallow-skin dough, sift the flour into a bowl. Add the salt to the boiling water and pour into the flour. Stir quickly with a wooden spoon. Add the lard and knead well on a board. Divide the dough into 2 portions and shape each into a long roll. Cut each roll into 12 pieces. Form each piece into a ball and roll out to 2 inches (5 cm) in diameter.

For the filling, finely chop the prawns. Boil all the pork for 5 minutes, then chop finely. Cut the bamboo shoots into matchstick-thin strips and add to the prawns and pork in a bowl. Add the salt, soya sauce, sherry, mustard, oil, sugar and pepper to taste. Place in the refrigerator for 30 minutes.

Divide the filling into 24 portions. Place the filling on one side of the dough skin and fold the other side over. Pinch the round sides together in the shape of a cock's comb. Place the 24 pieces on a greased ovenproof plate in a steamer. Cover and steam for 7 minutes. Serve immediately. Mix equal portions of vinegar and soya sauce as a dip.

# T'UNG CHING VEGETARIAN NOODLES

3 tablespoons sesame paste
1 tablespoon sesame oil
2 tablespoons wine vinegar
1 teaspoon monosodium
  glutamate (optional)
1 tablespoon sugar
2 tablespoons soya sauce

1 teaspoon chilli sauce
pepper
1 lb/450 g Chinese noodles or
  spaghetti
2 tablespoons finely chopped
  spring onion tops
1 tablespoon finely chopped garlic

Mix together the sesame paste, sesame oil, vinegar, monosodium glutamate, sugar, soya sauce, chilli sauce and pepper to taste. Divide the mixture among 5 separate bowls.

Boil the noodles or spaghetti for 15–20 minutes. Drain, and while steaming hot divide into equal portions and place on top of the mixture in the 5 bowls. Sprinkle the noodles with the spring onion tops and garlic. Each diner may then toss and mix the noodles or spaghetti with the ingredients and seasonings according to taste.

*Peking duck – a world-famous dish*
*(see page 279)*

# TOSS-FRIED RICE NOODLES

1½ lb/700 g rice stick noodles
8 oz/225 g lean pork
1½ oz/40 g dried Chinese
  mushrooms, soaked and
  drained
2 oz/50 g bamboo shoots
½ stick celery
1 small leek

2 cloves garlic
2 oz/50 g lard
2 tablespoons soya sauce
¼ pint/1·5 dl chicken or superior
  broth (see page 262)
1 teaspoon monosodium
  glutamate (optional)

Place the noodles in a saucepan of boiling water and boil gently for 5–10 minutes, or until soft and cooked. Drain and cool under cold running water and set aside.

Slice the pork, mushrooms, bamboo shoots, celery and leek into matchstick-thin strips. Peel and crush the garlic.

Heat three-quarters of the lard in a frying pan over high heat. Add the pork and bamboo shoots and stir-fry for 30 seconds. Then add the mushrooms, leek and garlic. Fry for 1 minute. Add the celery, soya sauce, broth and monosodium glutamate. Simmer for 2 minutes. Remove from the heat and pour the contents of the pan into a bowl.

Add the remaining lard to the pan. Place over medium heat for 30 seconds then add the cooked noodles. Stir-fry gently for 3 minutes. Add half the pork mixture and all its liquid. Continue to stir-fry for 2 minutes. By this time, the noodles should have absorbed all the liquid. Turn the contents on to a large, flat, heated serving dish. Heat the remaining pork mixture in the pan over high heat for 1 minute and use as a hot garnish or topping for the noodles.

# MEAT-FILLED MUSHROOMS

30 large Chinese dried mushrooms
4 oz/100 g lean pork
1 oz/25 g cooked ham
1 egg
1 tablespoon chopped onion
1 tablespoon ground dried
  shrimps
1 tablespoon cornflour

1 tablespoon soya sauce
½ teaspoon salt
for the sauce:
¼ pint/1·5 dl chicken broth
2 teaspoons cornflour
½ teaspoon monosodium
  glutamate (optional)
½ oz/15 g lard

Remove the stalks from the mushrooms. Soak the mushroom caps in warm water for 30 minutes. Mince the pork and ham and mix in a bowl with the egg, onion, shrimps, cornflour, half the soya sauce and half the salt. Spread the mixture over the inside of 15 of the mushroom caps and cover each one with a second mushroom cap. Put a board over them and press gently to flatten, keeping the insides of the caps together sandwich-style. Arrange these 'sandwiches' on a large plate. Place in a steamer, cover and steam for 20 minutes.

Meanwhile, prepare a sauce by mixing the remaining soya sauce, salt and chicken broth with the cornflour and monosodium glutamate. Bring to the boil and add the lard. Pour the sauce over the mushrooms and serve immediately.

# SPINACH BALLS

4 oz/100 g cooked fat pork
8 oz/225 g cooked lean pork
3 eggs
1 teaspoon chopped fresh root
  ginger
1½ tablespoons chopped onion
6 tablespoons water
1 tablespoon cornflour
½ teaspoon monosodium
  glutamate (optional)
1 teaspoon salt
pepper
2 lb/1 kg spinach
1 oz/25 g dried Chinese
  mushrooms, soaked and
  drained
2 oz/50 g bamboo shoots
1 oz/25 g cooked ham
½ pint/3 dl superior broth (see
  page 262)
1 teaspoon sesame oil

Finely mince the fat and lean pork and mix together in a bowl. Whisk the eggs for 1 minute and then mix well into the pork. Boil the ginger, onion and water in a saucepan. Remove from the heat and let stand for 6 minutes. Strain, discard the ginger and onion and pour the water into the pork mixture. Add the cornflour, half the monosodium glutamate, half the salt and pepper to taste. Beat the mixture for 1 minute. Form into small meat balls.

Wash the spinach, remove the stalks and add to a large saucepan of boiling water for a 10-second dip. Drain well and slice into matchstick-thin strips. Slice the mushrooms, bamboo shoots and ham into similar sized strips, mix together with the spinach strips and spread on a tray. Roll the meat balls over this to pick up the various coloured strips. Place on an ovenproof plate, cover and steam for 8 minutes.

Arrange the remaining spinach, mushrooms, bamboo shoots and ham in the bottom of a heated deep casserole. Place the meat balls on top. Meanwhile, make a sauce with the broth by adding the remaining monosodium glutamate, remaining salt and pepper to taste. Heat and pour over the meat balls. Sprinkle with sesame oil and serve.

# VEGETABLE RICE

1½ lb/700 g long-grain rice
1½ lb/700 g spring greens
1 oz/25 g lard
2 teaspoons salt
1 pint/6 dl cold water
¼ pint/1·5 dl boiling water

Wash the rice and let it soak in cold water for 3 hours. Wash the greens and discard the coarser outer leaves and stalks. Cut the leaves into 1-inch (2·5-cm) squares.

Heat the lard in a large heavy saucepan. When very hot, add the greens. Reduce the heat and stir-fry gently for 3 minutes, then add the salt and the cold water. Turn the heat to high. When the water starts to boil, add the rice. Continue to stir gently with a wooden spoon until the water reboils. Then lower the heat and cover tightly. When the water has nearly all been absorbed by the rice (after about 10–12 minutes), pour in the boiling water. Poke 4 holes through the rice to the bottom of the pan to facilitate steaming. Cover firmly and insert an asbestos mat underneath the pan. After 5 minutes, remove the pan from the

*Spinach balls*

heat. Allow the rice to steam in its own heat for 10 minutes. The vegetable rice should then be ready.

# LOTUS LEAF-WRAPPED RICE

| | |
|---|---|
| 1 lb/450 g short-grain rice | 1 egg |
| 2 teaspoons soya sauce | 4 oz/100 g peeled, cooked prawns |
| 1½ teaspoons salt | or crab meat |
| 1 teaspoon monosodium | 1 teaspoon sugar |
| glutamate (optional) | 2 teaspoons oyster sauce |
| 1 pint/6 dl water | ¼ pint/1·5 dl secondary broth (see |
| 3 oz/75 g lard | page 262) |
| 4 oz/100 g roast pork | 1 tablespoon cornflour |
| 2 oz/50 g dried Chinese | 2 tablespoons water |
| mushrooms, soaked and | 2 teaspoons dry sherry |
| drained | 6 large lotus leaves |

Wash the rice and place in a metal or ovenproof dish. Add the soya sauce, 1 teaspoon salt, half the monosodium glutamate and the water. Place in a steamer, cover and steam for 20–25 minutes until the rice is cooked. Stir in one-third of the lard. Set aside.

For the filling, cut the roast pork into ¼-inch (5-mm) cubes and dice the soaked mushrooms. Whisk the egg and make a thin omelette by cooking the egg in another third of the lard. Cut into ½-inch (1-cm) squares.

Heat the remaining lard in a frying pan. Add the remaining salt, pork, mushrooms, egg squares and prawns. Stir-fry for 20 seconds. Add the remaining monosodium glutamate, the sugar, oyster sauce and broth. When the mixture boils, stir in the cornflour blended with the water. Stir and cook for 2 minutes. Then add the sherry. Pour half of this mixture into the rice and stir. Set aside the remaining filling.

After blanching the lotus leaves quickly in boiling water, spread them out on the table. Divide the filling and the rice into 6 equal portions. On one side of the centre of each leaf place a portion of filling and over it a portion of rice. Wrap the leaf in envelope fashion and make it into a 'parcel', about 2 by 2½ inches (5 by 6 cm). Place in a steamer, cover and steam for 15–18 minutes. Pile the steaming 'parcels' on a heated plate and serve.

*Vegetable rice*

283

# SOUR AND SWEET CHINESE CABBAGE

| | |
|---|---|
| 2–3 lb/1–1·5 kg Chinese cabbage (or use a crinkly leaf type of Savoy cabbage) | 1 tablespoon dry sherry |
| | 2 dried chillies |
| 1 tablespoon cornflour | 3 tablespoons vegetable oil |
| 1 tablespoon water | 1 teaspoon salt |
| 3 tablespoons vinegar | 3 tablespoons secondary broth (see page 262) |
| 1 tablespoon soya sauce | |
| 1 tablespoon sugar | ½ teaspoon monosodium glutamate (optional) |

Discard the coarse outer leaves of the cabbage. Cut off the bottom and cut the heart and inner leaves diagonally into 1½-inch (3·5-cm) long strips. In a bowl, mix the cornflour, water, vinegar, soya sauce, sugar and sherry.

Sauté the chillies in the oil in a large frying pan for 1 minute then discard the chillies. Add the cabbage and stir-fry over high heat for 3 minutes. Add the salt, broth and monosodium glutamate. Continue to stir-fry for 5 more minutes over medium heat. Add the cornflour mixture and mix well with the cabbage. Stir-fry gently for 1 minute. Serve in a heated dish.

# RIOT OF SPRING

| | |
|---|---|
| 5 lb/2·25 kg cabbages (compact, with firm hearts) | 1 teaspoon cornflour |
| | ¾ pint/4·5 dl chicken broth |
| 1 chicken breast | 1 teaspoon salt |
| 1 thin slice cooked ham | 1 teaspoon monosodium glutamate (optional) |
| 1 oz/25 g winter bamboo shoots | |
| 8 dried Chinese mushrooms, soaked and drained | 1 tablespoon chicken fat |
| | vegetable oil for deep-frying |
| 1 egg white | 1 tablespoon dry sherry |

Cut off the stalks of the cabbages. Remove and discard the outer leaves until each heart stands out like an upstanding, firm green bud. Cut the chicken breast into thin slices 1 by ½ inch (2·5 by 1 cm). Slice the ham and bamboo shoots in the same manner. Cut the mushrooms into ¼-inch (5-mm) wide strips. Mix the egg white and cornflour in a bowl and dip the sliced chicken in it.

Bring the chicken broth to the boil in a large saucepan. Add half the salt, half the monosodium glutamate and half the chicken fat. Place the cabbages in this mixture and boil for about 1–1½ minutes.

Remove the cabbages and arrange the leaves to line the sides of a deep casserole, reserving the hearts. Use these to pack the middle with 3 or 4 layers of tender leaves. Deep-fry the chicken slices for 45 seconds. Arrange the chicken, ham, bamboo shoots and mushrooms in concentric rings on top of the layers of green leaves. Pour in the broth and dot with the remaining chicken fat. Sprinkle with the remaining salt and monosodium glutamate and the sherry. Place in a steamer, cover and steam for 25 minutes. Serve in the casserole.

# DRAWN-THREAD HONEYED APPLES

| | |
|---|---|
| 2 lb/1 kg apples | 4 tablespoons sugar |
| 1 egg | 2 tablespoons vegetable oil |
| 2 tablespoons plain flour | 3 tablespoons water |
| vegetable oil for deep-frying | 3 tablespoons golden syrup |

Peel and core the apples. Cut into potato chip-shaped pieces, 1½ inches by ½ inch (3·5 by 1 cm). Whisk the egg. Dip the apple pieces in the egg and dredge with flour. Deep-fry in hot oil for 2½ minutes, then drain. Heat the sugar and 2 tablespoons of oil in a flameproof dish. When the sugar has melted, add the water and then the golden syrup. Continue to stir gently over the heat until the liquid has become golden. Add the apple pieces to the hot syrup, turning the pieces over so they are well coated, and bring to the table in the cooking dish.

Each diner should be provided with a bowl of water with ice floating in it. Using chopsticks, a piece of apple should be taken from the dish and plunged into the water. The coating syrup will instantly cool into a brittle hardness. After the dipping, the apple should be placed in a saucer to cool for a few moments before eating. In the process of dipping, the apple should not be left for any length of time in the water or it will become sodden.

*Note:* This recipe can be applied with equal success to bananas, pears, oranges, pineapple or other fruit.

# ICE-MOUNTAIN FRUIT SALAD

| | |
|---|---|
| 1 lb/450 g apples | 1 lb/450 g strawberries |
| 1 lb/450 g pears | 1 lb/450 g grapes |
| 1 lb/450 g peaches | 8 oz/225 g water chestnuts |
| 1 honeydew melon | 1 small pineapple |
| 1 lb/450 g cherries | crushed ice (see recipe) |

Peel the apples, pears and peaches. Cut into quarters and place in iced water (to prevent browning) while preparing the other fruits. Halve the melon, remove the seeds and cut the flesh into similar-sized pieces. Rinse and stone the cherries and hull the strawberries. Peel and halve the grapes and remove the pips. Slice the water chestnuts. Peel and slice the pineapple, removing the woody centre core.

Make a bed of crushed ice on a very large serving plate. Arrange the pieces of fruit on top in an artistic pattern, interspersing the fruits with larger chunks of ice. Alternatively, a raised mound of ice may be piled in the middle of the large serving plate to give the effect of a miniature ice-mountain. Decorate the ice-mountain with the fruit.

*Note:* Small saucers of sugar, or a mixture of sugar and ground ginger, may be used as dips.

*Drawn-thread honeyed apples*

# FAR EASTERN

Nina Froud

*Photography by John Lee*

All good cooking in the Far East originated in China and India. But although the influence of these two countries continues to dominate oriental cookery, individual countries have succeeded in developing their own characteristic styles of food preparation and presentation.

The staple food of the Indian sub-continent is a cereal crop of one sort or another. In the north, wheat is made into excellent bread; in the south the people are rice-eating and to a great extent vegetarian. But it is difficult to define the differences between Indian, Pakistani and Kashmiri food. Eating habits throughout the sub-continent are dictated by many factors, not least by religion and economics. Religious influence and foreign occupations have also left their mark on the cooking of Sri Lanka – 'The Isle of Spices'. The staple diet is rice with curried vegetables, fish or meat, and *sambals* (called *sambols* in Sri Lanka) as accompaniments.

Rice is the staple food of Burma and vegetables, salads, fish and shellfish are very popular. A fish dish is served at all main meals. A delightful feature of Burmese cooking is their lavish use of fragrant flowers in soups, salads and other dishes.

Thailand is perhaps the most exotic of the Far Eastern countries. Colourful boats poled along the network of canals bring to Bangkok markets the vast variety of Thailand's superb vegetables, herbs, spices and fruit. In Thailand, as in Japan, the same meticulous care is taken with the presentation as with the preparation of food.

Malaysia has vast areas of dense forest and jungle, inhabited by primitive peoples. Singapore is a complete contrast . . . it is the great melting pot of South East Asia. The Chinese form the biggest community, followed by the Malays, Indians, Pakistanis and Singhalese. All have contributed to the cuisine, but a Malay cook interprets a dish in his own way, such as adding red chillies and *blachan* to accompany Chinese fried rice or serving a hot *sambal* with a bland noodle dish.

Indonesia is made up of thousands of beautiful islands, the principal ones being Java, Bali, Sumatra, Borneo and Celebes. A reminder of the lengthy occupation of Java by the Dutch is the famous Indonesian speciality, *rijstafel*. It consists of a basic rice dish accompanied by up to 40 side dishes, including satays, *sambals*, pickles and chutneys.

As befits the inhabitants of a rugged highland country, the Koreans are hearty eaters. Not for them the dainty Japanese morsels or the sophistication of Chinese *haute cuisine*. Three essentials of a Korean menu are rice, soup and *keem chee* (pickles), with fresh fruit to end a meal.

Filipino cooking is subject to many influences. Restaurant menus may offer you at one and the same time a noodle or rice dish of unmistakable Chinese origin, a Spanish speciality and a typically American dessert. Fresh fruit is abundant and the coconut palm plays an important part in the cuisine.

Japanese food is a fascinating reflection of the Japanese approach to life and talent for artistic expression. The use of seasonings is restrained in order to preserve the natural flavour of the original ingredients. Their predilection for purity of taste accounts for their simplicity of garnishing. Another characteristic is the smallness of the servings.

All the countries of the Far East share one talent – the ability to transform familiar fish, meat, fowl and vegetables into exquisite and exotic dishes.

# GLOSSARY

**Blachan or Balachaung**
A salted fermented paste made of shrimps or prawns, spices and chillies, much used in Burmese and Malaysian cooking. Anchovy paste may be used as a substitute.

**Bombay Duck**
A dried fish, served as a side dish to curries and particularly popular in southern India. It is available in cans. Bombay duck should be baked or fried until crisp and then crumbled.

**Cinnamon Bark**
Or cinnamon stick. Both are the dried bark of the cinnamon tree. Cinnamon bark is rougher and more uneven in appearance than the smooth curls or sticks of cinnamon that come from the inner bark of the tree. Either can be used where called for in a recipe. Remove from the dish before serving.

**Coconut Cream or Milk**
Coconut milk of a thick consistency is usually referred to as coconut cream. The cream is the result of the first extraction of liquid from the coconut flesh. If the process is repeated and water added, the slightly thinner liquid is referred to as coconut milk. To prepare coconut cream, proceed as follows: Have the top sawn off the coconut. Discard the natural liquid found in the coconut – this should not be confused with coconut milk. Remove the flesh and grate coarsely. (About 3 oz/75 g desiccated coconut may be substituted for freshly grated coconut.) Pour over boiling milk or water to cover and leave to soak for 1½–2 hours. Squeeze out through a fine strainer two or three times to get as much thick cream as you can. To obtain the thinner coconut milk, repeat the process. Coconut cream is also available in packets or cans. When using this dissolve 2 oz (50 g) coconut cream in ¼ pint (1·5 dl) hot milk. This makes a thick mixture which may be diluted according to taste. Dishes containing coconut milk should not be allowed to boil after the addition of the coconut milk.

**Coconut Palm Heart**
The tender inner heart of the coconut palm, white and cylindrical in shape. It is available in cans.

**Curry Leaves**
The aromatic leaves of a small tree or shrub of the orange family, used in India and Ceylon for flavouring curries, hence the name. Both fresh and dried leaves are used.

**Dhal**
Several kinds of split peas, described according to their colour. The commonest *dhal* is the lentil or red *dhal*. Some *dhals*, particularly white *dhal*, are ground into flour. *Dhal* is widely used in the East, particularly in India. Various kinds are obtainable from Indian food shops.

**Fenugreek**
An aromatic herb used in many oriental dishes to impart flavour, but mainly used to thicken gravies. If not available, the best substitutes are cashew nuts or peanuts, lightly roasted and ground to a paste.

**Garam-masala**
Indian mixture of curry spices and an essential ingredient of curries. For 6 oz (175 g), grind together in a mortar or coffee grinder: 2 oz (50 g) coriander seeds, 2 oz (50 g) black peppercorns, 1½ oz (40 g) caraway seeds, ½ oz (15 g) whole cloves, 20 peeled cardamom seeds and ½ oz (15 g) ground cinnamon. The powder may be used immediately or stored in an airtight container.

**Ghee**
Clarified butter which is available in cans. To make *ghee*, melt butter over very low heat until it begins to look like olive oil and a whitish deposit begins to form on the bottom of the pan. Strain into a clean jar, removing the deposit.

**Gingko Nuts**
Used as a garnish in many Japanese dishes. The canned variety is ready for use. The dried nuts must be shelled and blanched first.

**Gula Malacca**
Unrefined palm sugar, also known as 'Malacca sweet' and 'jaggery'. Usually sold molded into round cakes. It can be grated, shredded or chopped as required in a recipe. Maple sugar or soft dark brown sugar may be used as a substitute.

**Harusame**
Japanese noodles made from soy bean powder.

**Jalebi Powder**
A yellow powder used in India for coloring and in particular for making *jalebis*. Readily available in Indian shops. If unobtainable, saffron or turmeric may be substituted.

**Kamaboko**
A fish paste or steamed loaf made of fish for forcemeat. Sold in Japanese shops in the form of small flat cakes.

**Lemon Grass or Lemon Leaf**
The aromatic stems and leaves of a plant cultivated in most tropical countries and used as a flavoring. Lemon balm may be used as a substitute.

**Mien Chiang**
Chinese bean paste, used widely in Chinese and Korean cooking. Available from Chinese food shops.

**Mirin**
A Japanese sweet wine fortified with *sake* used for flavoring soups and sauces. Sweet white wine or sherry may be used as a substitute.

**Nam Pla**
Thai fish paste, with a piquant fishy flavor. Available in shops specializing in oriental produce. For a substitute blend equal proportions of anchovy paste and soy sauce, and use as directed in the recipe.

**Nori**
An edible species of marine algae. Sold in Japanese food shops in dried sheets or square pieces. It should be heated, then crushed, and the crumbs sprinkled over prepared dishes. Particularly good with fish recipes.

**Poppadum**
Poppadums are crisp 'breads' made of red lentil flour flavored with black pepper, assafoetida and various spices, and served as an accompaniment to curry. Before serving, they should be fried very quickly in hot fat, one at a time. Poppadums are sold ready-made in Indian food shops.

**Sake**
A Japanese rice wine for drinking and for use as a flavoring. As a drink it is usually served hot. In recipes, dry sherry, and in certain cases brandy, may be used instead.

**Shoyu**
This is the Japanese name for soy bean sauce. A universal flavoring agent for which there is no substitute. It is made from wheat and soy beans, mixed with malt seed and allowed to ferment; then pressed and filtered. Both salt and monosodium glutamate enter into its composition.

**Shrimp, Dried**
Sold loose in oriental food shops.

**Shrimp Paste**
A preparation similar to dried shrimp powder.

**Shrimp Powder**
Dried shrimp ground into powder.

**Tamarind**
The fruit of the tamarind tree. The pods are filled with an acid pulp which is used in many Asian countries in preference to lemon juice or vinegar. For cooking purposes use dry tamarind which should be soaked long enough to make it pliable. Remove the fibers before using. To make tamarind juice proceed as follows: Soak the tamarind in water, using 1 oz dried tamarind for every ⅓ cup water. Remove the fibers and strain the juice through a cheesecloth. Use the juice as directed in the recipe. Tamarind should be used for dishes to be eaten the same day. As a substitute, fresh lime or lemon juice may be used.

**Tiger Lily Bulbs**
Available in Japanese food shops. Shallots could be used instead but they are not really a substitute.

# India, Pakistan, Kashmir, Sri Lanka

## MULLIGATAWNY

*Serves 4*

6 oz/175 g red *dhal*
2 large onions
1 bay leaf
1 pint/6 dl water
1 clove garlic
1 oz/25 g *ghee*

1 tablespoon *garam-masala*
2½ pints/1·25 litres stock (meat, chicken, fish or vegetable)
salt and pepper
5 tablespoons coconut cream
1 lemon

Rinse the *dhal* under cold running water and place in a bowl. Cover with cold water and set aside to soak for 1½–2 hours. Peel and slice one of the onions. Drain the *dhal* and place in a saucepan with the onion, bay leaf and water. Bring to the boil over moderate heat. Reduce the heat and simmer for about 1 hour, or until the *dhal* is soft. Press the mixture through a sieve, or reduce to a purée in a liquidiser.

Peel and chop the garlic and remaining onion. Heat the *ghee* in a saucepan and sauté the onion and garlic until soft but not browned. Add the *garam-masala* and cook for 2–3 minutes. Add the *dhal* purée and mix well. Stir in the stock and season to taste with salt and pepper. Increase the heat and bring the soup to the boil. Boil for 2–3 minutes. Remove from the heat and stir in the coconut cream. Pour the soup into a heated tureen and garnish with thin slices of lemon.

## FISH PILAU

*Serves 6*

1½ lb/700 g hake fillet
12 oz/350 g long-grain rice
1 large onion
2 oz/50 g *ghee*
1 teaspoon turmeric
½ teaspoon ground coriander
pinch chilli powder

1 teaspoon *garam-masala*
1 teaspoon salt
1 tablespoon lemon juice
1½ pints/9 dl hot water
8 oz/225 g fresh or frozen cooked prawns, peeled and deveined

Rinse the fish under cold running water and pat dry with kitchen paper. Cut into pieces about 2 inches by 1 inch (5 by 2·5 cm). Rinse the rice in a sieve, then cover with cold water in a bowl and set aside until required. Peel and chop the onion.

Heat half the *ghee* in a saucepan. Add the turmeric, coriander, chilli powder, *garam-masala* and salt. Cook for 2 minutes. Add the lemon juice and continue cooking over high heat, stirring constantly, until the excess liquid has evaporated. Add the fish and cook on both sides for 3 minutes, taking care not to break the pieces. Remove the fish from the pan and reserve. Drain the rice.

Heat the remaining *ghee* in the saucepan. Add the onion and sauté until soft. Add the rice and sauté for 2 minutes. Add the hot water and bring to the boil. Reduce the heat, cover and simmer for 20 minutes. Stir lightly and place the fish on top of the rice. Cover and simmer for 10 minutes. Garnish with the prawns, cover and leave over very low heat for 2–3 minutes. Serve immediately.

*Mulligatawny*

# COD IN ALMOND AND YOGHURT SAUCE

*Serves 4*

2 lb/1 kg cod fillet
1 teaspoon turmeric
1 teaspoon salt
pinch white pepper
4 medium-sized onions
2 oz/50 g butter

1 piece cinnamon bark, about
    2 inches/5 cm long
¾ pint/4·5 dl milk
8 oz/225 g ground almonds
½ pint/3 dl natural yoghurt

Rinse the fish under cold running water and pat dry with kitchen paper. Cut into 2-inch (5-cm) pieces and sprinkle with the turmeric, salt and pepper.

Peel and chop the onions. Heat the butter in a frying pan and add the onions and cinnamon. Sauté until the onions are soft but not browned. Add the fish and sauté until lightly browned. Pour in the milk and bring to the boil. Lower the heat and simmer for 15 minutes.

Blend the ground almonds to a paste with the yoghurt and pour over the fish. Cover and simmer gently for 10 minutes. Transfer to a heated serving dish and serve hot with boiled rice.

# PRAWN DOHPIAZA (DRY CURRY)

*Serves 4*

1 lb/700 g fresh or frozen
    uncooked prawns, peeled and
    deveined
1 tablespoon ground coriander
6 medium-sized onions
2½ oz/65 g *ghee*
2 cloves garlic

1 green sweet pepper
1 teaspoon turmeric
small pinch cayenne pepper
1 teaspoon cumin seeds
1½ teaspoons salt
1 lemon

Rinse the prawns thoroughly under cold running water and place in a saucepan with just enough water to cover. Add the coriander and bring to the boil. Lower the heat and simmer the prawns for 2–3 minutes (overcooking will toughen them). Remove with a perforated spoon and set aside until required. Reserve the cooking liquid.

Peel 4 of the onions. Make two crosswise cuts two-thirds of the way through each onion so it is quartered but remains joined at the bottom. Heat the *ghee* in a frying pan and sauté the onions for about 5 minutes, or until lightly browned on the outside but uncooked in the centre. Remove the onions from the pan and set aside until required.

Peel and chop the garlic and remaining onions. Remove the seeds from the sweet pepper and shred the flesh. Heat the *ghee* remaining in the pan and sauté the chopped garlic and onion until soft but not browned. Stir in the turmeric, cayenne pepper and cumin seeds. Sauté for 2 minutes. Add the pepper and sauté for 3–4 minutes. Add the salt, the quartered onions and the reserved liquid. Simmer until the quartered onions are tender. Add the prawns and simmer until the excess liquid has evaporated.

Transfer the mixture to a heated serving dish and arrange the quartered onions on top. Garnish with slices of lemon and serve immediately with *puri* (see below).

# SAMOSAS (DEEP-FRIED PASTRIES)

*Makes 24–30*

**for the dough:**
10 oz/275 g plain flour
pinch salt
¼ pint/1·5 dl natural yoghurt or
    curds (see note)
2 oz/50 g melted *ghee*
**for the filling:**
1 medium-sized onion
2 teaspoons dried pomegranate
    seeds (optional)

3 large cooked potatoes
½ oz/15 g *ghee*
1½ teaspoons chopped fresh root
    ginger
1 tablespoon ground coriander
1 teaspoon chilli powder
1½ tablespoons sieved mango
1–1½ teaspoons *garam-masala*
1½ teaspoons salt
oil for deep-frying

Sift the flour and salt into a bowl and make a well in the centre. Add the curds or yoghurt and the *ghee*. Mix to a dough and knead well until smooth. Cover and set aside for 25–30 minutes.

To make the filling, peel and chop the onion. Pound the pomegranate seeds to a powder. Mash the potatoes. Heat the *ghee* in a frying pan and sauté the onion until soft but not browned. Add the ginger, coriander and chilli powder and cook for 2–3 minutes. Stir in the pounded pomegranate seeds, mashed potato, mango pulp, *garam-masala* and salt. Mix well. Continue cooking over low heat until the moisture evaporates and the mixture is quite dry and firm.

Roll out the dough to $\frac{1}{16}$-inch (1·5-mm) thickness. Cut into 3-inch (7·5-cm) squares and place 1 teaspoon of the prepared filling on each square. Brush the edges of the squares with milk and fold in half to make a triangle. Press the edges firmly together to seal in the filling.

Deep-fry the *samosas* in hot oil until golden brown. Drain on kitchen paper and keep hot. Transfer to a heated serving dish and serve with a chutney.

*Note:* Traditionally, curds are used in this recipe. They are obtained when milk becomes soured, either naturally or by the addition of an acid such as lemon juice. Natural yoghurt makes an excellent substitute for the curds.

# PURI (INDIAN DEEP-FRIED BREAD)

*Makes about 20*

8 oz/225 g wholemeal flour
1 teaspoon salt
½ oz/15 g slightly softened *ghee*

about ¼ pint/1·5 dl warm water
oil for deep-frying

Sift the flour and salt into a bowl and rub the *ghee* into the flour. Make a well in the centre. Add the water gradually and mix to a fairly stiff dough. Knead well until the dough becomes smooth and soft. Divide into about 20 pieces. Shape each piece into a ball and roll out each ball into a circle about 5–6 inches (13–15 cm) in diameter. Deep-fry in hot oil until risen and golden brown. Drain well on kitchen paper and serve hot.

*Samosas (deep-fried pastries)*

# ROGHAN JOSH (SPICY LAMB IN CREAM SAUCE)

*Serves 6*

2¼ lb/1·25 kg lamb fillet, or lean
  lamb cut from the leg
½ teaspoon finely chopped fresh
  root ginger
3 oz/75 g *ghee*
2 teaspoons ground coriander
1½ teaspoons *garam-masala*
salt

pinch chilli powder
1 pint/6 dl water
1 oz/25 g ground almonds
4 tablespoons double cream
1 oz/25 g pistachio nuts, chopped
1 oz/25 g blanched almonds,
  chopped

Wipe the meat with a cloth and cut into 1-inch (2·5-cm) cubes. Place on a shallow dish and sprinkle with the ginger. Heat the *ghee* in a frying pan and sauté the lamb until evenly browned. Add the coriander, *garam-masala*, salt and chilli powder, then gradually stir in the water. Bring to the boil, reduce the heat and simmer for 30–40 minutes, or until the lamb is tender and the water has evaporated.

   Mix the ground almonds with a little cold water to make a thick, smooth paste. Blend with the cream and stir into the lamb mixture. Cook very gently for 5 minutes. Transfer to a heated serving dish. Sprinkle with the chopped nuts and serve immediately with rice.

# LAMB QORMA

*Serves 4*

1½ lb/700 g lamb fillet, or lean
  lamb cut from the leg
1 tablespoon chopped mint
2 medium-sized onions
2 cloves garlic
2 oz/50 g *ghee*
1 tablespoon ground coriander
1 teaspoon chopped fresh root
  ginger

¼ teaspoon freshly ground black
  pepper
½ pint/3 dl natural yoghurt
few saffron strands
2 tablespoons lemon juice
½ oz/15 g blanched almonds
1 oz/25 g raisins
salt and pepper

Wipe the meat with a damp cloth and cut into 1-inch (2·5-cm) cubes. Place in a bowl, sprinkle with the mint and set aside for 1–2 hours.

   Peel and thinly slice the onions. Peel and chop the garlic. Heat three-quarters of the *ghee* in a saucepan and sauté the onions until soft and golden brown. Add the garlic, coriander, ginger and pepper and sauté for 5 minutes. Add the meat and sauté until well browned. Stir in the yoghurt. Cover the pan, lower the heat and cook the meat for 45–50 minutes, or until tender.

   Meanwhile, soak the saffron in the lemon juice. Soak the almonds in hot water for 2–3 minutes. Drain well and cut into thin slices. Heat the remaining *ghee* in a frying pan and sauté the almonds and raisins for 2–3 minutes. Drain on kitchen paper and add to the lamb with the saffron and lemon juice. Season to taste with salt and pepper. Transfer the *qorma* to a heated serving dish and serve hot with boiled rice.

*Kashmiri kebab*

# KASHMIRI KEBAB

*Serves 6–8*

2 lb/1 kg lamb fillet, or lean lamb cut from the leg
1 medium-sized onion
pinch saffron powder
2 tablespoons lime or lemon juice
1–2 cloves garlic
1 teaspoon chopped fresh root ginger
pinch ground cloves
pinch pepper
½ pint/3 dl natural yoghurt

Cut the lamb into thin slices, about ¼–½ inch (5 mm–1 cm) thick. Peel the onion, cut in half and rub the cut sides over the slices of meat. Pound the slices flat with a meat mallet. Cut each slice into strips ½–¾ inch (1–1.5 cm) wide and beat again to make thin flat ribbons with slightly ragged, very thin edges. Blend the saffron with the lime juice. Peel and chop the garlic. Mix together the garlic, ginger, cloves, pepper, yoghurt and saffron mixture. Pour over the lamb and set aside to marinate for 4–5 hours.

Wind the meat on to 6 to 8 skewers. Each strip should be wound round so that it overlaps, making a fat sausage shape (see photograph). The thin edges will make the meat stick to itself so there is no need to pierce it with the skewer. Press each sausage gently with the fingers into a lozenge shape. Cook under a hot grill until well browned and serve hot on the skewers accompanied by onion salad (see below).

# ONION SALAD

*Serves 4*

4 medium-sized onions
3 large tomatoes
1 teaspoon ground coriander
salt
chilli powder
¼ pint/1.5 dl white vinegar

Peel and thinly slice the onions and tomatoes. Arrange on a plate and sprinkle with the coriander. Season with salt and chilli powder to taste. Add the vinegar and mix well. Set aside for at least 1 hour before serving.

# SINGHALESE CHICKEN CURRY

*Serves 4*

1 chicken, about 4 lb/1.75 kg, with giblets (see note)
10 cardamom seeds
10 peppercorns
4–5 cloves
1½ tablespoons ground coriander
1 teaspoon ground cumin
pinch dried fennel
½ teaspoon turmeric
small pinch fenugreek
12 shallots
1–4 red chillies (according to taste)
2 tablespoons coconut oil or groundnut oil
2 pieces cinnamon bark, each about 2 inches/5 cm long
¾ pint/4.5 dl coconut milk
1 teaspoon salt
¼ pint/1.5 dl coconut cream
1–2 tablespoons fresh lime or lemon juice

Rinse the giblets well under cold running water. Dry with kitchen paper. Divide the chicken into 8 portions.

Lightly crush the cardamom seeds and peppercorns to release the flavours, and place in a frying pan with the cloves, coriander, cumin, fennel, turmeric and fenugreek. Heat gently over moderate heat for 2–3 minutes, stirring constantly to prevent the mixture from burning. Remove from the heat and set aside.

Peel and thinly slice the shallots. Remove the seeds from the chillies and chop the flesh finely. Heat the oil in a frying pan and sauté the shallots and chillies until lightly browned. Add the chicken, the giblets, the heated spices and the cinnamon bark. Sauté for about 10 minutes, or until the chicken changes colour. Add the coconut milk and salt. Cook very gently for 15–20 minutes, or until the chicken is tender. Add the coconut cream and simmer for a further 12–15 minutes, or until the excess liquid has evaporated. Remove and discard the cinnamon bark. Transfer the mixture to a heated serving dish, sprinkle with the lime juice and serve hot with rice, onion or cucumber *sambol* (see page 295), Singhalese chutney (see below) and hot sautéed cashew nuts.

*Note:* Beef or pork may be substituted for the chicken.

# SINGHALESE CHUTNEY

*Makes 3 lb (about 1.5 kg)*

4 oz/100 g stoned prunes
4 oz/100 g dried peaches
4 oz/100 g dried apricots
2 oz/50 g dried apple rings
1 pint/6 dl vinegar
1 piece green root ginger, about 1 inch/2.5 cm long
4–6 cloves garlic
1 oz/25 g dried chillies (see note)
1 teaspoon salt
1 lb/450 g castor sugar
3 oz/75 g sultanas
2 oz/50 g sliced cashew nuts

Place the prunes, peaches, apricots and apple rings in a bowl. Add a quarter of the vinegar and set aside for 45–50 minutes. Strain off the vinegar and reserve.

Cut the fruit into ¼-inch (5-mm) pieces. Peel and chop the ginger and garlic. Pound the garlic, ginger and chillies in a mortar and add 2 tablespoons of the vinegar. Pour the remaining vinegar and the reserved vinegar into a saucepan. Add the garlic mixture, the salt and sugar. Bring to the boil over low heat. When the sugar has dissolved, add the soaked fruit, the sultanas and the cashew nuts. Lower the heat and simmer for about 1 hour, or until the excess liquid has evaporated and the mixture has become fairly thick. Remove from the heat and set aside to cool. Pour into jars and seal. Store in a cool dry place until required.

*Note:* This is a very hot chutney and the quantity of chillies may be reduced by half, if preferred.

# TANDOORI CHICKEN

*Serves 4*

| | |
|---|---|
| 2 chickens, about 2½ lb/1·25 kg each | 1 teaspoon ground cumin |
| 1 medium-sized onion | 1 teaspoon chilli powder |
| 6 cloves garlic | 1 teaspoon ground coriander |
| 1 piece fresh root ginger, about 1 inch/2·5 cm long, or ¼ teaspoon ground ginger | 1–1½ teaspoons salt |
| | 5 tablespoons lime or lemon juice |
| | 1 teaspoon *garam-masala* |
| 6 tablespoons natural yoghurt or curds (see *Samosas*, page 290) | melted *ghee* (see recipe) |

Skin the chickens and prick all over with the point of a knife. Peel and chop the onion, garlic and ginger and press through a sieve. Add the yoghurt, cumin, chilli powder, coriander and salt and blend to a thin paste. Spread this mixture over the chickens and set aside to macerate for 5–6 hours, then sprinkle with the lime juice and half the *garam-masala* and set aside for 1 hour.

Cook the chickens for 1–1½ hours, or until tender (see note). If roasting, the oven should be moderately hot (400°F, 200°C, Gas Mark 6). Baste the chickens occasionally with melted *ghee* during the cooking.

When the chickens are cooked, remove from the oven, pour 1 teaspoon melted *ghee* over each one and set alight. Once the flames are extinguished, sprinkle with the remaining *garam-masala* and transfer to a heated serving dish. Serve with a green salad, onion salad (see page 293) and lemon wedges.

*Note:* This famous dish takes its name from *tandour*, the utensil in which it is cooked. Ideally this should be a clay oven, thus permitting heat to be applied from both below and above. The best Western alternatives are the barbecue and the spit rotisserie, but the chicken may also be roasted.

# CHICKEN BIRIANI

*Serves 4–6*

| | |
|---|---|
| 1 chicken, about 4 lb/1·75 kg | 3 cloves |
| 1 tablespoon lime or lemon juice | 1 piece cinnamon bark, about 2 inches/5 cm long |
| 1 teaspoon finely chopped fresh root ginger | pinch freshly grated nutmeg |
| 2 large onions | 1 pint/6 dl soured milk |
| 2½ oz/65 g *ghee* | 14 oz/400 g long-grain rice |
| 1 tablespoon ground coriander | 1 pint/6 dl water |
| 1 teaspoon ground cumin | 1 teaspoon chopped chives |
| ½ teaspoon ground fennel seed | **for the garnish:** |
| 1½–2 tablespoons poppy seeds | 8 shallots |
| 2 teaspoons salt | ½ cucumber |
| ¼ teaspoon freshly ground white pepper | 1½ lb/700 g tomatoes |
| | 1 green sweet pepper |
| 1 oz/25 g ground almonds | 6 slices pineapple |

Wipe the chicken with a damp cloth and chop into 2½-inch (6-cm) pieces. Sprinkle the chicken with the lime juice and ginger. Peel and thinly slice the onions. Heat three-quarters of the *ghee* in a saucepan and sauté the onions until soft but not browned. Stir in the coriander, cumin, fennel, poppy seeds, salt, pepper and half the ground almonds. Add the chicken, cloves, cinnamon, nutmeg and soured milk. Bring to the simmering point. Lower the heat, cover the pan and

cook for 30 minutes. Meanwhile, rinse the rice very thoroughly under cold running water. Place in a saucepan with the remaining ground almonds and the water. Bring to the boil and cook for 5 minutes. Drain well.

Take half of the rice out of the pan and pour the chicken stew on top of the remaining rice. Sprinkle with the chives. Replace the rice that was removed from the saucepan. Cover with a tight-fitting lid and cook over low heat for 10–15 minutes, or until the rice is tender.

Meanwhile, peel and slice the shallots and sauté in the remaining *ghee* until crisp and brown. Slice the cucumber and tomatoes. Remove the seeds from the sweet pepper and slice the flesh. Stir the rice and chicken mixture and transfer it to a heated serving dish. Garnish with the cucumber, tomato, sweet pepper and pineapple. Sprinkle with the shallots and serve immediately.

# DUCK VINDALOO

*Serves 4*

| | |
|---|---|
| 1 duck, about 5 lb/2·25 kg (see note) | 2 tablespoons *vindaloo* paste (see recipe below) |
| 2 medium-sized onions | 2 tablespoons lime or lemon juice |
| 3 cloves garlic | ¼ pint/1·5 dl water |
| 2 oz/50 g butter | salt |

Divide the duck into 8 pieces. Peel and chop the onions and garlic. Heat the butter in a saucepan and sauté the onion and garlic until soft but not browned. Add the *vindaloo* paste and lime juice. Simmer very gently for 5 minutes.

Place the pieces of duck in the saucepan. Add the water and salt. Cover tightly and simmer for 45–50 minutes, or until the duck is tender. If necessary, add a little extra water during cooking to prevent the mixture from sticking or burning. Adjust the seasoning and arrange the duck in a heated serving dish. Serve hot with rice.

*Note:* Pork or goose may be substituted for the duck.

# VINDALOO PASTE

| | |
|---|---|
| 1–2 cloves garlic | 1½ teaspoons ground coriander |
| 6 red chillies (see note) | 1 teaspoon ground cumin |
| ½ teaspoon chopped green root ginger | ¼ teaspoon turmeric |

Peel and chop the garlic. Remove the seeds from the chillies and chop the flesh finely. Place the garlic and chillies in a mortar with the ginger, coriander, cumin and turmeric. Pound until reduced to a smooth paste. Alternatively, this may be done in a liquidiser.

Store in an airtight container and use as required.

*Note:* The amount of chillies in this recipe may be increased or decreased, according to how hot the curry is preferred.

# ONION SAMBOL

*Serves 4*

| | |
|---|---|
| 2 large onions | 1 teaspoon salt |
| 2 tablespoons *ghee* or groundnut oil | 3–4 curry leaves |
| | pinch ground cinnamon |
| 1–2 teaspoons fresh shrimp paste | 2 tablespoons lime or |
| 1 teaspoon chilli powder | lemon juice |
| ¼–½ teaspoon turmeric | |

Peel the onions and cut lengthwise into very thin slices. Heat the *ghee* in a frying pan and sauté the onions for 5 minutes, or until slightly softened. Add the shrimp paste, chilli powder, turmeric, salt, curry leaves and cinnamon and sauté for 3–4 minutes. Sprinkle with the lime juice. Transfer to a heated serving dish and serve as an accompaniment to rice, as a side dish to curries or as a filling for *bouchées, vol-au-vents* or stuffed vegetables such as green sweet peppers.

# CUCUMBER SAMBOL

*Serves 4*

| | |
|---|---|
| 1 medium-sized cucumber | 2 tablespoons shrimp powder |
| 1 tablespoon salt | 2 tablespoons lime or lemon juice |
| 3 spring onions | 3 tablespoons coconut cream or |
| 1 green sweet pepper | natural yoghurt |

Peel the cucumber and cut in half lengthwise. Remove the seeds. Cut into thin slices and then into very fine strips; or grate coarsely. Place on a dry cloth, sprinkle with salt and set aside for 30 minutes. Trim and chop the spring onions. Remove the seeds from the sweet pepper and cut the flesh into thin strips.

Wrap the cloth around the cucumber and squeeze lightly to remove the excess liquid. Place it in a bowl and add the spring onions, green pepper and shrimp powder. Mix lightly. Add more salt, if necessary, and sprinkle with the lime juice. Just before serving dress with the coconut cream or yoghurt. Serve as an accompaniment to a hot curry.

*Cucumber sambol*

# AUBERGINE RELISH

*Makes 1 lb (450 g)*

2 large aubergines
salt (see recipe)
¼ teaspoon turmeric
1 head garlic
4 oz/100 g shallots
12 green chillies
2 tablespoons oil

1 tablespoon coriander seeds
12 dried red chillies
1 teaspoon mustard seeds
1 teaspoon ground cumin
3 tablespoons vinegar
2 teaspoons shrimp powder
1 teaspoon castor sugar

Cut off the stalks and rinse the aubergines under cold running water. Cut into ½-inch (1-cm) slices and arrange on a large plate in a single layer. Sprinkle liberally with salt and set aside for about 30 minutes to extract the juices. Drain and dry the aubergine slices and sprinkle with turmeric.

Meanwhile, peel the garlic and shallots. Remove the seeds from the green chillies and slice the flesh. Heat the oil in a frying pan and sauté the aubergine slices for 2 minutes on either side without browning. Add the green chillies, shallots and garlic and sauté for 3 minutes. Lower the heat to a minimum and cook for 10 minutes.

Meanwhile, place the coriander seeds, red chillies, mustard seeds and cumin in a mortar. Pound to a paste. Stir this paste into the aubergine mixture with the vinegar and shrimp powder. Cook for 15 minutes. Add the sugar and adjust the seasoning, if necessary. Set aside to cool. Pour into preserving jars, cover tightly and store until required.

# CHAPATTIES (UNLEAVENED INDIAN PANCAKES)

*Makes 16*

10 oz/275 g wholemeal flour
1 teaspoon salt
3 tablespoons vegetable oil

scant ½ pint/2·5 dl warm water
1 oz/25 g slightly warmed *ghee*

Sift the flour and salt into a bowl. Make a well in the centre and add the oil and water. Mix to a fairly stiff dough and knead well. Wrap in a slightly dampened cloth and set aside for 1 hour.

Knead the dough and divide into 16 portions. Knead each portion lightly on a floured surface; then roll out to a round about 5 inches (13 cm) in diameter. Pat the *chapatties* between the hands to make them thin.

Heat a griddle, or a heavy frying pan, over moderate heat and brush very lightly with *ghee*. Cook the *chapatties* for 1 minute on each side, or until very pale brown (overcooking will toughen them). Brush the griddle or pan with more *ghee* when necessary. Serve hot with curries.

# AUBERGINE FOOGATH

*Serves 6*

4 large aubergines
salt
3 medium-sized onions
2 cloves garlic
1–2 dried chillies (optional)
2 green sweet peppers

2 oz/50 g *ghee* or 3 tablespoons vegetable oil
1 tablespoon *garam-masala*
¼ pint/1·5 dl coconut milk
pinch dry mustard

Cut off the stalks and rinse the aubergines under cold running water. Cut into 1-inch (2·5-cm) thick slices, then cut each slice into quarters. Place on a large, flat plate and sprinkle liberally with salt. Set aside for 15 minutes, or until the bitter juices of the aubergines have been extracted.

Peel and thinly slice the onions. Peel and chop the garlic. Remove the seeds of the chillies and pound the flesh. Remove the seeds of the green sweet peppers and dice the flesh. Heat the *ghee* in a frying pan and sauté the onion and garlic until soft but not browned. Stir in the *garam-masala*. Drain the aubergines thoroughly and add to the cooked onion and garlic. Sauté for 1 minute, stirring gently. Add the chillies, sweet peppers, coconut milk and mustard. Cover and simmer for 30 minutes. Do not let the mixture boil. Add more salt, if necessary, and serve hot.

*Note:* Foogaths are curried vegetable dishes, usually fried with spices and often cooked with fresh shredded coconut. These dishes are acceptable to all Indian communities irrespective of religious taboos. They may be served independently or as accompaniments to other curry dishes.

# PARATHAS (FLAKY INDIAN PANCAKES)

*Makes 10*

8 oz/225 g wholemeal flour
½ teaspoon salt

¼ pint/1·5 dl warm water
4 oz/100 g *ghee*

Sift the flour and salt into a bowl. Make a well in the centre and add the water. Mix to a fairly stiff dough and knead well. Wrap in a slightly dampened cloth and set aside for 1 hour.

Knead the dough and divide into 10 portions. Knead each portion on a lightly floured board and roll into a 5-inch (13-cm) round. Spread the *paratha* thinly with *ghee*. Fold into quarters, roll out again, and repeat the process once more.

Heat a griddle, or a heavy frying pan, over moderate heat and brush well with *ghee*. Cook the parathas for 2 minutes, brush with *ghee* and turn over. Cook for a further 2 minutes, or until golden brown on both sides. Serve very hot.

*Parathas* may also be stuffed with *dahl* or a lightly curried vegetable. The filling is placed in the centre of a rolled out circle of dough. This is folded to enclose the filling and carefully flattened out into a circle.

*Aubergine relish*

# COCONUT ICE CREAM

*Serves 6*

| | |
|---|---|
| 1 pint/6 dl coconut cream | 4 oz/100 g vanilla sugar (see note) |
| 3 eggs | 2 oz/50 g cashew nuts |

Heat the coconut cream in a heavy saucepan over low heat, but do not allow it to boil. Beat the eggs and sugar until frothy and stir into the coconut cream. Remove from the heat and set aside to cool. Stir in the cashew nuts and pour into a shallow container. Place in the freezing compartment of the refrigerator until half frozen. Beat well, then return to the freezing compartment until frozen. Serve alone, or with fruit.

*Note:* If vanilla sugar is not available use 4 oz (100 g) granulated sugar and ½ teaspoon vanilla essence.

# MANGO ICE CREAM

*Serves 6–8*

| | |
|---|---|
| 3 egg yolks | 4 oz/100 g castor sugar |
| generous ½ pint/4 dl milk | 8 oz/225 g fresh or canned |
| 1 teaspoon vanilla essence | mangoes |
| ¼ teaspoon salt | ½ pint/3 dl whipped cream |

Blend the egg yolks with 4 tablespoons of the milk. Pour the remaining milk into a saucepan and add the vanilla essence, salt and sugar. Heat gently until the sugar has dissolved, then stir into the egg yolks. Pour into the top of a double saucepan, or into a bowl placed over hot water. Heat gently, stirring constantly, until the mixture is thick enough to coat the back of the spoon. Remove from the heat and stir until cool. Strain into a bowl and place in the freezing compartment of a refrigerator until thick but not completely frozen. Peel and slice the fresh mangoes or thoroughly drain the canned mangoes and fold into the semi-solid ice cream. Chill well and serve with the whipped cream.

# RICE DESSERT WITH CRYSTALLISED FRUITS AND NUTS

*Serves 6*

| | |
|---|---|
| 1 pint/6 dl milk | 4 tablespoons shredded fresh |
| 3 oz/75 g short-grain rice | coconut |
| 1½ oz/40 g castor sugar | ½ teaspoon orange flower water |
| ¼ teaspoon salt | 3 tablespoons chopped crystallised |
| ¼ teaspoon ground cinnamon | fruit (cherries, apricots, pears, |
| 1½ oz/40 g blanched pistachio | greengages) |
| nuts, chopped | coconut cream or *gula-malacca* |
| 3 oz/75 g ground almonds | syrup (see page 306) |

Pour the milk into a saucepan and add the rice, sugar, salt and cinnamon. Bring to the simmering point over moderate heat and simmer for 7–8 minutes. Add the pistachio nuts, ground almonds, coconut, orange flower water and crystallised fruit. Mix well, cover and cook very gently until the rice is soft and the milk has been absorbed. Pour into a serving dish and chill. Serve the rice with the coconut cream or *gula-malacca* syrup. For festive occasions decorate with gold and silver leaf, silver balls or silver sprinkles.

# JALEBIS (DEEP-FRIED SWEETMEATS IN SYRUP)

*Serves 4*

| for the batter: | for the syrup: |
|---|---|
| 6 oz/175 g plain flour | ½ pint/3 dl water |
| 2 teaspoons baking powder | 1 lb/450 g castor sugar |
| scant ½ pint/2·5 dl water | 1 teaspoon *jalebi* powder |
| 3 tablespoons natural yoghurt or | few drops rose water |
| curds (see *Samosas*, page 290) | *ghee* or oil for deep-frying |

Sift the flour and baking powder into a bowl and make a well in the centre. Gradually stir in the water and yoghurt to form a batter. Set aside overnight in a warm place to ferment.

To make the syrup, pour the water into a small heavy saucepan and add the sugar. Heat gently until the sugar has dissolved. Add the *jalebi* powder and rose water. Simmer the syrup until it thickens. Keep warm.

Beat the batter well. Heat the oil. Pour the batter through a funnel into the hot oil to form rings about 3 inches (7·5 cm) in diameter. Fry the *jalebis* a few at a time to prevent them from sticking to each other. When crisp and golden brown, remove from the hot oil and drain well on kitchen paper.

Place the *jalebis* in the hot syrup and set aside for 15 minutes. Drain and arrange in a heated shallow serving dish. Serve freshly made.

# CASHEW CANDY

*Serves 4*

| | |
|---|---|
| 1 pint/6 dl milk | 4 oz/100 g cashew nuts |
| 12 oz/350 g castor sugar | 1 oz/25 g butter |

Heat the milk in a saucepan until boiling. Add the sugar. Lower the heat and simmer very gently until the liquid becomes thick and syrupy. Add the cashew nuts, then stir in the butter, a little at a time. Continue simmering until a sugar thermometer registers a temperature of 230–240°F (110–116°C). If a sugar thermometer is not available, drop a little of the mixture into cold water; when the correct temperature has been reached it should mould into a soft ball. Remove from the heat and beat until thick. Pour into a 7-inch (18-cm) square tin and cool slightly.

While still warm, divide into small squares or diamond shapes and set aside until cold. Store wrapped in greaseproof paper and serve as required.

## Burma, Thailand, Malaysia and Singapore, Indonesia

## FRESH GINGER AND NUTS

*Serves 4–6*

6 oz/175 g fresh root ginger
½ teaspoon salt
4 tablespoons lime or lemon juice
4 oz/100 g white sesame seeds
pinch castor sugar

6 oz/175 g cashew nuts
6 oz/175 g peanuts
4 oz/100 g shrimp powder
4 oz/100 g shredded coconut, roasted

Peel and finely shred the ginger. Sprinkle with salt and set aside for 10 minutes. Rinse well under cold running water and squeeze dry. Place in a bowl and cover with the lime juice – this turns the ginger pink. Set aside until required.

Heat the sesame seeds in a frying pan until they begin to 'jump' and turn brown. Remove from the heat and cool. Drain the ginger and sprinkle with the sugar. Arrange the ginger, sesame seeds, cashew nuts, peanuts, shrimp powder and coconut in separate piles on a serving tray.

## LETH-OH (BURMESE MIXED VEGETABLES)

*Serves 4*

8 oz/225 g French beans
6 spring onions
4 oz/100 g okra
4 oz/100 g bamboo shoots
3 tablespoons sesame seeds

2 medium-sized onions
1 lb/450 g spinach
4 tablespoons vegetable oil
salt and pepper

Trim the beans and spring onions and cut into 1-inch (2·5-cm) lengths. Pare the stalks from the okra and slice the bamboo shoots. Cook the prepared vegetables separately in lightly salted boiling water for 5 minutes. Drain well and keep hot.

Meanwhile, heat the sesame seeds in an ungreased frying pan until they begin to 'jump' and turn brown. Remove from the pan and reserve. Peel and slice the onions. Rinse the spinach and dry well with kitchen paper. Heat half the oil in a frying pan and sauté the onions until soft and lightly browned. Remove from the pan and keep hot.

Heat the remaining oil in the pan. Add the spring onions and spinach and sauté for 2–3 minutes. Arrange the beans, okra, bamboo shoots and spinach mixture on a heated serving dish. Season with salt and pepper, garnish with the onions and sesame seeds and serve hot as an appetiser or a luncheon dish.

*Leth-oh (Burmese mixed vegetables)*

*Burmese fish soup*

# CHICKEN AND MUSHROOM SOUP

*Serves 6*

| | |
|---|---|
| 1 chicken, about 4 lb/1·75 kg, with giblets | ½ teaspoon chilli powder |
| 1 medium-sized onion | 2 tablespoons chicken fat |
| 4 pints/2·25 litres water | 2 teaspoons *nam pla* |
| 6 oz/175 g button mushrooms | 1 tablespoon *gula malacca* |
| 2–3 cloves garlic | salt |
| 1 teaspoon ground coriander | 1 teaspoon soya sauce |
| | 1 tablespoon chopped parsley |

Rinse the chicken and giblets under cold running water. Peel the onion. Place the chicken and onion in a saucepan and add the water. Bring to the boil over high heat. Cover, lower the heat and simmer for 45 minutes–1 hour, or until the chicken is tender. Remove the chicken from the stock and set aside to cool. Strip the chicken flesh from the bones and return the bones to the stock. Continue to simmer the stock until reduced to half the quantity. Remove the bones.

Meanwhile, slice the chicken flesh and giblets. Rinse the mushrooms under cold running water and simmer in lightly salted boiling water for 2 minutes. Drain before using. Peel the garlic and pound to a paste with the coriander and chilli powder.

Heat the chicken fat in a frying pan. Add the pounded mixture and the *nam pla*. Fry for 3 minutes, stirring constantly. Add the chicken and sauté for 2 minutes. Transfer the chicken mixture to the stock. Add the *gula malacca* and salt to taste. Bring to the boil and add the mushrooms and soya sauce. Simmer for 5 minutes. Pour into a heated soup tureen, sprinkle with chopped parsley and serve hot.

# BURMESE FISH SOUP

*Serves 4*

| | |
|---|---|
| 1 lb/450 g mackerel or sea bass | 2 pints/generous litre water |
| 1½ tablespoons soya sauce | 1 oz/25 g long-grain rice |
| pinch black pepper | 2 sticks celery |
| 1 onion | 4 oz/100 g white cabbage, finely shredded |
| 1 teaspoon salt | 1 teaspoon *balachaung* |

Scale and gut the fish. Cut off and reserve the head. Bone the fish and reserve the bones. Rinse the fish under cold running water and dry with kitchen paper. Cut into 1½-inch (3·5-cm) pieces and place in a dish. Sprinkle with the soya sauce and pepper and set aside while preparing the stock. Peel the onion. Place in a saucepan with the fish head and bones, salt and water. Bring to the boil over moderate heat. Lower the heat and simmer, uncovered, for 50 minutes.

Rinse the rice well under cold running water. Strain the stock into a clean pan and bring to the boil. Add the rice and simmer for 12 minutes. Add the fish and reboil. Lower the heat and simmer for 5–6 minutes.

Chop the celery. Add to the soup with the cabbage and *balachaung* and simmer for 5–6 minutes. Transfer to a heated soup tureen and serve.

# LOBSTER IN COCONUT

*Serves 4*

| | |
|---|---|
| 4 fresh coconuts | 3 oz/75 g butter |
| 1 pint/6 dl water | 1 teaspoon salt |
| 12 oz/350 g lobster meat | pinch pepper |
| 1 large onion | ½ teaspoon flour |
| 1 clove garlic | **for the flour and water paste:** |
| 2 green sweet peppers | 8 oz/225 g plain flour |
| 1 large tomato | ¼ pint/1·5 dl water |
| ½ pint/3 dl coconut milk | rum for serving |
| (see recipe) | |

Pierce the 'eyes' in each coconut and pour away the liquid. Saw the pierced end off each coconut and reserve to use as a lid. Remove the coconut flesh from each shell, without breaking the shell, and place in a large bowl. Add the water and set aside to soften for 2–3 hours.

Meanwhile, flake the lobster meat. Peel and chop the onion and garlic. Remove the seeds from the peppers and slice the flesh thinly. Peel and slice the tomato. Drain the soaked coconut, squeezing it well to extract as much thick milk as possible. Measure the required amount of milk. Shred, or coarsely grate, the coconut flesh.

Heat half the butter in a frying pan and sauté the onion and garlic until soft. Add the lobster and peppers and sauté for a further 5 minutes. Add the tomato, salt, pepper and coconut milk. Cover and simmer for 20 minutes. Blend the remaining butter with the flour and stir into the lobster mixture. Simmer for 2–3 minutes, then remove from the heat.

Stand the coconut shells upright in a deep cake tin or casserole. Fill the coconut shells just over half full with the lobster mixture. Fill to the top with grated coconut. Place the lids on top. Blend the flour and water together to make a thick paste. Press enough paste over each coconut to cover the holes and seal the lid. Add sufficient water to the baking tin to come a quarter of the way up the height of the coconuts. Bake in a cool oven (300°F, 150°C, Gas Mark 2) for 1–1¼ hours. Spoon a little water over the sealed coconuts from time to time to prevent them from burning.

When ready, remove from the tin and dry with a cloth. Place in a serving dish. Remove the lids, pour a tablespoon of rum over each coconut, flambé and serve.

# SPICED FISH FILLETS

*Serves 4*

| | |
|---|---|
| 1 lb/450 g red mullet | ½ teaspoon finely chopped chilli |
| or herring fillets | (optional) |
| 1 small piece tamarind | 1 tablespoon soya sauce |
| 2 medium-sized onions | 2 tablespoons water |
| 2 cloves garlic | 1 teaspoon soft brown sugar |
| 4 tablespoons groundnut oil | 2 tablespoons lime or lemon juice |

Rinse the fish under cold running water and dry well with kitchen paper. Rub the fish with the tamarind. Peel and chop the onions and garlic. Heat the oil in a frying pan and fry the fish for 2–3 minutes on each side, or until lightly browned. Reduce the heat and add the onions and garlic. Cook for 3–4 minutes. Add the chillies, if used, and fry lightly for 1 minute.

Mix together the soya sauce, water, sugar and lime juice and pour over the fish. Bring to the boil and cook for 3–4 seconds only. Transfer to a heated serving dish and serve hot.

# FISH WITH RICE NOODLES IN SPICY COCONUT SAUCE

*Serves 4*

| | |
|---|---|
| 1 lb/450 g white fish (cod, | 3 cloves garlic |
| haddock, halibut) | 4 large onions |
| ¼ pint/1·5 dl Burmese fish | ¼ pint/1·5 dl groundnut oil |
| sauce (see note) | 1¾ pints/1 litre water |
| 2 blades lemon grass, each 1 inch/ | ½ pint/3 dl coconut cream |
| 2·5 cm long, or ½ teaspoon | 1 oz/25 g rice flour (see note) |
| dried lemon balm (see note) | 1 oz/25 g *dhal* flour |
| 2 chillies | 2 hard-boiled duck or hen eggs |
| ¼ teaspoon turmeric | 2 lb/1 kg rice noodles |
| 1½ teaspoons chopped fresh root | |
| ginger | |

Gut the fish and wash thoroughly. Place in a saucepan. Add the Burmese fish sauce, one of the blades of lemon grass, one of the chillies, the turmeric and enough water to cover. Bring to the boil. Lower the heat and simmer for about 10 minutes, or until the fish is just cooked but still firm. Remove with a perforated spoon. Strain and reserve the stock. Remove and discard the fish skin and bones. Flake the fish into large pieces and set aside until required.

Peel and chop the ginger and garlic. Remove the seeds from the remaining chilli. Place the ginger, garlic, chilli and remaining blade of lemon grass in a mortar and pound to a paste. Peel and slice two of the onions. Peel and quarter the remaining onions and reserve. Heat the oil in a frying pan and sauté the sliced onions until soft. Add the pounded ginger mixture and cook gently for 2–3 minutes, stirring constantly. Add the fish and cook for 2 minutes. Remove from the heat and set aside until required.

Add the water and coconut cream to the reserved fish stock and bring to the boil. Blend the rice flour and *dhal* flour with a little of the boiling stock to make a thin paste. Pour the paste into the stock and bring to the boil. Cook, stirring constantly, until a thick sauce is formed. Lower the heat, add the quartered onions and simmer for 20 minutes.

Shell the eggs and cut into quarters. Add to the *dhal* sauce with the fish mixture. Heat gently for 2–3 minutes.

Meanwhile, plunge the rice noodles into lightly salted boiling water and boil for 1 minute. Drain thoroughly and transfer to a heated dish. Pour the fish mixture into a heated deep serving dish and serve immediately with the noodles. The traditional accompaniments are fried onions, lime wedges and chilli powder, served in separate dishes.

*Note:* Burmese fish sauce, lemon grass and rice flour can be obtained from oriental food shops. Ground rice may be substituted for rice flour.

# CURRIED EGGS IN COCONUT SAUCE

*Serves 4*

4 eggs

**for the sauce:**

2 small onions

2 cloves garlic

1 piece fresh root ginger, about 1 inch/2·5 cm long

3 red chillies

2 tablespoons coconut oil

5–6 curry leaves or 1 tablespoon *garam-masala*

1½ teaspoons turmeric

½ pint/3 dl coconut milk

5 tablespoons tamarind juice (see note) or 6 tablespoons lemon juice

¼ pint/1·5 dl coconut cream

Boil the eggs for 10 minutes. Plunge into cold water, shell and set aside in warm water until required.

To make the sauce, peel and thinly slice the onions, garlic and ginger. Remove the seeds from the chillies. Heat the oil in a frying pan and sauté the onions, garlic, chillies, ginger and curry leaves or *garam-masala* for 3 minutes. Add the turmeric and sauté for 1 minute. Lower the heat and gradually stir in the coconut milk. Simmer for 30 seconds and add the tamarind juice.

Drain the eggs and place in the sauce. Spoon the sauce over the eggs and heat gently for 4–5 minutes. The sauce should not be allowed to boil. Stir in the coconut cream and heat for 1 minute. Transfer to a heated serving dish and serve immediately.

*Note:* It is the tamarind juice that gives Malay curries their distinctive sour flavour.

# NASI GORENG (INDONESIAN FRIED RICE)

*Serves 4*

8 oz/225 g long-grain rice

¾ pint/4·5 dl water

8 oz/225 g cooked meat or fish

2 oz/50 g dried shrimps

2 medium-sized onions

1 clove garlic

1 chilli or ½ teaspoon chilli powder

generous ¼ pint/2 dl groundnut oil

3 eggs

salt and pepper

1 tablespoon vegetable oil

Rinse the rice in a sieve under cold running water. Place in a saucepan and add the water. Bring to the boil over moderate heat, then lower the heat and simmer for 10 minutes. Drain well. Spread on a large plate and set aside to dry.

Finely slice the meat or fish. Place the dried shrimps in a bowl with enough water to cover and soak for 10–15 minutes. Peel and chop the onions and garlic. Remove the seeds from the chilli and chop the flesh. Heat the oil in a frying pan and sauté the onions until soft but not browned. Add the garlic and sauté for 1 minute. Add the chilli and sauté for 3 minutes. Add the meat or fish and sauté for 2 minutes. Drain the shrimps and add to the pan with the rice. Sauté for 5–6 minutes, or until the rice is lightly browned.

Meanwhile, lightly whisk the eggs with a pinch of salt and pepper. Heat the vegetable oil in a large frying pan. Add the beaten eggs and cook gently to make a thin omelette.

Season the rice mixture to taste and transfer to a heated serving plate. Cover with the omelette and serve immediately with *atjar* (Indonesian mixed vegetable pickle, see page 305).

*Nasi goreng (Indonesian fried rice)*

# THAI NOODLES

1 lb/450 g Chinese rice noodles
  or fine egg noodles
1 medium-sized onion
4 cloves garlic
6 oz/175 g pork fillet or lean pork
  cut from the leg
8 oz/225 g boned chicken
4 oz/100 g crab meat
8 oz/225 g fresh or frozen
  uncooked prawns, peeled
  and deveined
4 oz/100 g bean curd

4–5 oz/100–150 g bean sprouts
4 spring onions
½ pint/3 dl vegetable oil
1 tablespoon soya sauce
1 tablespoon vinegar
1 tablespoon *nam pla*
1 tablespoon castor sugar
salt
4 eggs
pinch ground coriander
red chillies for garnishing
  (optional)

Break the noodles into 2½-inch (6-cm) pieces and drop into lightly salted boiling water. Simmer for 1 minute. Drain well and spread on a board. Set aside to dry for 30 minutes.

Peel and chop the onion and garlic. Thinly slice the pork and chicken. Flake the crab meat and chop the prawns. Cut the bean curd into ½-inch (1-cm) cubes. Rinse the bean sprouts under cold running water and drain well. Trim and chop the spring onions.

Heat three-quarters of the oil in a deep saucepan and fry the noodles, a few at a time, until crisp and golden brown. Drain on kitchen paper and set aside until required. Heat the remaining oil in a frying pan and sauté the onion and garlic for 3–4 minutes. Add the pork and sauté for 8–10 minutes, stirring frequently. Add the chicken and cook for 3 minutes. Add the crab meat, prawns and bean curd, and cook until the chicken and prawns change colour. Stir in the soya sauce, vinegar, *nam pla*, sugar and salt to taste. Whisk the eggs and stir into the meat mixture. When the egg begins to set, add the bean sprouts and noodles and cook for about 5 minutes, stirring frequently. Transfer to a heated serving dish, sprinkle with the spring onions and coriander and garnish with the chillies, if used. Serve immediately.

# BEEF OR VEAL SATAY

*Serves 4*

1 tablespoon ground almonds
1 slice fresh root ginger
1 teaspoon ground coriander
1 teaspoon turmeric
½ pint/3 dl coconut milk

1 lb/450 g rump steak or fillet of
  veal
salt and pepper
1 teaspoon soft brown sugar

Place the almonds, ginger, coriander and turmeric in a mortar and pound to a paste. Gradually add the coconut milk. Cut the meat into 1-inch (2·5-cm) cubes. Place in a bowl and sprinkle with salt and pepper. Add the flavoured coconut milk and set aside to marinate for 2 hours.

Drain the milk from the meat and reserve. Thread the meat on to 4 metal skewers and sprinkle with the sugar. Cook under a moderately hot grill for 4–5 minutes, turning frequently and basting with the reserved coconut milk. Serve hot, on the skewers, with satay sauce (see following recipe).

# SATAY SAUCE WITH OIL

*Makes ½ pint (3 dl)*

2 large onions
3 oz/75 g roasted peanuts
½ teaspoon chilli powder
2 tablespoons groundnut oil
¼ pint/1·5 dl warm water

1 teaspoon soft brown sugar
1 tablespoon soya sauce
1½ tablespoons lime or lemon juice
½ teaspoon salt

Peel the onions. Thinly slice one onion and finely chop the other. Pound the chopped onion, peanuts and chilli powder in a mortar.

Heat the oil in a frying pan and sauté the sliced onion until soft but not browned. Add the pounded mixture and sauté for about 3 minutes, stirring constantly. Stir in the water and sugar and cook the mixture for 3 minutes. Add the soya sauce, lime juice and salt. Serve hot with satay dishes.

# BURMESE MUTTON CURRY

*Serves 4*

1 lb/450 g lean mutton fillet or
  lean mutton cut from the leg
2 large onions
3 thin slices fresh root ginger
2 cloves garlic

½ teaspoon salt
¼ teaspoon turmeric
¼ teaspoon chilli powder
3 tablespoons groundnut oil
1 tablespoon soya sauce

Cut the mutton into 1-inch (2·5-cm) strips. Peel and finely chop the onions, ginger and garlic. Mix together in a bowl and sprinkle with the salt, turmeric and chilli powder. Heat the oil in a frying pan and fry the onion mixture for 2–3 minutes. Add the meat and sauté until lightly browned. Add the soya sauce and enough water just to cover the meat. Simmer for 25–30 minutes, or until the meat is tender. Serve hot with rice.

*Note:* Beef or pork may be substituted for the mutton, if preferred.

# INDONESIAN BRAISED PORK

*Serves 4*

1 lb/450 g pork fillet or lean pork
  cut from the shoulder
1 medium-sized onion
1 clove garlic
2 tablespoons groundnut oil

5 tablespoons soya sauce
2 tablespoons water
1 teaspoon lemon juice
1 teaspoon soft brown sugar

Cut the pork into 1-inch (2·5-cm) cubes. Peel and chop the onion and garlic. Heat the oil in a frying pan and sauté the meat until well browned. Add the onion and garlic and sauté for 3 minutes.

Mix together the soya sauce, water, lemon juice and sugar. Pour this mixture over the meat and simmer uncovered for 12–15 minutes. Transfer to a heated serving dish and serve hot.

# PORK IN ORANGES

*Serves 4*

| | |
|---|---|
| 1 clove garlic | 1 teaspoon *nam pla* |
| 1 oz/25 g peanuts | pinch ground coriander |
| 1 tablespoon groundnut oil | ¼ teaspoon chilli powder |
| 12 oz/350 g pork fillet or lean | 1 teaspoon salt |
|    pork cut from the leg, minced | 4 large oranges |

Peel and finely chop the garlic. Chop the peanuts. Heat the
oil in a frying pan and sauté the garlic for 1–2 minutes. Add
the pork and sauté for 5 minutes, stirring frequently. Add the
peanuts, *nam pla*, coriander, chilli powder and salt. Reduce
the heat and simmer for 10 minutes, stirring frequently.

   Cut the oranges into quarters without cutting right
through and open out to form a tulip shape. Place the
oranges in a casserole and spoon the pork mixture into each
one. Bake in a moderate oven (350°F, 180°C, Gas Mark 5)
for 10–12 minutes. Serve hot with boiled rice.

# COCONUT CHICKEN

*Serves 4*

| | |
|---|---|
| 2 chicken breasts | 1 teaspoon grated lemon rind |
| 1 small onion | pinch castor sugar |
| 1 clove garlic | pinch salt |
| 1 dried chilli | 2 oz/50 g butter |
| 1 oz/25 g ground peanuts | ½ pint/3 dl coconut cream |
| ½ teaspoon ground coriander | 1½ teaspoons soya sauce |

Remove and discard the skin from the chicken breasts and
slice each breast horizontally into 2 thin pieces. Pound the
slices lightly to flatten. Peel and chop the onion and garlic.
Remove the seeds from the chilli and chop the flesh. Place the
onion, garlic, chilli, peanuts, coriander, lemon rind, sugar
and salt in a mortar and pound to a paste. Spread this
mixture over the chicken slices.

   Heat the butter in a frying pan and fry the chicken for 2–3
minutes on each side. Reduce the heat, then add the coconut
cream and soya sauce. Simmer for 25 minutes, or until the
chicken is tender. Serve hot with boiled or fried rice.

*Pork in oranges*

# BURMESE COCONUT RICE

*Serves 4*

| | |
|---|---|
| 1 small onion | 1½ pints/9 dl coconut milk |
| 2½ oz/65 g *ghee* | pinch castor sugar |
| 8 oz/225 g long-grain rice | pinch salt |

Peel and chop the onion. Heat the *ghee* in a saucepan and sauté the onion until soft but not browned. Add the rice and fry for 2 minutes, stirring constantly. Add the coconut milk, sugar and salt and bring to the boil. Lower the heat and simmer until all the milk has been absorbed and the rice is dry and fluffy. Serve hot as required.

# PRAWN SAMBAL

*Serves 4*

| | |
|---|---|
| 2 chillies | 1 lb/450 g fresh or frozen |
| 1 medium-sized onion | uncooked prawns, peeled and |
| 1 clove garlic | deveined |
| 1 teaspoon crushed tamarind | ½ teaspoon ground ginger |
| ½ bay leaf | 1 teaspoon castor sugar |
| 2 tablespoons coconut oil | ½ pint/3 dl coconut milk |

Remove the seeds from the chillies and chop the flesh. Peel and chop the onion and garlic. Place the chillies, onion, garlic, tamarind and bay leaf in a mortar and pound to a paste.

Heat the oil in a frying pan and fry the pounded mixture for 3–4 minutes. Add the prawns, ginger and sugar and sauté for 3–4 minutes. Add the coconut milk. Cook for a further 4–5 minutes, without boiling, until the mixture thickens. Pour into a heated serving dish and serve hot.

# TOMATO SAMBAL

*Serves 4*

| | |
|---|---|
| 3 cloves garlic | 3 tablespoons groundnut oil |
| 1 small onion | 1½ teaspoons salt |
| 1 small piece tamarind | 1 tablespoon soft brown sugar |
| 2 red chillies | ¼ pint/1·5 dl coconut milk |
| 6 large tomatoes | 2 tablespoons prawn *sambal* |
| 2 leeks | (see preceding recipe) |

Peel and crush the garlic. Peel and chop the onion. Crush the tamarind. Remove the seeds from the chillies and shred the flesh. Peel and slice the tomatoes. Trim the leeks, rinse thoroughly under cold running water and slice thinly.

Heat the oil in a frying pan and sauté the garlic, onion and tamarind for 3–4 minutes. Add the chillies and tomatoes and sauté for 2 minutes. Add the leeks and sauté for 2 minutes. Sprinkle with the salt and sugar, then gradually stir in the coconut milk and prawn *sambal*. Simmer gently for 10 minutes and serve hot.

# ATJAR (INDONESIAN VEGETABLE PICKLE)

*Makes 2 pints (1·25 litres)*

| | |
|---|---|
| 2 green sweet peppers | ½ teaspoon chopped fresh root |
| 1 small carrot | ginger |
| 1 small cucumber | 5 cashew nuts or blanched |
| 4 oz/100 g French beans | almonds |
| 8 oz/225 g shallots | 1 teaspoon turmeric |
| 2 cloves garlic | 1 pint/6 dl malt vinegar |
| 3 teaspoons salt | ¼ pint/1·5 dl water |
| | 1 oz/25 g soft brown sugar |

Trim the peppers, remove the seeds and shred the flesh. Peel and thinly slice the carrot and cucumber. String and slice the beans. Peel the shallots and garlic. Place the peppers, carrot, cucumber, beans, shallots and 2 teaspoons salt in a saucepan and add enough boiling water to cover. Bring to the boil over high heat. Boil for 5 minutes, then drain well.

Meanwhile, place the garlic, ginger, nuts and turmeric in a mortar and pound to a paste. Add the vinegar, water, sugar and remaining salt. Pour into a large heavy saucepan and bring to the boil. Add the vegetables and boil for 10 minutes. Remove from the heat and set aside to cool. Transfer to jars, seal tightly and use as required.

# BURMESE CABBAGE SALAD

*Serves 4*

| | |
|---|---|
| 2 large onions | 1 white cabbage, about 1 lb/450 g |
| 2 cloves garlic | 2–3 tablespoons sesame or |
| 2–3 thin slices fresh root ginger | groundnut oil |

Peel the onions and slice into thin rings. Peel and chop the garlic. Chop the ginger. Remove the hard core and outer leaves from the cabbage. Wash and finely shred the rest.

Heat the oil in a frying pan and sauté the onions and garlic until transparent. Add the ginger and sauté for 2 minutes. Add the cabbage and heat gently for 2 minutes, or until coated with the mixture. Serve hot or cold as required.

# TOMATO FONDUE

*Serves 4*

| | |
|---|---|
| 6 large tomatoes | pinch turmeric |
| 2 oz/50 g dried shrimps | pinch salt |
| 4 medium-sized onions | 3 tablespoons vegetable oil |
| 2 cloves garlic | 3 tablespoons water |

Peel and quarter the tomatoes. Pound the shrimps to a powder in a mortar. Peel and slice the onions. Peel and chop the garlic. Place the tomatoes, shrimps, onions, garlic, turmeric, salt, oil and water in a saucepan. Heat very gently for about 45 minutes, or until the tomatoes and onions are very soft and the excess liquid has evaporated. Pour into a heated dish and serve as a relish with boiled rice or noodles.

*Burmese coconut cake*

# BURMESE COCONUT CAKE

*Serves 8*

2 oz/50 g plain flour
4½ oz/125 g semolina
pinch salt
1 teaspoon baking powder
4 oz/100 g butter
8 oz/225 g vanilla sugar
  (see note)
4 egg yolks

4 oz/100 g fresh coconut,
  finely grated
4 egg whites
**for decoration:**
¼ pint/1·5 dl double cream
3 tablespoons shredded
  fresh coconut

Sift together the flour, semolina, salt and baking powder.
Cream the butter and sugar in a bowl until soft and white.
Add the egg yolks one at a time, beating well after each
addition. Add the sifted ingredients and mix well. Stir in the
grated coconut. Whisk the egg whites until stiff and fold into
the cake mixture. Divide the mixture between 2 greased 8-
inch (20-cm) sandwich tins. Bake in a moderate oven (350°F,
180°C, Gas Mark 4) for 25 minutes, or until firm and golden
brown. Turn out on to a wire tray and set aside to cool.

Whip the cream until thick and spread one of the cakes
with it. Sprinkle with the coconut and place the second cake
on top to make one deep cake. Alternatively, pipe half the
cream and sprinkle half the coconut on each, and leave as 2
separate cakes.

*Note:* If vanilla sugar is not available add 1 teaspoon
vanilla essence to 8 oz (225 g) castor sugar.

# SAGO WITH COCONUT CREAM AND PALM SUGAR SYRUP

*Serves 6*

1 pint/6 dl water
8 oz/225 g sago
**for the coconut cream sauce:**
½ pint/3 dl thick coconut milk
pinch salt

**for the gula malacca syrup:**
4 oz/100 g *gula malacca* or soft
  dark brown sugar
¼ pint/1·5 dl boiling water

Measure the water into a saucepan and bring to the boil.
Add the sago and stir until the mixture forms a thick paste.
Remove from the heat and pour into 6 individual moulds
rinsed out with cold water. Set aside to cool.

To make the sauces, gently heat the coconut milk. Add the
salt and simmer until the mixture thickens. Remove from the
heat, pour into a jug and set aside to cool.

For the second sauce, cut the palm sugar into pieces and
place in a saucepan. Add the boiling water. Bring to the boil,
stirring to dissolve the sugar. Simmer, stirring all the time,
until the mixture thickens slightly. Remove from the heat
and set aside to cool.

Unmould the sago desserts on to individual serving dishes.
Pour a little of each sauce over them and serve.

## Korea, The Philippines, Japan

## CHRYSANTHEMUM PRAWNS WITH TEMPURA SAUCE

*Serves 4*

4 oz/100 g fresh or frozen cooked
  prawns, peeled and deveined
2 egg whites
pinch salt
1 tablespoon cornflour
pinch monosodium glutamate
¼ oz/15 g *harusame* noodles
oil for deep-frying

**for the tempura sauce:**
½ pint/3 dl *dashi* (see page 313)
4 tablespoons soya sauce
4 tablespoons *sake*
  or dry sherry
pinch monosodium glutamate

Finely chop the prawns, then pound in a mortar until reduced to a paste. Add the egg whites, salt, cornflour and monosodium glutamate. Mix well. Shape the mixture into 8 patties. Cut the noodles into pieces about 2 inches (5 cm) long and press one side of each patty on to the noodles. The patties should retain their shape and pick up as many 'petals' as possible. Deep-fry the patties until golden brown. Drain on kitchen paper and keep hot.

To make the *tempura* sauce, place the *dashi*, soya sauce and *sake* in a saucepan. Bring to the boil over moderate heat. Season with monosodium glutamate to taste.

Arrange the chrysanthemum prawns on a flat serving dish (a straw dish is ideal) and serve with the *tempura* sauce.

*Note:* The traditional garnish for this dish is edible chrysanthemum leaves.

## CRAB WITH HAM AND WALNUTS

*Serves 4*

1 medium-sized onion
6 oz/175 g lean cooked ham
1 small piece fresh root ginger
1 oz/25 g shelled walnuts
2 eggs
1½ tablespoons vegetable oil
2 teaspoons cornflour

4 tablespoons cold water
2 tablespoons soya sauce
1 teaspoon salt
¼ teaspoon freshly ground white
  pepper
6 oz/175 g white crab meat

Peel and chop the onion. Mince the ham. Peel and chop the ginger. Chop the walnuts. Whisk the eggs. Heat the oil in a frying pan and sauté the onion and ham for 7–8 minutes. Blend the cornflour with the water and soya sauce and stir into the ham mixture. Add the eggs, ginger, walnuts, salt and pepper. Cook gently for 5–6 minutes, stirring constantly. Add the crab meat and cook gently for 4–5 minutes, or until the crab is heated through. Pour into a heated serving dish and serve with boiled rice and a salad.

## STUFFED PANCAKE ROLLS WITH SWEET SOYA SAUCE

*Serves 4–6*

**for the filling:**
1 oz/25 g chick peas (optional)
4 oz/100 g pork fillet or lean pork
  cut from the leg
2 slices cooked ham
1 clove garlic
1 medium-sized onion
2 oz/50 g fresh or frozen cooked
  prawns, peeled and deveined
6 oz/175 g French beans
1 large carrot
12 oz/350 g cabbage
8 oz/225 g coconut palm heart
  (see note)
2 tablespoons vegetable oil
1 teaspoon salt

pinch pepper
12 crisp lettuce leaves
**for the pancake batter:**
2 eggs (duck eggs, if available)
3 oz/75 g cornflour
½ pint/3 dl water
groundnut oil
**for the sauce:**
generous ¼ pint/2 dl chicken stock
2 oz/50 g castor sugar
2 tablespoons dark soya sauce
1 teaspoon salt
1 tablespoon cornflour
3 tablespoons water
1–2 cloves garlic

To make the filling, soak the chick peas in cold water overnight. Simmer in lightly salted boiling water until tender and drain well. If using canned chick peas, drain well. Cut the pork into ½-inch (1-cm) cubes. Cut the ham into matchstick-thin strips. Peel and chop the garlic. Peel the onion and slice very thinly. Chop the prawns. Trim the French beans and slice thinly. Peel and grate the carrot. Finely shred the cabbage. Drain and shred the coconut palm heart.

Place the pork in boiling water and simmer for 5 minutes. Drain well. Heat the oil in a frying pan and sauté the garlic for 2–3 minutes. Add the pork and ham and sauté for 2 minutes. Add the prawns and chick peas and sauté for 2 minutes. Add the beans, carrot, cabbage, coconut palm heart, salt and pepper. Cook gently for 6–8 minutes, or until the vegetables are tender but still firm and crisp. Remove from the heat, drain off any liquid and set aside to cool. Wash and dry the lettuce leaves.

To make the pancake batter, separate the egg yolks from the whites. Whisk the egg whites until stiff. Add the yolks and whisk lightly. Blend the cornflour with the water and stir into the egg mixture to make a thin batter. Brush a 6-inch (15-cm) frying pan lightly with oil. Add 2 tablespoons of the pancake batter and tilt the pan until the mixture covers the bottom. As soon as the pancake is set, but not browned, remove from the pan and keep warm. Continue until all the mixture has been used.

Divide the filling into 12 portions. Wrap each portion in a lettuce leaf and then in a pancake. Arrange on a wooden serving dish and keep hot.

To make the sauce, pour the stock into a saucepan. Add the sugar, soya sauce and salt and bring to the boil. Blend the cornflour with the water and stir into the boiling stock. Simmer for 2–3 minutes, stirring constantly until the mixture thickens.

Pour the sauce into a heated bowl. Peel and chop the garlic and sprinkle on top. Serve the stuffed pancakes hot with the sauce.

*Note:* A combination of bean sprouts and spring onions may be substituted for the coconut palm heart.

# CHICKEN BUNDLES

*Serves 6*

6 oz/175 g boned chicken
1 tablespoon *shoyu*
1 tablespoon *sake* or
  dry sherry

½ sheet *nori* seaweed
1 beaten egg white
vegetable oil for frying

Remove and discard the skin of the chicken. Cut the chicken into strips about 2 inches (5 cm) long and ¼ inch (5 mm) thick. Place in a bowl and sprinkle with the *shoyu* and *sake*. Set aside to marinate for 1 hour.

Cut the seaweed into ½-inch (1-cm) strips and brush with egg white. Divide the chicken into bundles of 4 to 5 pieces and bind with the seaweed. Fry in shallow oil for 5–6 minutes, or until the chicken is tender and golden brown. Drain on kitchen paper and serve hot as an appetiser.

# RICE BALL PRAWN ZUSHI

*Makes 24*

4 teaspoons grated horseradish
4 teaspoons water
12 oz/350 g cooked *zushi* rice (see
  below)

24 fresh or frozen cooked prawns,
  peeled and deveined

Pound the grated horseradish to a paste, then blend with the water. Take a spoonful of the rice and press gently to form a shape similar to a prawn. Brush the top with a little of the horseradish mixture, then press a prawn gently into the rice. Mould the rice to the exact shape of the prawn. Place on a serving dish. Repeat until all the ingredients have been used.

# RICE FOR ZUSHI

*Makes about 1½ lb (700 g)*

8 oz/225 g long-grain rice
½ pint/3 dl water
1 tablespoon vinegar

pinch monosodium glutamate
1 teaspoon salt
1 teaspoon castor sugar

About 3 hours before cooking, rinse the rice thoroughly under cold running water and set aside to drain. Pour the water into a heavy saucepan and bring to the boil. Add the rice. Return to the boil, lower the heat and simmer for 10 minutes, or until the water has been completely absorbed and the rice is cooked but still firm. Transfer to a shallow dish and set aside to cool. Divide the rice in half. Mix one half with the vinegar, monosodium glutamate and three-quarters of the salt, and the other half with the sugar and remaining salt. Serve the two mixtures separately or together, depending how sweet or sharp you like your *zushi*.

*Sashimi (raw fish hors d'oeuvre)*

# SEA BREAM SASHIMI

*Serves 4*

| | |
|---|---|
| 1 lb sea bream or porgy | ⅓ cup *shoyu* |
| 2 teaspoons grated horseradish | 1 bunch watercress |

*Sashimi* is a famous Japanese specialty, justly considered an exquisite delicacy and completely free of any 'fishy' taste or smell. It usually consists of slices of raw fish but chicken can also be used. To render it more digestible, and to add flavor, it is usually served with grated *wasabi* (Japanese horseradish) and invariably with *shoyu*. Garnish and presentation are of great importance.

Scale and clean the fish and cut off and discard the head, tail and fins. Rinse well under cold running water, then soak in cold water for 30 minutes. Blend the horseradish with the *shoyu*. Fillet the fish (see Planked Lake Superior Whitefish, page 14) and remove the skin. Cut the fillets obliquely into 1½-inch wide slices. Place the slices, slightly overlapping each other, on a long narrow dish (see note). Garnish with watercress and serve with the horseradish mixture.

*Note:* If possible the fish should be arranged in the shape of a whole fish. The watercress garnish should give the impression of the fish seen through a growth of seaweed. For a variation of this recipe make fresh tuna fish *sashimi*, using parsley for 'seaweed'. Serve with a dressing made of 2 teaspoons freshly grated ginger and ⅓ cup *shoyu*.

# SOLE IN CHRYSANTHEMUM WREATHS

*Serves 6*

| | |
|---|---|
| 6 sole fillets | 1 tablespoon distilled malt vinegar |
| ½ cup soy sauce | dash sugar |
| 1 cucumber | 6 tablespoons *mirin* or sweet |
| salt | white wine |
| 1 tablespoon *sake* or | 1 red sweet pepper |
| dry sherry | |

Rinse the fish fillets under cold running water and pat dry with absorbent paper. Place in a shallow dish and add the soy sauce. Set aside to marinate for 3 hours.

Peel the cucumber and cut lengthwise into slices about ¼ inch thick. Cut the long cucumber slices on one side at brief intervals without cutting right through. At this stage each strip looks rather like a comb. Sprinkle with salt and leave to soften for 10–15 minutes, then moisten with the *sake* and vinegar and sprinkle with the sugar. Set aside for 1 hour.

Drain the fish fillets, reserving the soy sauce. Sprinkle with salt on both sides and thread them on to 6 skewers. Mix the reserved soy sauce with the *mirin* and dip the skewered fish in the mixture. Broil under a preheated hot broiler for 5–10 minutes, dipping the fish in the sauce 2 or 3 times during the broiling. Arrange the fillets on a serving dish. Roll up the cucumber strips and arrange cut side up on the fish. Using a chopstick or similar implement, open out the petals of each cucumber 'flower'. Cut small discs of sweet pepper and put one in the center of each 'flower'. Decorate the dish with chrysanthemum flowers.

*Beef sukiyaki*

# BEEF SUKIYAKI

*Serves 4*

- 1 lb/450 g rump steak
- ½ pint/3 dl *dashi* (see page 313)
- ¼ pint/1·5 dl *shoyu*
- 2 tablespoons *sake* or dry sherry
- 3 oz/75 g castor sugar
- 2 small onions
- 8 oz/225 g spinach
- 1 crisp lettuce
- 1 lb/450 g bean curd
- 16 button mushrooms
- ½ oz/15 g lard or suet
- 4 eggs

*Sukiyaki* is an excellent dish for a party because it offers the hostess an opportunity to serve a delicious, festive-looking meal with very little cooking. All the cooking, in fact, is done in batches at the table in front of the guests.

Cut the meat across the grain into slices about 5 inches by 1½ inches by ⅛ inch (13 cm by 3·5 cm by 3 mm). Mix together the *dashi, shoyu, sake* and sugar. Peel and quarter the onions. Rinse the spinach and lettuce under cold running water and dry well. Shred the lettuce by hand, not with a knife, into fairly thick strips. Cut the bean curd into squares about 1 inch by 1 inch by ⅛ inch (2·5 cm by 2·5 cm by 3 mm). Cut off the mushroom stalks, rinse the mushrooms under cold running water and drain. Arrange the vegetables and meat attractively on a large plate in separate groups and place on the dining table.

Melt half the lard or suet in a large heavy chafing dish over moderate heat. Add half the strips of meat and brown lightly on both sides. Place the meat to one side of the dish and moisten with 3–4 tablespoons of the *dashi* mixture. Add half the onions, spinach, lettuce, bean curd and mushrooms to the dish, but keep separate. Cook gently for 3–4 minutes, turning all the ingredients carefully to avoid mixing them. Moisten and season with the *dashi* mixture to taste. Serve immediately. Cook the remaining ingredients in exactly the same way.

The *sukiyaki* is accompanied by rice and raw egg, both served in individual bowls. Each diner helps himself to an ingredient and dips it into the beaten egg which cools it and serves as a dressing.

*Note:* To make chicken *sukiyaki*, substitute chicken for the beef and use chicken fat for greasing the chafing dish.

# KOREAN FIERY MEAT WITH SESAME SEED DIP

*Serves 4*

- 12 oz/350 g fillet of beef
- 4 shallots
- 1 clove garlic
- 1 leek
- 5 spring onions
- ¼ teaspoon castor sugar
- ½ teaspoon salt
- 4 tablespoons light soya sauce
- 1 tablespoon sesame oil
- pinch chilli powder or 3–4 drops Tabasco
- ¼ pint/1·5 dl groundnut oil

**for the dip:**

- 2 tablespoons sesame seeds
- ¼ teaspoon salt
- 1 clove garlic
- 3 spring onions
- ¼ teaspoon castor sugar
- 1 teaspoon *mien chiang*
- ½ teaspoon cayenne pepper
- 4 tablespoons light soya sauce
- 2 tablespoons vinegar

Cut the meat into thin slices about 3 inches by 1 inch by ¼ inch (7·5 cm by 2·5 cm by 5 mm). Pound lightly to flatten and place on a plate.

Peel and chop the shallots and garlic. Trim the leek and spring onions and rinse thoroughly under cold running water. Drain well and chop finely. Mix together the shallots, garlic, leek, spring onions, sugar, salt, soya sauce, sesame oil and chilli powder or Tabasco and pour over the meat. Mix well and set aside for 3–4 hours.

To make the dip, heat the sesame seeds in an ungreased frying pan until they begin to 'jump' and turn brown, then pound with the salt in a mortar. Peel and chop the garlic. Trim and chop the spring onions. Mix together the sesame seed mixture, garlic, spring onions, sugar, *mien chiang*, cayenne pepper, soya sauce and vinegar.

Heat the groundnut oil in a saucepan until hot. Dip the slices of meat into the oil for a few seconds, then drain on kitchen paper. Dip each slice into sesame seed dip and serve immediately with the remaining sesame seed dip, or vinegar and soya sauce dip (see page 313).

# KOREAN STEAMED DUMPLINGS

*Serves 6*

**for the filling:**

- 1 lb/450 g boned chicken
- 6 oz/175 g bean sprouts
- 6 cubes bean curd
- 2–3 oz/50–75 g fresh or frozen cooked prawns, peeled and deveined
- 1 oz/25 g lard
- pinch chilli powder
- pinch monosodium glutamate
- pinch freshly ground black pepper
- 1 tablespoon light soya sauce
- 1 tablespoon sesame oil

**for the dough:**

- 8 oz/225 g plain flour
- generous ⅓ pint/2 dl boiling water

Mince the chicken. Rinse the bean sprouts under cold running water, then place in a saucepan with just enough water to cover. Bring to the boil and cook for 2 minutes. Drain well and chop finely. Simmer the bean curd in a little water for 2 minutes. Drain well and cut into ½-inch (1-cm) cubes. Finely chop the prawns.

Heat the lard in a frying pan and sauté the chicken, bean sprouts and bean curd for 5 minutes, or until the mixture begins to change colour. Add the prawns, chilli powder, monosodium glutamate, pepper, soya sauce and sesame oil. Cook for 1 minute. Remove from the heat and set aside until required.

To make the dough, sift the flour into a bowl. Add the water, a little at a time, and mix to a soft dough. Knead well on a lightly floured surface. Divide the dough into 24 pieces and roll each piece into a 3-inch (7·5-cm) round. Gently press out a hollow in the centre of each.

Place a teaspoonful of the prepared filling in each hollow and moisten the edges of the dough with water. Fold in half to form a semi-circular dumpling. Steam the dumplings for 10 minutes. Serve hot with sesame seed dip (see Korean Fiery Meat With Sesame Seed Dip, above) or vinegar and soya sauce dip (see page 313).

# CHICKEN WITH SPICED PINEAPPLE SAUCE

*Serves 4*

4 poussins, about 1 lb/450 g each
4 pints/2·25 litres water
1oz/25 g fresh root ginger, finely chopped
2 teaspoons castor sugar
2 pints/generous litre pineapple juice
3 teaspoons salt
generous ¼ pint/2 dl chicken stock (see recipe)
oil for deep-frying
4 oz/100 g peanut butter
1 teaspoon Worcestershire sauce
few drops Tabasco
salt

Rinse the chickens under cold running water and dry with kitchen paper. Truss with fine string. Pour the water into a large saucepan and add the ginger, sugar, pineapple juice and salt. Bring to the boil and add the chickens. Simmer for 10–15 minutes, or until tender. Remove the chickens with a perforated spoon and set aside to drain and cool. Measure and reserve the required amount of stock. Deep-fry the chickens in the oil for 4–5 minutes, or until crisp and golden brown. Drain on kitchen paper and keep hot.

Heat the peanut butter in a saucepan. Add the chicken stock, Worcestershire sauce, Tabasco and salt to taste. Heat until simmering. Pour into a small bowl and serve as a dip with the chickens.

# YAKITORI (GRILLED CHICKEN ON SKEWERS)

*Serves 4*

6 oz/175 g boned chicken
4 oz/100 g chicken giblets
2 medium-sized onions
1 large sweet potato
2 tablespoons *shoyu*
2 tablespoons *sake* or dry sherry
1 oz/25 g castor sugar
4 oz/100 g Japanese radish or red radishes, grated
1 teaspoon ground ginger
pinch freshly ground white pepper

Cut the chicken and giblets into 1-inch (2·5-cm) cubes. Peel and thickly slice the onions and sweet potato. Thread the chicken, giblets, onion and sweet potato on to 4 bamboo or metal skewers.

Mix together the *shoyu, sake* and sugar. Brush this mixture over the skewered ingredients. Place the skewers over a charcoal brazier or under a hot grill and cook until golden brown, brushing frequently with the remaining *shoyu* mixture during cooking. Mix together the radish, ginger and pepper.

Serve the *yakitori* accompanied by the radish mixture as a dip.

*Yakitori (grilled chicken on skewers)*

# SPICED PORK AND CHICKEN

*Serves 6*

| | |
|---|---|
| 1 chicken, about 3 lb/1·5 kg | 3 teaspoons salt |
| 1 lb/450 g pork fillet or lean pork, cut from the leg | ¼ teaspoon freshly ground white pepper |
| 3 cloves garlic | 1 oz/25 g melted butter or 2 tablespoons oil |
| 3 small bay leaves | |
| 5 tablespoons vinegar | ½ pint/3 dl coconut cream |

Chop the chicken flesh into 2½-inch (6-cm) pieces. Cut the pork into 1-inch (2·5-cm) cubes. Peel and finely chop the garlic. Place the chicken, pork, garlic, bay leaves, vinegar, salt and pepper in a flameproof casserole. Set aside for about 15 minutes, stirring frequently to coat the meat with the seasonings.

Add enough boiling water just to cover the meat and bring to the boil over moderate heat. Lower the heat, partly cover and simmer until the meat is almost tender and the liquid has evaporated. Add the butter or oil and continue cooking until the meat is evenly browned and tender.

Heat the coconut cream gently and stir into the meat. Pour into a heated serving dish and serve with plain boiled rice.

# ROAST SUCKLING PIG

*Serves 8*

| | |
|---|---|
| 1 suckling pig, including the liver | ½ pint/3 dl boiling water |
| salt and pepper | 5–6 cloves garlic |
| 12 tamarind leaves or 6 thin, unpeeled lemon slices | 3 medium-sized onions |
| | 3 tablespoons lime or lemon juice |
| about 3 oz/75 g melted lard | ½–1 oz/15–25 g sugar |

Have the suckling pig ready for roasting with the head on. Reserve the liver, to be used for the sauce. Rub the inside of the pig with a mixture of salt and pepper. Put the tamarind leaves or lemon slices inside and brush the outside of the pig with 2–3 tablespoons of the melted lard. Protect the ears with oiled greaseproof paper or foil and roast in a moderately hot oven (375°F, 190°C, Gas Mark 5) for 2–2½ hours. Baste frequently with the meat juices. Meanwhile, slice the liver and brown lightly in 1 tablespoon of the remaining lard. Drain, then chop or mince. Add the water and rub the mixture through a fine sieve, or reduce to a purée in a liquidiser. Keep hot in a bowl over simmering water.

Peel and finely chop the garlic, and peel and slice the onions. Heat the remaining lard in a saucepan. Add the garlic and fry for a few moments to brown. Remove the garlic and reserve. Add the onions to the hot fat remaining in the pan and fry gently until soft but not brown. Add the liver purée and stir to blend. Sprinkle with the lime juice, season to taste and add the sugar. Simmer for 10 minutes over low heat, stirring frequently. Pour the sauce into a heated sauceboat and sprinkle with the reserved garlic. Serve with the roast suckling pig.

# VINEGAR AND SOYA SAUCE DIP

*Serves 6*

| | |
|---|---|
| 6 tablespoons vinegar | 1–1½ tablespoons chopped pine nuts |
| 1 oz/25 g castor sugar | |
| 6 tablespoons soya sauce | |

Heat the vinegar and sugar gently until the sugar has dissolved. Add the soya sauce and pour the mixture into 6 small individual dishes. Sprinkle some chopped pine nuts into each dish. Serve with Korean steamed dumplings (see page 311) or as an accompaniment to grilled and fried foods.

# DASHI (JAPANESE STOCK)

*Makes 2 pints (generous litre)*

| | |
|---|---|
| ¼ oz/7 g *konbu* seaweed (see note) | ¼ teaspoon monosodium glutamate |
| 2 pints/generous litre water | |
| 1½ oz/40 g *katsuobushi* (see note) | |

Put the *konbu* seaweed in a saucepan with the water. Place over moderate heat and bring to the boil. Remove from the heat and add the *katsuobushi*. Return to the heat and bring just to the boil. Remove from the heat immediately. Add the monosodium glutamate and set aside for 10 minutes. Strain and use as required.

*Note: Dashi* is the foundation of Japanese cooking. Both *konbu* seaweed and *katsuobushi* (dried bonito shavings) are available from Japanese food shops.

# KEEM CHEE (KOREAN PICKLES)

*Makes 2 pints (generous litre)*

| | |
|---|---|
| 2 lb/1 kg small cucumbers (see note) | 1 teaspoon Korean red pepper or chilli powder |
| 2 tablespoons salt | 1 tablespoon light soya sauce |
| 6 spring onions | 1 teaspoon monosodium glutamate |
| 3 cloves garlic | |
| 3 teaspoons chopped fresh root ginger | ½ pint/3 dl water |

Scrub the cucumbers gently under cold running water and drain well. Cut in half lengthwise, then into ½-inch (1-cm) pieces. Place on a tray or a large plate and sprinkle with half the salt. Set aside for 30 minutes.

Trim and chop the spring onions. Peel and chop the garlic. Rinse the cucumber under cold running water, drain well and place in a bowl. Sprinkle the cucumber with the spring onions, garlic, ginger, red pepper, remaining salt, soya sauce and monosodium glutamate. Add the water and mix well. Cover tightly and set aside for 4–5 days. Chill well and serve as required.

*Note:* The cucumbers may be replaced by cabbage, baby turnips, carrots or other vegetables.

# INDEX